IN THE HOME WORKSHOP

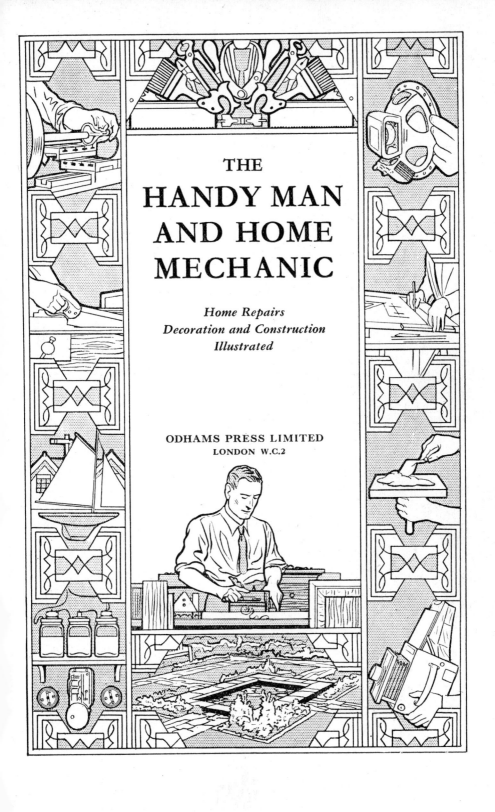

THE
HANDY MAN
AND HOME
MECHANIC

Home Repairs
Decoration and Construction
Illustrated

ODHAMS PRESS LIMITED
LONDON W.C.2

INTRODUCTION

THE Dictionary defines a handyman as "A man of all work." In these specialist days, the handyman has almost disappeared from business, but he lives on in the home in greater glory than ever.

There is something unusually satisfying—something that appeals to the fundamental instincts of husbandry—for a man to be a real handy man in his own home.

To the average man, there are few pleasures in life comparable to that of doing a job himself in and about his own home.

Was there ever a bookcase that gave a fraction of the satisfaction as the one fashioned by your own hands? Was ever paint more pleasing—distempering more delightful—a crazy path more happily laid, a greenhouse or a shed more worthily made—than that on which you have lavished your own care and time and skill? To be a craftsman—to create, with brain and hands, some of the necessities of life—to furnish one's home with comforts, gives a man a feeling of solid competency and achievement.

Only those who have experienced the thrill of making things know what the man misses to whom such things as wood and nails and hammers and saws and paint and varnish and wire and metal are things in a world apart. To the handy man, they are the stuff of which a thousand and one things are made.

Apart from the pleasure that being a craftsman brings, there is the business side. It makes a big difference to your pocket to be able to turn and do things for yourself—in the course of years it represents a very considerable economy and in these days that means a lot.

To you, whether you are a seasoned craftsman or just a beginner, this book is dedicated. It is written by practical men for practical men in plain and simple language that all can understand. To those who are already experienced we believe that in the pages of this book there may be found much that is useful. Even if there are jobs here you have done without instructions, there still remain the tips and wrinkles gained by long experience to ease the work and make difficult parts appear simple.

In any case, the wider a man's experience, the more anxious is he, as a rule, to extend his knowledge, and there is much in these chapters that follow that will be found of interest even to old hands at the game.

To those who are beginners, this book is intended to be *really* helpful. While its scope is wide, it assumes little previous knowledge—while it covers the activities of the handy man in the home from A to Z, it does not deal with the XYZ before it explains the ABC.

If you have hands that will obey your brain and a brain that will follow this book, you will have no difficulty. For here are instructions for the perfect completion of almost any household job. The simple writing of these instructions is supported by hundreds of plans, drawings and photographs that doubly clarify the problem in hand. And added to that is a series of beautifully printed working drawings, seven of which are on a large scale and separated from the book for easy and constant reference. The "Handy Man and Home Mechanic" is the epitome of experience. You are shown not only how to do a particular job, but how to do it in the easiest and quickest way, and the cheapest manner consistent with good results.

This book will fill your leisure hours with pleasure and profit. Aimless leisure is unknown to the handy man. He has a necessary job for every minute—he has a lifetime hobby inherited from time immemorial from his forefathers—that of making and doing *real* things.

Remember that the final charm of being an efficient handy man is that you can produce things that money cannot buy in the ordinary way. You may have an alcove in which shelves and a cupboard would look admirable, but no shop sells exactly the size and the shape of fixture you want. In making it yourself, you not only have a lot of pleasure, but you get precisely what you require. Unless you order things to be specially made for you —and the cost of that is sometimes more than you can afford—there is no other way in which you can achieve it.

THE EDITOR

CONTENTS

PAGE

WOODWORK

Timber 9
Selection and Use of Timber . 13
Tools and Their Uses . . 17
Saws and Sawing . . . 27
Planes and Planing . . . 32
Marking Out 38
Nails and Screws . . . 43
Chiselling 48
Boring 51
Rebating 57
Joints and Jointing . . . 60
Hinges and Locks . . . 72
Sharpening Woodworkers' Tools . 77
Glue and Gluing . . . 83
Cramps and Wedges . . . 86
Glass-papering 88
Wood Finishing 92
Plywood 99
Fretwork 103
Useful Workshop Appliances . 110
Arranging the Workshop . . 116

CONSTRUCTIONAL WOODWORK

A Work Bench 119
The Home Workshop . . . 123
Handy Shelves 132
A Plain Ledged Door . . 135
A Cabinet for Screws . . . 136
A Tool Rack 140
A Corner Table 141
A Medicine Chest . . . 143
A Useful Bookcase . . . 145
A Sectional Bookcase . . . 147
A Bureau Writing Desk . . 151
A Dog Kennel 154
A Cycle Shed 158
A Span-roofed Greenhouse . . 163
A Poultry House and Run . . 166
Household Steps and Ladders . 171
Radio Cabinets 176
Useful Cupboards . . . 179

BEDROOM FURNITURE

Chest of Drawers . . . 182
Dressing Table 184
Wardrobe 184

PAGE

CONSTRUCTIONAL WOODWORK—cont.

Bedstead 188
Bedside Cupboard . . . 190
An Invalid Table . . . 193
An Inexpensive Sideboard . . 196
A Kitchen Cabinet . . . 199

SIMPLE KITCHEN FITMENTS

Folding Clothes-horse . . 202
Hinged Scullery Table . . 202
Egg Stand 203
Airing Rack 203
Plate Rack 203
Food Safe 203
Draining Board . . . 203
A Portable Garage . . . 204

METAL-WORK

Metals and Their Uses . . 209
Metal-working Tools . . . 211
The Metal-turning Lathe . . 217
Files and Scrapers . . . 245
Measuring Instruments . . 249
Drills and Drilling . . . 253
Screws and Screw Threads . . 257
Rivets, Bolts and Nuts . . 262
Smiths' Work 265
Soldering 270
Hardening and Tempering . . 276
Shafting and Pulleys . . . 279
Workshop Foundations . . 288
Belts and Belting . . . 292
Gas Engine Overhaul . . . 295
Motor-car Adjustments . . 299
Motor-cycle Adjustments . . 323
Bicycle Adjustments . . . 326

ELECTRICITY

The Laws of Electricity . . 329
Alternating and Direct Current . 334
Dynamos 335
Electric Motors 339
Accumulators 341
Installing Electric Light . . 357
Electrical Heaters and Cookers . 392
Wiring for Electric Bells . . 397

PAGE

ELECTRICITY—*cont.*
Making an Electric Bell . . 404
Faults in Electric Bell Systems . 406
Electric Light Extensions . . 410
Installing an Immersion Water
Heater 412
Home Made Lighting Fittings . 415
Mending an Electric Iron . . 421
A Domestic Telephone . . 424

WIRELESS 427

HOUSE DECORATION AND REPAIR
Distempering 441
Paperhanging . . . 446
Indoor Painting . . . 455
Outdoor Painting . . . 461
Enamelling and Varnishing . 464
Fitting a Picture Rail . . 466
Mending Blinds . . . 469
Pelmets and Curtain Rods . 471
Plugging Walls . . . 477
Laying Linoleum and Carpets . 478
Simple Furniture Repairs . 480
Remedying Ill-fitting Drawers . 484
Household Repairs . . . 486
Overhauling a Sewing Machine . 488
Overhauling a Gramophone . . 490
Making use of a Recess . . 492
Fitting an Extra Door . . 497
Fixing a new Sash-line . . 502
Draught Prevention . . 504
Re-glazing a Sash . . 507
Laying a Tiled Hearth . . 510
Simple Gasfitting . . . 512
Gas Fires, Burners and Pipes . 513
Smoky Chimneys and their Cure . 516
Damp Walls and their Cure . 518
Dry Rot—Its Prevention and Cure 520
Burst Pipes . . . 521
Faults in Cisterns . . . 524
Faults in Water Taps . . 526
Making and Fitting a Shower
Attachment . . . 528
Hot Water Systems and Boiler
Troubles 530
Cleaning Pipes, Drains, etc. . 533
Roof and Gutter Repairs . . 537

PAGE

THE GARDEN AND SMALLHOLDING
Making and Edging Paths . . 541
Laying Crazy Paving . . 543
Concrete and Cement Work . . 546
Simple Bricklaying . . . 549
Garden Pools 554
Levelling and Draining a Lawn . 558
Wire Netting and its Uses . . 563
Fences and Fencing . . . 566
Trellis Work and Pergolas . . 569
Garden Gates 571
Useful Garden Appliances . . 574
Overhauling a Lawn Mower . 578
A Hose-reel 581
A Home-made Garden Roller . 582
A Wheelbarrow 584
A Garden Frame . . . 587
Garden Seats 589
A Rabbit Hutch . . . 592
A Child's Swing . . . 594
Window Boxes and Plant Stands . 595
Bird Boxes 599
Pigeon Cotes 602
An Outdoor Aviary . . . 605
Roofing Materials . . . 609

AMATEUR PHOTOGRAPHY . . 613

PREPARING WORKING DRAWINGS . 627

MODEL MAKING
Planning a Model Railway . . 643
A Wayside Station . . . 645
A Signal Box 648
Bridges 651
A Goods Depot 654
A Level Crossing . . . 657
Signals 659
SMALL ACCESSORIES:
Fogman's Hut . . . 662
Platelayer's Hut . . . 662
Coal Merchant's Office . . 662
Coal Stack 663
Telegraph Poles . . . 664
Gradient Post . . . 664
A Model Yacht 664
A Doll's House 667

*With this Volume is given an envelope
containing seven large working drawings.*

WOODWORK

TIMBER

WOODWORKING, from the handyman's point of view, includes carpentry and joinery, and cabinet-making. The former applies more or less to the erection of sheds, cupboards, fitting shelves and similar work, and refers more to the working of wood into useful objects rather than the beautiful; while the latter calls for workmanship that is a good deal more artistic and exacting. Having chosen woodworking as a means of occupying your spare time, the initial step is to learn something of the nature and peculiarities of the material upon which you are going to work. Unless you have some idea of the properties of the commoner varieties of timber, you will be at a loss to know the best kind of material to use for the work you wish to undertake. Thus, some woods, such as yellow pine, can only be used in dry situations, while others, such as oak and teak, can be used for outside purposes, exposed to all weathers. Some woods, especially yellow deal, can be used for either, but where it is used for outside purposes it should be carefully painted. Again, some woods can be finished to produce a brilliant polish, a typical example being mahogany; but others, such as teak, will not take polish.

Although there are dozens of different kinds of woods used by the professional craftsman, it would be sheer waste of time to go into details about wood you are not likely to use.

The descriptions given in the following paragraphs are intended to outline the characteristics of the commoner kinds of timber and the uses to which they are generally put.

Woods are usually classified under two headings, soft and hard, although some softwoods are really hard and some hardwoods soft.

Softwoods are obtained from coniferous trees—that is, trees having evergreen, needle-shaped leaves, the timber of which is more or less resinous. Hardwood is produced mainly from non-coniferous trees, whose broad leaves are shed annually, as the oak.

The commonest softwoods used principally in carpentry and joinery are pine and spruce. The hard variety include oak, walnut, mahogany and American whitewood, which, although soft in

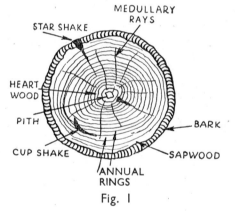

MEDULLARY RAYS
STAR SHAKE
HEART WOOD
PITH
CUP SHAKE
BARK
SAPWOOD
ANNUAL RINGS

Fig. 1

texture is usually known as a hard-wood.

All timber used in constructional work is cut from "outward growing" (exogenous) trees. If a cross-section of a tree (as illustrated in Fig. 1) is examined, it will be noticed that numerous concentric rings surround the pith. These rings, called "annual rings," are formed at the rate of one a year and provide a ready means of roughly estimating the

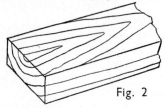

Fig. 2

age of the tree. This statement, however, does not apply to all timber, as in certain tropical trees there may be more than one ring per annum.

The lines seen radiating from the pith are called "medullary rays," and, when suitably cut, give the beautiful figuring of the wood.

During growth the inner parts of the tree fill up somewhat and harden and form what is known as "heart-wood." That portion of the timber which lies just beneath the bark is called "sapwood."

The following points should be noted when selecting timber: Always obtain well-seasoned wood that is straight in the grain, of uniform colour, smells sweet, and has its annual rings close together.

If the plank comes from the centre of the tree you may get a strip of pith-wood that will lift from the surface (as illustrated in Fig. 2). On the other hand, if a greenish-blue colour appears in softwood it usually indicates that the plank contains sapwood, which is not only weaker than other parts, but soon decays. The sapwood of most dark-coloured hardwoods is greyish-white in tint.

Fig. 3 shows another defect known as "waney edge," where what should be square corners become rounded. It is caused by the too economical cutting from the log; in fact, in some cases some of the bark appears on the waney edges.

"Heart shakes" and "star shakes" (Fig. 1) are also defects associated with timber. The former is usually found in wood cut from old trees, and the latter is generally caused by bad seasoning.

Here is a list of the most commonly used softwoods:

Yellow Deal.—Deal refers to the northern pine grown in Norway and Sweden and the Baltic region. It is sometimes referred to as Scotch fir and is the wood most used by the amateur woodworker. Timber obtained from this tree is known in the trade as yellow deal, but in the north of England it is called red deal. It is light in weight,

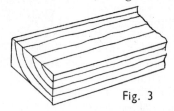

Fig. 3

fairly tough and easily worked; and when it is well seasoned can be relied upon. The advantage of using this wood, especially of the better quality known as "Archangel first," is that it is cheap, straight-grained, more or less free from knots, and can be planed to produce a smooth surface. It is suitable for all kinds of joinery work, such as doors, window-frames, cupboards, kitchen tables, etc.

White Deal.—Wood obtained from the spruce fir, grown in Norway, and generally known as white deal or common spruce, is unsuitable for joinery work because it warps and splits easily, is somewhat difficult to work, and generally has a large number of large, loose knots. For box-making and shelves, and similar common work, however, it answers the purpose very well and is cheaper than yellow deal.

Yellow Pine.—Yellow pine must not be confused with yellow deal, as it is lighter in weight, softer and less durable. It is a product of North America. The wood is almost entirely free from knots, straight-grained, and does not shrink or warp to any appreciable extent. It is unsuitable for outdoor work or for use in damp situations, but is durable when used in dry places. Yellow pine is easily worked, and is an excellent wood for joinery, mouldings, and work which necessitates the use of wide boards, such as panels, as it can be obtained in widths up to three feet. The disadvantage of this wood is its comparatively high cost.

Pitch Pine.—This wood is extremely strong, heavy and straight-grained. Its colour varies from a dark yellow to a light reddish-brown. It is very durable, on account of the large amount of resin present, which also makes it very difficult to plane and paint. It is used principally in the form of blocks for making floors, thresholds, treads of staircases and other indoor work that is subject to wear.

The following is a list of commonly used hardwoods:

Ash.—Ash is a whitish-coloured, close-grained wood. It is tough and springy and is used for cart shafts, tool handles, gates and furniture. It is durable if used in dry situations, but is unsuitable for ordinary constructional work.

Beech.—This wood is of a yellowish-white colour, very hard, and has a close and compact grain. Owing to this feature it is used largely for wood-turning. Beech is also favoured a great deal for making the wooden parts of tools, such as mallet heads, stocks of planes, etc. It is also employed for making chairs and other articles where a hard, durable material is required.

Box.—Boxwood is exceedingly hard, has a very even, close and compact grain and takes a fine polish. It is a very useful wood for the turner, and should you at any time acquire a lathe you will find it very useful for turning tool handles, chessmen, wooden chucks, etc. It is rarely obtained over about 4 in. in diameter.

Elm.—Elm is a very difficult wood to work as it is very tough and cross-grained. It warps badly, but takes nails better than any other wood. Elm is an excellent wood to use in damp situations and under water. It is for this reason that wheel-barrows, agricultural tools, stable fittings and numerous other articles subjected to dampness are made from it.

Mahogany.—This wood, of which there are several varieties, is the ideal one for the amateur woodworker who specialises in cabinet-making. That known as "Honduras" or baywood, from Central America, is inferior to "Spanish" from Cuba and Jamaica. The former is pinkish in colour. In the best quality it is easily worked, but the inferior kind sometimes planes up rough and spongy. It can be obtained in boards up to 5 ft. in width and, as it is cheaper than Spanish, it is more widely used. Its use is confined principally to cabinet-making and furniture. Spanish mahogany is of a deep red-brown colour and can be usually distinguished by a whitish, chalky substance which fills the pores. It is beautifully marked, takes glue better than any other wood, is remarkably free from knots and other defects, and has less tendency to warp than any other wood. It also takes a brilliant polish. Spanish mahogany is used for high-class furniture or cabinet making, and is cut into sheets for veneering inferior kinds of wood.

The amateur woodworker will find it a great advantage to make all appliances such as straight-edges, winding strips, etc., from this excellent and reliable wood, for by so doing he will not have to worry himself continuously over possible inexactitudes in his work due to untrustworthy tools.

Oak.—This wood is generally associated with England's might of the past.

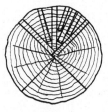

Fig. 4

Our old manor houses, farmhouses and even cottages boast of their oak beams that stand and smoulder even in a fire where steel girders crumple up. There are a vast number of species of oak, but all have the same main characteristics and vary in colour from light brown to dark brown. It is a close, compact, straight-, but more or less broken-grained wood; very hard and extremely durable and weather-resisting, though having a tendency to twist and warp. Oak is extremely useful for building construction, fence-making, and general outdoor work. It is also very much more used in these days than formerly for cabinet work, in the form of " wainscoat " or " quartered " oak. In the former, the tree trunk is run through the frame-saw set to cut the log right through to the thicknesses required (as shown in Fig. 4), but for beautiful effects an attempt is made to cut the log to show the grain-mark or figure.

Teak.—This wood is sometimes called " Indian Oak " as it resembles oak in grain and colour and has an even texture. It is easy to work when new, but more difficult when thoroughly seasoned. It is non-inflammable, does not shrink or warp to any great extent, and weathers well. Best quality teak is imported from Burma and Siam, while an inferior quality comes from Java. Teak does not take a polish but looks well when oiled. It is very durable, even when subjected to alternate wet and dry, and is therefore an excellent wood for outside work. It resists insects and does not corrode nails and screws, due to its natural oil. Teak is employed largely in shipbuilding, building construction, superior joinery, and for making the outside containers of electrical storage batteries.

Walnut.—This is another useful but expensive wood much used in these days for cabinet work. Its scarcity makes it inapplicable for general constructional work; but on account of its beauty and other good qualities it should appeal to the amateur craftsman who wishes to make something artistic to match existing furniture. It is tough and hard, easily worked, and takes a good polish. The American variety is darker and straighter in grain than English or Italian, the former having a grey-brown colour and the latter a dark, purplish tint.

Satin Walnut is a product of the United States of America. It is close-grained, easy to work and takes a good polish. The colour is a light reddish-brown, and the wood is obtainable in large widths. Satin walnut is exceedingly liable to warp and twist. The amateur should, therefore, think twice when planning to make anything with this wood. It was once used extensively for making cheap furniture, but seems to have lost favour during the last few years.

Plywood.—An extremely useful form of wood for both amateur and professional, known as plywood, has come into favour during the past few years. Briefly stated, plywood consists of a number of thin layers of wood so placed that the grain of each layer is across the grain of its neighbour. Each layer is glued, and the whole subjected to enormous pressure, resulting in a very tough board. It will be understood that by making the outside layers of more expensive woods and the inside laminations of a common variety it is possible to get practically the same result at a very much reduced cost compared with that of solid wood.

Plywood is valuable for making panels and work of a similar nature. It can be obtained in various sized sheets up to 60 in. by 48 in. and from 3 mm. to about 1 in. in thickness, faced with oak, mahogany and a number of other hardwoods.

Pulpwood.—The amateur will also find pulpwood boards extremely useful for numerous purposes, such as panels for doors, panelling a room, making partitions, etc. It is composed of wood-pulp and an adhesive which is pressed into large sheets. Some kinds are so heavily and closely pressed and treated that they become practically impervious to damp, and the texture is so fine and close that it can even be planed at the edge, provided a sharp tool is used. It saws readily and may also be cut with a sharp knife, while nails can be driven into it easily.

Pulpwood boards are sold in sheets of 6 ft. to 16 ft. in length, and 3 ft. and 4 ft. in width. These useful boards are sold under various trade names.

SELECTION AND USE OF TIMBER

THE characteristics of various kinds of wood used by the amateur having been dealt with, a few general remarks on the selection and the proper use of timber may be acceptable to those readers who have had little or no experience in this direction.

The old saying that "a little learning is a dangerous thing" does not apply in this case, as a little knowledge on this subject may be the means of a considerable saving in the cost of material.

The word "timber" generally refers to that portion of the felled tree which when deprived of its limbs forms a "log." The logs may be sawn squarely to form a "baulk," which may vary in size from 12 in. by 12 in. to 18 in. by 18 in. Logs are also then subdivided into "deals," "planks," "scantlings," "battens," etc., the sizes of which vary considerably.

For instance, a deal is the size of a piece of timber 9 in. wide, whose thickness varies from $2\frac{1}{2}$ in. to $4\frac{1}{2}$ in.; while a plank measures anything above 15 in. wide and over $3\frac{1}{2}$ in. in thickness.

A batten is narrower than a deal, and may measure anything from $4\frac{1}{2}$ in. wide and from $\frac{3}{4}$ in. to 3 in. in thickness.

Timber cut to a thickness of less than 2 in. and to any width from 6 in. upwards is called a "board."

The term "quartering" is applied to timber of square section, and varies in size from 2 in. by 2 in. to 6 in. by 6 in.

Scantlings are pieces of timber with sides varying from 2 in. to 5 in. and averaging about 2 in. in thickness.

Sawn softwood boards can be usually obtained in standard widths of 6, 7, 8, 9 and 11 in. in the following thicknesses: $\frac{5}{8}$, $\frac{3}{4}$, 1, $1\frac{1}{4}$ and $1\frac{1}{2}$ in. and up to about 24 ft. in length. These sizes may be a trifle smaller when purchased at the timber-yard as they may have shrunk a little during the process of seasoning.

When ordering softwood it is usual to specify either "sawn" or "prepared" stuff. The former means that the faces and edges are more or less rough and in the same condition as it left the saw; while the latter has its sides and edges finished by a planing machine. Thus, in ordering, say, a 12 ft. length of 2 by 3, ordinary sawn material is implied, and you will possibly receive a piece of wood whose sectional dimensions are of full size. On the other hand, these measurements may be smaller, especially if the timber-yard sawyer has cut two pieces of the material from a 2 in. by 6 in. batten. One piece measures a full 2 in. by 3 in., but the other piece may be smaller, due to the thickness and set of the circular saw.

When a length of 2 in. by 3 in. prepared stuff is asked for, you will receive a length whose sectional dimensions will measure only $1\frac{3}{4}$ in. by $2\frac{3}{4}$ in., as $\frac{1}{8}$ in. of the material has been removed from each face for planing purposes.

Prepared Boards.—The same applies to prepared boards. For example, a 6 in. by 1 in. floorboard planed on one face and two edges will only "hold up" to $5\frac{3}{4}$ in. wide and $\frac{7}{8}$ in. in thickness.

The effective width of tongued and grooved boards is usually $\frac{1}{2}$ in. narrower than the "nominal" width.

Planks, deals and battens, etc., when sold in large quantities are generally at so much per "Petersburg" standard, representing 165 cubic ft. From this it is simple to calculate the number of running feet of material of any sectional dimension contained in a standard of timber by applying the following simple formula:

$$FR = \frac{144}{N} \times 165$$

where FR = the number of feet run, and N = the sectional area of the material in square inches.

For example, how many feet run is contained in a standard of 4 in. by 2 in. timber?

Applying the above equation we have:

$$FR = \frac{144 \times 165}{8} = 2970 \text{ ft. run per standard.}$$

These quantities, however, are seldom if ever required by the handyman, and the above example is only mentioned as a point of interest.

The amateur generally buys his scantling and quartering at so much per 100 ft. run, and floorboards and matching at so much per 100 ft. super, which means 100 square ft., usually termed a "square."

Hardwood, such as oak, etc., is generally sold at so much per square ft. up to 1 in. in thickness, but timber above this thickness is frequently quoted at so much per in. thickness per square ft. For example, a piece of hardwood $1\frac{1}{2}$ in. thick at 4/– per in. would cost 6/–.

It may not be out of place here to mention that a price should always be asked before giving a definite order for timber as prices vary a great deal. For instance, it is often possible to get quite good quality, say, 2 in. by 3 in. stuff at some yards for practically the same price as that asked for 2 in. by 2 in. at others.

This is a point worth considering, especially when the material is to be used for constructing a workshop or a shed, because 2 in. by 3 in. studding makes a stronger job than 2 in. by 2 in., and in this case costs little if any more.

Before paying a visit to a timber-yard to place an order for wood it is a good plan to work out the quantities required, and make a note of them on paper, giving the size of each item. The reason for this is that the timber merchant, although generally willing to give every assistance, cannot be expected to sort out exactly what is asked for—if you expect it you may be disappointed.

If you require a number of varying short lengths, calculate them so that their added lengths are equivalent to the number of standard 12, 13 or 15 ft. lengths, as the case may be. This method of ordering is not only economical, but saves a great deal of time and puzzling when you come to cut the timber to the required sizes.

Do not be surprised if, after having ordered, say, 12 ft. lengths, you receive pieces 13 ft. long, for it often happens that material of a specified length is out of stock. In such cases the merchant usually sends the nearest longer size to that ordered, which is very often a blessing in disguise.

Tongued and Grooved Matching is a particularly useful prepared wood of great service to the amateur for covering workshops, sheds, etc. It can be obtained in listed widths of 4, $4\frac{1}{2}$, 5, $5\frac{1}{2}$, and 6 in., and in thicknesses of $\frac{1}{2}$, $\frac{3}{8}$, $\frac{3}{4}$, and 1 in.

There are two kinds of this material. One has a moulded bead on one edge and is known as beaded matching (illustrated at A in Fig. 1), and the other has both edges bevelled to form a V between the joint (as shown at B). The latter is recommended because it generally forms a stronger joint, and has perhaps a more pleasing appearance when erected.

When ordering matching it is necessary to specify which of the two kinds is required.

Do not overlook the fact that the thickness of matched boards is $\frac{1}{8}$ in. less than the listed thicknesses, that is, $\frac{5}{8}$ in. matching is only $\frac{1}{2}$ in. thick. Also, that a matched board when joined to its neighbour loses $\frac{1}{2}$ in. from its standard width. This is important, because if you estimate the number of boards required to cover a given length on the basis of listed widths—say, for instance, the back of a shed—you will find that you have an insufficient number of boards to complete the work.

For example, suppose you wish to cover a length of 12 ft. This would require 24 6-in. nominal sized boards; but as the true width of such boards is only $5\frac{1}{2}$ in., over 26 such boards would be necessary.

It follows from this that the narrower the board used the greater the deficiency

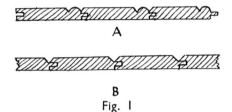

A

B

Fig. 1

will be. Thus, if 4 in. boards are substituted in the example quoted above, 36 boards of nominal width would be necessary, but as each board loses $\frac{1}{2}$ in. in width the 36 boards would cover only about 10 ft. 6 in.

Like all softwood, tongued and grooved boards shrink and swell an appreciable amount according to the state of the weather. If erected whilst in a wet condition the work will open out and possibly expose the tongues when it has had time to dry. This should be borne in mind when trying to make up your mind whether to use wide or narrow matching. The wide stuff covers the ground more quickly; and, as bought, loses less in width than the narrow material, as already mentioned; but it shrinks more as there is more substance to shrink. On the other hand, narrow boards do not shrink so much, but you lose a great deal more in covering capabilities.

It is false economy to use very thin matching as there is more risk of finding both tongue and groove broken, especially in the $\frac{1}{2}$ in. stuff. This comes to you only $\frac{3}{8}$ in. thick, and when you consider that this is divided into three —with the face edge a little thicker than the back portion—you will quite readily understand that some of the back part of the grooved edge, and also some of the fragile tongue often gets broken off in handling.

When nailing matchboards in a vertical position, always start with a grooved edge flush or just overlapping the vertical supporting member, so that the groove of the next board to be fixed fits into a tongue. This method not only ensures easier working, but presents a stronger edge should it be necessary to knock the succeeding board in place.

Do not strike the unprotected tongue of a board when using a hammer for forcing a board in position, as the tongue will either break or spread out and thus render the next board difficult to fit. This can be prevented by placing the groove of an odd piece of matching over the tongue of the board to be fixed, and striking this.

When fixing matching in a horizontal position out of doors, always keep the tongued edge uppermost, as it allows rain, etc. to run off. If the board is fixed with its groove to the top, water may lodge in the groove and remain there for some appreciable time, obviously damaging the wood.

As it is usual either to paint or creosote the exterior of matched boards used for covering sheds and other structures exposed to the weather, to preserve the wood, it is an advantage to apply a little of the finishing material to the joints as they are being fitted. This protects the wood at its weakest parts and helps to keep out the weather.

Weather-boards are used extensively for covering sheds, poultry-houses and similar structures.

In the common weather-board, sometimes called feather-edge board, the section is cut obliquely and produces a wide and a narrow edge—as shown in Fig. 2. They may be obtained either roughly sawn or sawn and planed, and with or without a rebate; the rebated board (Fig. 3) being easier to fix than the plain-edged one.

Weather-boards are, of course, used horizontally and when being fixed to the framework should be started from the bottom with their thick edge downwards.

When fixing plain weather-boards care must be taken to give sufficient overlap and to keep them level. A spirit-level comes in handy for levelling, but if such a tool is not available, the two end uprights of the framework can be marked at equal distances to suit the width of the boards.

Fig. 2

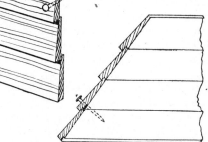

Fig. 3

The nails should be driven in so that they pass only through one board (as shown in the illustrations, Figs. 2 and 3).

The same remarks apply to fixing rebated boards, except that there is no need to mark the positions as the rebates keep them parallel. If a spirit-level is available it is as well to check parallelism after fixing, say, every fifth board.

The nails should be driven in at not less than ¾ in. above the thick edges to prevent them going through and perhaps splitting the thin edge of the previous board. This distance also allows a little latitude for expansion and contraction.

French nails about 2 in. long are useful for fixing weather-boards, as they have a fairly large head, and if driven on the slant ensure a strong fastening.

The effective width of a 6-in. rebated weather-board is only 5⅜ in., as the rebate is generally ⅝ in. deep.

Fig. 4 shows a modern type of weather-board introduced from Canada a few years ago. It makes a neat and

effective covering and offers a level outer surface, and like the ordinary rebated weather-board, gives a level

Fig. 4

inside face, which a plain feather-edged board does not.

It is hardly necessary to state that all timber should be stored in a perfectly dry place having a free circulation of air. Any timber required for outside work which cannot be conveniently stored under a roof should be kept off the ground and covered up with sacks, linoleum, or galvanised iron to keep out the weather as much as possible.

TOOLS AND THEIR USES

THE question of tools is as important to the woodworker as the materials they are to be used upon, for without a suitable equipment it is impossible to turn out neat and accurate work. It is said that a good workman can do good work with any tool, whatever its condition may be, but that is a myth and you can be assured it will be done more satisfactorily and expeditiously with a good tool kept in good condition.

A large number of tools is unnecessary at the outset, as the simpler kind of woodwork can be done by the skilful use of a few, but those few should be of the finest quality your pocket will allow.

The best and most economical way of getting a kit of tools together is to go to a reliable firm of tool dealers and purchase guaranteed tools. Buy the articles singly and gradually add to the equipment as necessity arises.

The purchase of good tools should be regarded as an investment, as they will soon pay for themselves and last a lifetime if properly used and cared for.

Take particular care that all cutting tools, such as chisels, planes, etc., are not allowed to lie about in a slipshod fashion on the bench, or put into a drawer with other tools, as their cutting edges are liable to be chipped. When a plane is finished with for the time being, place it on its side and not on its working face. Use only the tool intended for its particular purpose and do not be tempted to turn a screw with a chisel if a screwdriver is not immediately at hand. Another important point worth mentioning is always to keep your tools under lock and key and if tempted to lend a tool—which is bad practice—make sure that the borrower returns it.

The wooden parts of planes and chisels are sometimes french-polished to add to their appearance. It certainly does not add to their durability, but what would do so would be to soak the chisel handles in linseed oil for a day or two, rubbing them daily with a cloth. The same suggestion applies to a plane. Remove the plane iron, stop up the narrow opening at the base with paper or rag, fill the aperture with linseed oil, and put it by for a time to allow the oil thoroughly to soak in.

This treatment preserves and solidifies the wood.

The metal parts of all tools should be kept free from rust, as a sharp edge cannot be made on cutting tools after they have been allowed to get in a rusty condition. The simplest plan to prevent rust is to keep the tools in a dry place and give them an occasional rub with an oily rag.

For a start, the amateur woodworker is advised to obtain a claw-hammer, hand-saw, tenon-saw, brace and bits, screw-driver, bradawl, try-square, marking-gauge, rule, and a trying-plane. Although the general practice is to have a jack-plane at the outset, a trying-plane is perhaps the more useful tool, as the majority of the material employed, especially at the beginning, should be bought ready prepared.

The Hammer, three types of which are represented in Fig. 1, is perhaps the most frequently used tool. It is made in various forms, sizes and weights. A good hammer has a cast-steel head and when made by a reliable firm is a well-formed, nicely-balanced tool, with its striking-face made slightly convex to prevent damage to the timber when the hammer strikes the surface.

The Claw-hammer (shown at A in Fig. 1) is recommended as the amateur's first choice because, in addition to being a striking-tool, it is useful for extracting nails when pincers are not available. If the nail to be withdrawn is a long one,

it is advisable to place a piece of wood under the head to obtain a more direct pull, as a nail usually comes out straight. This method prevents the nails from being pulled, as it were, round a corner.

The Warrington Hammer (represented at B) is a favourite tool among woodworkers, and may be termed a general purpose hammer. It has a wedge-shaped edge opposite the striking face, which is useful for hammering in confined spaces or starting small brads and nails.

The Tack-hammer (C) is useful for light work, such as cabinet-making, and driving in small brads, panel pins and the like.

The Mallet (shown in Fig. 2) consists of a wooden head made of hardwood—usually beech, but better in apple wood—fitted to an ash shaft or handle. It is used principally for striking the wooden handles of chisels, gouges, etc., where the use of a hammer would damage the tool. The head is generally rectangular in form. As a rule the shaft is fitted to the head in a similar way to that used in the pickaxe; that is, the handle is made larger at the head end, which enables the shaft to pass through the hole in the head. This causes it to bind and grip the head firmly.

Mallets may be obtained in several sizes, but a medium-sized tool usually satisfies the needs of the amateur craftsman.

The practical man requires at least two saws, one for cutting large work and the other for smaller work at the bench.

The Panel-saw (an illustration of which appears at Fig. 3) is a general purpose saw and therefore a useful tool from the amateur point of view. It is usually about 22 in. in length and has from 6 to 8 teeth to the inch.

The Rip-saw is about 28 in. in length and has coarser teeth than the panel-saw,

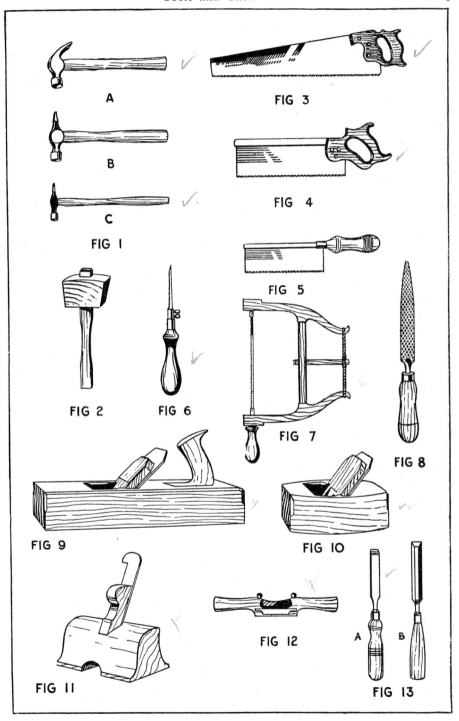

FIG 3

A

B

C

FIG 1

FIG 4

FIG 5

FIG 2

FIG 6

FIG 7

FIG 8

FIG 9

FIG 10

FIG 11

FIG 12

A

B

FIG 13

usually 3 or 4 to the inch. It is used for cutting in the direction of the grain of the wood.

Cross-cutting Saw.—For cutting across the grain a cross-cutting saw is used. One having 6 teeth to the inch is a useful type, as it can be used for sawing both hard and soft wood.

When purchasing any of the saws mentioned above, you are strongly recommended to get one of a reliable make, otherwise you are likely constantly to rue your purchase. A good saw should be made with an even temper throughout, springy and elastic. If badly tempered or soft it will soon get dull and consequently need frequent sharpening. An inferior saw usually buckles easily, and gets out of truth, which defies reasonably correct sawing. In a good saw the point end of the blade can be bent to touch the handle, and when released should fly back to its original position without showing any sign of distortion.

Tenon-saw.—Fig. 4 shows a tenon- or back-saw as it is sometimes called. It is much smaller than the hand-saw and is essentially a bench tool although sometimes used off the bench. As its name implies, it is used principally for cutting tenons. Tenon-saws vary from about 12 in. to 16 in. in length and have about 10 teeth to the inch. As the blade is very thin a thickened piece of steel or brass is attached to the back to keep it rigid.

The Dovetail-saw is a small edition of the tenon-saw and has about 12 teeth to the inch. It is used for fine work such as dovetailing, etc.

Brass-back Saw.—Fig. 5 shows a small brass-back saw, which is extremely handy and should find a home in every woodworker's kit.

Pad-saw.—Fig. 6 represents a pad-saw or, as it is sometimes called, a keyhole saw. It is fitted with a narrow,

tapering blade which makes it particularly useful for cutting curves, both external and internal, keyholes, etc. The blade is adjustable and slides in the handle. It is kept in position by two binding screws. This feature enables the blade to be shortened or lengthened as required. As the blade is rather soft it is liable to buckle, so care must be taken when being used to avoid twisting. In selecting a pad-saw get one with an 8-in. blade.

The Compass- or **Lock-saw** is very similar to a pad-saw, but as the handle is a fixture the length of the blade cannot be adjusted.

The Bow-saw (Fig. 7) is a sort of frame-saw with the blade held in tension by means of a twisted cord similar to that in the tourniquet. It has a very narrow blade which allows small curves to be negotiated. As a rule it is used when the curve starts from the edge of the wood. Its place, from the handyman's point of view, is easily taken by the pad-saw and the fretsaw.

Rasp.—As its name implies, a rasp is used for rasping or filing, and is handy for finishing off inside curved work after it has been cut out with a pad-saw. The amateur would be well advised to include one in his outfit. The form recommended is the shoemaker's rasp, of the half-round, medium-smooth type, as shown in Fig. 8.

A plane—one of the most important tools in woodworking—as its name signifies, is used for preparing plane surfaces. Planes can be obtained in either wood or metal, in various shapes and sizes, each of which is designed for its particular purpose.

Try-plane.—Fig. 9 shows a try-plane, which should be acquired by the amateur in preference to a jack-plane, as most of the timber used will be bought ready prepared. It consists of a stock or body—usually made of beech as this material is more or less free from twisting and warping—provided with a handle for propelling it along the work, a plane-iron, and a hardwood wedge to keep the iron in position. The bottom or sole of the tool is perfectly flat, and has a slot across it through which the cutting-edge of the iron projects. The thickness of the shaving it is intended to cut is regulated by the amount of cutting-edge exposed to the work, and is adjusted by means of the wedge. Plane-irons are made of steel and are fitted with a back-iron screwed to the blade. This extra iron gives additional support to the cutter and breaks the shavings when being cut. To loosen the iron the body of the plane is held in the left hand and struck smartly with a mallet on the top at the front end of the tool.

Smoothing-plane.—Fig. 10 shows a smoothing-plane, which is a much smaller tool than the try-plane. It is used for finishing a surface after it has been trued up with a try-plane. As the tool is held differently to the try-plane a handle is unnecessary. The iron is loosened by holding the body with the left hand and supporting the wedge and iron with the thumb and then smartly tapping the back end of the tool.

Router-plane.—Fig. 11 shows a type of plane called a router, or "old woman's tooth." It is not very often seen in these days, yet it is, nevertheless, extremely useful for finishing housing joints used in the uprights for shelves and partitions in drawers, etc. It consists of a narrow plough-iron fixed by a wedge in a suitably shaped piece of hardwood, and is held with both hands. When using the tool it is advisable to choose an iron of less width than the groove to be cleared. The groove is made in the ordinary way with the saw and chisel and then followed by the router, which is first worked from one edge of the wood towards the centre and then

from the opposite edge towards the centre.

Other planes include the rebate, the plough, and various beading and moulding planes, and others for special purposes.

Many of these planes are duplicated in metal. They are heavier, but they have the advantage that the sole does not wear away as in the case of a wooden plane. The plane-iron is adjustable to various cutting angles within its range, by means of a screw adjuster. This feature is very useful as it enables the plane-iron to be altered to suit soft or hard wood.

The Spokeshave (Fig. 12) is what may be termed a small double-handled plane and is used for finishing curved surfaces. There are several types, all of which work on the draw-knife principle, that is, a cut may be taken by drawing the tool over the work, or it may be pushed to obtain the cut. The blade can be set for fine or coarse cuts. The spokeshave is not a particularly easy tool to use and only light cuts can be taken.

In Fig. 13 (at A and B) are shown two types of wood chisels, known as the firmer and paring respectively.

The Firmer-chisel is the tool most commonly used and may be termed a general purpose chisel. They are to be obtained in sizes ranging from $\frac{1}{16}$ in. to about 2 in. The hardened steel blade containing the cutting-edge is generally fitted into an ash or boxwood handle having a brass ferrule to prevent splitting. For ordinary everyday work a set of chisels, $\frac{1}{4}$, $\frac{1}{2}$, $\frac{3}{4}$ and 1 in. wide, fitted with octagonal handles, should be included in the tool equipment.

A Mortice-chisel is used for cutting mortices, and has a thick blade, so formed to help to keep the mortice true. Like all chisels it has a bevel on its cutting face. If the flat side of the tool is not held firmly against the edge of the cut it usually cuts inwards, and if held with the bevel to the cut it will cut outwards. A mortice-chisel is not much used in these days by the amateur, as the brace and twist-bit is generally used for first removing the waste, followed by a firmer-chisel for finishing.

The Paring-chisel is similar to a firmer, except that the blade is not so thick and the front and side edges are bevelled. As its name suggests, it is used for paring wood.

To get the best results when using chisels they must be sharp, for good work cannot be done with blunt tools, as they tend to bruise the wood more than cut it. A chisel should never be struck by a hammer: the mallet is the correct tool to use for this. If a mallet is not available, use a piece of wood, say, 9 or 10 in. long and 2 in. square, thinned down at one end to form a handle.

Gouges are really chisels with a curved cutting-edge and are used for circular work. They are to be obtained with either externally or internally ground cutting-edges. For general work the internally-ground tool will be found useful. An internal- and an external-ground gouge are illustrated in Fig. 14 at A and B respectively.

Brace bits, gimlets and bradawls come under the heading of boring tools.

The Bradawl (illustrated in Fig. 15) is made in many sizes. It is a very simple tool and consists of a blade with a wedge-shaped cutting-edge, fixed into a handle. It is used mostly for making small holes for the insertion of nails or brads; hence its name. When using the bradawl the cutting-edge must be across the fibres of the wood, otherwise the wood will split. Force must be used when employing the tool, either by hand or tapping it with a hammer.

The Gimlet (Fig. 16) does not require force or pressure as it has a screwed point which draws the tool into the wood when turned by the handle. It is used principally for making holes for the insertion of screws, and can be obtained in many sizes. It is rather a dangerous tool, especially when used near the end of a piece of wood, as it is likely to split it. For such holes it is advisable to use a metal hand-drill fitted with a twist-drill (as illustrated by Fig. 17).

Bits.—Fig. 18 shows a number of boring bits in various forms extensively used by woodworkers. The bits are held in a brace, an illustration of which appears in Fig. 19. The object of the brace is to increase the speed of the revolutions of the bits and also to obtain leverage. The brace consists essentially of a crank fitted with a handpiece and a chuck for holding the tools. The bits are inserted in the jaws of the chuck and held tight by a screwed ferrule.

Bits can be obtained in a variety of shapes and forms for various purposes. The shell-bit shown at A in Fig. 18 is used mostly for boring small holes for screws, etc.; while the centre-bit at B is employed for making larger holes.

Braces.—There are two forms of braces, namely the plain brace and the ratchet. The former is being rapidly replaced by the latter as the ratchet brace embraces the two. The ratchet device enables the crank to be turned without the chuck, a feature which makes it particularly convenient when working in confined positions. The bit can be driven in (or extracted) by a partial turn of the crank, which when swung back has no effect on the bit, due to the sliding action of the driving pawl over the ratchet. A good type of brace to acquire is one having about an 8-in. sweep and fitted, of course, with the ratchet device.

The Centre-bit consists of a centre pin which guides the tool when cutting the hole, a nicker which severs the fibres of the wood, and a cutter which removes

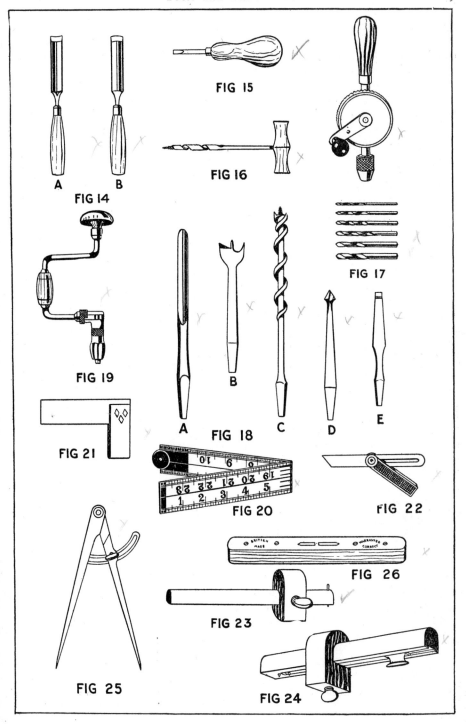

FIG 15

FIG 16

A   B
FIG 14

FIG 17

FIG 19

A   B   C   D   E
FIG 18

FIG 21

FIG 20

FIG 22

FIG 26

FIG 23

FIG 25

FIG 24

the waste. A centre-bit is used principally for making shallow holes, and makes a clean hole when sharp. When using this type of bit the work should be placed upon a piece of flat wood and the hole partially made until the point of the tool just appears at the back of the work. The work should then be reversed and the operation completed from the other side.

The Twist-bit is a very useful type of boring tool, and is illustrated at c in Fig 18. It is provided with a screwed tapered point, similar to that at the end of a gimlet, while the body of the tool is helical-shaped. When the boring operation is started, the screwed point draws itself into the wood and the cutter does its work without any perceptible pressure being applied at the top of the brace. Twist-bits can now be purchased quite cheaply, so it behoves the woodworker to include $\frac{1}{4}$, $\frac{1}{2}$, $\frac{3}{4}$ and 1 in. bits in his collection.

A Countersink-bit is used for removing the sharp edge of a screw hole to enable the head of the screw to lie flush with the surface. This tool is obtained in two forms. One called the snail-horn (as shown at D) is used for countersinking soft wood. The other, known as the rose or fluted head, is employed for hardwood.

A Screwdriver-bit (E) is another useful tool. In addition to its value in driving in screws it is also useful for removing obstinate ones, made possible by the extra leverage obtained by the brace.

Rule.—Among the many measuring tools employed by the woodworker the four-fold "two-foot" rule (illustrated in Fig. 20) is perhaps the most popular. It is hinged in three parts, which enables it to be conveniently carried in the pocket. A graduated scale in inches and fractions of an inch is engraved along each edge. Some rules are provided with a brass sliding piece with a projection at the outer end to enable the thickness of wood or the diameter of a screw to be easily gauged.

Try-square.—Fig. 21 shows a try-square used for marking work at right-angles. It usually consists of a blued steel blade riveted to a hardwood stock, the inner edge of which is faced with brass.

Bevel.—Another tool of a similar nature is the adjustable bevel (illustrated in Fig. 22). It consists essentially of a light hardwood stock, slotted at one end to take the blade, which is fastened by a clamping screw passing through the stock and the slot in the blade. This arrangement enables the blade to be set to any desired angle.

The Marking-gauge (Fig. 23) is used for marking lines or points parallel to the edge of the work. In its commonest form it consists of a hardwood bar about 9 in. in length, with a movable block sliding along it and fixed in position by a screw. The pointed end of a steel pin projects on the flat face at the end of the bar, which marks the work when the block is held in position and pushed along the edge. As the spike is often some appreciable distance from the end of the shank and therefore prevents its use for certain operations, it is advisable to get two gauges so that the end of one can be cut off close to the pin. This will be found extremely useful, for instance, when fitting hinges in awkward places.

The Mortice-gauge (as shown in Fig. 24), really a double marking-gauge, is constructed similarly to the marking-gauge. It is provided with two pins, one of which is adjustable to allow it to be set at any desired distance within its limits from the fixed pin. It is used when two parallel lines are required to be marked on the face of work when setting-out mortices and tenons, etc.

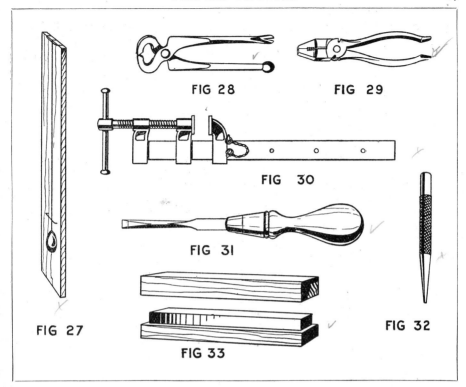

FIG 28   FIG 29

FIG 30

FIG 31

FIG 27   FIG 32

FIG 33

A **Cutting-gauge** is a tool similar to the marking-gauge, except that a cutting-edge takes the place of a pin. The cutter is held in position by a brass wedge to allow the depth of the cutter to be altered. The tool is handy for cutting thin strips of wood along the grain.

Dividers are used for several purposes, such as striking curves, transferring measurements from the rule to the work, marking out equal distances along work, etc. Fig. 25 shows a good type of dividers where to one leg is attached a quadrant, through a slot in which passes a screw on the other. When the legs are opened to the desired distance, a turn of the screw in the second leg presses upon the quadrant and locks them.

The Spirit-level (shown in Fig. 26) consists of a small glass tube containing methylated spirit set in a truly squared block of wood (sometimes metal), covered with a slotted brass plate exposing a short length of the tube. The plate is marked with a centre mark. When the instrument is placed on a truly level surface an air bubble appears which coincides with the mark. It is useful when fitting up shelves and other work where a truly horizontal position is required. When a long length of work is to be tested it is usual to interpose a length of trued-up wood between the work and the level.

Plummet-gauge.—Fig. 27 shows the plummet-gauge, used when it is required to fix a piece of work vertically, such as the uprights of a shed or garage. It consists of a metal plummet, a length of fine cord, and an accurately prepared strip of wood. A gauge-line is marked along the centre of the face, parallel with the sides, while the plummet is suspended by the cord from a saw-cut formed in the upper end of the rule and hangs freely in a hole made a few inches from the other extremity. In use, the long edge of the plumb-gauge is placed against the work, which is adjusted until the plumb-line coincides with the line on the rule.

Pincers.—Fig. 28 shows a pair of pincers commonly used for extracting nails. A good pair of pincers is made of forged steel. To prevent damage to the surface of the work a thin piece of wood should always be inserted between the tool and work.

Pliers.—Strictly speaking, pliers (Fig. 29) do not come under the category of woodworking tools, nevertheless such a tool should always be included in a woodworker's outfit. The tool is extremely useful for holding small articles and cutting wire, etc.

Iron Cramp.—Fig. 30 shows an iron cramp employed for drawing pieces of work together while gluing-up framing.

The Screw-driver (illustrated in Fig. 31) is used for turning screws. It takes many forms and sizes both with regard to the blade and handle. Many may be acquired in time, but for a beginning it is advisable to get one that corresponds as near as possible with the size of the slot of the screw used. If the end of the blade is larger than the screw-slot the wood round the screw-hole will be torn away. On the other hand, if it is too small, difficulty will be experienced in driving the screw home, and the edge of the tool perhaps destroyed. Ratchet screw-drivers are to be obtained at a reasonable figure, and have the additional advantage that they can be used in either a right- or left-hand direction as in the case of the ratchet brace.

Nail Punch.—One useful little tool which should not be overlooked is the nail punch—or nail set, as it is often called—shown in Fig. 32. It consists of nothing more than a tapered piece of hardened steel having a flat or a hollowed blunt point. It is used for sinking a nail below the surface of wood. If driven deeply, the hole is afterwards filled in with stopping, such as plastic wood.

Oilstone.—No tool equipment is complete without an oilstone for sharpening tools, an illustration of which appears in Fig. 33. It is used for producing a keen edge on cutting tools. There are several kinds of oilstone, among which Turkey, Arkansas, and Washita may be mentioned. The Washita stone, of medium hardness, is much favoured by professionals as it is close-grained, somewhat soft, quick cutting and produces a keen cutting-edge. A hard stone should be avoided, as it tends to polish rather than cut, and makes sharpening a tedious job. If the tool to be sharpened is badly chipped on its cutting-edge it should first be ground on a grindstone or an emery grinder; or, failing either of these, a coarse carborundum stone makes a good substitute. After grinding, the tool is finished on the oilstone after a few drops of thin oil have been applied to its surface. For general purposes, a stone about 9 in. by 2 in. by $1\frac{1}{4}$ in. should be obtained. Before being put into service the stone should be partially sunk into a solid block of wood about $\frac{1}{2}$ in. wider and longer than the stone, and a neat lid made in the same way to exclude dirt and grit. As oil is needed, a suitable oil-can should be obtained for its reception.

SAWS AND SAWING

THE types of hand-saws used by woodworkers for general use include a rip-saw for cutting timber along the grain, a cross-cutting saw for sawing across the grain, a panel-saw for general purposes, a tenon-saw, generally used on the bench, a pad-saw for cutting curves, and several others for special purposes.

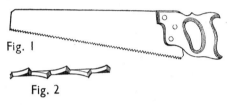

Fig. 1

Fig. 2

Fig. 1 shows an illustration of a saw blade from which it will be observed that it consists of a thin tapered blade of hardened and tempered steel having a number of triangular serrations on its lower edge. These teeth, as they are called, act like a number of chisels or cutters which sever the fibres of the wood when the blade is moved through it.

If you now look at Fig. 2, which shows a few saw-teeth enlarged, you will notice that they are not in the same plane as the rest of the blade, but are bent out alternately one side and then the other. The amount of this bending out is termed the "set" of the teeth. You will also notice that the fronts or faces of the teeth are sloped off to form points instead of edges. The reason for setting the teeth is to allow clearance for the blade, for if this was not provided for the blade would simply bind in the work.

Rip-saws are used for cutting along the grain and not across it. The teeth of these saws are comparatively large and shaped as illustrated in Fig. 3, that is,

the faces are usually at 90° to a line drawn through their tips, although in some intended for ripping softwood a slight amount of forward tilt is advisable. Rip-saws have four teeth to the inch in the usual practice for working softwood; while for hardwood a finer pitch of teeth is better—say, six to the inch, or even more.

Cross-cutting Saws are used for cutting timber across the grain and have a greater number of teeth to the inch compared with the rip-saw. For general purposes a saw having five to six teeth per inch is considered correct. The shape of the teeth is also different from the tool used for ripping. The faces of the teeth are set back, the amount depending upon the kind of wood to be operated upon. The harder the wood the more back slope is required. The tips of the teeth terminate in a fine point, due to the face and back being bevelled.

The correct way to hold such a saw is shown in Fig. 4, that is, with the fore-

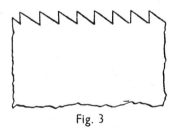

Fig. 3

finger extended along its handle and not through it, as seems the natural way of gripping the tool. This method is used to ensure control over the saw and accuracy when cutting along a guide line.

To saw correctly only comes with practice. The chief difficulty to over-

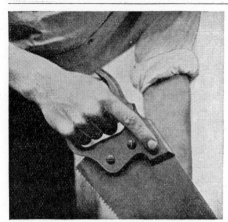

Fig. 4

come is that of keeping the saw square to the timber throughout the cut. Learn to cut squarely, and test with a square from time to time until you become proficient. Use as long strokes as possible and avoid sawing too quickly. A saw in good condition, that is, sharp, unbuckled, and correctly set, does not require pressure on the downstroke, so let it work by its own weight, simply pulling the saw slowly upward and pushing it slowly forward in long, even strokes. For easy cutting the saw should be nearly vertical.

Ripping.—When ripping, the board should always be supported on both sides of the cut to prevent the unsupported side from breaking off. A short board may either be laid along a sawing-trestle, or sawing-horse as it is sometimes called, with the end to be sawn overlapping the end of the trestle, or held in a vertical position in the bench vice, as shown in the illustration (Fig. 5). Start the cut by using the left thumb as a guide, as shown in Fig. 6, and push the saw blade very lightly against the wood so that it just nicks it, then continue until the slot is sufficiently deep to guide the saw. Keep the head well over the tool so that both sides can be seen. Move the saw to

and fro in a vertical plane, taking care to keep the cut parallel to the mark, not forgetting to leave sufficient waste for planing to size afterwards if this is necessary.

If the board is to be sawn into two or more equal widths, follow the marked lines so that the saw-cut divides the line equally on each side.

It sometimes happens that the saw does not follow the line, in which case give the saw a slight axial twist on the downstrokes until the desired result is obtained. Do not attempt to bend the saw blade over towards the line as such a procedure is useless.

One of the faults common to novices is that they try to saw far too quickly

Fig. 5

and do not use sufficiently long strokes. This is bad practice, as short strokes mean that some of the teeth are not doing their proper share of cutting, and are thus caused to wear unevenly.

It frequently happens, especially when ripping a long board from end to end, that the saw-cut closes and pinches the saw. This difficulty may be overcome by inserting a thin wooden wedge or the blade of a bradawl and following the saw up with it, as shown in Fig. 7. The wedge should be removed before finishing the cut to prevent the wood splitting.

Cross-cutting, or cutting across the grain of the wood, is not a difficult operation provided the cut is started in the right way. To do this, use the thumb as a guide for the blade in the same manner as in starting the rip-saw. Take two or three short upstrokes to get a start. Do not attempt to start

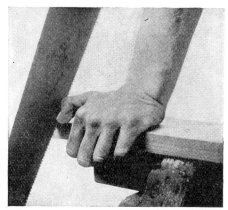

Fig. 6

on a downstroke as the saw is liable to jump, perhaps with disastrous results to one's hand.

To saw off the end of a board of given length, measure up the board and mark it with a pencil, guided by a square, to the desired size. If the board is a long one place the wood across two trestles—or boxes, if trestles are not available. Place the right knee upon the board to steady the wood. Start the cut just outside the line to allow sufficient waste for finishing off with a plane. The left hand can now be used

to help support the board. Cut across the wood, using long even strokes until near the end of the cut, when the strokes should be very light to prevent spoiling the edge.

If the amateur does not feel disposed

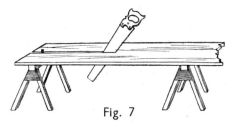

Fig. 7

to go to the expense of purchasing a rip-saw and a cross-cutting saw, the best equivalent to have is a panel-saw. Such a saw can be used for ripping, cross-cutting and, in a good many instances, for cutting wood where a tenon-saw would be normally employed. It is not, however, so efficient as the separate tools. A handy size to have is one with a 22 in. blade.

The Mitre- or Tenon-saw shown in Fig. 8 is a different type of tool from either the cross-cut or rip-saw, the blade being parallel and very thin. The upper edge is provided with a stiffened back of either brass or steel which somewhat restricts its use. The teeth are very much finer and more numerous, varying from 10 to 14 to the inch. It is usually employed on work held in the vice, or across a bench-hook, an

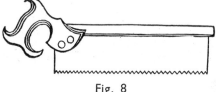

Fig. 8

illustration of which appears in Fig. 9. The bench-hook is a simple device for holding the work steady. It consists essentially of a flat piece of wood having a wooden block at the back edge of the top and a similar block fixed on the underside along the front edge. When a piece of wood is to be sawn, the bottom block of the bench-hook is placed against the front edge of the bench, and the material placed and pressed against the

Fig. 9

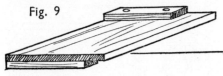

top with the left hand. The correct way to saw, when using the hook, is to start cutting with the saw gripped in the right hand with the index finger extended in the same way as the rip-saw is held, and the blade tilted up to an angle of about 30°, and as the sawing proceeds, gradually to bring the handle down until the saw is horizontal. An illustration of a bench-hook in use is seen in Fig. 10.

The tenon-saw is also used with a mitre-block for cutting mitres, etc.

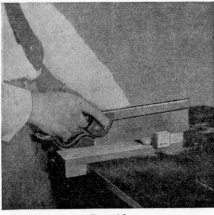

Fig. 10

For small work the mitre-block shown at A in Fig. 11 is employed, while for larger work a mitre-box illustrated at B is the correct accessory to use. The mitre-block is somewhat similar to the

bench-hook, the main difference being that the back block is provided with three vertical saw-cuts or slots, two at angles of 45° and the other of 90°, which serve as guides for the saw. The two angled slots are set in opposite directions for cutting mitre-angles, while the centre slot enables work to be cut perfectly true, at right-angles.

Mitre-block.—To use the mitre-block, first place a thin piece of wood on the base to prevent the saw damaging the surface when finishing the cut. Next place the work against the block and hold it firmly in position with the left hand. Gently saw down into the selected slot, taking care that the saw runs freely. Do not force the saw

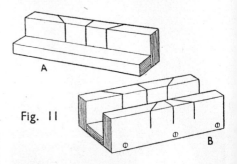

Fig. 11

against the sides of the slots or they will be enlarged, resulting in inaccurate work. Figure 12 shows a mitre-block in use.

The Mitre-box, as its name suggests, is box-shaped and is deeper than the mitre-block. It is used principally with the panel-saw for cutting mitres, etc., on deeper and larger mouldings than can be sawn on the block. Sawing is accomplished in the same way as with the mitre-block, and the same precautions should be taken to prevent forcing the saw and damaging the slots.

The craftsman would be well advised to drill two holes through the blade of his tenon-saw to enable a strip of wood to be screwed to the side of the blade, as

Fig. 12

shown in Fig. 13. This arrangement acts as a depth gauge, which will be found very useful when cutting shallow slots which have to be of uniform depth, such as grooves for shelves or partitions in drawers.

A **Dovetail-saw** is used for sawing small stuff. It is smaller than the tenon-saw, has an open handle, and usually has about 12 teeth to the inch. The tool is used in a similar way to the tenon-saw.

The Pad-saw is a very handy little tool for cutting curves either on the outside or inside of a piece of work. Fig. 14 shows such a tool. The blade is thin, narrow and tapered and is adjustable. It is held in the handle by

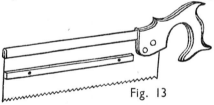

Fig. 13

means of two set-screws which allow the length of the blade to be adjusted at will. New blades can be purchased separately should you have the misfortune to break one. Fig. 15 shows the correct way to use a pad-saw. It will be noted that both hands are used for gripping the tool. The index finger of the right hand is extended to control the tool, as in using the hand-saw.

Owing to the fragile nature of the blade great care must be exercised to prevent buckling. This can be obviated to a great extent by exposing only sufficient length of blade, as may be necessary, and sawing with slow even strokes.

Bow-saw.—Another type of saw for cutting curves in wood is illustrated by Fig. 16, which shows a bow-saw. This type of saw is really a large fretsaw for working comparatively thick material. The blade is parallel, thin and narrow. It is fixed between the top and bottom arms of the frame, and is kept in tension

Fig. 14

by a strong, twisted string. When fitting the blade take care to insert it correctly, that is, in the opposite direction to that of a fretsaw, as the cutting strokes are made away from the operator.

To use the saw, grip the handle with both hands as shown in Fig. 17, and work the saw back and forth with steady

Fig. 15

even strokes. Avoid twisting the blade suddenly, otherwise you may break it, and always keep the blade at right angles to the work.

For cutting internal curves a small

hole must first be made in the work. One end of the blade is then unfastened and threaded through the hole in the same manner as a fretsaw.

When not in use it is a good plan to relieve the tension on the blade by untwisting the string.

As it is not a particularly pleasant

Fig. 17

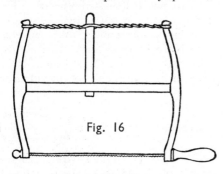

Fig. 16

job to resharpen a saw, steps should be taken to guard against the necessity. For instance, when sawing old wood

note well whether any nails are in the way of the saw-cut, as there is nothing like a nail to take the edge off the teeth. Avoid placing the saw teeth downwards on the bench; lean it on something at the back, teeth upwards; or, better still, hang it up when not in use.

PLANES AND PLANING

Planing, by which is meant finishing and smoothing work truly to size, is one of the most important processes in woodworking. It is for this reason that the amateur craftsman should be able to plane up a piece of work accurately, otherwise he will be seriously handicapped in the pursuit of his hobby. As with sawing, proficiency in planing is only obtained by practice.

The principal planes used by the amateur are the jack-, trying- and smoothing-planes; but for occasional use on special work he may find it necessary to employ a rebate, router, or one or more of the special planes suitable for the work in hand.

A plane (Fig. 1) is really a guided chisel, and usually consists of a stock

or body of hardwood which carries a cutting-iron held in position by a wedge, and in the case of a jack- and a try-plane a suitable handle for propelling

Fig. 1

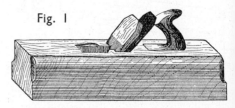

it along the work. The bottom surface, or sole as it is termed, is perfectly flat and has a slot through which the cutting-edge projects. The thickness of the shaving is determined by the amount of cutting-edge exposed below the face of the sole.

The irons employed in the jack-, trying- and smoothing-plane consist of two components, namely, the cutting-iron proper and a supporting iron, termed a back iron. The purpose of the back iron is to support the steel

Fig. 2

cutter and to break the shavings when being cut. (An illustration of a plane-iron appears in Fig. 2.)

If the rough sawn surface of a piece of wood has to be planed it is first rough-planed with a jack-plane to remove most of the waste material. This operation is followed by a trying-plane to obtain a straight and true surface, and lastly a smoothing-plane to give the material a smooth even finish.

The Jack-plane is usually about 16 in. long, fitted with a $2\frac{1}{8}$ in. wide cutting-iron. The edge of the cutter is slightly convex or rounded (as shown

A   B   C

Fig. 3

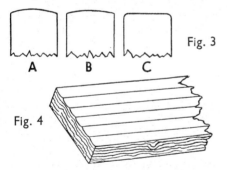

Fig. 4

at A in Fig. 3) to enable it to work freely and quickly. It produces a series of shallow grooves in the material (as illustrated in Fig. 4) which are afterwards removed by the trying-plane.

The back iron is usually set back about $\frac{3}{32}$ in. from the cutting-edge.

The Trying-plane is a similar tool to the jack-plane, the main difference being

2

that it is longer, usually about 22 in., which allows all the uneven or lumpy parts left from the jack-plane to be smoothed down. The cutter is about $\frac{3}{8}$ in. wider than the roughing tool and is ground slightly rounded (as at B in Fig. 3) but not so much as that of the jack-plane, while the back iron is set closer to the cutting-edge, usually about $\frac{1}{16}$ in.

A Smoothing-plane (an illustration of which appears in Fig. 5) is generally 7 to 8 in. in length and fitted with a $2\frac{1}{4}$ in. cutter. The cutting-edge is practically straight (C, Fig. 3), except at the ends, which are rounded off a trifle to prevent them scoring the work.

Fig. 5

The back iron is set nearly level with the cutting-edge, the distance being regulated according to the degree of finish required.

For the purpose of explaining the process involved in planing, it is assumed that a piece of rough sawn timber is to be finished, 3 ft. in length, 4 in. wide, and $1\frac{3}{4}$ in. thick for a certain piece of work.

Before beginning operations always examine the material to see that it is entirely free from grit or other foreign matter likely to dull the cutting-edge of the iron. Place the better side of the wood upwards flat on the bench-top, with one end against the bench-stop, taking care to see that the grain of the timber runs in the right direction, that is, the planing is done in the direction of the grain. Note also that the bench-stop is not allowed to project high enough to foul the plane when in use, especially if the stop is a metal one.

The first operation consists in making the work fairly smooth with a jack-plane. Grasp the handle of the tool with the right hand and place the front end of the stock flat on the work, putting the left hand on the front of the plane and keeping the thumb on the near side and the fingers on the other (as shown clearly in Fig. 6). Keep the fore end of the tool upon the work by pressing down hard on the stock. Now push the plane along the work until the

Fig. 6

cutter passes the farther end of the wood, gradually relieving the pressure as the tool approaches the end of the stroke. Draw the plane back to its original position, still keeping the left hand on the front, but, of course, without pressure, lifting the back of the tool a trifle to keep the cutter from touching the work. Continue the operation until the whole of the surface is planed. If the shaving is very thick and it takes a great deal of force to propel the tool it usually shows that the cutter is set too deeply, in which case the obvious remedy is to re-set the cutter so that the cutting-edge does not project so far below the sole. If, on the other hand, the shaving is too fine, one or two light taps on the top of the iron will generally have the desired effect.

Try to avoid the common error of removing too much at the farther end of the work, and also try to plane the timber perfectly flat, and not towards

Fig. 7

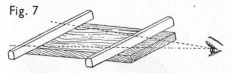

the sides as is often done by the un-initiated.

Testing.—The work should be tested from time to time, as one of the common faults found in timber is that it has a twist. This defect may be observed by holding the work on edge, closing one eye and looking over the near top edge. If it is seen that one end of the far edge stands up more than the other it must be planed down until it is level.

A more practical method of testing, however, especially when working narrow stuff, is the use of a pair of winding strips, which are simply two narrow strips of wood a foot or so in length with their edges planed perfectly parallel. The strips are placed on edge across the work parallel to one another, at convenient distances apart. A sight is then taken over their tops as indicated in Fig. 7, when any twist which occurs

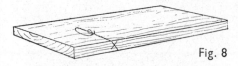

Fig. 8

is easily detected. The try-plane should be used for taking the twist out of work.

After a perfectly true surface has been obtained by the try-plane—which is used in the same way as the jack—a "face mark" should be pencilled on the face and edge you are going to true up next, as shown in Fig. 8. Now place the wood in the vice, better edge uppermost, with the face towards you,

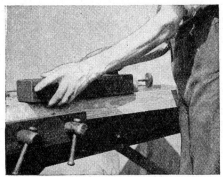

Fig. 9

as the next step is to square the edge. In planing the edge, grasp the handle of the plane with the right hand as already explained, but allow the finger-tips of the left to slide along the side of the work in the manner shown in Fig. 9. This procedure will help to steady the plane and keep it at right-angles to the already prepared face.

As the work progresses test for accuracy with a try-square. If the work is found to be out of square, correct the fault by tilting the tool a

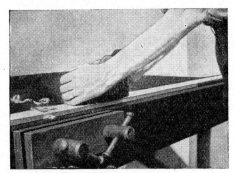

Fig. 10

trifle and remove the prominent parts. When the edge is finished pencil a **V** mark on it pointing to the face side.

Remove the work from the vice and mark out on the face side the exact width the work is to be, using a marking-gauge for the purpose. Set the marking-gauge and run the point along the face

by moving the stock of the tool along the face edge. When this edge has been planed down to size and tested for squareness from the face, the work should be placed prepared face downward, to enable the remaining face to be planed. Before this can be done, however, the exact depth must be gauge-marked on the sides, by running the gauge stock along the face - edges. When this has been planed to size, the whole may be skimmed over with the smoothing-plane.

The Smoothing-plane has no handle and it is used in the manner indicated in

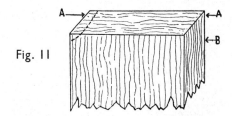

Fig. 11

Fig. 10. As this tool is essentially a finishing tool, the plane-iron should be very sharp, and set very "fine," that is, the cutting-edge should only project beyond the sole by the merest fraction of an inch, to produce a very fine shaving.

The work is now ready for cutting to length. Measure the distance with a rule, and mark the positions on the face of the work. Square a line across the face and round the edges at each end, and carefully saw on the *outside* of these lines. Fix the work end upwards in the vice, as the final operation consists of planing the ends, which are, of course, planed on end grain. Do not attempt to plane right across the end, otherwise the opposite edge will be damaged, but work first from one edge to the centre and then from the opposite side towards the centre as indicated at A in Fig. 11 or, in cases where the preservation of the edge is immaterial, first remove the far corner—shown

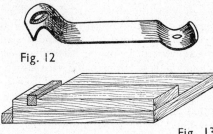

Fig. 12

Fig. 13

by the dotted lines—with a sharp chisel, and then plane across the surface in the direction indicated by the arrow at B.

As the long edges of work are usually sharp after planing, it is a good plan to remove the "arris," as the sharp edge is called, by either running the smoothing-plane held at an angle along the edges, or by using a cornering tool (illustrated

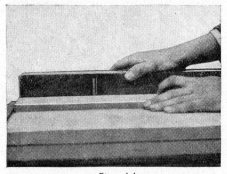

Fig. 14

in Fig. 12). Such a tool can be obtained from almost any tool-dealer for a few pence.

The Shooting - board. — Fig. 13 shows a useful planing device. It is used for shooting or planing the edges of comparatively thin material, both with the grain and across the end grain. The board consists of an accurately planed and trued wooden base about a foot wide, an inch thick, and varying in length from 24 in. upwards. On the top of the base is a narrower prepared board running lengthwise and flush with the front of the base, and kept in position by

screws driven in from the underside. A hardwood stop is grooved into the top member near the left-hand end, and as the base is liable to twist, a strengthening batten fixed on the underside at the ends is advisable.

In use the board is placed against the bench-stop, as shown in the illustration, and the work against the stop on the board. The plane is used with its side resting on the base and its cutting-

Fig. 15

edge towards the edge of the work to be prepared. The work is kept in position with the left hand while the right one propels the plane as pictured in Fig. 14.

When shooting the end-grain edge of a piece of work it is a good plan to insert a small piece of accurately prepared wood between the work and the stop, keeping the front edge of the piece flush with the edge to be planed. Its use ensures proper support to the corner of the work and prevents it from splitting off.

Always plane to a drawn line even

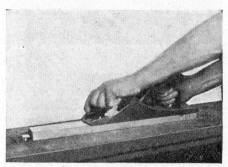

Fig. 16

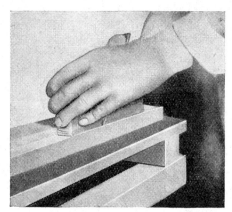

Fig. 17

useful planes for special purposes. These include the rebating and the plough plane.

The Rebating Plane is used for finishing rebates or shoulders along the edge of a piece of wood as shown in Fig. 17. The plane is fitted with a cutting blade as wide as the body in order to cut right into the angles.

The Plough Plane (Fig. 18) is used for cutting grooves in the edges or faces of work, as indicated in Fig. 19. The tool consists of a stock and a set of cutting irons of different widths. The depth of cut is regulated by means of a thumbscrew.

Fig. 18

Fig. 19

when using a shooting-board. If possible, mark the line with a scribing knife. A pencil line has the disadvantage that it can get planed out easily or otherwise obliterated, but a knife-scribed line leaves a clean, clear cut to work to.

Metal Planes, that is, planes having an iron stock as represented in Fig. 15 are becoming increasingly popular, especially in the smaller types. (Fig. 16 shows a metal plane in use.)

Although the jack-, trying- and smoothing-planes are the most generally used planes, there are one or two

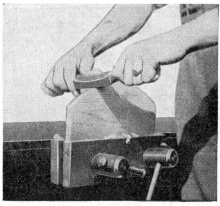

Fig. 20

A Spoke-shave is an elementary type of plane used for smoothing curved surfaces, either convex or concave. It consists of a cutting blade supported by a double-handled stock of either wood or metal. In the wooden type the blade is provided with two tapered square section projections, or pegs, which fit into corresponding holes in the stock.

The blade is adjusted by tapping the tops of the pegs. (Fig. 20 shows how the tool is used.) Care must be taken to work "with the grain," and in some instances it will be found an advantage to push the tool across the surface to be finished, rather than to pull it. For ordinary work a 9-in. tool will be found useful.

MARKING OUT

ACCURATE marking out is the first step in the production of good work. Unless the job in hand is carefully marked at the outset, and however skilfully the subsequent operations may have been done, there is little likelihood

Fig. 1

of the finished product being anything but a failure.

The actual tools required for marking out a particular piece of work naturally vary with the kind of work, but fortunately the tools necessary for marking ordinary "everyday" work call for only a few quite inexpensive items such as a pencil, scribing-knife, rule, squares, marking-gauge, and dividers.

A Lead Pencil is generally used for marking where no high degree of accuracy is needed, but in cases where great precision is necessary—as in setting out joints and cabinet making—it is better to use either a scribing-knife or a chisel edge, as the clean cut obtained by these tools leaves a fine definite line.

The lead pencil should be sharpened to a fine chisel point as shown in Fig. 1, as it produces a clear thin line. For marking a line for rough sawing this is, of course, unnecessary.

A Rule is indispensable for measuring. The most useful and handy type for general work is perhaps the 2 ft. fourfold rule, as it can be easily carried about in the pocket.

For rough measurements it can be used flat, but for exact marking it should be held edgewise direct on the work. This is necessary because it is extremely difficult to judge and mark accurately

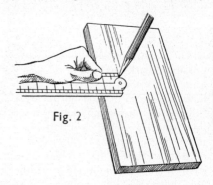

Fig. 2

the precise point required when the division lines of the rule are even only a small fraction of an inch above the work. You can prove this by trying it.

It is frequently necessary to draw a line parallel to a planed edge of a prepared board as, for instance, in marking out a strip preparatory to sawing. This can be done quite easily by adopting the method shown in Fig. 2. Place the work so that its long edge overlaps the front of the bench by an inch or so, and make a pencil mark at the desired distance from the long edge, near the end. Place the pencil point on the mark and bring the rule, held flatly in the left hand, up to the point, keeping the forefinger up to the edge of the work to act as a guide. Now draw the rule and pencil along the entire length of the board, taking great care to keep the rule at right-angles to the edge.

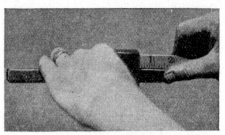

Fig. 5

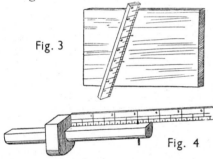

Fig. 3

Fig. 4

Marking into Equal Widths.—A quick method of marking a board into a given number of equal widths is shown in Fig. 3. Place the rule on edge obliquely across the surface with one end touching one edge, and at the other a number of inches which is a multiple of the required number of widths, and mark the wood opposite the division mark of each multiple. For example, if a 6-in. board is to be divided into four strips of equal width, then by placing the zero end of the rule against an edge and the 8-in. division on the other, the desired distances will fall at the 2-, 4-, and 6-in. divisions, which give four spaces each $1\frac{1}{2}$ in. wide. Parallel lines are then drawn along the board at these positions.

Similarly, in dividing the same board into three equal widths, the rule would be set across at the 9 in. division and the surface marked at the 3-in. and 6-in. points respectively.

The Marking-gauge (Fig. 4) is one of the most important tools in the setting-out equipment. It is used for marking parallel lines. The gauge is a very simple tool consisting of a hardwood stem having a steel pin near one end for marking the wood, and an adjustable fence which slides along the stem. The fence is set by sliding it along the bar until the distance between the pin point and the fence is equal to the width required, and then locked by a hardwood screw or other suitable device.

Fig. 5 shows the correct way to set a gauge. To do this, first slack off the screw to enable the fence to slide easily along the stem. Hold the bar with the left hand, placing the thumb on the edge of the fence to steady it, and then place the zero end of the rule

Fig. 6

squarely against the side of the fence, resting the long edge of the rule on the stem. Gradually push the rule along the bar until the required measurement appears opposite the marking point.

Fig. 7

Keep the fence in this position by pressing it with the left thumb and tighten the screw.

Test with the rule to make sure that the fence has not shifted. If it has, it can be altered a trifle by tapping one end or the other of the stem on the bench. Tap the marking end if the fence has shifted away from the pin, and the other end if it is too close.

A common method of holding and using a marking-gauge is shown in Fig. 6. Rest the end of the work on the bench, but if the wood is not of sufficient thickness to enable the fence to clear the bench-top, place it upon another piece. Hold the tool in the right hand, keeping the thumb behind the marking point, and place the forefinger over the fence to steady it. Now press the fence close up to the edge of the work and push the tool along the work in the direction of the grain, keeping the top of the marking pin tilted slightly forward, so that the point lightly marks the wood. Now repeat the process, applying a little more pressure on the

pin. The reason for marking it twice is that if a deep cut is made at the outset the point is liable to follow the grain and consequently mark an imperfect line. It is for this reason also that the fence must always be pressed hard up to the edge of the work.

It should be noted that a marking-gauge should never be used for marking wood across the grain.

A Mortice-gauge is really an ordinary gauge having an additional point which can be adjusted. This allows two parallel lines to be marked simultaneously.

As its name implies it is used for setting-out mortices, the second point being set at the required distance from the fixed one to suit the width of the mortice.

As the width of a chisel used in marking a mortice should be equal to the width of the mortice, the gauge is usually set from the cutting edge of the chisel in the manner shown in Fig. 7. The tool is used in the same way as the ordinary gauge.

The Try-square is used when marking right-angles to the trued edges of wood. In using the tool it is absolutely essential that the stock be held firmly against the work before the scribing-knife or pencil

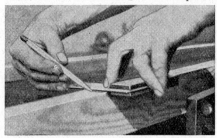

Fig. 8

is drawn along the edge of the blade, and that the edge of the work being marked be perfectly straight.

A square having a 6-in. blade will generally be found large enough for small work, but such a tool is obviously too small for marking across a 9-in. board.

Fig. 8 shows a square being used for marking a line across a piece of work. To do this, first mark the exact position where the line is to be scribed, then, still keeping the point of the pencil on the mark, slide the square along the edge of the work until the blade just touches the pencil point. Draw the line across, holding the left hand pressed against the back of the stock to keep it in position, as shown clearly in the illustration.

When several pieces of wood of equal size are to be similarly marked, as, for instance, in setting out the stiles or the rails for a cabinet door, it is much better to clamp them together and mark the lot than to mark them individually. This method not only makes for more accurate marking but also saves a great deal of time. When the preliminary guide lines have been marked it is an easy

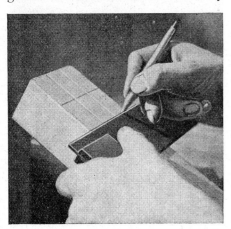

Fig. 9

matter to continue the lines round the work where necessary, with the aid of a try-square. Fig. 9 shows a number of pieces being marked simultaneously.

Do not always take the accuracy of a try-square for granted, because it is

2*

easily put out of truth if roughly handled or allowed to drop on the floor.

To Test the Accuracy of a Square, plane up a perfectly straight and true edge on a piece of wood. Scribe a line

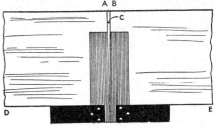

Fig. 10

across the wood in the normal way and then turn the blade over and scribe another line, as shown in Fig. 10. If the square is accurate the two lines should coincide. If the tool is inaccurate the error will be shown doubled by the difference between the two lines.

Thus, in Fig. 10, the line DE represents the true edge of the board, and a line is drawn with the square held in a normal position A, while that at B shows the position of the blade when turned over. The space at c indicates the amount of error doubled.

This error can be corrected by fixing the square, blade horizontal, in the vice and carefully filing the top of the blade from the stock to the other end, using a smooth file for the purpose. The first stroke should be short and each succeeding stroke a trifle longer. Do not make a heavy cut, and take care to keep the file almost parallel with the edge of the blade. Test frequently and when true, remove the tool from the vice, and finish off the edge on an oilstone or rub it gently, lengthwise, on a piece of fine sandpaper laid on a true surface. The same operation must be carried out if the blade is full at the other end,

Fig. 11

but, of course, that end gets most attention.

The Adjustable Bevel is used for setting-out and testing angles on work. The tool in use is shown in Fig. 11. It is similar to the try-square except that the stock is narrower and slotted at the top to accommodate a thin parallel-edged blade which is also slotted. The blade is held securely in position by means of a screw passing through the stock and the slot in the blade.

To set the bevel, first slack off the fastening screw a trifle so that the blade is not too slack in the stock; and adjust the blade to the desired angle, and tighten up the screw. Test for accuracy, as the blade may have shifted a trifle whilst being tightened up. Should any

Fig. 12

slight inaccuracy be detected, tap the blade on a piece of wood and again verify. The tool is then used in the same way as the try-square, care being

taken to keep the stock pressed tightly against the edge of the surface to be marked.

Dividers are useful for transferring measurements from one piece of work to another, and from the rule to the work. The tool is also handy for dividing the distance between two given marked points into equal parts, where it could not be conveniently done with a rule. To use the dividers for this purpose, the trial and error method is adopted. The legs are first opened to approxi-

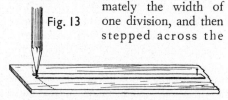

Fig. 13

mately the width of one division, and then stepped across the

work between the two marked points. If the distance between the points of the dividers does not exactly divide into the

Fig. 14

overall dimensions they should be reset and again tried until the number of steps does divide equally into the marked positions.

In the absence of compasses, dividers may be used for scribing circles and curves. The legs are first opened to correspond to the radius required and the point of one leg is placed on the centre-mark of the circle or arc to be described, as shown in Fig. 12. The tool is then held at the top and twisted round so that the point of the other leg lightly marks the work.

If the point at the centre is likely to make an undesirable mark on the work, a thin piece of wood should be interposed, taking care that it does not slip. If this is likely to happen, place a piece of sandpaper rough side down on the work and moisten the underside of the wood.

A Home-made Beam Compass.— The professional generally uses a beam compass or a trammel for scribing large circles or curves. This can be improvised out of a thin strip of wood a little longer than the desired length of the radius of the circle or curve. A notch is made at one end to guide the pencil point, and a thin nail is driven through the lath near the other, at a distance from the pencil-point equal to the radius required. To use the device, all that is necessary is to drive the nail lightly into the work at the desired centre, place the pencil point into the notch, and move the lath round. This simple yet effective contrivance is shown in Figs. 13 and 14.

It frequently happens that a number of small pieces of the same size and shape have to be marked out. In all such cases an enormous amount of time will be saved by making a template and using it as a guide in marking out. For instance, in marking out dovetail pins, a piece of thin sheet zinc or brass can be cut out with an old pair of scissors to the exact size and shape of the pins, as illustrated in Fig. 15. The template can then be used as a guide for the point of the marker so that each pin is exactly the same size. The same thing applies for larger work, or for the marking of awkward corners. In a great many instances stiff cardboard could be used with advantage instead of sheet metal.

Fig. 15

NAILS AND SCREWS

ALTHOUGH there are many methods of fastening pieces of wood together, such as gluing, dowelling, wedging, etc., nailing and screwing are possibly the ones most commonly used by the amateur.

Nails are made in numerous shapes and sizes, each designed to suit a particular purpose. The novice should, therefore, get familiar with the commonest sorts of nails and screws so that he will then be able to choose the correct fastener to suit his purpose.

Types of Nail.—Fig. 1 from A to I shows a few types of nails for what may be termed everyday use.

That shown at A represents an oval wire nail, so called because its shape is practically oval and it is made from wire. It is an excellent nail for general purposes, has good gripping power and does not split the wood, provided it is driven in with its largest diameter parallel to the grain. As it has a small head it can be punched under the surface without leaving an unsightly hole. Oval wire nails can be obtained from ½ in. to 6 in. in length, the thickness varying with the length.

The French or Round wire nail illustrated at B may be obtained from 1 in. to 10 in. in length. It is used for more or less rough work and has great holding power. A French nail has a larger head than an oval wire nail and as it is more robust it does not bend so easily. Owing to the large size of the head it cannot be sunk below the surface.

A Cut Clasp Nail is illustrated at C and, as will be seen, it is an entirely different kind of nail to the wire as it is punched from sheet metal. It is more or less rectangular in section and tapers in its width from the top of the shank downwards, terminating in a blunt unpointed end. Like oval brads, clasp nails are driven in parallel with the grain of the wood.

The nail shown at D is a floor brad specially designed for nailing down floorboards.

The illustration at E represents a wrought clasp nail and these were once made by hand. It has the advantage that it is more flexible than the cut nail, which makes it particularly useful for clinched work, that is, where a nail is driven through two pieces of wood and its end knocked over or clinched on the reverse side. Owing to the high cost of manufacture it is seldom used.

A Clout Nail (F) has a thin flat head which is larger compared with its length than any of the nails previously referred to. This feature makes it particularly useful for fastening down roofing felt. When used for outdoor work the galvanised kind should be employed.

Panel Pins are an extremely useful kind of fastener from the amateur's point of view. They are made from very thin wire and have a tiny head which makes them extremely handy for fastening small work, such as beadings, etc. They may be obtained in sizes varying from $\frac{1}{2}$ in. to 2 in. in length. A panel pin is shown at G.

Needle Points, shown at H, are used for fastening very small work. They

are headless and brittle. In use they are driven partially into the work and a tap on the side with a hammer breaks off the projection flush with the surface, which makes them practically invisible.

Tacks, represented at I, are a form of small nail with a very sharp point and fairly large head. They are used more for household purposes, such as fastening down carpets and the like, than for woodwork.

When nailing two pieces of wood together where the top piece is thinner than that at the bottom—as indicated in Fig. 2—a nail nearly three times as long as the thickness of the top piece should be employed. Thus if the upper piece is 1 in. thick, a nail at least $2\frac{1}{2}$ in. in length should be employed. This is an arbitrary figure, however, and cannot always be adhered to.

In cases where a piece of wood has to be fastened to another piece with the nail going into the end grain, in the manner shown in Fig. 3, a longer nail than that previously mentioned is necessary, as nails do not grip so well in the end grain. For example, if the thickness of the top piece is 1 in., a 3-in. nail would be the minimum size to use.

When fastening two pieces of wood of equal thickness together, a nail a little longer than the combined thicknesses can be used. This allows the ends of the nails to be hammered over or clinched, as shown in Fig. 4. The proper way to do this is to drive all the

A B C D

H

I

E F G FIG I

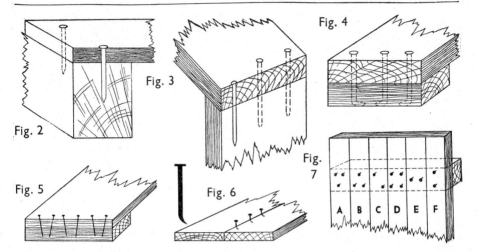

Fig. 4
Fig. 3
Fig. 2
Fig. 5
Fig. 6
Fig. 7

| A | B | C | D | E | F |

nails in first, turn the work upside down and hammer over the ends by striking them on their sides. To prevent the heads from being driven back, the heads should rest upon a piece of heavy metal, such as an anvil, or, failing this, a domestic flat-iron fixed sole upwards in the vice will generally answer the purpose.

In the event of the clinching method being objected to on account of its unsightliness on the back face, the nails should be driven in at an angle to form "dovetails," as indicated in the drawing at Fig. 5.

Fig. 6 shows a method of making a nailed butt joint. Before inserting the nails bend them at the tip as indicated.

Hammering.—When driving a nail do not forget that a series of smart taps at the finish is better than heavy blows and less likely to damage the wood. The hammer should be held near the end of the shaft and used from the wrist and not the arm.

Always bore holes where nails are to be driven in near the end of a piece of wood to avoid splitting. These may be bored with a sharp bradawl, but when using a bradawl see that its cutting-edge cuts across the fibres of the wood and

not with it. If the nails are large ones make the holes with a twist-drill, the diameter of which should be smaller than that of the nail. Nails should never be driven into hardwood at whatever positions they may be required without drilling holes first.

Fig. 7 shows three common methods of nailing boards to a supporting batten as, for instance, in fastening matchboards to a cross-piece or ledge of a door. The main object to be aimed at in dealing with work of this description is to arrange the positions of nails in such a way that they do not split the boards or the support, and to ensure that the whole width of the board makes good contact with the cross-piece.

From the above it follows that those at A, B, C, and D fulfil these conditions, while those at E and F do not.

In good work it is usual to sink the nail-heads a little below the surface and then fill the cavity with one of the various fillers, such as plastic wood.

A Steel Nail Set or **Punch** is used for sinking nails; illustrations of these appear at A and B in Fig. 8. Nail punches may be obtained in rectangular or in round section steel, the former

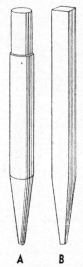

A   B

Fig. 8

having small flats on its tapered end while the end of the latter is cup-shaped to prevent it slipping off the head of the nail. It is a good plan to have two nail sets: one of the rectangular type for large nails and a round one for small.

The Punch is used by presenting the tapered end to the head of the nail and giving it a slight blow with a hammer, driven in the same direction as the nail. Fig. 9 shows a nail set in use.

Fig. 10 shows a method of hiding a nail head, called secret nailing. It is used in high-class work where a nail-head, even if punched below the surface and "stopped," is objected to. To

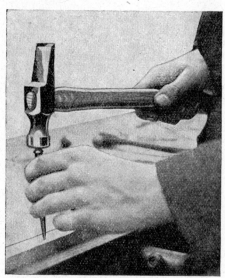

Fig. 9

carry out this process all that is necessary is first to lift a tiny portion of the surface of the wood in the direction of the grain

with a sharp narrow chisel, at a point where the nail has to enter. Then drive the nail in and bury the head by punching it down. Glue down the raised strip and, when dry, sandpaper the surface or run a very finely set smoothing plane over it.

In nailing, it sometimes happens that the hammer-head slips off the head of a nail and dents the wood. This is not always due to bad workmanship, but very often caused by the face of the hammer becoming greasy and dirty. When this occurs, clean the striking face by rubbing it on the floor.

Hammer Marks are difficult to remove, but if the dent is treated at once with water, allowed to dry thoroughly and then levelled over with sandpaper, the water may have swelled the wood sufficiently to make the fault almost invisible.

As it is sometimes necessary to withdraw nails, do not forget to use a piece of wood between the work and the jaw of the pincers, as illustrated in Fig. 11.

Screws are used where greater strength is required than that produced by nails, and where the parts to be fastened are likely to be taken to pieces at some future time.

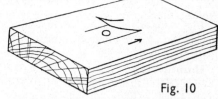

Fig. 10

The screw is very much more powerful in holding the parts together and drawing the parts tightly to one another. It is based on the principle of the inclined plane, one of the most powerful of the mechanical forces.

Screws, like nails, are made in numerous sizes, but the difference of shape is generally confined to the heads.

The commonest types of screws are

made of iron or brass, while copper and gun-metal are used for screws for special purposes.

The most frequently used screw is possibly the countersunk-headed screw, shown at A in Fig. 12. It is employed

Fig. 11

where a flush surface is required. The round-head screw illustrated at B is used mainly for fastening fittings, such as locks, door-bolts, etc., where countersunk-headed screws could not be conveniently employed, and in cases where the wood is too thin to countersink.

The raised head (c) is a sort of "half-way house" between the countersunk and the round head.

Wood-screws may be obtained in sizes ranging from $\frac{1}{4}$ in. in length, as used by the cabinet-maker for fixing small hinges, etc., up to 9 in. The diameters of screws are known by their gauge numbers; the thicker the screw the higher the gauge number. Thus a 1 in. No. 8 screw is thicker than a No. 6.

When fastening two pieces of wood together, as in Fig. 13, a clearing hole— that is, a hole a trifle larger than the plain part of the screw—should first be drilled in the top piece, and if the screw to be driven is small, it may be screwed direct into the piece to be joined.

In the event of a large screw being used, however, the piece to be joined should also be drilled with a drill a shade under the diameter of the screw at the bottom or base of the thread.

As the top of countersunk-headed screws are intended to lie flush with the surface of the work, the screw-hole should be countersunk to correspond. This is usually done with a special tool called a countersink bit, used with a hand brace. In some instances it may be found impracticable to use a countersink bit, in which case the depression may be scooped out with a gouge.

Screws, like nails, do not hold so well when used in the end grain of wood, so a thicker and longer screw than that normally employed in cross grain should always be employed.

In driving in a screw, use a screw-driver with a blade a trifle wider than the slot at the start and finish with one of equal width. This method will prevent damage to the slot and also obviate tearing the wood round the screw-head.

A small quantity of grease smeared on a screw will not only make it easier to drive but will also prevent it from rusting and enable it to be extracted easily at some future time.

Brass screws should always be used in oak as the tannic acid present in this wood has a detrimental effect on iron.

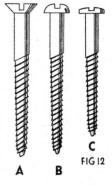

A   B   C

FIG 12

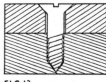

FIG 13

When a small screw has to be driven in such an awkward place as to prevent holding the screw in the normal way, the difficulty may usually be overcome by pushing the screw through a piece of folded paper and using it as a "handle." When the screw is nearly home the paper can be torn away and the screw finally tightened up. For larger screws a thin, narrow strip of tin or brass, with a slot cut in one end so that it can be easily withdrawn, answers the same purpose.

To Remove Screws always use as large a screw-driver as possible to obtain sufficient leverage. In the case of an obstinate screw, try tapping the end of the driver with a mallet at the same time as the driver is being turned. If this is ineffective, hold the end of a hot poker on the head of the screw. This causes the screw to expand slightly, forcing the wood out with it. When cool it contracts and so is loosened.

Coach-screws are invaluable to the woodworker as a substitute for ordinary large screws in positions where the appearance of the heads is immaterial. Holes are first prepared as in the case of the ordinary screw, a metal washer placed on the shank, and the screw is screwed into the wood by means of a spanner or wrench.

CHISELLING

THE three common types of chisels used by the craftsman are shown at A, B and C in Fig. 1.

That represented at A is a firmer-chisel, which is possibly the most used tool and

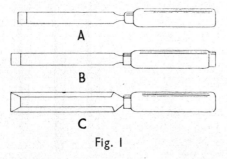

A

B

C

Fig. 1

may therefore be termed the handyman's chisel, as it can be used for cutting mortices in small stuff, paring, etc. The tool shown at B is a mortice-chisel and, as its name implies, is used for cutting mortices. It is more robust than the firmer, and is generally used on large work where it has to withstand the blows from a mallet. The paring-chisel (illustrated at C) is a more delicate tool and has a thinner blade than either of the two tools previously mentioned. It is used principally for finishing off work by hand, and is not struck with a mallet.

The Blade of a chisel is made of cast steel, one end of which is bevelled off to form a cutting edge, while the other end terminates in a shouldered tang which is driven into the handle. As the majority of chisels have to be struck with a mallet, a metal ferrule encircles the tang end of the handle to prevent it splitting, and in the case of the morticing tool an additional ferrule is generally fitted round the top.

For a start, the amateur craftsman should provide himself with a set of chisels comprising $\frac{1}{4}$, $\frac{1}{2}$, $\frac{3}{4}$ and 1 in. of the firmer type, as these will be found suitable for most purposes. The set can then be added to as circumstances demand.

Before a newly-purchased chisel can

be used it must be sharpened on an oil-stone, as the cutting edges of a new tool are only roughly finished on a grindstone, and therefore unsuitable for good work.

A sharp chisel is essential; a blunt one merely breaks the fibres of the wood instead of cutting them. From this it follows that when chiselling has to be done it is a good plan to keep an oilstone close at hand so that the cutting-edge may be touched up from time to time.

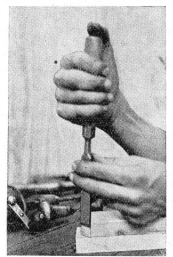

Fig. 2

Fig. 2 shows how a chisel should be held when cutting away a corner of a piece of wood. To do this, first place the wood to be prepared on a piece of flat waste wood—preferably hardwood —to prevent damage to the bench-top, and also to prevent splitting the grain on the underside of the work. Grip the handle of the tool with the right hand, keeping the thumb at the top. Press the left on the work to keep it from slipping and place the forefinger in front of the blade to act as a guide. Now force the tool downwards to remove the waste by making a series of sliding cuts as with a knife, slicing off only a small quantity at a time. A slicing action of the blade makes a cleaner cut than a cut taken straight down. If the work cannot be conveniently held down

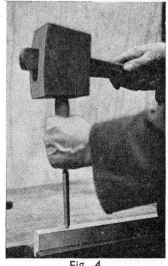

Fig. 4

with the hand, use a cramp.

It may be mentioned here that the greatest care should be exercised when using chisels to keep the hand holding the work as far away as possible from the cutting-edge, as there is every chance of the chisel slipping.

Fig. 3 shows the correct way to hold a chisel when removing the waste from a slot in a piece of work after

Fig. 3

having been cut down at the sides with a tenon-saw. The work is placed securely in the vice or cramped down to the bench-top, as near the front as possible, and the tool worked from one side of the wood to the middle, reversed, and worked from the other side towards the centre. This eliminates the risk of breaking off the edge of the far side if the cut is made straight through. When using the chisel, take a small sloping cut upwards and finish by holding the tool flat on the bottom and working it with a sliding movement, taking care to remove only a small shaving at a time.

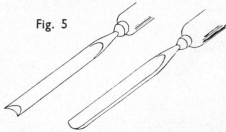

Fig. 5

The correct tool for cutting mortices is the mortice-chisel, although a firmer-chisel can be used on small work. The thick blade of the mortice tool is designed to keep the tool true to its work, so that when the mortice is finished the four sides are square with the face. The width of the blade should be the same as that of the mortice.

Fig. 4 shows the tool being used. After the mortice has been marked out on the top and bottom faces of the work it should be firmly fixed down on the bench, preferably over a leg, as this position is more solid, and therefore better able to withstand the shocks from the mallet. To cut the mortice, start at the centre and work backwards towards the marked line at the end of the hole. Take care to keep the chisel perfectly upright and drive the blade into the wood by striking it smartly with a mallet. *Never* use a hammer, otherwise the handle of the tool will be damaged, and avoid cutting too deeply, as the blade is likely to stick. Repeat the operation by making a series of small cuts until near the mortice line. Take care not to cut right up to the line, as the chisel tends to undercut. Next, start again from the middle and work towards the other end. Continue the process until a hole is formed half-way through the wood. The remainder of the work

is done from the other side, so it must be turned completely over. Before fixing it down to the bench, raise the work up on two pieces of wood of equal thickness. The pieces should be so placed as to form a gap under the mortice. By doing this the waste is allowed to fall through the hole on to the bench.

The method of removing the whole of the waste with a chisel, as explained above, is somewhat slow and tedious, and is rapidly becoming obsolete. Its place is being taken by the simple and more expeditious process of first removing as much surplus wood as possible by boring holes with a brace and twist-bit, and finishing the work with a firmer- or a paring-chisel.

A chisel is useful for marking out work and is, in the majority of cases, superior to a lead pencil. When marking out with a square, make sure that the stock is held tightly against the edge of the work and hold the chisel with its bevelled side against the metal blade of the square, away from the operator and

Fig. 6

also away from the square. The marking is, of course, made towards the worker.

The Gouge is really a chisel with a circular cutting-edge. Two kinds of gouges are in vogue, namely, the "internal ground," having a bevelled cutting-edge on the concave surface of the blade, and the "external ground," having the bevel on the outside. The two types are represented in Fig. 5.

Gouges are used much in the same way as chisels.

Fig. 6 shows how a gouge is held in forming a channel along a piece of wood.

It is hardly necessary to say that when using chisels and gouges on the long grain of wood the cut is made in the direction of the fibres, as in using a plane.

If you have the misfortune to split a chisel handle there is no need to discard the whole tool, as new handles can be purchased for a few pence.

To Fit a New Handle, first fix the handle ferrule end upwards in the vice, and carefully drill a hole sufficiently deep and a trifle smaller in diameter than the tang of the blade. After having removed the tool from the vice, insert the blade between the jaws, slip the handle over the tang, and give it a few smart blows with the mallet, until the shoulder on the tang prevents further movement. When drilling the hole, take particular care to keep the drill straight, otherwise the blade will not be parallel with the handle.

As the cutting-edges of chisels and gouges are easily damaged if allowed to come into violent contact with other metal tools, it is a wise plan to keep them wrapped up in a piece of baize, when not in use, or to make a proper rack for their reception.

Always keep them in a dry place, and if they are to be stored for a considerable time, smear them with vaseline.

BORING

THERE are very few jobs in woodwork that do not require the use of a boring tool, but although the actual process of boring a hole in wood is quite simple, the correct tool must be chosen to suit the work. Fig. 1 shows an illustration of the three principal boring tools for general work, namely, the bradawl (A), gimlet (B) and the brace and bit (C).

The Bradawl, or sprig bit as it is sometimes called, is the simplest, handiest and the easiest tool to use for boring purposes, but its employment is restricted to making small holes, such as those for the insertion of nails and very small screws. It consists essentially of a hardwood handle and a steel rod or shank, the lower end of which terminates in a double bevelled cutting-edge. The cutting-edge is purposely made sharp to enable it to cut across the fibres of the wood.

Bradawls, like other tools, can be obtained in several qualities. In the common bradawl the shank is simply held in the handle by the friction between the wedge-shaped tang and the

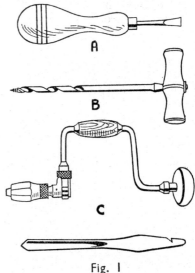

Fig. 1

wood, but in a better tool the shank is further secured by means of a pin driven into the handle and through a hole in the tang. The craftsman should therefore get the latter type unless he does not mind the inconvenience of constantly having the blade part company with the handle.

Fig. 2 shows the correct method of using a bradawl when employed as a hand-operated tool. As mentioned previously, the cutting-edge is used across the grain because if it be used with the direction of the fibres there is a danger that the wood may split, as the wedge-shaped blade forces the fibres apart.

In using the bradawl the blade should be forced lightly into the wood and twisted to and fro and then gradually withdrawn by holding the handle between the first and second fingers of the right hand, pulling upwards and still continuing the twisting movement.

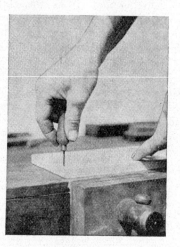

Fig. 2

In some instances it may be necessary to hammer the tool, in which case the top of the handle should only be tapped lightly and the tool twisted as previously mentioned. Great care should be taken not to force the blade to one side when making a hole in hardwood. Failure to take this precaution invariably results in a broken blade and it may also spoil the work, especially if the blade happens to break off short in the wood.

In the event of the blade breaking near the cutting end, do not discard the tool, as it is an easy matter to file or grind the blade to form another bevelled chisel edge. If necessary it can be hammered out slightly so that the edge is a trifle wider than the rest of the shank. As a rule the steel is soft enough to allow of this being done.

Bradawls can now be obtained with a hollow handle containing several different sizes of awls. The blades are held in the stock by means of a wing nut to enable it to be tightened with the fingers. The main objections to such a tool are that it is usually bulky and cannot very well be used with a hammer when one wishes to drive the blade into hardwood, such as oak.

As a bradawl—like every other tool with a round handle—is likely to roll about on the bench and to drop on the floor, it is a good plan to plane or file a flat on two opposite sides of the handle. Before applying a plane, however, make sure that the fixing pin (if fitted) is not likely to come into contact with the cutting edge of the plane-iron.

The Gimlet is a later production than the bradawl for boring holes. It has during its existence taken several forms and it was extensively used when it took on a taper screw-point and screws did not. The early type of gimlet had a groove or hollow with a sharp edge formed along the shank from the screw-point upwards, to rid the hole of chips and to cut the material. This type of tool, however, was not very effective, especially when boring a deep hole. The defect was remedied by forming a twist in the metal stem, as in the case of twist-drills and bits, which are more or less self-clearing.

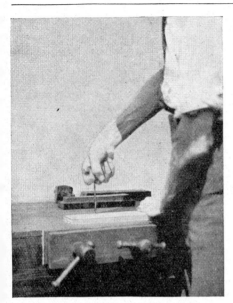

Fig. 3

is in the wood the fault is difficult to rectify. A gimlet cannot be used successfully when boring into end grain, as the screwed end cannot obtain sufficient grip. Like every other cutting tool the gimlet must be sharp if clean-cut holes are required.

Gimlets appear to be going out of fashion and their place taken by the more efficient hand-drill, mentioned later in this article.

The Brace and Bit may be justly termed the "king" of boring tools and is perhaps the most frequently used. The brace is the tool for holding and rotating the bit. It consists of the head for holding, the crank for revolving the bit and the chuck for holding the bit.

Although the bradawl and gimlet are useful tools within their limits, the

The screw-point of the gimlet only draws the tool into the wood and any cutting done is produced by the sharp edge of the groove or channel. There are several types and sizes of gimlets, but the one shown at B in Fig. 1 is a common form and will serve for general purposes.

Fig. 3 shows how a gimlet is held in boring wood. The point of the tool is applied to the work at the position required, pressed down and turned in a clockwise direction. When the point has once established itself in the wood it draws itself in and cuts the hole. The operation then consists in merely twisting the handle. The tool is withdrawn by simply pulling the handle, rotating the shank back and forth, as withdrawing a bradawl, to bring out the core or waste.

The main points to be observed when using a gimlet are these: Never use it for boring holes near the end of a piece of wood, as there is great danger of splitting. Always start a hole with the tool held upright, because once the shank

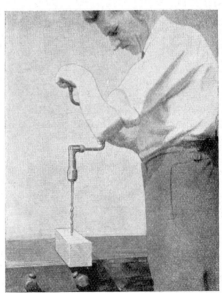

Fig. 4

brace and bit is a much handier and better tool because a constant, even rotation of the crank, coupled with a better form of boring tool, produces a better job more easily effected. The enormous leverage obtained by the

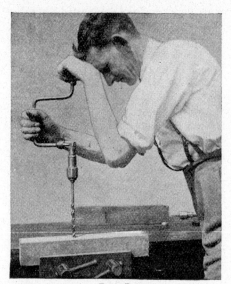

Fig. 5

sweep of the crank enables large, deep holes to be cut with the minimum of effort and the ratchet arrangement now fitted to most braces allows the tool to be used in confined places.

The brace is used in an upright position, as illustrated in Fig. 4, with the left hand placed on the broad top and exerting the necessary pressure while the right hand revolves the crank.

When greater pressure is required on the bit, as when boring large holes, it is generally an advantage to steady the tool by allowing the forehead to rest on the left hand (Fig. 5). If still greater pressure is necessary to operate the bit effectively, the brace may be used horizontally against the operator's chest (Fig. 6).

A common form of boring bit, known as a centre-bit, is shown at A in Fig. 7. Such bits are used for making holes up to about 3 in. in depth and are made in a number of sizes ranging from $\frac{1}{4}$ in. to $1\frac{1}{2}$ in. It will be seen from the drawing that the centre-bit consists of three main parts. The triangular centre point

acts as a guide when boring; the "nicker" or outside cutter cuts a circular groove, while the "router" cuts away the waste wood between.

When using the tool it is advisable to place the work on a piece of waste wood to prevent damage to the bench-top.

Place the centre point of the bit on the wood where the hole is to be and apply an even pressure on the top of the brace with the left hand and turn the crank with the right. Take care to keep the tool upright with the work. This can be tested by observing whether the first cut of the nicker cuts equally all round. Continue boring until the centre point appears on the back face, then turn the work upside down and continue boring from that side. Do not press heavily on the brace when finishing the hole, otherwise the remaining waste will probably break off in the hole and thus necessitate the use of a gouge to clear it out. If the work has been carefully done a straight clean hole will result.

In ascertaining the size of a centre-bit to cut a certain sized hole, do not

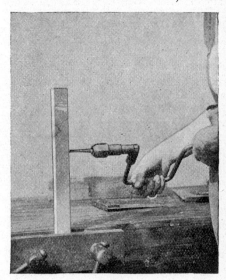

Fig. 6

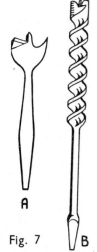

Fig. 7

A

B

measure its extreme width, as the hole produced will be a trifle larger in diameter. The hole produced by a centre-bit is equal to twice the distance between the centre point and the nicker, because the radius of the outside edge of the router is smaller than that of the nicker. This will be readily understood by referring to Fig. 8.

For producing deep straight holes there is nothing to beat a twist-bit, an illustration of which appears at B in Fig. 7. Like the gimlet, the twist-bit is provided with a screw-point which draws the tool into the wood and thus requires little or no pressure when boring holes. The spiral shank also helps in drawing the cutter into the wood and lifts the waste chips to the top of the hole.

Twist-bits.—There are numerous types, all of which work more or less on the combined principle of the gimlet and centre-bit. The chief point to observe when using a twist-bit is to see that the brace is held perpendicularly to the work, as once a small portion of the shank has entered the wood "on the skew" the fault cannot be rectified by leaning the tool over, as such practice would ruin the tool.

To ensure the tool being upright it is a good plan to place a try-square at the side of the work to act as a guide, as indicated in Fig. 9, or better still to get an assistant to tell you when the tool is in the correct position. A little practice will soon enable you to bore holes without such aids.

The general design of a closed-end twist-bit makes it particularly useful for boring holes in the end grain of wood, where the use of a centre-bit would be useless.

It sometimes happens that a number of holes of uniform depth has to be bored, as in dowelling. This necessitates a depth-gauge which may be either bought or home-made. A suitable gauge for a twist-bit would be a piece of sheet tin or brass encircling the shank at the desired distance from the cutting edge and fastened by means of a small bolt and nut. Or the shanks or centre-bits could be marked with a piece of chalk or by sticking on a piece of gummed paper at the desired distance.

There are numerous other kinds of bits used with the brace including such items as spoon-bits, countersinking-bits, screw-driver-bits, etc. Spoon-bits are to be obtained in sizes up to about $\frac{3}{8}$ in. in diameter. The countersink-bit is employed for countersinking the tops of screw-holes to allow the screw-head to lie flush with the surface

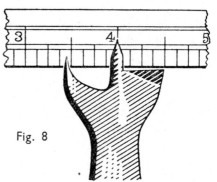

Fig. 8

of the work. The screw-driver-bit is useful for driving in large screws where a powerful leverage is required, extracting obstinate screws and driving in a number of screws rapidly.

The hand-drill shown in Fig. 10 is rapidly taking the place of the bradawl and gimlet. The twist-drill—the same

Fig. 9

kind as that used in metal work—is held in a small adjustable chuck and driven at high speed by means of a geared wheel operated by a handle. This enables a clean accurate hole to be cut in the minimum of time and with little risk of splitting the wood even when drilled near the edge. A standard-sized hand-drill usually accommodates drills from $\frac{1}{64}$ in. to $\frac{1}{4}$ in. in diameter.

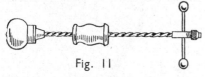

Fig. 11

The Archimedean drill (Fig. 11) is extremely useful for making very small holes.

Motion is imparted to the drill, which is held in a miniature chuck, by working a bobbin up and down a twisted stem which is free to revolve in the top by which the tool is held. In the old type of drill the rotation of the bit is reversed at every up and down stroke but these are being replaced by a

tool having a ratchet arrangement which allows the drill to revolve in a clockwise direction only.

The bits used with such a drill are usually spear-pointed and can be purchased in assorted sizes at a few pence per dozen, or, if the user feels disposed, he can make them out of knitting needles. To do this, cut off a piece about 2 in. in length and soften the steel by heating it up to redness and then allowing it to cool slowly in dry ashes. If necessary, file a flat at one end to fit the chuck.

Hammer the other end out more or less flat according to the size of the hole to be drilled and file it to a spear-point, using a fine smooth file for the purpose and taking care to get the cutting edges equal. The cutting edge should be "backed off" by filing the back edge, holding the tool on the slant. This will be reversed, of course, on the other cutting edge. The drill is ready for use when it has been hardened by heating it up to redness and plunging it into some grease to cool it rapidly.

Fig. 10

REBATING

REBATING, or rebetting as it is often called, consists of cutting a rectangular recess along the edge of a piece of wood. It is used as a means of setting glass, panels, etc. in a framework, as

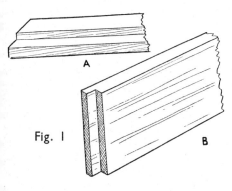

Fig. 1

shown at A in Fig. 1, and in some cases to form a joint with another piece at right-angles, as illustrated at B.

In the former, the rebate is generally formed on the long edge with the grain of the wood, while the latter is formed transversely to it. The transverse rebate is used largely in the construction of drawers and in cases where a simple yet effective joint is required though the outer faces of the pieces are to remain flush.

As a general rule a rebate is required on a piece of work already prepared, that is, it is already planed and trued up to size.

The first thing to do when making a rebate on the long edge of a piece of timber is to mark it out to the desired width and depth with the aid of a marking-gauge. Adjust the gauge to the proper width and run the stock along the front edge to mark the width on the face, then readjust the gauge to the correct depth, and mark along the edge by running the stock along the face.

The next process consists of removing the waste; there are several methods of doing this. If the recess is shallow, the rebate-plane may be used to advantage, but if it be deep, the plough or, failing this, a chisel, can be employed.

When the rebate-plane is resorted to it is a good plan to fasten a strip of wood along the sole, as shown in Fig. 2, to serve as a guide; the width of the strip being so adjusted as to expose only sufficient width of the cutting-edge of the iron to suit the width of the recess. Do not fix the guide directly to the sole with nails or screws as is so often done, as the marks left by them may damage the most

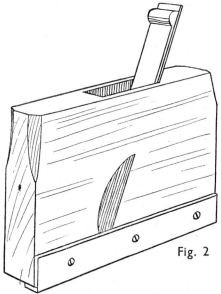

Fig. 2

important surface of the plane. A much better plan is first to fix the strip to another piece of wood and then screw it to the side of the tool, as shown clearly in the drawing.

The rebate-plane is used in the ordinary manner by taking long, even strokes along the edge of the work, taking care to keep the tool square.

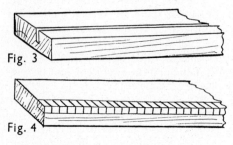

Fig. 3

Fig. 4

Fig. 3 shows a groove after having been partly formed with a plough. The plough is first used to cut the groove to the correct depth and the remainder removed with a chisel. When using the plough, start at the front end and work gradually backwards until the full depth is obtained from end to end, and finish off by giving one or two strokes right along the work. Take great care to see that the guide is kept against the vertical face, otherwise the groove will be cut out of square.

As the average amateur does not usually possess either a rebate-plane or a plough, he must be content to remove the waste with a chisel.

Fig. 4 shows an easy way of doing this. Make a series of saw kerfs (cuts) across the front edge of the work, that is, from the depth line to the width line, by tilting the edge of the saw upwards, taking care not to cut past the marks. Now remove the waste with a chisel held obliquely so that the cutting-edge near the wall of the rebate is a little in advance of the other.

A Cutting-gauge having a very sharp cutter, as shown in Fig. 5, is a handy tool for cutting narrow, shallow rebates in good straight-grained timber. It should not be used, however, where the width and the depth exceed about $\frac{1}{4}$ in.

Fig. 6 shows a stopped rebate, so called because it stops instead of running the full length of the work. The recess is formed by first ploughing a groove and then chiselling out the waste.

In cases where the rebate is made transversely to the grain, as indicated at B in Fig. 1, it is usual to have the material upon which the rebate is to be formed thicker than the piece to be joined. The depth of the recess is usually from one-half to one-third the thickness of the wood, and the width equal to the thickness of the piece to be joined.

After the gauge lines have been marked, the end is cut across to the correct depth with a tenon-saw, and the waste removed by one or other of the following methods.

For wide work the best way to remove the surplus, after cutting across the work at the gauge line, is to chisel it out (as shown at A in Fig. 7), and finish with a firmer- or, better still, a paring-chisel held horizontally as at B.

In cases where the wood is comparatively thick, first cut across it as pre-

Fig. 5

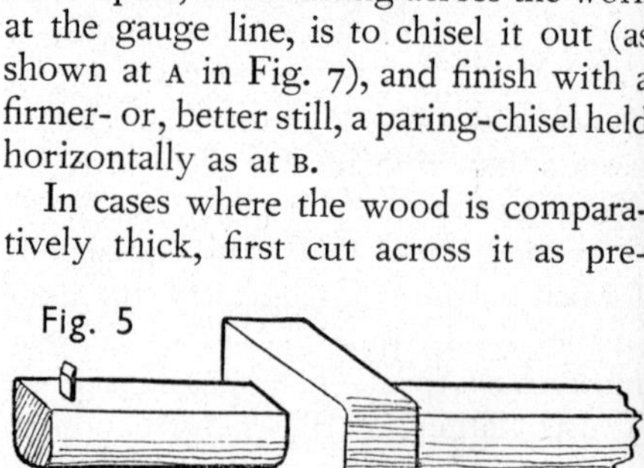

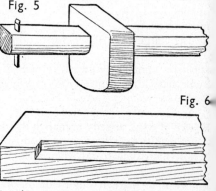

Fig. 6

viously mentioned and then place the work, narrow edge uppermost, on the bench and use the chisel vertically.

Chamfering is a term used when removing a sharp edge to form a narrow, flat face, as that seen at A and B in Fig. 8. The edges of the wood are usually planed to an angle of 45°, the width depending upon the nature of the work. A chamfer forms a neat, narrow, flat surface which greatly enhances the

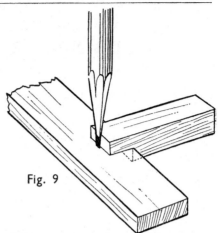

Fig. 9

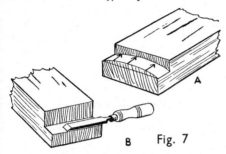

B **Fig. 7**

appearance of a piece of work, as instanced in panelled framework, etc.

The two chamfers in general use are known as the ordinary chamfer, where the bevel runs through the full length of the work, as indicated at A, and the stopped chamfer (B) which, as its name implies, stops before the ends are approached.

A Through Chamfer can be carried out with a jack or any other plane fitted with an iron whose cutting-edge runs

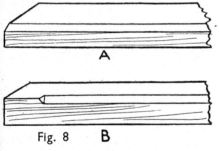

Fig. 8 **B**

straight across the sole, or with a proper chamfer plane. As the last-mentioned tool is seldom required by the amateur, there is no necessity to explain its function here.

To make a through chamfer, all that is necessary is first to mark a line parallel to the front edge on the face and side to be treated, and then plane down to the gauged lines.

When marking the lines do not use an ordinary marking-gauge as such, but remove the pin and substitute a short length of blacklead from a pencil. This will prevent damage to the edges of the work due to the sharp point of the pin. If this is not practicable, use a home-made gauge fashioned from a small piece of wood, as indicated in Fig. 9. A point to note when setting out the bevel is that the newly-formed face will be wider than the marked width at the edges.

In Forming a Stopped Chamfer, the stop is first sawn and chiselled out for a distance at least equal to the distance from the front of the plane to the cutting-edge of the iron, and then the intervening waste removed and finished with the plane. As it is unusual to stop the ends of the chamfers abruptly, one of the two common methods of finishing the stop, as shown in Fig. 10 at A and B, may be employed. They are, of course, prepared with a chisel.

Fig. 10

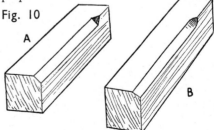

A

B

JOINTS AND JOINTING

WOODWORK joints may be classified under three headings, namely (*a*) angle joints, where the parts to be joined form an angle, as in the mortice and tenon joint; (*b*) those for increasing the width, as instanced in tongued and grooved boards; and (*c*) those employed for lengthening timber—usually confined to constructional work

In describing the joints, mention will only be made of those likely to be of use and which can be easily made by the novice.

Glued Butt Joint.—The glued butt joint shown in Fig. 1 is a good test for

Fig. 1

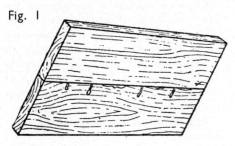

careful planing. To make such a joint, true up the top and bottom faces of the pieces to be joined, and test for winding with the winding strips as explained in the section under PLANES AND PLANING. Next, true up one edge by planing the wood held either in a vice or on a shooting-board, and test for straightness by using a straight-edge. Make a pencil mark on this edge. True up the edge of the other board in a similar fashion and mark it as explained above. Now, whilst one board is in the vice—trued edge up—place the other board on it, that is, marked edge to marked edge, and test with the straight-edge in the manner shown in Fig. 2. If inaccurate, and reversing the board

does not give a satisfactory result, the only alternative is to plane the edges again. If the joint is correct the boards may be glued together.

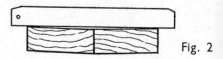

Fig. 2

Most softwoods take glue better than hardwoods, so when the latter are employed it is an advantage to draw the teeth of a tenon-saw down the face to be glued, to roughen it slightly.

To make a successful glued joint, warm the pieces to be joined and apply a small quantity of glue to each edge, then rub the two pieces together in the direction of the joint to exclude the air. It may be pointed out that it is not the quantity of glue applied to the joint that counts, but the amount that can be squeezed out.

After the joints have been glued, the work should be set aside for about 24 hours to dry, taking care to lean the work against something flat, as shown at A in Fig. 3, otherwise the joint is likely to assume the shape illustrated at B.

Dowelled Butt Joint.—The ordinary glued butt joint may be greatly

Fig. 3

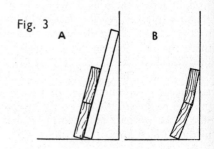

strengthened by using dowel pins (as described in a later section and illustrated in Fig. 4). When dowels are used the rubbing process for excluding the

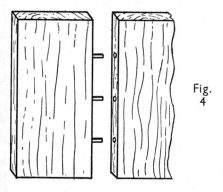

Fig. 4

air after gluing obviously cannot be accomplished.

Tongued and Grooved Joint.— Another method of joining the long edges of boards is by means of tongues and grooves as instanced in the tongued and grooved matchboards and floor-boards, as shown at A, B and C, Fig. 5, which can be purchased ready for use.

When dealing with plain-edged boards, the tongue and groove may be formed with planes sold in pairs to match, or by using a single

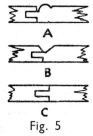

A

B

C

Fig. 5

grooving-plane. In the latter case, the edges of the boards to be joined are first grooved and then a separate tongue is inserted in the grooves. When a separate tongue is used it is advisable to make the tongue from a piece of wood cut across the grain, as this method is very much stronger than using a piece cut with the grain. This can be readily proved by trying to break the two tongues. The tongue should be of sufficient thickness to fit snugly in the grooves yet leaving enough

clearance for the surplus glue when gluing up.

The board from which the tongues are prepared should be planed to the required thickness before cutting to length, as difficulty will be experienced in planing across the grain if cut first and then sawn into strips. Fig. 6 shows the most economical way of cutting the tongues.

In some cases where the quality of the finish is immaterial, cross-pieces may be either screwed or nailed to the boards,

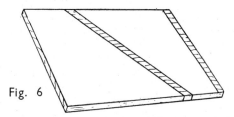

Fig. 6

not only to strengthen the joint but as an aid against twisting. This is shown clearly in Fig. 7.

Screwed Butt Joint.—Fig. 8 shows another method of joining the long edges of boards. In the example a depression

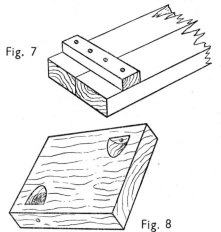

Fig. 7

Fig. 8

is gouged out near the edge of one piece, deep enough to take the head of a screw. A hole is then bored to take the screw, which is inserted and screwed tightly into place after the boards are glued together.

Joint made with Corrugated Fastener.—The handy little device illustrated in Fig. 9 is useful for making a butt joint. It is composed of a thin piece of corrugated steel having sharp edges. It is simply driven into the ends of the wood, the corrugations preventing the members from being pulled apart. Corrugated fasteners are used extensively for making packing-cases and articles of a similar nature where a good close joint is required but where there is no necessity to go to the trouble and expense of making, for instance, a glued butt joint.

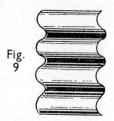

Fig. 9

Battened Butt Joint.—When making a drawing-board or an object of a similar character such as a dresser or a

A Fig. 10

B

table-top, where great care is needed to avoid possible shrinkage and twisting, the joint illustrated in Fig. 10 may be used with advantage. In the case of a drawing-board, the separate pieces to be joined (A and B) may be either butt-jointed or tongued and grooved, and further strengthened by carefully trued-up battens fixed on the underside by round-headed screws. The cross-pieces have a number of slots cut in them depending upon the width of the board, the slots being just wide enough to take the unthreaded part of the screw. Brass sockets, obtainable for the purpose, cover the slots and offer less friction to the screw when the board either shrinks or expands. In this way the battens are enabled to do their work as if they were screwed direct on to the boards they are intended to keep from twisting.

Simple Ledged Joint.—Fig. 11 shows a simple yet effective joint commonly used at the ends of boards to prevent twisting. The joint is used extensively in the making of cheap drawing-boards, pastry-boards, etc. The ends of the boards are tongued and fit

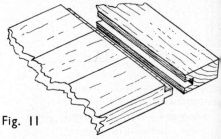

Fig. 11

into grooved battens which are fixed by either nails or glue, or both.

Another type of ledged joint is represented in Fig. 12. It is useful when a large surface, such as a table-top, is to be fixed to a framework, as it prevents twisting and shrinkage. The table-top is fastened to the framework in the usual way by gouging a recess—similar to that shown in Fig. 7—in the sides of the

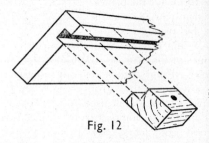

Fig. 12

framing and driving screws through it into the top. A groove is also provided near the top edge of the framing and small blocks of wood screwed to the underside of the table-top. The blocks can be made of any kind of hardwood such as mahogany, oak, etc., and should be shaped as indicated in the drawing.

The types of angle joints used by the woodworker are legion, but the most important from the amateur's point of view

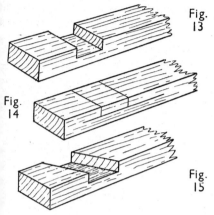

Fig. 13

Fig. 14

Fig. 15

are perhaps halving, housing, mortice and tenon, and dovetailing, although the latter joint is seldom required.

Halved Joint.—The halved joint is used for many purposes and takes many forms. As its name implies, the material of each piece to be joined is half cut away. In the cross halved joint illustrated in Fig. 13, one piece is cut away as shown. This piece is laid across the second piece, which is then marked and cut out in a similar way. The depth of the cut is marked with a marking-gauge, and the position of the cross-cuts squared across and marked with a scribing-knife. Care should always be taken to saw in the waste side of the mark, that is, the part of the wood to be cut away. The cross-cutting is sawn, of course, with a tenon-saw, and the waste removed with a firmer-chisel.

A good-fitting joint should be hand tight, that is, one piece will just hold the other by friction and yet can be easily separated by means of the hands.

To make the Joint, first plane up the timber truly square as tested by a straight-edge and square. Do not trust to timber purchased ready planed, as it may not be perfectly square. Measure up exactly where the joint has to be by laying one piece across the other, and scribe a line on each side with a scribing-knife or a penknife. Test these lines with a square. Now square down the edges of the wood. Take the marking-gauge and set it to half the thickness of the piece of wood. To prove accuracy of setting, make a gauge-prick on another part of the wood, first from one side and then the other. If the two indentations correspond you know you have the exact half. Gauge-mark both sides of the wood from one face. Fig. 14 shows the joint marked out.

Place the timber in the vice or on the sawing-stool and saw down to the proper depth, taking care not to cut below the depth-marks, otherwise the joint will be considerably weakened. The waste material may now be chiselled away by using a firmer- or a paring-chisel. Do not chisel right through to the farther side as you are likely to break the farther edge, but work towards the middle from each edge.

To test for accuracy of the chiselled surface, lay the long edge of the chisel across the bottom of the cut. If the chisel rocks easily it indicates that the

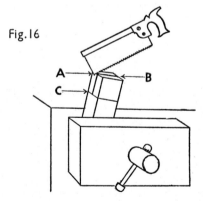

Fig. 16

A   B
C

base is high somewhere about the centre. This fault must be rectified, but in doing so be careful not to make it hollow.

This finished piece may now be laid across the other and tested for squareness with a try-square. The other piece of wood is treated in exactly the same manner.

Angled Halved Joint.—Fig. 15 shows a halved joint set at an angle. It is made in exactly the same way as

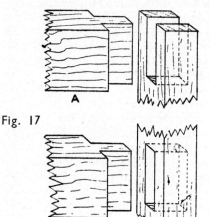

Fig. 17

the right-angled joint mentioned above, except, of course, that the faces are marked out and sawn to the required angle.

T Halved Joint.—In making a T-joint, where the end of one member is cut away to fit the piece forming the top of the T, it is a good plan to fix the tail-piece in the vice and saw out the waste in the manner indicated in Fig. 16. Gauge the piece as previously explained, and run the marking-gauge round the two sides and the end. Place the wood in the vice, with the top slightly sloping towards you. Start the cut at the top edge as indicated at A in the illustration, and saw along the end until the edge B is reached. Push the wood over, keeping the saw in the saw cut and saw down to the gauge mark at C. Now turn the work round and saw down the other side in the same fashion. The cut can then be made level and the waste piece cut off.

This finished piece can now be placed on the second piece for marking purposes, and when this is completed, the recess can be formed with the aid of the saw and chisel.

The same routine is carried out in making similar T-halved joints where an angle other than a right-angle is desired.

Mortice and Tenon Joint.—The mortice and tenon joint is one of the most important joints in woodwork where strength and rigidity are required. There are numerous forms of this useful joint, a good many of which are not likely to be used by the amateur wood-worker. The mortice and tenon joint is a much stronger and more satisfactory joint than the halved joint, and is formed by cutting a rectangular tongue on one member to fit a corresponding cavity in the other.

An ordinary simple slot or open mortice and tenon joint ready for fixing is shown at A in Fig. 17, and that at B represents a through T-joint.

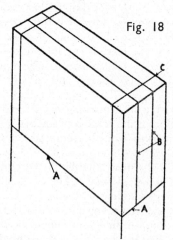

Fig. 18

For the purpose of describing the various operations for making a mortice and tenon joint it is assumed that a T joint with a shouldered tenon is to be made.

Before going into details, however, i

should be noted that a special tool called a mortice-gauge is necessary. This tool, already described elsewhere, is similar to an ordinary marking-gauge but has two marking points, one of which is adjustable to enable it to mark two lines at the same time.

Assuming that the pieces to be joined

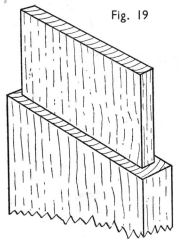

Fig. 19

have been planed up perfectly true, the first thing to do is to mark the position for the tenon, which is usually made a little longer than the finished size. Scribe a line round the faces where the shoulder of the tenon or projecting piece is to be, as shown at A in Fig. 18, and then set the mortice-gauge. As the thickness of the tenon is generally made one-third of the width of the timber, choose a chisel—mortice or firmer—of the desired width, and use the width at the cutting-edge as a guide to measure the distance between the two points of the gauge. Estimate either by eye or by rule a similar distance between the body of the gauge and the point nearest to it. Test for accuracy by first making pricks in the wood with the points of the gauge and then applying the gauge to the other side of the wood. If necessary, alter the gauge until the prick-marks agree. Now run the gauge round the timber to mark

the position of the tenon as shown at B in Fig. 18. Set the marking-gauge equal to the thickness of the tenon, and then mark the lines as indicated at C. Carefully saw away the two broad faces and then the narrow ones, keeping the saw on the outside of the gauge-marks. Fig. 19 shows the completed tenon.

Now lay the tenoned piece on its fellow member in the position it will eventually occupy. Make a pencil-mark on both sides, and then run the pencil round the face side and the two edges, using the square for the purpose. This indicates the position for the mortice. With the mortice-gauge, mark out from the face A the lines shown at B in Fig. 20, the actual position of the mortice on the two edges.

The next operation consists in removing the waste material. The simplest way to do this is first to remove the majority of the waste material with a brace and twist-bit and then remove the remainder and finish off with a firmer-chisel. Choose a suitable bit, that is,

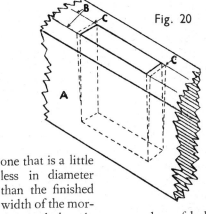

Fig. 20

one that is a little less in diameter than the finished width of the mortice, and then bore a number of holes about half-way through the timber. The wood is then turned upside down and the same operation repeated from the other face of the mortice.

When using the brace it is essential to keep the bit absolutely parallel with the

3

sides of the wood in which the mortice is being cut, otherwise the work may be ruined. When this operation is completed all that is necessary is to remove carefully the remaining waste with a sharp chisel.

When an extra-strong joint is required, the two narrow edges of the outer face are

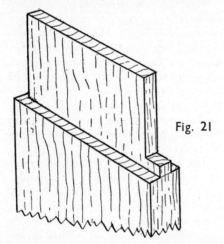

Fig. 21

cut away for about ⅛ in., and the walls of the slot cut downwards in a slanting direction to take two wedges, as shown by the outside dotted lines at c in Fig. 20. Such a joint is known as a keyed-through tenon. The wedges should be made to the same width as that of the aperture.

The joint is complete when a small quantity of glue has been brushed in the mortice and on the tenon, and the tenon either pushed or knocked into the mortice. If wedges are used, a spot of glue should be applied to each wedge before driving them home. As you do this, test for squareness, as one of the wedges may force the joint slightly out of truth. This fault can be corrected in most instances by driving in the other wedge before the glue sets. When sufficient time has elapsed to allow the glue to set thoroughly, the tops of the wedges and the tenon are sawn off flush, and the surfaces trimmed up with a plane.

Haunched Tenon.—Fig. 21 illustrates a square haunched tenon used in cases where the end of a morticed piece has to be flush with the tenoned member, instances of which are found in the joint connecting the top framing to a table leg, and the framing of a large panelled door.

The tenon is formed in a similar way to the plain tenon except that one end-piece is cut away as shown clearly in the illustration. The mortice is made to take the haunch which, of course, is shorter than the actual width of the tenon.

Stopped Tenon.—A tenon that does not pass right through the morticed member is called a stopped tenon or a stub tenon, an example of which appears in Fig. 22. The pieces are marked and cut out as previously described, except that the mortice is cut to a sufficient depth to suit the length of the tenon.

Where two stopped tenons meet in the timber, for example, where the sides of the frame meet at right angles at the tops of table legs, the ends of the tenons

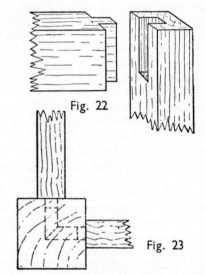

Fig. 22

Fig. 23

are mitred off as indicated in Fig. 23. The mitre gives a longer bearing and a larger gluing surface, which imparts additional strength to the joint.

Barefaced Tenon.—The barefaced tenon has only one shoulder and is used in cases where the interior of the framework, such as matchboards, is required to lie flush on the face side in the manner shown in Fig. 24.

The thickness of the rails or crosspieces is determined by the thickness of the material used between the uprights or stiles.

The members are marked with the aid of a single-pointed marking-gauge and cut out in the usual way.

As previously pointed out, a successful joint depends upon the accuracy of marking out and cutting. Great care should be taken to see that these conditions are complied with. Most faults arise through want of system and forethought, and hurrying to get the job finished. In cutting, the saw may be guided with the finger-tips of the left hand or by the use of a straight-edged strip of wood placed with its edge along the gauged lines. In marking out, use a knife in preference to a pencil—except, of course, in special cases—as its use tends to greater accuracy, and the marks do not get obliterated. As there is a

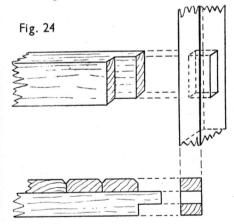

Fig. 24

tendency to cut in a slight curve, even with a tenon-saw, the curvature can be rectified with a chisel.

A good-fitting joint can be obtained by cutting the shoulders of the tenon a little out of square, as shown in Fig. 25.

Housing Joint.—Fig. 26 shows two types of useful joints known as housing joints. That shown at A illustrates through housing and that at B is called

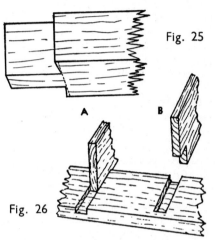

Fig. 25

Fig. 26

stopped housing. It is used extensively in fitting shelves, etc., into their uprights. The joint is formed by sinking the ends of the shelf, for instance, into grooves cut in the uprights for their reception. The depth of the groove is usually one-third of the thickness of the wood.

To make the through joint, first true up the wood and then mark the width and depth of the groove in the piece to be recessed, using a square for the purpose. The width of the groove is equal to the thickness of the shelf or board to be joined. Cut across the lines so marked down to the depth-marks with a tenon-saw, not forgetting to saw in the waste. The waste can then be roughly removed with a chisel and finished off with a router-plane.

When using the chisel, work from one edge to the centre, then turn the wood round and work from the other edge towards the centre.

In making the stopped housed joint,

the trench is stopped a short distance from the edge of the upright.

Square and mark out in the same way as previously mentioned, not forgetting to gauge the length of the stopped end. Cut across the lines with the saw held slantwise, that is, handle down, until the saw reaches the stop and is the correct depth at the other end. Remove the waste with a chisel and finish off with a router.

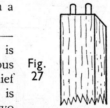

Dowelled Joint.— The dowelled joint is useful for numerous purposes, the chief of which, perhaps, is that for joining two or more boards together widthways, as shown previously in Fig. 4, and for making simple right-angled joints, as illustrated in Fig. 27.

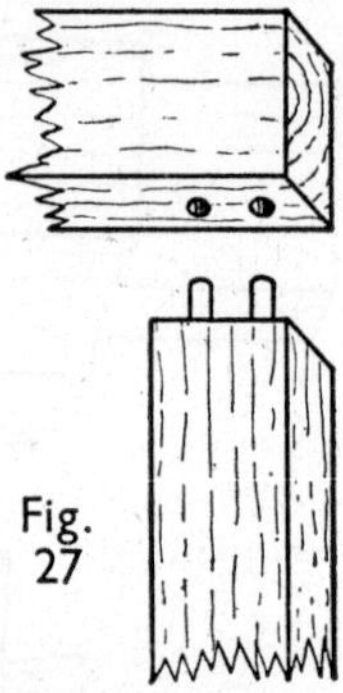

Fig. 27

The joint consists of a series of dowels or hardwood pegs glued into holes bored at right-angles to the surfaces to be joined. The dowels fit into corresponding holes bored in the other member.

The dowel is made of hardwood such as beech, and can be bought ready-made in various diameters from $\frac{1}{8}$ in. upwards, in lengths of about 3 ft.

The parts to be joined are prepared in the same way as the glued butt joint, and the holes to be bored are marked with square and gauge. A twist-bit of the same diameter as that of the dowel is used for drilling the holes. Fig. 28 shows the two members marked ready for boring.

Before boring the holes it is advisable to centre-punch each centre-mark to ensure even entry of the bit. Drill the holes to the desired depth, which will depend upon the size of the dowel used, taking care to keep the bit upright when boring, otherwise an unsatisfactory joint will result.

Having completed the holes, counter-sink the tops to remove the sharp edges. Cut the dowel-pins to the correct length, and make a slot or groove in them, as shown in Fig. 29, to allow the surplus glue to escape. This may be done by holding the pin in the vice and sawing a small channel along the length of the pin. Remove the sharp edges at the ends by rubbing them with glass-paper.

The joint is made by first gluing the pins and driving them into the holes of one board, gluing the edges of both, including the pins, and then knocking the parts into place by means of a mallet. As the edges cannot be rubbed together to extrude the surplus glue, it is a wise plan to use cramps. If the work is such a size that it prevents the use of ordinary cramps, the difficulty may be overcome by laying the work flat on the floor with one edge against a wall and the other edge wedged against a length of batten nailed to the floor. If this method does

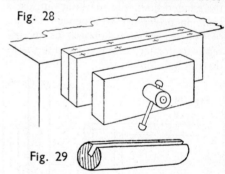

Fig. 28

Fig. 29

not answer the purpose, the worker must use his ingenuity as to the best way of overcoming the difficulty.

It may be mentioned that whenever it is found necessary to use a hammer or a mallet on the edges of work, a piece of waste wood should always be inserted between the work and the striking-tool to prevent bruised and damaged edges.

An improvised dowelled joint can be made by using nails and screws in place of wooden pins.

The work is prepared and marked as previously explained, and wire nails, oval brads, or screws are partially driven into the edge at equidistant spaces in one member. The heads of the "dowels" are then removed, and the projecting parts filed to a chisel-edge, care being taken not to loosen the pins. After the edges of the boards have been glued they are knocked into place and cramped. To facilitate the entry of the metal dowels, a number of holes should be drilled, in positions corresponding with those of the pins, in the edges of the board to be joined, using a bradawl a trifle smaller in diameter than that of the pins.

Another effective method of strengthening a glued butt joint is to drive a number of screws into the edge of one board, as indicated in Fig. 30, allowing the heads to project a trifle above the surface. Holes are bored at a distance of about $\frac{1}{4}$ in. in front of their actual final positions in the piece to be joined to take the heads of the screws. Narrow channels about $\frac{1}{4}$ in. in length are then cut in the second board, just wide enough to take the smooth shanks of the

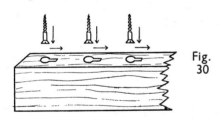

Fig. 30

screws. After gluing, this board is so placed that the screw-heads enter the holes in the other piece, and is then driven on from the end until it assumes its correct position. The heads of the screws tend to work upwards as they cut channels for themselves and thus tighten the joint.

The Dovetail Joint.—The dovetail joint is not a difficult joint to make, but the greatest care is needed in marking out and cutting. It consists essentially of one or more inverted wedge-shaped pins fitting into similarly shaped sockets which lock the joint.

Single dovetail joints are used mostly

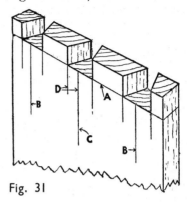

Fig. 31

in joinery, and multiple dovetailing is resorted to in cabinet-making, in the construction of drawers, etc.

The joint should be made just hand-tight, otherwise the angles of the pins and their sockets as well as the outer dovetails are likely to be broken off.

For the purpose of explaining the process of making a simple dovetail joint it is assumed that the front, back and sides of a box are to be prepared for dovetailing after the parts have been trued and the ends properly squared.

The pins are formed on the sides and the sockets on the front and back of the box. Start by marking out the sockets. As the two pieces are identical they can be marked at the same time by fastening them together with fine brads. Great care must be taken when doing this to see that the edges are flush.

Place these parts in the vice, working-end up, and measure the thickness of one piece. Scribe a shoulder line right round the work at a distance from the top edge equal to the thickness of the piece just measured. This is shown at A in Fig. 31.

The number of dovetails required in a given length is an arbitrary matter, although it is usual to have a larger number when hardwood is employed. It will be assumed that three pins and sockets are desired.

Mark off a distance equal to the full width of a socket at each end of the shoulder line, indicated by B in the illustration, and divide the space between these points into two, which gives the centre of the middle socket. Mark this point, as shown at c. From each of these centres, mark on both sides half the width of a socket. These lines are shown at D. For example, if the extreme width of the socket is 1 in., the distance to be marked on each side of the centres is obviously $\frac{1}{2}$ in. Now set the bevel to an angle of 10°—the angle must not be too acute, otherwise the joint will be weak—and mark the inclined lines by placing the stock of the bevel on the top edge of the work. Square the lines across the top and mark the angles on the back face.

The next operation consists in cutting the sockets down to the shoulder line by means of a dovetail-saw or, failing this, a fine-toothed tenon-saw. When sawing,

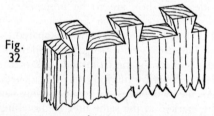

Fig. 32

great care must be exercised to keep the tool on the waste side of the guide lines.

To facilitate the next operation, which consists in removing the waste, it is an advantage to make a number of saw-kerfs in the waste down to the shoulder line before chiselling out.

When both ends have been cut, remove the work from the vice, and separate the pieces.

The waste is cut out with the aid of a very sharp chisel by first working from the top face, then reversing the work, and finishing off on the other side. When doing this, place the work on a piece of waste wood to prevent damage to the top of the bench.

The positions of the pins to be formed

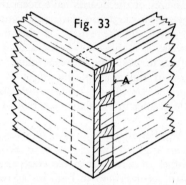

Fig. 33

on the back and front of the box may now be marked from a socketed member, in the following manner.

Lay the piece to be marked flat on the bench, and place a socketed piece on edge on top, so that it forms a right angle, taking care to keep the face of the socketed member flush with the edge of the other. Now mark out the angles by using the inside edges of the sockets as guides, using a finely-pointed pencil for the purpose. The remainder of the marking out is then completed in the same way as that adopted in marking the sockets.

The sawing and removal of the waste is then carried out in the same way as already explained.

An illustration of the finished pins appears in Fig. 32.

Fig. 33 illustrates a blind or lap dovetail, so called because the pins do not show on the face. It is used to a large extent in making drawer-fronts where the appearance of the ends of the pins would look unsightly.

In making a drawer-front it is usual

to have this part thicker than the sides and back, and to make the pins first. The length and width of the pins should be equal to the thickness of the sides.

To mark out the pins, set the marking-gauge to the thickness of the sides, and make a shoulder line on the inside face. Next, mark a line along the edge without altering the gauge, near the outside face, as shown at A in Fig. 33. Now set out the pins by marking off half the thickness

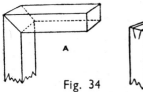

A   B

Fig. 34

of a pin from each end of the shoulder line and mark the centres for the pins in the intervening space by using either the dividers or rule. Set out the bevels as previously described.

The removal of the waste calls for careful work. Cut away as much waste as possible with the dovetail saw held at an angle, and clear out the remaining wood with a very sharp chisel.

Shoulder lines are now scribed on the ends of the side pieces, and then marked from the pins.

Mitre Joint.—The mitre joint, shown at A in Fig. 34, is commonly employed in picture-framing for joining the horizontal and vertical members.

The joint is made by first marking out the ends at an angle of 45°, planing them up true on the shooting-board, and then gluing the parts together.

A stronger joint than the plain mitre, used principally in cabinet-making and joinery, is obtained by the insertion of tongues or keys at the corners as shown at B in Fig. 34.

To make such a joint, mark and plane the mitred surfaces accurately and glue up as in the plain mitre. When the glue

is set, place the work in a vice and make two saw-kerfs across the corners with the saw held at an angle to form a dovetail, as shown clearly in the illustration. Insert a thin piece of glued hardwood with its grain at right-angles to the joint, into each slot, and allow the glue to dry. The ends of the hardwood pieces are then trimmed off flush.

End Lap Joint.—A joint commonly used for a quick, cheap job where accuracy and neat appearance are of little importance, is the end lap joint shown in Fig. 35. It is used principally for making packing-cases and boxes.

The wood is cut to lengths and either nailed or screwed at the sides. If nails are used, a better hold is obtained by driving them in slantwise, as indicated in the sketch. The bottom member is fixed after the sides have been assembled.

A modified joint of this type is shown in Fig. 36. Such a joint is useful when

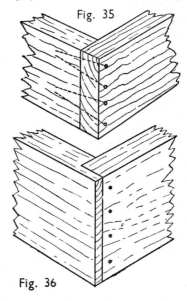

Fig. 35

Fig. 36

constructing common-type drawers, where a dovetailed joint is not deemed advisable. A rebate is formed on the inside face at each end of the front piece

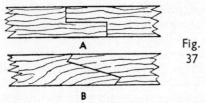

A

Fig. 37

B

to take the sides, which are fastened by glue and secured by nails or screws.

Lengthening Joints. — Joints for lengthening timber are used mostly in large constructional work, and therefore seldom attempted by the amateur.

Two typical examples of such joints are illustrated in Fig. 37. That shown at A represents a halved joint, and that at B, a scarfed joint. In both joints the members are usually bolted together.

HINGES AND LOCKS

HINGEING is the process of connecting two or more pieces of wood together in such a way as to allow one to revolve or move about the other. The connecting part that allows this free movement is called a "hinge."

There are many different kinds of hinges, each designed for a particular purpose. These include butt hinges, flap hinges, T-hinges—some plain and some ornamental—and others too numerous to mention.

The Simplest Form of Hinge consists of a strip of leather fastened to the faces of the stationary and moving parts. Although somewhat primitive, a leather hinge is remarkably durable and useful at times for hanging doors to poultry houses and similar objects.

Where such material is used, it is better to use round-headed screws in preference to nails for fixing purposes. Metal washers should be inserted between the head of the screw and the leather to prevent the screw-head tearing the material. If nailing is desired, it is a good plan to use galvanised clout nails as they have large heads and the galvanising coat prevents rust.

Another useful and simple type of hinge is found in the ordinary clothes-horse, in the form of pieces of cloth webbing fitted at the top and bottom

of the members, allowing the sections to be folded in both directions. These hinges are usually fixed by means of short galvanised clout nails for the reason stated above.

Metal Hinges.—Fig. 1 shows a few common types used for woodwork. The one shown at A is known as a "butt," and is a comparatively heavy hinge usually made of iron for common work and brass for furniture and cabinets. It is long compared with its width, and can be obtained in sizes ranging from $\frac{3}{8}$ in. to about 3 in.

Another handy form of a butt hinge,

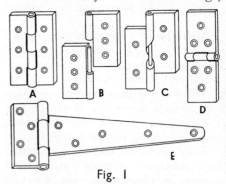

A   B   C

D

E

Fig. 1

known as a loose butt, is illustrated at B. The chief difference between the ordinary butt and the loose one is that the former has the two leaves forming the hinge locked together by the central pin, whereas one leaf of the latter can be removed from its fellow member. This useful feature enables a door, for instance, to be easily removed.

The Rising Butt Hinge illustrated at c has a loose leaf, which, when opened, rises on the centre pin and thus enables a door on opening to rise over a mat or a thick carpet and to close automatically.

The Back-flap Hinge represented at D is longer than its width, and can be obtained in either mild steel or brass. Such a hinge will often be found more useful than the butt type for certain amateur purposes, as it generally takes less cutting away to fit.

An extremely useful type of hinge, known as a T-hinge or cross-garnet, is depicted at E. This type of hinge is largely used on shed doors and garden gates, etc. where appearance is not the primary consideration. Cross-garnets require no great amount of skill to fix as they are generally fastened to the surface of the wood by countersunk-headed wood-screws.

Where cross-garnets are used on a shed door having a lock and key, one or two plain, round-headed bolts and nuts should be employed in place of ordinary wood-screws. The bolts should be fitted with their heads on the exterior of the door and secured by nuts

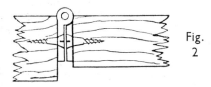

Fig. 2

on the inside. The screw-holes in the hinges may have to be enlarged for the purpose, in which case the tang end of a file can be used for reamering out the surplus metal. This will prevent unauthorised persons gaining access to the interior of the shed by removing the screws.

Butt hinges are used principally for

3*

hanging doors where it is necessary to fix the hinges on the edge. There are numerous ways of fixing such hinges, but whichever method is chosen it is necessary to sink the leaves into either one or both of the edges to be joined. This will be clearly understood by referring to Fig. 2, which shows a butt hinge incorrectly screwed to the face of the edge of the door and the supporting

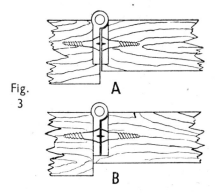

Fig. 3 A

B

frame. Such practice forms a gap as wide as the thickness of the two leaves, which is not only very unsightly but also allows dust to enter should the door be fitted to a cupboard.

The usual practice when hingeing a large door is to cut a recess in both the door edge and the jamb, to enable the leaves to lie flush with the respective surfaces in the manner shown at A in Fig. 3.

In the case of hingeing small doors such as those used on cabinets, furniture, etc. it is generally an advantage to cut recesses sufficiently deep to take both leaves in the edge of the door only. This arrangement allows one leaf to be fixed direct to the surface of the frame as illustrated at B in Fig. 3.

As a general rule it is best to allow the centre pin of the hinge to lie in line with the face of the door.

When fitting hinges to a large cupboard proceed as follows:

Place the door, edge to be hinged uppermost, against something to support it. Hold the hinge in the exact position required, keeping the pin in line with the front face of the door, and then scribe a line round the hinge by means of a sharply-pointed pencil. Repeat the process for the other hinge. If preferred, this marking can be done with a

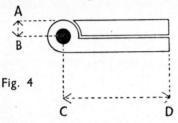

Fig. 4

marking - gauge by setting the gauge from the hinge itself, and gauging from the long edge of the hinge to the centre of the pin in the manner indicated by CD in Fig. 4. When the lines indicating the width have been marked on the edge of the door, mark off on these lines a distance equal to the length of a hinge. From these marks draw lines at right-angles to the long edge of the door and carry them over to the front face, using a square for the purpose. The next item is to gauge the depth of the recesses which, of course, is equal to the thickness of a leaf as represented at AB in Fig. 4. Set the gauge from the hinge and mark the depth lines on the front edge of the door. The waste is removed by first making a series of saw kerfs and then cutting it away by the use of a chisel.

Fitting the Hinges.—Great care should be exercised to see that they are not set too far in from the front, as this will prevent the door opening to its fullest extent; and if sunk too deeply the door either will not close or, if it does happen to close, it will spring open again because it is hinge-bound. In the latter case, the hinge can be brought up level by packing it underneath with cardboard.

Having fitted the hinges to the door, the next process is to hang the door to its frame. To do this, place the door in its final open position to enable the positions of the other leaves to be marked on the frame. If the door is a large one, a thin wooden wedge should be inserted under the bottom edge to raise it a trifle above the floor level and thus allow the door to swing freely. Care must be taken to see that the door is not raised too high, otherwise the top edge will foul the top of the frame.

The positions for the recesses in the frame are then marked by tracing the outlines of the leaves and marking the depth with a marking-gauge. The waste is then carefully removed with a chisel and mallet. Now place the door in position again (not forgetting to insert the wedge when so doing), and then drive a screw through the middle hole in each leaf into the frame, after having bored the necessary screw-holes with a bradawl.

If the door swings freely, as it should do after removing the wedge, the remaining screw-holes can be bored, the screws inserted and finally driven in.

Locks, like hinges, are to be obtained in many varieties and sizes, and may be classified under three headings: (*a*) those suitable for room doors; (*b*) those employed on cupboard doors; and (*c*) those used for boxes and drawers.

Fig. 5 shows three common forms of locks in everyday use. That illustrated at A represents a simple type of lock, known as a rim lock. Such a lock is useful for unimportant doors where appearance is of little consequence, and the use of a more costly lock is unjustified. A rim lock takes but little fitting as it is fixed on the inside face of the door.

To fit a rim lock, all that is necessary is to sink the projecting flange into the edge of the door, cut the keyhole, and bore a hole for the knob spindle to pass.

The first thing to do in fitting a rim lock is to prepare the recess in the front edge of the door to take the flange. The position for this is usually in line with the centre of the middle rail of the door. Mark this position and from it trace the outline of the flange, using a sharp-pointed pencil for the purpose. Mark a depth line by setting the marking-gauge to the thickness of the flange, and remove the waste with the aid of a chisel and mallet. Next, place the lock in position and mark the positions for the keyhole and spindle hole by pushing the blade of a fine bradawl through the centres of the apertures in the lock, taking care to hold the bradawl perfectly square.

Select a bit a trifle larger in diameter than the diagonal thickness of the spindle, bore the hole until the point of the tool just appears on the other side, and finish the hole from that side. Great care must be taken to keep the brace perfectly square when boring the hole, otherwise the lock will not work properly. Now prepare the keyhole by first boring a hole a trifle larger than the shank of the key and then making another just below to clear the bottom of the ward. Finish the keyhole by removing waste between the holes, using a pad-saw for the purpose. Now hold the lock in position, insert the key and the spindle from the outside to test whether they work freely. If satisfactory, bore the holes for the fixing screws by means of a bradawl, and drive in the screws.

Fix the small plate or " escutcheon " that surrounds the keyhole and the cover plate for the spindle hole, on the outside

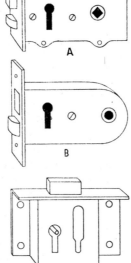

A

B

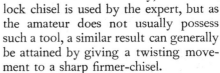

C

Fig. 5

of the door. Finally, screw the box staple that receives the latches to the frame, taking care to see that it is centred correctly.

A Mortice Lock (B in Fig. 5) is used for room doors where neatness of appearance is essential. Such a lock is not so easy to fit as the rim lock, as the body or box containing the mechanism is sunk into a mortice cut in the closing stile and centre rail of the door.

To fit a mortice lock, mark the position of the recess on the edge of the door by means of a rule, marking-gauge, and square. Next, select a twist-bit whose diameter is the same as the thickness of the lock, and bore a series of holes as deep as the lock is long, to remove as much waste as possible. Drill the holes as close to each other as convenient, as it is somewhat difficult to clean the end of the mortice. To clear the ends sufficiently, a mortice-lock chisel is used by the expert, but as the amateur does not usually possess such a tool, a similar result can generally be attained by giving a twisting movement to a sharp firmer-chisel.

Having completed the holes, remove the remainder of the waste by using either a morticing- or a firmer-chisel, and clear up the sides with a wide chisel so that the lock fits hand-tight in the recess.

Cutting a Recess.—As some mortice locks are fitted with an additional plate to cover the fixing plate, due allowance must be made for this—if fitted—when gauging the depth of the recess.

Insert the body of the lock into the mortice, trace the outline of the end plate with a sharp-pointed pencil, gauge the depth, and then chisel out the waste.

Now measure and mark the positions for the centres of the handle spindle and the shank of the key, on both sides of the door. Drill the holes through one side only and then slide the lock into the mortice to test the accuracy of the holes. If correct, bore the holes on the other side and finish the keyholes by cutting them down accurately with a pad-saw, taking care not to make the holes too large.

Fix the lock permanently in place by driving screws through the end plate.

Having fixed the escutcheon plates over the keyholes, the spindle plates and handles, the next thing to do is to mark accurately the position for the mortice and the cover plate to take the latches, on the door jamb. Cut the mortice a trifle deeper than the length of the latches and accurately chisel out the recess for the plate. The work is complete when the plate has been fastened securely with countersunk-headed screws.

Little difficulty should be experienced in fitting a drawer lock (c in Fig. 5).

The Keyhole.—Mark the position of the keyhole which obviously comes in the centre of the drawer front. From this point square a line up to the top edge and across it as indicated at A in Fig. 6, then set the marking-gauge from the top plate, to the centre of the pin over which the end of the key fits, and mark the point B. Fix a boring bit, a shade larger than the diameter of the barrel of the key, in the brace, and make the hole at this point. In doing this it is a good plan to hold a piece of waste wood at the back to

prevent the bit bursting through, and also to ensure a perfectly clean hole. Drill a smaller hole a little lower down

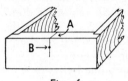

Fig. 6

with a bit a trifle larger than the thickness of the ward of the key, and then remove the waste between the two holes with a pad-saw. If, on trying the key, the aperture is found to be too small, enlarge the hole by means of a small flat file.

Now pass the key through the keyhole into the lock, and holding the lock in the exact position for its final resting-place, trace the outline of the back plate. Make sure that the lines so marked are perfectly square by testing with a square.

Carefully chisel out the recesses for the back and top plates and then mark and cut the deeper recess to take the body of the lock. Insert the fixing screws and screw all tightly home.

Shoot the latch out by turning the key, and smear the end with some grate polish, or some other substance that will mark easily. Return the latch into the lock, close the drawer, and turn the key as far as possible in an attempt to lock the drawer. Replace the latch, and on opening the drawer the exact place for the mortice will be clearly visible.

Chisel out the mortice a little deeper than that actually required, countersink the plate, and fasten it with screws. Finally, test to see that all works smoothly, and then fix the escutcheon.

SHARPENING
WOODWORKERS' TOOLS

WHATEVER tools the amateur possesses, whether few or many, the time comes when something or other needs to be done besides oiling the wood or steel to keep them in good condition.

The commonest requirement is sharpening, because wood-cutting tools lose their usefulness as soon as they become blunt.

Of course, the sharpening can be done for you at a fairly low cost by the local tool-dealer, but this generally means delay, as it is seldom that the necessary work can be undertaken at a moment's notice. It is much better to do such jobs for yourself.

Saws are generally considered difficult tools to sharpen, but this is really not so if one goes about the work in a careful and methodical way.

The tools required to sharpen saws include a saw-cramp, a suitable triangular or three-cornered file, a flat file, a saw-set, and the bench vice.

The tradesman generally uses a special type of saw-cramp, but this device is unnecessary for the amateur as one can be improvised by fixing the saw, teeth upwards, between two pieces of board with their outer edges chamfered off, in the bench vice.

The boards must be thicker than the shoulders formed by the handle of the saw, which, in all saws in general use, is just under ½ in. The length of the strips should be a little longer than the saw-blade.

When fitting the saw between the cramps for filing, the teeth should not project more than ½ in. above the level of the top edges. If the saw is allowed to project more than this amount, "chattering" will take place when the file is used. This does not apply when "setting" the teeth, because the height of the saw above the cramps will have to be adjusted to allow the setting tool to be conveniently operated.

It does not necessarily follow that because a saw cuts badly it requires sharpening; it may be that the tool only needs re-setting. If, on examining the teeth, the "points" appear to be a trifle rounded and dull, it usually indicates that the tool requires sharpening. On the other hand, if the points seem to be well defined and clean, it may be taken that re-setting will put the tool into serviceable condition. This should be borne in mind, because a saw generally needs setting more often than sharpening—sometimes as much as three settings to one sharpening.

Assuming that a saw requires a general overhaul, proceed in the following way.

Fix the saw securely between the cramps so that the teeth are parallel to and project ½ in. above the edges.

Stripping.—The first operation consists in filing the tops of the teeth perfectly level from one end of the blade to the other. This is necessary because the teeth usually get more wear in the centre than at the ends, causing the top edge to assume a slightly concave shape. A straight-edge placed on the top of the teeth will enable you to verify this, and indicate where most filing is required.

To strip the teeth, place the file lengthwise over the teeth, that is, the file and saw running in the same direction, and file lightly along the tops, using a smooth, flat file for the purpose.

Take care to keep the file perfectly horizontal so that it does not remove more metal on one side than the other. Press mostly at the ends if the middle happens to be a trifle concave. If you

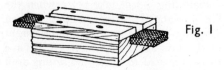

Fig. I

have difficulty in keeping the file straight, it is a good plan to sink the file squarely in a block of wood to act as a guide, as shown in Fig. 1.

If the stripping process has been properly done, all the points should appear perfectly level when tested with the straight-edge.

It may be that some of the teeth are a trifle flattened after filing, in which case it will be necessary to file them at the backs.

Setting the Teeth is the next process. This means that each alternate tooth on one side of the blade and each alternate tooth on the other is bent

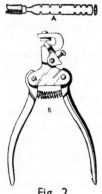

Fig. 2

outwards to an amount which depends upon the type of saw. Thus, the teeth of a rip-saw do not require so much set as a cross-cutting saw, and a tenon-saw is set finer than the latter. In any case it is essential that the same amount of set be given to each tooth of a particular saw, so that they are all alike.

The Saw-set.—Saw-setting is accomplished with a tool called a saw-set. A common type is represented at A in Fig. 2. It will be seen that the tool consists of a steel blade having a number of slots, and fitted with a suitable handle. The slots are of various sizes to suit different thicknesses of teeth.

The tool is used by fitting a suitable slot over a tooth and pressing it downwards until sufficient set is produced. This type of tool certainly has the advantage of being cheap to buy, but it is not recommended for use by the

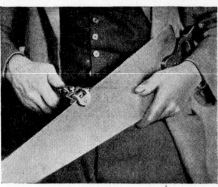

Fig. 3

inexperienced worker as a considerable amount of skill is needed to judge the amount of bending, and it is an easy matter to break the teeth if the work is not carried out properly.

The Mechanical Saw-set (Fig. 2, B) is an excellent tool for the handyman, because the amount of set can be regulated by a screw and this enables the teeth to be bent exactly alike. To use the tool the screw is first adjusted to give the desired degree of set, the jaws are fitted over a tooth, and the handles pressed together in the same way as a pair or pliers.

It should be noted that only the points of the teeth are bent over, and that the operation should not be attempted on a very cold saw. It is safer to warm the saw and the saw-set prior to operations, and to carry out the work in a warm room. During the winter the best place is obviously in front of a fire, not only for the worker but also for the saw. Fig. 3 shows the operation.

Filing the Teeth.—A tapered triangular file about 4 or 5 in. long will be required for treating hand-saws, while a smaller tool will generally answer the purpose for tenon-saws.

Fix the saw between the cramps as already mentioned, taking care to see that the teeth do not project more than ½ in. above the edges of the cramps.

Grasp the handle of the file in the right hand, keeping the thumb on top, and hold the point of the tool with the left, in the manner indicated in Fig. 4. File those teeth that have had their points removed during the stripping process first. When this has been done, file down into each alternate V-groove so that the back of each tooth and the face of the next is treated, then reverse the blade in the cramps and proceed with the other side.

In using the file give the same number of strokes—one or two only—to every tooth, and make the strokes of equal length and pressure.

If a Rip-saw is being Sharpened use the file horizontally and keep it square with the blade. In the case of a cross-cutting saw hold the file obliquely to the saw-blade and keep the point of the tool inclined upwards to an angle of about 15° or more to the horizontal. This can easily be done by following the angle of the original cut.

A good test for determining the accuracy of a cross-cutting saw after it has been set and sharpened can be carried out by holding the saw, teeth uppermost, and placing a needle lengthways in the groove formed by the bent points of the teeth. If the needle slides without interruption from one end to the other on tilting the saw, it is a sure indication that the work has been carried out satisfactorily.

Sharpening Plane-irons, chisels, gouges and similar tools is a much simpler process than sharpening saws, and usually only requires the use of an oilstone and the occasional use of a grindstone.

Two stones are recommended for sharpening these tools, one being a coarse carborundum and the other a good quality Arkansas or a Washita. The latter should be neither too hard nor too soft, but of a medium hardness. A serviceable size for these is 6 in. by 2 in. by ⅝ in. They should be sunk into a block of wood and provided with a cover to keep out dirt and grit.

If you neither possess a grindstone nor have easy access to one, the coarse carborundum stone previously mentioned will generally be found a good substitute.

Each time you sharpen the cutting-edge of a chisel, etc., rub down the bevel

Fig. 4

also. The bevel should be a little longer than the width of the cutting-edge in the case of a firmer-chisel, but in a paring-chisel it could be almost half as long again, bearing in mind that the sharper the angle the weaker the edge and therefore it will be more likely to notch and break, although a sharp angle means cleaner cutting.

Assuming that you wish to sharpen a chisel, and that you have a coarse stone and an oilstone as suggested, proceed in the following way.

Treat the bevel first by means of the carborundum stone.

Apply a few drops of thin oil to the surface, taking care that the oil is really thin. A thick lubricant tends to make the tool glide over the surface rather than "bite" on the stone and sharpen it.

Hold the chisel, bevel side down, with the right hand, and press the fingers of the left on the blade just above the cutting-edge, keeping the bevelled face flat on the stone. Now move the tool forward over the surface of the stone, applying a little pressure with the fingers. Relieve the pressure at the end of the stroke and draw the blade back to its original position, and repeat these movements until the bevel is perfectly flat.

Test the Squareness of the Edge by means of a square and if one corner is a trifle "high" more pressure must be exerted on that point when rubbed over the stone again. You will now have a clean straight bevel, as shown at A in Fig. 5, with probably a definite "wire" edge or burr projecting from the flat side of the cutting-edge of the tool. If such is the case place the plain face of the chisel flat on the stone and give it one or two light rubs, taking care to keep the tool perfectly flat.

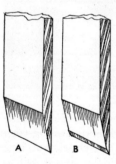

Fig. 5

The medium oilstone will now be required to finish off the cutting-edge. Apply a few drops of very thin oil, such as kerosene.

Hold the chisel in the right hand and lay the fingers of the left on the blade, keeping the thumb under the handle end of the blade, as indicated in Fig. 6. The tool is held at a slightly wider angle than

when treating the bevel to obtain a slightly more obtuse angle at the cutting-edge, as shown at B in Fig. 5. The tool is then moved back and forth over the stone in the manner already described.

Fig. 6

This operation is continued until a burr appears on the flat side of the tool, which is a good indication that the edge is sufficiently sharp. When this occurs, turn the chisel over and give the back one or two rubs to remove the burr, as already explained. Great care must be exercised whilst doing this to keep the blade perfectly flat on the stone, as any indication of a bevel on the flat side of the tool will ruin its cutting capabilities.

In sharpening chisels some workers prefer to "run" the cutting-edge parallel to the long edge of the stone, while others hold the tool at an angle to the edge of the stone, and some rub the tool along the surface, using a circular or curved stroke. The best plan is to try each method and then use the one you can manage best.

Plane-irons require frequent sharpening to keep them in serviceable condition, as a blunt tool, or the slightest notch in the cutting-edge, will mar the surface of the work.

Plane-irons, like chisels, are sharpened on an oilstone, and treated similarly.

Fig. 7

After having removed the iron from the body of the plane by holding the stock with the left hand and striking the front, as in Fig. 7, the back iron must be separated from its fellow member, the cutter. To do this it is advisable to place the component flat on the bench and then unfasten the screw, as it is dangerous to attempt to turn the screw while it is held in the hand.

Put a few drops of oil on the oilstone, and place the bevelled edge flat on the surface, and then raise it a trifle to obtain the correct cutting angle as in sharpening

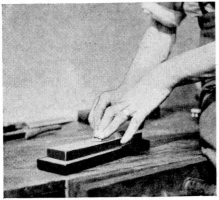

Fig. 8

a chisel. Move the cutter back and forth over the surface with a more or less circular sweep. If the stone is not

wide enough to take the whole of the cutting-edge when held at right angles to the edge of the stone, the iron should be held obliquely to ensure that the whole of the cutting-edge remains on the surface. This is an important point. Failure to do so invariably results in an unequal sharpened edge, and may also put it out of square. When a burr forms, showing that the edge is sharp, reverse the iron so that it lies perfectly flat on the stone and give it one or two rubs to remove the wire edge. Fig. 8 shows how the cutting-iron is held whilst being sharpened on an oilstone.

The Slip, a wedge-shaped oilstone

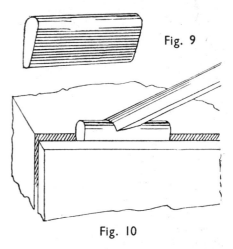

Fig. 9

Fig. 10

with rounded edges, is required for sharpening internally-ground gouges. Such an oilstone is illustrated in Fig. 9.

In sharpening an internally-ground gouge, that is, one having the bevel on the concave face of the blade, the stone may either be held in the vice, as indicated in Fig. 10, or in the hand in the manner shown in Fig. 11. The former method is perhaps better as the tool can be sharpened in practically the same way as a chisel by rubbing it up and down the curved face of the slip. The burr left on the outside edge is then removed on an ordinary oilstone, by placing the blade flat on the surface and giving it one or two rubs along the stone. The tool should be given a turning movement during the process to ensure that the whole of the edge comes in contact with the stone.

When using the hand method of holding the slip, the tool is held in the

Fig. 11

left hand and the slip in the right. The slip is then rubbed up and down against the cutting-edge, care being taken to see that the whole of the edge gets the same amount of treatment.

The oilstone slip is, of course, lubricated with one or two drops of thin oil as in the case of the flat stone.

An Externally-ground Gouge is sharpened by rubbing its cutting-edge back and forth on the oilstone, as shown in Fig. 12. The tool is held at an angle to the long edge of the stone and at a slightly larger angle than that of the bevel to obtain a fine cutting-edge.

The blade is given a circular turning movement as the work proceeds, to ensure equal thickness of the whole length of the cutting-edge. The burr formed on the inner edge is then removed with an oilstone slip.

Clean holes can only be produced by using sharp bits, because dull cutting-

edges simply break the fibres of the wood instead of severing them.

When any fibres are left on the walls of a hole after being bored it is usually a sign that the tool needs attention.

Sharpening a Centre-bit.—The centre-bit consists of three principal parts, namely, the "centre" or guide-point, whose object is to guide the bit in its passage through the wood; the "nicker" or outside pointed cutter, which severs the fibres at the outside diameter of the hole to be cut, and the "knife-cutter," whose purpose is to cut out and remove the waste.

If a bad hole is produced when using a centre-bit it usually indicates that either the nicker or the cutter, or both, require "touching up," as it is seldom that the point needs attention.

Should the guide-point happen to be blunt or the corners rounded, the fault may be rectified by filing the prong by means of a smooth file. This can be done either by fixing the tool upwards in the vice or by holding it in the left hand and placing it on a piece of wood on the bench, and filing each face until sufficient

Fig. 12

metal has been removed to form a new point. Care must be taken, however, when doing this not to take off too much metal, otherwise the point will be level with or below the level of the nicker and thus render the tool useless.

Any filing of the long edge of the nicker must be done from the inside, that is, between the nicker and the centre-point, because any metal removed from the outside will reduce its cutting diameter.

If the top of the nicker requires atten-tion, take care to see that the edge slopes back to give the correct clearance angle, otherwise the edge will merely scratch the wood instead of cutting it. It is also equally important to ensure that the cutting-edge of the nicker does not come below the level of the interior sloping cutter.

The inclined cutter for removing the waste wood is treated with a smooth, flat file, working it towards the cutting-edge in the manner shown in Fig. 13. The chief point to observe when dealing with this part of the tool is to maintain the original inclined angle.

Any burr thrown up after filing the various parts can be removed by the oil-stone slip or the ordinary flat oilstone.

The cutting-edges of twist-bits are so varied that one can only recommend the worker to note carefully how the cutting-edge is formed, and then treat them accordingly. In some cases a rat-tail file, in others a flat file, is necessary.

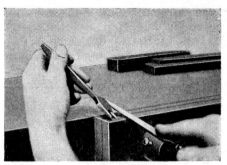

Fig. 13

It may appear curious to refer to sharpening a screw-driver, but this operation is often needed, especially when the working end of the blade has been burred over by careless usage.

A good method of reconditioning such a tool is to place it, blade uppermost, in the vice, and file the edge to a narrow level face. The edge can then be thinned down to the required thickness by rub-bing the bevelled faces on a coarse carborundum stone.

Hand-driven Emery Grinding Machines can now be obtained at a cost of a few shillings. They are particularly useful for grinding both woodworking and metal-working tools as the interchangeable abrasive wheels may be obtained in various forms and degrees of hardness.

GLUE AND GLUING

GOOD glue is one of the greatest aids to the woodworker, but if it is of poor quality it is worse than useless. A good quality glue can be distinguished by its clear amber colour, while its texture is hard, somewhat brittle, and it is practically odourless.

There are several kinds of glue, including English, French and Scotch. Scotch glue is the strongest. Then there are several varieties of proprietary glues, sold ready for use, all of which are excellent adhesives and generally used cold.

Before ordinary glue can be used it must be prepared and melted and, as it is applied hot, a suitable glue pot must be provided.

The Glue Pot.—Fig. 1 shows the type commonly used. It consists of an inner and outer vessel: the inner one to hold the glue, and the outer to contain the water. In these days such a pot can be obtained very cheaply at almost any ironmonger's shop.

A good substitute for a glue pot is a treacle tin placed in a saucepan, but as the bottom of the inner container must not touch the bottom of the outer one, something should be placed between the vessels to satisfy this requirement.

Fig. 1

Preparation.—Break a piece off the cake—it is usually sold in cakes of about 6 in. square, at so much per pound—sufficient for your requirements, remembering that glue swells considerably when soaked in water. Break the piece into small fragments by using a hammer. As this operation causes the glue to fly about in all directions, it is an advantage to wrap the glue in a piece of thick brown paper or a clean duster before applying the hammer. Place the "bag" of glue on a hard surface, such as a stone floor, and hit it smartly several times with the hammer. After removing any fragments of paper or other extraneous matter which may have adhered to the glue, put the glue into the inner vessel of the pot. Cover the contents with cold water and leave it overnight to soak. This will cause the glue to swell. After straining off the water, partially fill the outer vessel with clean water (taking care to see that the water is absolutely clean, otherwise it will

boil over) and replace the inner container. Put it on a lighted gas ring, and bring it gently up to the boil. Allow it to simmer for a time until the jellified glue has melted, stirring the mixture occasionally to remove lumps, and add more water as needed. Before use, remove any scum that may have formed on the surface.

Some glue pots have a notch in the lip of the water vessel to allow the steam to escape, others are not so provided. If you are using one of the latter, insert a match-stick between the lips of the containers, or, better still, file a notch when the pot is cold.

Before using the glue it is a good plan to stretch a wire across the centre of the container and fix the ends to the handle lugs. This arrangement allows any surplus glue on the brush to be conveniently removed by wiping the brush across the wire.

The glue is ready for use when it assumes the consistency of thin treacle. This can be tested by dipping the brush into the glue, holding it up over the pot and allowing it to flow back. If it flows from the brush in a steady easy stream, it may be taken as correct.

If you have never made glue before, and have plenty of time at your disposal a further test may be made which will

Fig. 2

enable you to judge its quality for future occasions.

Plane up the edges of two small pieces of wood, as in a butt joint, warm the pieces and apply a little hot glue to both surfaces. Rub the glued edges together and then cramp it up. Set aside for 24 hours in a warm room. If it breaks anywhere but at the glued joint after attempting to break the joint either by hand or by inserting the blade of a chisel into the end of the joint, you may be sure that the glue has been correctly made and properly used.

Glue Brushes.—Glue should be applied with a brush, the size of which depends upon the nature of the work. A paint brush about ½ in. wide will serve well for small jobs, such as gluing mitres of picture-frames and small mortices. A large brush should be employed on large work as the adhesive should be applied rapidly to prevent chilling, because chilled glue means an unsatisfactory joint. For this reason the work should always be warmed before applying the glue, and the process should be carried out in a warm room. When heating the wood be careful not to scorch or warp it.

Brushes after use should be washed in hot water to remove all traces of glue, and then allowed to dry.

It sometimes happens that a brush cannot conveniently be used for applying the glue, in which case the difficulty may be overcome by using an old teaspoon bent to shape as illustrated in Fig. 2. This forms a holder which, when filled with glue, can be poured into any odd corner of the work.

Cramps.—To ensure true fitting of the faces of the joint it is advisable to use two cramps as shown in Fig. 3. After the work has been cramped it should be placed flat down on an even surface and a heavy weight put on top.

Before fixing the cramps, however, any surplus glue adhering to the surface of the work should be removed by applying a rag dipped in hot water. This is a much better method than scraping it off, as it prevents damage to the surface, and ensures the removal of every particle of glue. This is particularly necessary should the work have to be stained or otherwise finished.

Reheated glue has not the adhesive power of fresh.

Liquid Glue.—If glue is only required occasionally, or if a small quantity is wanted, it will be found more economical and convenient to purchase a tube of liquid glue. The demand has reached such proportions that new makes of this form of glue are constantly appearing on the market. The prices vary considerably, but unless it is required for some important work the very cheap tubes sold at some of the numerous stores answer the purpose very well. A brush is unnecessary in applying the

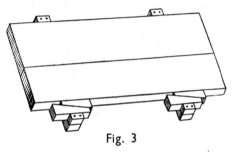

Fig. 3

glue, as all that is necessary is to place the nozzle of the tube directly on the work and squeeze the bottom until sufficient adhesive is forced out. The glue may then be spread evenly over the surface with the forefinger.

Re-gluing Old Work is not always a pleasant job, and cannot always be successfully carried out. It is useless to attempt to make a new joint by merely spreading glue over the old, putting it under pressure and hoping for the best.

The proper way to set about a re-gluing job is to remove the old glue first, using a sharp knife or chisel for the purpose, and then to wipe the surfaces with a cloth dipped in hot water. When the parts to be joined are perfectly dry they may be warmed, re-glued and put under pressure.

CRAMPS AND WEDGES

NEARLY all glued work is the better for being cramped whilst setting. This not only forces the parts together but it also defeats any tendency to break away whilst the glue sets.

Cramps are varied in form and are used for other purposes besides gluing.

An ordinary screw is in reality a cramp, but one left permanently in the

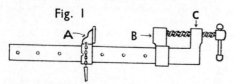

Fig. 1

job. It not only pulls the parts together but holds them in place.

A screw works on the same principle as an inclined plane and all cramps are based on this principle in one form or another—thus bought metal ones are fitted with a screw, while home-made

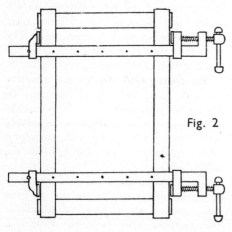

Fig. 2

clamping appliances generally rely upon the inclined plane in the shape of a wedge.

The usual type of joiner's cramp (shown in Fig. 1) consists of a long bar,

either of iron or mild steel, in which a number of holes are bored to take an iron peg that holds a sliding bracket A necessary to give the varying distances required. A second sliding bracket B, is worked by a screw passing through a fixed head C, at one end of the bar.

Two such cramps are usually necessary efficiently to cramp the work together. As joiner's cramps are rather expensive to buy, the cost generally precludes their use by the average home worker. The method of using such cramps is illustrated in Fig. 2, which

Fig. 3

shows a small door frame under treatment.

Cramp-heads can be bought separately and will be found of great service to those workers who have a fair amount of cramping to do from time to time. The heads are provided with swivelling iron straps that bind on a suitable length of timber. Their usefulness is limited only by the length of wood used for the bar. As this type of cramp is comparatively cheap it should appeal to the handyman. Fig. 3 shows this useful device.

The majority of work needing the use of cramps can usually be done by cramps made of suitable lengths of wood, with wedges to replace screws. They can be easily and quickly made of odd pieces of wood generally found in every workshop.

A typical example of a home-made cramp suitable for cramping, say, a small frame measuring 18 in. wide, is shown at A in Fig. 4. Such a cramp can be made from a piece of board, 2 ft. or more in length, 4 or 5 in. wide and ⅞ in. thick, by screwing a cross-piece flush with one end of the board, and another at a distance of 19 in. away. This leaves a gap of 1 in. between the work and the cross-pieces for the insertion of wedges.

The two wedges shown at B are prepared from a piece of rectangular wood ⅞ in. thick, by cutting it across diagonally. The wood for these should be straight-grained, and the taper should only be sufficient to obtain the compression desired. If angles are made too obtuse they may work loose.

If the frame is fairly long, it is advisable to use two cramps; they should be fitted as close as possible to the mortice and tenon joint of the framework.

An improvement on the home-made

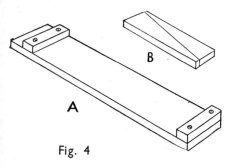

Fig. 4

wooden cramp just described is shown in Fig. 5. The illustration needs no description as it is self explanatory. If much use is going to be made of the device with boards of varying thickness, the following alterations are advisable.

Make the two inner blocks (A) slightly thicker than the work to be wedged, and fix them to the outer members by means

of bolts and wing-nuts, not forgetting to insert large iron washers between the heads of the bolts, nuts and wood.

The advantage of using this type of cramp is that the work is supported on

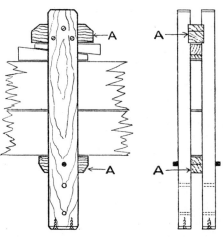

Fig. 5

all sides, and any tendency to rise at the joints is prevented by the side members.

In cases where short boards are to be cramped, the edges to be joined should be very slightly planed hollow. If this is done, a single cramp in the middle would suffice, as the slight concavity causes the ends of the boards to meet at once, and any pressure in the middle binds them together.

To keep the ends of the boards true laterally, a joiner's " dog " (illustrated in Fig. 6) may be called into requisition; or, if the boards are not thick enough for these, a corrugated nail driven partly home will usually answer the purpose.

A Cramping-board made on similar lines to that shown in Fig. 7 will be found very useful for cramping small work. A cheap pastry-board could be used for the base if it is not thought worth while to make one. Two accurately-planed strips of wood are either nailed or screwed at right angles to each other to the base, and two similar strips are fastened down at a slightly greater distance from the others than the length and width of the frame to be cramped.

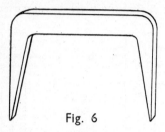

Fig. 6

The strips need not be as long as either the length or width of the frame.

The frame to be cramped is glued and assembled, one corner is inserted into one of the angles formed by the two strips, and wedges are driven between the frame and the other strip, which cramp all up tightly.

In making the device, care must be taken to fix the pieces at right-angles. Always test them with a square.

Cramping Floorboards. — While dealing with the subject of cramps it may not be amiss to give a method of cramping up floorboards, especially if a new workshop or other structure is in course of construction.

The tradesman generally uses special cramps for the purpose, but the amateur can cramp floorboards in the following way.

Nail down the first board, and at a distance of about $\frac{1}{4}$ in. less than the width of 4 or 5 boards, nail down a second board. Place the loose boards, with their edges butted together, in the intervening space. The middle joints will be raised, but by standing on them,

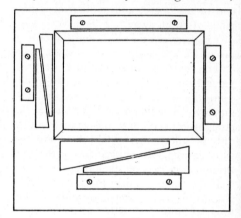

Fig. 7

the boards will be forced into place. It may need more than the weight of one person to do this. This method answers very well if each board extends the whole length of the floor.

GLASS-PAPERING

GLASS-PAPER is used principally for putting a final finish to the surface of wood where the plane has not left it as smooth as could be desired.

It is made by sprinkling powdered glass over the glued surface of tough paper by means of sieves having from 16 to 90 meshes per inch.

Fine, medium and coarse glass-paper are the grades commonly used by the amateur. No. 0 is the finest, and is employed for producing a fine finish;

No. 2 is coarse and therefore suitable for rough work.

Glass-paper is sold in sheets measuring 12 in. by 10 in., and can be obtained with a cloth backing instead of paper, which gives it exceptional strength. It can also be obtained with a waterproof backing which renders it invaluable for rubbing down paintwork with water.

In using glass-paper for finishing the surfaces of wood it is usual to start with a coarse grade and to finish with a fine, but this does not always apply, because much depends upon the finish desired.

When preparing work that is to be either french polished or varnished, the glass-paper should be rubbed along the grain of the wood, as any scratches left on the surface will show through the more or less transparent film of polish. This is not so important where the work is to be painted, as the paint will cover up any such imperfections. In fact, it is generally an advantage to glass-paper across the grain at an angle of about 45° when paint is used, as this makes for quicker finishing.

Flat surfaces treated with glass-paper should be kept flat on the work by means of a suitable rubber.

These appliances can be purchased at a cost of only a few pence, but one can be easily made by the worker himself from a piece of flat wood 4 in. in length, 3 in. wide, and $\frac{3}{4}$ in. thick. The bottom of the rubber is then faced by gluing on a piece of cork, such as that commonly used for teapot stands, or a piece of thick linoleum.

If cork is used, cut it with a wet knife, as when cutting rubber.

The Block can be used by folding the ends of the glass-paper over the sides and keeping it in position with the fingers.

A much better device for holding the glass-paper is that illustrated in Fig. 1, which, although not quite so simple to make as the plain block, is well worth the little extra time required for its construction. Reference to the illustration shows that it consists of two parts. A strip of glass-paper is held between the top and bottom members, which are fastened together by means of a $1\frac{3}{4}$-in. by $\frac{3}{16}$-in. Whitworth bolt fitted with a wing-nut.

The block is made in the following way. Get a piece of wood, preferably hardwood, and plane it up to a finished

size of $5\frac{1}{2}$ in. by $2\frac{1}{2}$ in. by $1\frac{1}{4}$ in. Round off the top long edges and form a hollow in the sides by means of a gouge. The hollow is not absolutely necessary but it enables the block to be conveniently held. Bore a $1\frac{1}{4}$-in. diameter recess, $\frac{1}{2}$ in. deep, in the centre of the top face, using a centre-bit for the purpose, and drill a small clearing-hole through the centre of the recess to take the bolt.

The finished size of the bottom piece is the same as the top except that its thickness is only $\frac{1}{2}$ in. Make a $\frac{3}{16}$-in. diameter hole through the centre, and cut a small recess round the hole on the bottom face to take the head of the bolt and allow it to lie flush or just below the surface. Now drive the bolt through the hole by giving it a few taps

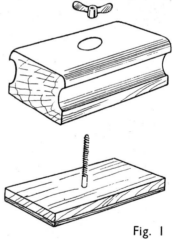

Fig. 1

with a hammer. The bolt will be prevented from turning when the nut is fitted by the small square shoulder under the head of the bolt. Glue either a piece of lino or cork on the bottom and allow the glue to dry. Cut a strip of suitable glass-paper, 10 in. in length and $2\frac{1}{2}$ in. wide; insert the ends between the top and bottom pieces of the block and pass the shank of the bolt through the hole in the top member. Slip an iron washer over the end of the bolt and tighten up the parts by means of the wing-nut. Fig. 2 shows the block in use.

When glass-papering concave-shaped surfaces such as hollows in mouldings, etc., it is an advantage to wrap the glass-paper round a suitably shaped

Fig. 2

piece of cork or wood. For treating convex surfaces a hollowed piece of wood is a great help. (*See* Fig. 3.)

The marks left on the flat surface of hardwood after planing are generally removed by means of a scraper before finishing the work with glass-paper.

A Scraper is merely a piece of steel about $\frac{1}{16}$ in. thick and 5 in. long by 3 in. wide, and can be purchased from most tool-dealers for a few pence.

Scrapers may be obtained with curved surfaces to fit various curved work such as mouldings, etc., but they are more costly than the rectangular ones.

The properly-sharpened scraper becomes an efficient tool and does not just scrape as its name suggests, but acts as a very finely-set plane. This makes it particularly useful for negotiating irregular grained hardwoods, where the use of a plane generally tears the fibres.

The cutting action is effected by turning the long edges over to form a "burr," as shown enlarged in Fig. 4, and the

secret of successful scraping depends in no small degree upon how well the burr has been formed.

In use, the tool is usually held at the ends by placing the thumbs at the back and the fingers at the front in the manner indicated in Fig. 5. It is held at an angle of about 60° to the surface of the work in the same way as a plane-iron is fixed at an angle in the stock.

Some workers prefer to push the tool forwards—in the direction of the grain, of course—while others pull the scraper towards them. It is sometimes a help to hold the tool a little obliquely instead of at right angles to the direction of scraping.

If the tool fails to do its work properly it should be sharpened. The formation of dust instead of tiny shavings is generally a sure sign of a blunt tool.

The scraper is regarded by many as a difficult tool to sharpen. This may be due to their lack of knowledge regarding the working principle of the tool, or it

Fig. 3

may be that they do not go about the work in the correct manner.

To Sharpen a Scraper, place the tool, working edge uppermost, in the vice, and file the edge perfectly clean and flat, using a fine flat file, held lengthways, for the purpose. Test with a square, and if there is any trace of hollowness or other irregularities, repeat the operation until a perfectly true flat face is obtained. Just touch the two corners with the file to round them slightly and prevent the corners scoring the work.

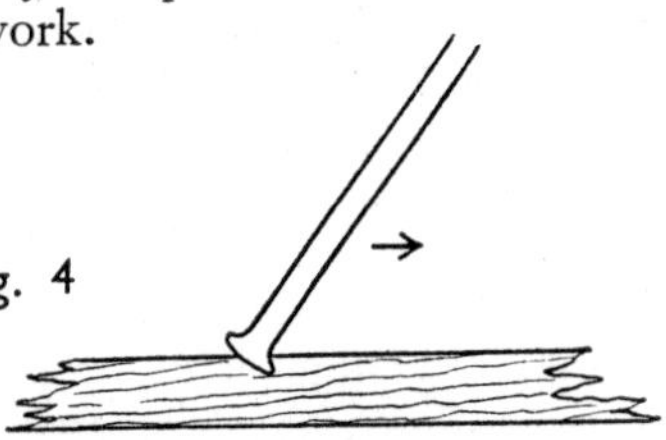

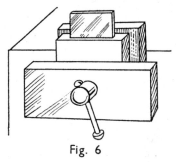

Fig. 6

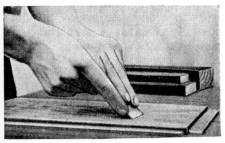

Fig. 4

Now fix the oilstone, long edge upwards, in the vice in the manner shown in Fig. 6. Rub the edge of the tool several times up and down the side edge—now the top—to remove the marks left by the file, using the wooden edge of the case as a guide. The burr thrown up at the edges by the file must

Fig. 5

piece of round hard steel or the back of a gouge, applying heavy pressure during the process, to turn up the burr. Reference to Fig. 7 will show you exactly how this is done. When rubbing the edge, keep the handle of the sharpener down to give the burr the necessary angle. When one edge is finished, turn the blade over and work the other edge in the same way.

It should be noted that if the tool has been allowed to get badly pitted with rust it is better to discard it, as an efficient edge cannot be produced and good results will be impossible.

A cleanly cut piece of window-glass is a good substitute for a metal scraper,

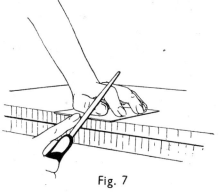

Fig. 7

now be removed by placing the working end of the blade flat on the oilstone, and giving it one or two rubs across the surface. Turn the tool over and repeat the process on the other side.

It is of the utmost importance that the foregoing preliminary operations be carefully carried out, because the better they are done the smoother the scraper will work.

Turning up the Burr.—Hold the scraper flat on the bench with the left hand, allowing the prepared edge to overlap the edge of the bench by about ⅛ in. Now rub back and forth along the edge of the tool several times with either a

and generally answers the purpose perfectly. If it is held at an angle of about 60° to the surface of the work it takes off a nice clean "shaving." Before using, it is a good plan to remove the corners of the working edge by rubbing them on the oilstone.

WOOD FINISHING

WOOD that has been used for any construction work is rarely left in its natural state but is "finished," as it is called, and this finishing consists generally in applying some coating protective or decorative, or both.

The commoner varieties of wood, including most softwoods, generally receive a protective coat, although before any such medium is applied the wood should be thoroughly seasoned.

Softwoods are generally painted, creosoted, or stained and sometimes varnished, while hardwoods of the more expensive kind are usually french polished.

Paint or other protective mediums are useless if applied to unseasoned wood, because they merely fill up the outside pores and confine the moisture in the wood, which causes it to rot.

Thus, the practice of tarring the bottoms of posts that are to be put into the ground is little better than useless if cracks are open or likely to open to allow the wet to enter the substance of the post.

A better procedure would be to put the bottom portion of the post into a metal container such as a dust-bin, or an old milk churn, partially filling it with creosote and then boiling it for about twenty minutes or so.

Painting is generally adopted for covering the commoner varieties of wood such as deal, spruce, etc., as paint if properly applied has both decorative and protective properties.

Before actually applying paint to new wood, the surface to be covered must be subjected to certain treatment, and the first and most important item is to see that the material is perfectly dry.

All holes and cracks should be "stopped" with a "filler." There are many wood fillers on the market, but for paint work the commonest is putty. Putty can be either made at home or purchased. It is made by mixing ordinary ground whiting with linseed oil and then kneading to form a plastic mass. Care must be taken when buying linseed oil to get the best quality, as a common grade has poor drying capabilities, with the result that it often works its way through the coats of paint and leaves an unsightly stain. This fault is particularly emphasised when whtie or any light-coloured paint is used.

As putty will not adhere to bare wood, it is applied after the first or "priming" coat of paint has been finished and allowed to dry. The reason for this is that the oil in the putty is absorbed in bare wood and consequently leaves a quantity of whiting only, which either flakes off or simply crumbles away.

A Useful Filler for bare wood can be made out of sawdust mixed to a thick paste with glue or gold-size. This compound will be found particularly useful for filling defects in hard or fancy woods, as the sawdust of the actual wood can be utilised.

Recently another form of filler has appeared on the market. It is known as plastic wood, and can be obtained in either tins or collapsible tubes. For the infrequent user, the latter is much to be preferred, as it not only means a smaller initial outlay, but the tubes are almost self-sealing and therefore exclude the air. If, however, a large amount of "stopping" has to be done, it is more economical to buy a tin; but the cover must always be refixed as soon as the material is withdrawn, because plastic wood loses its pliability when exposed to the air.

The special benefit obtained by the use of plastic wood is that it cannot be distinguished from the wood on which it is used. To use the preparation, all that is necessary is to fill the hole or crack by applying a small quantity in excess of the actual quantity required for filling the crevice; when dry, use fine sand-paper to level the surface. Plastic wood shrinks slightly and dries very rapidly.

Knots in wood present another difficulty to the painter. They exude turpentine and resin, or, on the other hand, they absorb the paint, leaving ugly marks on the finished surface. The knots are, therefore, "killed" by painting them over with "patent" knotting, which is a preparation of shellac and methylated spirit. Ordinary french polish or shellac dissolved in methylated spirit usually answers the purpose.

Paint is composed of a basic pigment consisting generally of either an oxide of lead or an oxide of zinc, a pigment to give the desired colour, and linseed oil and turpentine, to which is added a small quantity of "driers" which helps the paint to dry and harden.

The first coat of paint applied to the wood is called the "priming" coat, and should consist of a mixture of red and white lead, and either boiled or ordinary linseed oil. It is mixed in suitable proportions to allow it to dry quickly, and, if properly prepared, also helps the following coat to dry.

A good priming coat for outside work can be made as follows. Add ½ pint of raw linseed oil and the same quantity of boiled linseed oil to 4 lb. of white lead and ½ oz. of driers. Stir well and strain before use.

The time required for paint to dry depends to some extent on the temperature of the atmosphere. It oxidises rather than evaporates, so a good supply of warm fresh air would help to quicken the process.

If the paint thickens, its more liquid consistency may be restored by the addition of either turpentine or linseed oil—boiled oil in preference for exposed positions. Sometimes it is advisable to use both, as "turps" in excess dulls the surface and affects the durability.

Some paint manufacturers advise a special thinning compound of their own make to suit their paint which, when specified, should always be used.

As mentioned before, wood should always be in a dry condition before painting is attempted. If damp, the moisture is kept enclosed by the coat of paint, and the heat on a warm day vaporises it, causing blisters to appear. Surfaces that have had previous coats of paint burnt off are dried by the heat of the blow-lamp, consequently paint applied to the treated surface rarely blisters.

Painting.—No advantage is gained by brushing the paint on too thickly, and the idea that one thick coat is equivalent to two thin ones is a fallacy. Thin coats, properly applied, and the judicious use of sand-paper between each coat when thoroughly dry are the determining factor of a good final finish.

Sometimes the final coat is mixed with varnish to add brilliancy, or the last coat of paint is varnished afterwards. In both cases the previous coat must be thoroughly dry and hard; otherwise cracks will appear later.

It may be pointed out here that when a glossy finish is required, the previous coats must be carried out with a "flat" paint—that is a paint which dries without gloss.

Enamel or hard gloss paints are now obtainable. Some are specially prepared to withstand the effect of boiling water and are sold under the name of bath enamel. A coat of this applied to the wood, if carried out in a warm room and the enamel paint itself kept warm in a hot-water bath, produces a delightfully smooth and glossy effect. The finish may be to some extent compared to the stove enamelling used for finishing bicycles. One cannot, nor would it be advisable to, stove articles of wooden manufacture, as they would in all probability twist and shrink out of shape.

When a painted surface is intended to be for decorative as well as preservative purposes, "graining" and "marbling" is often resorted to.

Graining requires special tools to mark the final coat of paint, called the graining coat, which is painted to represent or imitate a particular kind of wood such as ash, oak, maple, etc.

Marbling is the process used to imitate natural marbles, and bears a close relationship to graining in the imitation of woods. Transfer papers can be obtained that enable one to produce these effects without having to rely on skilled workmanship.

Another popular medium for the artistic finishing of wood is found in cellulose brushing lacquer, of which there are numerous makes now on the market. This useful material can be obtained in various colours at most colour stores. It is applied with a brush like ordinary enamel. The advantages gained by using cellulose lacquer are that it dries very quickly without leaving any brush-marks, and produces a beautiful, glossy and durable surface.

Generally speaking, the number of brushes required for painting woodwork depends upon the nature of the work. For painting narrow surfaces a "sash tool" is the correct brush to use, but when larger surfaces are to be covered, a larger tool called a "ground brush" is generally employed.

It always pays in the long run to get a good brush. One bound with metal and rubber is much to be preferred to the more or less old-fashioned brush having the bristles fastened in with glue. Before using a new brush always soak it in water for two or three hours to prevent the bristles from becoming detached—a common occurrence if this precaution is overlooked.

A Good Brush is worthy of good treatment; it therefore behoves the amateur who does not use his brushes frequently, to clean them thoroughly after use. Wash them out with soap and warm water. The cheap soap containing an excess of soda answers well. Damp the brush and rub it on the soap, rinse out, and repeat until perfectly clean. A final rinse in turpentine will leave the brush in good condition for use at any later occasion.

On no account allow linseed oil to dry in the brush, as it is almost impossible to remove after oxidisation takes place.

When brushes are used frequently, it is a good plan to store them in an old paint pot or a jam jar, keeping the bristles covered with water. If, however, the brush is one with glued-in bristles, it is advisable not to use water, as this sometimes results in loose hairs. The bristles must not be allowed to rest on the bottom of the receptacle, otherwise the brush will be ruined. Drill a hole through the handle and suspend it from a piece of wire pushed through the hole and supported by the sides of the container.

For further particulars on the subject of painting refer to the section on HOME DECORATING.

If the worker is proud of his handiwork he will take care not to spoil it by bad finishing.

In cases where the joints are not quite what they should be, it is possible to hide the imperfections by means of fillers and paint, but where the work has been well done it is well worth while to try to retain the beauty of the wood and the workmanship also. This can often be done by calling into use one or other of the numerous stains that can be obtained ready for use or can be easily made as required. If a suitable stain is chosen, any beautifully grained wood, such as some kinds of oak, retains its beauty, which is very often greatly enhanced.

Staining.—Wood, then, is stained to improve the appearance of the more expensive kinds, or an inferior wood such as pine, birch, etc., is stained to represent or imitate a good quality wood.

Creosote, when used for outside work, acts as a decorative stain as well as a preservative medium. It can be used for interior decoration, but it takes longer to dry than the usual stains meant for such work. It may be obtained in various tints in the form of proprietary products, under various trade names.

The introduction of aniline dyes has opened up a vast field in the matter of stains. Aniline is a coal-tar product obtained by distillation, soluble in alcohol, ether, etc., but only slightly so in water. By treating it with various reagents, a range of colours is obtained of every conceivable tint. The green obtained from aniline has taken the place of the old poisonous green once obtained from arsenic; and the old-fashioned dyes extracted from logwood, tumeric, walnut shells, and other members of the vegetable kingdom are now scarcely ever used.

Oak.—The amateur may like to try his hand at staining oak, to produce artificially what would otherwise be produced naturally by age. This may be done by giving the wood several coats of liquid ammonia—the stronger the ammonia used, the darker the colour will be.

In the trade, the oak wood is encased in an airtight chamber and fumed with ammonia—hence the term "fumed" oak.

Mahogany may be given a richer, darker colour by means of several applications of bichromate of potash solution.

Pine and Birch can be stained to represent the beautiful and durable appearance of walnut by frequent applications of stain made by dissolving an ounce of permanganate of potash in $\frac{1}{2}$ pint of rain water. It can then be applied with a piece of flannel worked in the direction of the grain of the wood. After being left for about 10 hours to dry, it can be varnished if desired.

Stains may also be obtained ready mixed with varnish; they go by the name of varnish stains, and are useful for finishing floorboards, etc.

Any wood that is well oiled gets darker in time. If the amateur has oiled the wood of his planes, he will probably have noticed this action of linseed oil. This method of darkening wood may be used on more important work, and if well rubbed into the pores the oil produces a pleasing semi-polished finish.

Polishing, or, as it is generally termed, french polishing, is chiefly resorted to for finishing good quality furniture, cabinets, etc. This finish gives the wood a fine smooth glossy surface, showing, in the majority of cases, the colour and natural beauty of the wood.

French polishing is also employed to enhance the impression produced in woods that have been stained to imitate a better class of wood.

This process of french polishing consists in applying a solution of shellac in methylated spirit evenly and smoothly over the surface to be finished. The polish is distributed over the wood, until the pores are completely filled, by means of a "rubber" consisting of a wad of cotton-wool wrapped in a small calico "bag." Polish is applied to the cotton-wool which, when squeezed through the calico by light pressure, adheres to the surface of the work and produces the delightfully smooth hard glazed surface so well known and generally admired by everybody.

The brief outline just given makes

Fig. I

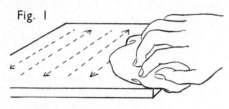

french polishing appear to be a much simpler process than it really is.

A good deal of practice is necessary before reasonable proficiency is attained. There is no reason why you should not try your hand at it, but you will be well advised to practise on small panels of wood before attempting to french polish an important piece of work.

One of the chief points which leads to success in french polishing is that the process should always be carried out in a warm room free from dust. Good work cannot be done in a cold or even a damp atmosphere.

The Grain.—If the surface of wood is carefully examined, it will be noticed that the grain stands out more in some woods than in others. Some woods are much "coarser grained" than others; for instance, oak is much more so than walnut. This grain must be filled in because polish alone would not give the brilliant finish that is desired.

The first work of the polisher is to get the surface of the wood as smooth as he possibly can. This operation necessitates the use of the scraper and glass-paper. Two or three grades of glass-paper may be necessary, the last one used being a very fine one. In using glass-paper for finishing, do not, on any

account, rub the paper across the grain, as such a procedure will almost certainly result in scratches which will show up more after polishing than before. Therefore, rub up and down the surface in the same direction as the grain.

Filling.—The next operation consists in filling the pores of the wood. The filling-in must be carefully done, as the filler forms the foundation for the polish. Any carelessness on the part of the worker in carrying out this important process invariably results in an unsatisfactory finish.

The amateur has the choice of several kinds of fillers. Plaster of Paris is the filler most commonly used, and it can be applied by one of several ways. One method is to make a pad by rolling up a piece of rag, moistening it with water, and then dipping it into the plaster of Paris, taking care to see that the latter is free from grit. Rub the filler well into the grain by working across it, as illustrated in Fig. 1, until the whole surface is well covered. Wipe off the surplus before it sets hard, but not so soon as to remove that which is intended to fill the pores. If the surplus is allowed to remain until it gets hard, great difficulty will be experienced in removing it with glass-paper. Having obtained a satisfactory result, allow it to dry thoroughly.

As the process of filling-in raises the grain of some woods, it may be necessary to give the surface another rub down with glass-paper. For this, use very fine glass-paper that has been used before or, if this is not available, rub the sanded faces of two new pieces together before applying it to the work in hand.

Some workers prefer to use turpentine for filling purposes instead of water, in which case the grain is not affected in the same way.

If preferred, the plaster of Paris may

be mixed into a paste with water and then applied to the work.

Another commonly used filler consists of plaster of Paris and melted tallow, the employment of which allows the polishing to be started at once; whereas fillers containing water must be allowed to dry before the work can be proceeded with.

Oiling the Surface is the next process whereby the surface previously made white by the filler is "killed," that is, completely obliterated. This is done with a rag moistened with linseed oil, and any surplus oil remaining is removed by rubbing the surface vigorously with a clean soft rag. Care should be taken not to leave any trace of oil, because the less there is, the more brilliant and solid the resulting surface will be. If too much oil is left on the work it may also eventually

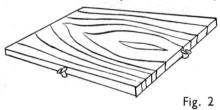

Fig. 2

cause trouble to the finished surface, due to "sweating."

If the wood is to be stained, the stain may be applied after filling-in. In some cases the stain is added to the polish itself.

Polishing Filled Wood.—Where plaster of Paris filling has been used, the surface may now have a preliminary or foundation coat of polish. If the work in hand is a small panel it is an advantage to fasten it down to a flat surface by means of screws in the manner shown in Fig. 2. Take a wad of cotton-wool and soak it full of polish. Fold it in a piece of used calico rag to form a rubber as shown in Fig. 3, and pass it over the surface to be polished, squeezing the

polish out slowly as the rubber glides over the surface. Take care to cover the whole of the surface, especially the sides and corners. Do not rub hard or attempt to polish whilst laying on this foundation coat, because a good base of

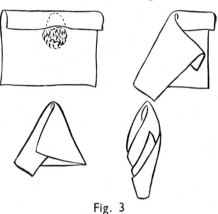

Fig. 3

polish is required for working on later. When this operation is finished, place the work aside to allow the surface to dry thoroughly and harden.

As the rubber will get hard and therefore useless by the time it is next required, due to the evaporation of the methylated spirit, it is a good plan to soak it in polish and then store it in a small air-tight tin or jar.

Fig. 4

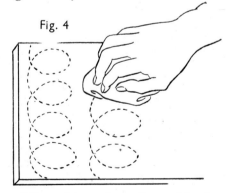

When the work is thoroughly dry, go over the entire surface with fine sand-paper—No. 1 grade paper should

4

answer the purpose well. If the foundation does not appear satisfactory after sand-papering, apply another coat of polish.

Bodying-in.—If all is correct, the actual polishing can be started. The rubber used for the first coat will do for this if it has been kept moist as suggested. Charge it with polish as before, but not so copiously, and fold the rag over the cotton-wool so that it is fully enclosed, and hold the loose ends in the hand.

Apply a spot or two of linseed oil (some prefer almond oil) to the face of the rubber. This acts as a lubricant which prevents the pad from sticking and dragging along the surface of the work. Failure to include this important item may possibly ruin the work. Do not use too much oil, otherwise it will subsequently cause trouble.

Method of Rubbing.—Apply the charged rubber to the surface and rub the pad in a circular motion over the face of the wood as indicated in Fig. 4, so that all parts are covered uniformly, taking care not to press too hard on the pad or you may possibly rub off the polish you have put on.

The rubber may need many applications of fresh polish until eventually a beautiful finish is seen following the course of the pad, but it may appear somewhat smeary.

Put the work aside to dry, which may take a day or two.

Subsequent examination will probably reveal that the polish has sunk somewhat, perhaps unevenly. Use the sandpaper lightly, and then give another bodying coat. Good work is often gone over three or four times in the manner described.

After these coats have been allowed to dry thoroughly and harden, give the work a good rub with a clean soft rag to remove any dust that has settled on the surface and also any oil that may have found its way through the coat.

The finishing coat is then given with the same rubber, charged with french polish and spirit in equal proportions. Be careful not to saturate the rubber; otherwise it will possibly destroy the hard surface that has been so carefully produced. If, on dabbing the pad on the back of the hand, it feels wet, squeeze some out and let the rubber dry off a little. It should feel only slightly damp.

Apply a spot of oil to the rubber, and then run it over the whole surface of the work, using horizontal strokes only. This application should be sufficient slightly to soften the surface and leave it ready for the final glaze, which is produced by the friction of this final rubbing. Careless work at this stage may undo a lot that has gone before, but the careful worker can finish off with a clean, hard brilliant surface at this stage.

Spiriting-off.—Should the surface appear to be a little bit smeary after this treatment, it should be run over in parallel sweeps along the full length of the work with a rubber charged with spirit only.

Such a rubber is sometimes called a "ghost" and the process is called "spiriting-off."

The pad is prepared as before with cotton-wool covered with a piece of calico, but the wool receives only a slight charge of spirit, and must on no account be wet. To verify the condition of the pad it is a good plan to test it on the cheek.

Sweating.—The rubber may then be applied to the work to enable it to take off any smear or oil that has exuded, causing what is termed "sweating."

It is claimed that almond oil does not cause sweating like linseed oil. It should be the worker's aim to use as little as possible and to clear away any excess during the latter stage of obtaining the final lustre. Some woods are naturally oily and this should be taken into account.

Furniture cream and polish-revivers are used to keep a polished surface in good condition.

An excellent reviver for dull surfaces can be made by mixing together 4 oz. of spirits of wine, 2 oz. of vinegar and 1 oz. of linseed oil. Rub well on and polish with a soft cloth.

A useful polish for stained softwood is made up as follows: Melt some beeswax, and add a small quantity of turps and linseed oil. Stir the mixture and then add a smaller quantity of kerosene. When cool it should form a thick paste, but if not, add a little more of each ingredient. The more often this mixture is applied and polished off the work, the finer the result will be.

A harder finish is obtained by using carnuba wax instead of beeswax. Allow it to soak in before polishing-off with a soft cloth.

PLYWOOD

THE advantages of using plywood in preference to ordinary wood are manifold. The most important of these are its freedom from shrinkage; its enormous strength; the large widths in which it can be obtained, and its adaptability to certain shapes and forms. Another great point in its favour is that it can be obtained with expensive woods such as oak, walnut, mahogany, etc., on one face cemented to a cheaper wood on the lower plys. In this way it is possible to get the beautiful effects generally associated with high-priced woods at a very much reduced cost.

Composition.—The freedom from shrinkage and the strength is obtained by the manner in which the material is built up. The first layer has its grain running in one direction and the next has the fibres at right-angles to the former, and this is carried on alternatively throughout the thickness.

In some makes of plywood the inner layers are slightly thicker than the outer ones to ensure a balance of strength in both directions, and the several layers are cemented together with a special cement which is claimed to be unaffected by damp.

A standard-sized sheet of plywood faced with walnut, mahogany, oak, etc., measures 60 in. by 48 in., while those faced with common woods such as birch and alder are to be obtained in sheets measuring 48 in. by 36 in., and 60 in. by 48 in.

There is no need to purchase a large

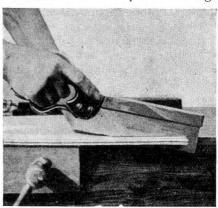

Fig. I

panel where only a small quantity is required, because panels as small as 6 in. by 6 in. and other convenient sizes suitable for the home carpenter, can now be obtained from any of the numerous shops, to be found in nearly every town, which cater for amateur woodworkers' requirements. It can also be purchased at most hardwood stores.

The thickness of plywood varies from

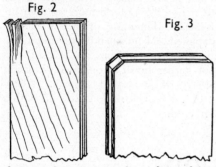

Fig. 2

Fig. 3

$\frac{1}{32}$ in. to $\frac{3}{4}$ in., having from three plys to as many as nine.

Varieties of Plywood.—Like ordinary wood, there are various qualities, the commonest of which is only suitable for packing-cases—but the better grades have an excellent surface. In the commoner varieties of plywood, that is, those faced with birch and alder, the best quality is good on one face only, while the third quality has slight defects on both faces.

The thinnest plywood ($\frac{1}{32}$ in.), which is not much thicker than average cardboard, can be cut quite easily with a pair of sharp scissors, or a chisel held at an angle and drawn across it, but for cutting thicker material a fine-toothed saw should be employed. Never attempt to cut plywood with a coarse-toothed saw, otherwise the lower layer will split away.

Fig. 1 shows an illustration of a piece of plywood being cut with a tenon-saw. In cutting, the material should be well supported on a flat surface, and the saw held at a small angle to the surface in the manner shown clearly in the drawing.

Care must be taken when truing up the edges of plywood because all edges have one or more layers exposing the end grain which are likely to split out as in

Fig. 2 if planed right across. Use a very sharp, finely-set plane, and plane from each end to the centre, as in planing the end grain of ordinary wood. Another method to prevent damage to the edges is first to remove the corner with a sharp chisel as shown in Fig. 3. This method, however, can only be adopted where the corners do not show, as for instance when it is sunk into grooved wood.

A fretsaw is an ideal tool for cutting small and comparatively thin pieces of plywood to shape, as the fine teeth produce a clean edge and are not likely to damage the outside laminations. For convenience in cutting it is an advantage to use a proper cutting-board having a V-shaped aperture for supporting the work, as explained in the article dealing with FRETWORK.

Owing to its exceptional strength, thin plywood is extensively used for making " frets " or ornamental openings in the fronts of loud-speaker cabinets. To make such a fret, all that is necessary is to mark out first of all the design on the face of the material, using a pencil

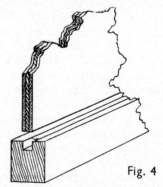

Fig. 4

for the purpose, and then remove the internal waste with a fretsaw.

Where a number of similar shaped pieces are required, a great deal of time will be saved and accuracy assured if a cardboard template of the exact shape is made and then used as a guide for marking purposes. This method simplifies marking-out and is very often the means of saving a considerable amount of material.

Plywood is exceedingly useful for making light furniture such as cabinets, chests of drawers, and other useful and ornamental articles.

There are several ways of using ply-

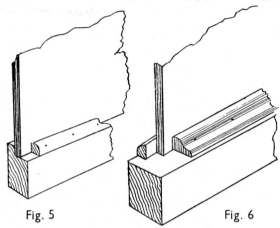

Fig. 5   Fig. 6

wood for this purpose. In one method —perhaps the best—the framing is grooved to take the correct thickness of the panel (as shown in Fig. 4), where the material has to be in place before the framework is fastened together. Fig. 5 shows the framing with a rebate cut sufficiently wide to allow for the thickness of the panel and a narrow moulding. In this case, the frame is put together first, the panel inserted into the recess, and kept in place by either gluing or pinning a moulding to the inner edge of the frame. Fig. 6 illustrates another simple way of fitting plywood panels. The inner edges of the frame are left square, and a narrow moulding is first fixed near the back edge to form a rebate. The panel is then inserted, and kept in position by the front moulding.

In some work the panels are left loose in the recesses, but in some cases it is advisable to fix them in with glue.

Grooved Framing.—Suitable grooved material of various sections and shapes for making the framework for thin plywood panels can now be obtained from most hardwood shops. The grooves are usually made to take panels $\frac{3}{16}$ in. in thickness, and are provided with recesses on one or more faces.

This useful material is of inestimable value to the home carpenter as it eliminates the somewhat tedious tasks of ploughing grooves and making rebates, and enables a first-class job to be accomplished with a minimum amount of labour by the use of a few ordinary tools.

On account of the non-shrinking and non-twisting characteristics of plywood, it is possible to make serviceable doors for cabinets, etc., without any orthodox framework, by simply gluing or pinning a plain or an ornamental moulding round the front edges of the panel, as illustrated in Fig. 7. Mitred joints are used, of course, at each corner of the moulding.

This form of door, however, is not so good as a door having a proper grooved frame surrounding the panel, the joints of which can be either a dowelled joint, or a stub

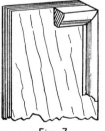
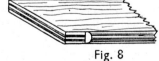

Fig. 7   Fig. 8

tenon cut in the top and bottom rails to fit the grooves of the stiles.

Some workers object to the use of plywood on certain work because the laminated edges have rather a rough and unfinished appearance. This difficulty, however, is easily overcome by fixing a small edge moulding over them, as indicated in Fig. 8.

When fixing such mouldings great care must be taken to drive the pins into the centre layer of the plywood, otherwise damage may be done to the outside faces by splitting them apart. Another important point is to use always long thin panel pins driven in at an angle to form "dovetails," because this method makes a stronger joint than pins driven in straight.

Panelling.—Plywood offers an easy means of panelling a room. The advantages gained by the use of this artistic material for decorative purposes are too well known to be mentioned. Only best quality plywood should be used, whether it be faced with oak, mahogany or any of the commoner kinds of wood.

If the walls to be panelled are perfectly dry and even, the plywood may be nailed directly to the surfaces, but should there be the slightest suspicion of dampness the panels must be mounted on battens to allow the air to circulate between the walls and the covering material.

Where the panels are fastened to the walls without any intervening battens, the first thing to do is to mark the walls to suit the spacing of the panels, and then cut the plywood to size. It is a wise plan to leave a small gap of about $\frac{1}{8}$ in. between each panel to allow nails driven in the centres of the covering strips to enter the plaster. The panels should be fastened with $1\frac{1}{2}$-in. oval brads driven in slantwise to obtain a good grip, care being taken to see that the nail heads are eventually hidden by the covering strips. Before fixing the covering strips, however, the whole of the panelling, as well as the strips, should be stained or otherwise finished to the desired shade, and then wax polished. The strips can be touched up after erection.

Should fixing battens be necessary, the walls are marked as previously mentioned, and the battens securely fixed to the walls. The wood used for this purpose need not exceed $1\frac{3}{4}$ in. in width and $\frac{1}{4}$ in. in thickness. The panelling is then fixed in the same manner as already explained.

A few years ago the writer wished to panel a room in oak-faced plywood. At the time, great difficulty was experienced in trying to obtain the chosen material, so a plywood having a face of Siberian ash was offered. This material had a beautiful figured surface closely resembling figured oak, but the size of each panel was 50 in. by 25 in., which meant a lot of cutting to waste.

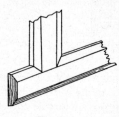

Fig. 9

To overcome the difficulty, the panels adjoining the skirting-board were laid and fastened longitudinally, while the panels above them were fixed in a vertical position. This left a gap between the upper and lower panels which was eventually covered by wide covering strips forming a useful chair rail. The panel joints were covered with bevel-edged strips of wood, the ends of which were cut to fit over the bevelled edge of the piece it had to join, as shown in Fig. 9. This was found the best and simplest method of solving a seemingly difficult problem.

FRETWORK

THE art of fretcutting is both fascinating and instructive and the necessary skill can be acquired with very little practice. Indeed, it is quite possible to become proficient in the course of a few days.

Such objects as cabinets, photo-frames, glove-boxes, and a hundred-and-one useful and beautiful articles can be made with the aid of a very limited number of inexpensive tools. The space required for carrying on the work need be no more than the end of a kitchen table to serve as a work-bench.

To commence work, all one actually needs is a saw-frame, saw-blades, drill-stock and bits, cutting-board, a supply of fretwood, and a pattern or design to work to, unless, of course, one goes in for the more expensive fretwork machine.

The Hand-frame.—This is the principal tool used for fretcutting, and is shown in Fig. 1. It consists of a light steel frame into which a fine saw-blade is placed, the clamping screws fitted at the top and bottom providing a means of gripping the blade. A handle is fixed to the bottom of the frame for working the saw up and down.

In a good type of frame, costing about 5/-, an adjusting device in the shape of either a lever or a special clamp having a screw thread and a wing nut is provided at the top for altering the tension of the blade, while a screwed arrangement in the handle allows further adjustment, that shortens and tightens the distance between the clamps.

These are very useful features, as they allow saw-blades, which one may be unfortunate enough to break, to be used again—provided, of course, that the break does not occur in the middle of the blade, and thus render it too short.

The sizes of frames, which refers to the distance between the back of the tool and the saw, vary from 12 to 18 in. The size recommended depends upon the size of the design likely to be cut, but when deciding upon the size required, the fact that the corners of the material have to be negotiated must not be overlooked.

Generally speaking, a 14-in. hand-frame is a very convenient size to get,

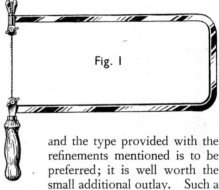

Fig. 1

and the type provided with the refinements mentioned is to be preferred; it is well worth the small additional outlay. Such a frame will answer well for most amateur purposes and is not too awkward to handle.

Saw-blades.—The secret of success in fretwork depends in no small degree upon the tiny saw-blade, so a hint or two as to suitable blades will not be out of place.

A good blade for rapid and clean cutting should have regular, sharp, hook-shaped teeth, spaced equally and not too close together. It should also be tempered to the correct degree.

To fulfil these conditions extreme care is necessary during the manufacturing process, and it is therefore obvious that an article of good quality will cost more than one that is inferior. Therefore, pay a reasonable price for your saw-blades.

One of the greatest mistakes made by many amateurs is to purchase cheap saw-blades, usually of Continental origin, which have none of the qualities referred to above.

The teeth, in the majority of cases, are irregular, blunt and without "set," and so close together that the blade simply gets choked with sawdust, thus rendering it quite unsuitable for the purpose for which it is intended.

A dozen good blades of British manufacture, costing about 4d. or 5d., will outlast a gross of the cheap variety, and will save you the annoyance and the utter waste of time occasioned by the continual stopping of work in order to replace a broken blade.

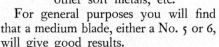

Blades may be obtained in about a dozen different thicknesses or gauges to suit all varieties of work. A No. oo is the finest and is only suitable for cutting wood up to $\frac{1}{16}$ in. in thickness. A No. 10 blade, however, is capable of sawing material $\frac{1}{2}$ in. thick. For cutting wood over $\frac{1}{2}$ in. in thickness a special blade called a toymaker's fretsaw is employed. Specially hardened and tempered steel fretsaw-blades can also be obtained for cutting brass, copper, and other soft metals, etc.

Fig. 2

For general purposes you will find that a medium blade, either a No. 5 or 6, will give good results.

Archimedean Drill-stock and Bits. —An Archimedean drill-stock for holding thin diamond-pointed bits is the correct tool to use for drilling holes in fretwood. Such a drill is shown in Fig. 2.

Drill-stocks range in price from 6d. to about 2/6. A good type to have is one fitted with weights at the bottom and a device which allows the drill to rotate in a clockwise direction only. The weights allow a smoother and better cutting action, and if kept revolving permit the drill to be easily withdrawn from the material.

Cutting-table.—In order to do fretwork comfortably you should provide yourself with a suitable table or board.

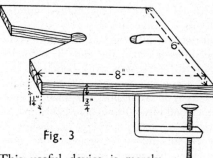

Fig. 3

This useful device is merely a flat piece of wood with a V-shaped slot cut in one end and a clamp for fixing purposes at the other, as shown in Fig. 3.

By clamping the board to the edge of an ordinary table a small projecting platform is formed which supports the work and prevents you knocking your knuckles against the table when operating the saw.

Another useful feature is that the board, being raised above the surface of the table, allows the material to be held tightly and swivelled round when required.

The cutting-table is one of those simple yet necessary articles which you can make for yourself, but if you prefer to buy one, you should see that it is made of wood and not metal. The latter kind is likely to injure the saw-blade should the teeth of the saw come into accidental contact with the edge of the platform.

To make a cutting-board, get a piece of perfectly flat planed board 8 in. in length, 6 in. wide and ¾ in. in thickness, and a small metal cramp costing only a

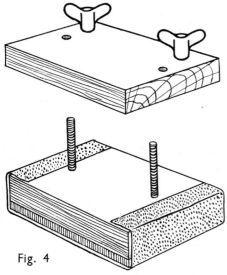

Fig. 4

Glass-paper Block.—A glass-paper block is used for smoothing down and finishing off the work when completed.

Such a block in a simple form is shown in Fig. 4. It consists of two pieces of flat wood which form the top and bottom members respectively. A strip of glass-paper covers the bottom surface of the lower member and the paper is cut long enough to fold over the two ends and partially over the top. The top piece is then screwed down tightly to the lower portion and serves to hold the paper in position. This accessory can either be bought ready-made or constructed at home. Suitable glass-paper strips for refilling the blocks are easily obtainable.

Fretwork Designs.—The requirements of the fretworker in the matter of designs are amply catered for. Excellent pattern sheets costing only a few pence

few pence. Draw a pencil line parallel to a long edge in the centre of the face of the wood, and mark on this line the positions for the holes. The centre of the front hole is $3\frac{3}{4}$ in. from the front edge, and that for the cramp is $2\frac{1}{2}$ in. from the back edge. Mark out the slanting lines to form the V-shaped recess to the dimensions shown in Fig. 3. Cut or bore the two holes, which should be ¾ in. diameter, and remove the waste from the recess. Cut a neat channel from the back hole to the back edge sufficiently wide and deep to allow the top of the cramp to lie flush with the top surface of the board.

An improvement on this board would be to use two cramps at the back.

If the board having a single cramp is inclined to twist round when in use, the difficulty can be surmounted by fastening a narrow strip of wood across the under-side to coincide with the edge of the table or bench.

4*

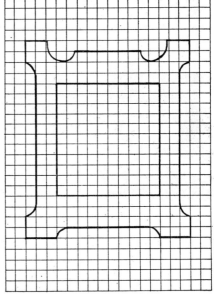

Fig. 5

can be obtained from dealers in fretwork material.

The range of designs covers practically the whole of the smaller articles one sees in and about the house, from clocks to stationery cabinets, and umbrella stands to overmantels, while designs of models, toys, and the like are also readily obtainable.

It is possible that you may want to make an article of your own design, in which case you must first of all make a drawing. The pattern can then be either stuck down to the face of the wood in the ordinary way or the outline can be transferred by means of a piece of carbon paper as used in typewriting, provided that the material is sufficiently light in colour to allow the outline to be easily seen. The latter method is resorted to when the design is required for further use.

When making one's own design it is an excellent plan to use thin square-lined paper, as the lines are a useful guide for drawing curves, etc. accurately. Such paper can be bought quite cheaply at most stationers' shops. Fig. 5 shows an

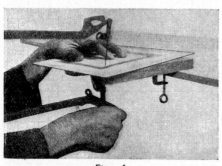

Fig. 6

example of a pattern drawn on square-ruled paper.

Where carbon paper is used, place the prepared side of the paper down on the surface of the wood and lay the pattern sheet on top; then fasten it securely at each corner with a drawing pin. With a sharp-pointed, hard lead pencil, or the end of a fairly fine knitting-needle, trace over every part of the pattern. If you

now remove the carbon paper you will find a well-defined outline plainly marked on the surface of the wood. Do not bruise the surface by pressing too hard.

Materials.—The material generally used in fretwork is thin hardwood, such as satin-walnut, mahogany, oak, etc. Deal and similar woods of a soft nature are not suitable for the purpose of the amateur.

Satin-walnut is perhaps the favourite wood for sawing as it is comparatively inexpensive, has a nice close grain, and is very easy to work. Its colour is a pleasing rich brown, and the boards can be obtained in wide dimensions, a distinct advantage when it is desired to fretsaw out a large design.

Plywood is also a useful material for the fretworker, but its use is somewhat limited owing to its rather unpleasing laminated edge.

Fretwood is generally planed up ready for use, the usual thicknesses being $\frac{1}{16}$ in. (planed on one side only), suitable for making delicate overlays, and $\frac{1}{8}$ in., $\frac{3}{16}$ in., and $\frac{1}{4}$ in., the latter being employed for heavier work. It is sold at so much per square foot (144 sq. in.).

Using the Saw.—Assuming that you have got the necessary tools together and a supply of fretwood to hand, and are ready to make a start, the first thing to do is to fix the blade, teeth downward in the hand-frame by slipping each end of the saw under the clamps and then tightening them up. The tension screw should be adjusted to pull the saw up tight, as a slack saw has a tendency to twist and break.

To gain a little experience in sawing and to accustom yourself to the " feel " of the tool, it is a wise plan to practise upon a few pieces of odd fretwork before attempting to cut out even a simple design. Pencil mark a few lines across the wood, some straight, some curved, and some with angles between them. Then try your hand at cutting along the lines in the following manner.

Place the wood on the cutting-table and hold the material down firmly with the left hand. Take the fretsaw and grasp its handle in the right, as shown in Fig. 6. Now bring the blade up against the edge of the wood where one of the straight lines begins, and work the saw up and down with smooth, even strokes, keeping the saw in a perfectly vertical position and, of course, cutting along the line. You will probably be astonished at the little effort required to propel the saw and surprised at the speed at which the fragile blade cuts its way neatly through the wood.

In curved work you should endeavour to turn the wood and not the frame, although you will find it an advantage at times to turn the saw, especially when working upon complicated designs.

One of the chief points to observe in cutting is to keep all angles sharp and

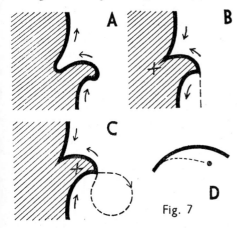

Fig. 7

well defined; otherwise they will probably appear as at A in Fig. 7. Two examples of negotiating angles are shown at B and C. In the one shown at B you saw from a drilled hole and arrive at the internal angle X from two directions as

shown by the arrows. In sawing the external angle formed at X in C, the saw follows the upward curve to the point and is then run into the waste and continued round until it meets and follows

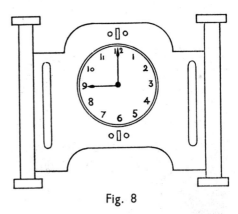

Fig. 8

the outline as shown by the dotted lines. By adopting these methods it will be seen that the angles are left sharp and clean.

In cutting a long curve as at D, the saw should take a gentle sweep to meet the curve to be cut. This is a much better method than sawing straight across the waste, and then making a very sharp angled turn with the tool.

Where it is found necessary to turn the saw, do it slowly, keeping the saw moving up and down the whole time.

It may be mentioned that if the saw is inclined to bind it generally indicates that it is too coarse, therefore, try a new blade. On no account should oil or grease be applied to ease the saw, as this may stain the wood.

Assuming that you can now cut the curved work out properly, and negotiate curves with ease, you will no doubt be anxious to take on something of a more ambitious nature. Buy or make a simple design such as a small bracket or other useful article as, for instance, that shown Fig. 8, before attempting to cut out a large complicated pattern.

Fixing the Pattern.—The first thing to do after having obtained a printed design is to read and carefully observe the instructions usually marked on the pattern sheet, as such instructions generally give details as to the best and most economical way to set the pattern

Fig. 9

out on the material. If these details are not given, proceed as follows.

Cut up the sheet into the various parts which go to make up the design, using a pair of sharp scissors for the purpose.

The pieces must now be fixed down to the wood. Before doing this, however, you should so arrange the parts of the design that the best use is made of the material without unnecessary waste, bearing in mind that the pattern should be fixed lengthwise to the grain of the wood.

When this has been done, apply a thin coat of paste to the surface of the wood and place the pieces of the design in position. Some workers prefer to paste the paper and fix it to the material, but this has the disadvantage of having to handle wet paper, which is not an easy matter. If this method is preferred,

apply the paste radially from the centre to the edges to ensure an adequate supply to the edges.

Take a piece of soft rag or a clean duster and gently smooth the pattern down, taking care to exclude all air-bubbles, and then flatten out any wrinkles that may have formed. Fig. 9 shows the process.

Do not use ordinary tube glue or gum as an adhesive as you will possibly experience great difficulty when the work is ready for finishing. A good bought paste or a home-made one will do admirably.

A good home-made paste may be made as follows. Mix a small quantity of flour or starch into a stiff mass, using only a small quantity of cold water for the purpose. On this pour boiling water until you see it " turning " or jellifying. The paste is ready for use when cold. If the mixture does not jellify when the hot water is applied it usually indicates that either too much cold water was used in the first instance, or that the supposedly boiling water that was added was not boiling. This fault can sometimes be rectified by boiling the whole of it up again. As paste in this condition will not keep for long and quickly turns sour, the addition of a few drops of oil of cloves will act as a good preservative.

After pasting, the work should be placed upon a flat surface, and be allowed to dry; a few weights on the wood will prevent it from warping.

Drilling the Holes.—The next operation consists in drilling the holes in those portions of the design which are to be removed. The holes are necessary in order to pass the blade through. The Archimedean drill is used for this—never a bradawl; otherwise the wood is liable to split.

Drilling must not be attempted until the pattern is perfectly dry; otherwise the paper will pull up, or get distorted, if not badly torn.

It is a mistake to make the holes too small, as difficulty will be experienced in passing the saw-blade through the wood.

The best way to carry out the drilling is first to place the work on a piece of waste flat wood to prevent the drill breaking the fibres on the underside, and then lightly fasten both the work and the support to a flat surface, such as a kitchen table-top. This allows both hands to be free to operate the drill, as illustrated in Fig. 10. The fastening can be achieved by partially driving in a few thin panel pins here and there in the waste part of the design.

After all the necessary holes have been carefully drilled, apply a piece of glass-paper to the back of the work to smooth down any lumps that may have been made by the bit.

Most saws are broken in one of two ways. One is the result of attempting to saw too quickly round corners, and the other is generally due to carelessness when inserting and fastening the blade under the fixing clamps of the frame, after the blade has been threaded through one of the drilled holes in the waste. In refixing the blade always see that the ends of the blade are perfectly straight and not bent before tightening the clamps. Failure to observe this simple precaution invariably leads to a broken blade.

Removing the Waste.—Cut out all the waste material from the interior of the design and then proceed to cut out the outline. This is a much better method than cutting the outline first, as the outside material greatly assists in strengthening the work whilst the interior is being cut. The sawing operation should be done very carefully to avoid risk of breakage.

Removing the Pattern.—Having completed the sawing out, the next thing

to do is to remove the paper pattern from the surface of the wood.

A certain amount of the paper may be pulled up with the fingers, but the remainder should be removed by means of the glass-paper block.

Do not use water on any account, as it will cause the wood to curl and buckle, and perhaps ruin your handiwork.

Put a piece of No. $1\frac{1}{2}$ glass-paper in the block, and when the pattern is rubbed off, finish the work with a finer grade of paper.

Give the back of the work a good glass-papering to remove the saw-kerf, and if any little lumps appear on the edges, rectify them by using a very small file of suitable shape.

Should the work be very small, as in the case of brackets for supporting shelves, it may be an advantage to fasten down a sheet of glass-paper on to the face of a smooth board and rub the work on

Fig. 10

the papered surface. The paper can be attached to the board by using drawing pins at the corners, or it may be glued down. Care is needed when this method is adopted to see that the supporting

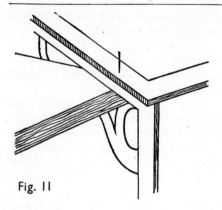

Fig. 11

surface is perfectly smooth and flat, because any little projection or unevenness may possibly force up a delicate part of the work and break it off.

Assembling the Parts.—The various parts of the article in hand may now be assembled in accordance with the printed instructions on the design sheet.

Special care should be taken when fitting the parts together, as a lot of trouble and disappointment can be easily avoided by taking simple precautions and exercising a little patience. All joints should be a nice, easy, hand-tight fit, and on no account must the pieces be forced together. If a slot is a little too narrow, ease it with either a fine file, or a piece of glass-paper wrapped round a small piece of wood. The same thing applies if the corresponding projecting pieces happen to be a little too " full."

Liquid glue is an excellent adhesive to use for fastening the parts together, as it is not only exceptionally strong, but is easy and clean to manipulate.

In some cases it may be found that glue is not sufficiently strong to make a firm joint, and it may be necessary to resort to the use of screws or nails.

When nailing or screwing, see that the part to be fastened is solidly supported. Fix a stiff iron bracket or something of a similar nature in the vice, and hold the solid part of the fret on this by allowing the projecting end of the metal to enter an opening in the fret close to the edge. The corner of a table may answer the purpose quite well provided the fret is a very open one, as shown in Fig. 11.

Fine veneer pins, or ordinary pins minus their heads, will generally suffice for nailing; but if screws are used do not forget to take the precaution to drill the wood before inserting them.

USEFUL WORKSHOP APPLIANCES

ONE of the first accessories the amateur should make for himself is a straight-edge, illustrated at A in Fig 1.

This device should be made from a piece of hardwood, preferably Spanish mahogany, as this wood can be relied upon not to twist and shrink like a good many hardwoods, such as oak.

A convenient size for general purposes is 2 ft. long, 4 in. wide, and $\frac{1}{4}$ in. thick.

Plane one edge perfectly true, and test this edge by first drawing a line on a clean piece of board, using the edge as a guide, and then turning the straight-edge over laterally. If the newly presented edge corresponds with the drawn line it indicates that the edge is true.

Bevel off the top corners, as shown in the illustration, so that no mistake will be made as to which is the true edge when it comes to be used, and bore a hole near one end to enable it to be hung up out of harm's way when not in use.

Never be tempted to use a straight-edge as a guide for a knife or chisel, but only for the purpose for which it is intended, that is, for testing planed surfaces.

If the appliance rocks on the surface being tested, it indicates that the surface is high somewhere near the middle; and if light can be seen between the working edge and the work it shows that the surface being planed is hollow.

Winding Strips have been mentioned elsewhere for testing whether a board or a framing has a twist in it or, as it is technically termed, gone into winding.

Two winding strips are needed which, like the straight-edge, should be made of mahogany.

Such winding strips, an illustration of which appears at B in Fig. 1, can be about 16 in. long, $1\frac{1}{2}$ in. wide, and $\frac{1}{2}$ in. thick.

In making this appliance great care must be taken to see that the long parallel edges are perfectly true. Gauge carefully and true carefully, and after preparing to satisfaction, turn them end to end to see if they coincide exactly as to width. Bevel off the top edge, as

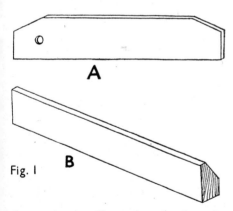

Fig. 1

shown in the illustration, leaving the full thickness of the bottom one to enable the strips to stand upright. The bevel should be planed to leave about $\frac{1}{4}$ in. on the top edges to sight along when in use.

A Sawing-stool is a very useful adjunct to the woodworker's equipment and is a much more satisfactory device than the usual makeshift box. If the worker feels so disposed he can make two sawing-stools, as the extra one will be found extremely useful when dealing with long lengths of timber.

The sawing-stool shown in Fig. 2 is

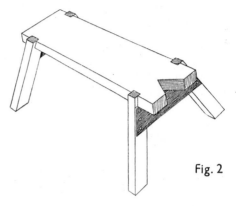

Fig. 2

quite simple to construct and will give a lifetime's service if properly cared for.

The top member is a piece of good-quality yellow deal, 2 ft. 6 in. long, 6 in. wide, and $1\frac{1}{2}$ in. thick. A V-shaped cut should be made in one end as the two projections so formed steady the material when the saw approaches the end of the cut.

The legs can be made from 3 in. by $1\frac{1}{2}$ in. material; and if these are made 20 in. in length, they will provide for a stool that can be used comfortably by the worker of average height. The tops of the legs should be marked and cut out to form a shoulder to support the top member, and let into the sides in the manner shown in the drawing. To strengthen the legs and prevent them from pulling outwards, a piece of 6 in. by $\frac{3}{4}$ in. board, cut to suit the splay of the legs, should be fitted across them at each end, and fastened by means of screws.

A Shooting-board is another useful appliance which the amateur can make for himself. A properly constructed home-made shooting-board is much to be preferred to the cheap ones that can be bought for a few shillings. As a rule such devices are merely made up of two boards screwed together, or from one thick piece having a rebated edge. This method of construction has the disadvantage that the wood easily twists and shrinks, and therefore soon becomes inaccurate.

Fig. 3 illustrates a shooting-board that is not at all difficult to construct and will give satisfaction for a lifetime.

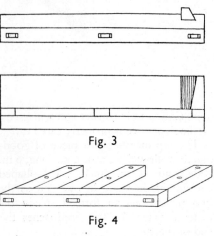

Fig. 3

Fig. 4

Obtain $5\frac{1}{2}$ ft. of 1 in. by $1\frac{1}{4}$ in. best-quality yellow deal, free from knots and other defects. Buy it ready planed, but test it before use and true up any little bit of twist that it may have acquired. This is absolutely necessary, because the material, although trued up and planed in all good faith by the timber merchant, may have developed a twist by the time the material is called upon for the job.

Cut the length into four pieces: one 3 ft. 1 in. long, and the remaining 2 ft. into three equal lengths. The extra inch on the long length is to allow $\frac{1}{2}$ in. at each end for safety when cutting the mortice, and can be trimmed off afterwards, if so preferred.

Mortice and tenon the pieces together to form a sort of framework, as shown in the illustration (Fig. 4), and when complete test for twist end to end and each end to middle. Then trim up with a plane to a finished thickness of $\frac{7}{8}$ in., and cut the legs to a length of 7 in.

True up a piece of faultless prepared yellow deal board, 3 ft. long by 5 in. wide and 1 in. thick. Drill two or three equidistant holes in each leg of the framing to take No. 8 countersunk-headed screws, $1\frac{1}{2}$ in. long. Countersink the tops of the holes fairly deeply on the underside to enable the heads of the screws to lie well below the surface to prevent them from scratching or catching anything.

Screw the parts together as shown in the plan—the lower drawing in Fig. 3.

A small space is left between the working edge of the board and the long member of the frame to allow shavings to slip away out of the course of the plane.

Next prepare the stop, which should be made from a piece of hardwood. Note the shape. On looking at the elevation and plan it will be seen that the stop has two bevels, but the front face, against which the work to be planed will rest, is left square. The height is of no great consequence as long as it provides a stop.

Having completed the stop, its position can be scribed on the board against a line drawn across the top with the aid of a square. When the recess has been carefully cut out, fit the stop by means of glue and screws, and trim off the front edge to allow free running of the plane.

The trying-plane is generally used on

a shooting-board. When using the board it is advisable to plane to a scribed line marked on the work even if the device is accurately made.

The Mitre Shooting-board shown in Fig. 5 is made on similar lines to the ordinary one just described, the main difference being that only two legs instead of three are necessary for the framework, due to its shorter length, and that two stops fixed at an angle of 45°, in the middle of the mitre shooting-board, take the place of one right-angled one.

To construct such a board, about 4 ft. of 1 in. by 1¼ in. deal is framed up as shown. The front member is 2 ft. long. The mortices can be made in it at a distance of about 2 in. from each end to take the legs, which are 9 in. in length overall. Screw the back part of the frame to a piece of trued-up board, 2 ft. in length, 7 in. wide and 1 in. thick.

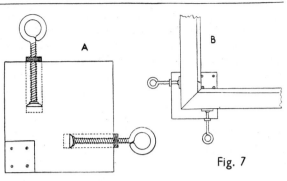

Fig. 7

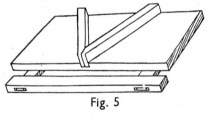

Fig. 5

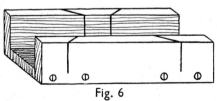

Fig. 6

From a centre line scribed on the front of this board mark off a distance of ½ in., and from these two points scribe lines at an angle of 45° to the front edge.

To make the stops, an 18 in. length of 2 in. by 1½ in. hardwood will be required.

From the lines already scribed, and using the narrow edge of the hardwood as a guide, scribe two more lines parallel to the first two, and remove the waste to form the recesses. These should be about ¼ in. deep and can be made either with a chisel or a router.

When this operation is finished, glue and screw the stops in position as shown in the illustration, finally trimming off any unnecessary projections.

The Mitre-box illustrated in Fig. 6 is looked upon by many workers as a better means of cutting a mitre than a mitre-block. In the case of the mitre-box the saw is guided on both sides of the material that is being mitred, consequently a more correct cut is obtained.

Such a box, suitable for cutting mouldings up to 3 in. wide, can be made with a prepared piece of yellow deal, 18 in. long, 4 in. wide, and at least 1 in. thick, to form the base, and two pieces of ¾ in. stuff, each 18 in. long and about 4 in. wide, for the sides.

True up the pieces and screw them together, using stout screws for the purpose, and then mark and saw the two slots at an angle of 45°, as shown in the drawing.

In fixing the positions of the screws, do not allow any of them to come in line with the saw-cuts.

The Corner Cramp.—Fig. 7 (A) shows this useful appliance, which will enable the handyman to overcome the difficulty of holding right-angled mitred work when gluing and nailing. Such a device will be found exceptionally useful for making picture frames, four cramps being necessary.

Fig. 8

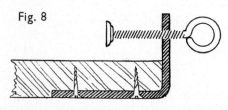

The principle upon which the cramp works may be gathered from a glance at B in Fig. 7, which is self-explanatory.

The base can be made out of a piece of oak, or other hardwood, about 4 in. square and $\frac{3}{4}$ in. thick. A small piece of $\frac{1}{2}$ in. hardwood, 2 in. square, is fastened to one corner of the base by means of screws.

The tightening screws on the two adjacent sides consist of small fretwork cramps with the long end opposite the screw removed. Two holes are drilled in suitable positions to enable these parts of the cramps to be screwed into recesses cut in the underside of the base, as shown in detail in Fig. 8.

A hacksaw can be used for removing the long leg of the cramp or, failing this, a file can be employed. If the latter method is decided upon, first cut a deep nick in the top and bottom surfaces by the aid of a half-round file used edgewise, and then give the leg a smart blow with a hammer. Complete the job by filing the end square.

To use the device, glue the pieces to be joined and place the mitred corners in the cramps so that the rebate (if a picture-frame) engages with the projection on the base. Insert slips of wood between the outer edges of the moulding and the ends of the screws to prevent damage, and tighten up the hand screws.

Another Form of Cramp for mitred work is shown at A in Fig. 9 in which four corner blocks made of hardwood, such as oak, beech, etc., are used. A corner block enlarged is shown at B in the illustration so that the method of preparing it can be better understood.

Each limb of the block is about 3 in. long by 1 in. thick, and is L-shaped. The corner forming the internal angle is recessed as shown. A hole is bored through the outer corner to take a stout piece of cord, which lies in a shallow channel formed in the two long edges. The hole and groove can be omitted if desired, but it is not advisable.

The tightening screw is an ordinary wood hand-screw and nut cut from a cramp, which can be purchased for about a shilling at most woodworkers' stores.

A hole is drilled near each end of the nut, and a piece of hardwood about 3 in. long, $1\frac{1}{2}$ in. wide, and $\frac{1}{2}$ in. thick takes the point of the screw, which is also provided with similar holes. One end of the cord is knotted, while the

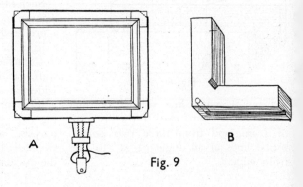

A   B

Fig. 9

other end passes through one of the holes in the nut and bearer, through the blocks and opposite holes in the bearer and nut where it is securely tied, after the blocks have been placed in position. A few turns of the screw tighten the cord and the resulting pressure on the blocks efficiently cramps the joints of the work.

The screwing may be eliminated if desired by substituting a block of wood or wedges between the frame and the tied cord, but this method of obtaining the necessary tension is not so satisfactory as the screw.

Fig. 10 illustrates a useful device for forming small depressions or beads along the edges of a piece of work. It consists of a cutter fixed in a suitable handle.

A piece of oak or other hardwood, 1 in. by 1½ in. and about 10 in. long, is sawn down the narrow edge for a distance of about 3 in., and a shoulder cut as shown, the remaining part being shaped to form a handle.

Suitable screw - holes are made at intervals along the side of the slotted portion to take ordinary wood-screws which, when tightened, hold the cutter firmly in place.

The Cutter or scraper—it is more of a scraping tool than a cutting tool—is made from an odd piece of steel, such as a piece of hacksaw blade filed to the desired shape after it has been softened by heating it to redness and then allowing it to cool slowly. After filing, the cutter should be hardened by heating it up to redness again and then quenching it in water. In filing the cutter it is necessary to "back off" the cutting edge in order to present a sharp edge to the work.

To use the device, insert the cutter into the slot at the desired distance from the shoulder, which acts as a distance guide, and tighten up the screws. Work the tool in the direction of the grain,

keeping the shoulder pressed up tightly to the edge of the work. Do not attempt to form the bead in one cut, but gradually develop the formation of the bead by taking several strokes, pressing the cutter a trifle deeper into the material at each subsequent stroke.

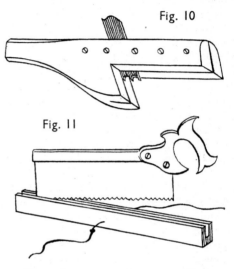

Fig. 10

Fig. 11

The illustration shown in Fig. 11 is of an accessory for protecting the teeth of a tenon-saw fitted with an open handle which does not allow of easy hanging on a nail after use. It consists of a strip of hardwood a trifle longer than the blade of the saw. A saw-cut about ½ in. deep is made in one of the long narrow edges, into which the teeth of the saw are inserted. A hole is bored through the centre of the strip through which a suitable length of cord is threaded and knotted at each side to prevent it from being pulled through.

When the saw is not in use, the teeth are slipped into the saw-cut and the cord tied over the back to keep it in place.

An ordinary household flat-iron firmly secured between the jaws of the bench-vice, so that the sole is uppermost, forms a convenient anvil.

ARRANGING THE WORKSHOP

IN estimating the size of a garden workshop much depends, of course, upon what it is going to be used for, remembering that it is poor economy to build the workshop too small.

If light woodwork, such as cabinet-making, fretwork, etc., is to be undertaken, a workshop about 10 ft. long by 7 ft. wide and 6 ft. high at the front and 7 ft. 9 in. at the back will generally answer the purpose, but where work of a larger nature is to be carried out, and perhaps a lathe installed, a more commodious structure is necessary.

Size.—A structure 18 ft. long by 10 ft. wide, built to a height of 7 ft. 6 in. to eaves and 8 ft. 6 in. to ridge, and fitted with double doors at one end, will give room not only for accommodating the usual woodworking equipment but also such items as garden tools, decorating material, and other apparatus commonly used by the practical man.

One of the most important considerations in planning a workshop is light, and this is where a home-constructed workshop scores against a ready-made one—the worker can arrange his windows where he wants them.

Lighting.—It is an advantage to have a number of windows running the whole length of the front of the workshop, where the workbench usually stands, while the inclusion of a skylight is one of those small items that make for comfortable working. If a skylight is included, a linen roller-blind should be fitted to eliminate the glare of the sun during the summer months.

Where possible, electricity should be used for the artificial lighting of the workshop, as it is safer and more efficient than gas or oil lamps.

In arranging the electric light points, do not forget to include a socket into which a portable light or any other useful portable electrical apparatus, such as a soldering-iron, can be plugged, and if a heating circuit is available a small port-

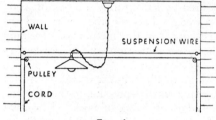

Fig. 1

able heater will give additional comfort during cold weather.

The light over the bench should not be a fixture, but be capable of being shifted from one end of the bench to the other. This can be easily arranged by fixing the light to a cord running over two pulleys fixed to the walls, in the manner shown diagrammatically in Fig. 1.

The possible general arrangements of the workshop are so great that only a few practical suggestions can be made.

For instance, the workbench—especially the working-end of it where the bench-stop and vice are placed—should be directly in front of a window, so that no shadows are cast upon the work. Some workers use a fixed bench while others prefer a portable type.

In some cases tools, such as chisels, files, bits, etc., can be kept in a rack at the back of the bench, but not at such a height as to interfere with the light from the window.

This arrangement may be quite satisfactory if no large work is intended, but it has the disadvantage that should at any time a fairly large door or frame be constructed, the rack would be obviously in the way, as the whole width of the bench is necessary for gluing, and planing after gluing.

Movable Wall Panels.—In cases where it is only possible to construct a small workshop, its capabilities can be greatly enhanced by making a movable panel in line with the bench-top, at each end, as shown in Fig. 2. This arrangement will be found of inestimable value when working upon long material, as the ends of the work can project beyond the ends of the workshop. Such panels can be easily arranged when constructing the framework. They can either be made to be entirely removed or hinged from the outside. If the use of loose panels is decided upon, they can be secured by turnbuttons operated from inside.

A similar movable panel could be arranged under a gable end of the roof to allow long lengths of timber to be easily inserted and stored upon a few pieces of scantling fixed across the workshop.

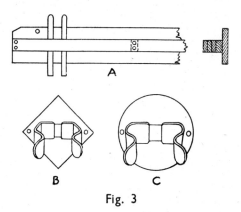

Fig. 3

Tool Racks and Shelves can be fastened to the walls at convenient points that will keep them out of the way yet leave them close to hand.

The racks can be made in various ways. Strips of wood, $\frac{1}{2}$ in. thick and about 2 in. wide, cut out in the manner indicated at A in Fig. 3, and either nailed or screwed to a broader piece screwed to the wall between the uprights, make excellent racks for chisels, gouges, screwdrivers, etc.

Another serviceable type of tool rack can be made by screwing a number of spring clips of the types shown at B and C to a board about 6 in. wide, such clips being obtainable at most tool shops at a low cost. Where a rack of this type is employed, centre-bits can be kept in place by hanging them with their points upwards so that their shoulders keep them in the clips, and chisels, etc., with their handles up for the same reason.

If racks are used, they should be so arranged that others can be added if necessary, as your list of tools increases.

Small tools, such as twist-drills, should be kept in a block of hardwood, drilled with a sufficient number of holes to accommodate their shanks.

This method of storing drills is to be preferred to the unprofessional way of

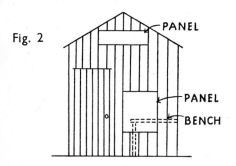

Fig. 2

PANEL

PANEL

BENCH

Tools need arrangement. Saws, as a rule, as well as the saw-cramp, straight-edge, and similar tools, can be hung on nails driven into the walls, within easy reach of the bench.

keeping them in a box, as it not only preserves the cutting-edges but also saves a considerable amount of time in selecting a drill of a particular size.

In preparing a block for twist drills, each hole should be bored with the same sized drill it is intended to accommodate, and the sizes should be plainly marked on the top of the block. An oak block about 3 in. long by 2 in. wide and 2 in. deep will hold over thirty small drills. A neat cover should be made to protect them from damp.

A Tool Cabinet.—Some workers may prefer to keep their tools in a cabinet or cupboard, in which case a receptacle made on similar lines to the one shown in Fig. 4 will be found to be serviceable and quite easy to construct.

The size of such a cabinet naturally depends upon the number of tools it is to contain and must therefore be left to the maker to decide.

The upper compartment contains a rack for chisels, etc., made by driving a series of nails or wooden pegs in the edge of a narrow support, as shown clearly in the drawing. The chisels lie between these projections and present a neat and orderly appearance. If wooden dowels are used, they should be sawn off so that they all project equally; and should nails be chosen, they should be driven in to an equal depth. To ensure this, a short piece of iron gas-pipe could be cut and placed over the head of the nail during the last stroke or two of the hammer, to act as a depth-gauge. This rack is, of course, made as a separate unit

and fitted after the completion of the cabinet.

The top section also contains a shelf for the accommodation of planes, etc., while the lower compartment can either be fitted with shelves or drawers; or a piece of wood could be fixed to divide the section vertically, one side of which could contain shelves and the other be

Fig. 4

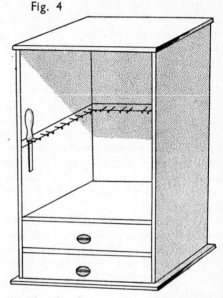

suitably fitted to accommodate saws, brace, etc.

If desired, the top section can be fitted with a door or a flap hinged from the bottom rail and fastened at the top by means of a hook and eye.

After the cupboard is completed it should receive a coat of stain to enhance its appearance.

CONSTRUCTIONAL WOODWORK

A WORK BENCH

A WORK bench should be rigid, without spring, and not too heavy to enable it to be comfortably moved about from place to place, yet heavy enough to prevent it from shifting from its position when in use.

The bench described in the following paragraphs fulfils these conditions, and as it is cheap and easy to construct it should appeal to those readers whose pockets are not too "well lined" and whose knowledge of woodwork is limited.

A general idea of the bench may be obtained by referring to the drawings in Working Drawing No. 1.

It will be seen that the space beneath the bench-top is made use of by the provision of two shelves for holding tools, etc., a feature not generally found in the ordinary type of carpenter's bench. This space is totally enclosed by means of three plywood panels, $\frac{1}{8}$ in. thick, fitted to the sides and back, and hinged doors at the front. This useful feature is optional and can be omitted if desired without interfering with the strength and general usefulness of the structure. Where possible it should be included, as the small amount of extra labour involved in its construction and the trifling additional cost will be well repaid by being able to keep your tools under lock and key. The overall dimensions of the bench are 4 ft. 6 in. in length, 2 ft. 2 in. wide and 2 ft. 9 in. high—a convenient size for general purposes.

One of the most important items in connection with a woodworking bench is the provision of suitable devices for holding the work. A useful type of vice suitable for use with a bench of this type can be either one of those handy metal tools which screw down to the top of the bench by means of four screws—as shown in the accompanying illustration in Fig. 1—or it can be one of the wooden variety having two adjusting screws and fixed to the front of the bench by means of two or three iron screws. Such a vice is shown in Fig. 2. The former costs about 7/6, while the latter is listed at about 3/-.

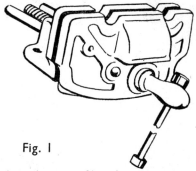

Fig. 1

As some sort of bench stop is required when planing the faces of boards, etc , an adjustable metal stop (Fig. 3), costing about eighteenpence, is an excellent one to have, and is much to be preferred to the old-fashioned stop consisting of a rectangular block of wood driven tightly into a hole in the bench-top. The metal stop is adjusted by means of a screw which raises or lowers the lip to the desired height and also allows it to lie flush with the top surface of the bench when not in use.

The following is a list of the finished sizes of the parts:

Description	No.	Sizes ft. in.	ft. in.	in.
Legs	4	2 7 ×	3 ×	3
End cross-pieces	4	2 0 ×	3 ×	2
Top front rail	1	4 6 ×	6 ×	1
Bottom front rail	1	4 0 ×	3 ×	2
Top back rail	1	4 6 ×	8 ×	1
Bottom back rail	1	4 0 ×	3 ×	2
Bench-top boards	2	4 6 ×	9 ×	2
Bench-top (middle)	1	4 6 ×	7 ×	1
Struts	2	3 0 ×	2 ×	1
2 shelves and bottom boards	7 (approx.)	2 0 ×	8 ×	$\frac{3}{4}$
Door stiles	4	1 10 ×	$1\frac{3}{4}$ ×	$\frac{3}{4}$
Door rails	4	1 $8\frac{1}{2}$ ×	$1\frac{3}{4}$ ×	$\frac{3}{4}$
Side panels	2	2 4 ×	2 0 ×	$\frac{1}{8}$
Back panel	1	4 0 ×	2 4 ×	$\frac{1}{8}$
Bearers	6	2 0 ×	2 ×	$\frac{3}{4}$

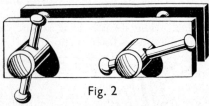

Fig. 2

The bench should be constructed of good quality yellow joinery deal, perfectly straight and free from knots and shakes. It is a good plan to purchase the timber ready planed and cut roughly to size, as the small extra

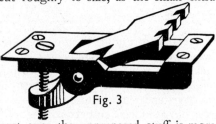

Fig. 3

cost over the unprepared stuff is more than compensated for by the great saving of time and labour.

Prepare the two end frames, as shown in Fig. 5 in the Working Drawing. Two end frames are required, one for the right hand and one for the left.

Each frame consists of two legs 2 ft. 7 in. long of 3 in. by 3 in. deal, and two cross-pieces each 2 ft. in length, 3 in. wide and 2 in. thick. The top rail is fixed flush with the tops of the legs, while the bottom one is placed with its lower edge 6 in. above the floor level. The joints used are halved joints—one of the simplest joints it is possible to make.

Mark out the positions on the legs where the joints are to be and remove the waste with the aid of a tenon-saw and chisel, taking care to make every saw-cut on the waste side of the line.

Having prepared all the joints, the members can be fixed together by using $2\frac{1}{2}$ in. No. 12 countersunk iron screws or, if preferred, by using glue and dowel-pins. In both methods it is advisable to draw the parts together tightly by means of a cramp before inserting the screws or the dowels.

Halve the ends of the two lower long rails which join the end frames at the bottoms of the legs. The corresponding top rails are formed of planed boards 1 in. thick, the front one being 6 in. wide and the back one 8 in.

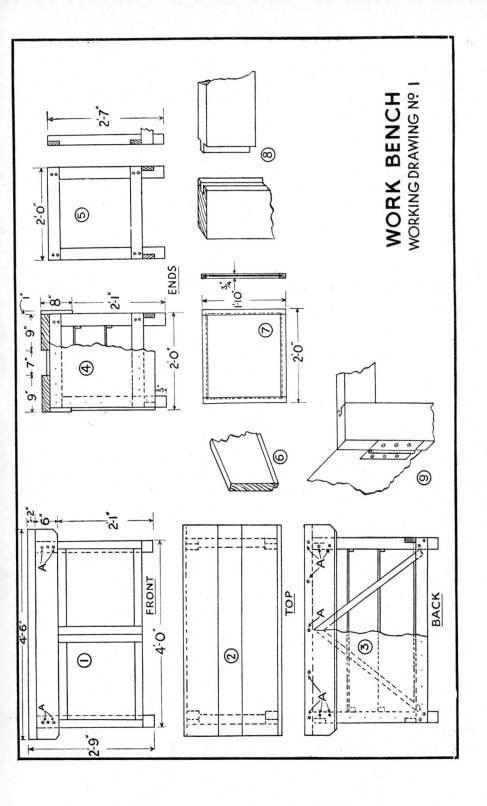

WORK BENCH
WORKING DRAWING № 1

Nail a strip of ¾-in. square wood along the bottom edge of the top back rail to form a rebate a trifle over ⅛ in. wide to take the top of the plywood panel, as shown in Fig. 6. Mark the positions of the fixing screws on the top rails, as shown at A in Figs. 1 and 3, and then drill holes a trifle larger than the diameter of the screws at these positions. Countersink the tops of the holes to allow the screw-heads to lie just below the surface. Mark and drill the bottom rails in the same manner. The position for these screw-holes is 2 in. from the ends.

Assembling the Framework.—The next process consists in assembling the framework. A convenient way to do this, if an assistant is not available, is to place the end frames with the back faces of the rear legs resting on the floor and the top rails against a wall. Place the top front rail in position and drive a screw partially into the left-hand leg; repeat the process at the other end, which will enable the framework to stand up without support. Now fix the bottom rail. When you have satisfied yourself that the work is perfectly square by verifying it with a large try-square, tighten up the screws already in and drive in the remaining ones.

Turn the frame over so that the back is now uppermost and proceed by fixing the back rails, bearing in mind that the top rail projects 2 in. above the end frames.

The next step consists in fitting the back struts, so the framework can now stand in its normal position, that is, of course, with the feet on the floor. Mark and cut the struts, which are made of planed batten 2 in. wide by ¾ in. thick, and fix them by means of screws in the positions shown in Fig. 3.

Now mark the positions and bore the screw-holes in the thick top board in a manner similar to that described

for the long top rails. When making the holes near the front edges, take particular care to keep the bit vertical, otherwise the screws may miss the comparatively narrow edge of the rail.

Screw the front and back top boards down to the framework and then fix the middle one, the latter being held down with 1½-in. No. 8 screws.

The main portion of the job is now complete, and if the work has been carefully done the structure should be perfectly stable and rigid. Make sure that the bottoms of the legs all stand perfectly level on the floor; if such is not the case now is the time to make adjustments.

Fit the bottom boards and the shelves. For supporting these, six pieces of 2-in. by 1-in. batten are required for bearers, which are fixed across the inside faces of the end frames. The bearers for supporting the bottom boards should be fixed so that their upper edges are flush with the tops of the long bottom rails. The supports can be fixed either with nails or screws.

Mark and cut the three bottom boards so that they are a nice fit between the bottom rails of the end frames, not forgetting to make the recesses to clear the corners of the legs and the struts.

The shelf supports, or bearers, and the shelves, which are 16 in. wide, are fixed in a similar manner in positions to suit the requirements of the user.

The Plywood Panels are quite simple to fix and no difficulty should be experienced from this source. They should be fastened to the frames by means of ¾-in. thin round brads driven in at intervals of about 6 in. The back panel is fitted by first sliding the top into the rebate or groove formed between the ¾ in. thick strip of wood on the bottom edge of the back board and the struts and legs. The top of the panel is fixed from the inside by driving brads through the panel into the wooden strip, the bottom and sides being "pinned" from the outside.

The bench stop should be fitted at about 6 in. from the left-hand end and in the centre of the first top board. Mark out the position for this and make the recess by first partially removing the waste with the aid of a brace and bit and then trimming up the edges with a sharp chisel.

Having fitted the vice, the bench may be put into commission, as it will be useful when constructing the doors.

Those readers who do not wish to go to the trouble of making panelled doors can use solid ones cut accurately to size from $\frac{1}{2}$ in. thick plywood. Plain plywood doors, however, do not have a particularly pleasing appearance, and as panelled doors are very simple to construct, the little extra time needed for their construction is not time wasted.

The framework of the panelled doors can be built up from standard-size plain hardwood moulding, having a groove already formed in one narrow edge for taking the panel. This handy material is quite inexpensive and can be purchased at most shops that cater for amateur woodworkers' requirements. For the two doors, two 8 ft. lengths of $1\frac{3}{4}$-in. by $\frac{3}{4}$-in. plain grooved moulding will be required.

Fig. 7 in the working drawing shows a detailed illustration of the method of construction of a door. First cut the stiles or vertical pieces, which should be 2 ft. in length—1 in. longer at each end than the finished size is to be. Next prepare the rails or cross-pieces. The overall length of these is 22 in., which allows $\frac{1}{4}$ in. at each end for forming the short strut tenons that fit into the grooves in the struts, as shown in Fig. 8.

Having cut the tenons, the parts can be assembled by first gluing the joints and then the edges of the panel, inserting the panel and keeping them together with the aid of cramps or wedges until the glue has set perfectly hard. The ends of the stiles are then carefully sawn off and, if necessary, the whole of the frame trimmed up with a very sharp, finely-set plane.

The Hinges.—Fix these as shown in Fig. 9. To prevent the doors being forced inwards and thus straining the hinges, a strip of wood should be screwed to the inner face of the top rail, allowing an inch to project below the bottom edge of the rail. A similar piece of wood screwed to the bottom board will answer the same purpose at the bottom. A couple of small sliding bolts fitted on the inside face of one of the middle stiles and a small lock fixed on the other, completes the work.

THE HOME WORKSHOP

THE workshop or garden shed, shown in the accompanying illustration (Fig. 1) and the Working Drawings Nos. 2 and 3, has been designed with the object of simplifying the construction to enable the man who can use a few carpenter's tools to erect it without difficulty. Such a workshop will last a lifetime, provided it is given a yearly coat of paint or creosote.

If the drawings are studied carefully, it will be seen that the structure is built in sections, a feature which enables it to be easily dismantled and re-erected.

Before starting the actual construction, a suitable site should be decided upon, bearing in mind that a dry position is essential and that the best situation is one that faces south, or south-west. A northern aspect is likely to be dark and depressing. It is a good plan to prepare the site before accepting delivery of the materials for, by so doing, the constructional work can then be proceeded with without delay.

If the site chosen is covered with grass, the turf should be removed, the ground made as level as possible and well rammed down.

Foundation.—An excellent foundation for a structure of this description can be made by using three disused railway sleepers, which can usually be obtained from the railway company for a few shillings. This method keeps the structure dry, well off the ground.

The use of railway sleepers is an improvement on the usual method of laying a few bricks on their large faces flat on the ground and spaced at intervals under long floor supports or "sleepers,"

as they are called. Bricks, owing to their comparatively small area, are liable to sink into the ground in the course of time and consequently upset the level and squareness of the building. If they have to be used, they should be placed transversely under the horizontal members supporting the floor joists, spaced at distances of not less than 2 ft. apart.

Tools required for carrying out the work include a good, sharp hand-saw, tenon-saw, 1-in. chisel, try-square, bevel, bradawl, brace and bits, straight-edge and a rule.

Before ordering the timber it is a good plan to study the list of sizes to enable you roughly to estimate the number of particular lengths required, as this will avoid a good deal of waste. If the material for the framework, let us say, is specified as so many feet of scantling, the timber-merchant will probably send odd lengths. For example, by referring to the following list you will see that six 7-ft.-long floor joists are required. This item should be ordered as three 14-ft. lengths, which will cut two joists out of each without waste.

The following is a list of the approximate sizes of the timbers, to which should be added at least 10 per cent. for waste.

Parts	No.	Size
FLOOR:		*ft. in. in. in.*
Sleepers, or joist plates . .	4 .	. 10 0 × 3 × 2
Joists	6 .	. 7 0 × 3 × 2
Flooring . . .	70 sq. ft.	. 6 in. × $\frac{7}{8}$ in. tongued and grooved flooring.
FRONT:		
Top and bottom plates . .	2 .	. 10 0 × 2 × 2
Studs	4 .	. 5 9 × 2 × 2
Cross-pieces	2 .	. 3 0 × 2 × 2
Top of window . . .	1 .	. 3 6 × 2 × 2
Bottom of window . . .	1 .	. 3 7 × 2 × 2
BACK:		
Top and bottom plates . .	2 .	. 10 0 × 2 × 2
Studs	4 .	. 5 9 × 2 × 2
Cross-pieces	3 .	. 3 $2\frac{1}{2}$ × 2 × 2

Parts	No.	ft.	in.	in.	in.
END:					
Centre stud	1	7	9½ ×	2 ×	2
End studs	2	5	6½ ×	2 ×	2
Bottom plate	1	6	8 ×	2 ×	2
Roof-pieces	2	4	0 ×	2 ×	2
Top cross-pieces	2	3	3½ ×	2 ×	2
Cross-pieces	2	3	2 ×	2 ×	2
DOOR END:					
Door studs	2	6	9 ×	2 ×	2
End studs	2	5	6½ ×	2 ×	2
Roof-pieces	2	4	0 ×	2 ×	2
Bottom plate	1	6	8 ×	2 ×	2
Top cross-pieces	2	1	10 ×	2 ×	2
Cross-pieces	2	1	8½ ×	2 ×	2
Cross-piece top of door	1	2	10 ×	2 ×	2
ROOF:					
Purlins	4	10	4¾ ×	3 ×	2
Capping-pieces for ridge	2	10	6 ×	6 ×	⅝
Gable ends	4	5	0 ×	6 ×	⅝
Battens	10	4	6 ×	2 ×	¾
WINDOW:					
Lining, horizontal	1	3	6 ×	2 ×	½
Lining, vertical	2	1	9½ ×	2 ×	½
Sill	1	3	10 ×	4 ×	2
Stiles	4	1	9½ ×	2 ×	1¼
Rails	4	1	8½ ×	2 ×	1½
Stops, horizontal	2	3	5 ×	¾ ×	½
Stops, vertical	2	1	9½ ×	¾ ×	½
DOOR:					
Ledges	2	2	7 ×	6 ×	⅞
Brace	1	5	2 ×	4 ×	⅞

Allowing for waste, this gives the following approximate quantities: 125 ft. of 3 in. by 2 in. scantling; 325 ft. of 2 in. by 2 in.; 2½ squares of matching for the front, back and ends; 80 sq. ft. for floorboards and 110 sq. ft. matching for the roof.

The following miscellaneous items will also be required. One pair of 14-in. cross garnets for hanging the door; two pairs of iron butt hinges for windows; one rim lock for the door; quantity of 2-in. and 1½-in. cut nails; 3½-in. and 4-in. wire nails; ½-in. galvanised clout nails for fixing roofing felt; 1½-in. galvanised wire nails for fastening roofing battens; eight 6-in. by ⅜-in. iron bolts, nuts and washers; creosote and roofing felt.

When the material is delivered it should be placed under cover to keep it perfectly dry or, if this is impracticable, the timber should be stacked on cross-pieces or odd wood and covered over with sacking or sheets of galvanised iron. Otherwise you may have difficulties not only in cutting but also when fitting the tongues and grooves in the matching.

The Floor.—When the material is to hand and the site and foundation have been prepared, a start may be made with the construction of the floor, as the walls stand on the edges of this.

Prepare the three long sleepers and floor joists by first marking and then cutting them to their correct lengths.

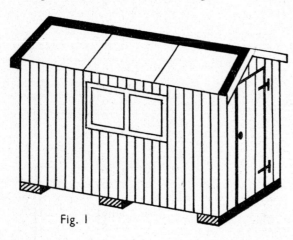

Fig. I

Give them a good coat of creosote and place the bottom members across the railway sleepers, making sure that they are at the correct distances apart and are perfectly level. To keep these in position for the time being, drive a nail obliquely through the members at each point of contact as shown in the elevation of the floor. Do not drive them right home as they have to be withdrawn after the joists have been laid.

Next mark out the positions for the joists on the two outer supports. Reference to the drawing will show you that the positions for these are 2 ft. apart. Fix the two end joists first, and then follow with the others. As these are fixed down with 4-in. wire nails which

are of a somewhat heavy gauge, it is advisable to bore holes for their reception by using a brace and shell-bit of small diameter.

The framework of the floor is now complete. It should be squared up and tested to see that it is perfectly level. The long bottom members should bear upon the railway sleepers at every point of support. If such is not the case, slips of wood should be inserted between them for this purpose.

The next procedure consists in cutting and laying the floorboards. If it has not been possible to obtain these in 10- or 20-ft. lengths, as previously suggested, the boards should be cut to such a size as to avoid any unnecessary waste. For instance, if the boards are supplied in 15-ft. lengths, a lot of waste would be avoided by putting in an extra joist in the middle of the floor frame to support the ends of the two half-lengths. In this case first nail a full-length board flush with the ends of the joists at either the back or the front, and then proceed by fixing another long board followed by two short ones, and so on until the whole of the joists are covered.

Before laying the first board, however, it is necessary to remove the tongue so that a plain edge is flush with the ends of the joists. This enables the tongue of the next board to be inserted into the groove of the first, which is much easier to accomplish than fitting them vice versa.

Fasten the first board down by driving in 2-in. cut nails at a distance of 1 in. away from the long edges, taking care to see that they are driven into the centres of the joists. Insert the tongue of the second board into the groove of the first and nail this down at the back edges only and proceed in a like manner until all the floorboards are in position. The remainder of the nails can then be driven in the front edges to complete.

If you experience any difficulty in fitting the tongues into the grooves, do not be tempted to hammer them in without first inserting an odd piece of tongued board to take the blows; otherwise the groove will be badly bruised and cause further difficulty when the following board is to be fitted.

Another important point to observe is that the edges of the boards must fit tightly against their fellow-members.

It sometimes happens that a board is not quite straight, in which case it can be forced into position by first inserting the tongue into the groove at one end, nailing it down, and then driving a chisel into the joist at the other end and prising the board into position, not forgetting to interpose the wooden block to prevent damage to the edges.

The floor is complete when any ends of the boards projecting over the end joists have been trimmed off flush.

The Construction of the Framework may now be put in hand. By referring to the drawings it will be seen that the top plates of the front and back are notched to house the ends of the vertical timbers. The notches are 2 in. wide and cut $\frac{1}{2}$ in. deep.

When the positions of the notches have been marked, the surplus material is removed with the aid of a tenon-saw and chisel.

Start with the front, the assembly of which is quite straightforward and should therefore present no difficulty. The members are simply fixed together by means of $3\frac{1}{2}$-in. wire nails. Like the floor joists, the members should be drilled to take the nails to prevent splitting the wood.

The back section calls for little comment as the construction is similar to that of the front. The nails for fixing the inner ends of the horizontal members to the uprights or "studs" should be driven in obliquely.

With regard to the end frames, it will be noticed that the top horizontal members are not notched at their outer ends but are merely nailed with 4-in. nails on top of the outer uprights, while the sloping pieces forming the roof supports are nailed to the horizontals.

The best way to deal with the roof supports is first to mark them at the ridge and eave ends to the correct angles, using a bevel for the purpose.

Details of the construction of the roof are shown in Working Drawing No. 3. Two roof sections will be required. Each section consists of $\frac{3}{4}$-in. tongued and grooved matching fastened down to two 3-in. by 2-in. horizontal members called "purlins."

The Roof Sections.—First cut the purlins to a length of 10 ft. 6 in. and the boards to 4 ft. 11 in., which allows an inch extra for waste at the ends. Nail the boards down so that their top edges project 3 in. from the outer face of the top purlin and 9 in. from the bottom one. When the boards have been nailed down, mark a line across them from one end to the other at the correct distance from the purlins, and remove the waste with a hand-saw. This method is to be preferred to cutting the boards to their correct lengths and then nailing them down to the members, as it ensures even and parallel edges.

Having completed the boarding, cut $\frac{5}{8}$ in. off the ends of the purlins to allow the barge boards to be fixed flush with the ends of the roof as indicated in the detail of the roof.

Before proceeding any further with the constructional work, it is advisable to give the exterior of the roof a good coat of creosote, and when sufficient time has elapsed to allow it to dry—this

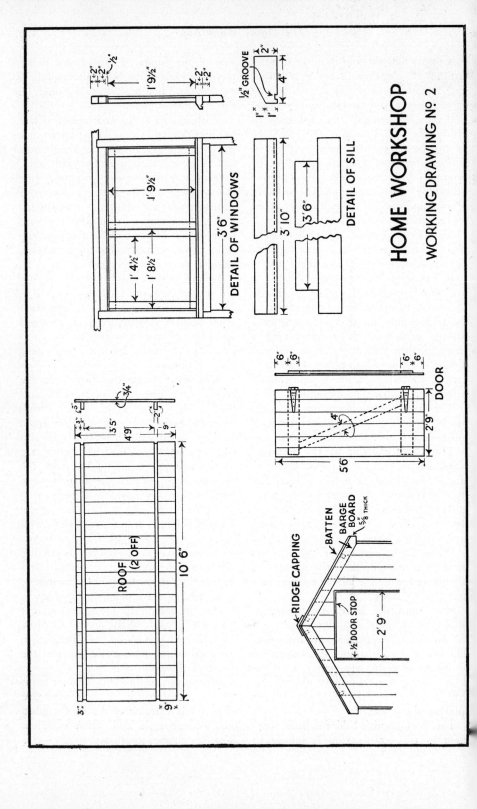

HOME WORKSHOP

WORKING DRAWING No. 2

½ GROOVE

DETAIL OF WINDOWS

DETAIL OF SILL

ROOF (2 OFF)

10' 6"

DOOR

RIDGE CAPPING

BATTEN

BARGE BOARD
⅝ THICK

½ DOOR STOP

2' 9"

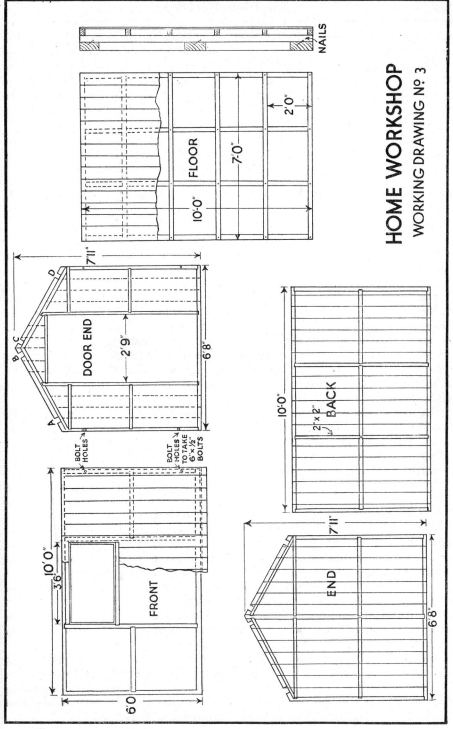

HOME WORKSHOP
WORKING DRAWING № 3

NAILS

FLOOR
10'0" 7'0" 2'0"

DOOR END
7'11"
2'9"
6'8"
BOLT HOLES
BOLT HOLES TO TAKE 6"x½" BOLTS
A B C D

BACK
10'0"
2"x2"

FRONT
10'0"
3'6"
6'0"

END
7'11"
6'8"

5

does not take long—to cover it with roofing felt.

Although some workers prefer to fix the roofing felt after the roof is in situ, it will be found easier to carry out the work on the level.

Covering the Roof.—The simplest and cheapest way is to use one of the many excellent proprietary brands of roof covering, which must not be confused with the old-fashioned tarred felt. It is sold in rolls 1 yd. wide, 36 ft. long. For covering the roof, two strips 11 ft. in length will be required for each section, which allows sufficient material for lapping the joint and for turning over the lower edges. Unroll the felt on a flat surface, taking care not to tear or otherwise damage it, and cut it to the required lengths by using a sharp knife and straight-edge. To lay the material, start at the top edge of the section and fasten it down with $\frac{1}{2}$-in. galvanised clout nails spaced at 2-in. intervals, taking care to see that it lies perfectly flat. Nail the second piece down after allowing the bottom edge of the first strip to overlap the second by 4 in. Bend the felt over the bottom edges of the roof timbers and nail it down to the bottom face. Now carefully cut the material to remove the surplus, after allowing a couple of inches for turning under.

The frames of the four sections may now be covered with matching, but before actually starting on the job it is absolutely necessary to see that all sections are perfectly square. This should be carefully checked and if any one is found to be incorrect, it should now receive attention. To keep the sections perfectly square it is a good plan to nail one or two strips of wood across the members at the angles.

The Matching is fixed in exactly the same manner as that described for the floor. Note that the first and last boards on the front and back sections overlap the frame ends by $\frac{5}{8}$ in. to cover the edges of the boards of the end sections. When cutting the boards to length do not forget that the bottom edges overlap the plates by $3\frac{3}{4}$ in. to cover the ends of the floor and joists.

The matched boards of the end sections project 3 in. above the tops of the sloping roof pieces. Fix the boards as shown in the drawings of the end and door end in Working Drawing No. 2, and then mark and cut off the waste after nailing them in position.

Having completed the boarding, cut the slots at the top of each end section in positions shown at A, B, C and D. The size of these is 2 in. wide by 3 in. deep. These recesses provide a simple and effective means of supporting the ends of the roof purlins, and keep the roof in position.

Now drill the bolt holes in the corner posts in the positions shown in the drawing of the front, using a $\frac{1}{2}$-in. twist-bit for the purpose.

Assembling the Sections.—The next step is to assemble the sections. If possible, get a friend to give you a hand with this.

Place the front section in position and see that the bottom plate rests flush with the sides of the floor. Your helper will now hold this in position whilst you place the plain end section in position. Having done this, insert the two bolts, not forgetting to fit the washers before fastening the nuts. Tighten up the nuts finger tight. The two parts will now be self-supporting. Place the door end in position and then the back, insert bolts, and screw all the nuts up tightly with a spanner.

Next put the roof in position by inserting the purlins into the respective slots at the top of the end sections, taking care to see that the ends of the roof overlap the walls equally.

Mark and cut the barge boards as shown in Working Drawing No. 2, then fix them to the ends of the roof by driving nails through them into the ends of the purlins, and also by a few nails driven in from the top edges of the roof.

When the roof capping, consisting of two 6-in.-wide boards, has been fixed, the roofing battens can be cut to length, creosoted and screwed down with 1-in. No. 6 screws.

The Door is of the ordinary ledged and braced type, dimensions of which can be readily taken from the details shown. The ledges should not be flush with the long edges of the door but cut back ¾ in. to allow the door to close when the door stopping is in position.

An ordinary iron lock—which is not an expensive item—should be fitted on the inside of the door at a height of about 3 ft.

Hang the door with a pair of 14-in. cross garnet hinges, and then fit the door stopping on the inner face of the frame.

The final constructional step consists in making the window and frames.

The Window Sill is formed from a piece of timber 3 ft. 10 in. long, 4 in. wide and 2 in. thick. Mark this out and plane a bevel between the front and top faces, as shown in Working Drawing No. 2, and make a ⅜-in. square drip-groove on the underside to prevent water from running into the joint. Screw the sill down to the bottom member of the window aperture, using

3½-in. countersunk-headed screws for the purpose. Line the remainder of the opening with planed strips of wood 2 in. wide by ½ in. thick.

The Window-frames are made of 2-in. by 1¼-in. planed joinery deal. As the windows are not very large, and therefore light in weight, an ordinary open morticed and tenoned joint can be used. The joints should be glued up and locked with dowels.

The rebate for the glass is formed by nailing ¾-in. by ⅜-in. strips of wood to the insides of the frames.

Before inserting the glass, the frames should receive a good coat of priming paint as putty will not stick to bare wood. When the paint is quite dry, glaze the windows in the usual way.

The Sashes are hung from the sides by means of 1-in. iron butt hinges. These are sunk half in the window frame and half in the lining and fixed with 1-in. No. 8 countersunk-headed screws.

Finish the window aperture by nailing strips of wood ¾ in. by ½ in. thick around the inside faces at the back to prevent the windows closing inwards, and fix a suitable window fastener.

The structure is now complete except that it should either be creosoted or painted. If paint is chosen, the building should receive a good primary coat of red lead in oil, followed by two coats of good quality lead paint of the desired colour. Creosote is an excellent preservative and is, of course, very much cheaper and easier to apply than paint.

HANDY SHELVES

S HELVES are a necessity in every house, and, fortunately, shelf-making and fitting is one of those comparatively simple jobs that the man who can use a few simple tools will find little difficulty in carrying out successfully.

Prepared deal boards varying from 5 in. to 11 in. in width and $\frac{7}{8}$ in. thick

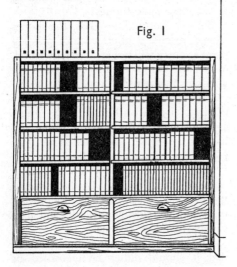

Fig. 1

are commonly used for shelves, whether they are for a humble apartment like the kitchen, for holding cooking utensils, or a more elaborate fitment for books in the study (such as the one illustrated in Fig. 1).

The Kitchen Shelf shown in Fig. 2, 9 in. wide is fixed between the walls of a recess in a kitchen or scullery. The ends of the shelf are supported by bearers $8\frac{1}{2}$ in. in length, 2 in. wide and $\frac{3}{4}$ in. thick, neatly shaped at the front ends and painted, if desired.

It is important that the boards forming any shelf are truly horizontal and square. To ensure accuracy, a guide-line should

always be marked upon the walls before the shelves are fitted. To do this, measure the height from the floor to where the tops of the bearers are to be, and make pencil marks at the points near the ends of the back wall. Draw a line across, cutting the two marked points, and trace the line round the adjacent walls by using a try-square, as indicated in Fig. 3.

If the walls are covered with ordinary plaster and the bricks are soft, the bearers may be fastened direct to the walls by driving in 3-in. nails at a distance of about 2 in. from the ends of the supports. Should the walls be cement-faced, however—as a good many walls are, especially in kitchens and sculleries—it will be necessary to drill and plug the wall to obtain a good fixing for the bearers, which are fixed by means of screws.

Having fixed the bearers, cut the board square and slightly chamfer the long sharp edges with a plane. Place the

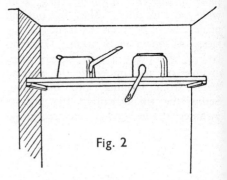

Fig. 2

board in position and test to see whether it is level by using a spirit-level for the purpose. If the shelf is not quite true, adjustments should be made to correct any errors. The shelf can now be fastened down to the bearers by means of either nails or screws—preferably the latter.

If the span of a shelf exceeds 4 ft. in length, it is advisable to fix an additional support at the back; otherwise the shelf is liable to bend when carrying a heavy weight. The extra support can be obtained by fitting a batten at the back, or an iron or wooden bracket could be fixed at the middle, as represented in Fig. 4.

One of the simplest methods of fixing shelves for supporting light weights to a wall is to use iron brackets, which can be obtained for a few pence. The brackets should not be fixed directly

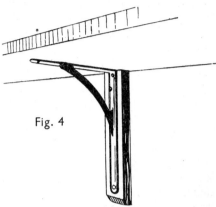

Fig. 4

Such a bracket is illustrated in Fig. 5. When it is desired to fit bookshelves in a recess of a living-room, the books should not be allowed to come in contact with the walls. In such a case it is better to make a self-contained fitment, as that illustrated in Fig. 1. A suitable height for such a fitment would be 6 ft. or so, but this is an arbitrary figure, as much depends upon individual requirements.

The shelves can be supported by means of narrow bearers about ¾ in. wide screwed to the inside faces of the uprights (as illustrated at A in Fig. 6),

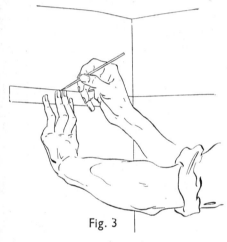

Fig. 3

upon the wall, as a much better job is obtained by first fixing two or more vertical battens to the wall and then mounting the brackets upon the battens.

The Uprights can be made from suitable lengths of 1½ in. by ¾ in. planed batten, cut to length and neatly finished by chamfering the front edges and rounding the corners. A recess should be cut at the back of the boards to allow them to lie flush with the wall.

Where extra strong shelves of over 10 in. in width are required, special wooden brackets should be employed.

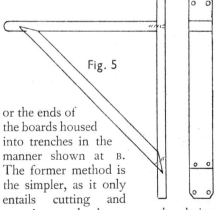

Fig. 5

or the ends of the boards housed into trenches in the manner shown at B. The former method is the simpler, as it only entails cutting and screwing on the bearers at the desired distances apart; but it has the disadvantage that extra head-room must be allowed to enable the tops of the books to clear the bottoms of the bearers supporting the shelf above. The housing method, although not so simple to accomplish, makes a much better job and allows the shelves to be fixed closer together.

An ordinary through-housed joint can be used or, better still, a stopped housed joint, which has the additional advantage that it forms a neater joint on the front edges.

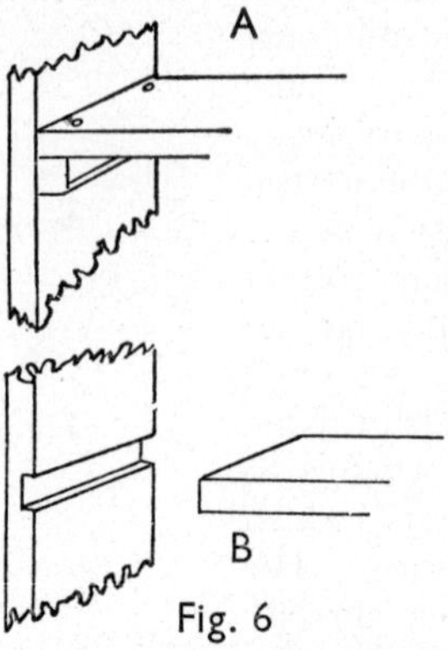

Where a stopped trench is employed, the grooves should stop at about ¾ in. from the front edges of the uprights, but should through-housing be resorted to, all that is necessary is accurately to

and as wide as the thickness of a shelf. If stopped housing be adopted, it will be necessary to cut the front ends of the shelves back for a distance of ¾ in., and when cutting the boards to length, an extra ½ in. must be added to their apparent lengths for insertion into the grooves.

In designing bookshelves of this type it should be noted that the bottom shelf should be raised about 2 in. above the floor, the intervening space being covered with a strip of wood or plinth about ½ in. thick.

A Useful Hanging Bookshelf for holding small books is illustrated in Fig. 7. The centre compartment between the top and middle

Fig. 6

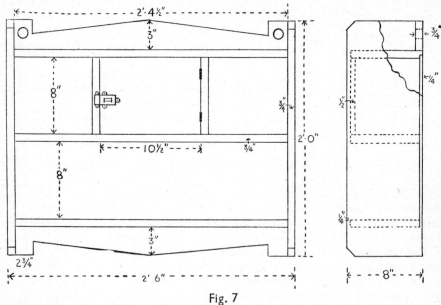

Fig. 7

mark the positions for the recesses, cut across the boards with a tenon-saw, and remove the waste with either a chisel or a trenching-plane. The depth of the trenches in both cases should be ¼ in.

shelves is fitted with a door, and will be found handy for holding oddments. Oak could be used with advantage for its construction, in which case it could be stained and wax polished.

A PLAIN LEDGED DOOR

THE door shown in Fig. 1 is the simplest type of door to construct, and is known as a plain ledged door. Its use is generally confined to work where appearance is of little consequence, as instanced in poultry - houses and structures of a similar kind.

The materials necessary to construct such a door include a few tongued and grooved V-jointed matched boards, three cross-battens and a few 1½-in. wire nails.

For a light door measuring 4 ft. 6 in. high by 2 ft. wide, six matched boards 4½ in. wide by ⅝ in. thick would answer the purpose and if they are kept together by means of three battens each 3 in. wide and ¾ in. thick, the resulting door would be suitable for a small poultry-house.

An Important Point to bear in mind.—In estimating the number of boards required for a given width of door of this description, do not overlook the fact that the effective width of a matched board is ¼ in. less than its listed width and it also loses ⅛ in. in thickness for planing purposes. Thus a board whose listed thickness is ⅝ in. only "holds up" to ½ in.; consequently, in the door under consideration, the width of each board at the joint will be 4 in. and the thickness only ½ in.

From this it will be observed that the total width of the boards when joined will be 2 ft. ½ in. and as it is necessary to remove the tongue of the first board, the resulting width is 2 ft.

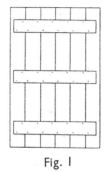

Fig. 1

Preparing the Boards.—The orthodox method of preparing the boards preparatory to fixing is to remove the tongue of the first and the groove of the last, but if the latter is done, its removal will make the width of the door ½ in. less than that required.

As the grooved edge comes on the hinged edge of the door and is therefore not likely to be broken off, its removal on a small door of this description is unnecessary.

The boards should measure an inch longer at each end than their final dimensions to allow for cutting off square after fastening to the battens.

In constructing the door, the first thing to do is to prepare the ledges, as the cross-battens are called. The length of these should be 1 in. less than the total width of the door to allow clearance for the usual ½-in.-thick door-stop which is fixed to the inside faces of the two uprights and top of the door-frame.

If the battens are made from rough sawn wood, clean it up with a plane and neatly chamfer the outside edges. A few minutes spent on small details of this kind, although of seemingly little importance, differentiate between a workmanlike job and a shoddy one.

To Assemble the Door, first plane off the tongue of the outside board and then mark the positions of the ledges on the board, not forgetting the ½-in. overlap

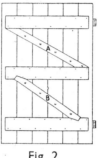

Fig. 2

as previously mentioned. Use the square in marking, and then screw the board to the ledges. Next turn the work over so that the face side is uppermost and place the remaining boards in position. Mark light pencil-lines across the boards to act as guide-lines for the nails.

As it is usual either to paint or creosote the completed door, it is a wise plan to give the joints a coat of the covering medium during erection, as it is obviously impossible to treat these parts afterwards.

Nail the boards to the battens, taking care in so doing to force each one tightly against its neighbour. Now clinch the ends of the nails. Square lines across the face at the top and bottom of the door and saw off the waste.

In cases where a stronger and more robust door is required, use thicker boards and stouter and wider ledges, and fix a couple of braces diagonally between the ledges, as in Fig. 2, A and B. The braces keep the door perfectly rigid and prevent it from sagging at the outer edge.

The method of construction is similar to that adopted in the plain ledged door, the braces being fitted to the ledges after the boards have been fixed. The ends of the braces can either be let in square with the ledges or at an angle. They should be cut accurately to obtain a perfectly tight fit and then fixed in position and secured by nails driven through the face of the door.

Doors of this description are usually hinged by means of T hinges, or cross garnets, as they are termed, screwed to the face of the door in such a position that the fixing-screws can be driven into the ledges.

A CABINET FOR SCREWS

A GREAT number of practical men who ought to know better store their nails and screws jumbled together in odd boxes, with the result that a considerable amount of time is wasted by having to search for a particular-sized screw. This state of affairs can be obviated by making the simple cabinet shown in the accompanying illustration (Fig. 1), and following the detailed drawings appearing in Working Drawing No. 4.

The construction of such a cabinet calls for no exceptional skill, and it can be made cheaply with the aid of a few simple tools in a few hours.

The main feature of the cabinet lies in the method adopted for supporting the drawers. This is attained by allow-ing the side edges of the bottoms of the drawers to project a trifle beyond the sides, the projections so formed sliding into narrow grooves cut on the inner faces of the sides of the cabinet. This method of construction, although not exactly orthodox, will be found very useful for constructing all kinds of cabinets where utility is of greater consequence than appearance.

The Drawers.—Another distinguish-ing feature of the drawers is that the fronts are provided with circular recesses, bridged across by narrow strips of brass, the ends of which are let in flush with the surface. This does away with ordinary projecting knobs or handles, saves space and allows the door to be easily fitted.

The following list gives the finished sizes, etc., of the parts.

Item	No.	Size. ft. in.	in.	in.
Top	1	1 0 ×	8½ ×	⅝
Bottom	1	1 0 ×	8½ ×	⅝
Sides	2	1 0¾ ×	7½ ×	⅝
Back	1	1 0¾ ×	9¾ ×	⅛ plywood
Back supports	2	1 0¾ ×	¼ ×	¼ stripwood
Door	1	1 0¾ ×	9¾ ×	½
Small drawer fronts	4	9¾ ×	2⅜ ×	⅜
,, ,, backs	4	9¾ ×	2⅜ ×	⅜
,, ,, sides	8	6¾ ×	2⅜ ×	⅜
Large drawer front	1	9¾ ×	2⅝ ×	⅜
,, ,, back	1	9¾ ×	2⅝ ×	⅜
,, ,, sides	2	6¾ ×	2⅝ ×	⅜
Brass handle strip	5	2¼ ×	3/16 ×	1/16
Brass butt hinges	2	1 ×	⅝	

The top, base and sides of the fitment can be made of either best quality deal, or better still, whitewood ⅝ in. thick, the back being a panel of plywood. The drawers are made of ⅜-in. stuff except the bottoms, which are cut out of ⅛-in.-thick plywood.

Start by preparing the cabinet sides.

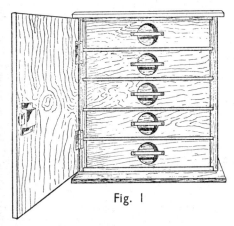

Fig. 1

Carefully mark and saw the ends perfectly square and from the top ends mark the positions for the grooves, as indicated in Fig. 1. (Working Drawing No. 4.) The grooves should be a trifle over ⅛ in. wide and 3/16 in. deep. Cut the grooves by first sawing across on the inside of the marked lines by using a fine-toothed tenon-saw and then remove the waste with a very sharp ⅛-in. chisel. As the grooves must be nicely finished to ensure the smooth running of the drawers, the recesses can be finished with glass-paper by wrapping the paper round a slip of wood and applying it edgewise into the groove.

The pieces forming the top and bottom are identical in size. When these have been carefully prepared by cutting them accurately to the dimensions shown in the drawings, chamfer the front and side edges to an angle of 45° as shown.

Reference to the drawing shows that the back panel is fitted flush with the back edges of the cabinet. This is attained by fastening pieces of ¼-in. by ¼-in. stripwood set ⅛ in. back from the long edges of the inside faces of the uprights.

The door is a plain piece of wood 1 ft. ¾ in. in length, 9¾ in. wide and ½ in. thick. Run the plane lightly over the front edges to remove the "arris," as the sharp edge is called.

The parts should now be thoroughly glass-papered and then assembled. Either nails or screws can be used for this purpose, but screws are preferable as they are stronger.

The best way to construct the four small drawers is first to prepare the material for the fronts, backs and sides, in one or two strips $2\frac{3}{8}$ in. wide, before cutting them to size.

The ends of the front pieces are cut away on their inside faces to house the ends of the sides, as shown clearly in the detailed drawing of a drawer. To make the housing, all that is necessary is first to mark a line across each back face $\frac{3}{8}$ in. from the ends and then scribe another line on each end $\frac{1}{8}$ in. from the front face. Saw across at the marked lines and smooth the recess with glass-paper if necessary.

The bottoms of the drawers are pieces of $\frac{1}{8}$-in.-thick plywood, cut accurately and squarely to size. Now prepare the parts for the large drawer, not forgetting that its depth is $\frac{1}{4}$ in. deeper than the smaller ones.

Next bore the recesses in the fronts for the handles, using a brace and $1\frac{1}{4}$-in. diameter centre-bit. Take care when making these, otherwise you may have the misfortune to cut right through the wood. It is a wise plan to stop boring when $\frac{1}{8}$ in. of the material has been removed and then to scoop out the remaining waste with an externally-ground gouge. Mark and cut out the shallow rectangular recesses on each side of the circular ones to allow the brass strips to lie flush with the surface.

Great care must be exercised in assembling the drawers to ensure that they are perfectly square. Nail the back to the two sides and then fix the front. One-inch oval brads are the best type of nail for this purpose as the heads should be punched down below the surface after assembly. Before attempting to fix the plywood bottom to a small drawer scribe pencil lines

$\frac{1}{8}$ in. from and parallel to the short edges to serve as a guide when nailing the bottom to the frame. The bottom can then be placed in position, using the marked lines as a guide, and fixed by means of $\frac{3}{4}$-in. panel pins driven in on the skew or dovetail fashion. The bottom edges of the large drawer are fixed flush with the edges of the frame.

The Handles are made of $\frac{3}{16}$ in. by $\frac{1}{16}$ in. brass strip. Cut these to the required length and drill a hole near each end to take a $\frac{1}{4}$-in. No. 3 brass countersunk-headed screw. Fit the prepared strips into the recesses in the drawer-fronts and fix them firmly with the screws.

Punch the heads of the brads in the sides of the drawers to a depth of about $\frac{1}{16}$ in. below the surface, as the drawers may have to be eased when fitted.

Remove the sharp square edges of the backs of the drawers by placing the drawers in a normal position and paring the edges with a chisel held vertically.

Now insert the drawers into their respective divisions in the cabinet and ease them if necessary by planing down the high parts. The drawers can be divided into a number of compartments if desired, to take screws and nails of various sizes, and other odds and ends. The divisions are made of plywood and fastened with liquid glue.

The final operation consists in fitting the door on the left-hand side. This is hung in the usual way by sinking the hinges half into the edge of the door and half into the edge of the upright. To keep the door shut a small hook fastened to the side, which engages in an eye screwed into the edge of the door is all that is required.

If a stained finish is desired, it is advisable thoroughly to smooth the surfaces with fine glass-paper before applying the finishing medium.

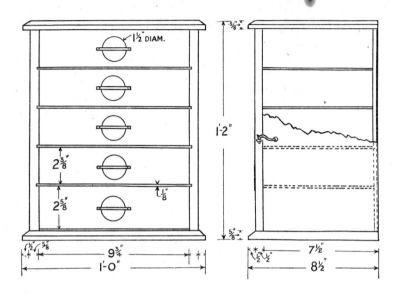

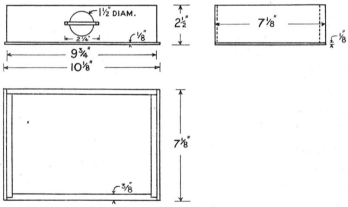

CABINET FOR NAILS & SCREWS

WORKING DRAWING Nº 4

A TOOL RACK

MUCH time is saved and annoyance obviated if the tools required are ready at hand and yet so kept in a safe place that their sharp edges are not injured.

A self-contained tool rack, which can be hung on the wall or screwed to the

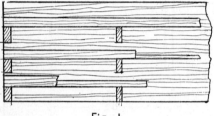

Fig. 1

back of the bench, is shown in the accompanying drawings. The rack may be of a length suitable to the position it may have to occupy or the number of tools to be accommodated.

Fig. 1 gives part of a front view and Fig. 2 an end view, while a perspective illustration is shown in Fig. 3.

The Back Board consists of two 9-in. by $\frac{3}{4}$-in. ordinary prepared deal boards, fixed together at the back by battens $\frac{1}{2}$ in. thick and 2 in. wide screwed to the two front boards.

If the rack is to be fastened to the back of the bench, the battens may be extended down for 9 in. or more to screw to the back board of the bench, in which case the battens should be 1 in. thick.

The Top Rack consists of two lengths of 1-in. by $\frac{1}{2}$-in. strip nailed to triangular brackets made out of $\frac{3}{4}$-in. deal, or hardwood for preference. The brackets are all alike and sawn out of a length of

wood 3 in. wide, as indicated in Fig. 4, which will thus cut up without waste. The angle is 45°. One edge of the bracket is 3 in. long (the width of the timber) and the other is 4 in. The 4 in. edges are screwed to the backboard and the 3 in. ones support the racks and shelves.

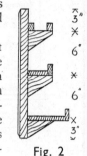

Fig. 2

It will be noticed that by sawing out the brackets, as shown in Fig. 4, the screws which hold them to the backboard do not enter the end grain, the shelves and racks being supported on the end grain.

The top rack, which is suitable for holding such tools as files, chisels, bradawls, etc., should not have the two rails parallel. They should be $1\frac{1}{4}$ in. apart at one end and $\frac{1}{4}$ in. apart at the other. This arrangement enables thick-handled tools to be accommodated at

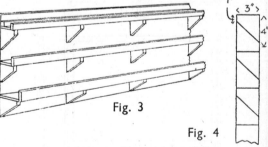

Fig. 3

Fig. 4

one end and ones fitted with thin handles—which would fall through the wider end—at the other end of the rack.

The brackets should be 18 in. apart.

The lower racks are really shelves with ledges. They are intended for holding such tools as do not conveniently fit in the top rack. They may be partitioned, if found desirable. The middle one is a board 3 in. wide by $\frac{1}{2}$ in. thick and the lower one of the same thickness, but 6 in. wide. The latter will hold such tools as planes, mallets, and odds and ends which may be more conveniently stood than hung.

If the two lower shelves are made shorter by about 18 in. from one end, the top rack can accommodate small saws and even a small-sized hand-saw.

Wire nails or oval brads should be used for fastening the shelves to the supports.

A CORNER TABLE

A SUBSTANTIAL corner table is a very handy piece of furniture to have in the kitchen or scullery, since it occupies very little room and has no corner projections. The one described in the following paragraphs is suitable for

Fig. 1

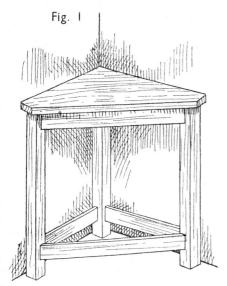

accommodating such things as a mincer or other small domestic machine requiring a good support.

Fig. 1 shows the table in position. The legs come $\frac{3}{4}$ in. away from the walls to allow for the skirting-boards, and the table-top projects $\frac{3}{4}$ in. to enable it to lie snugly against the wall.

The illustration shown in Fig. 2 is a plan view of the table with the top removed to show the general arrangement of the tops of the legs and frame. The legs are made of 2-in. by 2-in. yellow deal, 2 ft. 9 in. long and fixed at a distance of 2 ft. apart at the sides, measured over the width of the legs, as shown.

The top is made out of three pieces

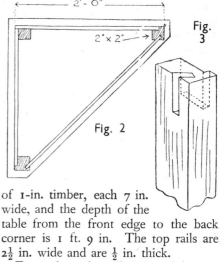

Fig. 2

Fig. 3

of 1-in. timber, each 7 in. wide, and the depth of the table from the front edge to the back corner is 1 ft. 9 in. The top rails are 2$\frac{1}{2}$ in. wide and are $\frac{1}{2}$ in. thick.

Fig. 3 shows how the tops of the two front legs are cut to take the side and front rails. The top of the side of the leg which faces the wall is cut out to a depth of 2$\frac{1}{2}$ in. and $\frac{1}{2}$ in. wide to a distance of $\frac{1}{2}$ in. from the front. On the opposite face, a $\frac{1}{2}$-in.-wide groove is cut at an angle of 45° to the back of the leg and to the same depth as the back cut, to take the front rail.

An alternative method is shown in Fig. 4, where the top front rail is not laid in an open-ended mortice (as in Fig. 3), but is just recessed for its thickness

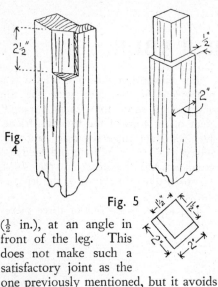

Fig. 4

Fig. 5

($\frac{1}{2}$ in.), at an angle in front of the leg. This does not make such a satisfactory joint as the one previously mentioned, but it avoids the necessity of making the open-ended mortice.

The left-hand leg will be set out, of course, the other way about.

The back (corner) leg supports the rails on a shoulder formed by sawing down adjacent sides to a depth of $2\frac{1}{2}$ in.—the depth of the rail—and is cut back $\frac{1}{2}$ in. from the face. This is shown in Fig. 5. As the leg is 2 in. square, this

leaves an upstanding piece $1\frac{1}{2}$ in. square to which the rails are nailed or screwed.

The bottom rails are housed into the legs at the back, the housing for the front leg being shown in Fig. 6, as viewed from the back. It takes the end of the 2-in. by $\frac{1}{2}$-in. lower rail. The housing or recess should be $\frac{1}{2}$ in. deep and 1 in. long. The rails are housed into the back leg in the same way as that adopted for the top ones.

The housing is made by cutting across the back two adjacent faces of the leg, cutting into each side for $\frac{1}{2}$ in. parallel with the face so that the rail lies snugly in.

The Table-top is cut 1 in. longer each side than the width of the frame. The short sides are 2 ft. 2 in. long. The end is cut square with the wall. The front ends are cut off square with the wall each side, and at 3 in. from the wall, measured square with it.

The top can be screwed down with large screws (3 in. No. 10), driven into the tops of the legs, and thinner ones into the frame. The addition of iron brackets screwed to the legs and underneath the table-top will greatly strengthen the fitment. All joints should be glued and screwed, but if preferred, dowel pins can be used instead of screws.

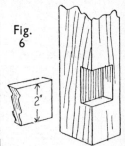

Fig. 6

A MEDICINE CHEST

A CABINET for storing ointment, bandages, and other first-aid materials should be included in the fitments of every home. Such a cabinet, the chief parts of which are constructed of whitewood, is represented in Fig. 1, and the working drawings in Working Drawing No. 5.

The Back is in one piece, 14 in. by $18\frac{1}{2}$ in., and $\frac{1}{2}$ in. thick, with the top and bottom edges shaped as shown. A pair of sides, also prepared out of $\frac{1}{2}$ in. thick material, is cut to the shape shown, each piece being 17 in. long by $6\frac{1}{2}$ in. wide. The two grooves for housing the top and bottom of the cabinet may be cut right across the width on the inside faces of the sides as indicated, or, if the joint is not desired to show, the ends of the grooves at the front should be stopped before reaching the front edge, and the top and bottom boards cut to suit, as indicated in the detail. The two boards for the top and bottom members should be prepared first, as it is easier to make the grooves to suit the thickness of these.

Plywood, $\frac{1}{4}$ in. thick, is used for the horizontal partition between the top compartment and the small drawer, and the sides and back may be grooved for the edges of this. To eliminate the trouble of grooving, a very small fillet could be used under the back edge for supporting the partition, provided the back of the drawer be cut away to clear it, and thus allow the drawer to go back the full distance. Fillets may also be used to support the side edges, behind the two $\frac{3}{4}$-in.-wide pieces at the front, at the sides of the drawer. These reduce the opening of this section, so that the drawer will pull out and clear the doors. Only a simple drawer is required, as

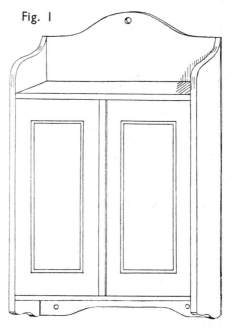

Fig. 1

it is used chiefly for storing bandages, etc. The front is $2\frac{1}{2}$ in. wide by $12\frac{1}{2}$ in. long, and $\frac{3}{8}$ in. thick, with drop-ring handles let in flush. The sides and back may be about $\frac{3}{16}$ in. thick material, glued and pinned, with corner glue-blocks used. A thin plywood bottom is glued and pinned to a light fillet inside the drawer, and fixed to the front and back.

One of the twin doors has a narrow length of beading covering the joint to act as a stop, although the drawer will prevent them from going back inwards. The overall thickness of the doors is $\frac{5}{8}$ in. and may be built up of $\frac{1}{2}$ in. thick by 1 in. or $1\frac{1}{4}$ in. wide wood as a frame, with $\frac{1}{8}$-in.-thick plywood backing, and a narrow moulding round the edge of the panels on the outside.

Mahogany, walnut or oak stain followed by polish are suitable finishes.

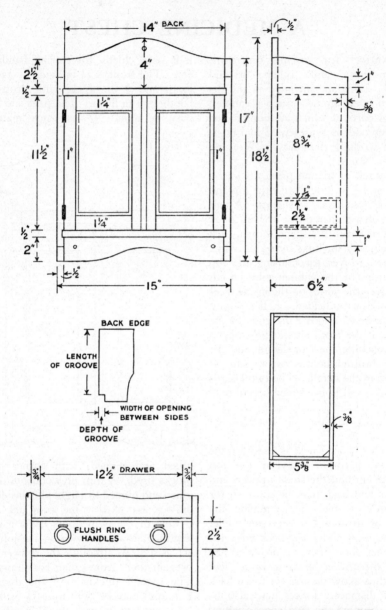

14" BACK

4"

2½"

½"

11½"

1"

1¼"

1"

1¼"

1"

½"

2"

½"

15"

17"

18½"

½"

1"

5/8"

8¾"

¼"

2½"

1"

6½"

BACK EDGE

LENGTH
OF GROOVE

WIDTH OF OPENING
BETWEEN SIDES

DEPTH OF
GROOVE

3/8"

5 3/8"

¾"

12½" DRAWER

¾"

FLUSH RING
HANDLES

2½"

MEDICINE CHEST
WORKING DRAWING № 5

A USEFUL BOOKCASE

THE bookcase illustrated in the accompanying sketch (Fig. 1) can be of oak, walnut, mahogany, or even whitewood. If oak is chosen it can be "limed" in accordance with the latest fashion or it may be wax polished. Walnut and mahogany, of course, need french polishing to bring out the natural beauties of the wood. In cases where whitewood is employed, it may be stained and varnished to imitate more expensive woods.

By referring to the detailed drawings

There is no need to use an expensive wood for the bottom member, as it is hidden, its edges being concealed by a moulding. Ordinary yellow deal can be used for this.

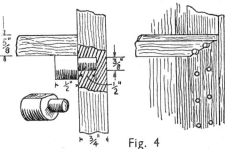

Fig. 4

Fig. 1

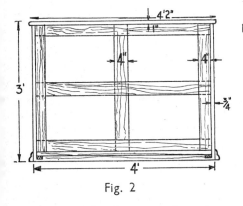

Fig. 2

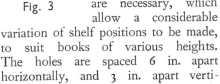

Fig. 3

The first thing to do is to prepare the parts for the carcass. Carefully mark, saw and plane up the top member to an overall size of 4 ft. 2 in. long and 1 ft. 2 in. wide. Plane the back edge perfectly square, and round off the front and end ones. Next prepare the bottom board and the sides. The former is 3 ft. 10½ in. in length by 11 in. wide and the latter 2 ft. 11 in. by 11 in.

Mark out the positions for the holes on the inside faces of the end members as shown in Fig. 3. The holes are for the plug supports which keep the shelves in position, details of which are given in Fig. 4. Eight rows of holes are necessary, which allow a considerable variation of shelf positions to be made, to suit books of various heights. The holes are spaced 6 in. apart horizontally, and 3 in. apart verti-

it will be seen that the principal members are the two sides and the top and bottom boards. The sides are of ¾-in. material and the bottom and top of 1-in.

cally. They should be bored to a depth of $\frac{1}{2}$ in., using a sharp $\frac{3}{8}$-in. diameter centre-bit for the purpose. Great care must be taken when making the holes to prevent the point of the bit penetrating the outer face.

The Back consists of a framing made of 4 in. by $\frac{1}{2}$ in. deal, with a vertical and a horizontal cross-member of the same size, as illustrated in Fig. 2. The parts are halved into each other and firmly held with screws. The frame is then faced inside with a sheet of plywood, which, when fixed into the back of the carcass, rigidly supports the whole of the structure. The size of the frame is 3 ft. $10\frac{1}{2}$ in. long and 2 ft. $8\frac{3}{4}$ in. high.

The parts should now be carefully assembled with the aid of screws.

The top face of the bottom board is fixed to the sides at a distance of $2\frac{1}{4}$ in. above the bottom edges, while the top board projects 1 in. over the front and sides and 2 in. at the back—the latter to fill the space occupied by the skirting board of the room and thus allow the top back edge to butt against the wall.

The Top Board should be screwed down firmly to the sides, the countersunk heads being covered, at a later stage, with a coloured filling to match the finish.

The built-up back should be driven in flush with the back inner edges of the carcass and fixed either by nails driven through at an angle from the back, or by means of long, oval brads driven in through the side members. If the latter method is adopted, the heads of the brads should be punched well below the surface and the holes filled in with stopping.

Fig. 2 shows how the frame, minus the plywood facing, fits in the back of the carcass, while the panel is shown distinctly in Fig. 3.

The carcass is complete when a suitable plinth moulding of any standard section has been sawn to length, mitred at the corners and fixed around the base.

The doors are framed and constructed of suitable material 4 in. wide and $\frac{3}{4}$ in. thick. The joint used is a combination of a mitred and a halved joint, which is not only exceptionally strong, but obviates the making of mortices and tenons.

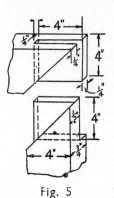

Fig. 5

To make the Frames, proceed in the following manner:

First cut the members a trifle longer than the finished sizes of the doors, which are 1 ft. $11\frac{1}{4}$ in. wide and 2 ft. $8\frac{3}{4}$ in. high. At the ends of the rails or cross members, scribe down two lines parallel to the wide face and $\frac{1}{4}$ in. from the edge, leaving a central space $\frac{1}{4}$ in. wide, i.e. dividing the ends into three thicknesses. Saw down these lines to a depth of 4 in. from the end, and cut the centre piece out with a chisel. Take a bevel-square and scribe the 45° angle on the front and saw through. The end of the rail with the prepared joint is shown in Fig. 5.

The ends of the stiles or side members are marked off in a similar way and sawn down at the back to a depth of 4 in. They are then cut squarely across as indicated in Fig. 5. The front face is marked for the mitre as before and sawn to a depth of $\frac{1}{4}$ in. on this line, and then sawn down from the end to meet it, thus leaving an upstanding flat piece with a halved back to join with the end of the top rail, and a tongue to fit behind the mitre. The mitre in front fits up against the mitre of the top rail.

This gives a very satisfactory joint. Viewed from the front it looks exactly like an ordinary mitred joint, but it has also the great advantage of having plenty of surface for gluing. The joints can be further strengthened if desired by means of brass screws driven in from the back.

Having completed the joints, they should be cramped after gluing until the glue has set perfectly hard, after which the faces should be lightly skimmed with a sharp, finely-set plane. The outer edges of the doors should also be planed to fit nicely when placed side by side in the front of the carcass.

The Glass.—A $\frac{3}{8}$-in.-wide fillet or bead should be cut, mitred, and fixed flush with the back edge inside each frame to hold the glass. A corresponding bead with rounded nose is placed in front of the glass and fixed in position with fine panel pins.

The front of the glass may be left plain or it may be decorated in the manner shown in the illustration (Fig. 1). The design can be built up of hardwood beading. The pieces forming the diamond pattern, struts, and outside beading must be jointed to fit each other, and then glued and pinned.

A simple way to do this is to cut a thin plywood panel exactly to fit the opening in the frame. The outline of the design is then traced on the panel. The parts are then cut to coincide with the design and pinned temporarily in position whilst being fitted. The pieces should be very carefully cut to the set-out angles to ensure a perfectly tight fit. Having prepared the parts, glue and pin them together and, when dry, stain and finish them to the colour and finish with either polish or varnish. The clean glass is then inserted into the frame and the ornamented overlay fixed to the glass with tube glue, the outside beading being fixed by means of very fine panel pins.

The doors should be hung with brass butts.

The left-hand door is prevented from closing inwards by means of hardwood stops, while the right-hand one has a $\frac{1}{2}$-in.-wide beading projecting $\frac{1}{4}$ in. beyond its long opening edge, which acts as a stop against the left-hand door. A couple of sliding bolts should be fitted to the inside face of the left-hand door and a lock and escutcheon fixed in the centre of the opening stile of the other.

The final operation—except finishing—consists in cutting and fitting the desired number of shelves.

A SECTIONAL BOOKCASE

AN expanding or sectional bookcase is a particularly convenient means of storing books. The construction of such a bookcase is a matter of simple carpentry and can be made by any handyman by following the detailed drawings on Working Drawing No. 6, to which all figure numbers appearing in the following paragraphs refer.

Fig. 1 shows a drawing of three complete units, identical in size, supported upon a base, and a top section to give the assembly a neat finish. The depth of each book unit is 1 ft., but this is an arbitrary measurement and sections can be built higher or lower as the case may be, keeping all the other dimensions the same. Since the ends are quite flat, additional units can be laid lengthways against each other so that the bookcase can be expanded sideways as well.

Fig. 2 shows the complete unit without its doors. The doors shown in Fig. 11 are hinged at the sides and close together in the centre. An alternative arrangement is to have one door hinged from the top. This would make no difference to the general construction of the bookcase.

Fig. 3 shows the front of a standard book unit; Fig. 4, a transverse section, and Fig. 5 an end view. The top or covering unit is shown in Figs. 6, 7 and 8, and the base in Figs. 9 and 10, while Figs. 11 and 12 show details of the doors. All drawings are fully dimensioned.

The Sides are of one piece of wood 1 ft. high and 10¾ in. wide. They are joined by the bottom board (or shelf) 2 ft. 6 in. long and 10 in. wide, which should be fixed by means of screws driven through the sides, using four long screws for the purpose. The bottom of the shelf is ½ in. above the bottom edges of the sides and forms the location for the member underneath; whether it be another book unit, top section or base. The back—partly visible in Fig. 3, which is a front view—consists of a frame made of 2-in. planed batten ¾ in. thick, halved at the four corners, and to it is pinned a three-ply panel 10 in. wide and 2 ft. 6 in. long. This panel fits exactly into the back, between the top back rail and the shelf, completely filling the inside of the back member as seen in Fig. 4.

Looking at Fig. 2 at A, it will be seen that the facia board projects ½ in. above the tops of the sides, and around the inside faces at the top is a rebated rail. This arrangement at the back and sides provides the location of the upper unit, whether it be for a top covering section or a book unit. The recess also provides a means of support for a plywood panel to keep out the dust, so that each unit is quite dustproof. The front of the unit is flush except for the moulding B,

which is fitted along the whole length of the front edge of the shelf and extends ½ in. below it, thus registering with the bottom of the end board or side.

The bottoms of the sides, moulding and the back board frame form a recess ½ in. deep into which the top of the unit below exactly fits. The moulding B should be glued and pinned to the edge of the shelf and the sides, using fine panel pins for the purpose. This completes the book unit.

The top covering section illustrated at Figs. 6, 7 and 8 is a frame of ¾-in. stuff, 2 in. deep round the sides and back, the front being a moulding. The moulding extends down a further ½ in. to register on the front of the facia rail A of the book unit. Fig. 8 gives a plan and top view with the covering board removed, and shows the corner stiffeners which should be glued and nailed in.

A plywood panel may be inserted and fixed to the bottoms of the corner pieces and the joint so formed covered with a ¼-in. quarter-round bead, to prevent the somewhat unsightly inside showing when the doors are open. The top board is a plain piece of ½-in. wood with a rounded front edge, the remaining edges being left square. The rounded edge imparts a neat finish when the bookcase is small and comparatively low in height.

The Bottom Unit or base is built up, as shown in the cross section (Fig. 9), to the dimensions given in the plan view (Fig. 10). The front member is a moulding, and the moulding B of the book unit rests on it and makes an attractive finish. The corners are strengthened by means of angle blocks 1 in. thick, which should be glued and screwed from the inside, while a brace 2 in. wide and ¾ in. thick is fixed across the middle to the undersides of the raised lining x (Figs. 9 and 10). The lining—made of ¾-in. stuff—beds down

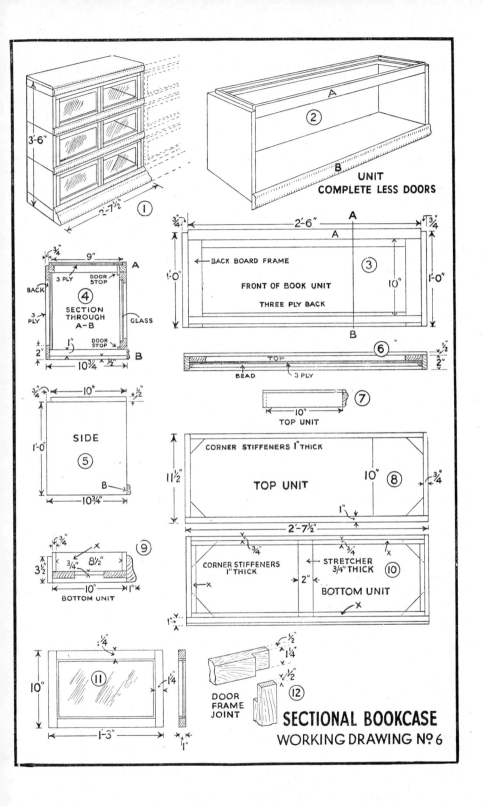

UNIT COMPLETE LESS DOORS

3'-6"

2'-7½"

① ②

3

BACK BOARD FRAME

FRONT OF BOOK UNIT

THREE PLY BACK

2'-6" A ¾"

A

1'-0" 10" 1'-0"

B

④

SECTION THROUGH A-B

¾" 9" A

3 PLY DOOR STOP

BACK

3 PLY GLASS

2" 1" DOOR STOP B

10¾" ½"

6

TOP

BEAD 3 PLY

½" 2"

7

10"

TOP UNIT

5

SIDE

¾" 10" ½"

1'-0"

B

10¾"

8 TOP UNIT

CORNER STIFFENERS 1" THICK

11½" 10" ¾"

1"

2'-7½"

9

¾" x

3½" ¾" 8½"

10" 1"

BOTTOM UNIT

10 BOTTOM UNIT

CORNER STIFFENERS 1" THICK STRETCHER ¾" THICK

¾" ¾" x

2"

x

1" x

11

10" ¼" ¼"

1'-3" 1"

12 DOOR FRAME JOINT

½" 1¼" ½"

SECTIONAL BOOKCASE
WORKING DRAWING Nº 6

on the corner pieces and is nailed through the inside into the frame and stands up $\frac{1}{2}$ in. above it to fit inside the under frame of the unit above.

All the joints can be nailed if desired, but a very much better result is obtained by fixing the members together by means of screws. The member requiring the most care in fixing is the facia rail A, as it has not much contact with the ends. It is therefore advisable to reinforce this piece by means of a couple of small right-angle metal brackets fixed inside with screws.

Each Door consists of a frame $1\frac{1}{4}$ in. wide and 1 in. thick, details of which appear in Fig. 11. The outside edges of the frame should be made $\frac{1}{16}$ in. over the dimensions shown to allow for fitting. The corner joints, details of which appear in Fig. 12, are plain halved ones which should be carefully made and accurately fitted. It is an advantage to glue and fasten the joints together with brass screws driven in from the back, care being taken to sink the heads below the level of the surface. The resulting depressions can be filled in afterwards with plastic wood. A sharp, finely-set plane should be run over the surfaces after the glue has set to ensure a perfectly smooth finish.

Each door is hung on two brass butt hinges. The leaves of the hinges should be sunk into recesses cut into the edge of the door and the inside edge of the side. A stop is necessary at the top and bottom, as shown in Fig. 4. The bottom stop can be of hardwood of $\frac{1}{2}$ in. square section, glued and pinned to the shelf board. The top stop should be of the same material 1 in. wide and 2 ft. 6 in. long, with recesses cut at the ends to receive the ends of the inner frame. This is fixed with screws to the inside face of the facia rail A. A piece of half-round beading should be fixed to one edge of each pair of doors to prevent dust entering the interior.

One door, preferably the left-hand one, should have bolts fixed on the inside face at the top and bottom of the opening stile; while the adjacent stile should be fitted with a lock, or a spring ball socket fitment let into the top and bottom edges of the stiles may be used if locking-up is not considered necessary or desired.

The Glass should be of good quality and fairly thick. It should not fit tightly within the frame and it should bed against a round-edged bead $\frac{5}{16}$ in. wide by $\frac{1}{4}$ in. thick, fixed to the inside edges of the frame, with the nose of the rounding flush with the front surface of the door or a trifle in front of it. The corners of the beading should be close-mitred and glued and pinned to the inside faces of the door framing. A corresponding bead at the back of the glass will make all secure and give a neat finish to both sides.

A Door with Mitred Corners can be substituted if desired. It may consist of rebated material and may be nailed and glued as in making a picture-frame, but owing to the unsupported weight of the door when open, it is better not to rely upon the mitred joint alone but to inlay a brass plate across the joint at the back and secure it tightly with brass screws. As regards material, it is better left to the discretion of the maker. Quite a presentable job can be made by using deal for the general construction and either oak or walnut for the door frames and the front mouldings between the units and the base.

If this method is adopted, a good finish can be obtained by staining the common wood to match the better kind, and finish with shellac varnish or french polish applied with a very soft brush.

In the event of a single door being preferred to double ones, the door may be hinged at the top or bottom. The latter is preferred by some, but there is a greater chance of breaking the glass. Such a door can be made in the same manner as those already described and using any of the joints suggested. It has less diagonal strain than a door hung vertically. A door hung from the facia rail has a distinct advantage over one suspended from the bottom one because in the latter case the moulding below the shelf would catch it and force the hinges if allowed to fall down beyond the horizontal position. In addition, it is awkward to withdraw a book from the case without injury, since the edge of the door rises its own width above the level of the shelf. Furthermore, the books must be lifted to withdraw them— another rather serious disadvantage.

A BUREAU WRITING-DESK

A CONVENIENT knee-hole writing-desk can be constructed from the simple design illustrated in the sketch and the working diagrams shown in Working Drawing No. 7.

It is of a size that will go into the usual recess at the side of a chimney-breast and yet has ample table and leg room—two necessary requirements sometimes overlooked.

The perspective sketch which appears in Fig. 1 shows the appearance of the desk in its open position. The pigeon-hole arrangement shown here can be easily modified to suit the taste of the user, and an alternative scheme is shown in Fig. 2 in the working drawings.

The Best Material to Use for its construction is oak, although a cheaper wood, such as whitewood, stained and brush-polished will make a presentable and durable piece of furniture.

Start by preparing the sides to the dimensions and shapes given in the diagram (Fig. 5). Two pieces of timber ¾ in. thick will be required, unless a board 18 in. wide can be obtained, which will be by far the best arrangement. But failing this, the edges of two boards, 9 in. wide, may be accurately planed and glued together to form a glued butt joint. The joint will then come below the top board of the desk and not in the slant upon which the lid lies when the desk is closed.

The Back can be built up of a cross framing and plywood, as described in the article dealing with the bookcase. The framing will be 3 ft. 4½ in. long and 3 ft. 2 in. deep and should be nailed in from the side boards and from the top board.

The Top of the desk is a board 10 in. wide and ¾ in. thick. Its front edge should be bevelled to the angle of the flap when closed, as the flap beds up against it, as will be described later. The top projects ½ in. beyond the sides and back and should have rounded edges at the ends and back to give it a neat finish. The front edge is shown clearly in Fig. 3.

The overall dimensions of the fixed desk-board are 3 ft. 4½ in. long and 1 ft. 6 in. wide, and it is fitted horizontally between the side-members at a distance of 2 ft. 3 in. from the floor level. It is constructed of two boards in the same manner as that employed for the sides. The board should be screwed in from the sides with long countersunk-headed screws and the tops of the screw-holes filled with a good kind of wood-filler, such as plastic wood. With the top, back and desk-board in position we have a solid framing and can begin to fill in the details.

At 1 ft. 3¾ in. from the inside face of the right-hand end is a division or partition extending from the desk-board to the floor level. It is of ¾-in. stuff, comes flush with the edge of the desk-board and the side-members, and joins the framed backboard at the back. The size of the partition is 2 ft. 2¼ in. high and 1 ft. 5¼ in. wide. It can be fixed by driving four 2½-in. oval brads through the desk-board into the top edge and by brads driven in from the back. The heads of the nails should be sunk below the surface and the holes filled in with plastic wood.

Two shelves, 1 ft. 2 in. deep and 1 ft. 3¾ in. long, are fitted between the partition and the right-hand side-member, while a footboard 2 ft. long and 1 ft. 5¼ in. deep is fixed on the other side. The latter may be fixed in any position convenient to the user. The shelves and footboard are fixed by driving brads through the partition and the side-members.

At the left of what may be termed the central board is a slide-box, its purpose being to house the slide that supports the flap. It is made of ¾-in. stuff and fixed to the underside of the desk-board by means of screws driven in from the top and by nails driven through the partition.

The Outside Member of the box is spaced 1 in. from the side of the central board and is 5¾ in. wide. The base of the box is a strip of wood ¾ in. thick and 1 in. wide.

The slide is 1 in. thick, 5 in. wide and 1 ft. 5 in. long and is shown in the side view in Fig. 3. It should be a nice fit, for it is to support, nearly at its centre, the desk flap which forms the writing-table portion of the desk.

A 3½-in. by ¾-in. rail is nailed between the slide-box and the left-hand side of the desk. It could be replaced by a drawer if desired. The object of the rail is to give the desk-board solidity and improve the appearance when the desk is closed by having a surface below the sloping flap to correspond with the front plane of the cupboard door.

The Footboard is nailed across the knee-hole at a distance of 2 in. from the floor and is supported by a front rail, as shown. This rail is 2 in. wide and ¾ in. thick and has a curved recess cut in the bottom for the sake of appearance. The footboard is constructed by gluing the long edges of two boards together, or the boards may be braced together by means of battens fixed across the undersides.

The footboard is supported on 2-in. by ¾-in. planed battens, screwed to the inside face of the left side-member and the left-hand face of the central board, and is held securely in position with screws driven through near the top edges. This cross-screwing greatly assists in strengthening the desk against distortion when moving it.

The Cupboard Door fits inside the cupboard and consists of two boards glued and butted together and further strengthened with cross-battens screwed on from the back. The cross-pieces should be about 1¾ in. wide and ¾ in. thick and fitted at a distance of about 3 in. from the top and bottom edges of the door. The overall dimensions of the door are 2 ft. 1½ in. high and 1 ft. 3¾ in. wide. It should be fitted with a suitable lock.

The desk-flap should be made of one piece of perfectly flat and well-seasoned timber. Its length is the full width of the desk, i.e. 3 ft. 6 in., and its width 1 ft. 3 in. The edges should be rounded, as shown in Figs. 2 and 3, and it should be hinged to the desk-board by two brass flap-hinges let into the desk-board

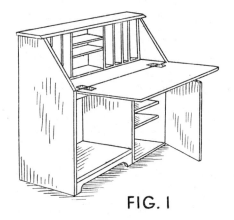

FIG. I

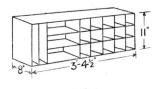

FIG. 4

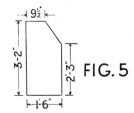

FIG. 5

FIG. 2

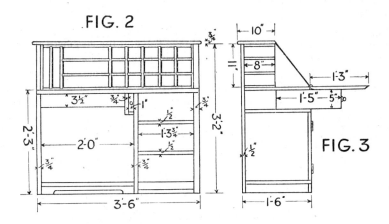

FIG. 3

BUREAU WRITING DESK

WORKING DRAWING № 7

and the flap and positioned approximately as shown in the perspective, Fig. 1.

The hinges should be of good quality cast brass (not stamped), and a suitable size is 1½ in. wide and at least 3 in. long when open. They are known as flap-hinges and should be fixed with brass screws, driven in tightly so that the heads lie flush with the surface.

The interior fittings consist of pigeon-holes and book racks. The form shown in the perspective view allows seven spaces for account books held vertically, two spaces for quarto note-paper, and a space for an inkwell, paste-pot, etc. An alternative arrangement is shown in Figs. 2 and 4, which has two quarto note-paper spaces, two book spaces and the rest square pigeon-holes.

Both fitments are built as a self-contained unit and slide into position at the back of the desk. If made to the dimensions shown in Fig. 4, they will fit accurately and are kept in place by means of screws or vertical fillets pinned to the inside faces of the side-members.

The frame for the unit should be of ¼-in. whitewood, with the vertical divisions made of the same material. The vertical pieces should be housed in grooves formed in the top and bottom boards, while the horizontal pieces can be of thinner material and supported by grooves cut in the vertical ones.

The best way to construct the unit is first to mark carefully and cut the various parts to size. Next mark the positions of the grooves on the top and bottom boards and cut the recesses with the aid of a tenon-saw, removing the waste with a sharp chisel.

In marking the uprights, sufficient allowance must be made at the ends for their entry into the grooves. The vertical pieces are then cut and grooved to take the ends of the horizontal pieces.

Assemble the frame, slide the partitions into the grooves and securely fasten them in position by driving oval brads through the top and bottom boards. Brush some glue into the horizontal grooves and slide the shelves into position as before, not forgetting to wipe off any surplus glue with a damp cloth. After sufficient time has elapsed to allow it to harden, trim the edges with a plane.

To improve the general appearance of the desk a half-round moulding ¼ in. wide could be fixed on the outside of the flap and the cupboard door to represent panels. The ends of the pieces forming the corners of the panels should be neatly mitred, and the parts fastened down with tube glue and ordinary pins, minus the heads. The moulding should be fixed at a distance of about 2 in. from the outer edges of both flap and door.

A DOG-KENNEL

A USEFUL type of dog-kennel which combines an inner and an outer compartment, the former cosy and draught-proof, and the latter having plenty of air by reason of the wired front, is shown in the perspective view in Fig. 1. Both compartments are readily accessible by full-opening doors, hinged at the top and buttoned at the bottom, and an end door is provided for cases where the dog must be kept inside. Good height—not always provided—is another important feature of the design.

The constructional details of the kennel are shown in Working Drawing

No. 8, to which the figure numbers mentioned below refer.

The framing is shown in Figs. 1 and 2, and consists of six posts 1 in. by 1½ in. and 16½ in. long, square at the bottom (where they form short legs to keep the kennel off the ground) and cut to an angle of 60° at the top to coincide with the slope of the roof. They are joined at the top by boards cut to an angle, the boards being 1 ft. 4 in. long, 5 in. high to the apex and ½ in. thick. They are cut into the tops of the posts, as shown in Fig. 1.

Cross bearers, 1 in. wide and 1½ in. deep, are nailed across the bottoms of the posts for supporting the floor, and

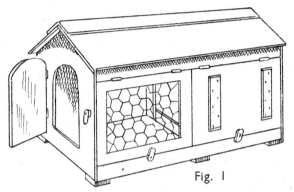

Fig. 1

at the middle division a 2-in. cross-piece is nailed close to the floor against the backs of the posts. A vertical board 2½ in. wide is nailed in front of it to reduce the size of the rear compartment to 10½ in. This board may be wider if desired to make a narrower opening to suit a smaller dog. The 2-in. cross-member at the floor is to keep straw and bedding in the inner compartment.

The floor consists of two boards ¾ in. thick, which are cut in at the sides to clear the posts. The boards should have a matched, tongued and grooved joint, as shown in the end view, Fig. 2, to keep out the draught. They are nailed to the three bottom bearers which join the posts.

The back and the closed end are covered with ⅝-in. (½-in. finished) matched boarding laid horizontally. Two rails, each 2 in. wide, are fixed along the front at the top and bottom. The top one is chamfered to correspond with the angle of the roof, while the bottom one has plain square edges. The two front doors are hung between these two members from hinges screwed to the top rail.

In making up the framing, the three transverse frames, which are identical, should be put in hand first. The timber should be of good quality deal and all parts should be planed for the sake of sanitation. Rough wood harbours dirt and, maybe, insects, and is uncomfortable for the occupant.

The parts are simply nailed together with the roof supports and the floor bearers in place and form the three transverse frames.

At this point the constructor can decide whether to make the kennel longer to allow for more space in the outer compartment. If this is desired, the longitudinal dimensions given in the drawing may be departed from by the addition of as many inches as are required for the extra accommodation.

Having completed the transverse frames the next item to claim attention is to cut recesses in the floor-boards to clear the posts and then nail the boards down to the bearers, after which the roof may be nailed on. Fig. 2 shows how the two upper edges of the roof overlap each other at the top. The width of the roof from eaves to ridge is 11 in. and as it is constructed of ½-in.-thick material one member will be about (not exactly) ½ in. wider than the other, due to the overlap, as shown in the end section at Fig. 2.

The roof-pieces project beyond the ends of the frames by 2 in., but may be more if desired.

The ridge is formed of two pieces of $\frac{1}{4}$-in. or $\frac{3}{8}$-in. strips, 2 in. wide, with the joint opposite to that of the roof. It makes a neat finish and effectively seals any chance gap between the joints in the top of the roof.

The roof-boards are best in one piece but two pieces of $5\frac{1}{2}$-in.-wide tongued and grooved boards may be used instead. To protect the wood and to ensure a watertight roof the boards should be covered with a good quality roofing material, or covered with one piece of thin zinc, neatly nailed on with galvanised nails, and the ridge-pieces could be put on over the material, in which case they would be for finish only.

The Two Side Doors.—Details are shown in Figs. 3 and 4. The long door of the fresh-air compartment is a frame of $1\frac{1}{2}$-in.-wide by $\frac{3}{4}$-in.-thick planed batten. The corners are halved one upon the other and nailed and clinched. The outside measurement is 2 ft. long and 11 in. wide. The drawing shows galvanised-wire netting as the confining medium, but vertical metal rods, or even close-joint electrical conduit of $\frac{3}{8}$ in. diameter, can be used if desired. These should be placed vertically and spaced $1\frac{1}{2}$ in. apart.

If wire netting is employed the back of the door framework should be recessed and the netting fixed in the rebate from the back by means of galvanised staples, which should not be long enough to project through the front. A thin beading may be fixed at the back to protect the dog from any loose ends of wire.

The Door is hung on a couple of iron butt hinges. Select a cast-iron hinge,

not a stamped-iron type, as the cast-iron ones last longer. One leaf of the hinge is sunk in the door frame and the other in the underside of the long top rail. A small wood stop nailed inside at each bottom corner prevents the door closing inwards and keeps it flush with the bottom rail.

The solid door for the sleeping compartment is made of two pieces of tongued and grooved board 6 in. wide by $\frac{3}{4}$ in. thick, sawn and planed to a finished width of 11 in., and two battens, $2\frac{1}{2}$ in. by $\frac{3}{8}$ in., with chamfered ends nailed on, as shown in Fig. 4. It is hung in the same way as the netted door, and both are fastened with hardwood turnbuttons.

The Rear End of the structure is of $\frac{5}{8}$-in. tongued and grooved matched boards, nailed to the roof support and the end framing; and the front is the same size and shape but should be of stouter material. The front can be made in two pieces, as shown in Fig. 5, and the door opening cut to the dimensions and shape indicated in the drawing.

The door for this is 1 ft. wide and made to the dimensions indicated by the dotted outline in Fig. 5. It can be hung on butt hinges—one leaf of each hinge fastened to the front of the kennel and the other cut into the back edge of the door.

A hardwood turnbutton is fastened to the front to keep the door shut.

The whole of the underside of the kennel should be treated with hot tar or creosote, liberally applied and well brushed into the joints. The exterior should have a good coat of lead priming paint, followed by two coats of any colour to choice, such as dark grey or green. It is not necessary to paint the inside but if desired it can be painted any suitable colour. The kennel may be kept cool in the summer by painting the outside of the roof a pure white.

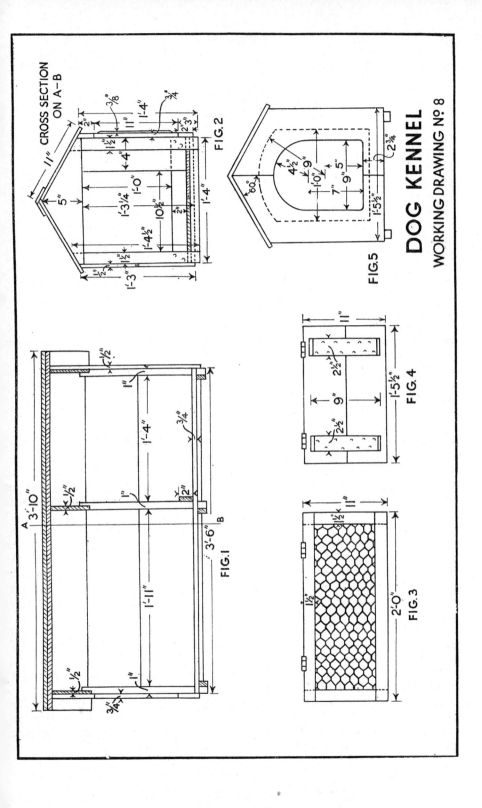

CROSS SECTION ON A–B

FIG.2

FIG.5

FIG.1

FIG.4

FIG.3

DOG KENNEL

WORKING DRAWING Nº 8

A CYCLE SHED

A SERVICEABLE type of cycle shed with double doors at the end is shown in the accompanying illustration (Fig. 1), the details of which are given in Working Drawing No. 9.

The size of the structure is approximately 8 ft. long by 6 ft. wide, which allows sufficient space for the easy accommodation of four or five cycles.

For its construction the following materials will be required: A trifle over half a square of tongued and grooved floorboards, 7 in. wide, for the floor. If the shed is to be clad with tongued and grooved matching, which is much to be preferred to ordinary weatherboards, 2¾ squares of this material will be necessary for covering the sides, end and roof, while the quantity stated will include sufficient boards for the doors. For the framework, etc., four 8 ft. lengths of 3 in. by 2 in. scantling will serve as bearers for the floor. The floorboards are fixed to four joists, each 6 ft. in length, of 2-in.-square section stuff. Two 5 ft. 6 in. lengths of 3 in. by 2 in. will also be required for the door-posts.

For the front and back sections, four 7 ft. 8 in. lengths of 2 in. by 2 in. scantling will suffice for the top and bottom horizontal members or plates, and eight vertical studs or uprights, each 5 ft. 8 in. long, will also be necessary. Several pieces of 2 in. by 2 in., 2 ft. 4 in. long, will be needed for the intermediate horizontal pieces and the top of the window aperture.

The End Frame section is composed of two 6 ft. lengths of 2 in. by 2 in. stuff which form the plates, and four studs each 5 ft. 6 in. in length, while three pieces a trifle over 1 ft. 9¼ in. will be required for the horizontal pieces, as in the front and back sections. The two sloping members or roof-supports are 3 ft. 9 in. long, fixed to a vertical centre-piece 18 in. long, to give the necessary slope to the roof.

The Frame for the Door-end merely consists of a top and a bottom plate, each 6 ft. long, of 2 in. by 2 in. stuff, and two pieces of 3 in. by 2 in. scantling for supporting the doors—as previously mentioned. The top plate is surmounted by an 18 in. length of 2 in. by 2 in. scantling and two sloping roof-pieces of the same lengths as those at the other end. Four purlins, or longitudinal members, each 8 ft. 8 in. long, of 2 in. square material, will be required for the roof.

A supply of nails will also be required —about 2 lb. of 2-in. floor-brads, 2 lb. of 4-in. wire nails for fastening the framework together and 3 lb. of 1½-in. cut nails for fixing the matching. Eight 4-in. No. 10 wood-screws will be needed for securing the sections down to the floor, while a pair of 2 in. by ⅞ in. butt hinges and two pairs of 10-in. cross garnets are necessary for hanging the window and doors, respectively. A couple of 4-in. shooting bolts and a lock and key or a good quality padlock and staples will give the necessary security.

A roll of waterproof roofing material will be sufficient to keep the roof absolutely watertight, and ½ lb. of ½ in. galvanised clout nails will be ample for fixing it.

A piece of 21-oz. glass, cut to suit the sash, and ½ gallon of creosote complete the list, except for odd pieces of timber, small screws, etc.

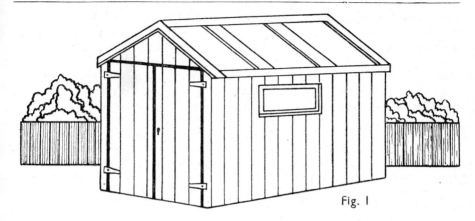

Fig. I

As it is undesirable to allow timber to come in direct contact with the ground, a few bricks should be laid flat at each corner and also at equidistant spaces under the floor-joist bearers. It is important that the bricks be laid perfectly level and that the wide faces of the bricks lie uppermost. If the bricks are not true with each other, pack some earth under the offending member or members, or remove some of the soil as the case may be.

Waterproofing.—When the foundation is completed, the first thing to do is to cut off the floor-joist bearers to length and give them a good coat of creosote mixed with tar. This mixture is an excellent wood-preservative and its use will greatly increase the life of the timber by preventing rot.

Cut as many pieces of roofing material as there are foundation bricks, place them on the tops of the latter and then put the bearers in position, narrow faces up, of course. The covering pieces will prevent any wet absorbed by the bricks rising to the wood. Mark the positions of the joists on the outside bearers and fix the joists down to them by using the 4-in. wire nails driven in from the tops. Creosote the joists before fixing. Details of the bearers and joists are shown in the drawing.

Cut the floorboards to length and creosote the undersides and joints. To lay the floor, rip off the tongue of the first board to be laid and smooth the edge with a plane. Place the prepared edge of the board flush with the ends of the joists and nail it down. Now take the second board and push the tongue into the groove of the first. If you find that it does not fit easily, on no account hammer the bare edge of the board, but get an odd piece of flooring about 8 in. long and cut off the grooved portion. Insert the tongue of this piece into the groove of the board to be laid and hammer on the small piece. Hammering directly on the edges of tongued and grooved boards ruins them and very often leaves them in such a deplorable condition that it is almost impossible to fit them together.

When you have fixed about half a dozen boards, test the back edge of the last board for parallelism by measuring the distance at each end that this edge is from the front edge of the first board. If the measurements are equal it may be taken that the boards are parallel. If such is not the case, a little "give and take" at the joints in subsequent boards will rectify the matter.

When you come to fit the last board you may find it too wide to come flush with the edges of the joists, in which case you will have to rip the board to the correct width.

Follow with the framework, starting with the front and back sections. Note that the length of these is 7 ft. 8 in., and not 8 ft., as the odd 2 in. at each end is made up to 8 ft. by the thickness of the end posts of the end sections. Carefully mark the positions of the studs on the top and bottom plates and then cut and fix the studs. These are 5 ft. 8 ins. long and simply fastened to the plates by means of 4-in. nails driven through the top and bottom plates. The "nogging," or short horizontal pieces which fit between the studs, are not fixed in line, but "staggered" as shown. This method allows the fixing nails to be driven in horizontally and not skew-nailed, as would be necessary if the pieces were in line.

Do not make the mistake of making both side-sections exactly alike. One section has two horizontal pieces to form the window-frame.

The End Posts of the End Sections are 2 in. shorter than those of the front and back sections, to enable the top faces of the sloping roof-supports to register with the front edges of the front and back corner-posts.

Having completed the frames, test them for squareness and, if found correct, they can be clad with the matching. In doing this it is a good plan to start with the front and back members, and for convenience it will be found better to fix the boards to the framework with the frame resting flat on the floor instead of fixing the frames in their vertical positions and then nailing the boards on.

The boards should be cut to a length of 6 ft. 3 in., that is, 3 in. longer than the height of the frame, the top edges of the matching being kept flush with the tops of the upper plates. This allows the

bottoms of the boards to overlap the lower edge of the lower plates by 3 in., and thus prevents rain water from percolating between the bottom plate and the floor. The 3-in. bottom overlap should also be provided for when cutting the boards for the end section, as well as a 2-in. overlap at the top to allow the purlins of the horizontal roof-members to rest on the sloping supports. The same amount of top projection must also be provided at the door-end for the same purpose.

The Roof is of the simplest character, and is not shown in the drawing. It is made in two sections, each of which is composed of matchboards nailed across two 8 ft. 6 in. lengths of 2 in. by 2 in. scantling.

In making the roof sections, the boards should be cut to project 6 in. beyond the sides and 4 in. at the ends. The edges of the boards at the roof ridge should project 4 in. beyond the long outside edges of the top purlins, while the other ends of the boards should project 12 in. from the lower ones.

Having completed the roof, give it a coat of creosote solution. When dry, fasten down the roofing material with galvanised clout nails and further secure it with four 1½ in. by ½ in. planed and chamfered battens, one at each end and two equally spaced between them. The top or ridge ends of the battens should be fixed 4 in. from the top long edges of the roof boards to allow sufficient space for the ridge cover, and they should be fixed with screws.

The next procedure consists in assembling the sections. Get a helper to hold a side section while you screw the end section to it. Take care to see that the inner faces of the projecting matchboards at the bottom butt up close to the edges of the floor. Now fix the other side section and then the front and fasten the bottom plates down to the

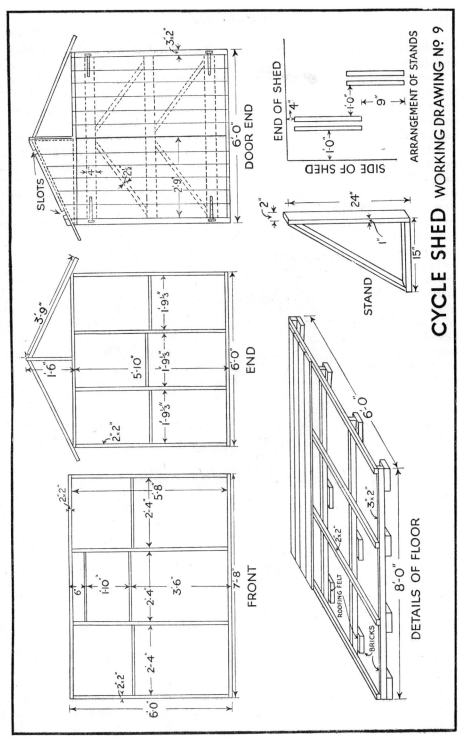

CYCLE SHED WORKING DRAWING № 9

DOOR END

SLOTS

3"×2"

4"

2½"

2'·9"

6'·0"

END

3'·9"

1'·6"

2"×2"

5'·10"

1'·9⅓"

1'·9⅓"

1'·9⅓"

6'·0"

FRONT

2"×2"

6"

1'·0"

2'·4"

3'·6"

2'·4"

5'·8"

2'·4"

2"×2"

6'·0"

7'·8"

ARRANGEMENT OF STANDS

END OF SHED

4"

1'·0"

9"

SIDE OF SHED

1'·0"

STAND

2"

1"

24"

15"

DETAILS OF FLOOR

ROOFING FELT

2"×2"

3"×2"

BRICKS

6'·0"

8'·0"

6

floor by means of 4-in. No. 8 counter-sunk-headed wood screws.

Place the roof sections in position and cover the small gap where the boards join at the apex with a 7-in.-wide strip of roofing material so that the long edges reach to the tops of the roof battens.

Then make the ridge capping with two 8 ft. 6 in. lengths of ½-in. planed batten. The width of the battens should be 4 in. and 4½ in. respectively. They are nailed together to form an inverted **V**, after one long edge has been planed to suit the angle of the roof. Give the capping a coat of creosote and screw it down to the roof, using 1-in. No. 8 screws for the purpose.

The doors are of the ordinary ledged and braced type, and to ensure a good strong job they should be fitted with three

Fig. 2

ledges about 4 in. wide, of 1-in.-wide material, while the braces should be at least 2½ in. wide. In fitting the braces, avoid the error of sloping them all one way—the braces of each door should slope upwards from the hinged edge to prevent the doors sagging. The ledges and braces are shown in the door end view.

The cross garnet hinges are fixed by screws driven into the door-posts and through the matching into the top and bottom ledges, keeping the centre pins in line with the joints formed between the edges of the door-posts and doors.

The Window has a sill projecting about 2 in. beyond the outside face of the matching. It is also necessary to line the sides and top of the window aperture with suitable lengths of 2½ in. by ½ in. planed batten. For a fixed window, all that is then necessary is to nail some 1-in.-by-½-in. strip round the frame to form a support or rebate for the glass. The lining and the rebate should receive a coat of priming paint before the glass is placed in position and fixed with putty. If an opening sash is desired, the stiles and rails should be constructed of 1½-in.-by-1¼-in. stuff, using either morticed and tenoned joints or halved joints at the corners. False rebates can be made with narrow strips of wood bradded to the inside faces of the frame in the same manner as that mentioned for supporting the glass in the fixed window.

When the door bolts and other fittings have been fixed, the whole of the exterior should be treated with a liberal supply of creosote, or, if preferred, two or three coats of good quality lead-paint.

The final operation is to construct and fix suitable stands in the interior for the accommodation of the cycles. These should be fitted at the end. Such stands can be easily and quickly constructed with ordinary 2 in. by 1 in. batten, cut and fixed together to form triangular frames as shown in detail in the drawing. Two frames will be required per cycle, because the front wheel is inserted between them as shown in Fig. 2. The frame parts should be screwed together. Each pair of frames is then fixed down to the floor by means of screws driven through the bases. The two members forming a frame should be spaced 2 in. apart, while the first pair of frames should be fixed at a distance of about 4 in. from the end wall and 1 ft. from a side wall. The next pair should be fixed 1 ft. away and 9 in. in advance of the first fixture, to economise space, as shown in the Working Drawing.

The little extra time and material involved in making the stands will be well compensated for by their convenience, and also by preventing damage to the enamelled surfaces of the cycles.

A SPAN ROOF GREENHOUSE

THE greenhouse shown in detail in the Working Drawings Nos. 10 and 11, presented separately with this book, is constructed of timber frames standing on a foundation of two courses of brickwork laid in "stretching bond." Damp earth inside and out is well below the level of any woodwork. To avoid having a step inside the doorway, the surface of the site is 3 in. below the top of the upper course of bricks. The floor may be of earth, with a centre pathway of bricks, flat stones, or concrete.

The Foundation.—The soft top soil over an area a little larger than the greenhouse should be cleared away to a depth of about a foot or more, the bottom well rammed, and the excavation filled with stones and broken bricks, each shallow layer being well rammed or rolled down firm and level. Fill up all the odd spaces until the whole site is well covered and firm. If this part of the work is put in hand early, while the timber-work is being made, it will give it time to settle, and a little more material may be added and rolled in from time to time, especially after rain.

Lines for laying the brickwork may be set out and indicated by means of thick string stretched between pegs set firm just beyond where the corners come, so that the strings at right-angles indicate the exact corners and the outer faces of the walls. The floor space *inside* the walls is 7 ft. wide by 10 ft. long, and the walls are one brick (4½ in.) thick. At the corners the courses interlock, and are laid in cement as described elsewhere. Wood plugs or blocks are inserted at intervals along the top course. To these the lower sill is nailed. Attention can now be given to the timber-work.

Much of the framework may be completed in sections to give two ends, one with a door-opening and the other with a central post 2 in. by 2 in. set back ⅞ in. on the sill with a barefaced tenon end as for the other intermediate posts.

The Door End consists of two corner-posts 3 in. by 3 in. stub-tenoned at the foot into the lower sill, and braced across the top by the 2½-in. by 1¼-in. head, let into the outer face of the post as detailed. This end of the post is cut to the slope of the roof, which is 30°.

Timber 3 in. by 2 in. is used for the lower sill, or plate, and laid with the 3 in. face on the top of the brickwork and 1¼ in. back from the front outside face of the wall on all four sides. The corners are halved and the mortice-holes cut for the stub tenons after the lower sill frame has been fitted together. The complete sill, ready to place in position, measures 7 ft. 6½ in. wide by 10 ft. 6½ in. long overall.

Door posts of 3 in. by 2 in. timber are fixed 2 ft. apart and central as shown, with a 2-in. face outside. The foot ends are cut as detailed, the outer 2-in. wide face of the lower sill being cut 2 in. wide by $\frac{7}{8}$ in. deep to allow the door post to go back flush with the sill. The top ends of the door posts are fitted behind the head as shown, the face of each post being cut back $1\frac{1}{4}$ in. by $2\frac{1}{2}$ in. to suit.

The Upper Sill, prepared from 4-in. by $2\frac{1}{2}$-in. material, is housed into the side of the corner and door posts, as detailed. The outer face is left solid to mask the joint. On the inner faces of both door and corner posts mortices are cut for the ends of each length of 1-in. square rail fitted under the upper sill to provide a background $\frac{7}{8}$ in. back to nail the vertical boarding to. A similar piece of 1-in. rail is nailed along on top of the lower sill for the same purpose, but is only fitted between the posts and not morticed in.

Battens 1 in. by $\frac{1}{2}$ in. are nailed to both inner faces of the door posts for stops.

Two lengths of sash-bar are required to make the window on each side of the doorway. The bottom end of each piece is cut as detailed, to make a tenon $\frac{1}{4}$ in. thick by $1\frac{1}{8}$ in. long to be let into the sill to a depth of $\frac{1}{2}$ in. At the top ends the front web which makes the $\frac{3}{8}$-in. division between the pieces of glass is cut away a full $\frac{5}{8}$ in. for a distance of about 2 in. from the end, thus leaving a flat face $1\frac{1}{8}$ in. wide to butt against the back face of the head-board. A fillet of $\frac{3}{8}$ in. thick by 1 in. wide strip is nailed to the under edge of the head, along the sill between the sash-bars, and down the edges of the door and corner posts, so that their surfaces behind the glass are all flush, making a rebate for the glass. The glazed space between door and corner posts is divided into three sections by two sash-bars. This gives a glass size of 9 in. wide. As near as possible lengths of 18 in. are used;

the middle piece overlaps the bottom piece, and the top one overlaps the middle pane, as indicated, so that the rain will not run inside. 21-oz. glass is used for all panes, and is secured by means of sprigs or brads driven partially into the wood, leaving part of the head bearing against the glass, and afterwards filling the angle or corner with putty. In the vertical sections above the bottom panes, sprigs driven into the wood will prevent them slipping down, or pieces of sheet zinc may be cut and bent to form hooks and nailed to the wood, for the same purpose. Where putty is to be used, the woodwork must be painted with red lead paint, otherwise the putty will not hold.

The door is 2 ft. wide by 6 ft. 6 in. high and may be obtained ready made, or home constructed, as desired. Builders often have odd used doors from which a selection can be made.

Each Side Frame consists of a 3-in. by 2-in. post at each end, with three intermediate posts of 2 in. by 2 in. in section, one placed central and the others on each side at 2 ft. $3\frac{1}{2}$ in., as shown. The foot ends are cut to form barefaced tenons, in mortices cut $\frac{7}{8}$ in. back from the edge of the lower sill to leave room for the vertical boarding. The top ends are cut on a 30° slope at the front and the $2\frac{1}{2}$-in. by $1\frac{1}{4}$-in. timber may be carried across in the same manner as the head-board used on the outside of the ends, and fitted in the same way. A rebated rail prepared out of $1\frac{1}{2}$-in. by $2\frac{1}{2}$-in. timber and cut to 30°, as shown at E in the detail of this part, is tenoned at each end into the posts.

The sash-bars are tenoned into the upper sill as before, and the top ends are cut with a tenon at right-angles, $\frac{7}{8}$ in. by $\frac{7}{8}$ in. in the under face of the rebated rail E, as in the detail.

The two end posts are fitted to the sill in the same manner as the door posts

IN THIS EXAMPLE THE BRICKWORK IS 3 ft. HIGH

in the end frame, by cutting the notch in the outer face of the sill and letting the post go back flush.

The cutting of the upper sill will have to be a little different at the intermediate posts, as shown in the detail. At the ends the housing is on the same lines as before, but as the post is 2 in. deep, the solid part of the sill on the front face will be 2 in. thick, and will overlap round the front face of the post by 1 in. as before. The intermediate posts will have the housing groove cut on the front face so that the sill is cut at the back.

Matched and V-jointed boarding, $\frac{7}{8}$ in. thick, is fitted all round the walls between the two sills. The front face is flush with the end posts, which are the only ones that show; the others are covered by the boarding.

The Eaves Board, marked D, is $\frac{7}{8}$ in. by 6 in. wide and extends the whole length of the house, and is fixed to the sloping tops of the posts. The ridge board A is fixed in the notched tops of the centre posts and a $3\frac{3}{4}$ in. by $1\frac{1}{2}$ in.

thick board is nailed to the ridge and carried over the eaves board, that end being reduced to $\frac{5}{8}$ in. thick for this, so that the $\frac{7}{8}$ in. board is underneath. Boarding, 3 in. wide by $1\frac{1}{4}$ in. thick, fixed on edge completes the gable end. This board also has its lower edge cut away to pass over the ridge board, although the latter could be made that $1\frac{1}{4}$ in. shorter at the end so that the gable board covered the edges of the timber behind it.

Two Ventilator Frames cover a framed opening in the roof, one as shown at two glass pane widths from the end, and the other at the same distance from the other end but on the opposite slope. The framing consists of 2 in. by $1\frac{1}{2}$ in. timber with the two horizontal members B and C fitted between, with mortice-and-tenon ends, or a stepped housing joint. If the ventilator is fixed farther along the roof, between the position of the intermediate posts, it would be three panes of glass wide, with a framed opening to suit. Hinges and a casement-stay fitting will be required for each.

A POULTRY-HOUSE AND RUN

THE poultry-house and run shown in the sketch at Fig. 1 is designed to give ample room for the accommodation of twelve birds.

It will be seen from the illustration that the roosting-house is raised two feet above the ground level. This feature serves three useful purposes. Primarily, it provides additional space to the run; secondly, it does not harbour rats and other objectionable vermin as so many houses do that are built only a few inches off the ground; and lastly, the floor of the house above provides a shade from the sun during the summer months.

It is a well-known fact that good

lighting has a beneficial influence upon fowls, and this has been provided for by the large aperture in the front, which is covered when not in use by a vertical sliding shutter.

Nest-boxes.—Another feature is the disposition of the nest-boxes in a detachable unit arranged to fit across the front of the structure. The position has not been chosen for the convenience of the egg-gatherer alone, but because it happens to be in the darkest part of the house, which, as is well known, is the best position for such boxes.

A door is provided at the side, but this position is optional. If there is not sufficient space to gain entrance from the side, the nest-boxes could be transferred to the side, and the door to the front; in which case it would be necessary to alter the general arrangement of the framework by shifting the window to either the right- or left-hand side of the front.

The small trap-door between the house and the run is operated from the outside by means of a cord passing through a couple of screw-eyes fixed in convenient

further protection in bad weather. The height should be a foot or so less than that of the roosting-house, and the slope of the roof made to correspond.

The framework of this part is constructed of 2 in. by 2 in. section deal, and is covered with planed and rebated weather-boards at the back end and part of the front, while the top is covered with $\frac{5}{8}$-in., V-jointed tongued and grooved matching.

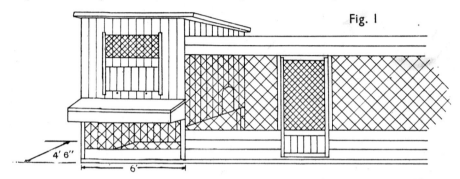

Fig. I

places in the side of the structure. This simple device saves the bother of entering the run every time the trap-door has to be opened or closed. It is kept in the open position by placing the looped end of the cord over a rail.

Two removable perches are provided, fixed at a height of 1 ft. above the floor-level. The width of these should be about 3 in. and the tops should be rounded.

The Total Length of the house and covered run is 18 ft.; 6 ft. being the length of the house and 12 ft. that of the run.

This measurement is necessarily an arbitrary figure because the length of the run can either be reduced by a couple of feet or added to, according to the amount of space available. It should be borne in mind, however, that it is better to increase the size than decrease it.

The covered run calls for no particular comment, except that it may be an advantage to add a hood in front, for

The Roosting-house is made in sections, each of which is framed with 2 in. by 2 in. section deal. Tongued and grooved V-jointed matched boards, $6\frac{1}{2}$ in. wide and $\frac{5}{8}$ in. thick are used for covering purposes.

Tongued and grooved floorboards 1 in. thick, placed across the narrow width of the structure, are used for the floor, and are purposely left loose for cleaning purposes.

The whole of the structure is supported on two 18 ft. lengths of 3 in. by 2 in. deal. This method of support will be found much more effective than the usual way of placing the uprights on bricks, which soon sink into the ground and thus throw the structure out of truth. The legs of the house are held in position by means of small metal angle-brackets screwed to the legs and foundation plates, an arrangement which allows them to be easily removed without damage, should the necessity arise.

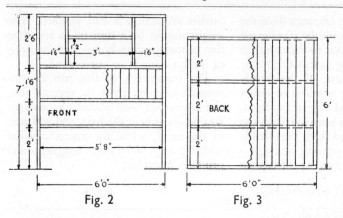

Fig. 2   Fig. 3

Mark each member as it is cut and keep the parts for each section in a separate pile to avoid confusion.

Next, assemble the parts. This is quite a straightforward job, as the members are simply butted together and fixed with 4-in. wire nails. To avoid splitting the wood, bore holes in the outside members to be joined by using a drill of slightly less diameter than that of the nails.

The following is a list of the necessary materials for constructing the roosting-house and run:

Framing—250 ft. run 2 in. by 2 in. deal.

Foundation plates — two 18-ft. lengths, 3 in. by 2 in. deal.

Matchboard—2½ squares V-jointed, tongued and grooved boards— 6½ in. wide and ½ in. thick.

Weather-board—1¼ squares planed and rebated, 6½ in. wide by ⅝ in. thick.

Batten—50 ft. run 3 in. by 1 in. and 32 ft. run 2 in. by 1½ in., both prepared deal.

Flooring—Twelve 4 ft. 6 in.-lengths, 6 in. by 1 in., tongued and grooved.

Miscellaneous—Eighteen 3-ft. plasterers' laths, a supply of 1¼-in. cut and 4-in. wire nails. 1-in. mesh, galvanised, wire netting—British make, not the cheap, foreign kind if durability is desired—and ½ in. galvanised staples for fixing it. Roofing felt and ½-in. clout nails (galvanised), for fastening it down. Half a gallon of creosote. Four 8-in. cross garnet hinges and four ⅜ in. by 5 in. round-headed bolts and nuts, etc.

Start by sawing up the scantlings for the framework for the house to the dimensions shown in the drawings (Figs.

Having completed each sectional frame, fix the matchboards to the front section. Start at the right-hand end and fix the first board, allowing ½ in. overlapping after having removed the tongue. The overlap covers the ends of the boards on the side section and

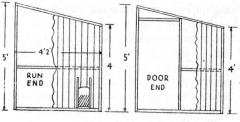

Fig. 4

consequently makes a neat flush finish when erected. A similar overlap is, of course, necessary at the other end.

When cutting the boards for the front section do not overlook the fact that the bottoms are fixed to the third horizontal rail and not the floor rail, as the space between these two members will be occupied by the nest-box.

When fitting the boards, it is a good plan to cover the whole area and then cut out the window aperture with the aid of a padsaw. If this is carefully done the waste can be utilised later. Fix a piece of 1-in. mesh wire netting over the aperture by fastening to the inside framing.

As creosote is much to be preferred to paint as a preservative medium for poultry-houses, owing to its excellent disinfecting qualities, each joint should receive a coat as the boarding proceeds.

Matchboard the back section in the same manner, not forgetting the ½-in. overlap at each end. The boards of this section extend from the top of the frame to the bottom.

The boarding of the sides calls for little comment except that care should be taken to see that they are covered on opposite sides and that the door-post must be perfectly square with the rest of the frame.

When all the sections are complete, give them a good coat of creosote on both sides and, whilst this is drying, proceed with making the roof.

The Roof fits on the top of the struc-

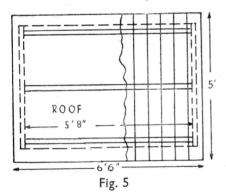

Fig. 5

ture like the lid of a box, as will be seen clearly by referring to the illustration (Fig. 5), the dotted lines representing the tops of the walls of the house.

It will be observed that each end board is only partly supported by the longitudinal rafters, but these boards are further supported by the top cross members of the sides when assembled.

6*

After the roof boards have been fixed, remove the sharp edges all round with a plane, to prevent them cutting the roofing material.

Give the roof a good coat of creosote on both sides.

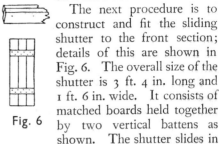

Fig. 6

The next procedure is to construct and fit the sliding shutter to the front section; details of this are shown in Fig. 6. The overall size of the shutter is 3 ft. 4 in. long and 1 ft. 6 in. wide. It consists of matched boards held together by two vertical battens as shown. The shutter slides in rebates or grooves formed by nailing pieces of 2-in.-wide batten over pieces of 1 in. wide, which are then fastened to the front by means of screws.

The Door is of simple construction, consisting of matched boards fastened to three ledges or battens. The length of the ledges should be ½ in. shorter than the total width of the door, to allow it to close against the door-stop. The latter consists of narrow strips of wood, ⅜ in. thick, nailed to the inside faces of the door frame.

When the holes for the fixing bolts have been accurately marked and bored, the structure is ready for assembly. Before this can be put in hand, however, the site should be prepared. If the ground is soft where the foundation plates are to rest, it should be well rammed down and more soil added if necessary to bring it up to the correct level.

Give the plates a thorough coat of creosote and, when dry, place them in position, wide face down, and test to see that they are perfectly level by means of a spirit-level.

The long outer edges should be 4 ft. 8 in. apart. They can be kept at this distance for the time being by nailing two or three pieces of batten across.

It will now be a wise expedient to obtain the services of a helper to assist with assembling and bolting the sections together and fitting the roof. When the four sections have been bolted together, test for squareness and verticality by means of a square and a plumb-bob. If correct, fit the roof, which is secured by driving 4-in. screws through the sides of the structure into the ends of the rafters.

Fit a small iron bracket to the inside face of each front leg and screw this down to the front foundation plate; the back is secured to its plate by driving in two 4-in. screws through the bottom of the frame into the plate.

The Roofing Felt.—Two 7-ft. lengths of standard width (3 ft.) material will be required, which allows 3 in. all round for turning under the edges and 3 in. overlap at the horizontal joint in the centre of the roof. Start fixing at the front edge and work towards the back, using ½-in. galvanised clout nails, spaced about 3 in. apart, for fastening purposes.

Fold the overlapping portion neatly over and under the edges of the roof and fix it securely by nailing home laths on the underside. Finish off the roof by nailing down the three battens—one in the centre and one at each end.

The Floorboards.—Cut and fit, but do not nail them down, and fix the door to its post and the door-stopping round the inside face of the frame. Make sure that the door closes properly against the stop and that the outside of the door is quite flush with the rest of the surface.

Now make the nest-box according to the details shown in Fig. 7, and fasten it to the structure by driving screws through the projecting ends into the two inside faces of the front uprights. The lid should be covered with roofing felt, and sufficient material should be left at the back to enable it to be fastened to

the front of the house and thus form a watertight joint. The cross garnet hinges can now be fixed in convenient positions.

Mark the position and cut the small aperture for the trap-door at the side with the aid of a padsaw, and then construct the door and the rebated side-pieces for keeping it in position. The side-pieces may be made in the same way as that suggested for the front shutter.

The Run.—Mark and cut the front and back uprights and mark the exact positions for these on the foundation plates. The back uprights are spaced equally apart, while the front ones can be either arranged to allow the door to adjoin the roosting-house or in any other

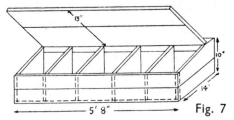

Fig. 7

position to suit the convenience and taste of the constructor.

Fix the uprights to the foundation plates by means of the iron brackets in the same manner as that mentioned for the front legs of the roosting-house. The front and back uprights adjoining the roosting-house should be fixed to it with screws.

Carefully mark the positions for the tops of the uprights on the long, horizontal top pieces and then fix these members to the uprights with 4-in. wire nails. Before driving the nails home make perfectly sure that each upright is absolutely vertical and square, as nothing offends the eye more than seeing an object which should be upright leaning over at an angle.

Having satisfied yourself on this point, the next thing to do is to fix the cross pieces. These are placed squarely across the horizontals and fastened with nails, the ends being cut off flush with the front after fixing.

Proceed by fitting the rebated weather-boards to the back and side, starting at an inch above the bottom of the foundation plate and working upwards towards the roof. Test the long edges of the boards with a spirit-level from time to time during erection in order to check any deviation from the horizontal, and do not forget to creosote the joint as each board is fixed.

Saw the matched boards for the roof to length, namely, 12 ft. 4 in., and when securely fastened down give the whole structure a good coat of creosote. When dry, cut and fasten down the roofing material in the same manner as previously described.

The Door is the next item to make. There are several ways of doing this. The best method is to use morticed and tenoned joints, but if this does not appeal, halved joints may be used at the top and bottom, and the middle rail fixed either with nails or screws, the latter being preferable. Another method would be to butt and screw the members together and reinforce the joints by using metal angle-plates. Such plates are to be obtained quite cheaply at most hardware stores.

Having completed the frame of the door, the lower portion should be filled in with matched boards, held in place by first nailing "fillets" or narrow strips of wood about $\frac{3}{4}$-in. thick around the inside faces of the frame to form a rebate, and then driving nails through the boards into the fillets. The fillets should be fixed $\frac{1}{2}$ in. back from the front edge of the frame to enable the boards to lie flush with the face.

Cross garnet hinges should be used for hanging the door which, of course, opens outwards, and a thin strip of wood fitted to the inside face of the door post will prevent the door from being forced inwards and thus straining the hinges.

The Wire Netting may now be fixed to the inside faces of the framework, etc., and the door, using galvanised staples for the purpose.

Fix wire netting to the bottom part of the roosting-house, fastening a short length of chain to the top of the front sliding shutter and a hook for its reception to keep the shutter closed; screw in one or two screw-eyes for guiding the cord operating the trap-door, and fit either turn-buttons or padlocks to the doors and nest-box cover.

HOUSEHOLD STEPS AND LADDERS

ONE of the most useful household articles is a pair of steps or, as they are called in the north, step-ladders.

The most durable and convenient form for amateur construction is that shown in the illustrations in Fig. 1, where A is a side view, B a front view, C an elevation of the back member, and D and E are details of the treads and sides.

The ladder when open stands 5 ft. 4 in. high, so that the ceiling of any room in a small house can be easily reached from it.

The timber for its construction should be of the best quality yellow deal obtainable, entirely free from knots, shakes, and other imperfections. The side pieces and treads are $\frac{7}{8}$ in. thick when planed or thicknessed and should be bought sized to finish. The back or strut member is $\frac{3}{4}$-in. thick.

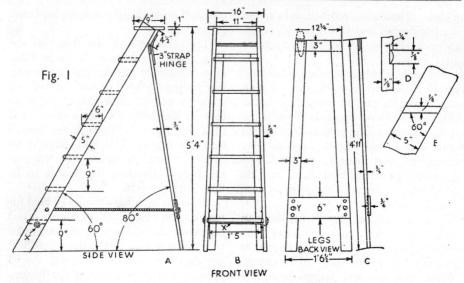

Fig. 1

SIDE VIEW   A   B   C

FRONT VIEW

Prepare the sides first. They are 5 in. wide by 6 ft. 3 in. long and provided with grooves to take the treads. (*See* E.) It is advisable to allow an extra 3 in. in the length to well inside the scribed lines, because the material for the treads may only be a bare $\frac{7}{8}$ in. thick, and it is important that the ends of the treads should be a tight driving fit in the grooves.

Trim off the ends of the side-members to the same angle as the grooves, as previously marked, that is, 9 in. from the top of bottom groove and 9 in. from the bottom of the top groove.

It will be understood, of course, that the two sides are right- and left-handed respectively.

As the distance between the side-members is greater at the bottom than at the top, each tread must be made longer than its neighbour from the top downwards.

The Treads.—There are six (excluding the top board) and as the width between the sides ranges from 11 in. to 17 in. there will be a difference of 5 in. between the top and bottom treads, so that each of the five intermediate treads will be 1 in. less in length than

its neighbour above. This gives the following widths between the sides—at the first tread (from the top) 12 in., at the second 13 in., then 14, 15, 16, and finally 17 in. at the bottom one. As the treads are sunk to a depth of $\frac{1}{4}$ in. in each side-member, $\frac{1}{2}$ in. must be added to each length, so that the overall sizes will be 12$\frac{1}{2}$ in., 13$\frac{1}{2}$ in., 14$\frac{1}{2}$ in., 15$\frac{1}{2}$ in., 16$\frac{1}{2}$ in., and 17$\frac{1}{2}$ in. respectively The treads are 6 in. wide and $\frac{7}{8}$ in. thick.

The Top Board is 16 in. long and 9 in. wide by 1 in. thick. It is recessed underneath with grooves $\frac{7}{8}$ in. wide, stopped 1 in. from the front, to take the tops of the side-members. The front edges of the treads may be rounded or squared to choice, and all bevelled off at the back to 60° to lie flush with the back edges of the side-members.

The parts are assembled by laying one side face-upwards on the bench, inserting the top tread into its groove and then fitting the bottom one in a similar manner. The other side-piece is then placed on top and fitted. The next step is to square up these parts and fasten them together with three 1$\frac{1}{4}$-in. clasp nails, driven through the sides into each end of the treads. Now place the frame on its back, drive the remaining treads into their respective grooves, keeping the back faces flush with the sides, and nail them in. Neatly bevel the projecting front corners, as shown in detail at D.

Now nail the top board on and then fix the back plate of $\frac{3}{4}$-in. stuff below the top board. This cross-piece is $4\frac{1}{2}$ in. wide, square at the bottom edge and bevelled to 60° to fit close under the top board. It should be screwed securely into the sides and also held by means of screws driven through the top board, as it holds the legs.

The Legs are shown at C, which is a back view. All is of $\frac{7}{8}$-in. prepared stuff, i.e. $\frac{3}{4}$ in. finished thickness. The top rail is halved into the tops of the legs, while the bottom one is 6 in. wide and is recessed at the ends. The shoulder fits against the inside faces of the legs and rests on the back of the legs, to which it is screwed.

Two strap hinges, 3 in. wide, of either wrought or stamped iron (not cast), should be screwed, with $\frac{3}{4}$-in. stout screws, into the back board of the steps and the top rail of the legs. They should be of the taper type, 4 in. long at the top and 6 in. at the bottom, as shown at C. If any difficulty be experienced in obtaining a hinge with leaves of different lengths, a 6-in. one could be cut down to the desired length.

The holes for cords can now be drilled in the sides and legs, and a piece of good quality sash cord fitted to each side and double knotted at each end. The length of the cords should be 4 ft. 2 in. between the knots, to allow the legs to be extended to their correct distance apart. When fitting the cords care should be taken to see that the bottoms of the step sides and legs lie level and square upon the floor.

In order to strengthen the steps and prevent any tendency of the sides to splay out from the treads, it is a good plan to fit a tension-rod underneath the bottom tread, as shown at X in A and B. This rod can be easily made of a piece of $\frac{1}{4}$-in. round iron with a screw-thread at each end. Clearing holes should be bored in the side-members, the rod slipped through them and firmly secured with nuts bearing on iron washers.

Obviously, the same method of construction can be followed for either longer or shorter step-ladders, but in cases of longer ones, it is advisable to make the legs of 1-in. thick material to avoid sag and twist due to the extra length and leverage. It is also a wise precaution to fit an extra tension-rod between the sides and under a tread at a distance of about two-thirds the length measured from the bottom.

A Loft Ladder.—Many a loft between the top-floor ceiling and the roof is unused because of the difficulty of getting to it. A loft ladder, which can be let down and pulled up again out of the way, will solve this difficulty. Such a ladder is easily arranged and constructed.

The drawings shown in Fig. 2 are not to scale, but will enable the reader to get an idea of the arrangement. The lengths and the position of the pulley will have to be made to suit particular situations.

The ladder is in two parts, A and B, of an equal length, the sides of which are made of good, sound timber $\frac{7}{8}$ in. thick and 3 in. wide. The rungs are let into the sides, as shown at 2, the rung being wider at the back than the front and bevelled upwards from the back at the bottom so that the rung has a tendency to lie back to the ladder when weight is put upon it. This is a valuable safety device.

Both ladders are of the same width and one lies upon the other. Their sides are parallel and the rungs of the lower ladder are a trifle below flush with the

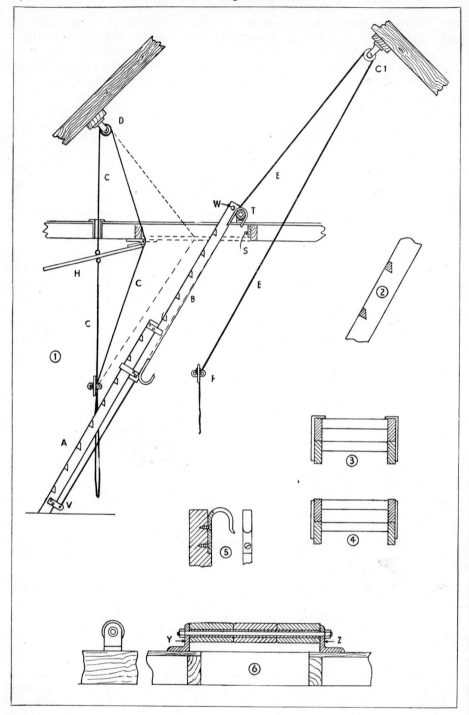

sides to enable the upper ladder to slide easily upon it.

To connect the ladders together so that they can slide one upon the other and yet remain firm when extended, ladder B has iron angle-straps, $\frac{1}{4}$ in. thick and $1\frac{1}{2}$ in. wide, screwed to its sides at the bottom and extending over the top ladder A, as shown in the section at 3. Ladder A has similar straps screwed to its sides at the top (shown in section at 4). It is not necessary that this strap should extend under B, since the tendency is to keep it down on B, and if returned it would cause an obstruction against the roller. These straps locate the ladders relative to each other and guide them as they are telescoped one on the other, when drawn up into the loft. Four curved steel hooks $\frac{7}{8}$ in. wide, of $\frac{3}{16}$-in. strip, are fixed to the ends of the ladder B. The hook has an inside diameter of 3 in.; details appear at 5. They are let into the narrow faces of the side-members and secured by means of three stout screws 1 in. long, with their heads well countersunk into the countersunk holes drilled in the shank of the hook.

Across the side of the trap-door opening a roller is fitted, as shown at 6. It is supported between two pieces of angle-iron, forming brackets Y and Z. These can be sawn with a hack-saw from any piece of angle-iron with a side 2 in. wide, and fixed to the loft floor or to boards fixed across the joists where there is no floor. The length of the roller must be 2 in. wider than the trap-door opening and it is made of three pieces of 2-in. iron barrel. The two end rollers should be 6 in. long, while the central piece will be of such length as, with the two end rollers, will make the overall length 2 in. longer than the width of the trap-door opening.

The three rollers are placed on a length of gas barrel, which fits easily in them, and the barrel is supported by an iron spindle whose ends fit into the holes in the brackets Y and Z, as indicated. They need not be an engineer's fit, but should be filled with grease. The reason for having three rollers instead of one is to allow the central roller to act as a frictionless guide for the operating cords.

The trap-door H should be taken off the top of the trap and trimmed to size to fit in the underside of the opening. It is hinged as shown to hang down, and is pulled up by a cord passing over a screw-on pulley D fixed to a convenient roof rafter. This cord is threaded through a hole in the side of the trap opening and can be fastened to a cleat fixed to the passage wall below the loft. A stop-piece S is nailed across the opening against which the door can be pulled up.

The ladder extended (with two rungs overlapping) should be of sufficient length to reach just above the roller down to the ground when at an angle of 60°.

In the loft, at a distance from the roller T, equal to the length of the closed ladder, a grooved pulley C, is fixed to a cross rafter or beam, or a cross board fastened across two rafters as shown.

A thin wire cable E, or a good quality plaited cord, runs up from an anchorage (which may be a cross bar) V at the bottom of ladder A and underneath its rungs and the rungs of ladder B, as indicated by the dotted line. It then passes over the central roller at T and up to pulley C, round it and back through a convenient hole in the ceiling and down to a cleat on the wall.

The action is as follows: The ladder being down rests with its top hooks on the roller and its foot on the floor. On pulling the end of the cable, the bottom of the ladder A is pulled up and slides along B until the top strap on A reaches a stop pin w projecting on each side of the ladder B, close to the top. Continuing, ladder B with A on top of it is pulled up until the hooks at the bottom of B engage with the underside of the roller. The cable is then secured tightly round the cleat on the wall at F. The trap-door is then pulled up by the cord C and all is neatly stowed away.

To Lower the Ladder release cord C from its cleat and let the trap-door H (shown closed by the dotted line) fall. Then pull the right hand bight of the cord till the slack is taken up round pulley D and the trap-door is pulled up into the position shown, so as not to obstruct passage up the ladder. Secure both sides of the bight round the cleat. Dotted lines show the position of the cord when the trap-door is closed. Next, release cord E from cleat F and let the ladder run down the rollers to the ground.

In cases where the roof is not high enough to obtain the necessary angle to start the ladder down by its own weight when released, a thick cord will have to be fastened to the bottom of the ladder and pass through a hole in the trap and be of sufficient length to be looped down and caught when the trap is lowered.

RADIO CABINETS

THE making of cabinets for radio receivers and loud-speakers offers exceptional possibilities for the ingenuity of the amateur craftsman who is interested in cabinet-making.

Fig. I

A very simple and inexpensive type of cabinet suitable for housing a three-valve set having an external loud-speaker is represented in Fig. 1. The cabinet is sufficiently large to accommodate the high-tension and low-tension batteries.

The base, sides, back and lid consist of plywood $\frac{3}{8}$ in. thick, while the front is of similar material $\frac{3}{16}$ in. in thickness. The latter is supported at the top by means of a horizontal piece of stripwood of $\frac{7}{8}$ in. by $\frac{1}{2}$ in. section. The sides of the lid are made from stripwood, $\frac{5}{8}$ in. wide by $\frac{3}{16}$ in. thick.

To construct the cabinet, mark and cut out all the parts to the dimensions shown in Fig. 1, in Working Drawing No. 12, presented with this book, and assemble the pieces, using brass counter-sunk-headed screws for the purpose. It is advisable to fix the sides and front of the lid with glue and fine panel pins, after which the top edges can be slightly rounded with the aid of glass-paper.

Before fixing the front of the carcass—which should be fastened with screws driven into the top rail, sides and base—the holes should be located and bored to receive the spindles of the various controlling knobs of the receiver.

A pleasing finish, contrasting well with the black dials, as shown in the illustration, is obtained by using white gloss enamel in lieu of the more orthodox french polish. Before applying the enamel, all screw-holes should be filled with plastic wood and the whole of the exterior of the cabinet thoroughly smoothed with fine glass-paper. Two undercoats of white, thin, flat paint should first be applied.

The Loud-speaker Cabinet repre-

Fig. 2

sented by Fig. 2 is of a suitable design to match the receiver fitment just described, and is of sufficiently large dimensions to accommodate a modern 8-in. diameter moving-coil speaker unit.

The carcass is finished in white enamel, with the exception of the overlay of the fret, which could be enamelled in black. This feature not only relieves the plain effect of a single colour, but greatly enhances the appearance of the cabinet.

Like the receiver cabinet, the carcass is built of $\frac{3}{8}$-in. plywood, dimensions of which are shown clearly in Fig. 2 in the Working Drawing.

The actual construction is quite a simple and straightforward job, and therefore calls for little explanation. The use of triangular-section strips, glued at the corners, adds considerably to the strength. The fretted front shown in the elevation should be accurately cut out with an ordinary fretsaw, and then

$\frac{1}{2}$-in. by $\frac{1}{8}$-in. overlay strips pinned and glued over the outline. Before fitting the front to the carcass, a piece of loud-speaker fabric, obtainable at most radio stores, is glued to the back of the fret. A $\frac{3}{8}$-in.-thick baffle-board, having a hole cut in it to suit the speaker unit, is then screwed to $\frac{1}{2}$-in. by $\frac{1}{2}$-in. fixing-blocks fastened to the sides of the cabinet as shown.

A Radiogram Cabinet.—Fig. 3 shows an illustration of an amateur-built radiogram cabinet which is a particularly handsome piece of furniture.

The cabinet is divided into three compartments; the top one for accommodating the gramophone turntable and pick-up; the middle one for housing the receiver; and the lower compartment for taking the loud-speaker, batteries, etc.

The fitment consists mainly of oak-faced plywood, supported in a framework formed by the legs and rails.

The legs are of oak and are 3 ft. 3 in.

Fig. 3

long by 1½ in. square section, a section sufficiently robust to allow of the making of strong mortice-and-tenon joints or, if preferred, dowel joints. The rails are of the same section, except the top back member, which is 5 in. by 1 in. Oak-faced plywood ½ in. thick is used for the lid, the unsightly laminated edges of which are hidden from view by means of ½ in. half-round section edge-moulding.

The door at the back is merely a framework upon which loud-speaker fabric is stretched and glued. A solid wooden door should not be employed, as it greatly reduces the tonal quality of the loud-speaker by imparting a muffled effect.

To make the Cabinet, start by sawing, planing and marking out the legs and rails to the dimensions given in Fig. 3 in the Working Drawing. It is best to make the top ends of the legs an inch or so longer than the finished sizes, as the extra material will enable the mortices to be cut without risk of splitting the wood. The surplus can be sawn away after the parts have been fitted.

Having completed the mortices in the legs and the tenons on the rails, the next procedure is to plough the ½-in. deep grooves to accommodate the side panels, and to cut the 5-in. wide and ½-in. deep recesses in the back faces of the rear legs, to take the top back rail, which is half housed into them.

Assuming that the parts are ready for assembly, start by gluing the side panels into their respective channels in the legs and rails and at the same time glue and fit the joints. Then cramp up the sides, test for squareness, and if correct, put the two members aside for the time being to allow sufficient time for the glue to harden. Next glue and fit the front and back rails to the sides, reinforcing the top back-rail joints by means of 1½-in. No. 10 countersunk-headed screws, taking care to keep everything square.

When sufficient time has elapsed to ensure that the glue is dry, fix a ½-in.-square section fillet round the two side faces and top of the front opening to form a fixing for the front panel. Fasten the fillets with No. 6 screws, 1 in. long.

The next items to receive attention are the shelves and door. The lower and middle shelves can be made of ⅜-in. birch plywood, which is considerably cheaper than oak-faced stuff, but the top shelf should be of the latter material. The bottom shelf or floor is supported by and screwed down to the projecting edges of the rails. The corners of the shelf will have to be recessed to allow the corners of the legs to clear. The front edge of this shelf should lie flush with the front of the side fillets, as the edge forms the bottom fixing for the front panel. Cross-pieces of ¾-in.-square section planed deal, screwed to legs, are used for supporting the other shelves. The distances between the shelves are, of course, determined by the depth of the gramophone equipment and the receiver. Quite a satisfactory door can be made by using 2 in. by 1 in. planed deal batten, dowelled and glued at the joints.

The Front Panel is ¼ in. thick. Holes should be bored to accommodate the spindles of the controlling knobs, switches, etc., and a number of holes drilled near the edges to take the fixing screws, which should be ¾ in. long, of the brass, round-headed type. A fret having a stripwood overlay is made in the lower portion of the panel. Dimensions for the fret can be taken from Fig. 2 (Working Drawing).

The remaining operations consist in hingeing the lid and door and glass-papering the whole of the external surfaces prior to staining and wax-polishing. A good effect is obtained by finishing the carcass a Jacobean oak colour and the front panel a light shade of oak.

USEFUL CUPBOARDS

CUPBOARDS are very necessary in every house and can be easily built by using the corners and recesses of the walls.

Recesses at the sides of chimney-breasts in bedrooms and kitchens are easily made into handy cupboards without having to build a very complicated framework—the walls providing a substantial fixing.

Such cupboards, being nailed or otherwise fixed to the building, become what are known as "landlord's fixtures," and may not, therefore, be taken away if the tenant leaves. If the householder is the owner of the premises he will, of course, be able to do as he likes. But even with the chance that the landlord may eventually claim the cupboards, they are well worth fixing, as they are easily constructed with inexpensive materials.

A Cupboard in a Recess.—Fig. 1 in Working Drawing No. 13 shows a useful type beside a chimney-breast. It is 6 ft. 6 in. high and 3 ft. 6 in. wide; the width, of course, depends on the width of the existing recess and the timbers must be cut to suit. In Fig. 2 a view is shown of the battens which support the shelves, the top member A holding the ½-in.-thick boards which form the top or cover. The battens are 5 in. wide and prepared from ¾-in. stuff, and the top member and shelves are of ½-in. deal nailed on to the battens.

As the chimney-breast is always constructed of brickwork, the wall should be plugged and screws used for securing the battens, but the wall opposite the side of the chimney-breast may consist of a lath-and-plaster partition, in which case the battens can be fixed by means of screws driven into the wooden "studs" or upright members of the wall, which are usually spaced from 14 in. to 18 in. apart.

In order to find the positions of the studs—which, of course, are invisible—take a light hammer and gently tap along the partition. The space between the uprights will sound hollow and the hammer-head tend to spring from the surface, while the sound produced when tapping on a stud is dull and it presents a solid resistance to the hammer. The position can then be verified by inserting a fine bradawl. Care should be taken not to damage the plaster by hammering too hard.

The door is surrounded by a framing of 4 in. by ¾ in. deal and can conveniently be 6 ft. 6 in. high. There is no bottom cross-member to the frame, the door extending down to the floor, which allows the bottom of the cupboard to be easily cleaned.

The top rail is halved into the side-members as shown at B in Fig. 3, and, to make a neat finish, flat strips, as indicated at C, 2½ in. wide, with bevelled edges and mitred joints at the top corners, surround the frame and are fastened to it by means of short oval wire brads. The overlay partly hides the longitudinal joints of the halved uprights and sides and is shown in section at C. The outside edges of the frame uprights are cut at the bottoms to fit the skirting board, as shown at D in Fig. 3, and the skirting boards round the recess are used to support a shelf of ⅝ in. stuff, below which shoes can be conveniently stored.

The frame beds up against the ends of the side battens shown in Fig. 2 and, in order to hold it firmly, one or other of the two fixings illustrated in Fig. 4 can be used. At D in Fig. 4 is shown a staple fixing. The staple (F in Fig. 4) has a tapered shank to drive between the bricks or into the wood. The circular-shaped end fits against the back of the frame and has a screw hole through which a screw is driven to secure the frame. Staples of this type can be obtained at most ironmongers, and are quite inexpensive.

The other fixing, shown in sectional plan at E in Fig. 4, is particularly suitable for a lath-and-plaster wall. A vertical post (G) is fixed to a stud by means of screws driven through the plaster, and the door-frame nailed up against it. A strip, H (Figs. 3 and 4), 3 in. wide and $\frac{1}{4}$ in. thick, is nailed around the back of the frame so that it projects $\frac{1}{2}$ in. beyond the edges to act as a door-stop.

The door-frame should be made up of ready-planed deal. The halved top corner joints should be well fitted, glued and screwed together from the back, using stout screws $\frac{5}{8}$ in. long. The frame should exactly fit the recess in width and should be temporarily held square and parallel by means of a batten nailed across the uprights at the bottom and strips lightly fastened diagonally across the uprights and the top rail to prevent the joints from springing out of position.

To fit the frame, it should be held temporarily in the recess by inserting thin slips of wood or wedges and set to vertical lines previously marked on both walls with a pencil and the aid of a plumb-line. The staples or the fillets (Fig. 4)—whichever method of fixing is adopted—are then fixed to the walls and the frame screwed to them from the back in the case of the staple fixing, and nailed through the front where the fillet fixing is employed.

The door shown in Fig. 5 is of the plain ledged type. It can be made of 6 in. by $\frac{3}{4}$ in. plain matched boards, i.e.

without any ornamental bead at the joint, fixed together by means of three 4-in. by $\frac{3}{4}$-in. battens. The boards should be temporarily held in position with thin strips of wood and fine wire nails and then cramped up tightly together. While cramped, the cross-pieces should be screwed securely from the back by using three stout screws at each joint. The width of the door will be the width of the framing plus $\frac{1}{8}$ in. for planing to fit—afterwards.

The front of the door should be carefully smoothed with a sharp plane and then glass-papered. The addition of a standard moulding, half-round in section and about $\frac{3}{8}$ in. wide, fixed to the face of the door to imitate panelling, will greatly improve its appearance. The beading strips should be neatly mitred at the corners, glued at the back and further secured by means of fine brads. The design is shown in Fig. 1, but any design of false panelling can be used to the choice of the maker.

The door is hung on two 2 in. cast butt hinges, recessed half in the frame and half in the edge of the door and arranged to open either hand, whichever is most convenient, although it is the usual practice for such doors to open against the wall.

Shelving can be fitted to suit individual requirements, but since the cupboard is 6 ft. 6 in. high there is ample room for a shelf 15 in. from the top. Such a shelf is handy for storing suitcases, hats, etc.

Below this shelf, side battens or rails of $\frac{3}{4}$ in. stuff, 5 in. wide, may be added. There should be two of them each side and one across the back. The upper set should butt up against the shelf batten and have a back batten for pegs. The under one should be 5 in. below the upper one. They hold the swivelling brackets which support the upper and lower members of the swing-arms used

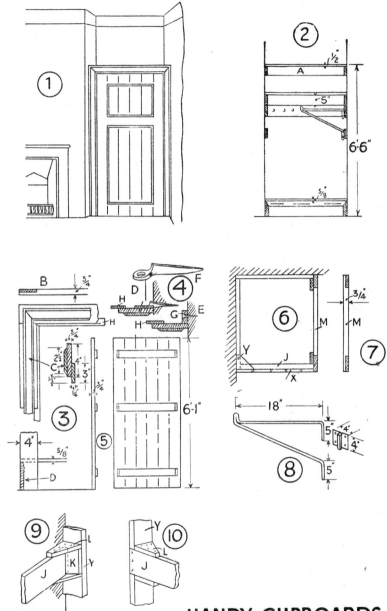

HANDY CUPBOARDS
WORKING DRAWING Nº 13

for suspending folded clothes (shown at Fig. 2).

The Brackets are made of $\frac{3}{16}$-in. iron rod, bent to the shape and dimensions shown, while the sockets for supporting the brackets are made by bending pieces of thin brass plate 4 in. deep and 4 in. wide when bent, as shown in detail in Fig. 8. The vertical ends of the brackets slip into the sockets and provide a substantial swivelling support. Four such brackets fitted on each side of the cupboard will give plenty of accommodation for hanging clothes.

Where a recess is not available for the construction of a cupboard, a corner fitment made on similar lines to the one just described can be used to advantage. Fig. 6 shows a plan view of the arrangement.

The Door-frame is of the same construction as the recess cupboard, and the door can be made to either wall, i.e. the cupboard may face in either of two directions. Battens (as in the recess cupboard) are nailed to the walls, and the outstanding side of the cupboard x, is of matched boards nailed to battens secured to a vertical post Y, which is screwed to the wall. As the side of the fitment has no outer support, the arrangement shown in Figs. 9 and 10 is used at the wall end of the battens. The side batten J is let into the wall-post Y, at the back of which is nailed a rectangular piece of wood K, 1 in. thick and the same

length as the width of the batten, J. The end of the batten is nailed into the recess in the post and, to strengthen the joint, triangular pieces are nailed to the batten J and the bearer-plate K. This makes a good, strong fixing to the wall.

The front frame M (Fig. 6) is exactly the same as that employed in the recess cupboard, and is halved into the top rail. It has, however, an additional rail, M, at the bottom, the same width as the top one and halved in the same way. This extra rail is to keep the projecting side of the cupboard perfectly rigid. This rail is shown in Fig. 7 and is of $\frac{3}{4}$-in. material. The door is exactly the same as the one previously described.

Shelves are supported on battens as in the cupboard (Fig. 2) and hangers are fitted in; to make the structure more rigid, the shelves should be screwed in from the outside of the side x and on the battens or bearers on the opposite wall.

The top member is made of material $\frac{3}{4}$ in. thick. The side x, should be screwed to four battens or rails J—one at the top and bottom and two equally spaced between.

The exterior of the cupboard should be carefully smoothed with glass-paper and all knots treated with knotting to prevent the resin from spoiling the surface when finished. A priming coat of paint followed by two further coats should then be applied; the latter to match the decorations of the room.

. BEDROOM FURNITURE

THE construction of the chest of drawers shown in Fig. 1 follows very simple lines. Oak-faced plywood plays an important part in its construction, with pleasing effect.

To make the chest of drawers, four legs are required, each 2 ft. $5\frac{1}{2}$ in. long,

cut from $1\frac{1}{4}$-in. square (finished) oak, as indicated in Fig. 2. The two back legs are grooved $\frac{1}{4}$ in. deep and $\frac{3}{16}$ in. wide as shown dotted in Fig. 2, to take the plywood panel, which is $18\frac{7}{8}$ in. from the top to the bottom edge, including $\frac{1}{4}$ in. let into the groove in the under edge of the top rail and the groove in the upper edge of the lower one. The front legs are grooved on one face only to the same width and depth as the back ones. The size of the side panels is 18⅞ in. long by 14⅜ in. wide overall.

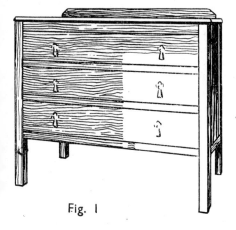

Fig. I

When preparing the legs do not attempt to true up more than the faces which butt against the ends of the rails; if these faces are dead square there is no need to worry too much about the outer faces.

The legs are secured to the rails by means of dowel pins, one at each end for a narrow rail and two for the wider ones. The back vertical piece is also dowelled. The diameter of the dowel pins is ⅜ in. When marking out the holes and dowel positions, care must be taken that those in the side rails do not run into those in the back rails. Do not forget to make a small groove down the length of each dowel before fixing, to allow any surplus glue to escape.

Each of the three dividing rails across the front opening is ¾ in. thick by ⅞ in. wide, fixed with the ¾-in. face to the front. Flush with the top surface

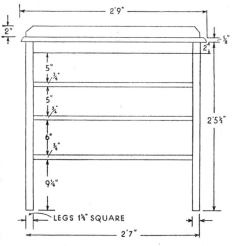

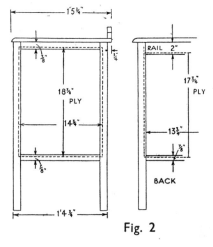

Fig. 2

The plywood for the back is in two sections, each measuring 17¾ in. long by 13¾ in. wide overall, divided by a vertical piece of wood 2 in. wide, grooved ¼ in. deep, ³⁄₁₆ in. wide, in both edges. This vertical member is fixed midway between the back legs and to the top and bottom back rails.

of each of these rails ⅝-in. square fillets are fixed to the sides of the legs at both sides. Each fillet has a strip of plywood tacked to the outer side and between the faces of the back and front legs and arranged to project ½ in. above the surface of the runner to act as a guide for the drawer.

The only difference in the sizes of the drawers is an extra inch on the depth of the bottom one. The fronts and backs of the drawers are $\frac{3}{4}$ in. thick, 2ft. $4\frac{1}{2}$ in. long by 5 or 6 in. as required, rebated at the ends to take the sides. The sides are $\frac{3}{8}$ in. thick and grooved $\frac{1}{2}$ in. from the lower edges to take the edges of the plywood bottom. Fillets of $\frac{1}{2}$-in. square wood are pinned and glued to the front and back below the bottom panel to support the long edges of the plywood. Six drop-handle fittings, or

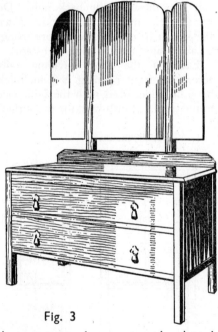

Fig. 3

the more modern rectangular-shaped wooden ones, will be required, and locks may be fitted if desired.

When assembling, the two ends can be finished complete with ply panels and drawer runners in correct position and the back made up into a complete unit. The top rail and drawer divisions can be eased into position on one side, the back unit treated in a similar manner and the other end-unit added last.

The top oak boards should be glued up, cramped and allowed to set before the edges are rounded off. The brads or small-headed screws used to fix the complete top to the body should be sunk well below the surface and the holes filled in with plastic wood. The surface should then be well rubbed down with glass-paper.

For finishing, a prepared grain-filler may be used, followed by two or three applications of brush polish.

The Dressing-table shown in Fig. 3 and Working Drawing No. 14 is made on similar lines and has $\frac{3}{16}$-in. plywood panels let into the grooved faces of the legs. Dowels are used for joining the ends of the rails as in the chest of drawers.

The back edge of the top does not overlap, but is flush with the back face of the legs so that the two vertical supports for the mirrors can be carried down the back as far as the bottom rail and secured by means of screws to the two rails. The lower part of the front edge of each support is cut away to the thickness of the backboard.

The mirrors are frameless and have bevelled edges. These are backed with plywood and are held in position by means of metal clips. The swivel movement for the centre mirror and suitable hinges for the side ones, as well as the mirrors themselves, can be obtained at most stores dealing in furniture fittings.

A Wardrobe to match the dressing-table and chest previously described is illustrated in Fig. 4 and the Working Drawing No. 15.

Large cupboard space is provided, a deep full-length drawer and a mirror. The wardrobe is made in two parts, the upper portion of which is detachable from the lower or drawer section.

The drawer section consists of two end frames formed by the legs and rails

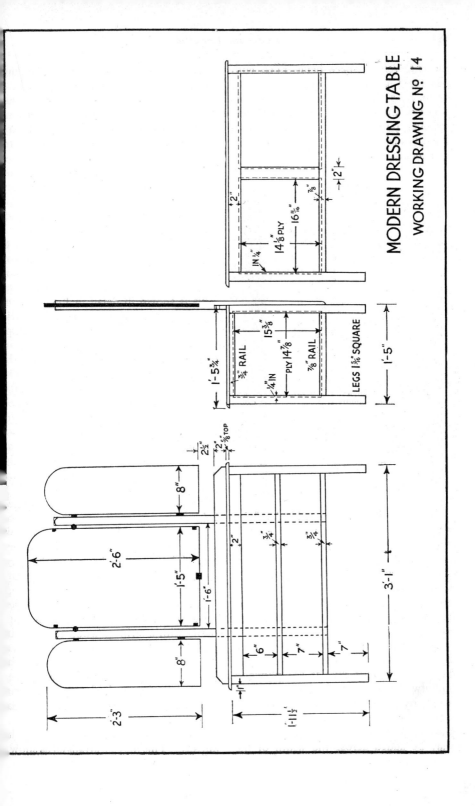

MODERN DRESSING TABLE
WORKING DRAWING Nº 14

the intervening space being filled with oak-faced plywood. The legs are of 1¾-in. by ¾-in. oak, grooved to take the edges of the panels, as also are the side member rails and the top and bottom longitudinal rails, which connect the end members together.

Fig. 4

All top rails are 2 in. wide by ¾ in. thick, while the lower ones are of similar thickness, but 3 in. wide. The joints used are simple dowel joints and ⅜-in. diameter dowel pins are employed. One dowel pin is used at the end of each top rail and two at the ends of the lower rails, as shown clearly in the front view.

An extra vertical member 2 in. wide by ¾ in. thick between the top and bottom back rails divides the plywood into two panels each 26¾ in. by 8½ in. wide overall. Side runners for the drawer are fitted to the inside faces of the legs. One or more cross-pieces may be added across the width of the

opening and dowelled into the front and back rails to give additional strength.

The drawer is made on similar lines to those described in the article dealing with a chest of drawers, but the plywood bottom should not be too thin and extra bearing strips fixed underneath across from back to front will give further support. The cupboard section consists of four corner posts of 1¾-in. by ¾-in. oak supporting the top, which overlaps all round.

At the lower ends the posts are cut to allow the back to pass behind the top front and back rails of the drawer section and thus keep the top section in position. This is shown in detail in Fig. 1 in the Working Drawing. The piece A is a strip of plywood 2 in. wide fixed to the uprights below the moulding, with its front face flush with the front of the top rail B of the lower section. The sides and back are treated in a similar manner and the main plywood panels forming the back, sides and front are screwed to the uprights. Lengths of corner moulding are fitted down all four corners to hide the edges of the plywood and the fixing screws as shown in detail in Fig. 2.

Extra vertical members are fixed behind the plywood front between the cupboard floor and the top to give support at the edges of the door opening. These are cut from ⅞-in. by ¾-in. material planed to leave a projecting fillet ¼ in. by 3/16 in. to act as a door-stop. As an alternative ⅞-in. by ½-in. planed batten could be used for the door uprights with a strip of wood to form the ¼-in. by 3/16-in. rebate as a separate piece secured by means of screws. The floor boarding is supported on bearers screwed to the inside faces of the posts and cut away where necessary to clear the posts.

A door frame is necessary to hold the mirror. This may be arranged as shown

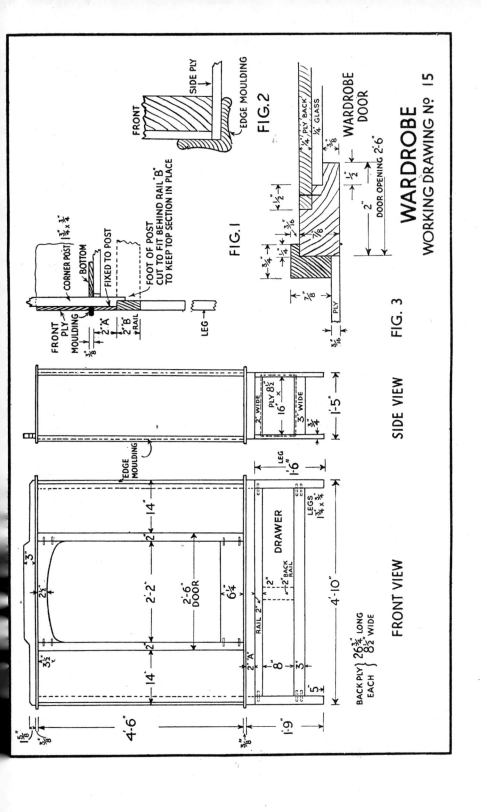

FRONT

SIDE PLY

EDGE MOULDING

FIG.2

¼" PLY BACK

¼ GLASS

³⁄₈"

WARDROBE
DOOR

DOOR OPENING 2'-6"

½"

½"

2"

³⁄₁₆"

⅞"

¼"

¾"

⁷⁄₈"

PLY

³⁄₁₆"

FIG. 3

CORNER POST 1¾" x ¾"

BOTTOM

FIXED TO POST

FOOT OF POST
CUT TO FIT BEHIND RAIL 'B'
TO KEEP TOP SECTION IN PLACE

FRONT

PLY

MOULDING

³⁄₈"

2" 'A'

2" 'B'

RAIL

LEG

FIG.1

EDGE
MOULDING

2" WIDE

PLY 8½"
16" x
¾"

3" WIDE

SIDE VIEW

1'-5"

1⅝"

³⁄₈"

4'-6"

3"

2½"

14"

2"

2"

14"

3½"

2-2"

2'-6"
DOOR

6¼"

LEG

1'-6"

DRAWER

RAIL 2"

2"

1-2" BACK
RAIL

LEGS
1¾" x ¾"

4'-10"

2" 'A'

8"

3"

5½"

1'-9"

³⁄₈"

BACK PLY 26¾" LONG
EACH } 8½" WIDE

FRONT VIEW

WARDROBE
WORKING DRAWING Nº 15

in detail in Fig. 3. The two side pieces or stiles are 2 in. wide on the outer face and the back is recessed in two steps each ½ in. wide. Assuming the mirror to be ¼ in. thick, the first step or recess is cut to suit and the next step behind this is cut another ½ in. back to take the ¼-in. thick plywood backing. The shaped top rail and the bottom one are recessed in a similar manner and small dowel pins may be used at the ends as a means of fixing the side members. Extra battens fixed across the back over the panel and into the uprights will give additional support.

Fig. 5

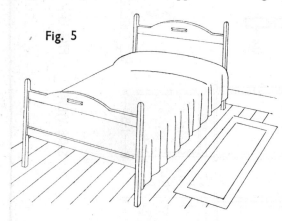

To give the structure a finished appearance a piece of oak 4 ft. 10 in. long by 3 in. wide and ¾ in. thick should be shaped and fixed along the front edge at the top.

The Bedstead illustrated in Fig. 5 is of modern design and can be easily constructed with a few ordinary tools to be found in most home carpenters' kits.

As will be seen by referring to the working details (illustrated in Working Drawing No. 16), the head part of the bedstead consists of two posts of $1\frac{5}{8}$ in. square section, into which the top and bottom rails are tenoned and glued, while the intervening space is filled with an oak-faced plywood panel ⅜-in. thick. The foot piece is constructed on practically similar lines, the main difference being that its height is lower.

The head and foot members are kept rigidly in position by means of longitudinal irons which fit into cast-iron dovetail fittings screwed to the back faces of the parts, as shown. These fittings can be obtained ready for fitting and are quite inexpensive. This method of support necessitates the use of a box mattress, which is placed over the supporting bars. Special wire mesh mattresses, complete with irons and dovetail fittings, can be used if desired. These mattresses are fitted with two screws which, when turned by a key, allow the tension of the springs to be adjusted.

Below is a cutting list of materials (oak):

ITEM	No.	ft. in.	ft. in.	in.
Head posts	2	3 8 ×	$1\frac{5}{8}$ × $1\frac{5}{8}$	
Foot posts	2	2 3 ×	$1\frac{5}{8}$ × $1\frac{5}{8}$	
Head top rail	1	4 $6\frac{1}{4}$ ×	7 × 1	
Head bottom rail	1	4 $6\frac{1}{4}$ ×	2 × 1	
Head panel	1	4 $4\frac{1}{2}$ × 2	$1\frac{3}{4}$ × ⅜ plywood	
Foot top rail	1	4 $4\frac{1}{2}$ ×	5 × 1	
Foot bottom rail	1	4 $6\frac{1}{4}$ ×	2 × 1	
Foot panel	1	4 $4\frac{1}{2}$ ×	$10\frac{3}{4}$ × ⅜ plywood	
Quarter round Moulding	50 ft.	¼		

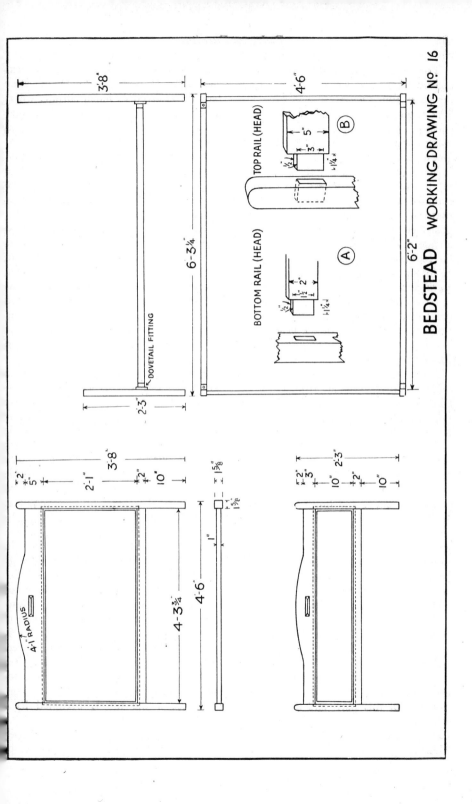

BEDSTEAD WORKING DRAWING Nº 16

To this list must be added one pair of bedstead bars and four dovetail fittings for same, four castors, screws, glue, etc. The tools needed include a tenon-saw padsaw, jack plane, grooving plane, chisel and mallet, square, rule and glue-pot.

Start by cutting the posts to the sizes in the drawings. These are shown rounded at the tops and square at the bottoms. If desired, the portions of the posts below the bottom rails can be made a trifle tapered, but the ends should not be reduced to a smaller section than $1\frac{1}{8}$ in. square, otherwise strength will be sacrificed.

Now cut and plane up a nice piece of oak 4 ft. $5\frac{3}{4}$ in. long by 7 in. wide and 1 in. thick for the top rail of the head of the bedstead, and a similar piece 5 in. wide for the top foot rail.

Mark out the positions for the tenons, taking all measurements from the lower edge, and scribe the top curve on the head rail to the radius shown in the drawing. If desired, the whole of the top edge can be one continuous curve, or even left straight, but if the latter be chosen, the overall width should not exceed 5 in.

Roughly saw out the surplus wood round the curve and finish it off neatly with a keen spokeshave, not forgetting to work it in the same direction as the grain. When finished, the curved portion can be laid on the foot rail and the curve traced on the latter, taking care to keep the ends flush with each other. Then cut out the curve as before.

Next prepare the two bottom rails. These are both the same size, namely, 4 ft. $5\frac{3}{4}$ in. long (allowing for the tenons) by 2 in. wide and 1 in. thick. Cut the tenons neatly with a fine tenon-saw to the dimensions shown at A in the detailed drawing of this part, and then proceed with the tenons in the top rails in accordance with the drawing shown at B. Mark the positions of the mortices in the

posts from the tenons, and then cut them accurately to a depth of $1\frac{1}{4}$ in. after having removed as much surplus wood as possible with a brace and $\frac{3}{8}$-in. diameter bit, taking every precaution to keep the bit square whilst so doing.

Cut the groove $\frac{3}{8}$ in. wide and $\frac{3}{8}$ in. deep in the centre of the inner side face of each post and also in the upper face of the lower cross-piece and the lower face in the upper rail.

Having cut the panels accurately to size, and cut the small ornamental pieces for the rails, the assembly can be put in hand. Use very hot glue at the joints, the edges of the panels and the ornaments, then cramp up the members and leave them to dry. Fasten the $\frac{1}{4}$-in. round beading round both sides of the panels, using $\frac{5}{8}$-in. fine panel pins driven in at a slight angle.

Give the whole of the woodwork a good smooth down with fine glass-paper, followed by a coat of glue size and stain to the desired shade to tone with other furniture in the room. The two members can then be varnished with a good quality oil varnish—not spirit varnish, as this has a somewhat brittle surface; therefore more likely to show scratches. If a duller finish is required, a good quality wax-polish will give the desired results.

The final steps consist in fitting the castors and screwing on the dovetail brackets for supporting the side rails.

The Bedside Cupboard illustrated in Fig. 6 and shown in Working Drawing No. 17 provides cupboard space of about 12 in. by 12 in. by 11 in. deep, in which a shelf may be fitted if desired. The top of the cupboard forms a shelf to hold a few books, and a pull-out slide for the morning cup of tea is a convenience if the top is occupied by a reading lamp.

Two sides, $27\frac{1}{4}$ in. long by 12 in. wide by $\frac{3}{4}$ in. thick, are reduced to $8\frac{1}{4}$ in. at the

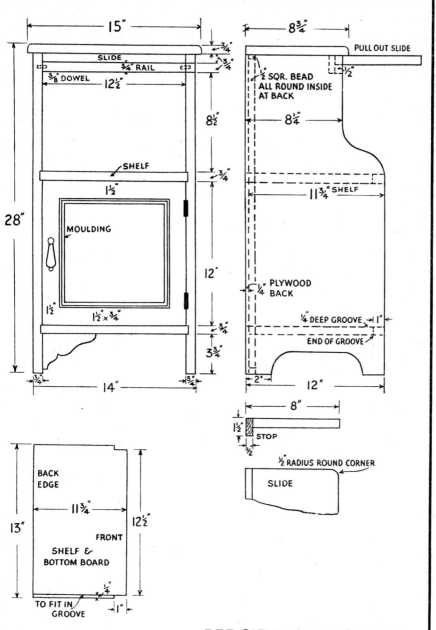

15"

SLIDE
¾" RAIL
³⁄₈" DOWEL
12½"

3/4
3/4

8½"

SHELF
1½"

MOULDING

1½"

1½" x ¾"

12"

3/4

3/4

3¾"

28"

¾"
14"
¾"

8¾"

PULL OUT SLIDE
½"

½ SQR. BEAD
ALL ROUND INSIDE
AT BACK

8¼"

11¾" SHELF

¼" PLYWOOD
BACK

¼" DEEP GROOVE 1"

END OF GROOVE

2"
12"

8"

1½"

STOP

½

½" RADIUS ROUND CORNER

SLIDE

BACK
EDGE

11¾"

13"

12½"

FRONT

SHELF &
BOTTOM BOARD

¼"

TO FIT IN
GROOVE

1"

BEDSIDE CUPBOARD
WORKING DRAWING № 17

top end and shaped as shown. On the inner faces mark off the positions of the two dowels in the slide rail, and also the two grooves for the book-shelf and cupboard bottom. If the grooves are not to show on the front, they must be stopped at about 1 in. from the front edge, and the sides of the shelf and

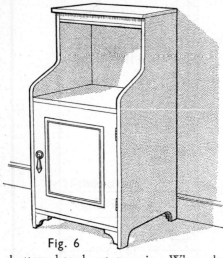

Fig. 6

bottom board cut to suit. When the extra cutting is not thought desirable, the grooves may be taken right across, but the joint will show on the front, as in the front view of the cupboard. In any case the shelf and bottom board should be prepared first, and the grooves in the side pieces cut wide enough to allow the parts to be fitted without being too loose. These two boards extend to within $\frac{1}{4}$ in. of the back edge of the cupboard, leaving room for the plywood back.

The front rail under the slide is $\frac{3}{4}$ in. by $\frac{1}{2}$ in. by $12\frac{1}{2}$ in. long, fitted with a $\frac{3}{8}$-in. dowel pin at each end, which does not show on the outside.

The top is 15 in. by $8\frac{3}{4}$ in. by $\frac{3}{4}$ in. thick, with all edges rounded off except the back one, which is flush with the back of the cupboard. The other edges overlap $\frac{1}{2}$ in. all round.

Material $\frac{3}{4}$ in. thick is also used for the slide, which is made $12\frac{1}{2}$ in. by $7\frac{1}{2}$ in. with rounded corners at the front. This piece should now be fitted to the opening between the cupboard top and the rail by easing the edges and under surface until it will slide easily without being too loose, otherwise it will drop at the front when pulled out. A recess should be cut on the under side to the front to provide a grip for the fingers. The stop piece, $\frac{1}{2}$ in. thick by $1\frac{1}{2}$ in. wide, may now be screwed to the back edge, and cut slightly less in length so that it will not hinder the movement.

When the cupboard is assembled the slide is put through from the back.

The door frame is made up of $1\frac{1}{2}$-in. wide by $\frac{3}{4}$-in. thick stuff, grooved for $\frac{3}{16}$-in. thick plywood panel. The joints may be either the usual mortice-and-tenon or dowelled butt-joints. Thinner wood may be used for the frame, if desired, in which case the plywood must be large enough to cover the whole of the back. This method of construction saves cutting grooves. A suitable moulding is added round the frame as indicated, and a drop-handle fitting with catch. This and the hinges may be fitted on the other sides to those shown if desired. Two shaped brackets are fitted in front below the door, more for finish than strength, and are secured by means of screws through the top face of the bottom board.

A fillet $\frac{1}{2}$ in. square is fixed all round inside the back edge, $\frac{1}{4}$ in. back. This with the edge of the shelf and bottom are required for fixing the plywood back, which is in one piece.

AN INVALID TABLE

LIGHTNESS, rigidity and simplicity of construction are the outstanding features of the invalid table shown in the accompanying illustration (Fig. 1), and the dimensioned drawings in Working Drawing No. 18.

Such a table can be easily constructed in a few hours by anyone familiar with a few ordinary woodworking tools. The outlay of only a few shillings for the materials shows an enormous saving over a ready-made article.

The table has been designed for use with a single 2 ft. 6 in. wide bedstead having a low foot end, and enables the table to be wheeled from this end up to the patient. The span between the legs is sufficient to allow at least 6 in. on either side for overlapping bedclothes.

The table-top consists of a plywood panel, $\frac{3}{16}$ in. thick, supported on a frame, the long members of which are 4 ft. long over all, and of $1\frac{1}{4}$-in.-square section yellow deal. These members are kept at their correct distance apart by means of two $\frac{3}{4}$-in.-diameter dowel rods—one at each end—which form convenient towel-rails, and $\frac{3}{4}$ in. by 1 in. battens housed near each end, as shown in the detailed drawing, A. Two cross-pieces of 2 in. by $\frac{5}{8}$ in. deal further support the panel near the centre, as indicated by the dotted lines in the plan view.

The long top members and end cross-pieces are rebated $\frac{1}{2}$ in. wide and $\frac{3}{16}$ in. deep to allow the top surface of the panel to lie flush with the frame, while the centre-supports are fixed flush with the bottom of the rebate for the same purpose.

Two rails, 2 in. wide by $\frac{5}{8}$ in. thick, are morticed into each pair of legs, as shown in the end view, the tops of the

legs being fixed to the top members by means of long screws. The legs are kept rigid by means of shaped plywood brackets $\frac{1}{4}$ in. thick, which are glued into recesses or grooves cut in the undersides of the longitudinal members and the tops of the side faces of the legs, as shown clearly in the detailed drawing B.

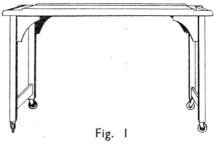

Fig. 1

Strips of $\frac{3}{8}$-in. by $\frac{1}{4}$-in. beading having a rounded top are pinned along the outer edges of the table-top, as shown in the front elevation, to prevent articles from slipping off.

To Construct the Table, start with the legs. These are 1 ft. $11\frac{3}{4}$ in. long, of $1\frac{1}{4}$-in.-square section deal. Cut them to length and carefully plane to true section. Mark each leg for the mortices, which are 2 in. from the bottom and $1\frac{1}{2}$ in. from the top, as shown. The size of the mortices is 2 in. long, $\frac{3}{8}$ in. wide, and $\frac{3}{4}$ in. deep. Cut the grooves $\frac{1}{4}$ in. wide and $\frac{1}{4}$ in. deep to a length of 6 in. at the top of the legs to take the plywood brackets, and then glue and pin the rails to the legs. Cramp them up tightly and leave to dry.

Next, construct the top frame. Mark and bore the holes for the dowel rods in the centre of the inside faces. The centres for these are $\frac{7}{8}$ in. from the ends, and the holes should be bored to a depth of $\frac{1}{2}$ in.

7

Mark out the positions for the $\frac{3}{4}$-in.-wide cross-pieces, and cut recesses $\frac{3}{4}$ in. wide, 1 in. long, and $\frac{1}{2}$ in. deep to take the ends. The top faces of these members should flush with the top faces of the long ones. Now mark the positions of the two middle cross members, which are merely cut squarely to length and fastened by means of screws driven through the sides of the long members. Mark and cut the grooves, $\frac{1}{4}$ in. wide and $\frac{1}{4}$ in. deep, on the underside of the longitudinal members to take the brackets, and cut a shallow recess $\frac{3}{16}$ in. deep, $\frac{1}{2}$ in. wide, in the top and inner faces to allow the plywood panel to lie flush.

Prepare the two end cross-pieces and cut them to a finished length of 18 in. and then cut four pieces of $\frac{1}{4}$-in.-thick plywood, $6\frac{1}{4}$ in. square, mark the curve approximately to that shown, and saw them carefully with a fretsaw.

The next step is to cut carefully the plywood panel for the top to a size of 3 ft. $4\frac{1}{2}$ in. by 18 in. Great care should be taken in preparing this, to see that it is perfectly square.

Drill the screw-holes through the sides of the long members to take No. 6 gauge countersunk-headed wood-screws for fixing the cross members, including the ends of the dowel rods. Countersink the tops of the holes sufficiently deep to enable the heads of the screws to lie well below the surface.

The parts may now be assembled. Get the glue-pot ready, and with plenty of hot glue join the parts together, starting with the end dowel rods, and secure these with $2\frac{1}{2}$-in. No. 6 screws, driven in tightly. Then glue the ends

of the end cross-pieces, screw up, and then fix the middle cross bearers.

Brush some hot glue in the shallow recess for the edges of the panel, and also on the tops of the middle cross bearers. Place the panel in position and fix it down with $\frac{3}{4}$-in.-long panel pins spaced at distances of 6 in.

Having glued up and fixed the end frames, consisting of the legs and their cross members, fix them to the table-top. These are fixed by means of $2\frac{1}{2}$-in. No. 8 screws, driven through the top frame into the tops of the legs. Brush some glue into the bracket recesses and slide the brackets into position, taking care to see that the legs are square with the top frame. When the glue has set perfectly hard, fasten the beading along the top long edges with glue and panel pins.

Stop up all the screw-holes with plastic wood and then smooth the whole of the table with fine glass-paper held in a wood block, and work it in the same direction as the grain. The constructional work is complete after having fixed the rubber-tyred castors.

To obtain a pleasing and durable finish, enamel is undoubtedly the best finishing medium. White, cream, or a light shade of blue is suggested; but the choice of colour must be left to individual taste.

Before applying the enamel, treat all knots in the wood with knotting, and then give it a good coat of glue size. When dry, give a priming coat of paint, followed by two further coats of flat undercoat paint, not forgetting to glass-paper the surface of each coat lightly before the next is applied.

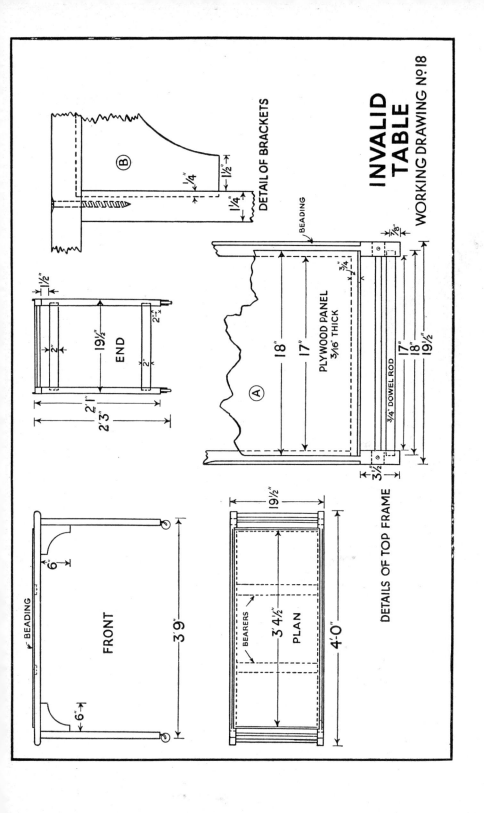

INVALID TABLE

WORKING DRAWING Nº 18

DETAIL OF BRACKETS

B

1/4"

1/2"

1/4"

BEADING

A

18"

17"

PLYWOOD PANEL 3/16" THICK

3/4"

1/2"

7/8"

3/4" DOWEL ROD

17"

18"

19 1/2"

3 1/2"

DETAILS OF TOP FRAME

END

19 1/2"

2"

2"

2"

2"

1 1/2"

2' 1"

2' 3"

FRONT

6"

6"

BEADING

3' 9"

PLAN

BEARERS

3' 4 1/2"

19 1/2"

4' 0"

AN INEXPENSIVE SIDEBOARD

THE sideboard pictured in the accompanying drawing has been designed to conform with modern conditions, namely, simplicity combined with utility. It has the straight lines so popular to-day but is, at the same time, as roomy as possible and suitable to any furnishing scheme.

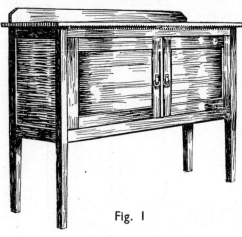

Fig. I

In order to keep down the cost as much as possible, plywood forms the major portion of the material. Thus, the top is built up of ½-in.-thick yellow deal board, covered with a 3/16-in.-thick oak-faced plywood, the edges being hidden from view by means of half-round beading.

The interior of the carcass is divided into two compartments by means of a centre partition, which not only serves as a bearing for the top but also provides two roomy cupboards, capable of being fitted with shelves if desired.

Fully-dimensioned drawings appear in Working Drawing No. 19, and if they are followed carefully no difficulty should be experienced in construction.

The materials, including such items as locks, hinges, screws, etc., can be purchased at most woodcraft shops, now to be found in nearly every little town.

The framework and legs are constructed from stock-sized material, ready planed and trued. The use of this not only considerably cuts down the cost by eliminating waste, but also dispenses with much tedious labour in the shape of sawing and planing.

Fifty shillings is the approximate cost of the material. The legs are formed of 1⅞-in. square section oak, 3 ft. long, costing 5s. per set of four. The rest of the main framework, door-frames, and the back board at the top are made from ⅞-in. by 2-in. section oak stripwood, costing 4d. per foot run. About 16 sq. ft. of figured oak-veneered plywood will be required for the top, sides, and door panels; this is listed at 9d. per sq. ft.

Ordinary birch-faced plywood of good quality will suffice for the back and the bottom of the cupboard, as they are hidden from view. These items involve the use of about 14 sq. ft., which is priced at 4½d. per sq. ft. Three 7-in. by ⅝-in. prepared (½-in. thick, finished) deal boards and the shelves will cost about 5s., and to this must be added 5s. for stripwood, beading, fittings, etc.

Having obtained the material outlined above, start by marking out and cutting the tenons of the front and side top rails as shown in detail at A in Working Drawing No. 19. The tenons are 1½ in. long by ½ in. thick, and are cut 1½ in. wide to form a ½-in. shoulder on the underside when fitted to the legs. The ends of the tenons are mitred, as shown in detail, to ensure plenty of surface for gluing.

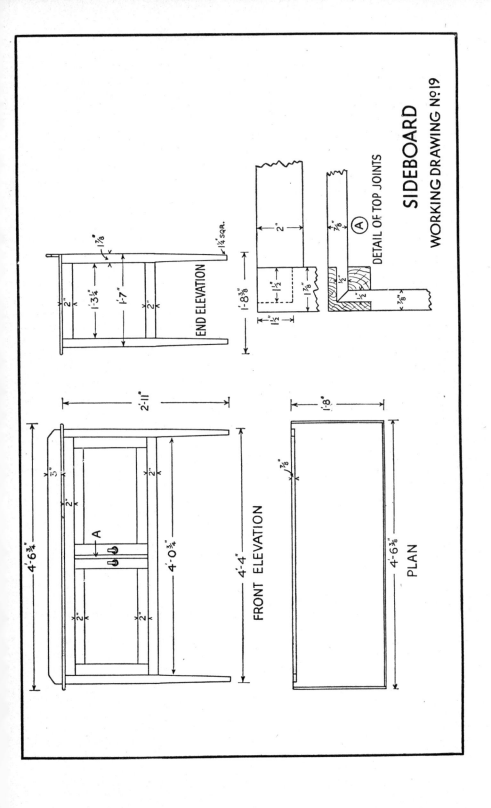

END ELEVATION

DETAIL OF TOP JOINTS

(A)

FRONT ELEVATION

PLAN

SIDEBOARD

WORKING DRAWING Nº19

The next procedure is to cut the bottom rails to exact length, square the ends and bore them to take $2\frac{3}{8}$-in.-diameter dowel pins, which are afterwards glued into corresponding holes bored into the sides of the legs.

Preparing the Legs.—Square the ends and cut them to an overall size of 2 ft. 11 in. This done, mark the tops for the mortices from the tenons already made in the top rails, and then carefully saw down on the inside of the marked lines to a depth of $1\frac{1}{2}$ in., removing the waste with a sharp chisel. Mark the positions for the bottom rails and the dowel pins on the side faces of the legs and bore the holes with a sharp $\frac{3}{8}$-in.-diameter centre-bit to a depth of $\frac{3}{4}$ in.

As the legs taper from full section at the lower edge of the bottom rails to $1\frac{1}{4}$ in. section at the feet, they should be carefully marked at this position and the ends, and carefully planed to size.

The next operation consists of assembling the frame and securing the joints with hot glue. When the glue is perfectly dry, fix a back and a front vertical piece to support the partition panel. The front one is indicated at A in the front elevation. These are fastened with screws driven through the top and bottom rails at the back and front. Fix a fillet of $\frac{3}{4}$-in.-square deal to the inner faces of the bottom rails to form a bearing for the bottom of the cupboard. The tops of the fillets should be flush with the tops of the rails. The bearers are fixed to the rails by means of $1\frac{1}{2}$ in. by No. 6 countersunk-headed screws, driven in from the inside.

Before fixing the long back and front fillets, however, a piece of 2 in. by $\frac{3}{4}$ in. planed batten should be cut and fixed between the long bottom rails at the centre to form a central support for the cupboard floor.

A number of suitable lengths of $\frac{3}{8}$-in. by $\frac{1}{4}$-in. stripwood should now be cut and pinned to the inner side faces of the rails and legs to form supports or false rebates against which the plywood panels fit. The horizontal strips should be laid flat with the narrow edge flush with the inside edges of the rails, keeping the vertical pieces—which are, of course, fixed to the legs—in line with them. Panel pins, $\frac{3}{4}$ in. long, may be used with advantage for fastening the strips.

At this stage the plywood panel for the bottom of the floor should be cut accurately to shape, not forgetting to cut recesses at the four corners to clear the corners of the legs, and two recesses in the centre to clear the partition uprights. The floor is fixed with $\frac{3}{4}$-in. panel pins, spaced about 6 in. apart. Cut the partition panel and fix in between the two vertical uprights by means of a $\frac{1}{4}$-in. stripwood, pinned to the floor and the inside faces of the verticals.

The side and back panels can now be cut to fit their respective rebates. They are kept in position by means of thin, round-nosed beading $\frac{3}{8}$ in. wide by $\frac{3}{16}$ in. thick, fastened down with fine panel pins $\frac{3}{4}$ in. long.

If shelves are desired they should now be fitted. They are supported by 1-in. by $\frac{3}{4}$-in. cross-pieces, screwed to the legs and the partition, and may be fixed so that the shelves come midway between the floor and the top, or any other convenient position. Two 7-in. by $\frac{5}{8}$-in. boards should be used for each shelf, which may be either bradded or screwed down to the supports.

The Preparation of the Top Board.—The 7-in.-wide ($6\frac{7}{8}$ in. finished) deal boards should be fitted together, long edge to long edge, with glued and dowel joints, and further strengthened with a couple of $\frac{3}{4}$-in. by 2-in. planed battens screwed to the underside, and spaced about 14 in. from the ends. When the glue is dry, the ends can be marked and sawn off squarely to length and skimmed over with a sharp plane. This operation should be followed by planing the long edges to true width, namely, 1 ft. 8 in.

The deal top is then fixed to the top of the carcass by means of 1¼-in. screws driven into the top rails, care being taken to countersink the heads well below the surface. Now cut the plywood overlay exactly to size and apply a good coat of very hot glue to the deal surface and the underside of the panel. Place the panel on top immediately, to prevent the glue chilling, and apply pressure all over to squeeze out as much glue as possible. Partially drive in a few panel pins here and there, place as many weights as possible on top and leave to dry.

When you are perfectly satisfied that the glue is quite set, remove the weights and pins, fix the edge-beading and the back board. The latter is simply held in place with dowels and glue.

The doors consist of simple panelled frames, the stiles and rails of which should be properly joined by means of accurately-fitted mortice-and-stopped-tenon joints, or, if preferred, well-made dowel joints. False rebates, as used for supporting the side panels, may be employed for securing the door panels, but the strips forming the rebate should be glued as well as pinned, and it is an advantage to apply a small quantity of glue to the edges of the plywood.

Brass butt hinges should be used for hanging the doors. One leaf of the hinge should be let into the edge of the stile and the other into the leg, to enable the doors to open and close properly.

A suitable ornamental lock of an oxidised finish should be fitted to each door, and a small door-stop consisting of a small strip of wood must be fixed vertically to the side face of the partition, opposite each opening stile.

The whole of the outside of the sideboard should be thoroughly smoothed down with fine glass-paper and given a good coat of glue size. Stain of a suitable shade to choice can then be carefully applied and, when dry, the whole can be polished with one of the many excellent proprietary polishing-waxes.

A KITCHEN CABINET

THIS useful piece of furniture for the kitchen may be made on quite simple lines by the average home carpenter having a certain amount of skill in the cutting and joining of timber.

The design shown in Working Drawing No. 20, presented with this volume, has eight compartments. On the left are two cupboards 2 ft. deep from back to front. These are fitted with full-depth shelves, three in the top cupboard (No. 1 in the drawing of the framework), and two in the bottom cupboard (No. 2). None of these need extend to the front unless required. Section 3 at the top consists of two small cupboards, side by side, suitable for small articles not in frequent or daily use, such as spare electric-light bulbs. An open front shelf is provided in section 4 and this may be fitted with glass bottles or other marked containers for tea, rice, etc. Section 5 is enclosed with a door to open downwards from the top edge, and when this is lowered the inner surface, fitted with an enamelled plate top for cookery work, exposes the two sections behind, used for housing a flour container and other materials required for cooking and pastry-making.

The bottom central section has four

drawers, each of different depth, and a cupboard on the right with only one shelf, for larger articles, such as bread bin, etc.

The last section, No. 8, is a full-length cupboard for brooms, mop, brushes, etc., and the inside of the door is used to accommodate an ironing-board.

The first stage of the construction is to make the frame, the six uprights of which are each 6 ft. 3 in. long, cut from 2-in. by $1\frac{1}{2}$-in. yellow deal. The three side-rails are also 2 in. by $1\frac{1}{2}$ in. thick, and set to the front and back uprights, 1 ft. 9 in. apart. Mortise-and-tenon joints will give a more robust construction, although dowelled joints are more simple to make, and quite satisfactory provided a suitable-sized bit is used so that the holes are not made too large.

All the frame members should be finished first, the dowels fixed into the rails and the uprights bored to receive them at the correct positions. The four uprights of the left-hand section may be assembled in stages, first the front pair with the three front rails, then the back pair with three rails. The rails at the sides, from back to front, are then added and the intermediate upright for the front of the centre section. The right-hand section of the frame is built up in the same manner, and the parts of the centre section added. The centre post and runners for the drawers should be fixed before the plywood sides are put in so that there is room to reach round. The fillets to support the bottom and various shelves are also fixed in each section while the framework is open, then the inner ply divisions between cupboards may be added, and lastly, the shelves. The outer panels of plywood are added when the majority of the work is finished, and the top is left until last.

In the two cupboards of sections 1 and 2 the shelves are $\frac{3}{4}$ in. thick, and supported on runners or rails of 1-in. by $1\frac{1}{2}$-in. stuff fixed between the uprights. Each complete shelf is cut away at the corners to clear the uprights, so that the shelf extends right up to the plywood sides and back. When several full-depth shelves are fitted, many articles may be hidden if the compartment is crowded, so some of the shelves need not be made to fill the space right to the front, but the remaining sections of shelving may be stored away, for use later as required. Shelf No. 6 and the bottom have smaller runners.

Each back section is filled in with a panel of $\frac{3}{16}$-in. plywood, so that the outer surface is flush with the face of the uprights. Beading of $\frac{3}{4}$-in. by $\frac{1}{2}$-in. section, for supporting the panels, is tacked to the uprights and rails by means of panel pins. The same section beading is used at the sides for the side panels of plywood, but the beading is set back to the edge of the rail. This leaves a space of $\frac{9}{16}$ in. on the outer face. The beading is fixed with its $\frac{3}{4}$-in. face to the side of the upright in each case so that there is ample surface for fixing the beading, and the plywood to the beading.

Sections 6 and 7 are divided by the centre bar and a plywood partition which is fixed more towards the catch side of the cupboard door to allow room for the side runners of the drawers. The front bars between each drawer are 1 in. thick by $1\frac{1}{2}$ in. wide. The side runners are of the same thickness and notched into the back uprights. A detail of this is shown in the Working Drawing. The shelf of cupboard No. 7 is $\frac{3}{4}$ in. thick and fixed to 1-in. by $1\frac{1}{2}$-in. runners, the same as the others. This shelf can be fixed, of course, at any desired height.

The Four Drawers.—Each is a different depth, but other dimensions are the same, as indicated in the detailed sketch. The shallow one at the top is lined with green baize and fitted with divisions for knives, forks, etc.

Sections 3, 4 and 5 are set back 9 in. from the front edge, and extra uprights are used between the back and front centre pairs, and fixed to the top or shelf, which is 1 in. thick. The lower compartment, No. 5, has a flap door 1 ft. 6 in. high by 2 ft. 6 in. wide, by 1 in. thick. At the back an enamelled plate is fitted, so that when this door is let down it makes a table for cookery purposes; the two compartments at the back contain the various materials and small appliances, such as rolling-pin, egg-beater, etc. A pair of strong butt hinges is required for this flap door, and a simple catch let into the outer surface of the wood so that no part projects. The top of this compartment is 1 in. thick, and also forms the shelf above. It is supported by 2-in. by 1½-in. rails fixed to the sides and back of the framework at that point. The two compartments at the top are enclosed by simple plywood doors.

A suitable moulding is fixed along the top edge, starting from the back, along the side, and following the framework round to the back of the right-hand side, the ends being cut with external and internal mitres as required.

The Door Frames.—All four are constructed in the same manner, dowels being used to join the members, which are made out of 2-in. by ¾-in. wood. To the back of each frame ³⁄₁₆-in. plywood is fixed by means of small brads. As the long door on the right may tend to twist, extra battens may be fitted at the back after the plywood has been fixed. From the outside the door looks the same as the pair on the left, except that it is not so wide.

Hardwood dowel rod ⅜ in. in dia-meter is obtainable, and cut to length as required. The holes for dowels are the same depth in both pieces to be joined, so the dowel is sunk into one piece the same length as the projecting part. Glue should be applied hot to the dowels and the holes before fitting together, and to prevent the wood from splitting when the glued dowels are forced in, each dowel piece should have a small groove cut along the side from one end to the other. This will allow the surplus glue to escape, otherwise it will fill the space intended for the dowel, and tends to split the wood.

Two butt hinges for each door should be fitted on the inside and let into the sides of the frame and the door so that only the centre part of the hinge round the pin shows on the front. This makes a neat and correct job. The appearance of many home-made cupboards is spoilt by putting the hinges on the outside. Four hinges should be used on the long door. Suitable catches and knobs may be obtained cheaply from any iron-monger.

The whole of the top is covered in with sheets of plywood, fixed before the moulding is added, so that the edges of the ply are covered by the moulding.

The design and construction shown may be adapted for a smaller cabinet by leaving out the right-hand long cupboard. Other alternatives are to build the centre sections only, that is, those marked 3, 4, 5, 6 and 7. This would be suitable for use in a recess. The two cupboards of the left-hand section, built as a separate unit, would make a very handy fitting for the scullery, and with an alteration to the shelves could be made to take brooms and brushes also.

7*

SIMPLE KITCHEN FITMENTS

THE various devices described here will be found illustrated in Working Drawing No. 21, presented with this volume.

The Folding Clothes-horse shown in Fig. 1 is made from any prepared wood, or rough timber of good quality planed to the sizes given and finished smooth with glass-paper, and may be left in this state or finished with white enamel for easy cleaning.

Three frames will be required, each consisting of two legs or uprights 1½ in. by 1 in. in section and 4 ft. long, braced across with three rails each 1 in. by ⅝ in. by 2 ft. 6 in. long over all. All six legs are cramped with the 1½-in.-wide faces together, and the mortice holes marked across them at the given distances from the lower end for the lower pairs, and at 2 in. down from the top for the top rails. Each mortice is ¼ in. wide and central on the 1-in.-wide face of the leg, passing right through. The nine rails may be marked out in the same manner in sets of three and the tenons cut as shown.

The bottom ends of the legs should be squared to stand firm, and the top ends rounded off with a chisel and rasp, and made smooth. When the rails have been fitted, glue and screw them firmly in place. Next hinge the three frames together, using stout upholstery webbing for the hinges.

Commence by nailing one end to the outer face of leg A, just below the top rail. Turn the webbing over the joint face, and nail it to the inner face of leg B. Use galvanised tacks with flat heads. Now fix the second piece below the first, to the inner face of leg A, pass it over the joint face and fix to the outer face of leg B. With two or three groups of webbing at each joint edge the horse may be turned in any direction and be folded flat.

The Hinged Scullery Table shown at Fig. 2 will prove very convenient where space is limited, as it only projects 3 in. from the wall when not in use. In the small modern house, fitments that fold out of the way when not in use are a boon to the housewife.

First make up the wall frame out of 2-in. by 1-in. finished ye'low deal. Cut two pieces 2 ft. 6 in. long, and two 1 ft. 10 in. long. At the ends of the latter pair cut the tenons ¾ in. wide as shown in the detail, and notch the ends of the horizontal members to correspond. Through the 1-in.-wide face of each horizontal member drill two holes for the screws for fixing the frame to the wall. These should just clear the size of screw used.

Cramp the two long pieces together and drill clearance holes through the 2-in.-wide faces for the pivot screws of the brackets. When the latter are folded in there should be enough space between the back edge of the bracket and the inside of the frame to allow the batten underneath the table-top to pass between when lowered.

Glue and screw the frame-joints firmly and use the finished frame for marking the position on the wall for the plugs, by passing a long bradawl point through the drilled holes when the frame is held against the wall. The height from floor to table-top is left to suit the convenience of the constructor. A pair of stout butt-hinges are fitted to the frame without hindering the movement of the brackets.

The brackets are made of 1-in. by 1½-in. material with halved joints. The back edge of the vertical member may be rounded off if necessary for clearance, and the whole made an easy fit without being too loose in the frame. The fixing, by means of long wood-screws passing through the frame into the ends of the bracket, is best done with the bracket in the closed position. The ends, after having been marked through for holes in the frame, may be drilled for part of the depth with a smaller diameter drill to prevent splitting.

The top consists of two boards, each 9 in. wide, with 1-in. by $1\frac{1}{2}$-in. battens screwed to the underside. The hinged top is covered with a piece of linoleum tacked on, and the remainder of the woodwork may be painted.

Egg Stand.—A safe storage for eggs is provided by the stand illustrated in Fig. 3, and may be made in two or more sections as required. The top is 5 in. wide by $13\frac{3}{4}$ in. long, and has 12 holes, each $1\frac{1}{2}$ in. in diameter, bored at the centres shown. Supporting pieces are required at the ends only. Each support has a slot cut for lifting purposes, and if more than one stand is to be used, dowel pins are fitted in the lower edge to fit into holes drilled in the top face.

Airing-rack.—Fig. 4 gives details. Two ends of $\frac{7}{8}$-in.-thick wood are required, $3\frac{3}{4}$ in. wide by 20 in. long, 5 round rods each $\frac{7}{8}$ in. in diameter being used (obtainable in lengths of 8 ft.). The position of the ceiling joists should be found before any attempt is made to suspend the rack in position.

Plate-rack.—The material required for the plate-rack (Fig. 5) is three pieces of wood $\frac{3}{4}$ in. thick, 7 in. wide by 18 in. long for the top, bottom, and shelf. The last piece is cut $1\frac{1}{2}$ in. shorter to fit inside the frame. Two sides, also $\frac{3}{4}$ in. thick, are 7 in. wide by $24\frac{3}{4}$ in. long. At about $1\frac{1}{2}$ in. back from the front edge on each piece except the sides, mark a centre line and space out

the positions for the $\frac{1}{2}$-in.-diameter dowel rods. The 12 rods may pass through the shelf and the top, but not right through the bottom. The finished rack may be secured to two metal brackets fixed to the wall with plugs.

The Food-safe (Fig. 6) is intended for use indoors in any cool, well-ventilated place. The back is covered in with ply or matchboarding.

For the safe, make up two frames 16 in. by 24 in. out of $1\frac{1}{4}$-in. by $\frac{3}{4}$-in. deal, fixing the top and bottom members into the verticals as indicated in the detail. The rails connecting the two frames to form the sides are also $1\frac{1}{4}$ in. by $\frac{3}{4}$ in., fitted with $\frac{3}{8}$-in.-diameter dowels at the ends for fixing into the frames. The centre rail on each side forms a ledge for the shelf-boards, which are removable for cleaning. Beading $\frac{3}{8}$ in. by $\frac{1}{2}$ in. is nailed all round inside the frame flush with the back face. To this the perforated metal is fixed and the edges are covered all round outside with a strip of wood, as shown. Both sides are treated in the same manner, and $\frac{1}{2}$-in.-thick bead is fixed round the door-opening to form a stop.

The bottom and top may be of matchboarding. The door frame is also of $1\frac{1}{4}$-in. by $\frac{3}{4}$-in. material and enclosed with similar sheet metal as the sides. When fitted on hinges the door should be an easy fit for opening.

The Draining-board (shown in the drawing at Fig. 7) is made to slip over the edge of the sink, so the piece under the front edge is fixed at an angle to give the top board a slope when in position. The gap between the back of this underpiece and the ends of the triangular pieces should be made to suit the thickness of the sink. Edging, $1\frac{1}{2}$ in. by $\frac{1}{2}$ in., is nailed along each side, and the top surface is grooved with a $\frac{3}{8}$-in. gouge to allow the water to drain away.

A PORTABLE GARAGE

THE motor-house described in the following paragraphs and illustrated in Fig. 1 with details in Working Drawing No. 22, presented with this volume, has been designed for the owner-driver who, as a practical man, is usually familiar with the use of tools.

The structure consists of a wooden framework clad with asbestos sheets, roofed with asbestos-cement tiles.

Such a garage will conform to the requirements of most public authorities. The size is 16 ft. long, 9 ft. wide, 7 ft. to eaves, and 8 ft. 9 in. to ridge. This size allows ample room for accommodating the popular small-sized car and leaves sufficient space at the end of the structure for a small bench.

When the necessary plans have been passed by the local authorities, the first thing to do is to mark out the site, remove the soil, and level the ground for the concrete floor. If possible, the floor should be arranged to have its top surface 4–6 in. above the ground level and not sunk below. This method allows the asbestos covering on the outside of the structure to overlap the sides of the concrete for a few inches and thus prevents any water finding its way, between the surface of the floor and the bottom plates, into the interior.

In constructing a building of this description it should be borne in mind that provided the structure is not fixed down permanently to the ground, it is classed as a temporary building and therefore a tenant's fixture which may be removed when desired. Thus, the building here described comes under that category, because it is merely fixed to the floor by means of bolts and nuts which can be easily unscrewed.

Having accurately marked out the site by means of four pegs driven into each corner at the correct distances apart, and removed the top layer of soil to a depth of 3 in., the excavation should be filled in with a layer of coarse clinker or with broken brick rubble and the whole either rammed down or rolled perfectly hard and level.

The next procedure is to enclose the floor space with thick boards set round the edges and level with the top surface of the concrete, which should not be less than 4 in. in thickness. In fixing the boards, make sure that their tops are perfectly level, as tested with a spirit-level, and drive in a number of stout pegs at distances of about 3 ft. apart, on the outside of the boards to prevent them bending outwards, when the wet concrete is poured in. The entrance end should slope down gradually for about a couple of feet to ground level to prevent the sharp edge of the concrete damaging the tyres.

The Concrete Floor consists of two layers. The bottom layer is 4 in. thick and is made of coarse stuff by mixing 1 part of Portland cement to 2 of clean sharp sand and 4 of aggregate, consisting of clean broken bricks, or shingle of about $1\frac{1}{2}$ in. diameter, while the finishing layer consists of cement mortar in the proportion of 1 of sand to 1 of cement. Sufficient time must be allowed to enable the bottom layer to set hard before adding the finishing layer, it being protected, in the meantime, against extreme weather.

When preparing the floor, bed in the holding-down bolts, not forgetting to apply a liberal supply of grease to the threads above the level of the floor, to prevent rust. The bolts should be 6 in. long and $\frac{1}{2}$ in. diameter and project

3 in. above the floor level, and a washer should be placed on the head before insertion. The positions for the bolts are $1\frac{1}{2}$ in. from the edges, two being required for each side and two at the back. Great care must be taken to see that the bolts are perfectly upright, otherwise difficulty will be experienced when fitting the bottom plates of the framework.

A hole about 4 in. deep and 4 in. square should be left near the front edge of the floor, at the door end, to accommodate the iron dowels which are fitted to the bottoms of the door-posts, as shown in the front view, the holes being filled in with "grout" or liquid cement after the posts have been fixed in position.

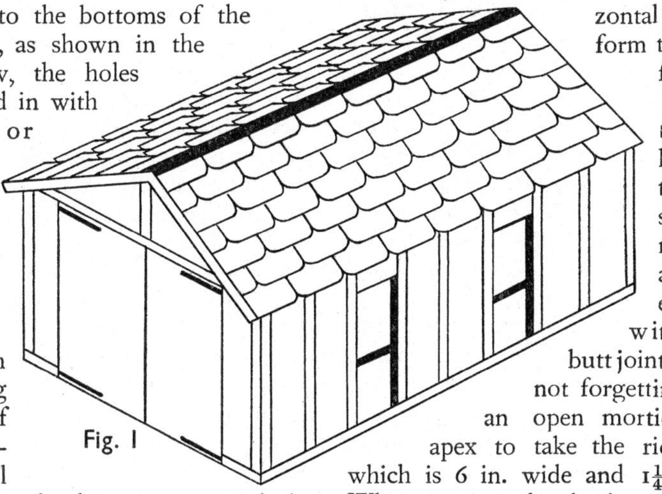

The main framing consists of 3-in. by 2-in. deal

Fig. I

scantling, and all joints are made by butting and nailing members together.

Cut off 4 16-ft. lengths for the top and bottom side rails and 18 7-ft. lengths for the vertical members or "studs." Lay one of the 16-ft. lengths flat on the floor and mark the exact positions for the ends of the studs, which must be 24 in. apart, centre to centre. Then by means of a square transfer the markings to the other rails. Drill two holes with a brace fitted with a $\frac{3}{16}$-in.-diameter spoon bit through the rails, in the centre of each marked position, keeping them 1 in. from the long edge. These are for inserting 4-in. long wire nails which fasten the studs and prevent splitting.

Now fix the uprights to the rails by nailing them together. As this cannot be conveniently done in a vertical position, the best way is to place the rails, narrow edge downwards, on he concrete; kneel on the uprights to keep them from shifting and drive in the nails.

Having fixed all the uprights, square up the frame and fix a 4-ft. long batten diagonally across each corner to keep it square. Mark, cut and fix the wind braces between the first, second and third studs at each end, as shown in the elevation, and then fit the short horizontal pieces to form the window frames.

Prepare the end or back section in the same manner, and cut and fix the end gables with nailed butt joints as shown, not forgetting to make an open mortice in the apex to take the ridge board, which is 6 in. wide and $1\frac{1}{4}$ in. thick. When cutting the back uprights, do not overlook the fact that they are 2 in. longer than the ones in the side members. The extra 2 in. on the height of these allows the ends of the roof rafters to rest on the top rails of the sides.

Having so far completed the framing, drill the holes in the bottom rails to take the holding-down bolts. These should be clearing holes bored with a $\frac{3}{4}$-in.-diameter bit to allow for slight adjustment. Two holes, $\frac{5}{16}$ in. diameter, should also be drilled in each side end upright, about 18 in. from the top and bottom, to take the fixing-screws.

The three sections may now be erected with the assistance of a helper. Lay one side flat on the floor, with the bolt holes opposite the bolts in the concrete, and lift up into position. In order to hold the side up whilst getting ready for erecting the opposite side, two lengths of 3-in. by 2-in. stuff about 10 ft. long should be used as supports. One end of each is nailed temporarily to the top rail near the ends and the other ends of the supports rest against heavy weights placed on the floor.

Follow the same procedure with the other side and then the back, and fasten them together with stout screws or coach bolts 4 in. long, driven in from the inside.

Place a washer on each holding-down bolt and screw on the nuts.

Next, prepare the front as shown in the front view in the Working Drawing. Cut two 7-ft. lengths of 6-in. by 3-in. timber for the door-posts, and drill a $\frac{3}{4}$-in. diameter hole to a depth of 4 in. in the centre of the bottom of both pieces. These holes are for taking the dowel pins, which enter the holes already prepared in the concrete floor. The "pins" consist of pieces of $\frac{3}{4}$-in.-diameter heavy-gauge electrical conduit, or as barrel of the same diameter. The tube is driven into the holes in the bottoms of the posts, allowing 4 in. to project.

Fix the door-posts to the end vertical members of the side sections by driving in three 6-in. stout screws from the outside. Cut and nail on the lintel or cross-piece above the door and then fix the gable as before. Fill in the holes at the feet of the door-posts with neat liquid cement and allow it to set.

Next fix a 17-ft. length of 6-in. by $1\frac{1}{4}$-in. deal between the morticed members of the gables, to form the ridge. The ends should project 6 in. at each end.

Now cut 14 roof rafters, each 5 ft. 2 in. long, and carefully mark and trim the ends to an angle to correspond with the slope of the roof. This done, fix them down to the top plates and the ridge

board, using 6-in. wire nails for the former and 3-in. ones for the latter.

When the rafters have been securely fixed, roof trusses consisting of 3-in. wide by $\frac{3}{4}$-in. thick battens should be nailed across each rafter in the manner shown in the diagram. The purpose of these members is to brace the sides of the roof and tie the walls to prevent them spreading out.

The whole of the roof should now be covered with $\frac{5}{8}$-in. thick roofing boards.

A facia board of 3-in. wide by $\frac{3}{4}$-in. planed batten should be fixed to cover the ends of the roof boards.

Now fix the external sheets of asbestos-cement. Four 8-ft. by 4-ft. sheets will be required for each side. Two similar sheets will partially cover the back, another is necessary for the doors, while an additional strip 8 ft. long by 1 ft. wide will be required to cover the centre space at the back. Two pieces 4 ft. 3 in. long by 3 ft. 9 in. wide can be cut diagonally to fit the front and end gables, while a couple of strips 7 ft. long by 9 in. wide for covering the door-posts completes the list of sheeting.

The asbestos-cement sheets should not be less than $\frac{1}{4}$ in. thick and they should be cut to allow a 3-in. overlap at the bottom of the floor plates all round. As the sheets covering the sides butt up against the underside of the roof boards, recesses will have to be cut in the tops of them to clear the ends of the roof rafters.

Having cut the sheets to length, offer up the first one at the door end, mark the positions of the rafters at the top edge and cut the recesses, bearing in mind that the long edges should come in the centre of the studs. Fix the sheets to the studs, including the intermediate ones, by means of $1\frac{1}{4}$-in. galvanised flat-headed nails spaced at intervals of 6 in. and not less than $\frac{1}{2}$ in. from the edges, leaving a small gap $\frac{1}{16}$ in. wide between each joint. Proceed in the same manner until both sides are complete.

The lengths of the end sheets are 7 ft. 5 in., which allows 3 in. at the bottom as before and 1 in. bearing on the top cross-rail. Fix the two end pieces first and then cover the gap in the centre with the 1-ft. wide strip.

Do not cut out the window apertures before fixing the sheets, as these may be easily cut out with the aid of a padsaw after the sheeting is in position.

The joints between the sheets are covered with planed and slightly chamfer-edged battens, 2 in. wide by $\frac{1}{2}$ in. thick, and for the sake of appearance a covering strip can be fixed over each intermediate stud. Before fixing the battens, give them a good coat of creosote, if this is to be the finishing medium, or, if paint is to be used, treat any knots in the battens with "patent" knotting and then give the strips a good priming.

Covering the Roof.—The "gauge," or the distance between one horizontal edge of one course to another, is, for centre nailing, half the length of the slate minus the amount of lap. This, with a standard slate, namely, $15\frac{3}{4}$ in. by $15\frac{3}{4}$ in., allowing $2\frac{3}{4}$ in. lap, which is the usual allowance for this type of roof, will be $\dfrac{15\frac{3}{4}\text{ in.} - 2\frac{3}{4}\text{ in.}}{2} =$ $6\frac{1}{2}$ in., or, in other words, this is the amount of each course that will be seen. From this it follows that each slate covers an area of $6\frac{1}{2}$ in. by $15\frac{3}{4}$ in., or $102\frac{3}{8}$ sq. in., and the number of slates to cover 100 sq. ft. will be $\dfrac{100 \times 144}{102\frac{3}{8}} = 140$ approximately.

As the area of the garage roof is 170 sq. ft. or, say, 175 sq. ft., the minimum number of slates required to cover the area will be $1\frac{3}{4} \times 140 = 245$. To this number must be added a sufficient number of slates to cover four extra courses—one at the ridge and one at the eaves on both sides of the roof.

The slates are laid upwards from the eaves and a double course, as mentioned above, should be fixed at this position, while the bottom of the slates should overlap the edges of the boards by 2 in. The overall length of the eaves slates, or lower course, will be gauge plus lap $= 6\frac{1}{2}$ in. $+ 2\frac{3}{4}$ in. $= 9\frac{1}{4}$ in. This course will be entirely covered by the next. The bottom course slates may be easily cut to size by scoring with a chisel and breaking over the straight edge of a piece of batten. Another double course will be needed at the ridge, which will be partly covered by the ridge.

The chief points to observe in fixing the slates are to keep each course perfectly parallel and the vertical joints of alternate courses strictly in line.

The best kind of nails to use for fixing the slates is the galvanised-wire type, $1\frac{1}{2}$ in. long.

Having completed the slating, a suitable roof ridge should be fixed. This article, made of asbestos-cement, can be had in various forms, and can be obtained from most builders' merchants. A triangular-shaped ridge having a slope of $25°$ is recommended, the standard size of which is 24 in. long plus 4 in. overlap, and 11 in. wide. The pieces are fixed by means of screws driven into the top of the ridge board.

The Doors.—All that remains to be done now is to make and hang the doors and windows.

A little care is necessary in making the doors, details of which appear in the Working Drawing, otherwise it will be found in a very short time that they will drop and bind on the ground. The distance between the door-posts is 7 ft. 6 in. and the height from the floor to the cross-rail is 7 ft. Therefore two doors, each 3 ft. 9 in. wide and 7 ft. high, will be required.

Cut off and plane up 4 stiles or uprights 7 ft. long and 6 rails 3 ft. 9 in. in length of 3-in. by 2-in. stuff, and make the doors with proper mortice-and-tenon joints, and cut in the braces after framing up. Plane off $\frac{1}{4}$ in. from the bottoms to allow for ground clearance, cover the frames with a sheet of asbestos nailed from the outside, and cut the edges flush with the framing.

Obtain two pairs of medium weight wrought iron reversible gate hinges and fasten them to the top and bottom rails by driving the fixing-screws through the asbestos covering. Offer the doors up into position and after allowing for ground clearance, mark the positions for the hinge cups on the side panels. Fix the bottom cups and drop the hinges into position and then finish by fixing the top cups. The object of allowing the stiles to project beyond the top and bottom rails will now become apparent —there would not be sufficient room for the hinge cups otherwise.

Nail a $\frac{3}{4}$-in. by $\frac{3}{4}$-in. fillet on the under face of the top cross-piece to act as a door-stop, and screw a 2-in. by $\frac{3}{4}$-in. planed batten to the long opening edge of the right-hand door. This strip should project 1 in. beyond the edge to overlap the other door when closed, and prevent the entry of rain water. Fix a shooting bolt at the top and a similar one at the bottom of the opening stile of the left-hand door, chip out the concrete to allow the lower bolt to shoot, and drill a hole in the cross-piece for the other. Finish the door by fixing a 9-in. hasp and a padlock.

The Windows should be made to open to give adequate ventilation when working within. The apertures in the framework, which are 1 ft. 10 in. wide, should be provided with sills 2 ft. 4 in. long by 5 in. wide and 2 in. thick. Each sill is cut out to fit between the uprights and allows a projection of 3 in. on both sides of the window frame. The tops of the sills should slope off towards the front and be channelled on the underside about $\frac{1}{2}$ in. or so from the front bottom edge to prevent water penetrating the joint.

Line the sides and tops of the window apertures with $3\frac{1}{2}$-in. by $\frac{1}{2}$-in. planed stuff and then make and fit the sashes. These should be made of prepared best yellow deal, 2 in. wide by $1\frac{1}{4}$ in. thick, and the rails and stiles should be fixed together with mortice-and-tenon joints. To save the labour of planing the rebates for holding the glass, false rebates consisting of $\frac{1}{2}$-in. by $\frac{7}{8}$-in. strips can be bradded to the inside faces of the sashes, keeping the back edge of the strips flush with the backs of the frames. The sashes should then be knotted and given a good coat of priming paint. When dry the sashes can be glazed with 21-oz. glass. They should then be tested and eased if necessary, and then hung from the tops by means of butt hinges.

METAL WORK

METALS AND THEIR USES

NEARLY everybody knows that a metal is an opaque substance which cannot be dissolved in water but is capable of being melted by the application of heat. An alloy is composed of two or more metals mixed together when they are in their molten state. A metal is said to be tenacious if it is tough, and ductile if it can be hammered to shape or drawn out easily without injury.

Cast Iron or **Pig Iron**, as it is sometimes called, because the iron is cast into moulds called "pigs," is impure iron, the chief impurities being such substances as sulphur and phosphorus. These elements in iron give different properties. Cast iron has an appreciable amount of carbon in its composition—over $1\frac{1}{2}$ per cent.—and is crystalline in texture. It is brittle and not at all ductile, which means that it cannot be hammered without injury. When the "pigs" are heated to a high temperature it melts—approximately at about $2750°$ Fahrenheit—and is then usually poured out into a mould, made of sand or other material, the resulting shaped metal being termed a casting. Cast iron is extremely strong in compression but very weak in tension, or in other words, it takes a much greater force—about six times—to crush it than to pull it apart. For this reason it is used largely for supporting pillars in constructional work and also for the framework of machinery, etc. Cast iron is useless for objects subject to bending.

There are two common varieties of cast iron, known as white and grey. White cast iron is smooth and white, while the grey variety has a comparatively rough surface, but has the advantage of being easier to work. Small iron castings should be made of grey iron.

Malleable cast iron is ordinary cast iron treated by burying the casting in an oxide of iron called red hæmatite. The casting is placed in a furnace and is kept red hot for a length of time according to the size of the casting.

Wrought Iron or **Malleable Iron** is made from cast iron after all the impurities have been removed. It is fibrous in texture, tenacious and soft, and is therefore easy to work. It can be forged into shapes, hammered, drawn or rolled into sheets when heated up to a cherry-red colour. Wrought iron contains not more than $0·25$ per cent. of carbon, and its strength is nearly equal in tension and compression; its melting point is $3250°$ F. This kind of iron is used extensively for ornamental work, horseshoes, etc.

Steel contains more carbon than wrought iron but has less carbon than cast iron. There are two common kinds of steel, called soft or mild steel and hard steel. The former has a fine, bluish-white colour and can be filed, drilled, or turned quite easily. Mild steel is used largely for making parts of machinery and engines, and for structural purposes. Hard steel or cast steel, such as that used in making tools, can be cast, forged, tempered and hardened by first heating it to redness and cooling it in water. As the amount of carbon in hard steel determines its hardness, the steel used in making a razor blade, which must have a very keen edge and is therefore hard and brittle, contains more carbon in its composition than that of the steel used for making a cold chisel, which does not require such a sharp edge but much greater strength. Hard steel is difficult to work, so that it is usually annealed or softened by heating the metal to a red heat and gradually letting it cool off before being worked upon. The more slowly the metal is allowed to cool, the softer it will be.

Copper is an extremely ductile and malleable metal, for it can readily be hammered to shape when cold. It can be rolled into thin sheets, and it can also be forged and cast but not welded. It is an excellent conductor of heat and electricity, and is extensively used for making electrical apparatus, electric cables, steam tubes and in making alloys. The melting point of copper is 1996° F.

Brass is a yellowish-coloured alloy made by mixing copper and zinc together when they are in a molten state. It has many different qualities depending upon the amount of copper and zinc the alloy contains. Ordinary common brass, for instance, contains about 65 parts of copper and 35 parts of zinc. Brass is malleable and ductile but harder than copper. It is specially useful for making small cast parts of machines. It is easy to drill, turn, file and solder.

Lead has a bluish-grey colour and is the heaviest and softest metal. It melts at a low temperature—620° F.—and has great resistance to the action of most acids. It is used largely for making cold-water pipes, coverings for electric cables, chemical tanks, and electric storage batteries. Lead is extremely ductile and can be easily cast.

Zinc is a bluish-white metal used principally for making alloys. It is also employed in the process of galvanising iron. The melting point of zinc is 785° F.

Aluminium is one of the lightest common metals known. It is ductile and quite easy to work, but it has a nasty knack of sticking to the tools. It can be drawn into wires and hammered into sheets; it can also be cast into shapes. Aluminium is a difficult metal to solder unless a special flux is used. It is not a particularly tough metal, but hardens a lot when worked and requires frequent annealing. The hardness and tensile strength of aluminium are equal to those of any metal except steel.

Duralumin is an alloy consisting of 96 per cent. aluminium, 3 per cent. copper and 1 per cent. magnesium.

Tin melts at a low temperature, 440° F., and as it does not rust it is one of our useful metals. Tin is chiefly used for making alloys, such as type metal, solder, etc., and also for coating thin sheets of iron, called tinplate.

Bronze or **Gun-metal** is a reddish-yellow coloured alloy, and is composed of about nine parts of copper to one of tin. It is used extensively for bearings of machinery and pinion wheels.

Phosphor Bronze is an alloy consisting of ordinary bronze with the addition of 2 per cent. to 4 per cent. of phosphorus. Its tensile strength is greater than that of ordinary gun metal.

Manganese Bronze is an alloy of bronze and ferro-manganese. It has about the same strength and toughness as mild steel and can be forged and rolled. As it resists the corroding action of sea-water it is largely used for ships' propellers.

Type Metal is an alloy of lead and antimony that does not shrink when cast. Clean and sharp small castings can be made quite easily by melting the alloy in a plumber's ladle over a gas-ring or fire.

METAL-WORKING TOOLS

METAL-WORKING tools can be divided under two heads—hand tools and machine tools. The former comprise all the various cutting and other tools which can be hand-applied to the work, while the latter include such machines as lathes, drilling machines, emery wheels, shapers, etc.

The following paragraphs give a brief survey of the tools most commonly used in amateur metal-work.

Hammers come first on the list. These are not the kind the carpenter uses. They are specially shaped for metal-working (engineering). The most useful are those shown in Figs. 1, 2, and 3. The cross-paned hammer (1) is the most useful of all. It should have an ash shaft, and it is advisable to have two sizes—one having a head weighing about ½ lb. and another with a 1-lb. head.

The round-paned hammer illustrated at 2 is extremely useful for riveting and hollow work. Such a hammer having a ¾-lb. head will be found serviceable for general work.

The straight-paned hammer (3) is not so much in general use as the tools mentioned above, but is very valuable for awkward jobs where a cross-paned tool could not be conveniently used.

If heavy work on the anvil is contemplated, a small sledge-hammer may be required. One of 4 to 6 lb. weight will be the most useful, and it should be fitted with an ash shaft of about 2 ft. to 2 ft. 6 in. in length.

An Anvil is an extremely useful tool in the metal-worker's shop but, unfortunately, such tools are expensive. A 28-lb. cast-iron anvil with a chilled face is handy for work of a light nature, if carefully used. A small wrought-iron steel-faced anvil is the proper tool for heavy work but will cost about twice as much as the cast-iron type. An anvil should stand on a solid block sawn from a tree-trunk. The latter should be at least 8 in. in diameter by about a foot high, standing on a foundation of sand. A serviceable type of anvil is illustrated in Fig. 4.

The Vice.—You will not be able to proceed very far with metal-work without the aid of a suitable vice, for if you wish to saw a piece of metal the material must be rigidly and firmly fixed to the bench.

Fig. 5 shows a useful type of engineer's parallel-jawed bench-vice. It consists essentially of two jaws, a screw, and a base. The back jaw is stationary and is in one piece with the base. The front jaw is the movable one and it can be either opened or closed by the movement imparted by the steel screw. Suitable holes are provided in the base for fixing the tool to the top of the bench. The work is placed between the jaws and the screw tightened up in the same manner as a carpenter's vice.

The jaws of most good parallel-type vices are fitted with hardened steel strips having roughened faces. The strips are let into the castings and secured in position at the tops of the jaws by means of countersunk-headed screws. This desirable feature ensures a perfect grip on the work and allows the pieces to be easily replaced when worn.

Quite a lot of useful work can be accomplished in a vice having jaws 3 in. wide which will open to about the same extent.

Smaller vices for screwing to a table by means of a wing bolt are to be obtained, and prove very useful for gripping very small work.

An important point to observe when using a vice is to fix a pair of soft metal clamps between the jaws when working upon finished surfaces, otherwise the work may be badly marked by the hardened jaws. Fig. 6 illustrates a pair of clamps suitable for the purpose, which can be easily made of tinplate, sheet lead, or brass.

When purchasing a vice do not be tempted to buy one of the fancy types which combine anvil, pipe-grips, bending jigs and a host of other devices. They are generally of inferior quality and are expensive. Avoid also "quick grip" vices. Only the best of these are good, and the extra outlay is only justified in cases where they are used on repetition work.

Files are to be obtained in a wide range of size, section and cut. The most useful are the "bastard" cut, in half-round, round, and flat; they should be from 7 to 12 in. in length. Small sizes can be had in the same sections and in three-square and square for small work.

Chipping-chisels, sometimes called cold chisels, will be found very useful for numerous purposes such as roughly shaping a piece of metal before finishing it off with a file, cutting off pieces of sheet metal, cutting grooves, etc.

There are several types of chisels, each useful for its particular purpose. The flat chisel illustrated at A in Fig. 7 will suffice for ordinary work, and for general roughing-out the cross-cut chisel represented at B will be most useful. Both types can be had in various lengths and widths of cutting edge.

Unlike the woodworker's chisel, the metal-worker's flat chisel has two bevelled faces which form the cutting edge; the angle formed is more obtuse than that of the carpenter's tool.

A Bench-drill (Fig. 8) should be included in every metal-worker's outfit. A useful size is one to drill holes up to $\frac{3}{8}$ in. diameter and having a $3\frac{1}{2}$ in. vertical travel. A machine having a self-feed is to be preferred to one fitted with a hand-feeding device only, and is well worth the little extra expense. The drill-spindle should have a self-centering drill-chuck for holding the drills, while an assortment of good quality twist-drills for iron and steel, and straight-fluted ones for brass should be provided.

A Hand Drill-stock, as illustrated in Fig. 9, should supplement the bench-drill, as it can be utilised on work where the use of a bench-drill would be impracticable. A hand-driven drill-stock is one of the most useful tools to have in the workshop and can be used for drilling holes up to $\frac{3}{8}$ in. diameter.

A good firm hacksaw-frame, with blades, is essential for cutting metal. This appliance consists of a frame into which a saw-blade is fixed and a handle by which the tool is held.

Hacksaw-frames can be had in several types, some being made so that they can be adjusted to suit different lengths of blades, while in another type an arrangement is provided for turning the saw in different directions to cut upwards, downwards or sideways.

A good type of hacksaw with blade attached is shown in Fig. 10. This type combines the two desirable features mentioned above. A glance at the illustration will show that the blade is held in position by means of short projecting pegs arranged at the top and bottom of the frame, the ends of the blades having holes made in them for the purpose. New blades can therefore be put in very easily and quickly. The nut at the top is for tightening up the blade as in a woodworker's fretsaw-frame.

Hacksaw-blades may be obtained in various qualities with either fine or

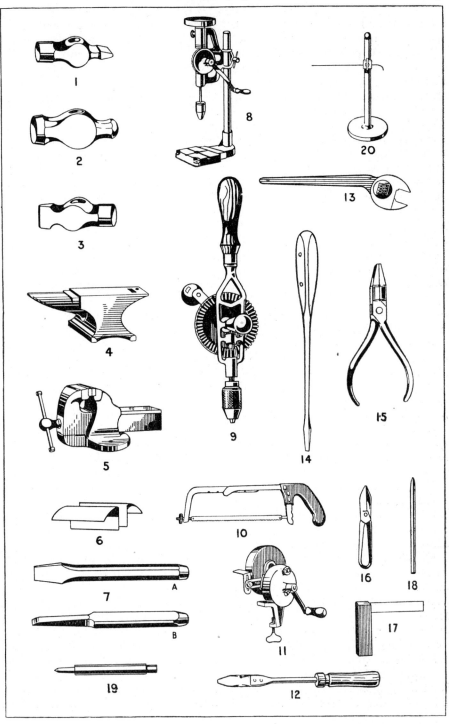

coarse teeth. There are many excellent ones on the market.

For general purposes, a 9-in. blade is a handy size to use. For cutting mild steel and cast irons, etc., choose a blade having about 14 teeth to the inch, while for sawing hard steel a finer degree of coarseness is recommended —say 24 to the inch. For all-round work a blade having 18 teeth per inch will be found quite suitable.

The way to use a hacksaw is to fix the work firmly in the vice—close up to the jaws to obviate vibration as much as possible—at about the height of the elbow when you are standing upright. Insert the blade into the frame so that the teeth cut on the outward stroke, that is, away from the operator. Tighten up the tension-nut tightly, as the blade should be rigid. Grasp the handle of the saw in the right hand and grip the other end at the top with the left, holding it perfectly straight. Now gently push the tool forward on the work, using a steady, even pressure right to the end of the cutting stroke; then relieve the pressure and draw the tool back to its original position. Repeat the process until the metal is nearly severed, when the pressure should be gradually relieved.

You will find it an advantage to make a nick in the metal with a file at the required position before beginning the cut, as this precaution will prevent the saw sliding sideways on the first stroke.

One of the chief points to observe when using a hacksaw is not to twist the blade, otherwise the inevitable result will be a broken blade, because hacksaw-blades are hard and brittle. Another observation to note is that the speed for cutting varies with different metals. When cutting iron or steel the number of cutting-strokes per minute should be in the neighbourhood of 75. Some workers prefer to lubricate the saw-blade. This is unnecessary and generally causes the teeth to slide over the work instead of biting into it.

For sharpening tools a wet grindstone is still the best tool, but it is expensive. A small emery grinder to clamp on the bench (as illustrated in Fig. 11) is now largely used. In selecting an emery grinder the essential point is to see that it can be easily rotated at a very high speed. The higher the speed the less the wear of the wheel. Foot-operated emery wheels are, of course, to be preferred to hand-operated ones.

Taps and Dies are the tools used for making internal and external screw-threads by hand. They can be had for cutting Whitworth, B.A. (British Association) and various other standardised screw-threads. A good way to go about the provision of these tools is to buy them separately as required. This method of buying as wanted is cheaper than purchasing sets, which generally contain a number of sizes never likely to be used by home workers.

The method of cutting threads with hand-operated tools is fully explained in a subsequent article.

Soldering-irons.—For soft soldering, a good-sized copper bit (Fig. 12) is necessary. The larger the better, as very small soldering-irons lose heat too quickly to be useful except for the smallest work. A copper bit weighing about $\frac{3}{4}$ lb. will suffice for general work, including most household repairs requiring an application of solder.

The bit should have an iron shaft, flattened, divided and riveted through the copper, and it should have a long beech handle. Avoid a soldering-iron where the shaft is screwed into the copper, as it invariably becomes loose and consequently very awkward to use.

For heating the iron a good clear fire can be used, but an eighteenpenny rectangular gas-heater with an inverted rectangular loaf-tin makes a better and more economical heater for the iron.

A blowlamp, using either paraffin or petrol, may be rigged up to heat the soldering-iron, with a little ingenuity.

Electric soldering - irons are ideal where current is available, as the bit is self-heating.

Spanners are necessary for amateur engineering work. The adjustable type of spanner is useless unless of good make. A useful wrench for awkward corners is the engineer's favourite "Clyburn," illustrated in Fig. 13. A 6-in. size has a span of $\frac{5}{8}$ in., while a 10-in. one has a span of 1 in.

It is advisable to have a set of thin double-ended spanners. A set of such spanners will fit eight sizes of nuts for Whitworth bolts from $\frac{5}{8}$ in. to $\frac{3}{4}$ in. diameter.

"Quick grips" are useful for pipe work, stud extractions and work of a similar nature. The "foot-print" grips are the best.

For the motor-car owner who carries out the majority of his own repairs a set of box spanners is almost indispensable. A set of four double-ended box spanners and a tommy bar for turning them will deal with nuts from $\frac{3}{16}$ in. to $\frac{5}{8}$ in.

Screwdrivers for engineering work should have extra strong handles. A suitable type where the blade and handle are in one, with wooden sides secured with rivets, is represented in Fig. 14. The ordinary joiner's screwdrivers are not suitable for engineering, neither are the various kinds of ratchet screwdrivers.

Fig. 15 illustrates a useful pair of square-nose pliers with side cutters for severing wire. At least two such tools should be included in the metal-worker's outfit, one about 6 in. long for dealing with large work and a lighter one for small work.

A Pair of Hand-shears is necessary for cutting sheet metal. This useful tool is shown in Fig. 16 and requires little explanation. It is very much like a pair of scissors, except of course that it is much more robust. Several patterns of shears are to be obtained, but you will be well advised to get a pair of straight "snips"—as the tool is often called—8 in. long, which will give a cut of about 2 in.

The Engineer's Rule is made of steel. This is necessary because very accurate measurements are generally required. Such rules are sometimes provided with metric as well as English scales. The metric scale is divided into centimetres and millimetres, while the English scale is in inches and subdivided into eighths, sixteenths, thirty-seconds, and sixty-fourths of an inch. A 6-in. rule is a handy size for small work, but for larger work a 12-in. rule will be required.

The Engineer's Square (Fig. 17) is also made entirely of steel. It is used, of course, for setting off lines on a surface at right-angles to a given edge, testing accuracy of work, etc., in the same way as a carpenter's square is used on wood.

A good type of square for general work should be provided with a thin blade about 4 in. long fitted to a thick stock.

The Scriber.—As a pencil cannot be conveniently used for marking metal, the necessary marks are made by means of a scriber such as that shown in Fig. 18. The tool, in its simplest form, consists of a thin rod of hardened steel, one end of which terminates in a sharp point. A scriber of this type is easily made with a length of $\frac{1}{8}$-in. diameter silver steel rod about 8 or 9 in. long, by filing or grinding one end to a sharp point and then hardening the tool.

Dividers suitable for metal-working have a spring head and side adjusting screw which provides a ready means of making accurate adjustments.

The Centre-punch (Fig. 19) although small in size is nevertheless an important tool. It is used principally for marking the centres of holes for drilling, marking out a piece of work preparatory to filing, sawing, etc.

Centre-punches are made of hardened steel, one end being ground to a point. For heavy work the point is ground to an angle of 45°, while a sharper pointed tool, having an angle of 60°, is used for work of a lighter nature.

iron casting having a perfectly flat and true surface. It is used for laying out work and for testing the accuracy of flat surfaces.

Surface-plates are very expensive to buy, and for this reason are seldom used by the amateur mechanic. A good substitute for such a plate is a piece of thick plate glass supported by a wooden framework or base.

The Bench, if possible, should be built into the wall of the workshop, since a deal of wrenching and bending is often necessary, which would pull a detached

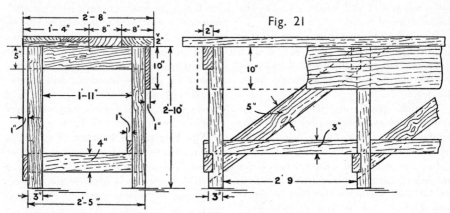

Fig. 21

The Scribing-block.—Where much fitting and turning is to be done, a scribing-block—or surface gauge—is necessary. It is generally used in conjunction with a surface-plate for accurately marking out pieces of metal previous to being worked upon. A simple form of surface-gauge is the one shown in Fig. 20. It consists of a vertical pillar—usually of mild steel—fixed into a circular base, the under surface of which is undercut to ensure a perfectly true bearing surface. A scriber is fastened to the rod by means of a clasping device provided with a wing-nut which allows the height of the scriber to be adjusted to any desired height and angle.

The professional engineer's surface-plate is generally in the form of a heavy

bench about the floor. If it is not possible or desirable to fix the bench to the wall, it may be screwed to the floor with strong angle-brackets. A suitable construction is shown in the drawing (Fig. 21), which illustrates the arrangement of the legs, bearers, rails, etc. Suitable dimensions are shown, except length, which will be such as to suit the space available. The little extra outlay in having stout frame- and top-members will be well invested. Finish is of no great importance except on the front and top, which should be planed. The rest could well be left rough as from the mill, but planed up if a neater finish is desired. Great strength is the prime importance, especially at the leg which supports the vice.

An engineer's bench should be of such a height that, with the vice fitted, the top of the vice will be 3 ft. 4 in. above the floor level. Since the vice will stand about 4 in. above the bench, the bench-top will be 3 ft. high.

Reference to the drawing shows that the legs are 2 ft. 10 in. long and 3 in. square. The top rails are 2 ft. 5 in. by 5 in. and 2 in. thick. They are let into the sides of the legs to a depth of 1 in. The bottom rails are 4 in. wide and of the same thickness and length as the top ones. The legs are placed at suitable distances apart to suit the length of space available. For a small bench three pairs of legs 2 ft. 9 in. apart will be suitable. 3-in.-wide rails are fixed against the legs behind and above the bottom rails along the full length of the bench, and diagonals are nailed on the back as shown in the side and front views. The diagonals are cut from 1-in. stuff and are 5 in. wide.

The top consists of two sound deal planks, 2 in. thick and each 8 in. wide, and two similar ones of 1 in. material. The front planks are laid direct on the top rails or bearers and screwed down. The 1-in. boards are fastened to strips of 1-in. stuff supported by the bearers to enable the tops of all four boards to lie flush when screwed down. The large members of the bench should be screwed together—not nailed.

The Front Board, which is 10 in. wide, may be dispensed with if desired, or a narrower one used in its place. It is an advantage to retain it as it stiffens the bench, gives a better appearance, and is useful for boring holes in which it may be handy to support work—pipes, rods, etc.—while being worked on in the vice.

The vice should be firmly screwed or bolted down over one of the legs. Generally, an end leg is found most convenient, but the question of light may prove the most important factor in deciding the best position.

THE METAL-TURNING LATHE

THE metal-turning lathe has been rightly designated the "King of Tools"; and as it is such an important machine tool in the art of metal-work, it is not surprising that a complete volume could be written about it. The present article, however, is only intended as a brief guide to the methods of using small lathes suitable for such work as model-making, small work in connection with motor-car repairs, and jobs of a like character.

There are numerous types and sizes of lathes—ranging from the tiny machine used by the jeweller to the huge tools employed in heavy engineering—varying in details but all possessing certain essential features such as the bed, head-stock and tool-rest.

In order to drive a lathe some form of driving-gear is necessary, which, for a small machine, is operated by foot-power, transmitted by a treadle. This method of driving the lathe answers the purpose quite well if the machine is only used occasionally, but when the lathe is constantly in service, a lot of labour will be eliminated by driving the lathe by means of a small electric motor.

Small lathes may be divided into three classes: the plain lathe, the back-geared lathe with a slide-rest, and the screw-cutting lathe.

The plain lathe, in its simplest form,

consists of a headstock and a tailstock mounted on a bed which is fixed either on a pair of legs or standards, or a suitable bench. The mandrel or spindle which imparts motion to the work is driven direct by a belt and pulleys without any intervening gear. A plain T tool-rest is generally provided for use with hand-operated tools.

A better and more useful type of plain lathe is fitted with a slide-rest, which allows the tool to be fixed rigidly in a holder attached to a slide which is movable in two directions by means

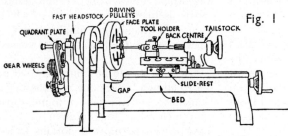

Fig. 1

of two screws and handles. This refinement greatly increases the scope of operations, and makes the production of accurate work a much easier matter than that entailed by the use of hand-operated tools. Such a lathe can be used successfully for light work in brass, gun-metal and steel.

Although good work of a light description can be turned out on a plain lathe, there is a limit to its use, for when heavy cuts have to be made, or work of a large diameter has to be turned, a back-geared lathe, which is usually provided with a gap in its bed, is essential.

The Back-geared Lathe differs from the plain lathe in having gearing incorporated in the fixed headstock to reduce the speed of the mandrel. This reduction in speed is a great advantage when the lathe is required for machining rough castings or other comparatively heavy work where a slow speed is

essential. The back-gear is adjustable so that it can be thrown out of action when the mandrel is required to be driven direct from the pulleys.

The Screw-cutting Lathe is the most useful kind of machine for all general purposes. It may be fitted with a back-gear, or it may not, but it certainly has the great advantage of being able to cut screw-threads and to impart a self-acting sliding motion to the tool in the slide-rest. These desirable results are obtained by means of a "lead"—or "guide" screw, as it is sometimes called —running along either in front of or within the bed of the machine, and operated by a suitable train of gear-wheels driven from the mandrel.

The rotation of the lead-screw, when it engages with a special nut on the saddle, upon which the slide-rest is mounted, causes the saddle to travel along the bed. This movement of the saddle can be varied in speed by manipulating various-sized gear-wheels driving the lead-screw. This alters the travel of the saddle in relation to the spindle, so that threads of any desired pitch may be cut upon the work. If the train of wheels is so proportioned to give a very slow action to the saddle, it follows that the lead-screw may be used for automatically traversing the tool for ordinary turning, or, in other words, the cutting-tool will be "self-acting."

Fig. 1 shows a useful type of small screw-cutting lathe, the various parts of which are shown clearly in the illustration.

The Foundation.—As the accuracy of the work depends almost entirely upon the accuracy of the machine— apart from any lack of skill on the part of the operator—it follows that the foundation or bed must be "dead" true. This high degree of precision is obtained in the main by accurately planing and scraping the working surfaces of the casting of which the bed consists, and enables the saddle to be moved along it without any play whatever. The inside edges of the channel or slot in the bed form a true guide for the tailstock when moved to any desired position.

Although the flat-section type of bed is not common to all lathes, it is a good type to have. Some makers of small lathes make their lathe-beds in the form of a round bar, but whatever the shape of bed may be, it must be dead true.

The Gap (shown clearly in the illustration), is one of those small details which makes all the difference in machine tools such as the lathe, as it greatly increases the capabilities of the machine by allowing short jobs of large diameter to be operated upon.

The Bed is usually supported either by a pair of short legs for bolting down to a bench, or a pair of standards forming an integral part of the lathe. In each case the foot-motor for supplying the necessary power is placed under the lathe.

The Fixed Headstock must be strong and rigid, for it carries the revolving spindle or mandrel, the driving-pulleys and the back-gear, if fitted. It is one of the most important parts of the lathe, and it may be a heavy iron casting fixed securely to the bed by means of a bolt or other locking device, or it may form part of the bed casting, as in the case of the lathe shown in the illustration.

The Tailstock—or poppet head, as it is sometimes termed—is also an iron casting, but capable of being moved to and fro along the lathe-bed to suit the length of the work. It is then screwed in position by a bolt passing underneath the bed. Its principal use is to carry

a hardened steel back centre, which is held in position by a tapered hole bored in the spindle. The spindle, which must be a perfect fit in the barrel and quite rigid when in use, can be adjusted backwards and forwards by means of a wheel or a handle operating a screw. A screwed locking-pin is provided for locking the spindle when it has been moved in or out to the desired position.

The Sliding-carriage which carries the slide-rest is known as the saddle. It is essential that this component move along the true surfaces of the bed without any play or rock, otherwise inaccurate work will result. The saddle is moved along the bed by either a guide-screw or by a rack-and-pinion-gear.

Fig. 2

The Slide-rest (shown in Fig. 2), consists of two main parts known as the cross- or bottom-slide and the top-slide. The former consists of a sliding member which can be moved to and fro across the width of the bed by a screw operated by a suitable handle. The cross-slide is usually provided with a number of ⊥-shaped slots running across it which serve a very useful purpose, for, when the top-slide is removed, it forms a convenient table upon which work can be bolted down. This is done by sliding the heads of the fixing-bolts into the slots. The top-slide is fastened down to the cross-slide, and carries the tool-post. Its normal move-

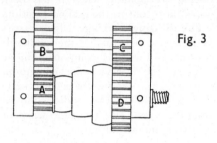

Fig. 3

ment is parallel to the length of the lathe-bed, but as taper-turning and boring is often required, it is usually made to swivel round to any angle. Movement to the top-slide is obtained by a screw operated by a handle.

The Tool-post is where the turning-tool is held, which, in the one illustrated, is fixed by means of two set-screws.

The Mandrel—or spindle, as it is sometimes called—is another important part of the lathe, for it must run perfectly true in its bearings, without any suspicion of shake. The spindle may be either solid or hollow—that is, with a hole bored right through. The hollow mandrel is a great advantage as it allows long pieces of rod to be inserted and held in a chuck. A three-step pulley is fixed to the spindle which revolves between the bearings in the fixed head-stock. The projecting part of the mandrel—professionally known as the "nose"—is bored out to form a tapered hole which holds the "live" or revolving centre. It is essential that the centre be truly placed or it will not run truly when the mandrel revolves. The nose is screwed externally to carry chucks

or other accessories it may be necessary to use.

In some lathes a driver-plate or catch-plate, consisting of a disc with a projecting pin, is screwed on the mandrel nose for driving work between centres, but in the lathe illustrated the same object is attained by a stud secured to a face-plate.

When large-diameter work is being turned or heavy cuts are being made, it is usual to reduce considerably the speed of the mandrel. This is accomplished in the best machines by a back-gear, a diagram of which appears in Fig. 3. It consists of a small pinion or toothed wheel, A, fixed to the belt-pulley, which meshes into a larger wheel, B, fixed to a spindle at the back of the headstock. This back-gear shaft carries at the other end another small pinion, c, which drives back on to a large-toothed wheel, D, keyed to the mandrel. The back

Fig. 4

pair of wheels are put in or out of gear by a back-gear handle. A locking device on the large pinion on the mandrel has also to be operated when the gear is changed.

The Train of Gearing, known as change-wheels, transmits motion from the spindle to the lead-screw. A full set of wheels—generally consisting of 22 wheels, ranging from 20 teeth to 120 teeth—is usually provided with the best kinds of lathes, but in the cheaper types a full set is not supplied. The wheels are fitted on an adjustable bracket or quadrant-plate, which is pivoted on the lead-screw. This plate carries a stud—or studs—to which the intermediate wheel or wheels of the screw-cutting gear are attached (as illustrated in Fig. 4).

It is sometimes required to cut a left-hand thread on a piece of work. To do this it is necessary to reverse the direction of rotation of the lead-screw. This is provided for by a slotted bracket projecting from the headstock. The bracket has an adjustable stud for carrying an extra pinion.

The Lead-screw.—The long screw which in some machines runs parallel to the front, and in others within the bed from one end to the other, is the leading-screw, sometimes termed guide-screw. Its purpose is—when in gear—to move the saddle along the bed, and so guide the tool along the work when cutting a thread. The screw, usually of steel, is provided with accurately-cut square threads, the pitch of which varies with the size of the lathe. Small lathes are usually fitted with lead-screws having four, eight or ten threads to the inch. In lathes provided with a lead-screw at the front, the saddle is put into motion or stopped by a handle which opens or closes a nut fixed to the saddle. The nut through which the lead-screw passes is split in two halves and obviously has a thread of the same pitch as the lead-screw. If the handle is operated when the lathe is geared and running, the nut closes and engages with the lead-screw, and the saddle travels along the bed, while an opposite motion imparted to the handle reverses the process by disengaging the nut, and so stops the traverse of the saddle.

The Rack.—To provide a convenient method for moving the saddle from one point of the bed to another, a tooth-rack or saddle-rack is sometimes fitted. The rack is fixed to the lathe-bed, and a small pinion carried on the saddle engages with the rack when the handle is operated, which causes the pinion to rotate and thus give motion to the saddle. This useful arrangement can only be used when the guide-screw is open, but when the lead-screw is in operation the handle rotates automatically. This "self-acting" arrangement is very useful when turning long pieces of work, for it not only enables the work to be performed in a uniform manner, but it also obviates the necessity of using the slide-rest screw.

The chief points to be observed when purchasing a lathe are as follows: For ordinary use it is not necessary to have a very heavy or expensive machine. A $3\frac{1}{2}$–$4\frac{1}{2}$-in. centre lathe should be large enough for all ordinary work of a small size. It should be of good design, robust and rigid, and provision made to enable the wearing parts to be easily adjusted. The lathe should be fitted with a gap, if possible.

Tools.—Although the use of an accurate lathe is essential for the production of high-class work, the proper use of correctly-shaped tools is almost, if not quite, as important.

A good turning-tool properly shaped and correctly applied to the work will cut easily into the metal, imparting an even and smooth finish. An incorrectly shaped tool, however, will give unsatisfactory results, and will tear the metal instead of cutting it, and at the same time will absorb a great deal more power in removing a given quantity of metal. The shape given to any particular tool is governed by the nature of the work it has to do, and the kind of metal to be operated upon. For example, a tool suitable for turning brass is quite unsuitable for turning steel.

The chief points associated with a good slide-rest tool are as follows:

1. The cutting-edge must be sharp enough to cut well and must be strong enough to stand the strain without fracture.
2. Sufficient "clearance" must be given underneath the tool to prevent it from rubbing the work.
3. It must have sufficient top relief to facilitate the removal of the cuttings from the tool.

By referring to the drawing (Fig. 5), which shows a tool for turning wrought iron and mild steel, it will be seen that the various angles have been represented by letters. A is the angle of clearance which has to be provided to prevent the tool rubbing the work; B is the cutting angle. This angle varies according to the metal being turned. For wrought iron, cast iron and mild steel an angle of

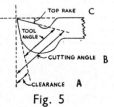

Fig. 5

about 58° is the usual practice, but if heavy cuts are to be taken in cast iron, the cutting angle is sometimes a little more obtuse, to give the necessary support to the point of the tool. c is the angle of "top rake," which slopes backwards from the front of the tool, forming an angle of about 28°. If the tool is used for cutting in one direction only, it is usual to provide side rake in addition, because such a cutting-edge cuts the metal much more easily and takes considerably less power.

Another important feature to be observed when using metal-turning tools is that those tools used in a horizontal position must have their cutting-points set level with the centre of the work to ensure the correct clearance and top rake.

Fig. 6 shows a series of drawings of a turning-tool in its right and wrong positions. A shows the tool correctly centred; B shows the tool set too high,

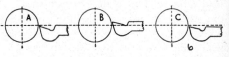

Fig. 6

with the obvious result that the work will simply rub against the metal; c— here the tool is wrongly placed as the cutting-edge is below the centre of the work. This is a very dangerous position, as the tool is liable to dig into the work and possibly ruin it. It is a mistake to elevate the tool by placing a piece of packing under the front of the body of the tool in order to raise its cutting-edge to the centre of the work. The result of this simply alters the angles of the tool in relation to the work, and causes the tool to rub the metal instead of cutting it. The effect of tilting the tool down results in having too much clearance and insufficient top rake.

From the above it follows that when it becomes necessary to raise the tool after it has become worn by constant regrinding, it is advisable to place a piece of flat metal underneath the whole of the body of the tool to keep it in its correct horizontal position.

A Set of Slide-rest Turning-tools, for general use with wrought iron and mild steel, consists of the following items, and is illustrated in Fig. 7. A front turning-tool, A, for turning work between centres and for cross-traversing cuts on work in a chuck or on a face-plate. A right-hand and a left-hand side cutting-tool, B, for coping with surfaces which cannot be reached with a front-tool. For facing the right and left sides of work, a right-hand and a left-hand knife-tool, shown at C, is necessary. These tools are used on such work as collars, making shoulders on shafts and for producing sharp corners. A parting-tool, D, is used for cutting channels, but little room available between the work and the face-plate. Proper clearance must be made under the cutting-point of the boring-tool, otherwise the tool will rub against the side of the hole. This precaution applies particu-larly to tools used for boring small-sized holes. This clearance is shown plainly at G.

V-thread Tools are used for forming internal and external V-shaped threads;

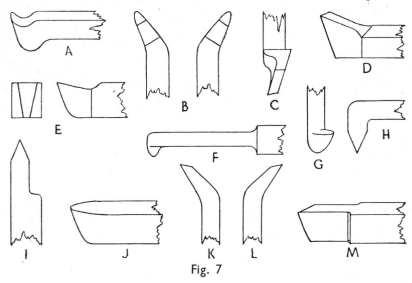

Fig. 7

and for cutting off the waste from work. Special attention must be paid to the clearance angles of this tool, for unless sufficient side clearance is provided, the tool is liable to stick in the work, which is likely to ruin both the work and the tool. These clearances are clearly shown at E.

An Ordinary Slide-rest Boring-tool, F, is used for turning internal sur-faces, such as cylinders, etc. This tool must have clearance at the cutting end to enable the tool to finish the cut to the end of the work. If this clearance is not provided, the tool will probably come in contact with the face-plate, or other device holding the work, should there be

such tools are illustrated at H and I respectively.

Tools for turning brass and gun-metal are different in shape to the fore-going and do not require top rake. A keen tool is not necessary for turning brass, for if the tool is too sharp it will tear the surface of the metal. To obtain a nice smooth finish on brass, a compara-tively blunt tool should be used. A front-tool suitable for brass is shown at J, while K and L represent a pair of side-tools. A parting-tool for brass is indicated at M.

The Slide-rest Tool-holder is illustrated in Fig. 8. This device, of which there are several types to be had, obviates the necessity of using several tools of the solid type previously described.

Small cutters of high speed or carbon steel can be obtained which fit into the head of the holder. The head of the tool-holder is designed to swivel round to any desired angle, and as the cutter is set at an angle it thus provides the necessary clearance and top rake.

As metal-turning demands a very high degree of accuracy—very often to within 1/1000th part of an inch—it follows that accurate measuring instruments are a necessity. A wooden rule suffices for measuring woodwork, where extreme accuracy is not required, but for metal-work of every description a metal rule should always be used. A 12-in. and a 6-in. steel rule, subdivided into eighths, sixteenths and sixty-fourths of an inch are handy sizes for general work.

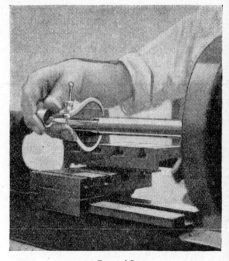

Fig. 10

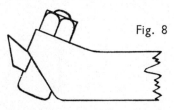

Fig. 8

For measuring external and internal diameters, several pairs of callipers should be included in every metal-turner's kit. A pair of callipers for measuring external diameters is shown at A in Fig. 9, and B illustrates a pair of callipers for ascertaining internal diameters. Another type of callipers, having odd-shaped legs—usually called "Moph" callipers (*see* Fig. 17)—is useful for marking centres on round material. For measuring the external

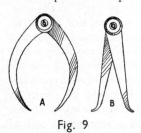

Fig. 9

diameters of screw-threads a pair of wide-pointed callipers is the correct tool to use. Vernier callipers and micrometer callipers are used when great accuracy is required. With these instruments it is an easy matter to take measurements as small as 1/1000th of an inch.

Measuring.—The best way of explaining how measurements are made with external callipers, is to give a typical example. Assume that it is required to measure the diameter of a circular metal bar, suspended between the centres of a lathe, as shown in Fig. 10. First open the legs of the callipers (A, Fig. 9) so that the distance between the points is a fraction of an inch larger than the diameter of the work. Now, with the callipers held loosely at the joint between the thumb and forefinger, gently tap the bottom leg on the work. This will cause the legs to close a trifle. Place the callipers squarely across the bar. If the points just lightly touch at the top and bottom of the work, that is, slide over it without any pressure whatsoever, you may assume that the operation has been properly done. If, however, the callipers close too much at the first trial, repeat the operation until the desired result is obtained. The next step is to read off the measurement with the aid of a rule. Place the point of one leg against the end of the rule and read off the measurement where the point of the other leg coincides with the figure on the rule. This is shown in Fig. 11.

The important point to be observed when using callipers is that the points must only touch the work lightly, otherwise inaccurate measurements will

Fig. 12

surface of the metal. Place a rule against a flat surface to keep one point of the tool level with the end of the rule, and read off the measurement, as illustrated in Fig. 13.

The Depth-gauge.—A simple tool which can be made quite easily is the depth-gauge shown in the accompanying sketch. (Fig. 14.) With this it is possible to measure depths of holes and recesses. It consists of a mild-steel stock

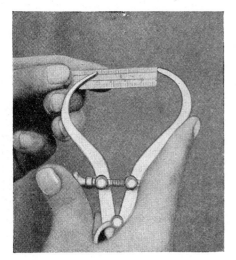

Fig. 11

result, owing to the natural spring of the tool. After some practice it is quite an easy matter to detect a difference in size as small as 1/1000th of an inch. Never use callipers on revolving work.

To Use Inside Callipers, proceed in the manner indicated in Fig. 12. Adjust the callipers by gently tapping the leg —not the point—as previously explained. Insert the callipers into the hole to be measured, keeping the bottom point stationary and rocking the upper leg to and fro. The measurement is correct when the top point just touches the

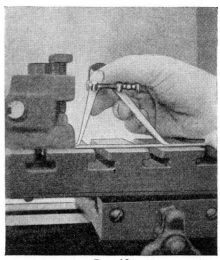

Fig. 13

8

drilled in the centre to take a $\frac{1}{8}$-in. spindle. The spindle is filed along its length to provide a narrow, flat surface. Another hole is made in the stock at right-angles to the spindle-hole in such a position that a portion of the hole passes through

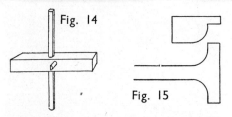

Fig. 14

Fig. 15

the spindle-hole. A small piece of steel of the same diameter is filed to produce a wedge-shaped surface which, when inserted into the aperture, locks the spindle.

Templates are useful yet simple devices used principally for gauging and testing the accuracy of curved work; two examples appear in Fig. 15. They can be made of thin sheet iron, or tinplate, or even of thin card, by first marking out the required shape and cutting to the marked lines, using either a pair of metal-shears or a pair of scissors, as the case may be.

Chucks.—We now come to the important subject of chucks and other devices for holding work in the lathe.

Although it is possible sometimes to do quite good work in the lathe with makeshift appliances ingeniously applied, it is far better to have the correct apparatus to hand when it is required, and so save a lot of valuable time.

As some chucks are expensive to buy, the best way to acquire them is to buy them separately, bearing in mind that the acquisition of good tools is a paying investment, and that they will give life-long service if properly treated and looked after.

The first indispensable item in the list is a driver-plate or catch-plate, used for driving such work as spindles, bars, etc.,

which are required to be turned between the centres of the lathe. Such a driver-plate is represented at A in Fig. 16. This accessory is sometimes supplied with the machine, and is quite a simple contrivance, consisting of nothing more than a flat plate fitted with a projecting stud which screws on to the mandrel nose. The stud engages with a "carrier" which is attached to the work to be driven.

An Independent-jaw Chuck is necessary for holding such work as heavy, irregular-shaped castings; an illustration of it appears at B. It should be large enough to take the largest work within the capabilities of the lathe. As its name suggests, the chuck is fitted with four jaws, each of which can be adjusted independently of the others, the adjustment being effected by turning

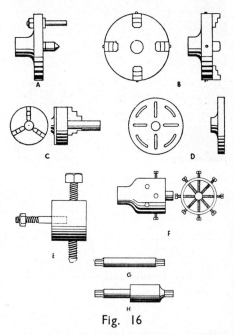

Fig. 16

the adjusting screws on the side of the chuck. This adjustment allows irregular-shaped work to be securely held in the jaws, and also allows holes to be bored in work where such holes are not central with the work. Reference to the drawing shows that the jaws are furnished with a series of steps which enable work of different diameters to be held. The jaws are also reversible to enable hollow work to be gripped from its internal surface.

Another type of chuck, with self-centering jaws, is shown at C. This form of chuck is usually provided with three jaws which all open or close at equal distances apart by the turn of a screw. This useful feature allows such work as rods, bars, small castings and drills to be held central. When acquiring a self-centering chuck it is advisable to choose one having two sets of jaws; one set for holding drills, rods, etc., and the other for holding castings and the like.

A Face-plate is a simple robust cast-iron plate having a dead true working surface with a series of slots and holes cast in it (as shown at D). The holes and slots enable bolts to be passed through them for fixing work to its surface.

" Dogs," furnished with adjustable screws, are obtainable or can be easily made. They are fixed to the face-plate and provide a good substitute for an independent jaw-chuck. These useful accessories are shown at E.

A Bell-chuck consists of a simple casting, usually having two sets of equally spaced set-screws fitted round the chuck (as shown at F). Such a chuck is useful for holding shafts, spindles and work of a similar nature.

A Plain Mandrel or "arbour," represented at G, is merely a round bar of metal used for mounting a piece of work for turning between centres which cannot be otherwise supported. This accessory consists of a bar of cast steel—although mild steel is often used with success—centred at the ends and turned to size. The two ends of the mandrel are usually turned to a smaller diameter

than that of the main portion, and are provided with a "flat" or a square to enable the working end of the screw of the carrier to secure a good grip. The centre portion upon which the work is mounted is turned slightly taper so that when it is driven on the work it forms a wedge and grips the work. A set of double mandrels (as illustrated at H) are useful appliances to have, and as they are quite simple to make, the craftsman should make a set for himself. Mandrels should be stored away in a box, and great care should be taken to see that they are not allowed to knock up against each other, otherwise their accuracy is likely to be seriously impaired. When fitting a mandrel into a piece of work, place the work face downwards on the open jaws of a vice and insert the mandrel after having applied a spot or two of oil to prevent binding. Place a piece of lead, brass or hardwood on the top end and drive the mandrel home, taking care not to force it too much.

Centering.—Before a bar of metal can be turned between the centres of a lathe, each end of the work must have accurately-centred and correctly-shaped centre-holes to suspend and to drive the work between the lathe centres. Before these holes are drilled, however, it is necessary to prepare the ends of the metal and correctly locate and mark out the positions where these holes are to be.

For the purpose of explaining these matters it is assumed that a piece of round material is required to be turned down to a certain size. The first thing to do, after having sawn off a piece of bar of the desired length, is to place it between the jaws of a vice and file the ends flat and square. Next, get a piece of chalk and rub it over the surfaces so prepared to enable the lines which are to be marked to be easily seen. Take a pair of odd-leg callipers, open the legs so that the distance between the points is just under half the diameter of the work. Place the point of the plain leg of the callipers in contact with the

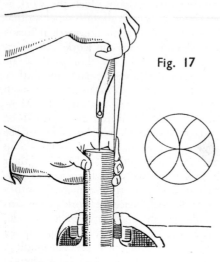

Fig. 17

Fig. 18

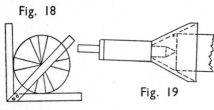

Fig. 19

edge of the material and scribe a mark near the centre of the chalked surface. Repeat this operation at four equidistant intervals round the circumference of the bar, as shown clearly in Fig. 17. Centre-pop the middle of the space made by the lines, using a centre-punch and hammer for the purpose. Remove the bar from the vice and repeat the process at the other end. Another way of centering a piece of round rod is by the use of a simple device known as a centering square (shown in Fig. 18). It consists of a metal square having a blade fixed on it so that one of its edges exactly divides the right-angle formed by the two sides of the square into two equal angles of 45°. To locate a centre,

all that is necessary is to place the square over the end of the work and draw a series of lines across the work as indicated in the drawing. The centre is obviously where the lines cut one another.

The Bell Centre-punch.—Another tool for automatically centering round metal rods is the bell centre-punch, illustrated in Fig. 19. The use of this simple device obviates the necessity of marking out the centres and thus saves a lot of time. The main point to be observed when using this tool is that the ends of the metal to be centred must be perfectly square. A glance at the drawing will show that this tool consists essentially of a cone-shaped holder the top of which is accurately bored to take a good-fitting centre-punch. To use the tool all that is required is to place the cup squarely over the work and give the punch a smart tap with a hammer.

Fig. 20 shows another method of centering round bars where a surface-gauge—or, as it is sometimes called, a scribing-block—is used in conjunction with a pair of V-blocks. When the ends of the work have been prepared as previously described, place the V-blocks on a perfectly flat surface such as

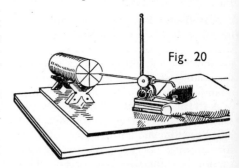

Fig. 20

the lathe-bed, or a piece of plate glass —which, it may be mentioned, comes in very handy for providing a flat surface for testing all kinds of metal-work— and lay the bar between the grooves in the blocks, as shown in the illustration. Set the point of the scriber of the surface-gauge approximately level with the centre of the work, and then mark a series of horizontal lines on each end of the bar, which should have been previously chalked. This is accomplished as follows. Hold the foot of the surface-gauge with the right hand and steady the work with the left, if necessary. Draw the tool along in such a direction that the point of the scriber marks the work. Next, revolve the bar a quarter of a turn and scribe another line and repeat this operation until a number of lines is produced as shown in the illustration. Centre-pop the work where these intersect.

Testing for Accuracy.—Suspend the work between the centres of the lathe using the centre-pops as centre holes, and spin the work round by the fingers. If the work wobbles, it is out of true. Hold a piece of chalk near the end of the bar in such a position that when the work is spun round, the side farthest from the centre will touch the chalk and thus mark the bar. Remove the work from the lathe, fix it end-up in the vice and draw over the defective centre-pop towards the chalk-mark. Replace in the lathe and repeat the operation until satisfactory results are obtained.

Having satisfied yourself that the centre-marks are as they should be, the next thing to do is to drill the centre-holes. These centre-holes are very important, for not only must they be shaped to correspond with the angle of the lathe centres—which is usually an angle of 60° in small lathes—but they must also be sufficiently deep to enable the points of the lathe centres to clear the work. To make these holes, place the work in the vice—end-up, of course—and with a $\frac{1}{16}$-in. drill make a hole about $\frac{3}{16}$ in. deep. This

hole will be deep enough for the lathe centre to clear the bottom. Now, with a larger drill having an angle of 60°, countersink the hole as shown in Fig. 21, which completes the job.

The Slocombe Drill.—The Slocombe drill is a drill and countersink combined. When buying one of these drills do not forget to mention the angle of the countersink, which must, as already stated, correspond with the angle of the lathe-centres.

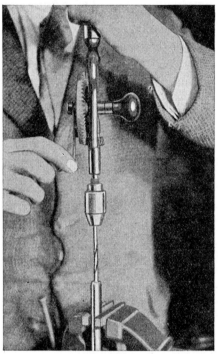

Fig. 21

The usual method of applying the centering drill is by fixing the drill into a small chuck held in the back headstock spindle. The drill is then fed up to the work in a self-centering chuck. An alternative method is to place the work against the back centre and feed it up to the revolving drill held in a self-centering chuck.

These two simple methods will

no doubt meet the general requirements for ordinary work done on small lathes.

Plain Turning.—The next step in lathe work brings us to the actual process of plain turning, and in order to describe the methods involved, step by step, in a simple manner, a typical example of such work will be given.

For this example it will be assumed that a mild-steel shaft, as shown by the dotted outline at A in Fig 22, is required for a certain piece of mechanism. The finished size of the job is to be 5 in. long; its largest diameter $\frac{7}{8}$ in., and its smaller one $\frac{5}{8}$ in.

Cut a piece of mild steel 7 in. long

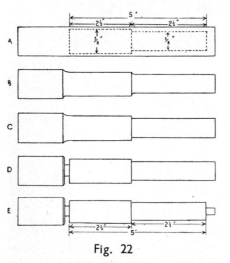

Fig. 22

from a piece of 1-in. diameter circular bar. The additional length included will give sufficient metal at each end over the finished size for the purpose of fitting the carrier, etc., and allow the slide-rest to be operated in a convenient manner. File the ends perfectly square, drill the centre-holes as previously explained, and fix a suitable carrier over one end. Fix the work between the centres of the lathe after

having put a spot of oil in the centre-hole where it is to revolve on the fixed centre. Test the work to see that it revolves easily and without any rock when turned with the fingers. Fix a suitable front turning-tool in the tool-post of the slide-rest, taking care to see that it is at the correct height. Start up the lathe so that it revolves in the right direction, that is, of course, towards the operator. Adjust the handle of the bottom slide so that the tool will make a cut deep enough to reduce the diameter of the work to about $\frac{1}{32}$ in. or so larger than the finished size is to be. The small amount left on will allow a light cut to be taken for finishing. Now turn the top-slide handle and traverse the tool along the length of the work until within a little under an inch of the end. Withdraw the tool a trifle by turning the bottom-slide handle whilst the work is still revolving. Make sure you turn this the right way. Bring the tool back to its original position and stop the lathe. With a rule set along the work, mark the position of the shoulder. Light centre-punch marks will come in handy for this. Start the lathe again and take another cut along the work until the centre-pop mark, indicating the position of the shoulder, is reached; withdraw the tool and repeat the operation until this part is about $\frac{1}{32}$ in. oversize. The work will now appear as in the illustration at B, and is known as "roughing out."

The finishing cuts may now be taken. If you have not a separate tool for this, see that the one being used is in perfect order. Start with the large diameter part by taking a light cut, and reduce its diameter to its exact finished size, namely, $\frac{7}{8}$ in. diameter.

Lubricating the Cutting-edge.—To obtain a good finish on mild steel it is necessary to lubricate well the cutting-edge of the tool with soap and water

It is also wise to lubricate the tool during the roughing-out process.

Having completed the main portion of the work, remove the front turning-tool from the tool-post and fix a knife-tool in its place to remove the surplus metal left in the shoulder. The work at this stage is shown at C.

Using the Parting-tool.—Measure the exact distance between the shoulder and the ends, which in this case is 2½ in. The position marked at the carrier end of the work gives the position where the right-hand cutting-edge of the parting-tool enters the metal for parting off.

Set the tool squarely in the post and take a cut (D), but do not make this too deep at present as the opposite end must now receive attention.

Take the parting-tool out and substitute the knife-tool again and face the right-hand end to size, taking care to leave a small portion round the centre-hole, as illustrated at E, as the work is not yet complete. With the parting-tool carefully set in position complete the cut previously started at the carrier end until there is just sufficient metal left to support the work. Now, with the work still revolving, just touch the edges of the shoulder and the ends of the spindle with a fine file to remove the sharp edges. This last operation should be done where all sharp edges are concerned, for it often prevents the fingers from being cut. Polish the work with a piece of very fine emery-cloth and oil. Take the work out of the lathe and remove the unwanted portions, with a hacksaw, finally smoothing down the rough surfaces left by the saw with a file.

In some jobs it is good practice to leave the centre-holes in the work so that it can be suspended between centres at any future time. This would apply, for example, in the case of an exhaust valve for a gas engine, which sometimes requires re-turning on the valve face.

Occasionally it may be necessary to use a file upon the revolving work to impart a good finish, in which case a sheet of paper spread under the work will prevent the filings from penetrating the various parts of the machine.

When turning a shaft or spindle to fit a hole, turn the work down to about 1/1000-in. oversize, and complete to the exact size with a fine-toothed file, finishing the surface with fine emery-cloth and oil.

The Steady.—When a long thin bar or spindle is to be turned, a "steady" or stay should be used to keep the work from bending and "whipping" when under the pressure of the cutting-tool. Failure to take this precaution will almost certainly lead to inaccurate turning, even if the work remains upon the lathe-centres. Such a steady can usually be obtained from the makers of the lathe. A common type of fixed stay consists of a casting, the foot of which is bolted down to the lathe bed. The top half of the upper portion of the stay is made to open to take the work, and has three sliding pieces which can be adjusted by means of the bolts to suit various sizes of shafts.

This type of steady is only used when the slide-rest is used for turning a short length of a long piece of work. When the whole length of the shaft is to be turned, a travelling steady fixed to the saddle is used. With this type of steady the work is supported rigidly, following the tool, which not only enables the self-acting motion to be used, but also allows comparatively deep cuts to be made. Care must be exercised in fitting a steady, and the bearing surfaces between the steady and the revolving work must be well lubricated.

Turning Tapered Work.—The two simplest ways are either to set the tail-stock over, or to use the compound slide-rest. In the former method the dead centre A and the live centre B are thrown out of line, as shown in Fig. 23. The amount by which the back centre is moved across the lathe is determined by the amount of taper required. To quote an example, suppose it is required to turn a bar 12 in. long by 2 in. diameter at the large end and 1 in. diameter at the other. Now the total taper is 1 in. to the foot, therefore it will be necessary to set over the tailstock $\frac{1}{2}$ in. because the taper on one side of the work is only $\frac{1}{2}$ in. This method of taper turning is limited in practice to work where only a small degree of taper is desired, as it will be readily understood that neither of the centres really fit the centre-holes.

If a large degree of taper is wanted, the compound slide-rest must be brought into operation. The top-slide carrying the tool-post is swivelled round to the proper angle to produce the desired taper, which means that the slope of the front of the top-slide in relation to the

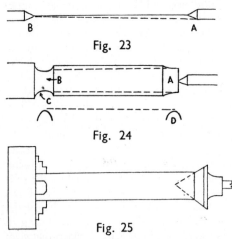

Fig. 23

Fig. 24

Fig. 25

axis of the work should exactly correspond with the required taper. Fig. 24 shows how this method of setting the slide-rest is applied. For the purpose of illustration, suppose it is desired to taper turn a piece of metal from 1 in. at A to

$\frac{3}{4}$ in. at B. First turn the end at B down to $\frac{3}{4}$ in. diameter, and also turn the work at A to 1 in. Next, swing the top-slide round to approximately what seems to be the correct angle. Bring the point

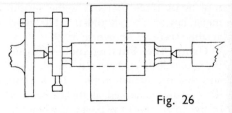

Fig. 26

of the tool opposite A and measure a distance of, say, $\frac{1}{2}$ in. from the surface of the work to the point of the tool D. Move the tool along by turning the handle until the point of the tool is opposite C. If these distances so measured are both equal, then it follows that the angle of the top-slide is correct. One of the most important points to be observed when turning tapers is to see that the cutting-edge of the tool is set exactly level with the lathe centres.

Turning Hollow Objects.—Fig. 25 shows a common method of supporting hollow objects for turning. The tube is fixed in a jaw chuck and the other end is supported by a large cone-shaped centre. The cone revolves on a centre-pin which fits into the tapered hole in the loose headstock barrel. When such a centre is not available, the difficulty may be got over by inserting a piece of hard wood to fit tightly in the end of the work and centering it in the usual way.

Fig. 26 shows how a pulley-wheel casting is turned between centres. Here, the centre-hole of the wheel would first be bored and then it would be mounted upon a short mandrel. The work is driven by the catch-pin of the driver plate, catching against the carrier in the usual manner. The use of mandrels for turning work between centres is not limited to circular objects, for in a great many cases it is convenient to turn irregular-shaped objects in this manner. When this is resorted to, be careful to see that a weight is fixed on the driver-plate to counteract the weight of the work, which may be out of balance. If this precaution is not carried out it may cause the work and tool to chatter.

Although a great number of turning jobs can be successfully carried out by either suspending the work directly between the lathe centres or by mounting the work on mandrels, there are numerous jobs which cannot be conveniently turned by these methods. For turning short work and such work as boring and drilling in the lathe, chucks and face-plates are used. As to what type of chuck or whether a face-

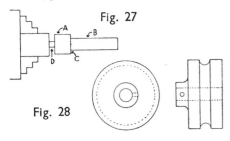

Fig. 27

Fig. 28

plate is used naturally depends upon the shape of the work and the operation to be performed on it.

A typical example of the use of a self-centring chuck, where a piece of round mild steel is to be formed into a special bolt, for a certain purpose, is shown diagrammatically in Fig. 27. The overall length of the bolt is to be $1\frac{1}{2}$ in.; the diameter of the head is to be $\frac{7}{16}$ in. and its length $\frac{3}{8}$ in.; the shank $\frac{1}{4}$ in. diameter and $1\frac{1}{8}$ in. in length, and threaded with a $\frac{1}{4}$-in. Whitworth thread.

If the lathe has a fixed headstock, fitted with a hollow mandrel, a convenient length of $\frac{1}{2}$-in. bar can be inserted into the tube, allowing 2 in. of the metal to project beyond the jaws of the chuck. If, however, the lathe is not so fitted, then a piece of the rod, about 3 in. long,

8*

should be cut off the bar, the extra length being necessary for holding-purposes.

The subsequent operations are then carried out in the following way: first, turn the head—which is the largest diameter—to size, as shown at A. Then follow with the shank, as at B. Next, form the shoulder C, finally parting off the pin, as shown at D. The screw-thread is then cut in the shank with a suitable hand-operated die, or, if the thread is to be cut in the lathe, the screw-cutting operation would be done before using the parting-off tool.

Turning a Small Grooved Pulley. —The following is the order of operations, as illustrated in Fig. 28.

A piece of solid mild-steel bar is inserted between the jaws of a self-centring chuck, and the largest diameter forming the top of the pulley is roughed out first. This is followed by roughing out the boss. The next process consists in drilling the hole for the shaft, and, when this is completed, the groove is roughly turned to shape. The work is then parted off and mounted upon a mandrel in order to take a light finishing cut all over. The job is complete when it has been polished with emery-cloth and oil, and a hole drilled and tapped in the boss to receive a fixing-screw.

Turning Irregular-shaped Objects where the use of a self-centring chuck is impracticable:

Fig. 29 shows an irregular-shaped piece of work in the form of a flange and guide inserted between the jaws of an independent-jaw chuck. It may here be stated that a certain amount of skill and practice is required in setting work of this description squarely and centrally in position before any operation upon it can be successfully carried out. When the work has been roughly set in position, start up the lathe, and if the work is out of centre, it will wobble when rotated. Hold a piece of chalk close to the work as it revolves, and where the work is marked, it indicates

Fig. 29

that part of the work which is set too high, or out of centre. Correct this error by adjusting the jaws and, if necessary, repeat the process until the work is revolving centrally and squarely.

Sometimes it is necessary to hold a piece of work exactly true in a chuck or on a face-plate, as, for instance, when a hole has to be bored out to a marked line. In such cases a scribing-block placed on the lathe-bed, and used in the manner indicated in Fig. 30A, is a convenient method of testing the accuracy of the chucking or mounting. As an alterna-

Fig. 30 A

tive, a scriber can be fitted in the top slide of the slide-rest and the work adjusted so that the scriber just touches the line all round, as shown in Fig. 30B.

The usual way of fixing work to a face-plate is by the use of metal clamps bolted through the slots or holes in the plate. Fig. 31 shows a piece of work set up on the face-plate ready for boring. It will be observed that one end of each clamp rests upon the work while the opposite ends are supported by hardwood blocks or packing-pieces.

Fig. 30 B

To set up a job of this description, place a washer on each bolt and pass the shanks through the slots from the back of the plate. Slip the clamps over the bolts and twist on the nuts for a few threads down to prevent them from sliding out of the slots. Now place the work as centrally as possible on the plate, and if the plate happens to be one with a series of concentric rings marked upon its surface, so much the better, for these lines will enable you to gauge the centre. The next step is to place the hardwood blocks in position and to tighten up the nuts. As this operation may prove awkward without the use of three hands, the difficulty may be overcome by using the back headstock as a support to the work. Slide the back headstock along the bed and fix it in a position near the work. Place a flat piece of wood across the work and feed up the back centre to the work, and lock the spindle. This will enable both hands to be used for placing the blocks in position and tightening up the nuts. If the work does not run centrally, relieve the pressure on the clamps by slackening off the nuts a trifle. Give the "high" part a light tap with a hammer, not forgetting to place a piece of wood between the work and the hammer when doing this. If this is done it generally has the desired effect.

The Angle-plate.—Fig. 32 shows this device. It is used in conjunction with the face-plate where the shape of the job precludes it from being

Fig. 31

conveniently fixed in a jaw-chuck or direct on to the face-plate.

On referring to the illustration it will be seen that slots are provided on each surface similar to those on the face-plate. These are needed to enable fixing bolts to be passed through them for attaching the work to the angle-plate and the angle-plate to the face-plate.

The method adopted for mounting a job on an angle-plate is shown clearly in Fig. 33. When using an angle-plate, a

counterweight should always be fixed on to the face-plate in such a position as to counterbalance both the work and the angle-plate. The reason for this has

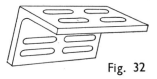

Fig. 32

already been explained. Always run the lathe at slow speed when using an angle-plate.

The capabilities of a lathe are almost unlimited, for not only is it possible to turn all manner of external surfaces accurately and true to size, but it can be used to equally good advantage for drilling and boring.

Drilling consists in making a hole of a desired diameter in a piece of metal in one operation by the use of a drill, and is confined to work where holes of small diameter are required. The process of boring—or internal turning—is really the operation of enlarging holes already provided in the work and is generally accomplished by the application of a boring-tool.

As the process of drilling consists in the removal of a comparatively large

Fig. 33

Fig. 34

quantity of metal at one operation and consequently absorbs a large amount of power, its application is limited in small lathes to the making of holes up to about ¾ in. diameter. On the other hand, boring being a process where the hole is gradually increased in size and therefore only a small amount of metal is removed at a time, holes can easily be made which are only limited in size by the size of the work operated upon.

There are numerous methods of drilling holes by the use of a lathe and Fig. 34 shows a method commonly used. An ordinary twist drill is held in a self-centering chuck and the work is fed up against the drill by means of the back centre, as will be seen from the detailed illustration. The work is placed against a drilling-plate, which is nothing more than a simple circular plate with a tapered shank at the back to fit the barrel of the loose headstock. A hole made in the centre of the plate allows the drill point to clear when it comes through the work. To drill a hole by this method, all that is necessary is first to make a deep centre-pop on the work where the hole is required—this operation should always be done where drilling is concerned. Fix a suitable-sized drill in the chuck, remove the back centre and fit the drilling-plate in its place. Move the loose headstock to a

convenient position along the bed, not forgetting to fix it. Place the work flat against the plate, holding it in place with the left hand, and feed the work up to the drill with the right, taking care to see that the point of the drill corresponds with the centre-mark in the work. Start the lathe and gradually feed the work forward until the drill has cut its way through the metal.

The utility of a plain drill-plate will be greatly improved if it is provided with three screw-holes in its surface to enable a block of flat hardwood to be fastened to its surface. This will allow small pieces of work to be fixed to the surface of the wood, which would otherwise be difficult to hold with the hand. The wooden fixture is also very handy when drilling thin metal, as it prevents the work from bending when under the influence of the tool.

Fig. 35

A hole may be drilled through a round rod by the same process as that mentioned above, but instead of having a flat piece of hardwood to support the work, a V-shaped slot should be cut across the surface to suit the diameter of the work.

A handy method of drilling holes in jobs held in a face-plate or chuck is shown in Fig. 35. Here, the drill used, which must be one of those having a centre-hole at the end of its shank, is fixed in an ordinary lathe-carrier, which is held in the hand to prevent it from turning round, and fed up to the work. The drill must, of course, be firmly pressed against the back centre whilst drilling is in progress.

Fig. 36 illustrates a drill held rigidly in a small, adjustable chuck which fits into the back centre hole of the tailstock spindle.

For Enlarging Holes already made in a piece of work or for enlarging "cored" holes in a casting, the two methods generally used, employing flat drills, are shown in the illustration (Fig. 37). That shown at A represents the method adopted for using the drill in the slide-rest, and B that where the drill is fed by means of the back centre.

When a cored hole is to be operated upon, the following points must be carefully observed. Where the method shown at A is adopted, the tool must be rigidly fixed in the tool-post of the slide-rest. The drill must also be fixed in a central position and at the correct height corresponding to the height of the lathe-centre, otherwise the tool will follow the course of the cored hole, which is usually out of truth. When all these conditions have been satisfied, the drill can be gently fed up to the work by the feed-screw of the top-slide.

The alternative way of using a flat drill for enlarging holes is shown in Fig. 37 at B. On referring to the illustration, it will be seen that instead of the drill

being rigidly held in the slide-rest, it passes through a slotted bar, as represented at x, which is held in position in the top slide of the slide-rest. The back end of the drill has a centre-hole to enable the tool to be placed against the back centre and fed up to the work. To keep the drill steady, a piece of flat iron in the shape of a hook is used at the back end.

To operate the drill, the back holder is pressed downwards either by the left

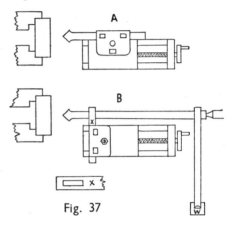

Fig. 37

hand or by means of a weight (w), suspended from the end, while the back centre is fed up to the work by using the right hand.

Boring is one of the most important processes applicable to metal-turning, and as so many jobs have to be bored, some general information on the subject will no doubt be useful.

There are two common methods used in the process of boring, the first—which is the one usually adopted for general work—where the cutting-tool is stationary and operates upon the revolving work held in a chuck or face-plate; the second, where the work is stationary and is operated upon by a revolving cutter, applicable to lathes fitted with a self-acting saddle.

Fig. 36

Fig. 38 shows a piece of work

mounted upon a face-plate, with an ordinary slide-rest boring-tool fixed in position ready for boring.

In preparing such a piece of work preparatory to the actual process of boring, there are one or two points to be carefully observed. The boring-tool must be of the correct shape to suit the metal to be turned, and it must also have sufficient clearance to enable the end to clear the work at the end of the cut, should there not be sufficient space behind the job being operated on to allow for this. The tool must also have proper under-clearance, otherwise the tool will rub against the work. When mounting the work in either a chuck or a face-plate, see that it is placed centrally as already explained, and furthermore, if it is possible to keep the work clear of the flat surface of the holding-device, so much the better, for this will allow the point of the tool to clear at the end of the work. Sometimes it is possible to interpose packing-pieces between the end of the work and the face-plate, as shown in Fig. 39.

Fig. 38

Having fixed a suitable boring-tool at its correct position and height in the slide-rest—which, of course, is parallel to the lathe-bed—the tool can either be fed through the work by hand, by using the top-slide, or by the self-acting feed, if the lathe is so provided. Start up the lathe and, if the work be a casting, take a fairly heavy roughing-cut to enable the cutting edge of the tool to get right under the "skin" of the metal, otherwise the point of the tool will almost certainly get ruined owing to the grinding action of particles of sand on the surface of the casting. When the tool has reached the bottom of the hole, withdraw the tool and stop the lathe. If the operation has been properly done, the hole should be found perfectly true and parallel when tested with a pair of inside callipers. If the hole is found to be tapered either way, the slide-rest, if this is being used, must be set over a trifle in one direction or the other as the case may be. Now take a light cut, and, if the hole is found to be parallel, a further light finishing cut may be taken to complete the job.

Here a word of warning may be opportune. If the work being bored is of a light nature, it may be necessary to slack off the jaws of the chuck, or the clamps, where a face-plate is used, before taking the finishing cut. This will relieve the pressure on the work and allow the work to resume its normal shape, which may have become a little distorted due to the gripping pressure of the holding device.

The Boring Steady is illustrated in Fig. 40. It is used in conjunction with a jaw-chuck for supporting the ends of tubes, pipes, or work of a similar nature where the ends are required to be bored or threaded. The device can be made of two pieces of flat hardwood, 1 in. thick, fixed at right-angles to each other by means of substantial angle-brackets, as shown.

The upright piece is bored out to fit the outside diameter of the work, and the steady is held in position across the lathe-bed by means of a bolt running through the base, between the bed, and a clamping-plate underneath.

Fig. 41 shows a method of boring work in a self-acting lathe by means of a boring bar carrying a cutter, driven between the lathe-centres. Here it will be seen that the work is bolted down to the saddle after the removal of the slide-rest. This method of boring is adopted when the job is too awkward in shape or too heavy to be properly held in a chuck or face-plate.

The first thing to do when this method

Fig. 39

of boring is used, is to mark out accurately the position and the finished size of the hole at each end of the work. This can be easily done if pieces of flat wood are inserted at each end of the work to obtain a flat surface. With a pair of compasses mark on the work a circle of the exact diameter the finished hole is to be, and make a series of centre-pop marks on this circle. Now bolt down the work in position on the saddle, leaving the fastening nuts slack. Pass the boring-bar through the work and suspend it between centres. Next, fix a

scriber in the cutter hole of the bar by means of a wooden wedge, in such a position that when the bar is revolved by hand the point of the scriber describes a circle of the same diameter as that marked on the work. Adjust the work until the scriber-point just touches the circle

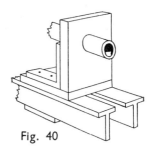

Fig. 40

on the work at every point on each end. When this is accomplished, the nuts of the holding bolts may be finally tightened up.

The Cutter.—In Fig. 42 at A is shown a common form used in a boring-bar. It consists of a small piece of round tool steel which fits into a hole in the bar and is kept in position by a small set-screw. This type of cutter is used for boring comparatively small holes. For boring holes of large diameter, the boring-bar is sometimes fitted with a boring-block, which is indicated at B in the illustration. This device has the advantage that it enables the tool to be well supported. It consists of a collar keyed to the bar, and the cutter

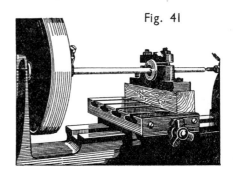

Fig. 41

is held in the collar by a set-screw as indicated in the sketch.

Another form of tool for special use with a boring-bar is a double-ended cutter, made of cast steel, suitably hardened and tempered. As this type of cutter cannot be adjusted, it follows that it will only cut a hole of the same diameter as that of the cutter. Such a tool produces excellent holes, but is rather

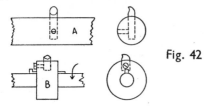

Fig. 42

difficult to make, and therefore generally outside the scope of the amateur.

As modern lathes are nearly all equipped with suitable apparatus for cutting screws, the arrangements of this extremely important process and the tools necessary for carrying out the work will now be examined.

Screw-cutting.—Many amateur craftsmen are deterred from "trying their hand" at screw-cutting for no other reason than that they are under the impression that screw-cutting is an extremely difficult and mysterious operation and calls for a vast number of mathematical calculations. This is quite an erroneous idea, for screw-cutting demands very little more skill than ordinary turning and boring, and once the principles involved are grasped and a little practice obtained, screw-cutting becomes both a fascinating and interesting operation.

To cut a screw in a lathe some arrangement must be adopted to move the tool along the bed at a perfectly uniform rate. This is obtained by means of a lead-screw and a system of change-wheels which are fitted to the lathe-spindle and the lead-screw. As

stated elsewhere, the saddle has a split nut, which, when closed, engages with the threads of the lead-screw, and when revolved causes the saddle to move along the lathe-bed at a definite speed in relation to the spindle.

The lead-screws of some lathes are provided with threads having a pitch of $\frac{1}{4}$ in., or what is the same thing, four threads to the inch. Now, it follows that when the split nut is engaged with the lead-screw and the lead-screw makes one revolution, the saddle will travel along the bed a distance equal to the pitch of the lead-screw. If a bar of metal is suspended between centres and a fine tool inserted in the tool-holder so that it just touches the work, and the gearing so arranged as to cause the lathe spindle to revolve at the same speed as the lead-screw, then the tool will trace a spiral of exactly $\frac{1}{4}$-in. pitch on the work. It will thus be seen that if the work is revolved at the same speed as that of the lead-screw a thread will be made equal in pitch to that of the lead-screw. Now suppose that the work makes two revolutions to one of the lead-screw, then the saddle will move only $\frac{1}{8}$ in. during one revolution, and the tool will trace eight spirals of $\frac{1}{8}$-in. pitch in the length of one inch.

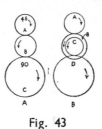

Fig. 43

Such variations of speed between the lead-screw and the lathe spindle are obtained by means of a train of toothed gear-wheels.

From the above it is easy to see that a train of gear-wheels driving the lead-screw will result in a screw of a definite pitch. The diagram at A in Fig. 43 shows a simple train of wheels set up for cutting a right-handed thread. Here,

A represents the mandrel wheel which gears into an intermediate wheel (B), which in turn transmits motion to the lead-screw wheel (C). In this particular instance, suppose a screw having eight threads to the inch is required. As the lead-screw is assumed to have four, it follows that the work must revolve twice as fast as the lead-screw and produce a thread on the work of the desired pitch. To obtain this ratio of speed, a 45-tooth wheel is shown driving a 90-tooth wheel through an intermediate wheel, which may have any convenient number of teeth, as it is simply used to transmit motion from A to C.

The rule for calculating the size of the change wheels to cut threads of different pitches is as follows:

$$\frac{\text{Pitch of lead-screw} = \text{PL}}{\text{Pitch of screw to be cut} = \text{PS}}$$

$$= \frac{\text{Wheel on mandrel (driver)} = \text{WM}}{\text{Wheel on lead-screw (driven)} = \text{WL}}$$

The following example will make this clear:

What change wheels are necessary to cut a screw having eight threads per inch, assuming that the lead-screw has a pitch of $\frac{1}{4}$ in.?

Here
$$\frac{\text{PL}}{\text{PS}} = \frac{\text{WM}}{\text{WL}}$$

substituting values we have:

$$\frac{\frac{1}{4}}{\frac{1}{8}} = \frac{\text{WM}}{\text{WL}} = \frac{4}{8} = \frac{1}{2}$$

Therefore any two wheels having the proportion of 1 : 2 will answer the purpose. Thus a 20-tooth wheel on the mandrel and 40-tooth wheel on the lead-screw would do, or a 30 and 60 and so on.

These wheels would be geared together by inserting an intermediate wheel of any size to fit conveniently.

Here is another example. A screw-thread having nine threads per inch has to be cut in the same lathe, what change wheels are necessary?

Here the proportion is $\frac{4}{9}$ so that a 40 and a 90 will serve, as also will a 20 and 45, as these wheels are in the same ratio.

Suppose the same thread is cut in a lathe having a lead-screw of $\frac{1}{2}$-in. pitch, then the ratio would be $\frac{2}{9}$, so that a 20 and a 90 would suffice.

It frequently happens that a simple train of wheels such as those mentioned above cannot be used owing to not having the necessary sized wheels available. In such a case a compound train of wheels would be used. This contingency usually arises when it is desired to cut threads of fine pitch. For instance, if a thread of 35 threads per inch is required, and the lead-screw has four threads per inch, the proportion is 4 : 35. As the smallest change wheel has only 20 teeth and the largest 120, it follows that to use a simple train would involve using a wheel of 20 teeth on the mandrel and one with 175 teeth on the lead-screw.

An arrangement of a compound train of gear-wheels is shown in diagram B, Fig. 43. The wheel A is attached to the mandrel, wheels B and C are keyed together and mounted on a stud on the bracket, wheel B being geared with A, whilst wheel C is in mesh with D on the end of the lead-screw. Wheel A is known as the first driver, wheel B, the first driven wheel; wheel C the second driver and wheel D the second driven wheel.

The following examples show how to select change wheels when it is necessary to use a compound train.

Calculate a set of change wheels to cut a screw of 35 threads per inch, with a lead-screw having four threads per inch.

Here the ratio is worked out in the same manner as that used for a simple train.

The ratio, in this case, will be:

$$\frac{\frac{1}{35}}{\frac{1}{4}} = \frac{4}{35} = 4 : 35$$

Both the numerator and denominator of this ratio can be multiplied by any number without altering the ratio. As the two smallest in the set is 20 and 25, it is no use to have a numerator less than 500. Multiply both the numerator of the fraction 4/35 by 200; thus $\frac{4}{35} \times \frac{200}{200}$

This will give $\frac{800}{7000}$ Now split the numerator and denominator into factors, as follows:

$$\frac{800}{7000} = \frac{20 \times 40}{70 \times 100}$$

Thus, a set of wheels having 20 teeth and 40 teeth as drivers, and 70 teeth and 100 teeth as the driven wheels would be a perfectly satisfactory combination to use because these sized wheels are usually available.

These wheels would be set up in the following way. The 20 wheel would be fixed to the spindle driving the 70 on the stud; the 40-toothed wheel would be keyed to the 70 on the stud to drive the 100 wheel on the lead-screw.

If both the numerator and denominator in the above example had been multiplied by 300 instead of 200, the resulting combination of wheels would have been as follows:

$$\frac{4}{35} \times \frac{300}{300} = \frac{1200}{10500}$$

This fraction split into factors is $\frac{30 \times 40}{100 \times 105}$ which would suffice equally as well.

Here is another example. What sized change wheels are required to cut a thread 7/24-in. pitch if the lead-screw is $\frac{1}{2}$ in.?

The ratio $= \dfrac{\frac{7}{24}}{\frac{1}{2}} = \dfrac{7}{12}$

In this case it will be observed at once that a simple train consisting of a 70 wheel on the spindle and a wheel of 120 teeth on the lead-screw would answer the purpose.

Note carefully when fixing up a train of gear-wheels to see that the tops of the teeth on one wheel do not foul the bottoms of the wheel it is in mesh with. Failure to observe this precaution may result in broken teeth. Another point to observe is that it is good practice always to arrange a train of wheels with wheels as large as possible, and where it is necessary to use wheels of small diameter they should be fitted as near to the source of power as possible, that is, the spindle.

Cutting a Screw Thread.—The actual operation is not a very difficult job, but a certain amount of care is required.

When the necessary train of screw-cutting change wheels has been set up,

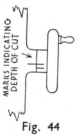

Fig. 44

mount the work between centres and fix a suitable tool in the slide-rest. Start up the lathe and give sufficient inward feed to the tool to give a light cut. A heavy cut should not be attempted as there is danger of breaking the somewhat fragile tool. Note the amount of cut given by marking the shoulder of the cross-slide handle, using a piece of chalk for the purpose, as shown in the illustration (Fig. 44). This will serve as a guide for judging the depth when making succeeding cuts. Next, engage the split nut and take a trial cut along the work; withdraw the tool and disengage the nut from the lead-screw and run the saddle back to its original position. Feed the tool forward to give the same depth of cut as the previous one—providing, of course, that it is satisfactory—using the chalk-mark as a guide, and mark the new position on the feed handle as before. Repeat the operations until the threads are cut to the correct depth.

If the lathe is of a modern type which is usually provided with graduated scales on the slide-rest handles, it is obviously unnecessary to chalk-mark the position for the depth of cut.

Before going any further it is necessary here to point out that the tool must, of course, always follow the same path at each successive cut, that is to say, the tool must always follow in the thread at every cut. If this is not so, the point of the tool would not be opposite the bottom of that part of the thread already cut, with the obvious result that the partially made thread would be ruined. Caution, however, need only be observed where threads are being cut which are not an exact multiple of the threads on the lead-screw, for the tool will always follow the thread when the threads being cut are an exact multiple of the leading-screw threads.

When the threads per inch to be cut on the work are not an exact multiple of the threads per inch of the lead-screw, after the first cut, the clasp-nut must only be engaged at certain instants.

To enable the tool to follow the thread at the proper time when cutting such a thread it is a good plan to bring the saddle right back so that it touches the back headstock, or, if this is impracticable, to bring the saddle back to a line marked across the lathe bed. It is also necessary to make a chalk-mark on the top of the lead-screw, or, better still, the gear wheel attached to it, and a similar chalk-mark on either the holding device or the first driving wheel on the mandrel spindle. After the first traverse, the clasp-nut should be released and the saddle moved back to the back head-stock (or other marked position), and then when the two chalk-marks come into their original position, the clasp-nut may be closed and the next cut made.

Multiple-thread Screws are generally used to replace a single thread of coarse pitch where the bottom diameter is too shallow for practical purposes. The depth of the threads of double-thread screws is only one-half that of single threads, while that of triple-thread screws is only one-third. The pitch of the screw, of course, remains the same, and the change wheels are calculated in the usual manner, as already described.

To Cut a Double-thread Screw, first cut a thread of one-half the depth and width of a single thread of the same pitch. Next, find the correct starting-point for the second thread, which obviously comes midway between the threads already cut. Make a chalk-mark on a tooth of the first driving change wheel—which should have an even number of teeth—and also mark the space occupied by the tooth in the follower or driven wheel. Now mark the tooth exactly opposite the one already marked on the driver. Lower the bracket or swing plate a trifle and turn the lathe spindle half a revolution so that the second marked tooth engages with the marked space on the follower. Start the lathe and cut the second thread, which will be in the correct position if the foregoing instructions have been faithfully carried out.

To Cut a Triple-thread Screw, proceed in a similar manner to that described above, but as three threads are required, three equal divisions are necessary on the driving change wheel. The number of teeth in this wheel should be a multiple of three, such as 30 or 45.

Sometimes it is necessary to cut a left-handed screw. In this case the lead-screw must revolve in the opposite direction to that of the work. The cut is started at the left-hand end of the work. The change wheels are calculated in the usual way. The reverse motion is imparted to the lead-screw by inserting an extra wheel in the train of gear wheels between the mandrel and the lead-screw, as shown at A in the diagram (Fig. 45).

Tools for screw-cutting are of special shape.

For Cutting V-thread Screws a single-pointed tool is generally used. Fig. 46 shows such a tool. If the threads to be cut are Whitworth threads, the straight sides of the thread are included in an angle of 55° with one another, and

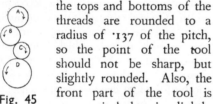

Fig. 45

the tops and bottoms of the threads are rounded to a radius of ·137 of the pitch, so the point of the tool should not be sharp, but slightly rounded. Also, the front part of the tool is not vertical, but is slightly canted over to prevent the tool rubbing the sides of the threads. Top and bottom rake, and clearance at each side, similar to that in a parting tool, are, of course, necessary.

From what has already been said it would appear that one cutting tool would only be suitable for cutting one particular pitch of thread. This is not necessary in practice, where small pitched threads are concerned, the reason being that the clearance angle of the cutting-edges of the tool is usually sufficient to allow for small variations in the rake of the thread.

In order to finish off a thread to its exact shape—that is, with the correct radius at the top and bottom of the thread—a chasing tool (shown in Fig. 47) is generally used. As this tool is only used for very light finishing cuts, it is usually fitted with a handle and used by

hand. To do this, fix a square bar in the slide-rest parallel to the axis and as close up to the work as possible, and run the chaser along the threads, using very light pressure only. A chasing tool is made for one particular pitch of thread, so it

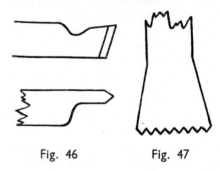

Fig. 46   Fig. 47

is necessary to have a separate chaser for every pitch of thread it is desired to cut. Chasers can also be obtained for finishing threads on internal work.

A Tool for Cutting Internal V-threads is shown in Fig. 48. It is similar to an ordinary boring tool except that it is provided with a cutting point made to the correct angle of the thread, as in the external V-threading tool.

An extremely useful little tool in the form of a screw-cutting gauge, which can be purchased for a few pence, is pictured at A in Fig. 49. By its use the correct angle of the cutting tool can be easily tested, and it serves as a useful guide when setting up the tool in the

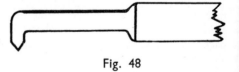

Fig. 48

slide-rest. The method of using the gauge will be readily understood by referring to B and C in the illustration, which shows the gauge being used for setting the tool for cutting external threads and internal threads respectively.

In using slide-rest tools for cutting external and internal square threads, it is important to see the front slope or rake is made to correspond with the pitch of the screw to be cut. The width of the tool for cutting a single square thread is equal to one-half the pitch of the thread, while that of a tool for producing a double thread is one-quarter of the pitch, and one-sixth for a triple thread.

Before bringing this brief survey of metal-turning to a conclusion, it would be incomplete if a few words on the important subject of speeds, feeds, and lubrication were omitted.

The speed and size of cut in metal-turning depend upon the material, tools, and the efficiency and rigidity of the machine being used. Thus, for turning cast iron, using tools of high-speed steel, which are now usually adopted, the approximate cutting speed would be in the neighbourhood of 25 ft. per minute; mild steel 60; cast steel 35, and brass 120. If carbon steel tools are used, then the above speeds would be reduced by about 25 per cent. When boring the above metals the speeds should be reduced from 25 per cent. to 50 per cent., and for screw-cutting 40 per cent. to 60 per cent.

In turning a piece of work it is more economical to take a moderately heavy cut at medium speed than a light cut at high speed, and also a deep cut with small traverse is better than a light cut with a rapid traverse.

Lubrication. — Some metals are turned dry and others require a lubricant. Mild steel and wrought iron require a good supply of soap and

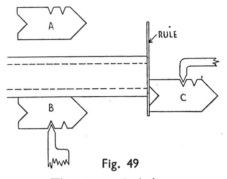

Fig. 49

water. This is particularly necessary when taking a finishing cut. Paraffin is a good lubricant for aluminium, although turpentine is better. Cast steel may be lubricated with engine oil. Cast iron, brass, copper and gun-metal are turned without any lubricant.

FILES AND SCRAPERS

FILES are as important to the metal-worker as the plane is to the carpenter, for just as a woodworker first uses a saw for cutting the material roughly to shape and then planes the wood to the desired size, so the metal-worker first applies a chisel or a hacksaw for roughing out the metal and then uses the file to finish the work.

Files are made of hardened cast steel, and their faces are provided with cutting teeth as shown in Fig. 1. They are used essentially for reducing a piece of metal to a smaller size, smoothing down uneven surfaces, and for giving a smooth finish.

Files are generally classified by their shape, cut, and the degree of coarseness of the teeth.

To go into details of every kind of file is unnecessary here. We will therefore strictly confine our attention to those tools you are likely to need.

Fig. 2 illustrates a few of the most useful shapes of files, and the kind of

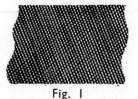

Fig. I

work on which they are intended to be used is as follows:

A.—The hand or parallel file. This is used for all kinds of flat work such as slots and shoulders which are required to be filed parallel. This type of file usually has one plain edge without teeth—known as a safety edge—the object being to allow the teeth to be

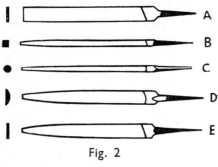

Fig. 2

used in a corner without risk of damaging the adjacent surface.

B.—The square file is used for filing square holes, slots, and between narrow surfaces.

C.—The round file is used for enlarging holes and rounding slots, etc.

D.—The half-round file is employed for working on concave or hollow surfaces, enlarging holes, etc.

E.—The flat file with bellied sides is used principally for roughing out flat work.

All the above-mentioned tools, with the exception of the hand or parallel

file, taper towards their ends; a parallel portion is provided, however, near the tang or handle end.

A file may be either single cut or double cut as in Fig. 3, at A and B.

In the former the teeth are made at an angle across the face in one direction only, while in the double-cut file an extra set of teeth is formed across the other, the result being a surface consisting of sharp points.

Single-cut Files are used mostly for working the softer metals such as brass, copper, lead, etc. For

Fig. 3

general work and filing iron and steel the double-cut file is the correct tool to use.

With regard to the degree of coarseness or fineness of the teeth, this must be determined by the nature of the work in hand. If it is desired to remove a large quantity of metal, a large rough file should be used, while if only a finish is required, then a smooth file is the tool to use.

When a new file is brought into operation it should first be used on brass or gun-metal; it can then be used effectively on steel and wrought iron, but a file that has been used on steel will not cut brass efficiently.

Never use a new file to remove the scale off castings. Do this with an old file, and when the "skin" has been removed a new file may be brought into action.

The Art of Filing correctly requires a considerable amount of skill which can only be obtained by practice. You will find it by no means a simple operation to file a surface perfectly flat, the tendency being to produce a more or less rounded surface.

For the purpose of explaining the process of filing let us take as a simple example a piece of mild steel 2 in. × 1 in. × 1 in. which has to be reduced in size to 2 in. × $\frac{7}{8}$ in. × $\frac{7}{8}$ in.

After having carefully marked out the material by means of a scriber and centre-punch (as indicated in Fig. 4), fasten the work securely in the vice with the marking-off lines just above the top of the jaws and about level with the elbow. Take a rough file and grasp the handle —a file should never be used without a handle—with the right hand, keeping the knuckles downwards; grip the opposite end of the tool with all fingers of the left hand as shown in Fig. 5, which indicates the correct way to handle a file.

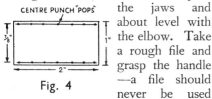

Fig. 4

Place the end of the file in a horizontal position upon the surface of the work, and push it forward, applying pressure with the left hand and gradually transferring the pressure to the right hand as the file advances towards the end of its

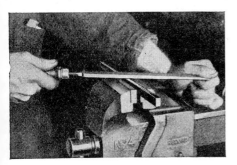

Fig. 5

stroke. This completes the cutting stroke, and it is well to remember that a file only cuts on the forward stroke as the teeth are shaped to cut in this direction. Failure to observe this will result in a ruined file. Now relieve the pressure and draw the file back over the work to its original position. Any

pressure exerted on this stroke will only wear the teeth out. Continue the rough filing, as it is called, until nearly all the waste metal is removed on both faces, leaving about $\frac{1}{64}$ in. clear above the marking-off lines for finishing purposes. Take a second-cut (medium teeth) file and remove the marks left in the work by the rough file, taking care that you do not file below the marking-off lines, and then finish off dead to size with a smooth file by drawing it across the work. This process is known as drawfiling, an illustration of which appears in Fig. 6. If any clogging of the teeth takes place when using the

Fig. 6

second-cut and smooth files, apply some ordinary chalk to the surface of the tool. This will usually have the desired effect.

If you have marked off the work and used the files correctly you will find that one-half of each centre-pop has been removed while the other half remains. To complete the work, polish it with fine emery cloth wrapped round a square block of hardwood and apply a few drops of oil to the emery cloth.

Scraping is resorted to in cases where a higher degree of accuracy and finish is required than that produced by filing, etc. The process consists in removing minute amounts of metal with a tool called a scraper.

Scraping is very skilled work. The method of handling the tool itself can be quickly learned, but the actual scraping, that is, the removal of the right amount of metal at the right place, needs great care and experience. The latter can be obtained more quickly if the principles underlying the operation are thoroughly grasped at the start.

Fig. 7 shows a handy type of scraper suitable for treating bearings of motor-car and gas-engine crankshafts as well as big ends of connecting rods. It can also be used for flat work.

Such a scraper can be easily made from an old half-round file. It should be annealed by heating it to a bright red colour and allowing it to cool in the ashes of the fire while the fire goes out. When cold, it should be roughly filed, to remove all tool-marks, for a distance of 2 or 3 in. from the working end. The remaining teeth need not

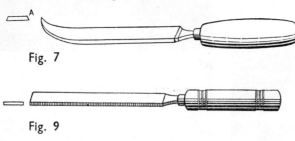

Fig. 7

Fig. 9

be quite so fully removed, but sufficiently to enable the tool to be held comfortably without roughing the hand. The blade should then be turned up slightly at the end as shown, and ground slightly convex on the flat side.

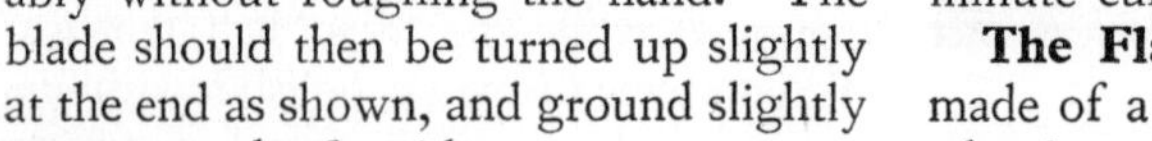

The scraper must now be hardened and tempered by heating it to a full red colour, as before, and plunging it vertically into a pail of swirling, clean, cold water in which a handful of salt has been dissolved. This will make the tool dead hard and very brittle. It should then be cleaned bright and heated with

a blow-lamp and tempered. The heat should not be applied directly to the cutting end but at a distance of about 3 or 4 in. from it.

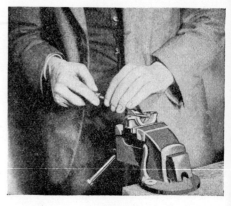

Fig. 8

To use the tool it should be held in the manner indicated in Fig. 8. The right hand keeps the tool steady but exercises little movement, while the fingers and thumb of the left hand hold the scraper near the work. The tool is then drawn steadily towards the operator, at the same time exerting slight pressure on the work to enable the cutting-edge actually to cut the metal, which should come off in minute curls.

The Flat Scraper (Fig. 9) can be made of a wide, flat file. The forward edge is used and in this case the tool is pushed away from the operator. The left hand is used for applying the pressure—as before—and the right hand for holding the tool at the correct angle and propelling it along the work. This tool has flat sides and edges and the working end is ground square with the sides and edges.

When scraping a bearing the working surface should be lightly smeared with a mixture of the finest red lead moistened with linseed oil. The journal should then be laid in the bearing and the shaft slowly revolved. The places where the journal touches the bearing will be clearly indicated by the "marking" (red lead) being rubbed. These are the places to be very lightly scraped in short, narrow "scrapes." When the high places have been removed, the remaining marking should be rubbed off, a fresh supply of red lead applied, and the journal revolved in the bearing, as before. On removing the journal it will be seen that the shaft has marked a larger surface of the bearing than previously, and this area should be scraped, and so on until the journal marks the whole of the surface when rotated. When this occurs the bearing is said to be "fitted," and having reached that stage it can be cleaned and assembled. The same procedure is followed in scraping flat surfaces such as the bed of a lathe, the slides of a slide-rest, or the face and bed of a steam engine slide-valve.

One part is marked and the other gently rubbed on it. The high places indicated are then scraped and the process repeated till a flat smooth surface in contact all over is produced.

For very fine work, finely-ground lampblack can be used instead of red lead, and for extremely fine work Prussian blue scholar's oil colour supplied in collapsible tubes may be used.

The vital point about scraping is to remove only a small quantity of metal at a time between subsequent markings, otherwise a large surface may have to be scraped to get down to a part scraped too low. In the case of scraping bearings, always make sure that the journal of the shaft is quite smooth and clean, and at each trial marking, scrape every spot which shows high, otherwise the next marking will be deceptive.

MEASURING INSTRUMENTS

As many branches of metal-work, such as turning and fitting, require a very high degree of accuracy, it is obvious that measuring devices, such as rules and ordinary simple callipers, are out of the question, and it is therefore necessary to employ instruments of a much finer degree of precision.

The instruments commonly used for measuring these minute fractions are known as sliding-gauges and micrometers.

It is unnecessary to go into details of ordinary simple callipers here as these measuring instruments are dealt with in the section on METAL-TURNING, but before going into details of vernier gauges and micrometers it may be an advantage to mention one or two instruments which, strictly speaking, do not come within the category of precision instruments, but are nevertheless extremely useful.

The first of these is shown at A in Fig. 1, which illustrates a registering calliper. It is useful, where extreme accuracy is not required, because the size of the work measured between the legs is indicated on a divided scale engraved on a quadrant attached to one of the legs. The other leg carries a pointer which indicates on the scale the measurement taken. It will be seen that the scale has a zero mark in the centre of the quadrant. This enables the index to swing on either side of the zero mark, depending upon whether the legs are being used upon external or internal work.

The illustration at B shows another

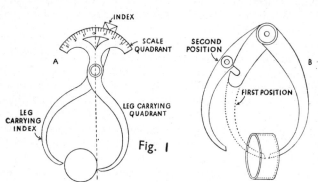

Fig. 1

just touches it. The locking screw is then tightened to keep the jaw in position and the dimension required is read off the scale where the thin edge coincides with a figure on the scale. An illustration of the method adopted is shown in Fig. 3.

The type of slide-gauge shown at A in Fig. 2 can only be used for determining external measurements.

A better type of slide-gauge, which can be used for external and internal measurements, is shown at B in Fig. 2. In this instrument small projections are provided on the ends of the jaws to allow them to enter the hole to be measured. Two index marks are engraved on

special type of calliper which is very handy, as the legs can be finely adjusted by means of a milled screw. It is also fitted with a detachable leg, which allows measurements to be taken as shown in the drawing, where ordinary callipers could not be used.

A Simple Form of Slide-gauge, where the object to be measured is placed between the jaws, is pictured at A in Fig. 2. It consists of a thin metal bar or stock having a projecting piece at the end which forms the fixed jaw. A suitable scale either in inches and fractions of an inch, or a metric scale, is engraved on the bar. The sliding jaw fits over the stock and is provided with a thin edge which moves over the graduated scale, while an adjusting screw allows the jaw to be locked in position when a measurement has been taken.

To take a measurement with a slide-gauge, all that is necessary is to place the object on the fixed jaw and slide the other jaw up to the work until the jaw

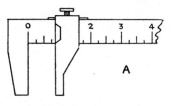

A

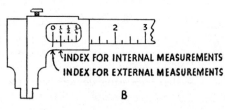

INDEX FOR INTERNAL MEASUREMENTS
INDEX FOR EXTERNAL MEASUREMENTS

B

Fig. 2

the sliding jaw for indicating outside and inside measurements respectively, the extra index being necessary to allow for the thickness of the projections on the jaws. It will be observed that inside measurements of under $\frac{1}{4}$ in. cannot be taken with this instrument.

We now come to those instruments

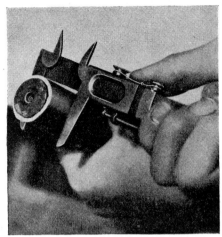

Fig. 3

To use the vernier, first note the number of inches, tenths and fortieths of an inch—the zero mark on the vernier is from the zero mark on the bar—then note the number of division lines on the vernier which exactly coincides with some division line on the bar scale. This will indicate the number of thousandths of an inch to be added to the distance read on the scale of the bar.

To make this clear let us take an example.

Assuming that the o or zero mark on the vernier has moved through two-inch divisions, three-tenth divisions, and three-fortieth divisions on the bar scale and that the line seven on the vernier coincides with a division line on the scale. The total will then be:

$$2 + \cdot 3 + \cdot 075 + \cdot 007 = 2 \cdot 382 \text{ in.}$$

An ordinary screw micrometer callipers,

which are commonly used for taking measurements as small as $\frac{1}{1000}$ of an inch, namely, the vernier calliper and the micrometer.

Fig. 4 shows an illustration of the business end of a vernier calliper, with the bar scale A and the vernier scale B clearly indicated.

On the bar of this instrument is a scale of inches, each of which is sub-divided into ten parts and each tenth into four parts, thus making a total of forty divisions per inch; thus each division on the scale represents $\frac{1}{40}$ in., which in decimal notation is $\cdot 025$ in. On the moving jaw is a vernier scale which is exactly equal in length to twenty-four bar divisions but is divided into twenty-five equal parts. If the end lines of each scale exactly coincide, the first division on B will fall short of the first on A by $\frac{1}{25}$ of $\frac{1}{40}$, which equals $\frac{1}{1000}$ or $\cdot 001$, the second will fall short of the second on the bar scale by $\cdot 002$ and so on. If the vernier is moved to the right until the fifth sub-division agrees with the first on the scale, the vernier has moved $\cdot 005$. No other pairs of gradations then coincide.

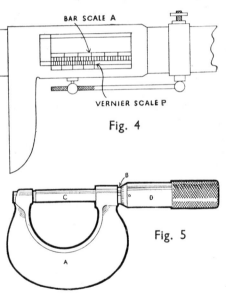

BAR SCALE A

VERNIER SCALE P

Fig. 4

Fig. 5

or micrometer as it is usually called, is shown in Fig. 5.

There are many types of micrometers, some fitted with a locking device to lock the spindle when a measurement has been taken, others fitted with a ratchet for gauging the correct pressure between the jaws; but of whatever type the micrometer may be they all work on the same principle, based on the screw-thread.

If a screw of, say, eight threads to the inch is fitted into a fixed nut and rotated through one revolution, the amount of

Fig. 6

the advance of the screw will be equal to the pitch of the thread, viz. $\frac{1}{8}$ in. Similarly, if the screw is rotated through one-half a revolution then the travel of the screw will only be one-half the pitch, or $\frac{1}{16}$ in., and if rotated one-tenth of a revolution the movement of the screw will be $\frac{1}{10}$ of $\frac{1}{8} = \frac{1}{80}$ in. It will thus be seen that the screw-thread offers a ready means of making fine measurements.

In Fig. 5, A represents the frame, in which is incorporated the barrel B. This is internally threaded for a portion of its length with threads of a pitch of forty to the inch. The partially threaded

spindle C is attached to the back end of the hollow sleeve D, which engages with the internal thread in the barrel. The horizontal zero line seen on the barrel is graduated into tenths of an inch which are further sub-divided into quarters, so that every small division is equal to $\frac{1}{40}$ in. The bevelled front edge of the sleeve or thimble is divided into twenty-five equal divisions numbered at 0, 5, 10, 15, 20. When the sleeve is rotated through one revolution, the spindle will move through one scale division or ·025 in. When the jaws are closed the zero mark on the scale should agree with the zero mark on the sleeve. If the sleeve is now twisted in an anti-clockwise direction until the first sleeve division

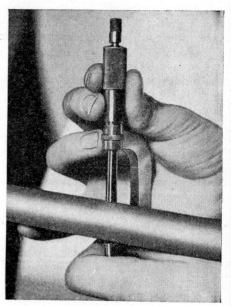

Fig. 7

coincides with the zero line on the barrel, the point of the spindle will move away from the anvil $\frac{1}{25}$ of $\frac{1}{40} = \frac{1}{1000}$ of an inch.

Fig. 6 shows a convenient method of holding a micrometer when taking the dimensions of an object. Excessive pressure must not be exerted, otherwise a false measurement will result, due to the spring of the instrument. Conversely, if the jaws do not quite touch the work the instrument will record a larger measurement than the object really has. The proper amount of pressure to adopt will soon be acquired by practice.

Fig. 7 shows a micrometer being used to measure the diameter of a piece of work suspended between the centres of a lathe.

DRILLS AND DRILLING

To the uninitiated the mere operation of making a hole in a piece of metal seems but child's play.

Admitted that the mechanical operation of drilling is a simple matter, there are other considerations to be taken into account before an accurate hole can be obtained.

A truly accurate-sized hole can only

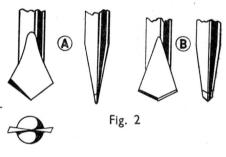

Fig. 1

be produced by the proper manipulation of accurate tools.

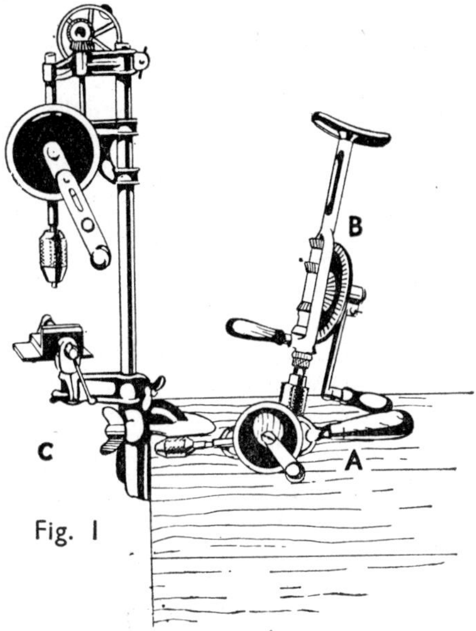

Small-sized holes are sometimes made by drills rotated either in a small hand-driven drill-stock for holes up to about $\frac{1}{4}$ in. diameter, or for larger-sized holes by a geared breast drill-stock, also driven by hand. A much better method, however, is that obtained by using a drilling machine, which can be driven by hand, foot or mechanical power.

A Hand-driven Hand Drill is shown in Fig. 1 at A, while at B a hand-driven breast drill-stock is indicated. A small drilling machine is shown at C.

Fig. 2, A shows an illustration of a flat drill made from a piece of circular bar steel flattened out at the end and ground to a point. To enable an accurate hole to be made with such a drill the follow-

Fig. 2

ing procedure must be conformed to. The point of the tool must be exactly in the centre of the drill; the two cutting-edges must be equal in length, and they should be backed off to an equal amount to provide the necessary clearance. If one cutting-edge is longer than the other, the drill will make a larger hole than the diameter of the drill. The angle of the cutting-edges of flat drills of this type is 120°; and the angle of clearance about 3°. This type of flat drill can only be revolved in one direction.

Another Type of Flat Drill is shown at B in Fig. 2. Here the cutting-edges are so shaped as to enable them to cut in either direction. Flat drills are not very satisfactory but are useful for rough work where extreme accuracy is not necessary.

The best kind of drill for all general work is the fluted twist-drill represented at A in Fig. 3. This type of drill produces a clean, smooth, accurate hole

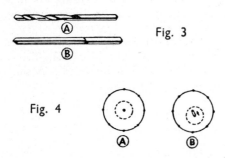

Fig. 3

Fig. 4

and clears itself from the cuttings. Twist-drills are not expensive to buy and can be obtained in sizes from ·01 in. up to 3 in. diameter with either parallel or tapered shanks. The twist-drill is made from round steel and has the spiral flutes slightly backed off from the cutting-edges in order to prevent the tool from binding. Twist-drills can be had in either high speed or carbon steel. The former are more expensive, but they are able to remove a given amount of metal at a much higher speed than the latter, as high-speed steel twist-drills do not lose their temper so readily as the carbon variety.

The usual method of procedure when it is required to drill a hole is first to "mark off" on the surface of the work the size and position of the hole. To do this, make a centre-punch mark in the centre of the material where the hole is to be, and with a pair of compasses describe a circle of the desired diameter, using the "pop" for supporting one leg of the compasses. Next, make several punch-marks on the circle to serve as a guide, as clearly indicated at A in Fig. 4. The work is now ready for the drill. Bring the drill point down on to the corresponding centre-mark in the metal and make a light preliminary cut to ascertain whether the drill is centering itself properly. If the circle cut by the drill is concentric with the marked circle, the drilling may be proceeded with. If this is not so, however, the centre must be drawn over. To do this, make a nick with a small cold chisel in the direction the drill should go, as shown in the sketch at B in Fig. 4. Make another test with the drill and repeat the foregoing operation if necessary, remembering that once the body of the drill enters the metal it is not possible to correct an error.

When comparatively large holes have to be drilled it is good practice first to bore a hole of a smaller diameter—about one quarter the size of the large diameter will do—to act as pilot. This will not only take the strain off the point of the large drill but will also save a large amount of power in driving it.

When Using Twist-drills it is important that they should be driven at the correct cutting speed, which varies according to the nature of the metal being drilled, and that the amount of "feed," or the distance the tool advances per revolution, should not be exceeded. If the cutting speed is exceeded, the corners of the drill will soon be worn away and therefore rendered useless. Excess of speed is generally indicated by a squeaky noise, and excessive speed, too, will be almost sure to result in a broken drill.

The following table of approximate

speeds and feeds will serve as a guide when carbon steel drills are used.

Diam. of Drill in ins.	Revs. per min.			Feed per rev.
	Steel	Iron	Brass	
$\frac{1}{16}$	1830	2140	3660	$\frac{1}{200}$ in.
$\frac{1}{8}$	915	1070	1830	
$\frac{3}{16}$	610	710	1220	
$\frac{1}{4}$	450	530	915	
$\frac{3}{8}$	300	350	610	$\frac{1}{140}$ in.
$\frac{1}{2}$	225	265	455	
$\frac{3}{4}$	150	175	300	$\frac{1}{110}$ in.
1	110	130	225	$\frac{1}{90}$ in.

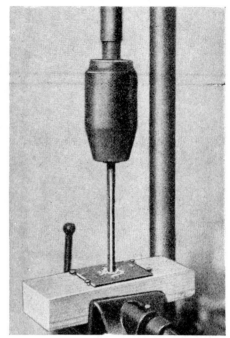

Fig. 6

The use of high speed steel drills will enable speeds and feeds to be taken of approximately double those given in the above table.

When drilling wrought iron or copper, soap and water may be applied for lubricating purposes; ordinary lubricating oil can be applied when drilling steel. Cast iron and brass do not require any lubricant.

Twist-drills should only be used when in first-class condition. As soon as a drill shows signs of being blunt it should be re-ground.

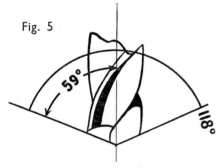

Fig. 5

Fig. 5 shows the cutting-edges of a twist-drill, which should be for ordinary purposes 59° with the central axis of the drill. It is important that both cutting-edges are equal in length and that the point is in line with the axis, otherwise an irregular-sized hole will result. It is also necessary that both cutting-edges are properly backed off or sufficient clearance provided so that only the edges come in contact with the metal. If the surface of the cutting-end of the drill is allowed to come in contact with the metal, it will not cut; on the other hand, if too much clearance is provided, the drill will undoubtedly catch in the metal—with disastrous results.

To Grind a Twist-drill properly is not a difficult job if a proper drill-grinder is available. The tools are somewhat expensive and therefore generally beyond the scope of the amateur. "Touching up," however, can be easily accomplished on an ordinary carpenter's oilstone.

Twist-drills are unsuitable for making holes in sheet metal, as they have a tendency to catch when breaking through the hole, with the result that a drill is very quickly broken.

For drilling holes in sheet metal the correct type of drill to use is the straight fluted drill, a drawing of which appears at B in Fig. 3. When drilling holes in thin metal it is a good plan to mount the work on a piece of hardwood to prevent the metal from bending. A few tacks driven into the wood (as in Fig. 6) will prevent the work from rotating.

A **Pin-drill** (illustrated at B in Fig. 7) is useful for producing a flat surface round a hole in a casting or other piece of work where it is necessary to provide a flat bearing surface for a nut, bolt head, or cheese-headed screw. The pin enters the hole, previously drilled, and steadies the drill, while the cutter trues up the surface.

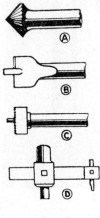

Fig. 7

When using such a drill a good supply of oil should be applied to the pin.

For countersinking or recessing the mouths of holes to take countersunk screws, a countersink drill (as shown at A in Fig. 7) is the tool to use.

A Bottoming or Arbouring Drill is shown at C. It is used when a flat surface is required at the bottom of a hole previously drilled with a cone-pointed drill. It will be seen from the illustration that the tool is in the form of a circular cutter having a series of cutters set at an angle with the edges, the cutting-edges being backed off in the usual way to provide the necessary clearance.

For cutting large holes in sheet metal, as for instance a water tank, a combination cutter-drill is generally used. Such a drill is illustrated at D in Fig. 7. It consists of a spindle or shank with an adjustable horizontal bar which holds the cutter. At the bottom end of the shank is a guide pin, similar to that in the pin-drill previously described.

To cut a hole, first drill a hole in the work of the same diameter as the pin of the drill. Set the cutter-bar to the desired radius, insert the pin into the pilot hole in the work and rotate the cutter.

Fig. 8 shows a marking-off template which is a handy device to have for rapidly marking the positions of holes when a number of similar parts are to be drilled. Such a template can be easily made with a piece of flat, thin sheet iron provided with a small hole (A) or holes, to coincide with the holes desired in the work, to enable the point of a centre-punch to protrude. The

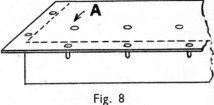

Fig. 8

template is held in position on the work and is prevented from slipping by a series of small pins, as indicated in the drawing. The point of a centre-punch is then placed in the hole and a smart tap on the head of a punch with a hammer locates on the work the position required.

SCREWS AND SCREW THREADS

BEFORE going into the methods adopted for making screw threads it is necessary to know the technical terms used to define the various parts of an ordinary single-thread screw.

Reference to the diagram at A in Fig. 1, which illustrates the parts of a screw thread, shows that P is the pitch, or the distance measured between the centre of one thread to the centre of the next; H represents the height; T the top of the thread; R the root, or bottom of the thread; and S indicates the slope of angle of the sides.

The form of thread most frequently used in this country for general engineering work is the Whitworth or English Standard thread shown at B in Fig. 1. The angle between the two sides is 55°. The depth of the thread is equal to ·64 of the pitch, and $\frac{1}{6}$ of the height is rounded off at the top and bottom of the thread to prevent damage to the top and also to strengthen the root of the thread.

The British Association thread illustrated at C is a finer-pitched thread than the Whitworth. It is employed for small screws used in electrical apparatus, wireless parts, etc. The angle of the thread is 47½°, rounded at the top and bottom of the thread to a radius of $\frac{2}{11}$ of the pitch.

The main difference between the American Standard or Sellers thread shown at D and the English Standard

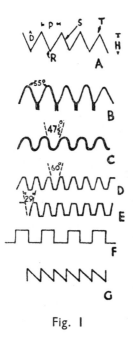

Fig. 1

lies in the shape of the thread. Instead of the top and bottom of the thread being rounded off, they are cut off to form a flat $\frac{1}{8}$ of the pitch in width. The angle formed between the sides is 60°.

Another thread, used largely in machine tools, such as the lead screws in lathes, is shown at E. It is known as the Acme thread. The angle between the sides is 29°.

An ordinary square thread is represented at F. The depth and width of the thread is equal to $\frac{1}{2}$ the pitch. The thrust is at 90° to its axis. This type of thread is weak at the bottom of the thread owing to the absence of metal.

The buttress thread shown at G has one side at an angle of 45°, and the other side vertical. It is stronger than the square thread when the thrust is in one direction only, owing to the extra amount of metal supporting the thread. It is used largely in vice-screws and in cases where pressure is required in one direction only.

There are several methods of making screw threads, which include the use of special threading machines, lathes, and hand-operated tools. The former process does not come within the scope of the amateur, and as screw-cutting in the lathe is dealt with in another article there remains the last-mentioned process of using hand tools.

This is accomplished by the use of stocks and dies for forming external

9

threads and "taps" for cutting threads on internal diameters.

Fig. 2 shows a stock and dies for producing one particular size of thread. The hardened steel die which cuts the thread is made in two halves and is placed in a holder or stock which is provided with an adjusting screw. Pressure is applied

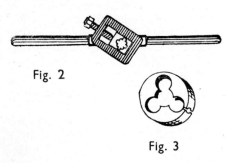

Fig. 2

Fig. 3

to the two holes of the die by means of the screw.

A set of dies usually consists of a suitable stock with a number of interchangeable dies. In some sets, especially those in the smaller sizes, the stock is designed to take several sets of dies. This method of arranging the latter has the advantage of obviating the necessity of constantly changing the dies when operating with different-sized threads.

Perhaps the most handy and useful pattern of stock and dies for small work, such as model engineering, making wireless parts, and work of a similar nature, is that fitted with spring dies (Fig. 3), which, as their name suggests, are circular in shape and split half-way across to obtain a certain amount of spring. A circular-shaped stock for holding the die is provided with a set-screw which allows the split die to be opened or closed, thus causing the diameter of the thread to be cut to be slightly increased

or decreased as the case may be. This feature is a distinct advantage, because it sometimes happens that either a tight or loose screw is wanted and the desired diameter may be easily obtained by adjusting the set-screw. As these dies may be bought separately there is no need to purchase a full set to begin with, but more may be added as required.

The most useful sizes for model engineering and work of a similar nature are $\frac{1}{16}$ in., $\frac{3}{32}$ in., $\frac{1}{8}$ in., $\frac{3}{16}$ in., and $\frac{1}{4}$ in. for cutting Whitworth threads, and Nos. 2, 4, 6, 8, for making B.A. threads.

To Cut an External Thread on a piece of round rod is an easy matter. Fix the work vertically in the vice and file up the end to be threaded to remove the sharp edge and to form a slight taper. Open the die until the work to be screwed can be entered; place the die on the prepared end of the rod and twist the stock round very gently in a clockwise direction, taking care that the die is kept at right angles to the work, or a bad thread will result. When the die has begun to cut, twist the stock backwards and forwards, taking a little more cut at each forward stroke, and continue until the desired length of thread is obtained. Twist the die back to bring it to its original position. Now close the die a trifle and proceed as before and if necessary repeat the operation until the correct-sized thread is obtained.

If the rod being screwed is of iron, mild steel or hard steel, the dies must have a plentiful supply of oil, but if brass is being threaded, no lubricant is needed. Fig. 4 shows an illustration of the process.

To cut an internal thread requires a little more care than that required for forming an external one.

Fig. 5 shows the hand tools necessary for cutting an internal thread. The thread-cutting component is known as a "tap," and the detachable handle a tap-wrench.

Taps are usually made from a rod of cast steel of suitable diameter upon which a thread is cut, after which they are, of course, hardened and tempered. Three or more equal grooves or flutes are provided lengthwise down the tap, which form cutting edges for the remaining portion of the thread, while at the top or shank end of the tool four "flats" are usually provided to enable a suitable wrench to be fitted for twisting purposes.

To produce a full-sized thread two taps are usually employed, called the taper and finishing taps respectively. A third tap, known as a plug tap, is generally used for special purposes.

The threads of the first or taper tap taper gradually from its lower end to within a few threads of the top, the threads on the lower end being ground

Fig. 4

away to enable the point to enter the hole. In the case of the second or finishing tap, the taper is more gradual and starts from the point to about only one-third up its length, the remainder being left full size.

The plug tap is generally used for tapping holes which do not extend right through the metal, and has a full-sized thread nearly the whole of its length.

A very useful holder for small taps is

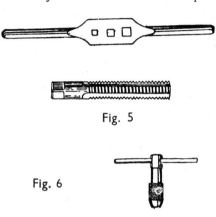

Fig. 5

Fig. 6

shown in Fig. 6, and as it is inexpensive it should be included in every metal worker's tool kit. It has a chuck which can be adjusted to take various-sized tools within its capacity.

To Cut an Internal Thread in a piece of metal it is necessary first to drill a hole of the correct size and then cut the thread with the taps. The size of the hole must be equal in diameter to that of the diameter of the bottom of the thread of the screw it is intended to fit. Thus, if it is desired to fit a $\frac{1}{4}$-in. Whitworth screw or bolt, the drill must only be $\frac{3}{16}$ in. diameter. Such a drill is called a "tapping-size" drill.

The following is a table of screw threads giving the corresponding tapping-size drills. It will be found useful for ascertaining the correct drill to use for all usual sizes of Whitworth and British Association threads. The worker who cannot afford a complete stock can therefore buy what he wants without risk of error.

SIZES OF TAPPING DRILLS FOR WHITWORTH THREADS

Diam. of Screw in.	Diam. of Tapping Drill in.	Diam. of Screw in.	Diam. of Tapping Drill in.
$\frac{3}{16}$	$\frac{9}{64}$	$\frac{3}{4}$	$\frac{5}{8}$
$\frac{1}{4}$	$\frac{3}{16}$	$\frac{13}{16}$	$\frac{11}{16}$
$\frac{5}{16}$	$\frac{1}{4}$	$\frac{7}{8}$	$\frac{47}{64}$
$\frac{3}{8}$	$\frac{19}{64}$	$\frac{15}{16}$	$\frac{51}{64}$
$\frac{7}{16}$	$\frac{23}{64}$	1	$\frac{27}{32}$
$\frac{1}{2}$	$\frac{13}{32}$	$1\frac{1}{8}$	$\frac{61}{64}$
$\frac{9}{16}$	$\frac{15}{32}$	$1\frac{1}{4}$	$1\frac{1}{16}$
$\frac{5}{8}$	$\frac{33}{64}$	$1\frac{3}{8}$	$1\frac{11}{64}$
$\frac{11}{16}$	$\frac{37}{64}$	$1\frac{1}{2}$	$1\frac{19}{64}$

SIZES OF TAPPING DRILLS FOR B.A (BRITISH ASSOCIATION) THREADS

Diam. of Screw	Diam. of Tapping Drill	Diam. of Screw	Diam. of Tapping Drill
0	No. 10	5	No. 37
1	No. 17	6	No. 43
2	No. 24	7	No. 46
3	No. 29	8	No. 50
4	No. 32		

Having decided upon the proper-sized drill to use, place the material in a vice and drill the hole in the usual manner. Fix a taper tap in the wrench or holder and screw the tap into the hole. When the tool starts to cut, work the tap gently backwards and forwards, gradually making a little more cut on each forward stroke. The tap must on no account be forced or wrenched sideways or it will break. Continue cutting until the top threads of the tool are level with the top of the hole, not forgetting to apply a liberal supply of oil if working with wrought iron or steel. When tapping cast iron do not lubricate as it causes the chips to adhere and often produces a faulty thread. Remove the tool by twisting it out of the hole and follow on in the same manner with the finishing tap. Fig. 7 shows an internal thread being cut.

One of the most important points to observe when using taps is that equal pressure must be used on both sides of the wrench when being twisted. Failure to take this precaution will undoubtedly lead to a broken tap, which if it breaks in the hole is a very difficult job to extract. Another point to watch is to see that the cutting edges of the tap are in good order, as it is useless to try to form a good thread if any of the cutting teeth are broken. In the event of broken teeth the teeth should be ground down before using. Special care is also necessary when tapping a thread in a blind hole—that is, a hole with a bottom to it. In this case the taper and finishing tap may be driven very gently down to the bottom of the hole and then followed by the plug tap, which will cut a full thread right down to the bottom. When using the plug tap, take very small cuts and see that the chippings are cleared as often as necessary so that the tool can be screwed right to the bottom.

Fig. 7

If you have the misfortune to break a tap and have not a spare one at hand, it is not a very difficult matter to make one.

For a plug tap, cut off a piece of tool steel of the proper diameter and length. File the metal for a distance of about three threads to form a slight taper. If a lathe is available this is an easy matter, for the metal can be fixed between the jaws of a self-centering chuck and filed as the metal revolves. Now cut a thread with a suitable die opened slightly larger than the finished thread is to be, and then take a second finishing cut, using plenty of oil as a lubricant. If the tap has to have flutes, take a triangular file and rough file where the flutes are to be. Now take a round file and finish off the flutes, remembering that the hollows are deepest at the lower end and gradually get shallower at the shank end of the thread. When the lower tapered threads have been backed off and a square is filed on the shank to fit the wrench, the tap is ready for hardening.

To Harden the Tap, heat it up to a bright cherry red by either holding it in the flame of a blow-lamp or Bunsen burner and quench it in cool water. When doing this, plunge the tap vertically into the water and stir it in circles to ensure even cooling. The tap is now hard and brittle and therefore must be tempered. Polish the tool with emery-paper so that it is perfectly clean and bright. Twist a length of wire round the lower end of the tap to form a holder. Now pass the whole tap horizontally through the flame, allowing the shank end to get the most heat. Watch carefully the change of colours as the heating proceeds and when the end of the tool attains a straw colour, plunge it vertically into cold water.

The method of making taper taps is the same as that just described but the taper tap has the lower end filed or turned taper up to about eight threads and from there up to the shank is parallel.

To make a die, get a piece of tool steel of the same diameter as the outside diameter of the die is to be and file up both faces to the thickness required. Mark out the exact positions where the clearing holes and the centre hole are to be. Drill out the clearing holes first and then plug them by driving in small mild steel plugs. Next, drill the centre hole to the exact size, which must be the root diameter of the thread. Countersink one end of the centre hole to a depth of about three threads and do likewise at the other end to the depth of one thread only. Grip the die firmly in the vice, keeping the tapered end uppermost, and tap the hole, using a taper tap for the purpose. Do not forget to use plenty of oil in so doing. Repeat the process with the finishing tap. The next operation consists in cutting the adjusting slot. Drill a small hole near the edge of the die in such a position as to leave a thin wall of metal between the edge of the hole and the edge of the die. This will leave sufficient metal to prevent the die from warping when undergoing the heat treatment; this is removed by a file when the die has been tempered. Cut the slot by using a small metal-piercing saw and drill two small shallow countersunk recesses to receive the fixing set-screw and the adjusting screw respectively. Drive out the metal plugs from the clearing holes and back off the rear of the cutting teeth with a small flat file. The die must now be hardened and tempered. Proceed in the same manner as that described for the tap, not forgetting the wire for holding purposes. Heat up the die to a cherry-red colour and then quench. Remove the metal in the slot and polish the die with emery cloth, then draw the temper, which should be a deep straw colour.

RIVETS, BOLTS AND NUTS

W E come now to the consideration of how best to fix two pieces of metal together, for, unlike wood, they cannot be glued or nailed. Often, too, the pieces must still be capable of movement.

The holding together of two pieces of metal in such a manner that they can be adjusted relatively to each other, or separated when required, is accomplished by bolts and nuts and screws. When two pieces require to be permanently attached, or where there is no necessity for separation, or where cheapness, neatness and great strength are required, rivets are used.

Rivets, bolts, nuts and screws are of a very wide variety. Something about their various adaptabilities and how to use them will be useful for reference by the amateur metal worker.

As mentioned elsewhere in this volume, there are several standard screw threads used in this country which have been developed as suitable for various classes of engineering and mechanical work. The best known is the "Whitworth" standard, which is used for screws and bolts and nuts from $\frac{3}{16}$ in. to 6 in. in diameter. It is in use for practically all general engineering and mechanical purposes. It has a comparatively coarse thread, so the angle of the thread to the axis is rather wider than any of the other threads. But it is very strong and only where great vibration is present need a finer thread be used. The "British Standard Fine" screw thread has a finer thread—more threads to the inch for a given diameter—than the Whitworth. Thus a Whitworth $\frac{1}{4}$-in. screw has 20 threads to the inch. A British Standard Fine $\frac{1}{4}$-in. screw has 26 threads to the inch. This thread is used very largely for motor-vehicle purposes,

motor cycles, etc., while for bicycles the thread standard developed by the Birmingham Small Arms Co., and adopted by the Cycle Engineers' Institute (before it became the Institute of Automobile Engineers), has been largely adopted. This is a fine thread and the nuts and heads are much smaller relatively to the bolt diameter than in the case of the Whitworth standard.

For small work, instruments, small accessories, such as carburettors and electrical apparatus, necessitating the use of small screws, the standard thread which the amateur will most commonly need is the "B.A." or British Association Standard thread. The range of threads goes by numbers, not fractions of an inch, and is based on the metric system. The largest size in the standard is denominated "o" and is 6 mm. in diameter, with a pitch of 1 mm. The sizes downwards go by numbers upwards up to No. 25, which is ·25 mm., or a quarter of a millimetre in diameter.

Tables of these threads are to be found in all mechanics' text and pocket books, and space need not be devoted to them here. These tables give the sizes of the nuts and of the heads as to their thickness and their measurement across the flats of the hexagon in the case of hexagon-headed bolts and screws. They also give, as well as the diameter over the thread (which would be the diameter of a clearance hole), the diameter at the core, i.e. measured at the bottom of the threads.

This core diameter is important, as it provides data as to the size of hole to be drilled for tapping to the correct size for the screw selected. But here some advice is needed. If a hole of the core diameter is drilled in wrought iron and an attempt is made to tap it with a standard tap, to take a standard screw, the tap will most likely jam and break. In any case the hole, when tapped, would be very tight on the screw—probably too tight to allow the screw to be screwed in, or so tight as to hold and seize the screw, which would be broken off in the hole in an attempt either to screw it in or out. On the other hand such metals as cast brass will not "flow" in this way, and the tapping size drill will make a hole which will allow the tap to cut a screw-thread to suit the bolt or screw. Cast brass will not flow. Copper will flow. Cast iron will not flow. Drawn brass—as rods (squares, rounds, etc.)—sometimes flows a little. Therefore, for cast iron and cast brass it is sufficient to drill a hole of the specified tapping size, but for wrought iron, copper, brass, etc., the hole should be slightly larger than the tapping size specified. The metal will flow towards the centre of the hole and give a good thread.

In the case of aluminium great care should be exercised, because it is of a very tenacious nature and "holds on" to the metal of the tap. Often the tap will "seize up" in the hole, at other times it will not feed in freely, and will rip all the thread out after the tap has been turned for a few rotations. More clearance should be given as regards the tapping size of the hole in aluminium than in the case of any other metal. If you are drilling and tapping large-sized holes—say, anything above $\frac{1}{4}$ in.—in aluminium, it is a good plan to grind away every third tooth on the tap on each of the three rows of teeth—the blanks to alternate. Such a tap will cut a clean unbroken thread in aluminium, where a full-toothed tap will simply jam up or tear out all the thread from the hole.

Lubrication is essential in the case of tapping some metals and should be avoided in others. All the ferrous metals—steel and iron—should be lubricated with oil when being threaded. Copper and brass and copper alloys should be tapped without lubricant and aluminium should be lubricated with turpentine—not lubricating oil. The use of turpentine on aluminium is very essential. In turning aluminium in the lathe, for instance, it will often drag and tear on the edge of the tool, thus spoiling the work. Sometimes the tool will get hold of it and embed itself so far as to pull the work from between the centres or out of the chuck. Turpentine used as a lubricant when turning, sawing, cutting or tapping aluminium will result in the avoidance of these troubles.

Nuts should be an easy fit on bolts. They should run down the whole length of the threaded portion by being rotated by hand, but they should not be "rocking" loose at any part. In using nuts, always lubricate the bolt with oil before applying the nut. This will result in allowing of a much farther turn at the final tightening up; furthermore, the nut will be less liable to slack off. This may seem a contradiction, but experience proves its truth. In dealing with any machinery, always lubricate the threads of studs, bolts, etc., before applying nuts. Even in the case of small instrument screws this holds good and will lessen the risk of breakages of screws in holes when tightening up. Dip them in vaseline.

Many machines have studs screwed into one part, with nuts to hold another part to the part with the studs. Trouble sometimes arises from the studs unscrewing with the nuts. This fault can be avoided by making the hole for the stud deeper than necessary, and tapping it with a taper tap so that the stud binds on the threads when it is screwed down. This happens, of course, just before the end of the thread and the plain part reaches the face of the metal. On occasions difficulty is experienced in withdrawing a stud. The use of hand-grips is to be avoided, since the jaws damage the surface of the plain part of the stud causing difficulty in getting the adjoining piece over the studs again. **To Withdraw an Obstinate Stud,** use two nuts and two spanners. Screw down the first nut nearly as far as it will go, and then screw down the second nut on top of it. Hold the bottom nut with one spanner and screw the second nut down hard upon it with the second spanner. Then screw the stud out by using the first spanner on the under nut. In very obstinate cases soak the metal round the stud with paraffin oil overnight. The stud can generally be withdrawn in the morning.

Where a stud or screw is broken in a hole, drill it down the centre with a drill of a diameter less than the tapping size of the stud. Take a hardened, square, taper reamer and tap it gently into the hole and turn. This procedure generally has the desired effect. In bad cases drill the full tapping size of the hole. This will leave only the threads of the screw in the threads of the hole. Be careful to drill straight and central. Then use a taper tap, which will generally strip the metal out without injuring the thread in the hole, especially if the tool is withdrawn and cleared a few times, and the loose metal (which it turns out of the thread) picked away from the thread with a pricker or steel scriber. Small screws which have broken in the holes may often be removed by using a flat drill, ground left-handed and turned left-handed. After a few turns of the drill the screw will possibly begin to turn out of the hole as drilling is continued.

When fitting bolts to holes always slightly countersink the edge of the hole. If this is overlooked, the head,

instead of lying flat on the metal, will only really be holding by the slight rounding in the corner where the shank of the bolt meets the head. It may seem to be tight down, but the under surface of the head is not actually resting on the metal, and such a bolt, under working strain, will certainly loosen and slack off, due to vibration.

Use a spring washer under all nuts and bolts of machines subject to vibration and on motor-car and motor-cycle work; and on all engine work use castle nuts and split-pins passing through holes in the bolt ends. Do not use a split-pin smaller than the hole it occupies. A sloppy-fitting split-pin is dangerous, because it gives a nut a chance to loosen and, in so doing, it may shear the pin. Let the split-pin fill the hole in the bolt.

In the case of rivets always have the holes in the two parts to be joined together dead in line with each other. On particular work especially, drill two pairs of holes first to locate the parts and then bolt them together with bolts which fit the holes tightly. Then drill the rest of the holes through both pieces. Always, on important jobs, slightly countersink the holes in the surfaces which meet. This prevents shearing and makes a stronger joint.

When Drilling through Two Plates together for riveting, the drill invariably pushes tiny twists of metal between the plates, which, when they are riveted up, prevent close contact and therefore weakens the job. After drilling, unfasten the two parts and slightly countersink the holes on their adjacent sides. This operation, trifling as it may seem, often makes the difference between a good fit and a bad one, especially in small work. The rivet should fit the hole. Badly-fitting rivets may seem tight through the riveting, but the parts will move eventually, because the holes are bigger than the rivets, and the friction of the heads is the only thing which is preventing the parts moving endways. When there is doubt about the holes being dead in line, or the job is a very particular one, reamer the holes in situ, and see that the rivets are a tight fit before riveting.

When riveting see that the head is tight up to the surface and the hole slightly countersunk. Let the first blow be a smart one, dead in line with the axis of the rivet—and let nothing but the head of the rivet rest on the anvil or block or vice or whatever you are using as a "hold up" for the rivet head.

Then, begin with the round peen of the hammer, to drive the edges down, going round the rivet with about eight or ten blows to the circle. Hit the edge of the rivet at 45° to the flat of the metal being joined. The idea is to drive the metal down at the top so that it spreads at the bottom. Practice will enable one to give a good finish with the hammer; but a rivet snap (a tool with a half-sphere indented in its hardened end) may be used to give a uniform appearance—as in the case of closing rivets on the seam of a model steam boiler. When flush riveting, i.e. when the plain end of the rivet is to be spread out in a countersunk hole, use the round peen of the hammer and strike the rivet vertically, dead in the centre so as to swell it sideways. Then, when the rivet has spread to the diameter of the outer edge of the countersunk hole,

drive it down with the flat face of the hammer. Let the rivet project far enough to ensure that it will spread the full width of the countersink, and if it overlaps when riveted, file it down.

Avoid having the rivet too long. Under such conditions it may bend, rendering a good sound joint impossible to make. A bent rivet should always be drilled out and a new rivet used.

Few amateurs will require to do any hot riveting, but some points about it may be mentioned. The rivets must be a trifle smaller than the hole so that, when red hot and expanded, they can be pushed just easily through the hole. The rivet should be a red heat, but not a glowing one, and it should be "closed" quickly. It must have its head held up tight to the surface of the metal by means of a heavy piece, such as a large hammer, otherwise it may expand in the hole when hit, and the rivet head may not come down on the outside surface of the piece. Consequently it will then be holding only by friction, and will be loose when cold. The procedure is the same as in cold riveting, except that the hammer blows, when closing the rivet, should not be so hard.

Splitting of cold rivets is due to tapping at them instead of hitting them hard. The outer surface of the metal is hardened and cracks by tapping, while the mass is unaffected. Always use good rivets and throw out rivets which have a "fin" below the head or along the shank. They cannot make a sound job.

SMITHS' WORK

S MALL smithing jobs can be done on a hearth which is made to stand on a bench and supplied with air blown from a portable foot-bellows. Such a device

will generally be big enough for any work the amateur may have in contemplation. The bellows shown in Fig. 1 will supply a continuous blast of

9*

air of sufficient volume to reduce steel
or iron of $\frac{1}{2}$-in. section to a welding
forging (fusing) heat.   The size is 14 in.
measured across the base which should,
preferably, be screwed to the floor.   It
should be coupled to a portable hearth
(shown in Fig. 2).   This can be made of
$\frac{1}{16}$-in. black sheet iron cut to the shape

ends of the hose should be copper-wired
to the bellows and the hearth tuyère.
A 56-lb. wrought iron, steel-faced
anvil should be procured.   Often one
can be picked up in a reasonably good
condition at a second-hand tool stores.
If an old motor-grease drum is cut in
half and filled with sand it will form an

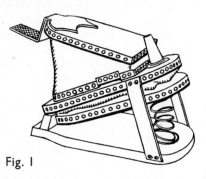

Fig. 1

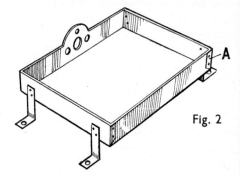

Fig. 2

and dimensions shown at Fig. 3.   The
front, back and sides are bent up at
the dotted lines, and the edges neatly
bent down to give strength and a finish.
The V gusset pieces, A, act as overlapping
plates riveted through the sides.   The
blast nozzle, known as the "tuyère,"
should be of cast iron and of large size.
It is cast from a wooden pattern (Fig. 4)
and then drilled through with a $\frac{1}{2}$-in.
or $\frac{3}{4}$-in. hole and three holes are drilled
through the flange to bolt it to the back
plate of the forge.   Four legs of 1-in.
by $\frac{1}{4}$-in. iron are riveted as shown
(Fig. 2) to the sides of the hearth, and
may be drilled for bolting to the bench
or other suitable support.

A length of rubber and canvas motor-
car water-circulation hose will couple
the bellows to the forge.   The hose
can be reinforced by winding 18-gauge
hard-drawn steel wire round a thin
broom handle in a spiral of about 6
turns to the inch, securing the ends,
inserting the broom handle and the wire
into the hose, releasing the wire and
withdrawing the broom handle.   The

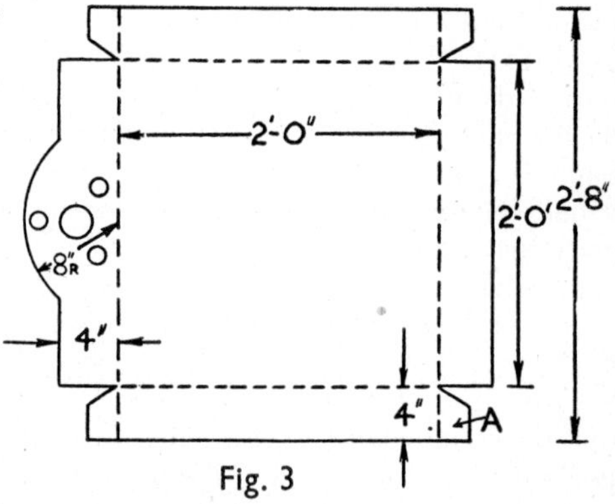

Fig. 3

ideal support for the anvil and will
deaden noise and shock.   This item is
shown in Fig. 5.

The Fire is the most important point
about smith's work, for the success of
the job depends upon properly heated
metal.   Small coal, known as "smith's
breeze," should be used.   A hardened
mass of caked coal is arranged around
and at the back of the tuyère, and may
be made by slacking the coal with water
sprinkled on.   An iron rod is pushed
through the tuyère iron while this is

being done, and when withdrawn leaves a channel for the air. The fire is prepared by first placing small pieces of wood (or shavings) soaked in paraffin into the cavity formed by the packed breeze, lighting this, and then blowing very gently. As the coal burns, the fire should be banked up with moist coal, and the draught continued. The work is inserted from the side and at a point about 5 in. from the blast orifice. A rake is used to draw the coal into position; the idea is to keep the work unexposed to the atmosphere. Coal is

Fig. 6. This nicks the material without cutting it, and the depressions so made around it should be of a depth to equal the outside measurement of the part to be reduced, as illustrated at Fig. 7. The flat of the hammer is then used on the still red-hot end of the bar and the metal reduced in thickness, beginning at the end and working to the depressed position, turning the piece over between every two or three blows, and gradually working back. If a round bar is being worked upon, it should be continually turned by hand (or by the tongs if it is

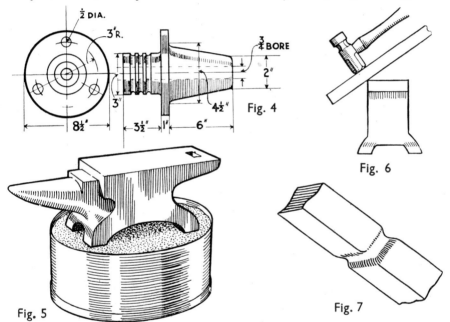

Fig. 4

Fig. 6

Fig. 5

Fig. 7

drawn from the front to make up for that burnt—and not from the back, which should be kept packed tight.

Forging consists in drawing down, upsetting and welding; but the various operations merge into each other.

In drawing down (from a large to a small cross-sectional area) the red-hot bar of iron is laid diagonally across the edge of the anvil and a blow given it with the flat peen of the hammer as in

of small length). In the case of square bars, hammer opposite faces alternately.

Reducing a round bar, as for a bearing, is done in a similar way and finished with a swage. For single-handed working a spring swage (as shown in Fig. 8) is most handy. It can deal with three or four sizes. Bottom swages (Fig. 9) fitting into a square hole in the anvil can be used with a flat-peened hammer for much reducing and rounding work.

A top swage can be used for finishing if an assistant is available.

In making such simple things as brackets, some smithing experience is needed. To make a good job the work should be thick at the bend. Fig. 10

jumped up and down vertically on the anvil, which causes the metal to swell out at the hot point. The jumping process should be discontinued as soon as the metal does not appear to swell easily, and the heat should be restored.

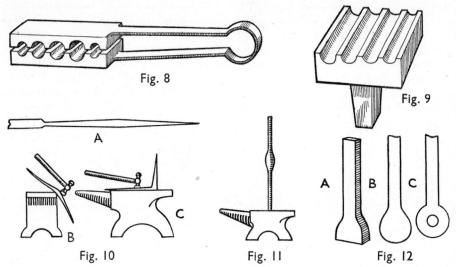

Fig. 8

Fig. 9

A

B

Fig. 10

A   B   C

Fig. 11

Fig. 12

shows the operations in sequence. At A the bar is hammered down to a taper at each end, meanwhile hammering it sideways so as to prevent it spreading in width. It is then bent over the anvil edge by hammering near the middle as at B, and finally it is hammered from the inside of the bend on the top of the anvil as at C, and squared up. Bending always reduces the strength unless the method shown is adopted.

If a head or a shoulder is wanted on a shaft or bar, the metal can be "upset." The easiest way of upsetting the metal is "jumping" it on the anvil. Fig. 11 shows the process. The metal is heated to a good yellow heat at the part where the "swell" is required. When taken from the fire it should be slaked each side of the heated part to confine the heat to where the bulge is to be. This can be done by pouring water over the ends. The bar is then up-ended and

A flat bar can be bumped out endways and hammered round to form an eye as shown at Fig. 12. At A it has been jumped up, at B it has been hammered round, at C it has had the hole punched through it while hot. This latter is done by means of a cold, flat-ended punch of taper form, which is driven into the hot metal from one side. If the metal is turned over it will appear dark where the punch has come partly through. As soon as this happens the punch is applied to the dark part and punched down again, the metal being, of course, red hot. The piece is then held over the hole in the anvil, and the punch driven through and out. A taper-punch enlarges the hole, and the metal is flattened and surfaced with blows of the flat peen of the hammer.

Welding is easy if sufficient heat can be obtained. To weld two pieces of iron together they should be jumped up to give excess of metal, as the subsequent hammering during welding will reduce the cross-sectional area. Fig. 13 shows two forgings as they appear before they are welded together. At A the ends have been jumped up, and at B the ends have been either sliced with a knife tool or driven down, white hot, to an angle on the anvil.

The ends are then placed in the fire together and raised to a welding heat— bright crackly sparks flying from the

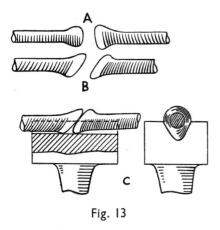

Fig. 13

dazzling white ends. To get the correct welding heat and prevent scale forming, dry sand is sprinkled on the job, which becomes molten, thus keeping the air away and so preventing oxidization, which would prevent the fusion of the two parts together.

When both are of a sparkling white heat they are removed, the faces brushed quickly with a wire brush and laid together, in a V block as at C, on the anvil or in a swage block, and quickly hammered down. The faces should be slightly rounded, as shown, so that the

first blows consolidate the metal in the middle of the weld. Then they are hammered down as the metal is slowly rotated by hand, the scarfed ends being very carefully closed down while at yellow heat, i.e. before they get red as they will do quickly, since they are the thinnest part of the job and therefore lose heat rapidly.

The job can be finished with top swages or top and bottom hand swages.

The following points will be of assistance in all forging and welding work:

1. Err, if anything, on the side of too much heat. Working at too low a heat cracks and disintegrates the fibre of the iron.

2. Confine the heat to the part to be worked.

3. Brush or knock off all scale before hammering.

4. Build up the metal by jumping wherever the metal has to be worked in a way which would reduce its cross-sectional area.

5. In welding, have a dazzling sparkling heat, get the two pieces together rapidly to prevent oxidization and scale (which would prevent the welding of the metal) and hammer at once.

6. In all forge work keep air from the work when in the fire by building the coal breeze around it.

7. Visualise every operation and its sequence before taking the metal out of the fire, and have all tools, setts, punches, swages, etc., ready at hand so that no second of time is wasted. Do as much at one heat as possible, but stop as soon as the glow gives signs of waning.

SOLDERING

IT is impossible to progress very far in metal working without a practical knowledge of soldering, for there are innumerable jobs in the shape of repairing household utensils, motor repairs, model making, and wireless which call for the joining of metals by this process. Indeed, in many cases, soldering is a vital part of the construction of an article.

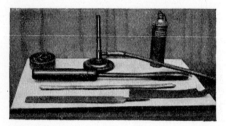

Fig. I

Briefly stated, soldering is a process of joining metals together by means of an alloy having a lower melting point than the parts to be united.

There are two distinct classes of soldering, known as soft soldering and hard soldering. The former is used where a joint of medium strength is required, and is usually attained by the use of alloys of lead and tin, which have a comparatively low melting point. The latter requires a very much greater degree of heat, and is employed where an exceptionally strong and heat-resisting joint is wanted.

As the majority of jobs the amateur is likely to encounter call for the simple process of soft soldering, this method will be dealt with at some length, while hard soldering, that is, silver soldering and brazing—which necessitates a considerable degree of skill but is only likely to be required for special purposes —will therefore only be briefly surveyed.

The equipment associated with soft soldering, as illustrated in Fig. 1, is inexpensive and consists of the following items:

Copper bit, commonly called a soldering iron.
Heating apparatus for heating the bit.
A supply of tinman's solder.
A suitable flux.
Blowpipe for special work.
File.
Emery cloth.

Fig. 2 shows a common form of soldering iron suitable for all ordinary purposes. It consists of nothing more than a piece of copper shaped nearly to a point, held by a straight piece of iron terminating in a wooden handle. Its purpose is to hold the heat which causes the solder to melt.

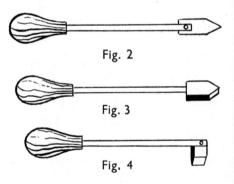

Fig. 2

Fig. 3

Fig. 4

It is a good plan to have two such bits, one for heavy work and a lighter one for work of a more delicate nature.

Another form of tool is illustrated in Fig. 3, known as a hatchet bit. It is used principally for soldering heavy lead pipes.

For Internal Soldering and for work where great local heat is required, the bit illustrated in Fig. 4 is a convenient tool to use.

If a supply of electric current is available an electric iron with its self-contained heating element is an ideal tool to have, for it rules out the necessity of having a separate heating device associated with ordinary soldering bits. Moreover, absolute cleanliness, so essential to the process, is assured. The

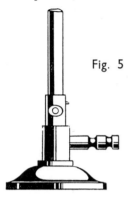

Fig. 5

type recommended for small work is one consuming about 60 watts, which is equivalent to the energy consumed by a medium-sized lamp. If such an iron is run off the power supply with current at one penny per unit, fifteen hours' service can be obtained for this small sum. The electric soldering-iron is simply plugged into a convenient socket which will heat up the bit to the desired degree in about four or five minutes.

Assuming that the ordinary copper bit is to be used it is essential to have some means of supplying the necessary heat, and as a coal fire is not always satisfactory, owing to its associated dirt, etc., it is advisable to employ either a Bunsen gas-burner or a petrol or paraffin blow-lamp.

The Bunsen Burner shown in Fig. 5 is particularly good for heating copper bits, as the heat produced is intense and the flame is clean. It is quite a simple device, and consists of a metal tube, at

the lower end of which a small gas-jet is provided. Holes are made near this end through which, when the gas is ignited at the top, a draught of air enters the tube by suction. The air mixes with the gas and produces a very hot, non-luminous flame. The air supply can be regulated to the correct degree by turning the loose sleeve fitted for the purpose. It is connected up to the gas supply by means of a flexible tube.

The Petrol Blow-lamp (Fig. 6) gives a very hot flame and heats a copper bit very quickly. It consists of a container for holding the spirit, a Bunsen burner, and a regulating valve.

To operate the lamp it should be filled about three-quarters full of petrol and the filler cap screwed down tight. A small quantity of methylated spirit is then poured into the flanged receptacle which is fitted just below the burner. The spirit is now ignited, and the burner allowed to heat up for a minute or so, the valve, of course, being closed. The regulator is now turned on a trifle, when

Fig. 6

the tiny spray of petrol vapour issuing from the nipple of the burner will ignite and burn with a bluish flame. If the petrol issues from the jet in the shape of a long smoky flame, it indicates that the petrol has not been sufficiently vaporised and it is therefore necessary to close the valve and heat the burner up again.

One of the chief points connected with blow-lamps is that they must always be kept perfectly clean. If the nipple becomes choked the obstruction can usually be dislodged with a small piece of fine steel wire, and should the orifice become too large, due to constant cleaning or any other cause, it must be replaced by a new one, which may be

Fig. 7

obtained for a few pence at most iron-mongers. Owing to the highly inflam-mable nature of petrol, great care should be exercised to keep all naked lights away when filling the container.

A Stand for Supporting a Solder-ing Iron whilst being heated is shown in Fig. 7. It consists of two pieces of stout tinplate, about 3 in. wide, and high enough to allow the business end of the tool to enter the flame of the heating apparatus. A recess is cut in each upper edge to receive the iron shaft of the tool, to keep it in place. The end pieces are then nailed or screwed to a wooden base which should be about 1 in. thick, in the manner shown in the illustration.

If an ordinary household gas-ring is used for heating the tool, the heater should not be placed directly upon a table, but should stand upon a suitable piece of sheet asbestos, otherwise the table may be badly scorched.

A Holder for the Iron that retains heat is a useful accessory for use with an ordinary gas-ring. It is shown in Fig. 8. It can be made from sheet iron bent to shape and fastened with rivets.

Fluxes.—Soldering calls for a suitable "flux" which must be applied to the parts to be joined, to prevent oxidisation of the surfaces.

There are many kinds of fluxes suitable for soft soldering, the principal ones being "killed spirit" (zinc chloride), resin, sal-ammoniac and several pro-prietary products, including a non-corrosive flux in a convenient paste form. For tinned iron (tinplate), wrought iron, steel, copper and brass, zinc chloride is generally used, but when this flux is employed, any surplus liquid left on the work should be washed away as it is corrosive and likely to have a detrimental effect upon the metals if not so treated. Acid fluxes should there-fore not be used upon such work as electrical apparatus, scientific instru-ments, and objects of a like nature.

Killed spirit is quite easily made if the following instructions are carefully carried out.

Procure a small quantity of com-mercial spirits of salts (poison) from an oilshop; pour it into a clean earthenware jam jar, and add some clean zinc cuttings. Directly the zinc clippings are immersed

Fig. 8

in the acid the solution will commence to effervesce and give off dense suffocat-ing fumes. It is therefore better to do this job out of doors where the fumes can pass quickly away. Add zinc bit by bit until the bubbling action stops.

Strain off to rid the liquid of surplus zinc, add a pint or two of sal-ammoniac, and when cool place the liquid into a distinctive bottle. Do not forget to label the bottle, and mark it POISON.

For soldering zinc, raw spirit of salts is used, but it is essential to wash away all traces of the acid directly the operation is complete, or else the acid will eat right through the zinc.

Suitable fluxes for tin—not to be confused with tinplate, pewter, and lead are tallow, resin, and resin oil.

Ordinary soft solders are alloys of lead and tin. The higher the proportion of tin the lower the melting point. A good-quality solder for use with a copper bit for general purposes should contain one part by weight of lead and two of tin. Such a solder melts at about 350° F. The quality of solder can easily be tested by bending it. If it crackles slightly you may rest assured that the solder is of good quality, that is, there is plenty of tin in its composition. Soft solder is obtainable in two forms, known as wire and bar. Solder in wire form is very convenient for small delicate work, while stick or bar material is useful for larger work.

Solder containing a small proportion of bismuth is useful for soldering pewter, zinc and tin.

Cored Solder, that is, wire solder having a core of a suitable flux such as resin, is very handy where small work is done with the aid of a blow-pipe.

The secret of successful soldering depends almost entirely upon absolute cleanliness of the parts to be joined and the correct temperature of the soldering iron. Before any soldering can be done with a new soldering bit it must be "tinned," which means that a thin film of solder must cover the whole of the lower portion of the bit. The first thing to do when a bit is being used for the first time is to file the faces perfectly

smooth. This operation is necessary because the surface of a newly-purchased iron is very often rough and pitted.

To Tin the Bit, pour out some killed spirit into an old saucer or other shallow earthenware pot. Place the bit in the flame of the heater so that the flame impinges upon the thick part of the copper and not on the working end, and heat it up to such a degree that the bit can be held about a couple of inches from your cheek without feeling any discomfort. On no account must the bit be allowed to become red hot, for a full black heat only is required. While the tool is getting hot, cut a piece of tinplate and place a small fragment of solder and a drop of flux in the centre. When the bit is hot enough, clean the surfaces with a smooth file, dip the end of the bit in the flux for a moment, and then melt the solder. Rub each face well in the molten metal until the nose of the bit is completely covered with a thin film of solder. If this operation has been successfully carried out the bit is now ready for use.

Before attempting to do work of any consequence it is a good plan to practise with the bit on different metals in order to get the "hang" of the operation, which, once learned, is seldom forgotten.

For the purpose of describing the process, it will be assumed that it is desired to repair a leaky domestic kettle.

First clean and remove all traces of dirt and grease from the surface to be repaired by rubbing it with fine emery cloth, bearing in mind that this surface should not be touched by the fingers after the cleaning process is done, otherwise the natural grease from the fingers will spoil the surface and thus prevent the solder from adhering. The cleaned surface must now be fluxed. This can be done by applying the flux with a small brush or by using a piece of pointed wood. Heat up the tinned soldering bit to the correct temperature, taking care not to let it get red hot or you will burn off the tin, in which event the bit will have to be re-tinned. When the bit is hot enough, wipe the surfaces quickly with a slightly damp rag and then put the nose of the tool into the flux for an instant. Place the end of the stick of solder on to the point of the bit so that a "blob" or spot of the molten metal sticks to the nose. Next, quickly place the tool to the prepared

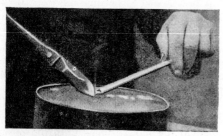

Fig. 9

portion of the work and keep it there until the solder adheres, which, if the bit is sufficiently hot, is a matter of only a few moments. This operation is indicated in Fig. 9. Remove the bit and allow the molten metal to set—which will only take a few moments—and cool off naturally, and then wash off any surplus flux.

Another simple example of soft soldered is shown in Fig. 10, where two pieces of sheet brass are required to be joined together by means of a soldering lap joint, that is, a joint where the edge of one piece overlaps the edge of the other. In this case it is necessary first to tin the faces between the joint. Clean and flux the surfaces to be joined in the same manner as that already described. Load the heated bit with solder and run it down the edge and underside of A to form a tinned surface about $\frac{3}{16}$ in. wide. Repeat the opera-

tion on the edge and top surface of B, which will complete the tinning process. Place the tinned surfaces together so that the edge of A overlaps that of B by $\frac{1}{8}$ in.; load the bit with solder and apply a spot of solder here and there along the edge to "tack" them together. Then draw the bit and solder very slowly together down the joint, allowing sufficient time to enable the tinned surfaces to unite.

In doing work of this description it is an advantage to tilt the work so that the molten metal will travel downhill with the point of the bit as illustrated in Fig. 11, which clearly shows the operation.

It frequently happens that when working on large objects, sufficient heat cannot be retained by the bit to allow the solder to flow easily, owing to the heat of the bit being rapidly absorbed by the work. In such cases it is necessary first to heat up the work and then proceed in the usual way, when it will be found that the solder will flow normally.

In some jobs it will be found that the use of a soldering iron is impracticable, in which case a small blow-pipe can very often be used to advantage. By means of a blow-pipe and spirit lamp a thin jet of intensely hot and clean flame can be directed on the joint until the solder fuses. This method will be found satisfactory in making joints in lead, tin, etc.

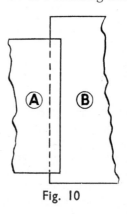

Fig. 10

We now leave the simple process of soft soldering with its comparative weak joint, and pass on to hard soldering, which includes silver soldering and brazing.

Unlike soft soldering, where heat at a comparatively low temperature is usually derived from a copper bit to make the solder run, hard solder requires a much more intense heat applied to the work to effect the same purpose.

Hard Solder, or silver solder, is an alloy of silver and brass, the brass being required to reduce the melting-point. It can be obtained commercially in various thicknesses in either wire or sheet form, and can very often be obtained at a jeweller's or silversmith's shop.

In small work it is usual to support the job on an asbestos or charcoal block in order to conserve the heat.

The flux used is borax, but before being applied to the work it should be prepared as follows. Heat the borax on a clean piece of iron plate over a clear fire or, better still, a Bunsen burner, until it melts. This will get rid of the water with which it is incorporated and leave pure borax. Get a piece of ordinary slate, about 4 in. or so square, and see that it is perfectly clean. Sprinkle a few drops of water on its surface, and mix some of the prepared borax with it to form a semi-liquid of the consistency of thin cream. Thoroughly clean the surfaces to be united, as in soft soldering, and then apply the flux. Cut a small square of solder and place it in position on the work. Now heat the work with a blow-pipe to a bright red heat, but do not allow the flame to play on the solder, otherwise it will melt before the work is hot enough, and consequently will not adhere. When the solder begins to fuse, add more flux and solder, any surplus of which can be removed by a file when the work is cool.

As silver soldering requires a high degree of skill to obtain a satisfactory joint, especially with regard to the application of heat, it is suggested that

numerous experiments be made before attempting more important jobs.

Brazing with brass solder, called "spelter," is a reliable method of uniting joints in brass, copper and iron articles. It is not a difficult process to acquire, provided sufficient heat is available. This usually necessitates the use of an iron receptacle containing small blocks of asbestos or pieces of fire-brick to retain the heat. The work is placed in position and the blocks built round it. A powerful blow-lamp will be found useful for supplying the heat. Like other methods of soldering, it is absolutely necessary thoroughly to clean the surfaces to be joined. This is best done with a file and then finishing off with emery cloth. A borax flux is

Fig. 11

used as in silver soldering, and a plentiful supply should be applied to the joint.

Direct the flame on the flux for a moment to get rid of the moisture, and then heat up the work to a white heat, but if the work is thin, take great care not to burn it. Dip the end of a stick of spelter in the flux and apply it all round the part to be united. When the spelter is seen to run, cut off the heat and allow the work to cool.

The small asbestos blocks previously referred to are made from pure asbestos. Pieces of asbestos-cement sheeting or tiles should not be used as they simply fly to bits when subjected to the intense heat from a blow-lamp.

HARDENING AND TEMPERING

THE tempering of steel for tools, etc., and the hardening of iron and steel for parts of mechanism which are subject to much wear—such as the cups and cones of ball bearings—are operations which can be easily accomplished by the amateur, and if proper precautions and procedure are adopted, good results can be obtained.

The process of hardening will be dealt with first.

In the case of cast steel or carbon tool steel, as it is often called, the hardening merely consists in heating the material to a bright red heat and plunging it into clean, cold water. This will make it "dead" hard and extremely brittle. Consequently it will easily crack and break, and therefore be useless for tools.

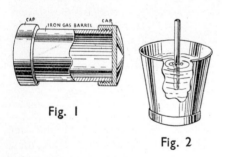

Fig. I

Fig. 2

Indeed, there are very few occasions where dead-hard steel can be used. To render it suitable for use it must be "tempered," or, in other words, the hardness must be reduced to a point where the metal will be sufficiently strong to withstand the shock of cutting the material for which it is intended, and yet be hard enough not to be easily blunted in use.

Mild steel and wrought iron cannot be hardened by heating and suddenly cooling, because they have not sufficient carbon in their constituents. Both of these metals must have carbon added to them before they can be made hard, and they cannot—except in expensive muffle furnaces—be hardened right through as in the case of cast steel, but only to a small depth from the surface.

Case - hardening.—This kind of hardening, rendered possible by the addition of carbon to mild steel or to wrought iron, is known as "case-hardening."

To add the extra carbon to the metal it is necessary to heat the metal in contact with the carbon to a very high degree of temperature. This can be easily done by enclosing the article to be treated in a piece of gas barrel charged with bone dust, scraps of leather, etc. (as illustrated in Fig. 1), and heating it to the right degree. The bone dust and leather become calcined by the heat, and the glowing iron, having an affinity for the carbon contained in the bone or leather, absorbs it into its surface.

The length of time during which the glowing metal remains in contact with the carbon determines the depth to which the carbon is absorbed into the surface of the metal. Four or five hours would give a depth of about $\frac{1}{16}$in. The iron actually assumes a "casing" of steel, and this casing may be hardened by heating the material to a red heat and plunging it into cold water, in the same way as hardening cast steel, but with this difference—the core of the metal will remain soft.

There is no need to temper the hardened surface, because the piece cannot crack, if certain precautions are taken, on account of the mass of comparatively soft metal within.

The heating of the metal in contact

with the carbon (bone dust, etc.) must be very thorough.

If the work is urgently required, cooling may be done at once by tipping the contents of the red-hot receptacle into cold water, but if time is of no consequence, a better way is to let the whole cool down gradually, when the metal (core and case) will be quite soft. Its surface can then be hardened by heating to a full cherry-red and plunging it into cold water.

Kasenit.—To avoid the necessity of packing the metal in bone dust and heating it in an iron receptacle, case-hardening to a lesser depth may be carried out by the use of a hardening compound known as Kasenit. This substance is in the form of a powder which is sprinkled on the red-hot iron while in the forge or under the influence of the blow-pipe. The Kasenit immediately melts on the surface of the iron and seems to be absorbed by it.

The process should be continuous, keeping the metal glowing hot and ladling the Kasenit powder on with a flattened rod, as one would apply spelter in brazing. After this treatment has been carried out for, say, twenty minutes to half an hour, the metal, still red hot, should be plunged into a bucket of clean, cold water to which a handful or so of salt has been added.

Kasenit is one of the most useful materials for amateur use. By its aid small screws as well as larger parts can be easily and quickly case-hardened, and as there is practically no distortion, a piece of iron or mild steel can be turned or otherwise shaped to finished size and hardened afterwards.

An important point to be observed when carrying out hardening and case-hardening is that the red-hot metal must always be immersed end-first. Failure to take this precaution will generally result in warped and bent material when cool. If the article is case-hardened the "casing" will crack on the outside of a curve. Fig. 2 shows the correct method.

Always use a large-sized bucket or similar circular vessel, so as to have a sufficient volume of water to prevent its temperature rising quickly. Swirl the water round and plunge the article being treated in the vortex. This will ensure a constant surface contact of fresh water on the piece being cooled.

As previously mentioned, dead-hard cast steel is practically useless unless it has been tempered, that is to say, its hardness reduced to a degree consistent with strength.

Tempering is done by re-heating the metal after hardening until it assumes a colour which would indicate the degree of hardness suitable for the work, and then quenching it in water.

Take a lathe tool, for example. It is first heated up to a bright red colour and then plunged into cold water, which hardens it. The next process is to clean the surfaces quite bright with a piece of pumice stone or with emery cloth. Then take a blow-pipe or a blow-lamp and apply the flame to the shank of the tool at a point about midway between the two ends. A colour will be seen to creep gradually up the tool from the part being heated. First it will be a light straw colour, then a golden yellow, and as the temperature increases, a dark brown, followed by purple and blue. These colours gradually follow one another from the heated part to the end of the tool. Observe the colour-changes carefully and when the dark straw hue reaches the cutting-edge, quench the tool quickly in clean, cold water.

If a chipping chisel is being tempered, let the colour continue up the tool until a straw-purple colour reaches the cutting end and then quench.

Quenching at a very light colour will give a very hard tool, with a tendency to brittleness; a full golden yellow gives a hard tool sufficiently tough to prevent breakage, and is the most useful temper for metal-working tools for cutting.

Woodworking tools may be "let down," as the process is called, to a yellowy-purple or brown colour. They need not be so hard as metal-working tools, and hold a finer edge at this temper, and will hone up on the oilstone, forming a "wire edge," which is the correct thing for plane-irons, firmer- and mortice-chisels, gouges, etc.

When tempering steel, avoid direct sunlight on the work, as it prevents one seeing the colour-changes accurately. A shady corner of the workshop is obviously the best for this kind of work.

Fig. 3

In the case of hardening taps, reamers, etc., where the cutting-edges are formed along the greater portion of their lengths, the best way to "draw the colour" is to make the tool dead-hard by quenching in a swirl of water as described and, having brightened it all over, to insert it in a piece of iron gas-barrel previously heated to a dull red heat. The tool should be held inside the tube with a pair of pliers, moving it backwards and forwards down the centre, but on no account allowing it to touch the wall of the tube. An illustration of this appears in Fig. 3.

The tool should be withdrawn occasionally to test the colour, and when the whole of the cutting-teeth assume a deep straw colour, the tool should be quenched.

A convenient method of tempering a screw-die is to hold the die by a pair of tongs or pliers over a red-hot piece of flat iron and keep turning the tool over. The die, having been polished, should be held at a distance of about $\frac{3}{16}$ in. away from the hot bar. When the colour assumes a very deep gold, nearly approximating purple, on each side, it should be quenched quickly by immersing it, flat side downwards, in cold water.

Another convenient method of tempering is to immerse the piece in molten lead, drawing it out occasionally for inspection till the required colour is obtained, and then quenching.

Quenching Colours.—The following is a short list of colours at which to quench when tempering various tools:

Taps and dies—full golden yellow.
Reamers—light golden yellow.
Lathe tools—golden yellow.
Wood chisels—gold with a touch of purple.
Plane irons—gold with a touch of purple.
Punches—purple.
Cold chisels—purple.
Knives—light blue.
Screwdrivers—dark blue.

For small tools such as the little cutters used in lathe-tool holders, a method which eliminates ordinary tempering is to heat the tool to a cherry-red colour and then swirl it in a bath composed of the following:

1 gallon rain or distilled water.
1 oz. cyanide of potassium (poison).
8 oz. saltpetre.
3 oz. lime.
Small pinch of permanganate of potash.

Pieces hardened in this way are very tough, will withstand considerable pressure before breaking and will take a good cutting-edge.

SHAFTING AND PULLEYS

WHERE a workshop is equipped with several machine tools, such as a lathe, drilling machine, universal wood-working machine, hack saw, circular saw, band saw—or any three or four of these machines—it becomes convenient to arrange shafting and pulleys so that a

In the accompanying drawings are given the design and construction of three different types of hangers and brackets which can be developed to suit any amateur's workshop, no matter what type of building it is.

The shafting is 1 in. in diameter and

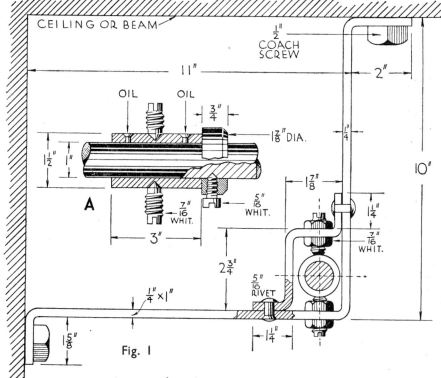

Fig. I

gas engine, an oil engine, or an electric motor can be employed to drive the plant or any part of it.

For the amateur's workshop nothing very elaborate is required, but it should be strong and easily constructed and applicable to varying conditions as to walls, joists, ceilings, etc.

can be bought at any machinery dealer's. Two kinds are standard stock, the bright-drawn steel and the turned steel. The former, for the 1-in.-diameter size, costs about eightpence a foot and the latter about sixpence a foot more. In the drawings 1-in.-diameter shafting is shown throughout, and readers can decide for themselves whether to use bright-drawn or turned. The latter is worth the extra sixpence since its accuracy makes for easy fitting and easy running.

In all the three kinds of brackets and hangers shown in the drawings the same arrangement of bearing is used. It is a plain casting of brass or gunmetal, 3 in. long, with a hole 1 in. (just full) to take the shaft, and $1\frac{1}{2}$ in. external diameter. It is shown in section, carrying the shaft, at A, in Fig. 1. Two

end will provide a seating for a core which will leave the hole $\frac{7}{8}$ in., so that only a small amount of metal will have to be taken off when boring.

The foundry will make the core (which is a simple sand cylinder) without a core box.

While making the pattern for the bearings, the reader may like to make also the pattern for the hub of the tinned-plate pulley shown at c in Fig. 4, and to be referred to later.

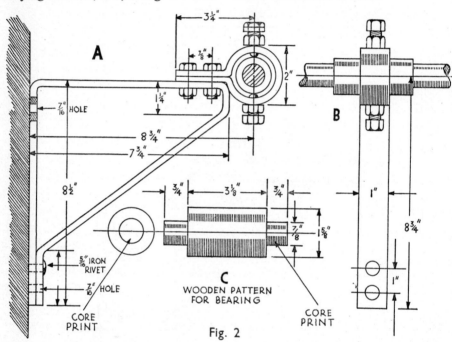

Fig. 2

oil-holes, with flared upper mouths are drilled to allow of easy and effective lubrication, or they can be tapped to take oil bottles or screw-down greasers.

A Pattern should be turned in hardwood to the dimensions shown at c, Fig. 2. These dimensions allow for machining, although there is no real necessity for doing any machining other than boring the hole; but it will look better turned on the outside and faced up at the ends. The core prints at the

The Bearing (A, Fig. 1) should be mounted in a three-jaw chuck, with a slight space left at the inner end so that the boring tool can be pulled in at the end of the bore to take off the sharp edge. Cut 4 in. off the shafting and remove the burr at the edge with a file, and use this as a plug-gauge when taking the final cut up the bore. It must be ascertained beforehand that the lathe is cutting parallel in the chuck (not between centres). To do this, chuck a piece of

½-in. mild steel rod in the chuck well back and projecting 2 in. Then take a fine cut along, using the top-slide of the compound rest, and calliper each end with a micrometer and see if both are exactly alike. If they are, the hole in the bearing casting will be parallel. Do not alter the top-slide till all bearings and all wheel-hubs have been bored out, and do not use the self-acting feed, which may not be parallel for boring, although parallel for centre-work. It is also better to use the top-slide because a finer

of dividers or "moph" callipers, and scribe a line across the end passing through the centre. Lay the bearing in a V-block and scribe, with the scribing block, a line along each side coinciding with the ends of the line across the ends. The points at which these lines cross the central circumscribed line around bearing are exactly opposite points. Here drill a ⅛-in. hole to the depth of just under ¼ in. and open it out to an angle of 90°, using a rose countersink, or a slightly more acute angle if you have a

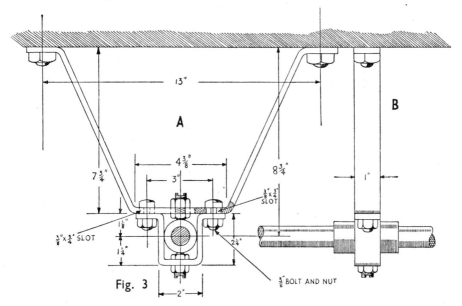

Fig. 3

finishing cut can be made with it than the self-feed.

The piece of shafting used as a gauge should push into the hole easily without any shake when lubricated. Then face off the end and remove the bearing from the chuck. Drill the two holes for oil and countersink them or tap them for lubricators. Then stand the bearing upright on the surface-plate or lathe-bed and scribe a line round it at the centre. Plug the end with a piece of flat hardwood and find the end centre with a pair

suitable countersink. The outside may now be turned—just skimmed up, if desired. It is probably better to leave it in its rough state, that is, as it left the moulding sand. In any case it should only just be cleaned up with the tool, and to do this it should be driven lightly on to a 1-in. mandrel between lathe-centres.

Steel Collars are used for keeping the shaft in position. Two collars are necessary for one shaft, and they may be placed at either side of any one of the bearings. If a pulley-wheel hub happens —in the laying out of the shafting and the machine or machines it drives—to come with its hub close to a bearing, one collar at the other side of the bearing will be sufficient to locate the shaft.

The collars are of standard size and can be bought with the shafting, but should the reader prefer to make them he can follow the dimensions on A, Fig. 1, which shows all necessary details. The collar is fixed on the shaft by a $\frac{5}{16}$-in. Whitworth screw, which should, of course, be case-hardened. Its end is pointed at a right angle and it screws through the collar into a slight counter-sunk depression made with a twist-drill in the shaft. This need not be more than $\frac{1}{8}$ in. to $\frac{3}{16}$ in. deep.

Figs. 1, 2 and 3 show clearly how the bearing is held by the pivot screws (shown at A in Fig. 1). They have Whitworth threads and may have hexagon heads or slotted heads, as desired.

The Hanger shown in Fig. 1 is the simplest. Like the other arrangements (illustrated in Figs. 2 and 3), it is made of bar iron 1 in. wide and $\frac{1}{4}$ in. thick. To make the hanger, bend the iron at right angles 2 in. from the end (top right corner), then at right angles the opposite way at 10 in., and then at right angles again at 11 in. We then have the hanging bracket shown, which is screwed to the beam or ceiling at one end and to the wall at the other end.

The bearing is held in a rectangular loop formed by a piece of the same stock as the bracket, bent $1\frac{1}{4}$ in. up, $1\frac{7}{8}$ in. along, $2\frac{3}{4}$ in. down, and $1\frac{1}{4}$ in. along, and riveted into the corner of the bracket as shown—with $\frac{5}{16}$-in. mild steel rivets —one each end.

Drill holes in this rectangle, on a line which halves it vertically. These are tapping-size holes for $\frac{7}{16}$-in. Whitworth screws, so they must be $\frac{11}{32}$ in. diameter. The hole in the strap corner piece should

be drilled before it is riveted in. Tap the holes with a $\frac{7}{16}$-in. Whitworth tap.

Prepare twice as many of the $\frac{7}{16}$-in. screws (pointed to fit the holes in the bearing and case-hardened) as you are going to make bearings. Case-harden them with "Kasenit" and fit them with nice, firm-fitting hexagon nuts and lock-nuts. The way the bearing is held in the brackets and hangers is quite plainly seen in all the drawings. The screws are screwed up to align the shaft when in position. When correct for height of bearing they are tightened up and locked with the lock-nuts. This will be dealt with later, when we come to fitting-up and aligning in position in the workshop.

With this hanger it will be necessary to assemble each bracket around the shaft with pulleys and bearings inter-vening, as required, before bolting up the hanger to the wall and ceiling or roof beams.

The hanger is attached by $\frac{1}{2}$-in.-dia-meter coach screws if a good depth of solid wood is available—say, at least 3 in. If not, ordinary bolts and nuts can be used. The holes are drilled at a suitable position at the ends. In some positions it might happen that one or both ends could be left straight and be bolted up to the sides of beams or along the top of walls.

The iron will have to be heated to a good red heat, and chalked beforehand where the bend comes. Then it is bent in the vice with a hammer to square up the corner. Do not "pull" the metal more than you can help or it will reduce its thickness and make it weak, and do not have the square corner bends too sharp. The amount shown in the drawings will give a strong construction.

In Fig. 2 at A and B is shown the ordinary type of wall bracket made out of quarter-by-inch stock. Here the bracket consists of one piece bent to a triangle and riveted at the bottom left corner with a $\frac{5}{16}$-in. iron rivet, and further held by the $\frac{7}{16}$-in. bolts or screws which secure it to the wall, the bottom one of which goes through both thicknesses of the metal.

The bearing is held in a separate circular-shaped lug, formed out of similar stock as the bracket, and turned round a mandrel while hot, to 2 in. outside diameter. It is bent, while hot, round the $1\frac{1}{2}$-in. bar, and the ends closed up on each other in the vice and then cut off at $3\frac{1}{4}$ in. from the centre of the loop.

The loop holds the bearing, and has the $\frac{7}{16}$-in. Whitworth holes drilled through it and tapped to take the bearing screws—a feature common to all the arrangements. The loop is attached at the top of the bracket by $\frac{3}{8}$-in. Whitworth bolts and nuts in $\frac{3}{8}$-in. holes spaced $\frac{7}{8}$ in., centre to centre, apart. These holes are filed to form slots $\frac{3}{4}$ in. long, to enable an adjustment to be made along the bracket of $\frac{3}{8}$ in. With the vertical adjustment by the pointed screws which hold the bearing, and the fact that the bearing can swivel around the vertical axis of the pointed screws, it will be seen that the bearing is adjustable in three directions for alignment.

A front view is shown at B, and the dimensions of the bracket are clearly seen on both drawings. The bracket itself stands $7\frac{3}{4}$ in. from the wall, but the bearing loop takes the centre of the shaft out to $8\frac{3}{4}$ in. from the face of the wall.

In this drawing at c is shown the pattern, turned from hardwood, for making the brassfounder's mould for the bearing. It can be turned, with its two core-prints, out of one piece of wood. It is essential not to exceed the $\frac{7}{8}$ in. for the core or a casting may be obtained which will not bore out so as to give a surface in the inch-diameter hole.

Fig. 3 shows a more conventional hanger suspended from the roof, ceiling or beam; or used upside-down as a

pedestal in those cases where it is convenient to have the shafting on the floor for machines driven below the table, such as fretsaws, circular saws, etc.

In this case the bearing is between the bottom horizontal member of the bracket and a dropped U-shaped frame bolted up to it. Both are of inch-by-quarter iron. The U-piece is fastened to the bottom of the hanger by two bolts in slots, which allow of adjustment sideways. The top pivot screw passes through a slot in the frame and is held in position by a nut and lock-nut. This can be adjusted to come vertically over the bottom pivot screw after the loop has been adjusted correctly.

Pulleys can be bought or made. Very light pulleys can be made of ordinary sheet tinplate of fairly heavy gauge.

Fig. 4 shows the construction of a 10-in. pulley with a 2-in. belt face. The same construction is, of course, used for larger or smaller and wider or narrower pulleys.

The Hub is a brass casting, cast from a hardwood pattern made to the dimensions shown at c, to which sufficient allowance has been added for machining. The casting is bored out to 1 in. diameter to fit snugly on the shaft, and has one shoulder a little longer than the other to take the grub-screw which fixes the pulley to the shaft.

The Sides of the Pulley are cut from fairly thick gauge tinplate to $10\frac{1}{2}$ in. diameter. There are two of these, the edges of which are knocked down to leave a ridge or lip, $\frac{1}{4}$ in. wide, square with the flat sheet. This can be done on the edge of a piece of 3- or 4-in.-diameter round stock, held in the vice, if the circle is first carefully scribed. The sheet should be held so that it lies on the top of the cylindrical block and the edge gradually hammered down all round to the scribed mark which indicates the outside edge of the corner. The disc is then cut across to the centre to form a V or gusset, as shown at E, and the edges of the V-shaped slot overlapped till the dishing is to the depth of $\frac{1}{2}$ in., plus $\frac{7}{16}$ in., as shown on the sectional drawing at D, the hole $1\frac{1}{2}$ in. diameter having previously been cut in the disc.

The disc is held temporarily in the dished position by means of a thin pin inserted into a hole drilled in the overlapping portions of the gusset. A permanent joint is then made by efficiently

the soldering process and their outer back edges should be touching.

The work should now be tested for truth. To do this, mount the hub on a piece of shaft on which it can rotate easily, without shake. Grip the shaft in the vice and spin the double disc to see that it does not wobble sideways at the edge. If it does, correct it by bending till it runs true.

The rim is now to be attached. Take a piece of moderate-gauge tinplate and

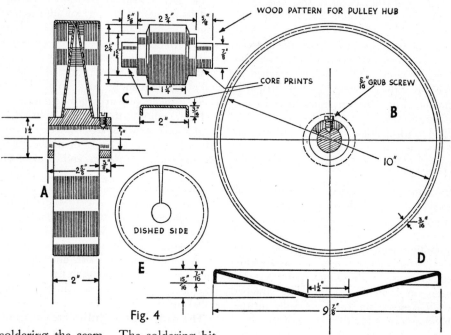

WOOD PATTERN FOR PULLEY HUB

CORE PRINTS

$\frac{5}{16}$" GRUB SCREW

DISHED SIDE

Fig. 4

soldering the seam. The soldering bit should be applied to the back and front of the gusset, allowing sufficient time to enable the solder to run well between.

The two discs are then fitted back to back on the hub, which has previously been tinned with solder, and they are soldered to the inclined double shoulder on the hub, the position of the two discs being shown at A—a sectional view. A couple of thin brass taper pins driven into holes made in each side will hold the discs to the shoulder on the hub during

cut a strip $2\frac{1}{4}$ in. wide and 32 in. long. Bend this round the flattened peripheries of the discs. It will overlap by about $\frac{1}{2}$ in. Tack it with solder at the edge where it overlaps and cut the strip across at the joint of the overlap, using a pair of tinman's snips for the purpose. Bend a piece of tinplate 1 in. wide and solder it underneath both ends of the strip when they are butted up close together, and cut the piece off $\frac{1}{8}$ in. inside each end. The strip will be $1\frac{7}{8}$ in. long.

Thus a hoop is formed with a joint flush on the outside and of a diameter to fit on the double disc.

Take the piece of round stock used for flanging the discs and bend both edges of the hoop down at right angles for a distance of $\frac{1}{8}$ in. each side. This forms a stiffening edge smaller in inside diameter than the diameter of the flanged edges of the discs, but the hoop can be sprung over the disc and then centred on the flange face of the discs by using the piece

$\frac{1}{4}$-in. yellow deal are cut $10\frac{1}{2}$ in. in diameter and a central hole just under $1\frac{5}{16}$ in. is bored in each with a centre-bit. They are then glued together and when quite dry are threaded on a 1-in. gas nipple 3 in. long, which has a standard flange screwed to its end and sweated with solder on the threads to prevent it turning. This is seen clearly at the right-hand end in the sectional view. Another standard flange is then screwed as tightly as possible at the other end of

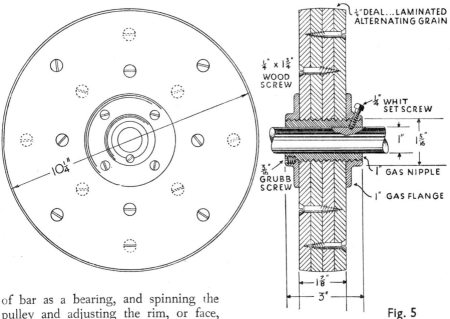

Fig. 5

of bar as a bearing, and spinning the pulley and adjusting the rim, or face, sideways on the double discs, as required. When true, the flanged periphery of the discs is soldered to the inside of the ring or hoop, which now forms the belt face.

A grub-screw driven into a threaded hole in the boss and into a corresponding depression in the shaft keeps it in position.

A Laminated Wooden Pulley may be used, as an alternative to the built-up sheet-metal one, and some amateurs may find it more convenient to make. One is shown at Fig. 5. Four discs of

the nipple, and the four $\frac{1}{4}$-in. laminations are further secured together by means of sixteen wood-screws driven in the flat faces of the pulley—eight in one side and eight in the other, in positions indicated by the full and dotted lines respectively, in the side view of the pulley.

The left-hand flange is screwed up tight by holding it in the vice, and a hole is drilled and tapped half in the flange and half in the nipple to take a $\frac{3}{16}$-in. Whitworth grub-screw.

The screw-hole for the fixing-screw in the right-hand flange is drilled at an angle, as shown, and passes through the boss of the flange and through the nipple and into a depression in the shaft. The rough interior of the nipple is cleaned out to 1 in. (to fit the shaft snugly), either in the lathe or with a reamer. The gap is removed from the lathe-bed, the pulley driven on a shaft between lathe centres and the belt-face turned slightly

pulleys can be built to any desirable width and any diameter by following the instructions given.

In erecting the shafting, one end hanger or bracket should be fixed in position, at a given distance from wall and roof and at right angles to it. Then the other end bracket should be placed temporarily in position. The bearings should be fitted along the shaft and located by the pointed set-screws in the hangers or brackets. A long spirit-level on a straight-edge should be laid along

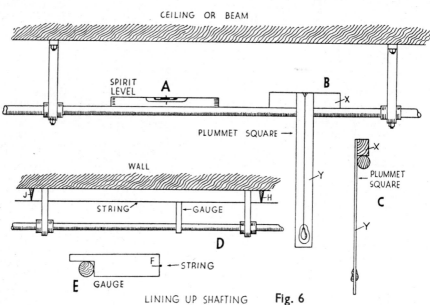

LINING UP SHAFTING   **Fig. 6**

convex. The convexity is slightly exaggerated in the drawing. It should be to a radius of about 12 in.

It must be understood that the idea of four laminations is to get the grain of the wood lying in four different (and equidistant angular) directions. This prevents splitting and offers an end grain of the wood to the belt at any part of its circumference, thus ensuring a non-slip "bite."

Both the tinplate and the wooden

the shaft as at A in Fig. 6, and the bearings adjusted, up or down, till the bubble stands central.

In place of a spirit-level the device shown at B and C may be used. It can be rigged up in the workshop roughly but accurately. It is a piece of wood of square section X, about 2 ft. long, with a wooden blade Y, about 4 ft. long, and is shown in the side view at C. The blade has a marked plummet-line and a plumb-bob and string, as shown in the front view at B. It is hung on the shaft as indicated, and the plumb-line shows whether the shaft is horizontal, i.e. square with the vertical—the blade Y being square with the stock X.

Having got the adjustment correct, so that the shaft is truly horizontal, the other brackets or hangers (if there are others required, owing to the length of the shaft) should be erected. They will have been strung on the shaft if of the type which has no detachable bearing-holder (as Fig. 1). They are adjusted for height to suit the position of the shaft, but left loose sideways. As the shaft is now resting in all the bearings and quite level (as tested again by the spirit-level or plummet), the necessary sideways adjustment, i.e. to or from the wall, can be made.

At D is a plan view of the wall (in section) and the shaft. Two nails or wooden plugs (H and J) are driven into or attached to the wall and a tight string is stretched between them. The string is at the same distance from the wall at each end and provides a straight line to work to.

Now make a gauge of a piece of hardwood as at E. It has a square recess at one end to locate it on the shaft and a scribed line (F) at the other, and its length between the inner edge of the recess and the square end is equal to the distance of the shaft from the string at H and J, less $\frac{1}{32}$ of an inch. You should just see daylight between the end of the gauge and the string when the mark (F) is placed opposite the string and the gauge held square with the shaft. If the shaft is bent sideways, by reason of an intervening hanger or bracket-bearing between the end ones being out of position, the daylight gap between the gauge-end and the string will be closed or widened. Whichever it is, make the lateral adjustment (by means described

in the case of each method of supporting the bearing) till the shaft is parallel to the line all along. Then tighten all up.

Pulleys should be left loose on the shaft till the shaft is fitted and adjusted, as directed, for alignment. Each pulley can then be moved along to the correct position to line up with the pulley on the machine it has to drive, and a counter-sink made in the shaft to take the end of the fixing-screw of the pulley.

The diameter of the pulley which takes the drive from the engine or motor will depend on the engine or motor speed, the diameter of its driving pulley, and the speed at which it is desired that the shaft shall run. A suitable speed for the shaft for operating woodworking machinery would be too fast for metal-working machines, so a compromise must be adopted in cases where amateurs do woodwork as well as metalwork.

The ratio of the diameter of the driving pulley to the driven pulley is the ratio of the speed. The circumference can be neglected. If the engine or motor runs at 1,000 revs. a minute, has a 4-in. pulley and the driven shaft has a 12-in. pulley, the shaft will run at $\frac{1}{3}$ of 1,000 or 333·3 revs. per minute, which would be a very useful speed. The speed of the machine which the shaft drives will again be varied by the ratio of the pulley on the shaft and the pulley on the machine. If we gear down again from the shaft in the same proportion we get a speed of 111·1 revs. per minute at the machine-driving pulley. Therefore, with the 12-in. maximum pulley on the shafting and the 4-in. minimum pulley on the power, it is possible to get variations suitable for metalworking or woodworking.

As a rough approximation, it may be taken that woodworking machines require to be driven at three times the speed of metal-working machines.

WORKSHOP FOUNDATIONS

IN installing a workshop with tools that may be reckoned as plant and machinery, the first thing to consider is the arrangement. Light is an important factor. Artificial light may be placed to suit the tool, but to get the best results from daylight the tool must be fixed to get the light in the right direction. In the case of a lathe the light should come from over the user's right shoulder, so as to fall naturally on the face-plate or chuck and on the front edge of work which is being turned between centres. Better, more accurate and quicker work is produced, with less strain of hand and eye, if the light falls directly on the edge which is cutting off the metal. The ideal is overhead lighting—a glazed roof or skylight. The next best is a high window with the lathe at right angles to its left-hand side and with the head-stock at the end of the bed away from the window. These are the ideals to be arrived at, but they must, in most cases, be modified by particular circumstances, such as the positions of doors, fireplaces, etc. A little trouble and effort, in re-arranging things, will have a lasting effect on the ease of working and the quality of the work turned out.

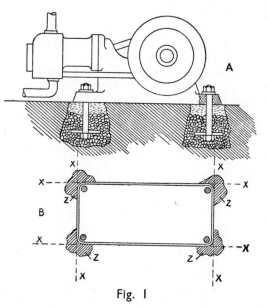

Fig. I

In the article on SHAFTING AND PULLEYS we have dealt with the methods of installing them. Machines require equal care in their fixing and arrangement, and should be rigidly attached to floor or wall to prevent vibration. Especially is this so where they are power-driven.

For the purpose of showing suitable ways of forming fixings and foundations for tools, etc., examples have been made of a small gas engine, a shaper, a lathe and a drilling machine, showing different arrangements for different conditions. Obviously, the different fixings could apply to any of the machines shown, or one method of fixing could apply to all of them, except the wall fixing of the drill.

In Fig. 1 is shown the most suitable arrangement for fixing machines which stand on a concrete, brick, stone or other solid floor.

Holes are dug in the floor for each holding-down bolt; and it is of importance that these holes should be deep, and wider at the bottom than at the top. To find the positions of the holes and the right location of the holding-down bolts is very simple if the following procedure is adopted.

When the shafting is in position, the

machine (we will take the gas or oil engine in this case) is placed on the floor and lined up with the shafting and turned by hand to see that the belt does not run off or travel along the sides of the pulleys. The engine should be as far away from the shaft as the possibilities of the small workshop allow, and should drive at an angle nearer the horizontal than the vertical, if practicable. The best possible position having been decided upon and the engine (or other tool) standing in that position, lines are traced on the floor of the outline of the base of the machine. These lines are marked x–x, x–x, x–x, x–x in the drawing. The lines should extend well beyond the machine so that, if the outline becomes obliterated in the course of breaking into the concrete and digging the holes, their **ends** will still be visible and new lines can at any time be scribed, chalked or chiselled to locate the engine or tool when we come finally to lay it down.

Next, with a narrow chisel placed through the holding-down bolt-holes, and rotated as it is struck with the hammer, mark the positions for the bolts. This marking will soon become obliterated, but it will have served its purpose of ensuring that the hole will be made in a position necessitating the least amount of removal of earth or concrete.

Then move the tool, machine or engine away, and dig holes far enough towards the centre of the machine to reach the points where the bolts will come, reaching out sideways, or cross-ways, as at z, z, z, z, to enable the bolt-head and washer to be inserted from the underside up into its place after having moved the machine back into its working position. The holes should be about 9 in. or a foot deep for a small engine of about $\frac{1}{4}$ h.p., and deeper for a heavier engine or machine. The depth

will also depend on the nature of the floor. If of good sound concrete the depth of the hole need not exceed 6–9 in. below the floor-level. On the other hand, should the foundation consist of nothing more than loose earth, with a thin concrete crust, the depth of the excavation should be a foot or more and it should extend well underneath on all sides. This will be a matter requiring judgment on the conditions obtaining in each individual case. The hole should be undercut, that is, it should be wide at the bottom and only wide enough at the top to facilitate digging the stuff out and getting the ballast (to be referred to later) and the bolt, nut and washer in.

The handiest tool for removing the debris is a garden trowel. The shape of the holes will be as shown in the sectional view at A in Fig. 1, and the mouths of the holes will be as shown in the plan view at B, where the engine has been replaced over the holes and, with the edges of the base lined up truly with the marks x–x, x–x, x–x, x–x, is now in position. Place a spirit-level across the top of the flywheel rim to see that the crankshaft is horizontal. If it is not, pack the engine bed up on the side necessary to make the adjustment. Pieces of broken slate are most useful for this purpose.

Now flood the floor round the engine with water and let the water soak thoroughly into the holes so as to have all in a moist condition. Prepare the bolts by substituting pieces of plate iron behind the heads instead of ordinary round washers. These plates should fit the bolts loosely and be about 4 or 5 in. square. Their shape is not important provided there is plenty of area. Any odd piece of $\frac{3}{16}$-in. or $\frac{1}{4}$-in. plate will do, with a hole drilled through of the same diameter as the hole in the engine or machine-tool bed.

10

Slip the plate, with the bolt through it, into the excavation and push the bolt up through the hole in the engine bed. Then, having greased its thread well, place a washer and a nut on to the thread and let it hang down vertically in the hole, allowing the end of the bolt to protrude about ¼ in. through the top of

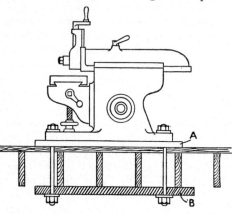

Fig. 2

the nut when the nut is down on the washer and the washer is down on the bed of the engine.

Now fill the hole loosely with pieces of broken brick, cement or stone. These pieces should not be larger than 1½ in. diameter and not smaller than ½ in. They should be clean and wetted before putting into the hole, and should be pushed down below the plate and fill the hole to within ¼ in. of the top. When adjusted, the nuts should stand vertical and square (flat) on the bed of the machine.

Now mix some fresh Portland cement to the consistency of fresh cream, and add a little clean, fine sand (not sea sand, which would sweat) in the ratio of one of sand to three of cement. Mix enough to fill all four holes and pour it in quickly, stirring a little with a piece of rod while so doing, to ensure the cement penetrating around all the brick

pieces, etc., and filling the whole of the orifice, to the level of the floor.

If the engine has to be raised, to bring its shaft horizontal, swill liquid cement in the space between the bed and the floor. Do this all round the corners and sides to ensure that, when set, the engine (or tool) rests everywhere on the cement. Then smooth off and leave for at least 48 hours to set, occasionally swilling water over it to assist in the hardening and toughening. Do not on any account touch the bolts or nuts till the job has stood for at least a week. The cement, when thoroughly hard, will hold the square head of the bolt, but, if an attempt is made to turn the nut before that, the bolt may turn and make a round recess for its head, making it difficult or impossible to tighten the machine down by the nut.

Where a workshop has a wooden floor, supported on joists, the arrangement shown in Figs. 2 and 3 should be used. The machine should stand on an iron plate A (Fig. 2) a little larger than the base of the machine. It could be about ³⁄₁₆ in. thick for a small machine.

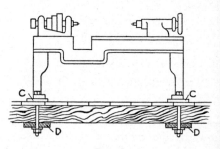

Fig. 3

And on this the tool should be laid in the right position so that the bolt-holes miss the joists. Each pair of the four bolts should go through an iron bar, B, underneath the joists. The bar should be of ¼-in. flat stuff, 2½ in. wide and long enough to reach well past the outer edges of the joist. Long bolts (which may have the nuts below or above or at both ends as convenient) hold the machine firmly to the joists when all is tightened up.

When the joists run in the direction of the length of the machine, as at Fig. 3, which shows a lathe so disposed, hardwood battens, c, c, twice the width of the feet, may be used, and, underneath, $\frac{1}{4}$-in. iron bars 2 in. wide, marked D, should be employed to take the pull of the bolts and brace the lathe firmly to the joists. It is bad practice to bolt a machine direct to floor-boards as it tends to loosen boards and joists. The methods shown actually increase the strength and rigidity of the floor and are well worth while; they will be fully appreciated when it comes to running the machine in actual work.

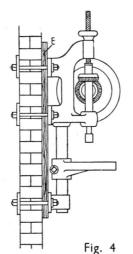

Fig. 4

Fig. 4 represents a post drill bolted to a 9-in. brick wall. Such a machine should not be placed against a lath-and-plaster partition. The wooden back-plate E should be of oak and at least $1\frac{1}{4}$ in. thick. Bolts $\frac{1}{2}$ in. diameter are used. They should go through the wall at points corresponding with the interstices between the bricks, if possible.

To fit up the machine, mark out the back-plate for the holes and drill them to take the $\frac{1}{2}$-in. bolts. Then lay the plate up against the wall, fixing it temporarily by means of one or two 3-in. wire nails, and mark on the wall the positions of the bolt-holes. Arrange them to come, if possible, at a vertical or horizontal brick-joint. Then drill the corresponding holes $\frac{3}{4}$ in. diameter through the brick, using a tool consisting of a piece of iron, gas or steam barrel with one end serrated by means of a three-square file. The tool is used by striking it on the head with a hammer and rotating it slowly with the hand. The particles of brick which enter the tube and sometimes choke it should be removed from time to time to prevent jamming and impeding cutting. This is best done by holding the tool vertically and tapping it with the hammer. The drilling machine and its back-plate are bolted up with 4-in. wide bars of iron plate at the back, under the nuts or heads as the case may be. A channel should be cut in the brickwork from a position above these back-plates to meet the hole, in the case of each bolt-hole. When all is bolted up fairly tight the back-plate of the drill should be tested with a plummet-line to see that it is vertical. Then pour liquid Portland cement into the channels at the backs of the iron plates to fill the space around the bolts. When dry, the bolts will be perfectly rigid and thus prevent the machine shifting. This extra rigidity of the bolts is particularly necessary when drilling a piece of work which can only rest on the floor. This is often very convenient, but if the bolts were not cemented into the wall as described, the pressure of drilling would force the drilling machine upwards, loosening things and straining the bolts. When the cement sets the nuts are tightened.

BELTS AND BELTING

THERE are many kinds of belting used for driving machines from a line-shaft, but for the small workshop there is nothing to equal the old-fashioned flat leather belt. It should be thin and, so, supple enough to enable it to hug the face of the pulley, for it is on the frictional resistance against the belt slipping on the pulley that the drive depends. If the belt is stiff it will not lap closely round the face and the area in close contact will be insufficient to transmit the drive without slipping.

The width of the pulley should be

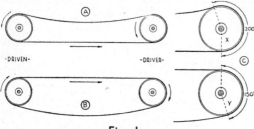

Fig. I

one-fourth greater than the width of the belt. In the description of workshop SHAFTING AND PULLEYS we have shown pulleys of 2 in. in width. On such pulleys 1½-in. belting will run nicely without fear of overlapping the edges. If the belt overlaps the edge of the pulley the leather will be stretched along the flat and not at the edge, and there will be a tendency for the belt to become distorted, which may cause it to run in any direction and therefore be liable to slip off the pulleys or ride with its edge in the centre of a small pulley—for instance, that of an electric motor, which has a slight surface curvature.

In actual practice, certain pulleys should have a slight camber. It is general practice to have a rise of ⅛ in. in

1 ft. of width, so that a pulley with a 12-in. face would be ¼ in. bigger in diameter at the centre than at the edges. A pulley with a slightly convex face has the effect of causing the belt automatically to centre itself, but the pulleys on machines, lathes, etc., and the pulley on an electric motor or small gas or oil engine may possibly be flat or have a very slightly convex face and if so it will be sufficient, presuming the pulleys are accurately in line, to ensure that the belts stay on. In the case of a sudden excessive strain the belt may leave the pulley, but this is not always a disadvantage because the sudden cessation of drive may conceivably avoid damage either to the tool being used or to the work on which it is being employed.

A wide belt running slack is preferable to a narrow belt running tight. There should be no need to run belts tightly. A tight belt absorbs a great deal of power which should be used in doing useful work. It also has the effect of wearing shafts and journals rapidly. This applies to both the bearings of shaftings and the bearings of machine spindles, such as lathe mandrels, saw spindles, etc. To obtain a good frictional contact between belt and pulley, the direction of the drive should be carefully considered. The whole efficiency and economy of the drive may depend on this simple problem.

A Vertical Drive is the worst of all drives for belts and should be avoided wherever possible. A horizontal drive is good if the slack side of the belt is upper-most so that the weight of the belt tends to wrap it farther around the pulleys.

A Horizontal Drive.—In Fig. 1, at A, is shown the correct arrangement.

The driving pulley pulls the driven pulley from the underside. This keeps the belt taut on the underside and its weight sags it down on the upper side so that it encircles more than half the circumference. The illustration at B

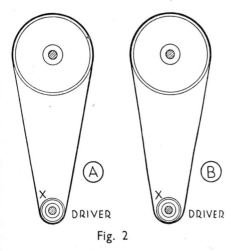

Fig. 2

shows the arrangement with the belt pulling on the upper side. The sag due to the under weight of the belt is pulling the belt away from the pulley, and the amount of surface of the face in contact with the belt is less than half the pulley circumference. Diagram C in Fig. 1 shows, at X, the arc of surface contact of a belt running as at A, and at Y the arc of contact of a belt running as at B. The difference is particularly noticeable as it represents the condition in both driving and driven pulleys. In one case the arc of contact is 200 degrees; in the other it is only 150 degrees.

Fig. 2 shows an inefficient vertical drive as from an electric motor to an overhead shaft. The whole weight of the belt is tending to keep it out of contact at both sides and bottom with the driving pulley X. A belt drive for an electric motor should be so arranged to have a good angle from the vertical. It should be at an angle of at least 45°,

as shown in Fig. 3, and it should pull from the bottom as indicated by the arrow. As the armature of an electric motor is small (on account of the high speed necessary to obtain a given power) every advantage should be taken of the weight of the bight of the belt, Y, to get the maximum amount of sag to enable the belt to embrace as much of the circumference of the pulley as possible. It may even be found advisable to place a spring or weight-loaded jockey-pulley at the back of the driving pulley, as in Fig. 4, at X, to keep the belt in close contact with the driving pulley for a greater surface of its circumference. The jockey-pulley should have a slightly concave belt-surface to match the convex surface of the driving motor pulley.

In a small workshop, using very small power, this would hardly be necessary, the best procedure being to increase the width of the pulley-face and use a wide belt. If the belt is soft and flexible and kept well dressed with colon oil or belt dressing (which can be had from

Fig. 3

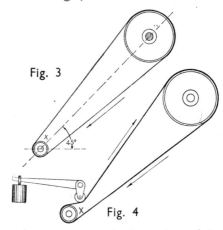

Fig. 4

the motor-car supply houses), and is wide enough, it will transmit all the power required if the angle of the drive is 45° or less from the horizontal. In cases where short pulley drives are essential the best way is to arrange the drive as nearly horizontal as practicable by mounting the motor on brackets fixed to the wall opposite to the one supporting the shafting. This would drive the shaft by the top weight of the belting being in tension, as in Fig. 5.

In all belt drives efficiency and absence of slip without strain on the bearings can only be obtained by keeping the pulley centres as far away from each other as possible. No short drive can be efficient.

In dealing with belts in general remember that tensioning up absorbs a lot of power. A lathe can very quickly be made inaccurate if driven constantly with a tight belt. A slack belt sagging on to the pulleys and not away from them gives the best results, i.e. least slip and least power absorbed in the drive and least wear and tear on shafts and machine bearings.

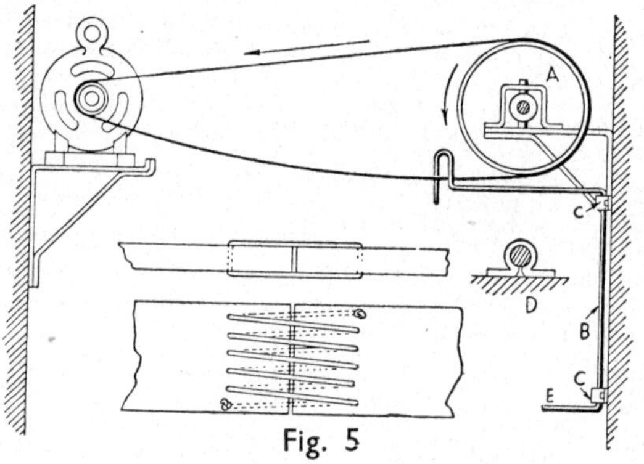

In the case of a lathe driven from a main shaft, a countershaft is necessary so that a three-step cone pulley may be used to drive the lathe-mandrel at various speeds. In some cases, where the shaft is driven by a slow-speed prime mover—such as a gas or oil engine—the three-step pulley could be mounted on the shafting direct and changes made as wanted by hand, but this is not advised as it is not only very inconvenient but also dangerous, because it means throwing off the belt to stop the lathe.

For a small workshop the arrangement shown at Fig. 5 will provide means of getting over the difficulty. In this case the pulley on the motor armature is made 6½ in. long for a 3-in. belt, and two 3-in. wide pulleys are used at A. One is screwed to the shaft and the other free to revolve on it, so that its face rides close to the face of the fixed pulley.

A Simple "Striker" for shifting the belt from one pulley to the other is made of a piece of ½-in. iron rod B, placed vertically and kept in position on the wall by means of bent strip loops c (shown separately at D). The handle is bent horizontally at E, and at the top is a horizontal arm bent upwards, and down over the belt at the other side.

By pulling lever E the belt is led from the fast to the loose pulley. If the lathe is fixed down to the floor and to the wall—as it will have to be —the lever E can be placed in such a position as to make the stopping and starting of the shaft easy and accessible, and the arrangement does away with the necessity for a fast and loose pulley countershaft, as the three-speed cone pulley is mounted on the shaft which carries pulleys A.

In the small shop it will probably never be necessary to run other machines while the lathe is being used: and so stopping and starting the whole shaft will be no particular disadvantage—none at all if the workshop-owner is the only workman.

For small belts which have to go over small pulleys and do not have to transmit much power the belt joint should be such as to easily bend round the small pulley and not to give a shock or blow in running. There are numerous kinds of belt fasteners on the market. They all

Fig. 5

give a little irregularity to the belt as it rides over the pulley. In a small machine and on small work such shocks are to be avoided. The raw-hide thong lace for making belt joints is the best. Thread the lace through the belt as shown in Fig. 5, and knot the ends. The ends of the belt are cut square so that their edges butt together. It should be laced up very tightly so that the two ends of the belt more than butt up close: any thickening is then hammered down with a flat hammer on a flat iron surface. The ends will then bed down flat and square to each other, and the raw-hide will be embedded in the leather. This makes an excellent joint for light work such as that under consideration, and if the belt stretches it is an easy matter to unlace it. In dealing with a stretched belt, cut off ½ in. or 1 in. and scarf the ends to match, then lace the belt with the raw-hide lacing again. Use a proper belt punch for making the holes for lacing;

holes made with a knife or solid punch are unsuitable. Have a punch of just sufficient size to cut out holes of the same diameter as the lace. The knots at the end of the lacing should lie on the outer surface. Another method is to start the lacing in two adjacent end holes with the same amount of lace coming through each hole and then cross the laces as each pair of holes are threaded, finishing on the outside of the belt. Note that the outside is the smooth side, and the side next to the pulley the flesh side of the leather.

The driving side of a belt should be kept clammy, as this condition allows the belt to drive, when a little slack, without slip. Thin wide belts drive better than narrow thick ones, and a thick belt will not hold to a small pulley at the bottom of a vertical drive. A highly polished pulley usually indicates a slipping belt, which should be treated with one or other of the numerous belt compositions.

GAS ENGINE OVERHAUL

A GAS engine will become inefficient and expensive to run unless occasionally overhauled. It is not a long job nor an intricate one.

Take off the cap nuts of the big-end bearing. Draw back the end cap carefully, taking care not to pull it sideways or it will jam on the bolts. Then push the connecting-rod and piston back by turning the crank. Let the crank come round forward and down to six o'clock, and then the piston and rod can be removed. Clean the piston-head by chipping and scraping off the carbon or

coke. Examine the rings. If much wear is apparent, new rings are indicated, which are best got from the makers. The rings should spring out to a good $\frac{3}{16}$ in. all round when the piston is

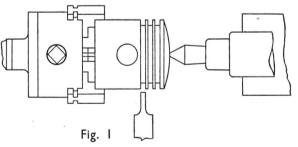

Fig. 1

clear of the cylinder. If the rings have good pressure outwards, but have worn thin in their slots, the slots will also be worn with a shoulder in the sides. Chuck the piston carefully in a three-jaw lathe chuck, using the back centre to support the crown of the piston, and, with a wide parting-tool, turn down the grooves square, and take off just enough metal to leave the sides of the grooves flat and without shoulders. This is shown in Fig. 1. Do not touch the outside of the piston.

To Make New Rings, turn a wood pattern $\frac{1}{4}$ in. larger than the diameter of the cylinder-bore and 4 in. long. It should be cored out to 1 in. in diameter below the cylinder-bore size, so will have core-prints at the end 1 in. less than the cylinder-bore diameter. It is a simple pattern and the foundry will make you a hard cast-iron ring from it.

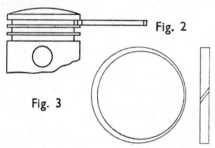

Fig. 2

Fig. 3

Place the casting into the three-jaw chuck and bore it out to the inside diameter of the old rings when fully closed. Then pack brass strip under one jaw so as to throw the ring of iron eccentric by the same amount as the old ring. It will be a very small set-over —$\frac{1}{16}$ in. probably. Now turn the outside to the exact diameter of the cylinder-bore, and then remove the packing from under the jaw, keeping the ring in the same place, and close the jaws again. The outside will now run eccentrically and the inside concentrically. The next procedure is to cut off the rings, one after the other, with a parting-tool which should have a square front edge and

should taper back each side for clearance—as in the setting for the piston grooves shown in Fig. 1. Since the inside is running concentrically the parting off can be done without injury.

The rings should, before splitting, be rubbed on emery cloth on a surface plate and smoothed on each side and tested by rolling them round the pistons in the ring groove till they will roll perfectly all round, going to the bottom of the groove and touching firmly all round, as shown in Fig. 2. Then the thin part of the ring is cut diagonally with a thin hack-saw as indicated in Fig. 3. The ring should be gripped with the edge just protruding above the vice-jaws—using lead clamps —while cutting the slot. When released, the ring will fly open, and the sawn ends should then be smoothed accurately with a thin warding file.

Try the ring in the cylinder with the joint flush both sides and the cut closed. If the cut closes before the edges of the ring come flush with each other at the slot, it will be necessary to smooth-file a little off one end.

When testing, the ring should be fitted squarely into the cylinder with edges flush. If found to be in order the ring can then be slipped on to the piston and the piston fitted into the cylinder.

The Gudgeon-pin.—Examine the gudgeon-pin when you take the piston off the connecting-rod, and if it is at all shaky, turn a new one out of cast steel bar, which should be very carefully annealed before working and again before the final cut is taken in the lathe.

First reamer out the holes in the gudgeon-pin bosses to ensure they are round and in line, and make the new gudgeon-pin to fit them. It will be a little bigger than the old one, and the bush in the small end of the connecting rod can be reamered out to fit the pin so that when the rod is fitted to the piston the latter will turn just a little stiffly on the new pin. It must not on any account be at all loose.

The Caps.—Take the caps off the two crankshaft main bearings and lift the crank and fly-wheel clear. Wipe the brasses and journals and look for scoring

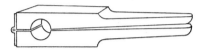

Fig. 4

on either. If scored, carefully scrape the bottom brasses and polish the crankshaft journal with a strip of emery cloth held in a wooden holder as in Fig. 4. It is made out of hard wood. A hole the size of the journal is bored through, and it has a butt-hinge screwed on the end. It is then sawn down the centre to form a clamp as shown. Lay the emery cloth in the holder and with oil applied to the journal press the two handles together and pull the tool backwards and forwards round the shaft or crank-pin till the surface is smooth. Measure with a micrometer and if found larger one way than the other, concentrate on the thick side till round to within one and a half thousandths of an inch.

When the journals are perfectly round and the crank-pin similarly true, apply the bearings. Lay the crankshaft in the bottom bearings, all clean, after having marked the journal with red ochre oil-colour as used by art students, and supplied in tubes. Observe where it touches, and scrape the part very carefully with a scraper (Fig. 5) made out of an old half-round file heated and bent round and carefully tempered to dark straw-colour and ground to the shape shown. The angle is a little

10*

more acute than 90° and the bottom is flat (*see* end section).

When the shaft, after repeated trying, and each time wiping the brass and redistributing the red ochre colour on the journal, marks the bearing all over, the job is done for half the bearing. Then place the top half on the lower one and similarly mark it for scraping. The top half may not close on the shaft (or crank-pin, as the case may be) and therefore requires treatment with a file across the face. It should bed down on to the lower brass tightly while being just right on the shaft. A proper marking cannot be had if it rests on the bottom brass before it touches the crank or crankshaft journal. Mark and scrape and clean and mark again, till the shaft or crank-pin marks all over the bearing. Then tighten all up as tight as possible. The crankshaft should be capable of being turned stiffly by hand. If it is easy, take a light cut off the brass face, first seeing which is tight by loosening one bearing and trying; but tightening up between tests. If it is still tight you know it is the other one which is loose. Slack off the first and tighten the other. It will be found not to close tight on the crank. Take a light cut over the face with a very

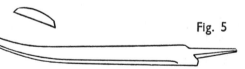

Fig. 5

smooth file, and screw down tightly again.

Examining the Valves.—Remove the cotter and the spring and withdraw the valve. If the seat and the head of the valve are badly pitted or the valve shows black at any part of its face, it must be ground in. Scrape the valve and seat and rub with coarse emery, treating the valve stem endways. Clean the valve-stem guide and oil it. Then make a spring of tough, springy wire to surround the upper portion of the valve guide and the valve stem, and have it of such a length that it will lift the valve from its seat as indicated in Fig. 6. Smear the valve-face with a coarse valve-grinding compound, and work the valve in an oscillating manner half a turn at a time backwards and forwards with a screwdriver. The spring will lift the valve when pressure is taken off the screwdriver. The valve should be allowed to come

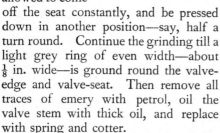

Fig. 6

Fig. 7

•003 IN.

off the seat constantly, and be pressed down in another position—say, half a turn round. Continue the grinding till a light grey ring of even width—about $\frac{1}{8}$ in. wide—is ground round the valve-edge and valve-seat. Then remove all traces of emery with petrol, oil the valve stem with thick oil, and replace with spring and cotter.

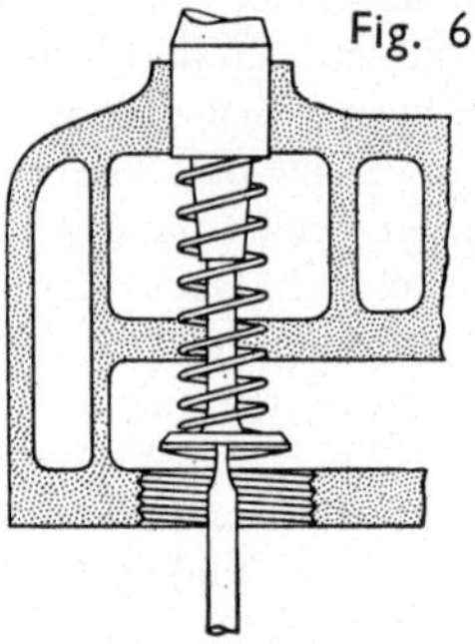

The Rocker Lever which operates the valve has its adjustment at the end, where it lifts the valve stem; and the adjustment should be made so that when the engine is warm, the valve seated, and the roller at the end of the rocker in contact with the low side of the cam, there is a clearance between the abutment screw and the valve stem of three thousands of an inch, as indicated in Fig. 7.

In some gas engines there is a timing valve which opens the combustion chamber to the hot-tube chamber. This valve works under bad conditions and sometimes hangs up, entirely preventing the engine starting or running. It gets gummed up with solidified oil. Ease it regularly with petrol and then use paraffin, and then, when dry, apply only the finest light motor-oil. It only requires a very little, and a pint would last a year. But it should be kept clean and always lubricated. Sometimes the helical toothed two-to-one gear has too much back-lash and the engine makes a lot of noise. The bracket which carries the horizontal shaft to the valve gear may be lifted very slightly to bring the big wheel on the camshaft a little nearer the half-size wheel on the crankshaft. It is usually dowelled for position and held by a couple of studs. Withdraw the bracket, knock out the dowel, draw the stud-holes with a round file ($\frac{1}{32}$ or $\frac{1}{16}$ in.) and bolt the bracket back with the stud units and tap with a hammer up to nearer the crankshaft wheel. Tighten up and run the engine, and if it runs silently, drill a new dowel-hole and drive a new dowel-pin to locate it.

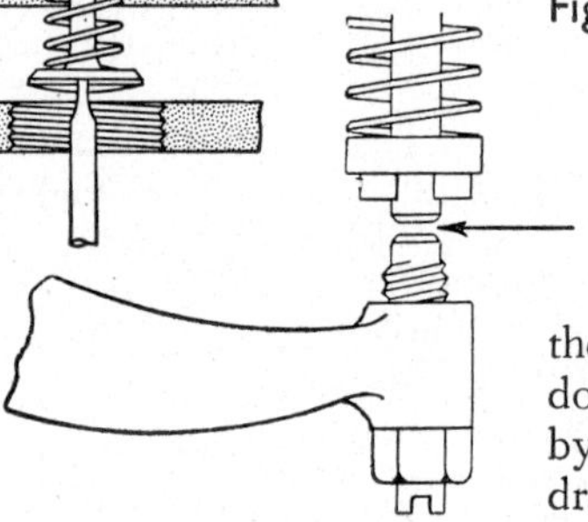

Look at the Rubber Gas-bag.—If it is perished get a new one. A new bag or diaphragm is worth while, for the gas engine, without the governing effect of the gas bag, will run jerkily, waste gas and make your whole gas-supply jumpy.

See that oil can actually get to the big end bearing while the engine is running.

Swill out the water-jacket with hot soda water left in for a day (or longer if possible) and clear the water-pipes and tank entry and exit. Also send a scraper brush along and up the exhaust pipe. Dismantle the silencer and scrape clear of carbon and see that nothing chokes its exit. If the engine exhausts into a pit, make sure that water can get away easily.

MOTOR-CAR ADJUSTMENTS

IN these days, when motoring is common both for business and pleasure, it behoves the owner to know something about the mechanism of a car in order that he may be in a position to execute certain repairs without the necessity of taking the car to a garage every time a little trouble is experienced. By carrying out one's own repairs, not only is a great deal of time often saved, but the running costs of the car are reduced to a minimum.

A motor-car may be said to be made up of eight distinct parts, excluding the body, which may be summarised as follows:

1. The engine, or power generator.
2. The clutch for connecting the power unit to the transmission.
3. The gearbox, forming part of the transmission.
4. The propeller shaft and rear axle for transmitting power to the road wheels.
5. The brakes.
6. The front axle and steering gear.
7. The electric installation.
8. The frame, including the springs.

The following paragraphs contain a brief description of these parts, how, and for what they function.

The power of the engine is obtained by the explosion and the resultant expansion of a gas in the cylinders of the engine. This "mixture" is produced by means of a carburettor, and exploded by an electric spark generated either by a magneto or a battery and coil. A definite sequence of events occurs in the engine to produce this power; in most engines it is that known as the "Otto" principle or cycle. This cycle is comprised of four strokes of the piston, namely, (1) The suction or induction stroke, (2) the compression, (3) the explosion or ignition, and (4) the exhaust, respectively. So for every two revolutions of the crankshaft we only get one power-stroke. These strokes are shown diagrammatically in Fig. 1.

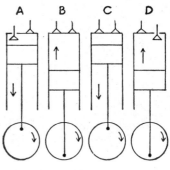

Fig. 1

As the piston starts to move down the cylinder on the suction stroke (A) a valve, called the inlet valve, is opened by means of a cam, allowing the gas mixture to be sucked into the cylinder from the carburettor. This valve shuts when the piston gets to the end of the stroke. In general practice, the inlet valve actually closes when the piston starts to go up on its next stroke. The next stroke (B) is the compression stroke and is upwards, and, as its name suggests, the piston compresses the gas into a very small space ready to be fired. At the end of this last upward stroke a spark occurs in the compression space at the top of the cylinder, exploding the gas. The explosion and the resultant expansion of the gas forces the piston down as at C, thus creating the force or power to turn the crankshaft. Nearly at the end

Fig. 2

of the power-stroke, a valve, called an exhaust valve, opens by means of a cam, thus allowing the exploded gas and the gas which is still expanding to escape. On the upward or exhaust stroke (D) the remainder of the exploded gas is forced out through an exhaust port, exhaust pipe, and silencer, into the open air. At the end of this stroke the exhaust valve closes and the sequence of the cycle is repeated, and so on.

As can be readily understood, the one explosion has not only to give power to propel the car but also has to overcome the resistance of the other three strokes. To assist in this work a flywheel is fitted to the crankshaft, which, after the explosion has taken place, stores enough energy in it to carry the crankshaft round through the other three strokes.

The cranks, valve openings, and the spark are so arranged that all cylinders

fire or create power during the two revolutions of the crankshaft, so the more cylinders there are, the more even the force or torque, and the more continuous the turning movement imparted to the crankshaft.

The explosion naturally generates excessive heat and, to keep the metal parts from burning or seizing up through expansion, the moving parts have to be lubricated with oil, generally supplied by means of an oil pump driven by the engine, although in some instances splash lubrication is employed. The cylinders are kept cool with the aid of water supplied from a radiator which circulates through a jacket surrounding the cylinders.

The Radiator is situated in the front of the car, and is designed not only to cool the water, but to keep it at its correct temperature. This is necessary because a petrol engine being a heat engine is most efficient when kept hot. One of two methods is adopted to circulate the water round the cylinder-jacket and the radiator. That known as the thermosyphon principle derives its circulating effect from the physical fact that the heated water rises to the top, while the cold sinks, and in so doing causes the water to circulate. This method is the one used on modern petrol-driven car engines. A pipe connects the top of the cylinder-jacket or head to the top of the radiator (as illustrated in Fig. 2), and a similar one from the bottom of the radiator connects to the bottom of the cylinder-jacket. Large-bore pipes are used to allow free movement of the water. As the water absorbs the heat from the top of the cylinder it rises up the pipe to the top of the radiator, where, on being cooled, it descends to the bottom, and so back to the water-jacket. The whole mass of water is soon heated up and is kept at a more or less uniform heat.

In the other method, a circulator or pump, driven by the engine, is installed in the water-system to force the water round, drawing it from the cylinder-top through the radiator, where it is cooled, and forcing the cooled water into the bottom of the water-jacket and so to the cylinder-top. In this arrangement smaller pipes can be used.

A fan, driven by the engine, is sometimes used with either of the above-mentioned systems to draw air through the radiator apertures, to assist in cooling the water.

The Carburettor.—Mention has been made of the carburettor, which might be termed the heart of the engine. Its function is to convert the liquid petrol into a mixture of petrol vapour and air in suitable proportions to produce a highly explosive mixture. The carburettor is in direct communication, through an induc-

tion or inlet pipe, with all the inlet valves of the engine. The principle upon which the carburettor works is based upon that of a garden sprayer, where air at high velocity is drawn or forced past or over a tube having a small outlet or hole in the top, the tube being full of liquid. The liquid is drawn out in the form of a very fine spray or vapour.

In the interior of the carburettor, the tube mentioned above is represented by a small device called a jet. The petrol is supplied to the jet through a float-

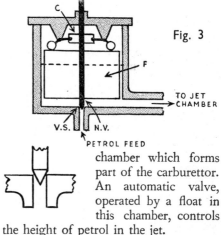

Fig. 3

chamber which forms part of the carburettor. An automatic valve, operated by a float in this chamber, controls the height of petrol in the jet.

The automatic device is simple and effective and consists of a float (F, Fig. 3), needle valve (NV), and valve seating (VS). Resting on the float are the weighted ends of two hinged levers, the other ends fitting loosely into a collar (C), which is fixed to the needle-valve spindle. The other end of the spindle is accurately pointed and fits into a corresponding chamfered hole through which the petrol is fed.

The action of the valve is quite simple, for when the petrol is drawn from the float-chamber by the action of the engine, the float naturally goes down, the weighted ends of the levers fall while the opposite ends rise, and in so doing lift the needle off its seating, allowing more petrol to flow into the chamber. The reverse action then takes place, the float rises, its needle-valve drops and shuts off the supply.

The Choke Tube.—In the chamber containing the jet, the necessary air-speed is obtained by surrounding the jet, as shown at J in Fig. 4, with a Venturi, or a choke, tube. This tube is tapered at both ends, the narrowest part being on a level with and surrounding the orifice, B, of the jet. The sizes of the jet-hole and choke tube are designed to give the correct power-mixture. As the piston travels down the cylinder during the suction stroke it sucks air through the choke tube, thus imparting great velocity at the narrowest part of the tube, which converts the petrol into a very fine spray, mixing easily with the air—a highly explosive mixture. The amount of vapour mixture drawn in is controlled by a butterfly valve or throttle, which in turn is controlled by a hand-lever and an accelerator-pedal operated by the driver.

There is also another jet, termed the "pilot," which is separate from the main or power-jet. It is used solely for slow engine speeds and, therefore, for starting.

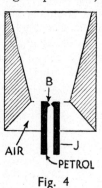

AIR

B

J

PETROL

Fig. 4

This auxiliary jet is necessary because the main jet and choke tube are too large to obtain the necessary air-speed for vaporising the petrol when the engine is running slowly. The pilot is installed together with a very small choke tube to give only sufficient power to start the engine and to keep it running at a slow or idling speed. The mixture obtained from this jet can be varied on the majority of modern carburettors by giving more

or less air as required, the adjustment being made when the engine is warm. Another point is that this mixture is not directly controlled by the driver, once it has been finally adjusted.

Although the above arrangement may be quite efficient for starting a warm engine, something else is required on most carburettors for starting a cold engine, for when the engine is cold, the petrol vapour has a tendency to condense or turn back into a liquid on entering the cold cylinders. Two devices are in general use to overcome this difficulty, one of which partially stops up the air-inlet, thus creating a sucking effect direct on the jet and therefore drawing a greater proportion of petrol to air. This is called an air "strangler." The other method adopted is to increase the size of the jet-orifice by means of a variable jet.

One of the latest types of carburettor consists of two carburettors in one. One of these is designed to give a very rich mixture on starting, which automatically weakens as the engine starts and gathers speed. As the engine-speed increases, the air-suction decreases in the starting carburettor, thus weakening the mixture, and the suction gradually increases in the power carburettor until the engine reaches a certain speed, when the whole of the mixture is drawn from the power carburettor. When the engine has warmed up, the starting carburettor is put out of action by hand control.

The electric spark for firing the explosive charge is obtained by utilising the principle of electro-magnetic induction, the theory of which need not be gone into deeply here. Two coils of wire are used, one called the primary and the other the secondary. The former consists of a comparatively few turns of thick, insulated copper wire, wound on soft iron core, while the latter is composed of a great many turns of very fine wire, as illustrated diagrammatically in Fig. 5. The ends of the primary coil are joined to an accumulator or a generator, and a suitable automatic device called a "contact breaker," for

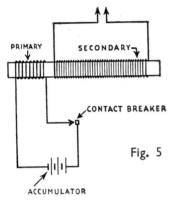

Fig. 5

rapidly interrupting the current, is included in the circuit. It is a well-known fact in electrical work that when an electric current flowing round one coil—in this case the primary—is suddenly stopped, or, in other words, is broken by the breaker, another current is induced in the other coil. The thickness and lengths of wire in both coils are so calculated that the current induced in the secondary is of an extremely high voltage, so high, in fact, that it causes a spark to jump or pass through an air-gap. The voltage of the current used in the primary coil is generally six or twelve volts when supplied by an accumulator, and roughly eight volts when a magneto is used.

Two methods are commonly employed for producing the high-voltage spark: one known as the magneto system and the other, battery ignition, the principle of the two coils mentioned above being used in both.

The Magneto (Fig. 6) is a self-contained low-voltage generator, combined with a high-tension coil, that is to say, in addition to the usual primary winding

on the armature for the actual production of the current, the secondary coil is superimposed on the primary. The method of breaking the flow of current is by means of two cams (c) and breaker (B), as indicated in the diagrammatic sketch Fig. 7. The cams are stationary and the breaker rotates on the end of the armature. One of the ends of the primary coil is connected to the centre piece (A), which is mounted on insulating material, and the other end is connected through the metal frame of the magneto to the breaker (B). In order to obtain good electrical contact at the place of breaking, special contact-points are used as at P, one point being riveted to the breaker-arm (B), and the other fixed to an adjusting screw in A, and locked in position with a nut. To obviate excessive sparking, which would otherwise take place when these contacts break the

Fig. 6

circuit, due to the current trying to jump the gap, a condenser is connected across A and B. The current, instead of trying to jump the gap, flows into the condenser, which also tends to make the current stoppage more sudden.

One end of the secondary winding is connected to an insulated brass ring, called the slip ring, mounted on the armature, and the other end to the metal frame of the magneto via the armature spindle. Pressing on this slip ring is a carbon collector brush mounted in insulating material, and kept in position by means of a coil spring. In turn, this brush is connected to another brush in the rotary part of the magneto, called the distributor, which is driven by geared teeth on the armature spindle. The distributor brush is pencil-shaped and is housed in a metal tube inserted in insulating material. This carbon pencil rotates in a fixed insulated block having four metal plates (in the case of a four-cylinder engine) cast in it, the plates having heavy leads connecting them to terminals fixed to the outside of the distributor block. The magneto is so designed that when the contact-points break the circuit, the distributor brush in contact with one of these plates conducts the current to a sparking plug in the particular cylinder to which it is connected, and thus fires the charge. To switch off the ignition, the primary current generated in the armature is earthed, by means of a hand-operated switch.

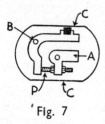

Fig. 7

A sparking plug of standard modern type (Fig. 8) consists of a metallic centre rod of special material to resist burning, encased in a high-class insulating material —such as porcelain, or mica— fastened in a steel or a brass body. The body forms the part which is screwed into the cylinder-head. The centre spindle is continued to level with the bottom of the threaded part of the body, which has a metal point—sometimes three —projecting towards the centre. The width of the gap between the centre rod or electrode and the metal

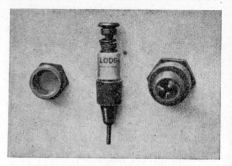

Fig. 8

point or points across which the spark jumps should be ·015 in.

In the battery system of ignition, an accumulator is used for supplying the initial current, and a separate ignition coil consisting of a primary and secondary winding, as mentioned before, for producing the high-voltage spark. In addition to this, a distributor is also necessary in order to distribute the high-tension current to the cylinders. This

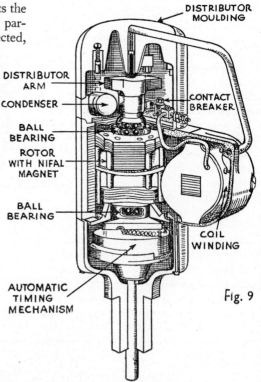

Fig. 9

DISTRIBUTOR MOULDING

DISTRIBUTOR ARM

CONDENSER

BALL BEARING

ROTOR WITH NIFAL MAGNET

BALL BEARING

AUTOMATIC TIMING MECHANISM

CONTACT BREAKER

COIL WINDING

device is shown clearly in Fig. 9. The distributor is driven by the engine, and has breaker-points like those of the magneto. The breaker itself is stationary, but the points are operated by means of a rotating cam. A condenser is, as in the magneto, connected across the contact-points to prevent sparking.

This system is cheaper to produce, and is now widely adopted, as it is quite as effective as the magneto. Its one weak point is liability to failure due to overtaxed accumulators. To switch off the ignition, the low-tension current from the accumulator is cut off by means of a hand-operated switch.

To obtain the action of advancing and retarding the ignition, which should be adjusted to suit the speed of the engine, the cams on the magneto are mounted in a housing, which can be moved backwards and forwards round the axis of the armature, while in the battery distributor system the contact-points are mounted so that they can be moved in a similar manner round the cam axis. In both cases the adjustment is obtained by hand, which causes the contact-points to break sooner or later, as the case may be. Automatic advance of the ignition is now used on a number of engines.

The Clutch is a frictional device for gradually and smoothly transmitting the power given out by the running engine to the road wheels of a stationary car in order to propel it, and also changing gear when once the car is started. It is purely a coupling between the engine flywheel and the gearbox, one part being the flywheel itself, and the other part—having a friction lining—connected to the gearbox shaft, but capable of sliding backwards and forwards on it. The two parts are generally kept pressed together by means of a spring, or springs. To disconnect the power, the springs are compressed by pushing down the clutch pedal, which allows the surfaces to slip.

The horse-power of an internal combustion engine is a combination of speed (engine revolutions) and force, so that when full throttle is used, the one varies directly as the other. To make full use of this power when force is required at the road wheels, as instanced in starting or climbing hills, the engine speed must be geared down to obtain the necessary force and to do this a gearbox is used. To start the car moving, the first gear (low) must be used so that the full power of the engine can be utilised, and therefore the maximum force at the road

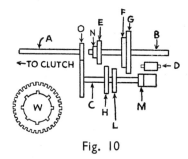

Fig. 10

wheels. Then, when less force or turning effort is required, more speed can be utilised by changing to the next higher gear and so on until the top gear is reached, which is a direct drive from the engine to the rear axle through shafts A and B (Fig. 10) being connected by wheels O and N.

The Gearbox is composed of four disconnected shafts (A, B, C and D) parallel to one another, all running in suitable bearings. The shaft A projects outside the gearbox and carries on its splined end the driven part of the clutch. On the opposite end inside the box is a wheel (O) with internal and external teeth, as shown at W. The teeth on the outside of this wheel mesh with a wheel fixed on shaft C, called the layshaft, and as these teeth are always in mesh, the wheels are called constant-mesh gears. Distributed along shaft C and keyed to it in permanent positions are three other wheels in a four-speed gearbox, and two in a three-speed box, each wheel decreasing in diameter. On shaft B, which is in line with shaft A, are two sets of gear wheels, E and N, and F and G—the latter usually being butted together—which slide along this shaft on splines or keyways. One end of the shaft B has a bearing in shaft A—called the spigot bearing—and the other projects through the box and is coupled up to the shaft which transmits motion to the road wheels. These sliding gears, which are controlled and moved at will by means of a gear-lever, effect the changes of gearing by G sliding into mesh with M, F with L, E with H, and N—which is part of E—with teeth on the inside of the constant-mesh wheel O.

Referring to the diagram, it will be seen that on shaft D is the "reverse" pinion, which engages with the bottom sliding gear in its normal position on the

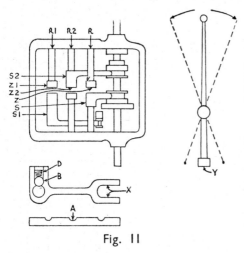

Fig. 11

top or secondary shaft and the bottom gear-wheel of the layshaft.

To enable the first gears to mesh when the car is stationary and the engine running, the shafts A and C must be prevented from revolving as A is directly coupled with the crankshaft through the

clutch. This is done, of course, by depressing the clutch pedal.

It has been mentioned that the sliding gears can be controlled at will by means of a gear-lever. There are two methods of accomplishing this: one by means of a "centre ball change," where the gear-lever moves on a ball fulcrum, and the other by using a "gate change," where the lever slides sideways and works in guides. The action in the gearbox is the same in both cases.

In the case of the ball-change system, which is the one usually adopted in private cars, the hand-lever is generally in one piece. Fig. 11 shows the movements of this lever. The sliding gears are held in position by selectors S, S1 and S2, which are able to slide along their respective rods R, R1 and R2. These rods are rigidly fixed in the gearbox casing. Each selector has a ball (B) and spring (D) (or a similar device), and each rod for forward gears has three grooves. The combination of these grooves and the ball and spring lock the sliding gear in its correct position. The centre groove (A) is for the gears when they are in their neutral positions; that is, when they are not required for driving. The other grooves are employed when the gear is moved into its driving position. Each selector has a fork (X), which engages in a machined circular groove on the sliding gear, and a slot (Z, Z1 and Z2) into which the end of the selector lever (Y) fits. The reverse selector rod has only two grooves, one for the neutral position and the other for the working position. As can be understood, all gears have to be brought back to the neutral position and locked there by means of the ball before another gear can be used, this being entirely automatic in action. The bearings used in a gearbox are generally ball bearings.

The Back Axle is used for three purposes. First, to transmit the power from the engine, through the gearbox, to the rear or driving wheels; secondly, to carry the rear part of the body by means of springs attached to the frame and the axle casing; and, thirdly, to carry the road wheels. For transmitting the power either a bevel or a worm gearing is used. The bevel type is shown in Fig. 12, from

The Differential, briefly stated, consists of a casing shown at E in Fig. 14, in the centre of which is fixed a shaft (H). On this shaft are two or more (according to the design) bevel wheels (L), which are free to rotate. A bevel wheel (G), called a crown wheel, is also bolted to the casing, which is turned or driven by a smaller bevel wheel (N), termed the driving or crown pinion. If the crown wheel be turned, the whole casing (E), shaft (H), and the bevel wheels (L) will turn with it. Two axle shafts (M and MI) are fitted into this casing, with bevel wheels (O and OI) —shown black— fixed to one end of each shaft, which mesh with the bevel wheels

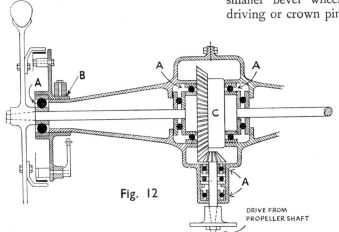

Fig. 12

DRIVE FROM
PROPELLER SHAFT

which the method of transmission can be clearly seen. The gears and shafts run in either ball or roller bearings, in positions marked A, while the springs are fixed to the casing at B, and the road wheels fixed to the shafts as shown. The part indicated by C is called the differential, which is a device to allow one road wheel to move independently of the other, and yet to receive power from the engine. This differential arrangement is necessary because the wheels have to move independently of one another when going round corners. The reason for this will be readily understood by referring to the diagram Fig. 13. Here, the outside wheel D, having a farther distance to travel than wheel W, has to revolve faster than the inner one. If the differential were omitted, and both wheels fixed to one shaft, the outside wheel would be partly dragged round, causing considerable wear on the tyre.

(L), and on the other ends are fixed the road wheels. Now, if there is equal resistance on both axle shafts (M and MI), and the crown wheel (G) is turned, the shaft (H) will go round with the casing (E), taking the bevel wheels (L) with it, which, in turn, move the bevel wheels (O and OI), the shafts (M and MI) and so the road wheels. Should

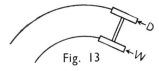

Fig. 13

there be more resistance on one axle shaft than on the other, the bevel wheels (L) will rotate slightly on the shaft (H), thus turning the bevel wheel (OI) a trifle faster than O. From this it can be understood that if one road wheel be jacked up it can be turned quite easily without moving the other wheel because the bevel wheels

(L) rotate on shaft (H) (rolling round the stationary bevel O1 or O), taking the shaft, casing and crown wheel with them.

On each end of the axle casing is fixed a special fitting for supporting the rear springs and for carrying the brake shoes. In the centre of the saddle is a hole into which fits the circular head of a bolt,

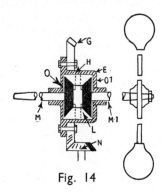

Fig. 14

termed the spring centre bolt, which secures the spring leaves together. Incidentally, this bolt locates the position of the rear axle in relation to the frame, the two ends of the spring being fixed to the frame by means of shackle bolts and plates, as illustrated in Fig. 15. Usually, the forward end of the spring fits into a fixed part in the frame, while the rear end is suspended between shackle-plates (G), which can swing backwards and forwards. This swinging movement allows the springs to adjust themselves as the road wheels pass over a bump or a hole in the road, as the shock tends to flatten the spring and so lengthen it.

The general method of fixing the brake shoes to the axle-casing is shown in Fig. 12. One end of each shoe is bolted to the fitting, but free to turn on the bolts; the other ends have flat faces as illustrated at F in Fig. 16. These flat faces butt up against a flat plate which can be rotated. When a turning movement is given to the plate by means of a lever, the flat ends of the shoes are forced

away from each other, thus pressing them against the brake-drum surface. When the lever returns to the "off" position, the springs pull the shoes back to their original positions.

All early experiments with braking systems were based on the external contracting system. This form, indeed, holds good to-day for many forms of wheeled traffic and is largely employed for slowing down shaftings and internal wheels, as opposed to the road-wheels.

Its use, however, for wheels which are called upon to perform efficiently in every kind of weather and road condition, was soon abandoned. The closed-drum with internal expanding shoes came into being and was soon developed into an efficient and powerful braking system, rising superior to almost any conditions of weather and acting with a silence and smoothness never known before.

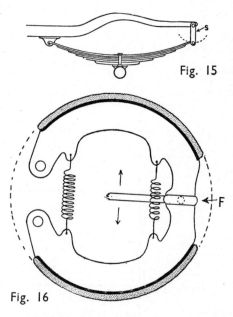

Fig. 15

Fig. 16

The Propeller Shaft is the connecting link between the gearbox and the back axle. There are two types in general use—the open and the enclosed. The open type simply transmits the drive, but with the enclosed type the casing surrounding the propeller shaft holds the axle in position, as this casing is rigidly fixed to the back axle. The use of an enclosed shaft necessitates the employment of shackle plates for suspending the fronts of the rear springs as well as those at the back.

Special driving couplings have to be used on the propeller shaft, because the

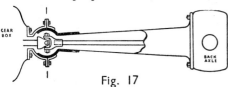

Fig. 17

gearbox is fixed rigidly to the frame, but the rear axle is fixed to the frame through the medium of springs which move more or less vertically in relation to the frame.

With the open type of propeller shaft, flat, round, flexible couplings made of strong, rubber-proofed canvas are generally employed. The coupling disc has six holes in it, three alternate ones being bolted through to a fixed coupling on the gearbox shaft, and the other three holes to a similar coupling on the propeller shaft. The same method is used at the back-axle end of the shaft.

In some instances a trunnion and universal coupling is used. The universal type is only employed at the gearbox end in conjunction with the enclosed drive. The trunnion type consists of a coupling with two slots in it, fixed to the back axle, driving the pinion shaft, and a coupling to the propeller shaft end having two round projections on it at right

angles to the shaft, upon which fit two square blocks—called trunnion blocks—which are able to rotate.

With the enclosed type of propeller shaft no flexible coupling is required at the back-axle end, but a universal coupling and a special ball-fixing is necessary at the gearbox end, as shown in Fig. 17. All the movement of the back axle is allowed for by the ball-mounting. As can be seen from the diagram, the ball-mounting holds the axle in position, taking at the same time all the push and braking effort from the rear wheels, as both ends of the rear springs can swing. In the open-type drive, the rear springs alone take this push or braking effort.

The function of the front axle is to carry the front part of the car by means of springs fixed to it and the frame. One end of each spring is fixed to a stationary part of the frame (called the forward dumb iron), and the rear end is fixed by means of shackle-plates to the frame. This axle also carries the front wheels,

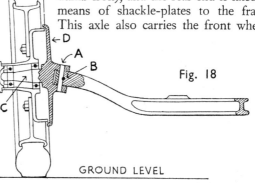

Fig. 18

which are fixed to it by means of "king" or swivel pins as shown at A in Fig. 18. These pins are fixed in the axle and kept in position by means of a cotter (B) and nut. Around the king-pin swings the stub axle (C), which is controlled by a steering arm fixed to it and coupled up by steering rods and box to the steering wheel. The brake shoes are fixed upon a back plate (D) which forms part of the stub axle, and are operated in a similar way to those on the rear axle. The wheel hub is mounted on ball-races as shown, while the brake drum and wheel are bolted to the hub flange.

It will be observed that the wheel is shown at an angle to the ground. The wheel is purposely set at an angle for two reasons, the first, to facilitate steering, and the other, to reduce the severe bending moment on the stub axle, caused by road shocks.

Steering is generally effected by means of a worm and sector in the steering box (A, Fig. 19; upper), the drop arm (B) fixed to the sector shaft giving motion to the pull-and-push rod (C), which, in turn, moves both wheels together by means of a tie-rod (D). The tie-rod is adjustable in order to set the front wheels; the setting of these varies according to the make of car. Generally speaking, the wheels should "toe" in or

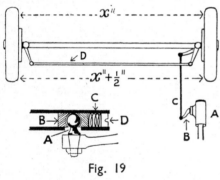

Fig. 19

be closer together in the front than at the back by about $\frac{1}{2}$ in. All the steering-rod joints are of the ball and cup type, as shown in the lower illustration (Fig. 19). A ball-headed bolt (A) is fitted to each various lever. The ball-heads fit into cups (B) in the rods, and are kept in position by a spring (C) and nut (D). The springs are very stiff and are employed to absorb road shocks.

The Electric Installation is one of the most important and often one of the most neglected features of a car. The equipment consists of a dynamo to generate current, and accumulator to store it; a cut-out to control it, and a switchboard to distribute it. Electricity is widely used on cars: for starting the engine by means of a starter in the form of an electric motor, lighting outside and inside lamps, operating horns, screen-wipers, petrol-pumps, ignition, clocks, cigarette-lighters, etc., all of which create a big demand on the accumulator, should the dynamo fail to charge. The charging rate of the dynamo should be about zero with the engine running and all lights, etc., switched on.

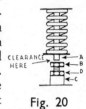

Fig. 20

Minor Engine Repairs.—Having briefly explained the functions of the most important parts of a motor-car, the following paragraphs will be devoted to a few notes on how to keep the car in good order and how to execute numerous minor repairs to the engine.

In order to keep the engine in first-class running condition, and therefore to obtain the maximum amount of power from it, it should receive attention after every distance run of, say, five hundred miles by executing the following adjustments and repairs:

First of all, check all valve clearances and adjust to the correct clearances as advised by the makers. Clean and adjust the ignition breaker-points of either magneto or battery units, including the magneto collector-brush and holder.

Clear out the float-chamber of the carburettor, filter, and jets, and inspect all oil, petrol, and water-joints, stopping leaks, if any. Take out the sparking-plugs, clean and adjust the points, if required. Examine all wire connections, and give a general inspection to the controls, their joints and bearings.

To check off the valve or tappet clearances, proceed as follows: Turn the engine slowly by means of the starting handle until you see that both valves have closed or stopped moving. Then insert a feeler gauge of the correct thickness, between the end of the valve stem (A) and the top of the tappet-adjusting screw (B), as illustrated in Fig. 20. If the feeler goes through very easily it indicates that the clearance is too much and requires reducing. To do this, hold the tappet (C) (if it goes round) with a spanner and unscrew lock-nut (D), then, holding D and C with suitable spanners—

generally supplied in the car tool-kit—screw up B until the correct clearance is obtained. This clearance is correct when the feeler can only just be pushed backwards and forwards in the clearance without forcing it. When this amount of clearance is obtained, hold B and C with the spanners, and screw the lock-nut down tight on C. Adjust the valve clearances of each cylinder before rotating the crankshaft for the next pair of valves. If you cannot get the feeler into the clearance, proceed as above, but screw B down. It should be noted that the correct valve clearance is of the utmost importance to the correct running and efficiency of the engine.

With regard to adjustments to the breaker-points of either the magneto or battery unit, proceed in the following way: Open the points with the fingers by pressing the end of rocker-arm in the direction of the arrow as shown at B in Fig. 21, and inspect the surfaces of the points C and D. These surfaces may be dark or nearly black, and also may not be level, as at E, one point having a depression and the other a distinct lump. This defect is caused by the slight sparking which always occurs at these points,

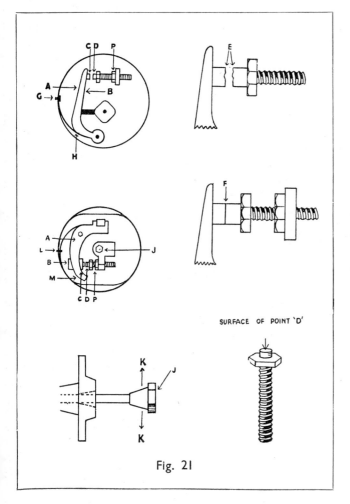

SURFACE OF POINT 'D'

Fig. 21

in spite of the use of a condenser. If the points are flat and come together squarely, as at F, and are only dark on the surfaces, clean them with the finest emery-cloth folded round a thin, flat file. A file alone will not generally be found of any use on the material used for the points, as this metal gets quite hard on the surface after use. If the surfaces are very uneven, as at E, the points will have to be removed. To do this, first remove the rocker-arm which is shown at A,

Fig. 22

in Fig. 21. In the case of the battery unit, release nut G, and lift up the rocker-arm with spring (H) attached. A little more work is necessary to remove the rocker-arm of a magneto. Unscrew the centre or contact screw (J), and remove it; then just push it back into its hole again and move it up and down as indicated by the arrows at K, exerting a slight pressure. The contact-breaker will then come away from its shaft. Hold the thumb on the breaker-spring (L) and unscrew the holding-screw (M), taking care not to drop the short spring underneath the long one—or the screw. Next, turn back the retaining spring and lift off the rocker-arm. Next remove the other point (D) by slacking off the lock-nut (P), and unscrew the point.

The next operation requires delicate handling. Hold the point downwards between the first finger and the thumb and rub the point surface on a fine carborundum stone as illustrated in Fig. 22, using a small quantity of paraffin oil as a lubricant. After a few rubs, give the point a quarter turn with the fingers and repeat the rubbing. Carry on this procedure until the surface is perfectly flat and square. Replace the point, and then rub the rocker-point on the stone, but before the surface is quite flat replace the point temporarily in position to see whether the two faces meet squarely. If not square, alter the position of rubbing, and keep repeating the operation until satisfactory results are obtained, and then replace the parts.

When dealing with a magneto, see that the key on the contact-breaker engages properly in the keyway. Now turn the crankshaft and watch the contact-points. When the cams have opened the points to their extreme opening, check the gap with a feeler gauge. The opening should be ·020 in. for a battery-unit breaker, and ·015 in. for a magneto.

The Collector-brush and Holder of a Magneto.—Remove the cover (A, Fig. 23) and then the holder (B), which is held in position by screws (C). Take

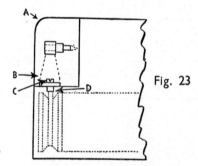

Fig. 23

care not to break the carbon brush (D) when lifting the holder. Carefully wipe the holder with a clean rag to remove all loose carbon deposit and then replace the parts.

Cleaning the Carburettor is quite a straightforward job. Do not use a fluffy rag for general cleaning, and use only thin, clean wire for cleaning the jets. Remember to clean the filter, which is best done by violently swilling it about in petrol.

The Sparking-plugs should be removed and taken to pieces, care being taken not to lose the small gland-washers. Carefully scrape away any carbon deposit from the plug body and points but only wipe the centre, and then reassemble the parts by screwing them tightly together. Examine the gaps and, if necessary, adjust them to ·020 in. for battery ignition and ·015 in. for a magneto. The gap can be altered by tapping the outside strip of metal. On no account must the centre electrode be altered. When replacing the plugs see that the plug-washers are in good condition and in their proper positions.

All control rods and rod joints should be carefully examined to see that they are working freely and in their proper positions to give their correct range of movements. All joints should receive a few drops of suitable oil.

After the car has travelled about 2,000 miles, the oil in the engine base should be drained off, and the filter in the base carefully cleared. In some cases it may be necessary to renew the filter to the maker's instructions. A good plan for cleaning out the various oilways, bearings, and the other parts in the engine is to run a proper flushing oil, or a cheap medium-body oil, into the base, and run the engine for about five minutes. Then draw off this oil, and fill up with oil of the correct grade.

Decarbonising.—The engine should be decarbonised after having run for about 5,000 miles—although no great amount of carbon deposit may be present —the valves, after this mileage, generally requiring attention. Your car instruction book will tell you the way to remove the

cylinder-head as, with different makes of engines, numerous fittings may have to be removed before the cylinder-head can be taken off. After having unscrewed the cylinder-head nuts, but before removing the sparking-plugs, squirt a few drops of paraffin oil round each head stud, and turn the engine sharply with the starting handle. This will ease the head up off the joint. Lift

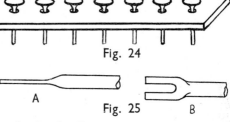

Fig. 24

Fig. 25

A   B

the head off, keeping it parallel in so doing, otherwise it will jam in the studs. Then remove the valves (as per car instruction book), keeping them in proper order. If the valves are not numbered on the heads, place them in a piece of cardboard with holes punched in it, as in Fig. 24. Number the holes, marking the first one No 1, which should hold the valve nearest the radiator, and so on.

If a proper valve-lifter is not available, the following method will be found quite a good substitute. Out of a piece of, say, $\frac{5}{8}$-in. round steel about 12 in. long make a rough lifter by heating one end and flattening it out as at A in Fig. 25. Then cut a slot in the flattened end as at B. The slot should be made wide enough for the valve cotter to pass through. Obtain a length of old cycle chain and fit it up as illustrated in Fig. 26, looping it over a convenient cylinder stud. Pass the lifter (L) through the bottom loop, and the flattened end under the valve-spring collar. With one hand press the lifter down, which will lift the collar up, and, with the other hand holding the valve down, lift the spring collar off the cotter, which can then be removed. The valve can then be lifted out.

Remove the sparking-plugs from the head and also the carburettor and induction manifold from the cylinder

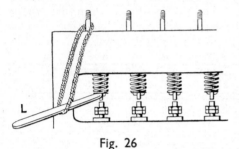

Fig. 26

block. Scrape off the carbon deposit from the head and cylinder tops, taking care not to scratch or cut the aluminium piston-tops. The piston-tops should be finished off bright by polishing them with a small quantity of metal polish. Carbon will also be found in the valve pockets, which must be carefully scraped off and thoroughly blown out afterwards, as on no account must any loose carbon or dust be allowed to remain in the pockets and passages. The head of the cylinder-block joint faces must be carefully scraped clean, and also the bottoms of the head studs; after which, all parts should be finally wiped once with a paraffined rag.

The Valves are the next items to receive attention. Scrape off all carbon from the stems and heads, taking particular care to remove any scale which may have accumulated round the exhaust valve stems. Finish off the valves with very fine emery cloth. Next examine all valve faces. If the exhaust valves are just blackened all the way round the faces, they can be put aside for grinding in, but should one portion of the valve-face be very rough and badly pitted, as at D in Fig. 27, which usually

indicates that the valve is burnt—probably caused by the valve not closing properly, or the head being distorted—replace with a new one. If the face is covered with small holes or slightly pitted all round, it should be refaced. This can be done in a lathe, or by using a special cutter, or, if neither of these two methods can be utilised, by inserting the valve stem into a drill brace, fixing the brace between the jaws of a vice and getting a helper to turn the handle of the drill while you carefully file the valve-face, keeping the file at the same angle as that of the face until the holes disappear. This process is shown in the illustration, Fig. 28. The holes can be ground out, if desired, by placing the valve on its seating and applying a small quantity of grinding compound between the faces and working the valve back and forth, but this

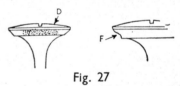

Fig. 27

method takes a considerable time, and uselessly grinds away the valve-seating in the cylinder block. If either the inlet or the exhaust valve-faces are hollow, as at F in Fig. 27, they must be refaced before grinding in.

The next process consists in grinding each valve face into its respective seating in the cylinder-block, in order to obtain a perfect gastight joint. Before actually starting to grind the valve in, turn the crankshaft so that the tappet is in the down position to enable the valve to be properly on its seating.

It sometimes happens, especially after a valve has been refaced, that, although the tappet is in its down position, the valve is not properly seated. In such cases it is necessary to lower the valve

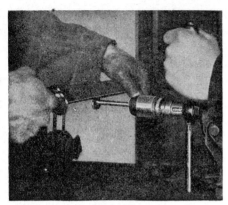

Fig. 28

by means of the adjustment on the tappet; but if there is no adjusting device, the end of the valve stem must be shortened a trifle with a file.

To Grind the Valve, smear a small quantity of valve-grinding compound (carborundum paste) on the valve-face, and dip the valve-stem into paraffin oil in order to clean the valve guide. Place a convenient length of light spring under the valve-head to enable the valve to be easily lifted off its seating when required, and insert the valve into its correct guide. Press the valve down on its seating and twist the head back and forth a few times by inserting the blade of a large screwdriver into the slot provided for the purpose on the head of the valve. Then release the pressure on the valve—the spring under the valve-head will lift it up—and turn the valve round about a quarter of a complete turn, and continue the twisting motion or grinding in. Remove the valve now and again and clean off the grinding paste from the seating, using paraffin oil for the purpose. Then inspect the seatings, and if they show a clear, even, matt surface all round, you can put the valve aside for the time being. When all valves have been treated in this manner, carefully clean the surfaces with a non-fluffy rag,

smear a very thin coating of blue marking (this can be obtained in small tubes) on the valve-face, and place the valve very carefully into its guide so that it does not turn on its seating. Then, with a screwdriver, press heavily on the valve-head and twist it backwards and forwards once or twice for a distance of about $\frac{1}{16}$ in. and again remove the valve. If the valve-seating shows blue all over, it indicates that the valve is correct, if not, more grinding is required until the desired result is obtained. Now thoroughly clean all parts with a paraffined rag, oil all the stems, replace and refix the cotters.

The next thing to do is to refix the head. To do this, place the head gasket in position, taking care to see that all the holes in the gasket correspond with the holes in the cylinder block. If the holes do not coincide, it will probably be found that the gasket is the wrong way round. Then replace the head. The writer recommends that a new head gasket be used every time the engine is decarbonised. If the gasket is a trifle too tight to pass over the studs, use a piece of metal tubing, or a box spanner, but be careful to push the gasket down, bit by bit, keeping the gasket parallel with the cylinder block.

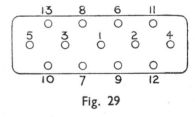

Fig. 29

Screw on the head nuts, in the order shown in Fig. 29, by first placing them in position, and then, using a box spanner, screwing them down evenly in rotation, exerting only a small pressure on this first tightening down. When all the nuts have been screwed down, start again at No. 1 nut, and tighten down again, repeating the process until all the nuts are dead tight. Replace all the dismantled parts and then adjust the tappet valve clearances. Fill up the radiator with water and start the engine Run the engine slowly until properly warmed up; then go over the nuts for a final tightening down. After about the first fifty-miles run, check over the tappet clearances, because the valves settle down a trifle after running.

At the end of about 20,000 miles, or maybe before, the engine will, no doubt, require a complete overhaul, especially if heavy knocking is heard when pulling up hills. This usually indicates worn bearings. Oily smoke issuing from the engine base through the oil filter, and thick, heavy, smoky exhaust generally signify worn pistons, cylinder bores, or piston rings. This trouble is also associated with heavy oil consumption.

Overhauling a Motor-car Engine is quite a big operation, necessitating the removal of the engine from the frame; but there is no reason why an attempt should not be made to carry out the work, especially if the owner has sufficient time at his disposal and has acquired some skill in carrying out some of the minor adjustments and repairs.

Before starting on the job it is a wise plan to make a list of noticed noises and defects in order that they may be dealt with in due course.

The first thing to do is to draw off the oil from the engine base and the water from the jacket and radiator. Disconnect the radiator and remove it. Then disconnect the main cables from the accumulator and all wires connecting to the engine, labelling them carefully for future reference when reassembling. Remove all external pipes, manifolds, carburettor, dynamo, starter, and any other external fitting. On most modern cars the engine and gearbox are in-

corporated in one unit, so disconnect the driving shaft behind the gearbox, also the footbrake, and any other controls. Next remove the engine fixing-down bolts, marking the positions of the engine bearers, noting any packings under the bearer arms. Lift the engine out and place it in a convenient place to enable it to be worked upon comfortably.

Before stripping down, retard the ignition, turn the crankshaft until No. 1 cylinder, that is, the one nearest the front of the engine, is on the firing stroke. Stop turning when the breaker-points just start to open, and make a clear distinguishing mark on the flywheel opposite to a similar mark on the crank case. Now turn the crankshaft again until the inlet valve of the same cylinder just starts to open, and also make a mark on the flywheel opposite the crank-case mark as before; then treat the exhaust valve in the same way, except that the marks should be made just as the valve closes and not as it starts to open. The marking for the exhaust valve is only necessary when two camshafts are used.

Unbolt and remove the gearbox from the engine, and start to dismantle the engine by removing the cylinder-head, engine sump (that is, the lower half of the crank case), timing-case cover, cylinder block (if detachable), valves, valve springs, internal oil pipes, oil pump, water pump. Before removing the timing-chains, examine them to see whether they are worn too much to be used again. As a rule the ignition driving-chain can be adjusted, but if the chain be exceedingly slack, it should be discarded and a new one substituted.

Support or fix the top portion of the crank case, upside down, mark all main bearing caps, if not already marked; a centre-punch is commonly used for this purpose. Make one mark on the cap and another to correspond on the crank case; then make two punch-marks on the second bearing, and so on. Remove the pins, nuts and caps, noting whether any "shims" (thin metal packings) are used, and if so, replace them on their respective studs. Now carefully mark all connecting-rod big-end caps and connecting-rods as shown in Fig. 30, making the mark on the side of the web facing the front of the engine and the marks on the caps to correspond. Remove the big-end pins, nuts and caps. We must repeat our warning that it is vital to watch for any shims, as these must be kept on their respective studs.

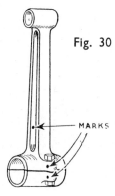

Fig. 30

MARKS

Now lift out the crankshaft, connecting-rods and pistons, and clean all parts thoroughly with paraffin oil, using only non-fluffy rag for drying off. All bearing-caps, shims, bolts and nuts should be replaced in their respective positions after dismantling. Unbolt and remove the flywheel from its flange, taking care to mark its original position on the flange. The pistons should be marked before removal from the connecting-rods, preferably towards the front of the engine in the same manner as the connecting-rod.

Make a thorough examination of the bearings and journals to ascertain whether they are round or oval. First calliper journals as shown in the illustration (Fig. 31). If found to be oval they can be corrected by hand, but the writer advises having them ground, as the hand method requires great skill and is not always satisfactory. The re-grinding of journals also necessitates the remetalling and boring out of the bearings to fit the new sizes of the journals. The regrinding should be entrusted, of course, to a reputable engineering firm.

Now see that all the bearing-shells or liners are a tight fit in the crank case, connecting-rods, and caps; if they are loose, new ones will be required. See that all main bearings fit down snugly in position by tapping them lightly with a hammer and a soft piece of wood; then smear the journals evenly and thinly with marking material. Lift the crank-shaft, keeping it parallel with the crank case, and carefully place it into the bearings. Apply a downward pressure on each end of the shaft, at the same time turning it backwards and forwards, and then remove the shaft, placing it on a clean piece of paper, as dirt must not be allowed to collect on the journals. Inspect the bearings, as some or all of them will have been marked. These marked places have to be scraped away by means of a scraper, which can be bought, or made from a half-round file.

Fig. 31

If a file is used it will have to be softened, ground smooth, bent to shape, and then rehardened, the cutting edges being ground and finished on an oilstone.

Scraping the Bearings. — The method is illustrated in Fig. 32. It con-

Fig. 32

sist in scraping away the bearing-surface which has been marked, thus bringing the marked portions down to the level of the unmarked. All the main bearings must, of course, be scraped after the one marking. Having accomplished this, clean all the bearings, re-mark the crank-shaft and repeat the above work—which will take some time—-until all bearings are marked all over, or, perhaps at least 75 per cent. of the surface. The main bearing-caps can now be fitted—one at a

Fig. 33

time. Mark the crankshaft as before, lay it in position and bolt the cap in place. Rotate the crankshaft, using a drilled bar (shown in Fig 33) and remove the cap. Probably it will not be marked.

If shims are fitted, remove one shim from each stud and replace the cap. In cases where there are no shims, file the flat surfaces, as illustrated in Fig. 34, taking the utmost care to keep the faces perfectly level and flat. Another method of treatment is shown in Fig. 35, which is self-explanatory. It consists in

Fig. 34

rubbing the cap-faces backwards and forwards on emery cloth charged with paraffin oil and supported on a piece of thick glass. Whichever method is employed, only a very small quantity of metal must be removed. Replace the cap and tighten up—taking care to see that the same nuts are fitted to their respective studs—until the crankshaft cannot be turned. When this happens, ease the nuts back, rotate the crankshaft, remove the bearing-cap and scrape away

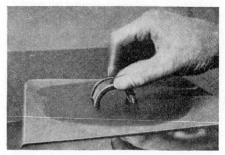

Fig. 35

the marked places. Repeat the process until the bearing is marked all over, when the nuts are screwed down tightly so that the crankshaft can only be turned by an effort to start it moving, but can be kept rotating with much less force. Treat the other main caps in the same manner, and when all the caps are as they should be, clean the crankshaft and bearings, replace the crankshaft after having oiled the surfaces, place the caps in position and tighten all down firmly. Turn the crankshaft, and if a decided effort is required to keep it rotating, ease off one cap and try again. If still too tight, tighten this one down and ease off another in order to locate the tight one. Although no marking is used this time, bright spots will show up on the surface, which can be scraped very carefully until the crankshaft requires some effort to start it rotating, but little effort to keep it on the move. The amount of tightness mentioned above only applies to white-metal bearings. If bronze bearings are being worked upon, they

Fig. 36

must, of course, have the same bearing finish; but the shaft must be quite easy to turn, that is, no effort should be necessary to start it rotating.

To Fit the Connecting-rods, hold one end of the crankshaft in the vice and support the other by means of a piece of wood, as shown in the illustration, Fig. 36. Each rod must be fitted to its respective crank-pin and the right way round. This should present no difficulty, provided the rods have been

marked as suggested. Fit the bearings—after having placed some rag round the rod inside the piston to save damaging the piston skirt—in the same way as the main bearings were fitted, except, of course, the final tightness test. When the bearing is deemed finished, oiled,

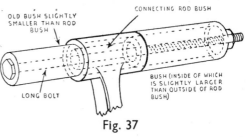

Fig. 37

and on the crankshaft, a sharp downward thrust should carry the connecting-rod round once, although apparently tight to move at first.

The Gudgeon-pins and Bushes will perhaps be found to have worn. If such be the case, they will have to be renewed. As piston gudgeon-bosses are generally not bushed, they will have to be reamed out until round, because they frequently wear oval, in which case an oversize gudgeon-pin must be fitted. Obtain the oversize pins first, and ream the bosses to fit them. In dealing with aluminium pistons, ream the bosses to somewhere near the finished size, dip the piston in boiling water, and try the pin into the holes. For the finished-size hole the pin should slide in comfortably when the piston is hot, but it will be quite tight when cold. The small-end bush may not have worn much, and will probably stand reaming out to take the new oversize pin. If it does not ream out circular, a new bush is necessary. To remove the old bush, draw it out as shown in Fig. 37 and draw in the new bush by the same method, at the same time making sure that the oil-holes in the bush coincide with the holes in the small-end. If oil-holes are not provided in the bush, be sure to drill them when the bush is in position. When reamed out, this bush must be a fairly easy fit on the pin.

Piston-rings.—It is quite possible that new piston-rings may be required. Place the old rings into the cylinder-bores, one by one, pushing them down the bore with the top of the piston. If the gap is too large, a new ring is required. To remove the rings from the piston, insert three strips of thin metal under the rings, as shown in Fig. 38, working them into position until the rings can be slipped off. Remove all traces of carbon from the

Fig. 38

ring-grooves, oil the return hole (if any) and the inside of the piston. Fit new rings to the ring-grooves, allowing a clearance of about ·002 in. in the grooves. Then try them in the cylinder-bores. Push the ring down the bore with the piston-top and test the gap. If the ends butt together, carefully file the ends of the rings and test again. The gap should be about ·0015 in. per inch bore of the cylinder. When fitted, place the rings on their respective pistons.

Treat the valves in the same way as that explained for decarbonising. If

the valve stems are very slack in their guides, remove the old guides and fit new ones by applying the same method as that suggested for the removal and fitting of the gudgeon bush. A badly-worn stem allows air to be sucked into the inlet, and exhaust fumes to blow out of the exhaust.

Testing the Bores of the Cylinder-block.—If a ridge is felt at the top of the bores, no further inspection is required, because the cylinder will have to be rebored. For further test, insert a pair of inside callipers into the bore and ascertain whether the bore is oval or tapered, that is, whether the bore is larger at the top than at the bottom of the stroke. If the bore is found to be oval or tapered, or both, reboring is necessary. This operation must, of course, be done by a firm which specialises in this class of work.

While the engine is out of the chassis, dismantle the clutch and clean out all dust. If the clutch-linings are worn down to the fixing rivets, or the plates buckled or blued, renew them. The thrust clutch-race should be inspected for roughness, and if rough, renewed. Also inspect the clutch spigot-bearing inside the flywheel. Wash out the gearbox with paraffin oil and test the bearings by pulling the shafts up and down. If badly worn they should be replaced. The gear-teeth should be examined for wear. Slight burrs will probably be found on the teeth, which, for quiet running, should be ground off. The gearbox parts will have to be dissembled for this job, as they will also have to be if new bearings have to be fitted.

Assuming that all the parts are now in proper order, the next task is to rebuild the engine. Great care should be taken to see that all parts are perfectly clean and devoid of any rag-fluff.

To replace the piston and rings in

the cylinder, first remove the rings from the piston, taking care to keep them in their correct order. Push the piston through the bore so that the grooves show out at the top; replace the rings and oil them. Then place a clamp (as shown in Fig. 39) round the piston and tap the piston down lightly with a piece of wood.

Bolt the crankshaft into its bearings, and the connecting-rods to the crankshaft. When the nuts are screwed down tight, look for the split-pin holes. A little more pressure on the nuts may, or may not, line up the hole with the castellation. If they do not line up, on no account slack the nut back, but remove the nut and carefully file away a small quantity of metal from the bottom, and try again. Replace the flywheel, making sure that the surfaces bolted together are clean.

Replace all parts, fitting new joints in place of the old ones, bearing in mind that most joints can be cut from thick brown paper.

To replace the timing-chains, turn the crankshaft until the inlet-valve mark on the flywheel corresponds with the mark on the crank case. Turn the camshaft in its working direction until the inlet valve only just starts to open. Having obtained these two positions, put the driving-chain on and connect the ends up. Do not insert the split pin yet, but turn the crankshaft round to test this setting. If a separate camshaft is used for operating the exhaust valves, fit the chain in a like manner, but with the exhaust valve just closing at the end of the exhaust stroke. Verify the setting. Now insert the split pin into the connecting pin. Set the piston into its firing position, and with the ignition retarded, turn the breaker for firing No. 1 cylinder. Set the breaker-points just opening, the flywheel mark in the right position, and fit the chain.

Test the setting and insert the split pin into the chain pin.

Fit up the clutch and gearbox and fix the engine into the frame, replacing any packing strips that may have been used before, under the bearer arms. Connect up the controls and clean out the carburettor and jets.

When assembling, oil all parts which require oiling, and see that all nuts are tight. Fill up with oil, water and petrol

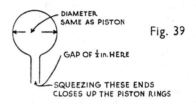

Fig. 39

and start the engine. The engine will possibly be hard to start on account of tightness, but with one turning on the starting-handle and a friend—who knows how—operating the starter motor, this stiffness will be overcome and the engine will start up. Run the engine quite slowly for quite a considerable time—some six to eight hours for "running in" purposes. Should the engine get too hot, put a hose with running water into the top of the radiator and open the drain tap at the bottom, and then run the engine. After the period stated above, the engine will be able to be turned by hand but will still be a trifle stiff.

Give the car a run on the road for a distance of about 250 miles (collectively) not exceeding a speed of 25 miles per hour in top gear and, of course, much slower speeds in other gears. On no account whatever must the engine be allowed to be raced or speeded up, especially when starting with a cold engine. This holds good for any petrol engine, new or old. After 250 miles the engine should be all right for any speed, except its maximum, which really should not be attempted until about 1,000 miles have been run.

Whenever play or excessive wear occurs in the steering-gear, the parts should be carefully examined. Excessive play in the steering-rod joints usually indicates a broken shock-spring. Steering-box play can be taken up in most cases by suitable adjustments applicable to the type of box used.

The front springs may be loose on the axle or a spring may even be broken. Front-wheel bearings may require adjusting and play taken up.

Faults and Noises.—A very common fault is one or more cylinders of the engine misfiring, causing loss of power, which may be due to several causes. The first thing to look for is a defective sparking-plug. Locate the faulty plug by short-circuiting two plugs at a time, and testing either, one at a time. When the apparently faulty one is found, change it with one of the others, and if still faulty you may be sure it is the plug. If the misfiring in the cylinder just tested is not due to a defective plug, check the leads to the plug, as the trouble may be due to damaged insulation allowing the conductor to short-circuit. Examine the contact-breaker clearance, and if this is found to be in order it may be taken that the trouble is not due to faulty ignition.

Misfiring may be caused by a valve not closing through sticking in its guide, or a bent valve-head, or no clearance between the tappet and valve stem. Try the compression by turning the starting-handle slowly. Poor or no compression will be noticed if the valve is faulty. Check the valve clearances, and if the clearances are correct it indicates that one or both valves are in bad condition.

Other faults which will produce misfiring and bad compression are a faulty or "blown" head gasket, and a burnt-through piston crown. In cases of very bad gaskets water comes out of the carburettor and exhaust.

If the Engine Fails to Start, after making sure that there is plenty of petrol in the carburettor, test the accumulator and examine the terminals and connecting wires. In the event of not having a proper tester to hand, switch on the lights. Normal glowing of these generally shows that the accumulator is charged; on the other hand, if the lights are dull, it indicates that the battery is nearly exhausted. Check the breaker-clearance and the main high-tension lead from the breaker to the coil. Turn the crankshaft so that the breaker-points make contact, switch on the engine and open the points with the finger. If sparking takes place at the points, the wiring to the breaker is in order, but if no such spark be obtained, carefully examine the wires. Another fault when no spark occurs is due to badly-burnt point surfaces, or faulty condenser and short-circuiting. A common fault associated with a magneto is a defective switch caused by chafing, which wears away the insulation and sets up a short-circuit. Stuck-open breaker-points and sparking-plug gaps too wide, are also common defects.

Apart from faulty accumulators, poor contact-points, etc., difficult or non-starting may be due to an air leak between the carburettor flange and the induction manifold, or the screen-wiper tubing being fractured.

It sometimes happens that the engine runs slowly and will not accelerate although firing correctly. This defect can usually be traced to a choked main-jet in the carburettor, or the fault may be due to a cold engine, in which case a richer mixture should be given by closing the choke a trifle.

"Popping" in the carburettor when the engine is warm is due to choked jets, or to very bad flooding of the carburettor, caused either by dirt getting under the needle valve, or a stuck-up needle. Stuck-up valves, or an overheated sparking-plug also cause popping. The former may very often be overcome by dropping oil from an oil-can over the air inlet of the carburettor whilst the engine is running (shown in Fig. 40), while the obvious remedy for the latter is to fit a new plug. Popping in the exhaust when decelerating is often due to a choked pilot-jet. A badly leaking exhaust manifold-joint has the same effect.

Fig. 40

Knocks or Tapping in the Engine when it is cold, but disappearing when warm, indicate worn pistons or defective cylinder bores. A persistent tapping in the engine points to badly-adjusted valve clearances—too large. Tapping or "pinking" on forcing the engine or overloading it, indicates excess of carbon, or maybe, worn gudgeon-bushes. Dull thudding and vibration in the engine at speed is a symptom of worn mainbearings. A peculiar noise, between that of a tap and a thud, when the engine is under load, indicates worn big-end bearings of the connecting-rods. To test this defect speed up the engine in neutral gear, and suddenly decelerate. A distinct rattle will be heard if the big-ends are worn.

Overheating of the engine can be caused through a blocked radiator or its connection, pump-spindle broken, or vane-key sheared. The thermostat regulator in the water system may not be functioning. Other causes of over-heating may be a clogged silencer, petrol mixture too rich, spark too much retarded; or the ignition-drive may have slipped.

MOTOR-CYCLE ADJUSTMENTS

SOME general points about motor-cycle adjustments and repairs though not covering the whole subject, may be condensed to include a few of the most common causes of defects in operation and inefficiency generally.

Loss of Power is the most important trouble, and may come from a wide variety of causes. Overheating and lack of lubrication may have resulted in undue piston and cylinder wear. If this is so a new piston and a new surface inside the cylinder are necessary. It is no use trying to cure, or even improve, a cylinder which has worn in use, because the wear is not radial but across the axis of the cylinder, which becomes oval and so cannot possibly fit a new, round piston.

A good plan for the amateur who has a workshop and lathe is to lap the cylinder. It is a rather long job, but it gets the result, and time is perhaps not of such moment as money.

Take a round iron rod (A, Fig. 1), about 10 in. long and 1 in. in diameter, and cut rough grooves along it with a chisel, cutting the metal so that it stands up as a pronounced "burr." Bore a hole in a piece of hardwood about 5 in. long (B), and roughly hew with a chopper to about 3 in. in diameter. With an auger bore a hole down its centre and drive the iron rod through, letting it project about 1½ in. at one end and 7 in. at the other. Then chuck the rod between the lathe-centres and turn the long end of the rod parallel, just taking off the rough. Next, turn the wood block quite parallel and of a diameter to just push easily into the cylinder. Mount the wood block by the long end of the rod in the three-jaw chuck of the lathe, and use it as a lap. To do this make a paste of coarse carborundum powder and gold size,

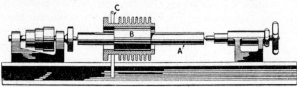

Fig. I

and smear a goodly thickness on the wood block.

Use this as a lap with water as a lubricant, and while it is running at a good speed push the cylinder backwards and forwards along it, holding the cylinder from rotating by a strap of iron (c) around it and engaging with the lathe-bed. As the lap becomes free, add more carborundum paste and continue, occasionally taking the cylinder off and wiping it and examining the inside surface. It can be seen directly when the worn part of the cylinder has been reached. That all is true and round, measurement with an inside micrometer (or even a pair of callipers carefully used) will give the necessary conformation.

If the cylinder head is removable, the lap may be on a much longer bar and between the lathe-centres, and the support of the three-jaw chuck will not be necessary. In this way a new round and true bore may be made. There will have to be a new piston and new rings. The fitting of a gudgeon-pin and the making and fitting of piston rings is described under the section dealing with the gas engine and the instructions there given will apply

to the same job on a motor-cycle engine.

Modern motor-cycles have ball and roller bearings to the big-end of the connecting-rod and the main bearings of the crankshaft. These wear and need renewal. Older plain bearings are out of fashion, but the small-end still has a phosphor bronze bush working on a case-hardened gudgeon-pin, the renewal of which we have referred to in the case of the gas engine.

The Big-ends and the Main Bearings need renewal only after much wear, or great neglect. They can be removed by taking off the cylinder-block, and dividing the crank case by undoing the bolts or studs which hold the two halves together. The separation cannot be effected till the drive sprocket has been removed from its taper end of the crankshaft and the pinion driving the cam-gear from its end of the crankshaft. A wheel-drawer will be required for this, such as the simple one shown at Fig. 2. It consists of two cast steel hooks (BB), a cross-bar of the same metal (C) and a central hardened screw (D), with a head drilled for a tommy bar. The hooks are adjustable to three positions along the bar, and, the screw being driven against the end of the shaft, the hooks or dogs, getting a hold behind the sprocket, withdraw it from the shaft.

This tool may be quite rough but it will be exceedingly powerful and if the edges of the dogs are turned in a little, and hardened, they will hold securely on a collar, or ring, or other shaft fitting.

Timing wheels should be marked so that they can be put back in the same position. If put back wrongly a great deal of time will be wasted in re-timing the valves and the ignition. Always mark wheels with a dot on one tooth and a dot on each of the two teeth on the other wheel which engage with it. This is shown clearly in Fig. 3. There will be four teeth marked on the crank-shaft wheel and one on each of the cam wheels. Where there is an intermediate wheel all must be marked.

roller bearing races into recesses in the crank case, the big ends of the connecting-rod, and the ball race sleeves on crank-pins. The ideal is something which will hold one part square and push the other part square into it or upon it. By the use of sleeves, ball races can be pushed right along a crankshaft spindle, as can wheels on their shafts in the timing gear.

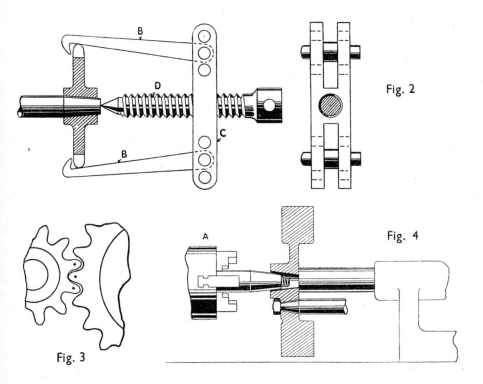

Fig. 2

Fig. 4

Fig. 3

If there is no press available, the back headstock-barrel of the lathe makes a good press for pushing a toothed wheel on to a shaft, or a crank-pin into a fly-wheel, as illustrated in Fig. 4.

The Crank-Pin is chucked in the four-jaw chuck (A). The fly-wheel is offered up against it, and the barrel of the back headstock is run up to press the pin into the fly-wheel. Similar methods may be used in pressing in new ball or

The Dog Clutches of two- and three-speed motor-cycle gears sometimes—through bad usage—get badly " chewed" on their faces and so worn that they incline the wrong way and slip out. Fig. 5 shows a dog clutch which will slip. It can be cured by dismantling and grinding the teeth back at an angle as indicated by the dotted line (AB). Do not attempt to soften the dog or the wheel teeth because in some cases they cannot be softened, and in any case the amateur cannot hope to restore the hardness combined with toughness which is essential for any mileage which would be useful. Grinding on the emery wheel is the only method; and if an emery wheel thin enough is not available as a grinder, mount a small disc emery wheel on a spindle in the lathe and use it to get into the corner of the roots of the dog teeth. In Fig. 5 the dogs on the left-hand pair are as new; on the right they are shown badly

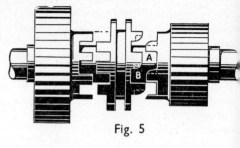

Fig. 5

worn, and the dotted lines indicate the shape to which they must be ground.

BICYCLE ADJUSTMENTS

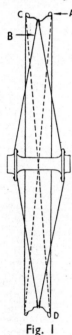

Fig. 1

THE modern cycle is so well made that little adjustment or repair is required under many miles of travel; but accidents and neglect may cause damage which the amateur worker may put right himself if he is skilled in the use of simple tools and appliances.

Wheels, where rim-brakes are used, must be true and, unfortunately, they never remain dead true for any long period. They are easily trued by inverting the machine on its handlebar and saddle (on a piece of sacking so as to protect the plating and the leather) and using the fork sides (back and front) as guides. Fig. 1 is a diagrammatic drawing of a wheel. If a piece of chalk is held against the fork side and the wheel rotated, the chalk will mark the place on the wheel rim which is out of truth. Supposing the chalk showed a mark at A, it would mean that the rim

was out sideways at that point. To true up, slack off the nipples of the spokes on the A side—one on each side of spoke B—a turn, and screw up spoke B two turns. This will bring the rim over to the other side a trifle. Test with the chalk, and if not enough, slack off the spokes on A side again and screw up spoke B. Do not tighten a spoke without slightly slackening the two (one on each side of it) belonging to the other side of the hub. Proceed in this way, using the chalk each side of the rim, till the wheel runs true. It may then not be running centrally with the hub, but otherwise running true. Take a string and pass it across the hub from opposite sides of the rim as at C and D in Fig. 1. It should cross the centre of the hub. If the rim has pulled over on one side, screw all nipples on the opposite side of the wheel an equal turn or turns, to bring the rim over to that side, and true again.

The defect shown in Fig. 2 is common. The fork-ends A and B have been strained out of parallel with each other and this has put a bending strain on the spindle. Its proper straight line would be X-Y, but it now assumes a position as at X-Z.

In the diagram this is grossly exaggerated. One could not actually see the distortion, but it results in the ball races being out of parallel planes with each other, causing the cones to wear badly. The fork-ends should be measured with a pair of inside callipers to see that they are quite parallel with each other. The best way to set the forks is to grip the whole length of the fork-end in the vice and pull the forks (back or front) round. The vice-jaws thus ensure against bending of the surfaces against which the ends of the cones rest.

The Chain Drive will be hard and power-consuming if the condition shown

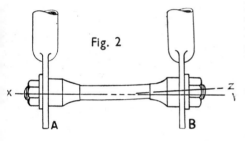

Fig. 2

in Fig. 3 is allowed to arise. The chain has worn and stretched. The teeth of the chain-ring have worn also, so that the worn hollow portion on the driving side of each tooth hangs on to the chain at the bottom and tries to carry it round, as at Q. The trouble here is that the chain link-joints have worn and the chain has elongated (chains do not stretch in their individual units), and a new chain is the remedy. But it would be useless putting a new chain on the wheel worn as shown. The chain sprocket should be removed from the hub and the individual teeth ground back on the emery wheel, the line of grinding being indicated by the dotted line z–x in Fig. 3. Front chain-wheels can be similarly ground back on their teeth if much worn.

Frame Defects, caused through

charging endways into an obstruction, are shown at Fig. 4. The top tube A and down tube B are bent and buckled below the head lugs. The fork-stem

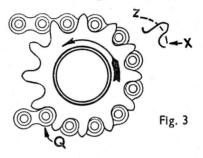

Fig. 3

inside the head is bent above the crown, exposing the bottom ball-race at D gaping in front, and the front-fork sides are bent back at C. The fork should be removed and the ball-race at D unsweated from the crown and removed. Then the fork-stem should be heated to a good red heat just at the ball-race seating, put in the vice and the bend straightened by pulling the fork-blades. Test with a straight-edge—such as an

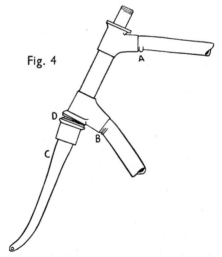

Fig. 4

engineer's steel rule. The bends at C are straightened in a similar way by dealing with one fork-blade at a time, sighting along it to see that it is in line with the column tube, and then bending the other blade to correspond.

The frame cannot be straightened by bending if buckled as at A and B, as it will be similarly buckled at the seat lug and the bottom-bracket forward lug. Cut the two tubes across in the middle. Then file the sides of all four lugs to find the brazed pin and drill this out. Then proceed as for brazing. Heat the head lugs and the seat and bottom-bracket lugs separately in the forge and with the blow-pipe (apply-

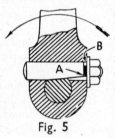

Fig. 5

ing boron compo. to flux the brass). When the brass is fluid pull the tubes out quite straight and with a twisting motion, so as not to bend the very thin and now red-hot lugs. Brush

the spelter away with a brazing wire brush, and fit and braze new tubes, filing them to fit those around the head tube and seat tube and pinning them with wire nails. Then braze and brush and file up.

At Fig. 5 is shown the fitting of a cotter holding the crank to the bottom-bracket spindle. The cotter should (when the spindle is not in the hole) be capable of being pushed right through the hole in the crank. This is important.

Its flat should bed on the flat of the bracket-spindle and the end of the flat at A should be past the end of the flat on the spindle. This is important too. Put a spot or two of oil on spindle and cotter when driving it in, and when tight there should be a space B between the shoulder and face of the crank. To drive a cotter tight, support the side of the crank with a heavy hammer and drive the cotter-head into place. Then pull the nut round with a spanner while blows are made on the head of the cotter.

Fig. 6 shows a bottom-bracket spindle which has worn at A and B. To effect a repair it must be softened by heating to a blood-red colour and cooled, after which the curve can be just skimmed up in the lathe to take out the wear at A and B. Before use it must be polished, and then be case-hardened. Heat it a full yellow heat and douse liberally with a case-hardening powder, letting the powder melt and flow for ten minutes or more, and then quenching in the vortex of a pail of swirling salt-and-water solution, immersing the spindle vertically.

New Cups and Cones should be fitted in hubs if worn and new cups in bottom brackets. But cones on spindles may be softened and re-turned, as in the case of the bottom-bracket spindle, and re-hardened with a case-hardening powder. Get a glowing yellow heat, keep applying the powder and letting it melt and flow all over the bearing face and, after a thorough soaking, quench at full heat.

Whenever fitting new cups or cones or

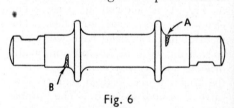

Fig. 6

bottom-bracket spindles always use new balls. Never put a new ball into a bearing which has worn balls in it, because the new ball will destroy the ball-race surface.

The ball-races in the head should be fitted with the full number of balls they will take. If a less number is fitted a wedging strain is set up in use which elongates the metal of the column tube, causing it to become crystalline. When this happens the tube will eventually break above the fork crown.

ELECTRICITY

THE LAWS OF ELECTRICITY

ELECTRICAL work opens up an enormous field of possibilities and scope for the practical home-worker, for not only is the subject intensely interesting, but many a pound can be saved by carrying out numerous jobs upon the domestic electrical installation and its appurtenances instead of calling in a qualified electrician every time a fault needs remedying or an alteration making.

An expert knowledge of electricity is not required in order to carry out such work; but as some knowledge is better than none, the following paragraphs will enable you to gain an elementary idea of some of the principles involved.

Although it is usual to speak of two distinct kinds of electricity, namely, static and current electricity, they are virtually the same thing, the only difference being that static electricity is electricity at rest, and current electricity is electricity in motion, in much the same way as one might call water in a pipe with the tap turned off, static water, and the water when the tap is turned on, current water.

It is current electricity or electricity in motion that causes the armature of a motor to revolve, works an electric bell, or causes a powerful light to illuminate a room at the mere flick of a switch.

The most important sources of current electricity are the dynamo, alternator and battery. The dynamo and alternator require a prime mover in the shape of a steam, oil or gas engine, or some other motive power to drive them, and the current thus derived is used for operating the heavier current-consuming devices, such as motors, heaters, cookers, domestic electric lamps, etc., while the current derived from primary batteries is useful for working telephones, bells, and other devices where only a comparatively small current is required.

In many respects a current of electricity is analogous to a flow of water, but the analogy only holds good up to a certain point. Thus water is conducted in pipes in order to prevent its escape and also to lead it to the desired spot. In much the same way electricity is conducted along insulated wires or conductors.

All metals are good conductors, some being better than others. Silver is the best conductor, but its high cost precludes its general use. Copper seconds the list, and as this metal is comparatively cheap it is perhaps the most extensively used metal for conducting purposes.

The Conductor is generally in the shape of a wire, and may be likened to the bore of a water-pipe. The larger the bore the greater the quantity of water that will flow for a given head or pressure. The larger the sectional area of a conductor the greater the quantity of electric current it will carry for a given pressure, or, as it is termed in electrical parlance, voltage.

In a similar way, as the friction of the walls of a water-pipe offers a resistance to the flow of water in direct proportion to its length, so also does an electric conductor impede the flow of an electric current, and this resistance is also directly proportional to its length, or, in other words, a conductor of a given size 20 yds. in length offers twice the amount of resistance of that of one 10 yds. long.

The resistance offered to a current of electricity produces heat, and this feature is made use of in a practical manner in the electric stove.

The electrical term used for expressing resistance is the ohm, named after Professor Ohm, a distinguished engineer who discovered the most important electrical laws governing the relation between current, resistance and pressure. **Ohm's Law** states that the current measured in amperes flowing in a circuit is directly proportional to the voltage (pressure), and inversely proportional to its ohmic resistance. Thus:

$$C = \frac{E}{R}, \text{ or } E = C \times R, \text{ or } R = \frac{E}{C}$$

where C = current in amperes, E = pressure in volts, and R = resistance in ohms.

From this simple formula it is quite an easy matter to find out the value of an unknown factor provided two others are known. For instance, suppose it is necessary to ascertain the amount of current flowing in a circuit whose resistance is 6 ohms and the pressure 12 volts. By applying Ohm's law $C = \frac{E}{R}$, $C = \frac{12}{6} = 2$ amperes.

Similarly, suppose the value of the resistance is required of an electric-light bulb taking $\frac{1}{2}$ ampere at a pressure of 200 volts. Here, $R = \frac{E}{C}$, $R = \frac{200}{\frac{1}{2}} = 400$ ohms. As a final example, what voltage must be applied to a circuit, whose resistance is 20 ohms, to enable a current of 5 amperes to flow through it? In

this case, $E = C \times R$, $E = 5 \times 20 = 100$ volts.

Ohm's law, as stated above, only applies to electric currents flowing steadily in one direction, as that produced by batteries and direct-current dynamos. It does not take such a simple form where alternating currents are employed, as certain other factors called capacity and inductance are introduced which somewhat complicate matters; but these will not be dealt with here.

Besides producing a heating effect, an electric current has two other remarkable properties. When a current flows through a conductor, a magnetic field is set up at right-angles to the direction of flow, and further, when the wire is coiled on a piece of soft iron, the intensity of the magnetic field is enormously increased. This valuable feature is made use of in nearly all electrical apparatus such as bells, telephones, transformers, dynamos, and a host of other devices too numerous to mention.

When a current is caused to flow through certain chemical solutions it splits them up into their constituent parts. This is easily demonstrated by immersing two pieces of lead, separated from each other, in diluted sulphuric acid. The action of the current deposits a film of oxide on one of the pieces, the oxygen having been obtained from the sulphuric acid. This useful property of a current is made use of in primary batteries, storage batteries, and electro-plating.

Mention has been made of the resistance offered to the passage of an electric current, and that some metals conduct better than others. Dry glass, ebonite, glazed porcelain, mica, india rubber, etc., offer an enormous resistance to the passage of an electric current and are known as insulators, or the converse of conductors. In comparing the resistance of metals, silver is used as a basis; that is, silver is adopted as unity. Annealed copper has a resistance 1.05 times greater than silver; hard-drawn copper, 1.07; aluminium, 1.64; annealed iron, 6.5; mercury 6.3; and carbon, which is not a metal, but an element used largely in electrical work, varies from 2,500 to about 6,000. A rise in temperature has the effect of increasing the resistance of metals but decreases the resistance of carbon, and of a good many insulators.

The amount of electrical energy used in a circuit is found by multiplying the voltage by the current flowing, and the result is expressed in so many watts. Thus, a domestic electric iron supplied at a not uncommon pressure of 200 volts and taking a current of $2\frac{1}{2}$ amperes, consumes 500 watts.

Electric energy is usually supplied at so much per Board of Trade Unit—or, as it is commonly termed, a unit, which represents 1,000 watts for an hour, or 1,000 watt-hours. From this it follows that if the electric iron just mentioned be used for 2 hours, its consumption would be $500 \times 2 = 1,000$ watt hours, or 1 unit. At the customary rate of 1d. per unit, the cost of running such an iron would, obviously, be $\frac{1}{2}$d. per hour.

As the majority of modern domestic electrical appliances are fitted with a metal label giving particulars of the current, voltage, or wattage, it is only a matter of simple arithmetic to calculate the cost of running such devices.

Meters.—The number of units consumed is generally registered on a meter situated near where the supply-cable enters the premises.

A great many people are under the impression that it is a difficult matter to read a meter, but this is quite a mistaken idea, and its apparent complication can be mastered in a few minutes' study. The great advantage of being able to read a meter is that a check can be kept on the cost of running the lights and

other apparatus, and this tends towards economy.

There are numerous types of meters used throughout the country, but the ones shown at A and B in the diagrammatic sketch in Fig. 1 are extensively employed. Both are known as ampere-hour meters. The registering mechan-

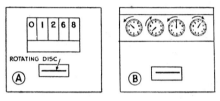

Fig. 1

ism is operated by a minute electric motor or disc, which revolves faster or slower in strict accordance with the amount of current passing its terminals. The instrument illustrated at A has a cyclometer dial and five sets of figures which, when read from left to right, indicates ten thousands, thousands, hundreds, tens and units respectively, so that it is quite a simple matter to read such a meter. In the case of the multiple-dial meter shown at B, four separate hand-indicating dials are used, registering units, tens, hundreds, and thousands of units. Reference to the sketch will show that the hands rotate in different directions as indicated by the arrows.

To read such a meter, start at the right-hand dial and note the figures, taking particular care, when the hands point between two figures, always to take the smaller one, except when reading the units-dial, when the higher figure should be noted. In cases where a hand is between 9 and 0, 9 should be recorded, and if the pointer be so near a figure that the correct reading is likely to be misjudged, observe the adjoining right-hand dial, which will indicate whether the figure has been passed or not. If the hand of this dial has started a new revolution, record the figure or not, as the case may be. The number of units recorded on the meter-dials illustrated in Fig. 2 is 765.

Most meters of the above-mentioned types have a plate attached to them giving particulars of their current-carrying capacity, voltage, periodicity, and the number of revolutions of the motor-

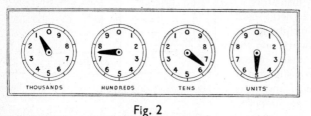

Fig. 2

disc per unit. The motor-disc (Fig. 1) is mounted behind a small glass window in the front of the meter to enable it to be clearly seen. A distinguishing mark is painted on the disc so that the number of revolutions can be counted and checked. This useful feature enables the current-consumption of lamps, domestic apparatus, etc., to be ascertained in a few minutes by simply counting the number of revolutions in a specified time and then working out the result of the observations by simple arithmetic. For example, suppose an electric heater, when plugged into circuit alone, causes the disc to revolve 50 times in 5 minutes. Assuming that the disc makes 600 revolutions per unit—a common figure—it follows that the heater, if kept on for an hour, will make $50 \times 12 = 600$ revolutions, or consume 1 unit. To calculate the amount of current taken by the heater, all that is necessary is to divide the number of watts by the voltage which, in this instance, assuming the voltage to be 200, is $\dfrac{600}{200} = 3$ amperes.

Before carrying out a test such as that

instanced above, certain precautions must be taken, the chief of which is to see that the apparatus is designed to suit the voltage of supply, and also to ascertain that the current taken by the device does not exceed the normal current-capacity of the particular circuit to which it is connected. For instance, a heavy current-consuming device such as a large electric stove must only be connected to a proper power-circuit having sufficiently large cables and suitable fuses for such apparatus, and not to a lighting-circuit, which is commonly fitted with smaller conductors and lighter fuses. No harm will be done, however, if a small heater, electric iron, kettle, etc., whose consumption is not more than 500 watts at 200 volts or over, is connected to the lighting-circuit.

Circuits. — There are numerous methods of connecting up electrical apparatus to form circuits, the simplest of which is shown in Fig. 3.

Here, a simple lamp is connected to a source of current—a battery or a dynamo for instance—with a switch in

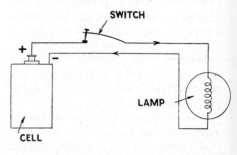

Fig. 3

the circuit in order to stop or continue the flow of current at will. In electrical work it is customary to assume that the current flows from the positive terminal, marked + (the recognised sign for positive), to the negative, marked −, via the switch and lamp, as indicated by the arrows.

Fig. 4 shows a common method of connecting up batteries such as those used for working electric bells, etc., where the positive terminal of one cell is connected to the negative of the next, and so on. Such a circuit is termed a series-circuit. In this arrangement the voltage

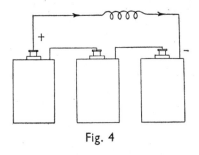

Fig. 4

of one cell is added to the next. Thus, if the pressure of one cell is 1·5 volts, the total voltage will be A + B + C = 4·5 volts. If the internal resistance of such a cell is 1·5 ohms, the total resistance will be the sum of the separate resistances, that is, 1·5 + 1·5 + 1·5 = 4·5 ohms. The current available at the terminals neglecting the resistance of the external circuit will be, according to Ohm's law $C = \dfrac{E}{R}$,

$$C = \frac{4·5}{4·5} = 1 \text{ ampere.}$$

The arrangement shown in Fig. 5 represents a parallel-circuit. In this case all the positive terminals are connected together, and all the negative ones. The total voltage available in such a circuit is that of one cell only, namely 1·5 volts, but the total internal resistance is reduced and consequently a larger current can be taken than is possible in the series arrangement. To find the

resistance of such a circuit, one need only apply the following simple formula:

$$\frac{1}{R} = \frac{1}{R} + \frac{1}{R} + \frac{1}{R} \dots. \text{ where R is the}$$

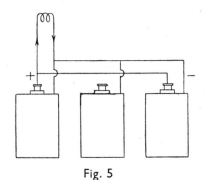

Fig. 5

total resistance and is the resistance of each unit. Working out the above:

$$\frac{1}{R} = \frac{1}{1·5} + \frac{1}{1·5} + \frac{1}{1·5} = ·66 + ·66 + ·66$$

$$= \frac{1}{1·98} = ·5 \text{ ohms approximately. The}$$

current available will be $C = \dfrac{E}{R} = \dfrac{1·5}{·5} = 3$ amperes.

This type of circuit is commonly used in electric lighting circuits, where all

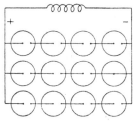

Fig. 6

lamps are connected in parallel across the supply-mains.

Another useful arrangement, known as a series-parallel circuit, is illustrated in Fig. 6. In this circuit three groups, each consisting of four cells connected in series, are connected in parallel. The total voltage of such a circuit is the number of cells in series which, in this case, is 6 volts, and the resistance of each group is equal to the sum of the separate resistances, namely, 6 ohms.

Applying the formula for calculating resistances connected in parallel we have:

$$\frac{I}{R} = \frac{I}{6} + \frac{I}{6} + \frac{I}{6} = \cdot 16 + \cdot 16 + \cdot 16 = \frac{I}{\cdot 48}$$

= 2 ohms, approximately, and the current available $C = \dfrac{E}{R}$, $C = \dfrac{6}{3} = 2$ amperes.

From the above it will be observed that it is possible to obtain any desired voltage and current by simply connecting up a number of cells in series to obtain the voltage and then arranging them in parallel groups in order to get the required current.

ALTERNATING AND DIRECT CURRENT

THE current produced by a primary battery, accumulator, or dynamo, as distinct from that obtained from an alternator is termed direct current (D.C.). It flows in one direction only and does not change in value. That produced by an alternator, whose function is to generate alternating current (A.C.), rapidly alters both in magnitude and direction in a given time.

The difference between direct and alternating current can be better understood by referring to the diagrams shown at A and B in Fig. I. That shown at A is a straight line and represents the characteristic of direct current, while

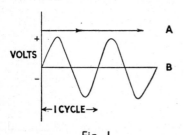

Fig. I

that indicated at B is a double curve which starts from zero, reaches a maximum in a positive direction, decreases to zero, and then reverses in a negative

direction to a maximum and decreases to zero. This complete series of changes is termed a cycle or period, and the number of such changes per second is known as the periodicity of the current. In practice a common periodicity for domestic purposes is 50 cycles per second.

Both kinds of current have their special advantages. One of the advantages of direct current is that it can be used for such purposes as electroplating, charging storage batteries, etc., where it is impossible to employ alternating current (unless the latter be converted into direct). On the other hand, alternating current has an enormous advantage over direct current in so far as transmission is concerned. Alternating current can be transmitted cheaply and easily over great distances by utilising its magnetic effect. This is done by means of a static transformer, which, as its name suggests, is a stationary piece of apparatus without moving parts. With such a transformer it is possible to step up the current given by a low-voltage alternator to an enormous tension, transmit the current at this pressure and then reduce it by means of a step-down transformer to a safe and suitable pressure for working all kinds of domestic apparatus, lighting, and so forth.

A huge commercial transformer delivering a current at 100,000 volts pressure works on exactly the same principle as that which operates a miniature electric-bell transformer off the A.C. supply mains. The principle involved is based on Michael Faraday's epoch-making discovery that if a conductor carrying a varying current is placed near a second conductor having a closed circuit, a current is induced in that conductor.

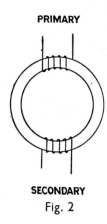

PRIMARY

SECONDARY

Fig. 2

Fig. 2 shows a diagrammatic sketch of a transformer in its elementary form. It consists of two separate coils of insulated wire, wound round a soft iron ring which forms a closed magnetic circuit. The two coils are known as the primary and secondary respectively. When alternating current is passed through the primary coil a current is induced in the secondary. The voltage available at the ends of the secondary winding depends upon the voltage impressed upon the primary terminals and upon the number of turns of wire as compared with that of the primary. Neglecting a very small loss of output which occurs in practice, it may be taken that the voltage of the secondary is equal to that of the primary, provided the number of turns and thickness of the wire on both coils are equal. For example, if the primary winding consists of 20 turns of wire and is supplied with a current of 2 amperes at 20 volts, the secondary will deliver 2 amperes at 20 volts if it has 20 turns. If, however, the windings on the secondary coil be doubled, then twice the primary voltage will be available at the secondary terminals, but the current will be reduced to one-half, namely, 1 ampere. Similarly, if the secondary windings be halved, the voltage will be 10 volts with a corresponding increase in current amounting to 4 amperes.

From what has been stated it will be observed that the power output in watts is equal to the power input in watts (neglecting inefficiency).

Continuous or direct current cannot be used for working a static transformer, as it lacks the rapidly fluctuating characteristic of alternating current.

A high voltage can be produced by direct current, however, by rapidly making and breaking the primary circuit of an induction coil; but this means is limited to more or less scientific apparatus.

DYNAMOS

ALTHOUGH primary batteries, such as the Leclanché cell, dry cell and numerous other types, are capable of producing sufficient electricity for such apparatus as small electric bulbs, bells, telephones, etc., which only need a l'ght current to operate them, electrical devices taking larger currents, such as electric stoves, motors, house-lighting, etc., are supplied by means of dynamos producing direct current alternators generating alternating current, driven by a prime move, which may derive its power from steam, oil or water.

Alternators are usually employed for generating large quantities of current at high pressure and their use is therefore generally confined to public supply power stations and other large commercial undertakings. Direct-current dynamos, although used in a good many instances for public supply, are also extensively used for operating small privately-owned lighting plants, charging accumulators, electro-plating and other purposes, and are therefore of more general interest to the amateur electrician than alternators.

The alternator and direct-current dynamo both work on the same principle, discovered by Michael Faraday in the early thirties of the nineteenth century. He found that when a closed conductor is moved across the lines of force of a magnetic field a current of electricity is induced in the conductor. It is safe to say that had it not been for

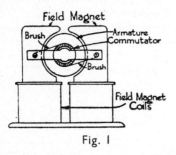

Fig. I

Faraday's remarkable discovery, civilisation would have been a different thing from what it is.

Although the theory of induction is an intensely interesting subject, it is unnecessary to go into its details here.

The Essential Parts of a Dynamo are shown in Fig. 1, and consist of an electro-magnet system to produce the necessary magnetic field, an armature or iron former carrying the conductors, which, when rotated in the magnetic field induces currents in the conductors, and a commutator and brush-gear,

Fig. 2

(Fig. 2), whose function is to change the alternating current generated in the armature coils into a unidirectional or continuous current.

The voltage available at the terminals of such a machine is proportional to the number of conductors on the armature, the speed at which they rotate and therefore cut the magnetic field, and the strength or intensity of the magnetic field. In other words, the quicker the armature rotates, the more conductors the armature contains; and the greater the strength of the magnetic field, the higher the voltage will be. This is only true up to a certain degree, however, because certain restricting factors come into being which limit the output. One of the most important of these is that the magnetic field is only capable of being strengthened to a certain maximum flux, called its saturation point, in much the same way as a sponge is only capable of absorbing a maximum amount of water. The speed of a dynamo armature is also restricted within certain limits, and if this limit were exceeded the armature conductors would fly off, due to centrifugal force, in the same way as a flywheel would burst if allowed to revolve at a greater speed than that for which it was designed.

In order to obtain the necessary magnetic flux across the armature, the iron cores of the machine are wound with insulated wire, through which a current passes, the strength of the field depending upon the number of turns of wire and the amount of current flowing through them.

The armature core is generally slotted to receive the armature coils and is built up from a number of thin iron stampings, or laminations, as they are termed, insulated from each other in order to prevent loss by eddy currents which would otherwise flow if this means of checking them were not adopted.

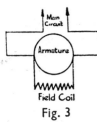

Fig. 3

A diagrammatic sketch appears in Fig. 3 showing the method of connecting up the field-coils of a shunt-wound dynamo.

The field magnets of this machine are wound with a very large number of turns of comparatively fine wire to produce a high resistance, and the ends of the coils are connected directly across the collecting brushes.

The Shunt-wound Dynamo is a self-exciting machine, that is to say, when the armature is speeded up from rest, the strength of the field gradually increases and in so doing also increases the voltage or electromotive force (E.M.F.) which, in turn, causes more

current to circulate round the field-coils. This is possible because the magnets of a dynamo at rest have a small amount of residual magnetism in them which is generally sufficient to build up the voltage. When the armature has reached

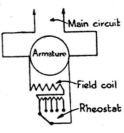

Fig. 4

its correct speed its full voltage is available at the terminals. This open-circuit voltage is slightly above that which is available when a current is taken from the armature, other than the exciting current, the drop in pressure being due to several causes, one of which is the small demagnetising effect which occurs.

The shunt-wound dynamo is admirably suitable for charging accumulators, as the main current can easily be regulated by altering the strength of the magnetic field. This is attained by inserting a suitable adjustable resistance in series with the field-coils (as shown in Fig. 4), which allows more or less exciting current to pass through the coils as the case may be.

Fig. 5 shows a diagram of a series-wound dynamo whose field windings consist of a

Fig. 5

smaller number of turns, but of much thicker wire than that employed in a shunt-wound machine, as the whole of the current of the main external circuit flows round the coils; consequently this circuit must be closed in order to excite the magnets.

In order to compensate the voltage-drop occasioned when a shunt-wound machine delivers current, an extra winding, consisting of a few turns of thick wire, is connected in series with the main external circuit as shown in the diagram, Fig. 6. The current flowing in this circuit increases the strength of the magnetic field and consequently enables a current of constant voltage to be obtained. Such a machine is said to have compound windings and is therefore called a compound - wound dynamo.

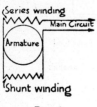

Fig. 6

This useful feature makes the compound-wound machine particularly suitable for running electric lamps where a storage battery is not included in the equipment. The lamp circuit is connected directly to the output terminals of the machine.

To keep a dynamo in good serviceable condition it should, in the first place, be installed on a rigid foundation in a perfectly airy situation. It should be kept perfectly clean, and proper attention given to the lubrication of the bearings, using a suitable oil for the purpose. Particular attention should also be given to the brushes and the commutator to avoid sparking. In these days, the brushes are invariably of carbon. Their bearing faces must bed correctly to suit the curvature of the commutator, as any inequality in this direction causes sparking, which burns and pits the commutator. The springs of the brush-holders should

be adjusted to obtain the correct degree of pressure—neither too much nor too little.

The Commutator should be kept perfectly clean, and as soon as it shows any signs of discoloration the brushes should be removed and the surface smoothed with fine glass-paper—never emery cloth. The abrasive should be held in a block of hardwood shaped to the same curve as that of the commutator and lightly held against the commutator as the armature revolves. In the event of the commutator becoming very pitted or worn, the armature should be withdrawn and placed between the centres of a lathe to enable the commutator to be lightly skimmed over, using a very keen turning tool for the purpose.

Where a dynamo is driven by means of a belt it is important to see that the belt is not too tight and that it is fitted with a suitable fastener to allow the joint to pass over the pulley without vibration or bump. A tight belt invariably causes excessive wear in the bearings, while a hammering joint has a similar effect. As a special adjustable bed-plate is generally used in conjunction with a belt-driven dynamo, it does not require much trouble to obtain the correct degree of tension on the belt.

In calculating the horse-power of an engine or other prime mover for driving a dynamo, it is a good rule to allow 2 horse-power per kilowatt output. For example, a dynamo having an output of 30 amperes at 50 volts, or 1,500 watts, would require an engine developing 3 horse-power to drive it comfortably.

ELECTRIC MOTORS

An electric motor is a machine for converting electrical energy into mechanical power, that is, its function is the converse of that of a generator, although a shunt-wound dynamo can be used as a motor if supplied with suitable current.

There are numerous types of electric motors, each designed for its particular purpose, but for convenience they are usually classified under two groups, namely, those suitable for use with alternating current, called alternating current motors, and those deriving power from direct current termed direct or continuous current machines.

The Direct-current Motor is identical in nearly all respects with the direct-current dynamo, inasmuch as it has a field magnet system, a rotating armature, brushes and a commutator.

When current is applied to the terminals of such a machine, the armature gathers speed and in so doing gradually builds up an E.M.F. (voltage) in the armature windings, due to the conductors cutting across the magnetic field, in the same manner as that of a dynamo when driven by a prime mover. The E.M.F. so induced, however, is in opposition to the E.M.F. of the input current.

If the motor is running without any load, the counter-, or back-E.M.F., as it is called, is practically equal to that of the supply, consequently only sufficient current is drawn from the mains to overcome certain small losses, such as that produced by the friction of the bearings, etc.

When a load is put on the pulley, however, the speed of the armature drops, which lowers the back-E.M.F., and as the supply voltage is constant, more current is allowed to flow, consequently more power is available at the pulley.

The Series - wound Motor has its field magnet excited by the whole of the current flowing through the armature, and adjusts its speed to the load taken from the pulley, that is, the speed increases as the load is reduced and decreases with an increase of load. A series-wound motor can be used to advantage where the load is more or less constant and without sudden variations, and, as the machine has a powerful starting torque or turning effort, it is more generally used for traction purposes.

Shunt-wound Field Windings.— Motors fitted with these are particularly useful where a practically constant speed is required at all loads, but its starting torque under load is small compared with that of a series-wound machine.

The Compound-wound Motor combines the advantages of both a series- and a shunt-wound machine in so far as it has a larger starting torque than a shunt machine, and does not tend to race on light loads, as does a series motor. These features enable the machine to deal effectively with widely fluctuating loads, such as those of compressors, machine-tools, etc.

All direct-current motors above about $\frac{1}{4}$ horse-power should be fitted with a proper starting switch in order to limit the supply current to a suitable value when starting.

This is necessary because the resistance of the armature windings is very low and would enable a very large current to flow through them, which would in all probability burn out or otherwise damage the conductors, or at least "blow" the protecting fuses every time an attempt was made to start the machine.

This difficulty is overcome by connecting a suitable adjustable resistance in series with the armature, which limits the current to a safe value until the armature attains enough speed to generate a counter-electromotive force, or voltage, sufficiently high to check the incoming current.

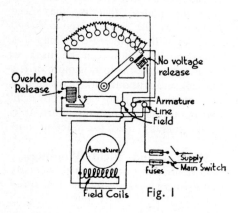

Fig. I

Fig. 1 shows a diagram of a starter suitable for use with a shunt-wound motor. The device consists of a series of coils of resistance wire wound upon insulated and fireproof formers, enclosed in a ventilated iron case. The coils are connected to a number of metallic contact-studs mounted upon a slate base. A radial switch, provided with a contact, slides over the contact-studs of the resistance coils and cuts out a certain amount of resistance wire at each step as the handle is operated and the armature gathers speed. In order to prevent the motor from being restarted without any resistance in circuit, the handle is fitted with a small armature which holds it in the running position by means of a small electro-magnet, called a "no-voltage release." In the event of the circuit being broken, this loses its magnetism and releases the handle, causing

it to fly back immediately to the starting position by means of a spring. Another important feature of the starter is the overload release, whose function is to interrupt the main current in the event of its increasing dangerously. This safety device is also an electro-magnet, with the main current passing through its winding. Should the current exceed the value to which the armature of the magnet is set, the armature lifts and short-circuits the no-voltage release coil, thus causing the handle to fly back to its starting position.

In wiring up an electric motor a double-pole main switch and fuses should always be included in the circuit, and, in switching off, the main switch should be used —not the starter handle. It is also necessary to connect the whole of the apparatus, including the conduit or other metallic sheathing protecting the cables, efficiently to earth.

Direct-current motors fitted with laminated magnet cores can be used on a single-phase alternating current supply of any frequency, provided the voltage of the machine is of the same voltage as that of the supply. A large number of small-powered motors, called universal motors, can now be had at a reasonable cost. They can be used with either alternating or direct current.

The most commonly used motors using alternating current are those known as induction motors, which can be obtained for use with single-, two-phase and three-phase current. The single-phase type is extremely simple, as no external connection is needed to the rotor or rotating part, the stator or magnet system being the only part connected with the supply. The alternating nature of the current produces a rotating field which reacts on the stator and drags it round, as it were.

Types of Induction Motors.—There are two types. One, known as the squirrel-cage type, has a number of copper bars placed along the rotor and these have their ends short-circuited by means of a copper ring. The other type has a wire-wound rotor, connected through slip-rings and brushes to adjustable resistances.

Electric motors in general are extremely efficient and give very little trouble provided that they are examined, cleaned, lubricated and adjusted periodically and not allowed to become permanently overloaded.

Before installing an electric motor it is always a good plan to consult the supply authorities in order to obtain particulars of any rules relating to such machines which may be in vogue in the district.

ACCUMULATORS

THE electrical accumulator, or storage battery, as it is sometimes called—although an accumulator does not actually store electricity—is one of the most important electrical devices of modern times. Its uses range from supplying the comparatively small currents for operating wireless sets to producing the huge currents in conjunction with the generating machinery of central power stations.

The current produced by an accumulator is obtained by chemical action in much the same way as current is derived from a primary cell. But there is an important difference between an accumulator and a primary cell, inasmuch as the former can be recharged when exhausted, by means of passing a direct current through the elements which constitute the cell, whereas the latter cannot be recharged by this means. Briefly stated, a lead accumulator cell in its simplest form consists of two lead plates constituting the positive and negative elements. The plates are usually cast in the form of grids which support the active material. When fully charged, the positive plate or element consists of lead peroxide, while spongy lead or lead in a finely divided state forms the negative. The

plates are immersed in a dilute solution of sulphuric acid, known as the "electrolyte," and contained in a suitable container of glass, celluloid, ebonite or other acid-resisting material. Fig. 1 shows the parts of a small cell.

The Capacity of an Accumulator depends upon the amount of active material on both sides of the positive plate, and in order to keep the size of the cell within reasonable limits, it is usual in all but the smallest type of cell to

Fig. 1

connect several plates of like polarity together by means of a connecting lug fitted with a suitable terminal, as shown clearly in Fig. 1.

The average voltage of a single lead

accumulator cell is 2 volts, irrespective of the size and the number of plates it may contain, so that to obtain a pressure of, say, 100 volts, 50 cells connected in series, that is, the positive terminal of one cell connected to the negative of the next and so on, would be required. Such an arrangement of cells is termed a battery.

The total capacity of such a series-connected battery is only that of one cell, but if the cells are connected in parallel, that is, all positive terminals connected together and all negatives similarly connected, the capacity of the battery will be equal to the sum of the individual capacities, though the voltage will only be that of one individual cell, viz. 2 volts.

The capacity of a cell is measured in ampere-hours; the ampere-hour being the amount of current represented by one ampere flowing for one hour, or, in other words, the number of amperes multiplied by the time it is flowing in hours.

An accumulator-cell is generally rated on its ten-hour rate, that is to say, that a cell having a capacity of 100 ampere-hours will deliver a current of 10 amperes for a period of 10 hours. At higher rates of discharge the capacity is lessened, and at slower rates it is increased. For instance, if the cell be discharged at only 5 amperes it will probably deliver this current for 25 hours, which gives a capacity of 125 ampere-hours, whereas if the current taken is 20 amperes, the cell will become exhausted after delivering this current for 4 hours, thus giving a total of only 80 ampere hours.

The capacity of a cell is also influenced by temperature, the capacity rising with an increase of temperature above 60° F. and decreasing as the temperature falls.

The chemical action which takes place in a lead accumulator may be summarised

as follows: In a fully-charged accumulator the active material of the positive plate consists of lead peroxide and assumes a rich, deep chocolate colour, while the active material of the negative plate is composed of spongy lead and has a pleasant light-grey hue. The electrolyte, consisting of sulphuric acid and water, is at its maximum strength or density. On discharge, the hydrogen in the acid combines with some of the oxygen in the lead peroxide and forms water which weakens the acid and causes its specific gravity to fall. The displaced oxygen from the positive element is replaced by lead sulphate, while on the negative plate lead sulphate is also formed. The reverse action takes place during recharging; the sulphate on the positive and negative plates is reabsorbed in the electrolyte, strengthens it and causes the specific gravity to rise. The variation of the specific gravity of the electrolyte is a valuable means of determining the state of charge or discharge.

The Density of the Acid of a fully-charged accumulator varies from about 1·200 to 1·250 according to the type and make of cell, while that of a discharged cell may be as low as 1·100 or as high as 1·170.

The correct degrees of density are usually supplied with all other necessary instructions by the makers, and on no account should the value specified be exceeded, otherwise the life of the cell will be considerably curtailed.

Fig. 2 shows an illustration of an inexpensive instrument for determining the specific gravity of the electrolyte of small cells. It is known as a hydrometer, and consists of a transparent, suitably weighted float, the upper part of which contains a scale that is graduated in degrees of density. The float is contained in either a celluloid or glass container, fitted with a rubber bulb at one end and a flexible nozzle at the other.

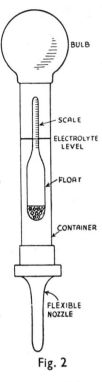

Fig. 2

All that is necessary is to squeeze the bulb, insert the nozzle into the electrolyte, release the bulb, which draws up sufficient liquid into the container, and read off the figure on the scale at the position where the scale-division coincides with the level of the electrolyte. The operation is illustrated in Fig. 3.

There are numerous types of hydrometers, each suitable for its particular purpose, but hydrometers of the floating-ball type should be avoided, as they do not give a precise indication of the condition of the electrolyte—so necessary with accumulators.

When testing with a hydrometer, the following points should be observed, otherwise a false indication as to the state of the cell will result.

Do not add acid instead of water to the cell, for by so doing the hydrometer reading may indicate the cell to be fully charged, whereas such may not be the case.

If the electrolyte requires some readjustment, charge up the cell until the S.G. remains constant.

Should the acid be found too strong, pour some of the electrolyte away, and replace with distilled water only. A further slow charge should be given to mix thoroughly, a further reading taken, and the electrolyte adjusted, if necessary, until the desired result is obtained.

On no account must tap-water be used, as it may contain elements such as iron, which is very injurious to the cell. It is also important to use a clean china jug or other non-metallic vessel for holding the water.

If the S.G. of the acid is found to be low in a normally healthy cell after it has been given a full charge, empty out the electrolyte and replace with fresh of the correct strength.

Always make sure that the hydrometer is in good order, because a cracked hydrometer-float will often give incorrect readings, due to some of the fluid entering the interior and thus adding to its weight.

Another important point in connection with hydrometer tests is the tem-

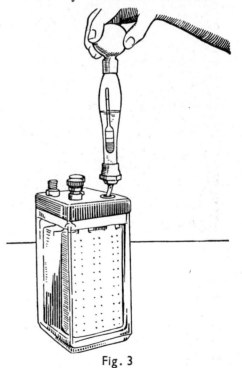

Fig. 3

perature of the electrolyte. The specific gravity of the acid is usually based upon a normal temperature of 60° F. Thus, if an electrolyte at the normal temperature of 60° F. is 1·125, the S.G. at 61° F. will be 1·218 and 1·212 at 59°.

It may be mentioned here that the maximum permissible temperature of the electrolyte at any period of the charge is generally 110° F. If this temperature is exceeded it may seriously shorten the life of the cell.

Although correct hydrometer readings give a reliable indication of the state of charge, it is usual to supplement the results so obtained by the use of an accurate high-resistance voltmeter whilst the cell is discharging, bearing in mind that a fully-charged cell, immediately off charge, will probably register 2·5 volts,

Fig. 4

and then rapidly fall to 2 volts, remaining at this voltage for the greater part of the discharge, after which it falls rapidly to zero. When the minimum voltage-drop permissible is reached, viz. about 1·8 volts, the discharge should be stopped. The illustration (Fig. 4) depicts the operation of taking a voltmeter reading.

When new lead accumulators are put into service they must be filled with diluted sulphuric acid of the specific gravity specified by the makers. The ordinary commercial sulphuric acid must not, on any account, be used, as it usually contains impurities highly detrimental to the plates. Pure brimstone sulphuric acid broken down to the desired density can be obtained ready for use, or concentrated acid of 1·840 may be diluted by the addition of distilled water.

The Acid.—Great care must be exercised when handling and mixing acid, as it is extremely dangerous if handled incorrectly. *Pour the acid slowly and carefully into the water.* If this operation is reversed, that is, if the water is poured on to the acid, great heat is generated, accompanied by violent "boiling" which may not only cause ruined clothes, but also serious personal injury.

The liquid must be thoroughly stirred with either a piece of clean wood or a glass rod to mix the electrolyte, and sufficient time should be allowed for the liquid to cool before being poured into the cell.

Fill the cell or cells with the mixture to the acid-level line, if the container is so marked, or to a height of not less than ½ in. above the tops of the plates, unless stated otherwise by the makers. In small cells this operation is best done with a glass or celluloid funnel to prevent the acid from splashing over the top surface of the cell and the terminals, and thus prevent corrosion of the latter.

Small cells of the wireless type should be left for a period of 24 hours to allow the electrolyte to soak thoroughly into the pores of the plates. If the cell has wooden separators, a quantity of the acid will be absorbed by them which will possibly cause the level of the acid to fall below the tops of the plates after a time. It will be necessary, therefore, to keep an eye on this and to replenish with more acid to make up any deficiency.

The cells are now ready for their first charge. This must be very carefully applied, for the life of accumulators depends to a great extent upon their primary charge.

Accumulators can be charged only with direct or continuous current, that is, a current flowing in one direction only. Alternating current cannot be used for charging purposes, because such a current, as its name suggests, alternates in direction first one way and then the

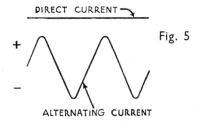

DIRECT CURRENT

Fig. 5

ALTERNATING CURRENT

other at a speed or periodicity of generally 50 cycles per second.

From this it is obvious that chemical action cannot take place, since the cell would be charging during the positive half of the cycle and discharging on the negative half-cycle of the current. This can be readily understood by referring to Fig. 5, a diagram illustrating the difference between alternating and direct current.

It is possible, however, to convert alternating current into continuous current by simple apparatus, details of which will be dealt with later on.

Assuming that a source of direct current is available, it is necessary to ascertain the positive and negative poles of the supply, because the positive terminal of the accumulator must be connected to the positive wire of the supply.

The positive terminal is usually marked with a +, or it may be painted red, while the negative pole has a − sign, or is painted black. To ascertain the

poles of the supply current, either of two methods may be used.

Partially fill a glass with cold water; add a teaspoonful of common salt, and connect up as shown in Fig. 6. Dip the bared ends of the charging wires or "leads" into the solution. Gas bubbles will form on the negative wire, while the positive lead will be unchanged. An alternative and more distinctive method is obtained by connecting up, in a similar manner to that described above, two pieces of clean lead and immersing them in dilute sulphuric acid. The lead connected to the positive wire will assume a brown colour, while the negative will evolve gas bubbles. On no account omit the lamp from the circuit.

When a new battery of accumulators, such as that used for a lighting installation, is being put into commission, it is usual to charge the battery at its normal rate for about 35 to 60 hours according to the type and design of the cells. This charge should be continuous for at least three-quarters of the period, after which the charging may be discontinued for a very short time, if necessary, and then

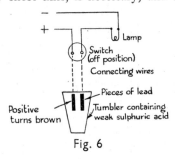

Fig. 6

continued until the cells gas freely; but it is much better practice to give the cells an unbroken charge. It is most important that no current be taken from the battery until the first charge is complete. The temperature of the electrolyte should be taken at intervals during the charge, and if the acid is found to exceed a temperature of $100°$ F., the amount of charging current must be reduced or, if necessary, charging stopped until the temperature falls. Failure to take this precaution may seriously injure the plates.

The Charge is considered complete when each cell shows a voltage of 2·5 to 2·7 volts and the specific gravity has risen to the value stated by the makers. The colour of the positive plates of a fully-charged cell should be a rich chocolate-brown and of the negatives bright silver-grey. Both positive and negative plates should gas freely, bearing in mind that the positives will give off gas some time before the negatives. The voltage and specific gravity should show no rise over a period of five or six hours.

The above observations are of a general character only, and in all cases where the first charge of a battery is concerned the makers' instructions should be carried out to the letter.

It is a simple matter to charge accumulators when a source of direct current is available, as no special apparatus is necessary other than a suitable resistance

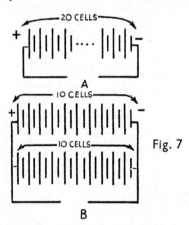

A

B

Fig. 7

to check the flow of current down to the correct charging-rate of the cells.

The charging can be accomplished by using the public electricity supply, or by means of a dynamo. Charging accumulators from the house supply is

an extremely convenient method for treating small cells of the motor-starter type and wireless accumulators. For charging accumulators of lighting plants, traction batteries, etc., taking a comparatively heavy current, a dynamo is generally resorted to.

The Voltage (E.M.F.) or pressure of the current for accumulator charging must necessarily be in excess of the total voltage of the cells to be charged, or in other words, the impressed voltage of the supply must be greater than the back or counter E.M.F. of the cells, for if the voltages are equal, obviously no current can flow.

Thus, the voltage necessary for charging a battery of, say, 20 similar-type cells connected in series, as shown at A in the diagram (Fig. 7), allowing a maximum voltage of 2·5 volts per cell, must be at least $20 \times 2·5 = 50$ volts.

Assuming that the capacity of each cell is 30 ampere-hours, and taking the maximum safe charging-rate at $\frac{1}{10}$th of its actual capacity, the charging-rate will be $30 \div 10 = 3$ amperes.

If necessary, these cells could be arranged in two groups of ten series-connected cells and both groups connected together in parallel as shown at B. In this case the supply voltage necessary would be only 25 volts, but the total current required would be doubled, that is, 6 amperes. Three amperes would flow into the A group, and three into B. Such a combination is called a series-parallel group.

A series-parallel combination is generally used when the supply voltage is not sufficient to enable the cells to be charged solely by the series method.

Assuming that the battery under review is to be charged by the usual series method, using the public supply at a pressure of 100 volts—a pressure it will be noted which is fifty volts in excess of that of the batteries to be charged—

it will be necessary to dissipate this surplus voltage by inserting a suitable resistance in series with the cells, and so regulate the current to the correct charging-rate, in this instance, 3 amperes.

If the battery was connected directly across the 100-volt mains, an extremely large excess current would flow which would quickly ruin the battery.

To calculate the value of the resistance required is a simple matter, and only requires the application of Ohm's law, which states that:

$$C = \frac{E}{R}, \ E = C \times R, \ R = \frac{E}{C}$$

where E is the voltage or E.M.F.

C is the current in amperes.

R is the resistance in ohms.

In the case under review, the values of E and C are known and the value of R has to be found.

Substituting values we have:

$$R = \frac{E}{C} = \frac{100 - 50}{3} = \frac{50}{3} = 16 \cdot 2/3 \text{rd}$$

ohms.

Therefore a resistance of 16·2/3 ohms must be connected in series with the cells to charge them at their correct rate.

By referring to a table of Resistance Wires it will be seen that a No. 18 S.W.G. Eureka resistance wire will safely carry a current of 3 amperes, and as it has a resistance of ·37 ohms per yard, the necessary length required is $\frac{16 \cdot 6}{\cdot 37}$ = 45 yards approximately, which weighs just under 1 lb. If German silver wire be substituted for Eureka, it will be seen that about three times the amount is necessary, as the German silver wire has a lower specific resistance.

A Suitable Regulator Resistance-frame or rheostat is easily made by coiling the wire into open spirals and mounting them between two pieces of slate or other incombustible insulating material. By tapping the wire at suitable intervals and connecting them to the studs of a radial switch, as shown diagrammatically in Fig. 8, the necessary regulation can be easily obtained.

Such a rheostat, and indeed all electrical apparatus of a like nature, should not

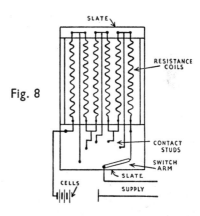

Fig. 8

be fixed directly upon a wall, but should project from the surface to enable a free current of air to circulate for cooling purposes. It is also a wise plan to fix a sheet of asbestos between the apparatus and the supporting medium, especially if it be a wooden partition, or material of an equally combustible nature.

It may be pointed out here that an ammeter should always be included in a charging-circuit to ascertain the amount of current flowing through the cells. It is also good practice to insert a suitable fuse in both poles of the charging-circuit, automatically to break the circuit in the event of short-circuits or mishaps of a similar kind.

A similar result to that produced by a wire regulating resistance can be obtained by means of a bank of 50-volt lamps.

The old-fashioned carbon filament lamps are generally used for this purpose because they take a great deal more current per candle-power than those with metallic filaments.

TABLE OF CURRENTS PASSED BY VARIOUS TYPES OF ELECTRIC LAMPS

Type	Candle Power	Current in Amps. at 100 v.	Current in Amps. at 200 v.	Current in Amps. at 240 v.	Current in Amps. at 50 v.
Carbon Filament	8	·28	·14	·117	·56
(3·5 watts per C.P.)	16	·56	·28	·22	1·12
	32	1·12	·56	·47	2·24
Metal Filament	25	·32	·16	·13	..
(1·25 watts per C.P.)	40	·5	·25	·21	..
	60	·75	·37	·31	..
	Watts				
½ Watt Gas-filled	20	·4	·2	·17	..
	40	·6	·3	·25	..
	100	1·0	·5	·41	..
	150	1·5	·75	·62	..

A glance at the table of currents taken by various lamps will show that a 32 C.P. carbon filament lamp passes 2·24 amps. at 50 volts, and an 8 C.P. lamp ·56

Fig. 9

amp., giving a total current of 2·24 + ·56 = 2·8 amps. This is ·2 amp. below the normal charging-rate of 3 amps., but this value is near enough for all practical purposes, for it errs on the right side, that is, it does not exceed the maximum

charging-rate. The small deficiency in the amount of current can easily be made up by allowing a little more time for the cells to charge.

From what has been stated above, it follows that the lamp method provides a convenient means of charging cells, as all that is necessary to vary the current passing is to substitute lamps of different candle power.

A simple way of making a bank of lamps is shown in Fig. 9. It consists of nothing more than a few ordinary batten lampholders mounted on a plywood board, and connected, as indicated in Fig. 10, with an ammeter, four terminals, two fuses, and a switch, which complete the outfit.

A handy method of charging a small wireless cell is indicated in Fig. 11. In this case, the lamp used for illuminating the apartment is made use of. Having ascertained the polarity of the switch terminals, a lead is taken from each terminal of the switch and connected to the accumulator, as shown in the diagram (Fig. 12).

The switch-knob must, of course, be kept at the "off" position or else the accumulator will be short-circuited.

Assuming that a 200-volt, 100-watt gas-filled lamp is used, a current of ½ ampere will pass. If the cell is of 20 ampere-hour capacity, it will take about 45 hours to charge.

An alternative to this arrangement is shown in Fig. 13, where an electric light pendant is made use of. This arrange-

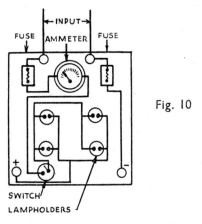

Fig. 10

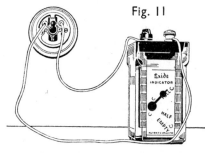

Fig. 11

Fig. 13

ment has the advantage that the accumulator cannot be short-circuited by the accidental "switching on" of the switch.

It is sometimes necessary to "boost-up" a motor-car starter battery for a short period. This can be easily done by inserting it in the lighting mains, in the manner indicated by Fig. 14. As the charging will possibly be done in the evening, the charging current obtained will be of a fluctuating nature, due to the increase or decrease of number of lamps being brought into operation. Provided the total number of lamps does not pass a current in excess of the normal charging rate of the battery, this method is quite satisfactory.

It is a good plan to insert a small terminal board, or a large cut-out, minus the fuse, operated by a switch in one of

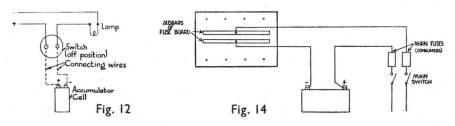

Fig. 12

Fig. 14

the supply mains, so that when the battery is taken off charge, the terminals are short-circuited, thus closing the lighting circuit without reconnecting wires and causing undue delay. This

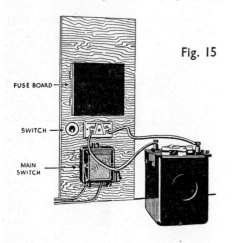

Fig. 15

FUSE BOARD

SWITCH

MAIN SWITCH

arrangement is shown in Fig. 15. When connecting up or disconnecting, do not forget to switch off the current at the main supply switch.

Fig. 16 shows a diagrammatic sketch of a liquid resistance which is sometimes used as a temporary measure to reduce the supply voltage for charging accumulators. It consists of an ordinary glazed-earthenware drain-pipe closed at one end. A thick lead disc is fixed at the bottom end, connected to a terminal. A similar lead plate, which forms the other pole, is suspended from a pulley by means of a thick, flexible cable, which, when operated by the handle, allows the distance between the plates to be adjusted. The cylinder is filled with water to which a little common salt is added. By putting the plates nearer together the resistance is reduced and by increasing the distance, the resistance is increased, which, of course, alters the amount of current flowing. The amount of current can also be adjusted by increasing or decreasing the amount of

salt; the more salt used, the greater conductivity of the fluid, hence a greater flow of current.

When other means are not available, it is sometimes necessary to resort to primary batteries for charging a small accumulator. When this method is used, it is important to choose a primary battery of sufficiently low internal resistance to deliver a moderately steady current. Such a cell is found in the Daniell cell, which has a voltage of 1·2. Cells of the Leclanché type are useless for charging purposes, owing to their inability to deliver a constant flow of current. This latter is due to their high internal resistance, coupled with the rapid polarisation, which takes place as soon as a current is taken from them, and further increases the internal resistance.

The voltage necessary for charging a 6-volt accumulator is about 8 volts. A battery consisting of seven Daniell cells

Fig. 16

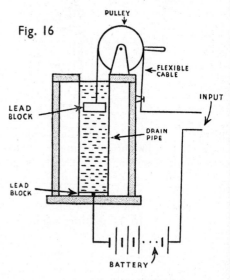

PULLEY

FLEXIBLE CABLE

INPUT

LEAD BLOCK

DRAIN PIPE

LEAD BLOCK

BATTERY

of three-pint capacity, connected in series, would therefore be necessary to obtain the required E.M.F. It is not necessary to use a resistance with this combination as the difference between the voltages is not sufficient to cause an excess current to flow.

In charging accumulators such as those of country-house lighting plants, a shunt-wound dynamo driven by an oil-engine is generally used to supply the charging current. A shunt-wound dynamo is necessary because a series-wound machine is likely to reverse its polarity, which would possibly ruin the cells. As a shunt-wound dynamo is a constant-speed machine, the amount of charging current is regulated by an adjustable resistance inserted in its field circuit. By increasing the resistance a decrease in the field current results, which

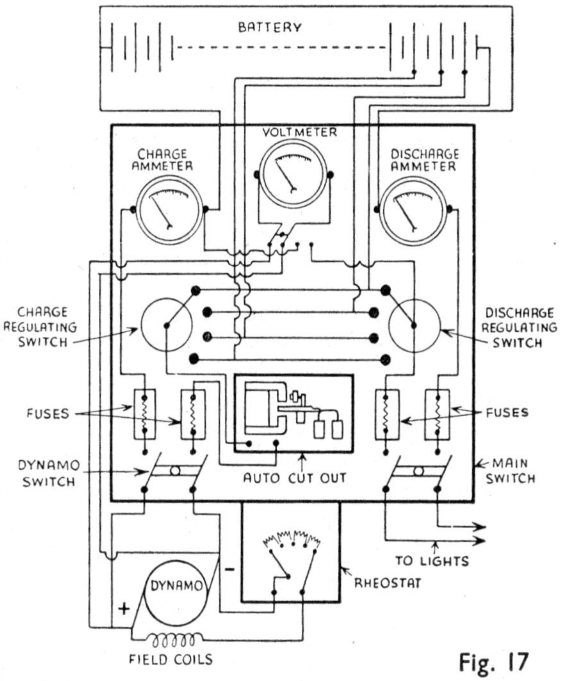

discharging the cells of a self-contained electric-lighting plant. It will be seen that it consists essentially of two circuits, one for charging and the other for discharging.

It will also be noticed that an automatic cut-out is inserted in the charging circuit. This device is to prevent a reversal of current should the speed of the dynamo fall or the engine stop. Ammeters are inserted in both the charge and discharge circuits, for registering the charging current and discharge current respectively. A single voltmeter with a two-way switch indicates the charging voltage and discharging E.M.F. The two radial switches seen in the centre of the switchboard are for regulating the discharging voltage by adding one or more cells to the discharge circuit. This is necessary to compensate for the drop in voltage, which falls as the load increases, or, in other words, as more and more lamps are switched on. As the regulating cells do not have to deliver a current for the same period of time as those in the main circuit and consequently do not require the same amount of time to recharge, the other regulating switch is used to cut them out of circuit, otherwise the cells would possibly be ruined by overcharging.

To charge such a battery is a simple matter. Run the engine up to its normal speed and adjust the voltage of the dynamo by the field rheostat until it stands a little in excess of that of the battery. Close the main charging switch, which, if the voltage is correctly adjusted, will cause a small current to flow and will close the automatic switch, thus

Fig. 17

reduces the voltage; similarly, by cutting out resistance the magnetic field is strengthened, with a corresponding increase in voltage.

Switchboard Connections.—Fig. 17 shows a typical example for charging and

Fig. 18

completing the circuit. The charging current is now brought up to its normal value by further adjustment of the field rheostat.

It has already been stated that accumulators cannot be directly charged by means of alternating current. There are numerous devices, however, for converting the alternating current into a unidirectional current. These include motor-generators, and chemical, mechanical and electrical rectifiers.

Fig. 18 shows a small but useful type of motor-generator suitable for use with current taken from the public electricity supply at 240 volts, 50 cycles. It consists of a synchronous motor directly coupled to a small D.C. shunt-wound dynamo. The supply current is fed to the motor through a double-pole switch, and protected by a fuse in each conductor. An automatic centrifugal switch is incorporated in the motor, which obviates the necessity of having a special external starter, the motor being started by simply operating an ordinary tumbler switch. Dynamos of various outputs to suit the number and size of the cells to be charged are fitted, while a shunt field regulator, an ammeter, and an automatic gravity-type cut-out mounted near the machine complete the outfit.

A Mechanical Rectifier consisting of a synchronous motor fitted with a recti-

fying commutator at one end of the shaft is shown diagrammatically in Fig. 19. The motor is fitted with an automatic starting switch and is started in the same manner as the motor previously referred to. A second circuit from the supply is connected to the primary terminals of a step-down transformer to reduce the voltage of the current to be rectified. The secondary winding is tapped to produce 25, 37 and 50 volts, and is connected to a radial switch to enable these voltages to be conveniently used. The secondary current, now reduced in pressure, is led to a pair of brushes on the commutator where the current is rectified. A separate pair of brushes collects the rectified current, which is fed to the main input terminals of the switchboard.

The switchboard consists of a slate panel upon which is mounted the following apparatus: a polarity indicator;

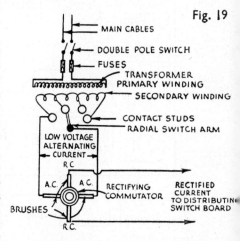

Fig. 19

MAIN CABLES
DOUBLE POLE SWITCH
FUSES
TRANSFORMER PRIMARY WINDING
SECONDARY WINDING
CONTACT STUDS
RADIAL SWITCH ARM
LOW VOLTAGE ALTERNATING CURRENT
R C
A.C.   A.C.
BRUSHES
RECTIFYING COMMUTATOR
RECTIFIED CURRENT TO DISTRIBUTING SWITCH BOARD
R C.

a double-pole throw-over switch; a single-pole fuse for the motor; an automatic cut-in and cut-out; an ammeter; a series-regulating resistance for adjusting the charging current; a single-pole fuse for the output circuit, and a tumbler switch for making or breaking the charging circuit.

To use the apparatus, first select the approximate voltage necessary to charge the cells by placing the radial switch-arm on the corresponding stud on the transformer. Close the motor switch, and when the machine has run up to normal speed, close the polarity changer switch. If the polarity indicator needle points to "right," the main charging switch can be closed. If, however, the needle points to "wrong," the polarity changer

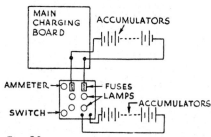

Fig. 20

switch must be switched over to the opposite contacts. This will cause the indicator needle to swing to the "right" position, and thus ensure the correct

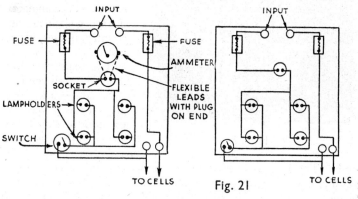

Fig. 21

polarity of the charging terminals. The cell switch can then be closed and the resistance adjusted to give the desired amount of current. To stop the motor, open the cell switch first and then operate the motor switch.

Owing to the high efficiency and flexibility of this type of charging apparatus, it is particularly suitable for use in wireless charging stations and motor garages.

With such an apparatus, it is a simple matter to connect the output terminals of

the switchboard to feed several independent charging circuits, as indicated in Fig. 20. Thus, one circuit can be arranged to charge at, say, 3 amps., for charging cells of 30 or 40 ampere-hour capacity; another circuit to charge at 2 amps., while other circuits of 1 amp. and ½-amp. respectively, are useful for charging cells of the "monoblock" type.

The regulation of the current in each circuit can be obtained by either a wire regulating rheostat or a suitable bank of lamps.

As the ammeter in the main circuit will register the total current flowing through all the circuits, another ammeter should be included to enable the value of the current to be ascertained in each sub-circuit. To avoid the unnecessary expense of having a separate ammeter permanently connected in each circuit, a single ammeter common to all sub-charging circuits can be arranged by using an ordinary electric wall socket with a short-circuited plug top in each circuit. The ammeter is connected to one end of a twin flexible lead, while a plug top is fitted to the other. To take a reading, all that is necessary is to remove the "shorting" plug in the circuit and substitute the ammeter plug. When the reading has been taken, the "shorting" plug is then replaced into its

12

socket. This arrangement is clearly shown in Fig. 21.

Figs. 22 and 23 show the front and interior of another rectifying device for charging accumulators for use with alternating current. It is a very simple apparatus consisting essentially of a rectifying valve, a transformer and a reactance enclosed in a substantial ventilated case.

The Rectification of the Current is obtained by a valve which operates in a similar way to a wireless valve, and allows current to flow in one direction

Fig. 22

only. The bulb is filled with an inert gas and contains a low-voltage tungsten filament, called the cathode. The anode consists of a special electrode or plate. When the filament is heated, a discharge of electrons takes place between the two, and a current passes only from the anode to the cathode. This is one of its most important features, as it is impossible for the accumulators to discharge back. Another salient feature is that it is noiseless in action, and does not interfere with nearby wireless receivers.

A metal rectifier is an extremely simple device and consists of a number of discs or washers of copper and copper

oxide, which allows the current to flow in one direction only. A number of metallic fins are fitted to the apparatus for cooling purposes. As the rectifier cannot be connected directly across the A.C. mains, a suitable transformer must be connected to drop the voltage to suit the particular rectifier to be used.

Rectifiers of this type are inexpensive, efficient, noiseless in running, and can be obtained in the following outputs:

Max. Input Volts	Output Volts	Amps.
9	6	·25
11	6	·5
11	6	1·0
22	12	1·0
11	6	2·0
14	9	2·0
9	6	3·0

The installing and erection of a small battery of accumulators, such as are used in self-contained lighting plants for country houses, is not a very difficult matter.

The battery room should be dry, light, and well ventilated.

Suitable racks or stands must be provided as the cells should stand above the floor level. Timber of suitable size and strength must be used for the stands, and they should be well supported to take the weight of the cells, while a couple of coats of good lead paint should be applied to the woodwork after completion.

The layout of the battery stand must, of course, be governed by the shape and size of the battery room. Suffice it to say that if the accommodation available necessitates the use of two tiers, sufficient head-room must be allowed to obtain easy access to the cells. There should be a space of at least the height of a cell for this purpose.

When the whole of the cells have been unpacked, cleaned, and checked to make sure that all items, such as insulators separators, connecting bolts, etc., have been included in the consignment, the plates can be carefully inserted into the glass boxes, and as each cell is completed, it should be placed in position on the stand.

If the plates are of the hanging type, which they usually are, great care must be exercised not to bend or strain the plates, connecting bars, and the supporting lugs. Should there be a mishap in this direction they must be bent back to shape before attempting to place them in the box. Failure to attend to this may perhaps crack the glass container, owing to the supporting lugs not bearing evenly on the top edge of the jar. The plates should be so arranged in the box that one end plate is in contact with the inside of the glass box, and the positive and negative should be equally spaced. The glass separators—the type usually employed—should now be inserted between the plates, care being taken to keep them in a vertical position, equally spaced, and neatly in line, finally inserting the corrugated lead strips in the remaining space between the outer negative plate and the glass container. The strips should be adjusted so that they bear evenly on the outside plate and the box, and they should be arranged in line with the separators. The cell is now ready for erection on the stand.

Place the insulators on the stand and space them so that an insulator supports each corner of the box, or tray, if used.

The glass insulators are usually in two pieces, the smaller one being placed in position first and partially filled with resin oil. The upper halves are then placed on top.

If trays are provided for the cells, a tray should be fitted with sawdust and then placed in position on the insulators. It is important that the trays should bear evenly on the insulators and if any "rock" is perceived, it must be remedied

by inserting thin slips of wood for "packing" purposes where necessary.

The cell may now be placed carefully and squarely on the tray.

When erecting cells it is, of course, important to see that the positive lug of a set of plates (painted red) connects to the negative (painted black) of the adjoining cell, and it is also essential that the surfaces of the connecting lugs be perfectly clean and making good contact when connecting up. If the last item is overlooked, heating will be almost sure to result, perhaps with serious consequences.

Fig. 23

It is a good plan when all the cells are connected together to smear some vaseline over the connecting lugs and terminals.

When all these things have been attended to, the battery is ready to receive the acid.

Assuming that the engine and dynamo are in perfect running order and that all connections have been carefully checked and found in order, the cells can be filled with acid, but if these things are not as they should be, the filling must be delayed until they are, because it is essential that the cells should be charged soon after the acid has been added, otherwise the plates will be seriously damaged by sulphating.

The cells should be filled with acid of the correct density, to cover the plates by no less than ½ in., and the spray-arresting plates placed in position.

It is good practice during the first few weeks, only to discharge partly a new battery before recharging fully ; it can then be discharged and charged normally.

The chief defect to which an accumulator is liable is "sulphating" of the plates, especially the negatives. This sulphate is insoluble and must not be confused with the sulphate formed in the course of the normal chemical reactions during discharge.

The insoluble sulphate is an insulator and forms on the positive and negative plates, preventing the plates from receiving their normal charge, and causing warping and other troubles.

The Sulphate formed on the negatives is easily distinguishable, as it is in the form of a white scale. Sulphated positives assume an unpleasant greyish-brown colour. The sulphate may be in patches or on the whole surface. The cause is usually undercharging or over-discharging.

In an excessively sulphated cell, the best thing to do is to take out the plates, scrape off the deposit with a piece of wood, and wash the plates with weak sulphuric acid. When the plates have been replaced in the container it should be filled with fresh electrolyte and given a long charge at a slow rate. If the plates are only slightly sulphated, charge the cell at about one-half the normal rate for about eighty hours. After several charges and discharges, the battery will usually recover and give its full capacity.

Another common defect in accumulators is the buckling of plates, generally due to overcharging or allowing them to become sulphated. The plates usually buckle and bulge out of place and very often to such an extent that a short-circuit is formed between the positives and negatives.

If the plates are only slightly buckled, they may be straightened by placing a board, equal in thickness to the distance between the plates, between each plate and applying gradual pressure to the outside ones until they are flat.

A letter-copying press is handy for this purpose. The plates should be very carefully handled and on no account must they be jarred, otherwise the paste is liable to fall out. Badly buckled plates will seldom stand up to this process, as they generally crumble away. In this event the only remedy is to replace them with new ones.

Corrosion of the terminals is another failing common to accumulators, especially to batteries of the small type. This is very often due to want of care when refilling the cell with acid in allowing the electrolyte to splash over the terminals. Corrosion may also be due to "creeping" of the acid up the lugs of the plates to the terminals, commonly caused by leakage between the lug and the top cover of the cell.

To Prevent Corrosion, wipe away all traces of acid by means of a cloth dipped in ammonia, and apply a coat of vaseline to all metal parts, taking care not to put too much between the contact faces of the terminals, as this may cause bad connections. In cases of bad corrosion due to leakage of acid between the lugs and the cover of a motor-car accumulator, scrape the lugs and cover and apply some Chatterton's compound at the faulty joint.

INSTALLING ELECTRIC LIGHT

IN these progressive days no home is considered complete unless it has its installation of electric light and power; such an installation is now looked upon as almost as important as a water supply. This observation is verified by the fact that the estimated number of houses in the British Isles now taking a supply of current from the public authorities exceeds the enormous figure of five millions, and is increasing rapidly year by year.

This extraordinary growth is due in no small degree to the cheapness of electric current—it has never been cheaper than at the present time—the high efficiency and general excellence of modern domestic electrical equipment and appliances, and the greatly reduced cost and improved methods of wiring the premises.

The advantages of electric light are almost too well known to be mentioned; suffice it to say that there is no healthier, more convenient and cleaner method of illumination, and it is therefore recognised as the best possible means of lighting the home.

Electric-light wiring is not really the formidable job it was looked upon as being a few years ago, for it is now possible to wire a house with comparatively little disturbance and damage to existing decorations, due to the many excellent systems in vogue and greatly improved methods of carrying out the work.

It is not a difficult matter to install electric light and power in the house, and any practical man of average intelligence, having a slight knowledge of electricity, and handy with tools, can carry out the work with confidence that the installation will be a success

when completed. At the same time, it is essential that the work be done to a certain standard of excellence and that the materials used should be of a certain quality. Faults in a wiring system can be both dangerous and annoying.

The following pages have therefore been written to enable the practical man to gain some knowledge of the principles involved in house-wiring and to enable him to fix up an electric-light system; or, if he is fortunate in having the electric light already installed, to carry out extensions and other work of a similar nature without having to call upon the services of an expert electrician.

Before going into details of the practical side of the work, it is as well to point out here that there are certain definite rules and regulations regarding house-wiring which must be complied with before the supply authorities will give a supply of current to a consumer. This is as it should be, as it is done entirely in the interests of safety and efficiency and is also a check on slipshod workmanship.

From the above observations, if the reader contemplates installing the electric light, it is advisable first to obtain a copy of the rules and regulations appertaining to the supply, from the local electricity supply authorities, who are always willing to give helpful advice and any information required.

The rules and regulations insisted upon by the various supply authorities are usually based upon the recommendations of the Institution of Electrical Engineers.

When going into these preliminary matters it is also a good plan to notify the fire assurance company interested in the insurance of the property, giving details of the proposed installation.

The rules regarding house-wiring apply chiefly to such items as the mechanical protection of conductors; the size of conductors; the maximum permissible current per sub-circuit; the testing of installations after completion; earthing, etc., etc., and certain other items. All look formidable in print but are really very easy to carry out.

The Nature and Voltage of the Supply varies in different districts. Thus, in some places alternating current is used, while in others the direct-current system is in vogue.

In the former, the current alternates first in one direction and then in the other at a certain frequency—usually 50 cycles per second. It is used chiefly because it is cheaper to transmit alternating current than direct. In the direct-current system the current flows steadily in one continuous direction as already explained elsewhere.

With the completion of the grid scheme of electrical transmission, however, the whole of the current supplied for electric lighting and domestic use will be standardised throughout England, Wales and Scotland to alternating current at a pressure of 230 volts and a frequency of 50 cycles per second.

The maximum voltage or pressure allowed for electric lighting and domestic purposes in the country is 250 volts.

The voltage of current supplied at present to the consumer varies in different localities; it may be as high as 240 volts in one district and as low as 100 volts in another.

The charge for electric current for lighting purposes is not at present standardised. In some places it may be as high as 10d. per unit.

The energy used is charged at so much per unit (Board of Trade Unit), a unit representing 1,000 watt-hours, that is, the number of watts (1 volt × 1 ampère = 1 watt) consumed, multiplied by the time in hours. Thus, if ten 60-watt lamps are in use for 1 hour they will consume 10 × 60 = 600 watts, and assuming, that the cost of energy is 4d. per unit, will cost $\frac{600}{1000}$ or $\frac{3}{5}$ of a unit at 4d., or $2\frac{2}{5}$d., to run. Similarly, if one 60-watt lamp is used for 10 hours the cost will be the same.

There are numerous systems of charging for current. One method commonly adopted is known as the flat rate, whereby the energy consumed is charged up at a definite fixed price per unit for lighting and another fixed rate for domestic purposes, such as heating, etc.

Another system, favoured by some supply authorities, is called the rebate system. Here all current supplied up to a certain maximum number of units is charged up at the maximum rate and surplus units used are charged up at a greatly reduced figure.

In small installations the prepayment system has certain advantages. This system necessitates the use of a prepayment meter, which, when a shilling is placed in the slot, a certain amount of current is allowed to pass and then cut off the supply automatically.

One of the most popular methods of charging for current is that known as the "all in" tariff for domestic supplies. It is an inclusive rate for electricity supplied for lighting, heating, cooking and all electrical domestic appliances. An annual fixed charge is made, payable quarterly in advance, according to the dimensions of the premises to be supplied, plus a charge of about a penny per unit consumed. With this system no meter-rent is charged as is done with the flat and rebate systems.

Service mains laid on consumer's property are generally charged for, and all service cables laid on public or private roadways in excess of 60 ft.

from existing mains are also generally charged for.

When an installation of electric light is contemplated it is a wise plan to get an estimate from the supply authorities for carrying out this work. The approximate cost of service cable is 2/6 per foot including laying, for a twin-core cable, and 3/6 per foot for a triple-core cable.

Having ascertained the necessary details and filled in the application form for a service, the next point to be considered is the choice of a system of wiring.

One of several methods can be used, the principal systems being:—

The Conduit System, which is both reliable and inexpensive and is used mainly in new houses in the process of erection or in old houses which are going to be redecorated. The wires and cables are run in enamelled steel tubing which affords complete and efficient protection to the wires.

The Metal-sheathed System.—This has become a very popular system for domestic installations, especially in existing houses and all such places where the conduit system cannot be conveniently used owing to its somewhat unsightly nature and liability to cause too much disturbance and damage to existing decorations.

Cable Tyre-sheathed System.— This system is carried out with a cable having a stout, tough yet flexible vulcanised rubber covering which is difficult to injure mechanically. It is used principally for surface work. Its chief advantage is that it is inexpensive, and it is only used on the cheapest type of installation.

In the conduit system the insulated conductors are run in enamelled steel tubes of which there are several kinds, namely, close-joint, brazed, welded, as shown at A, B and C in Fig. 1, and solid-drawn. Close-joint conduit consists of a strip of thin steel formed into a smooth and perfect tube, the

edges of which meet in a close joint, hence its name.

Close-joint tube is employed extensively where cheapness is one of the chief considerations. If properly installed it affords an excellent mechanical protection to the conductors, but it should not be used in damp situations, as the open seam does not render it impervious to moisture.

Brazed Conduit is a light-gauge tube having the seam brazed to form a solid joint, and is more expensive than the close-joint tubing.

Heavy-gauge Welded Conduit has a welded seam and is of sufficient thickness to enable it to be screwed.

Solid-drawn Conduit is a heavy-gauge tube and, as its name implies, is

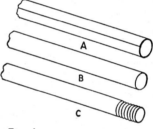

Fig. 1

drawn from a solid billet of steel. It is the most expensive kind of tube and is only used on the very best type of installation, being now seldom adopted for small private-house work.

In all electrical installations using metal tubes or other protective devices it is essential that electrical and mechanical continuity shall exist throughout the system, and that the whole of the tubing shall be efficiently connected to earth. This is a necessary precaution in the interests of safety, because in the event of the metal becoming "alive," due to a fault or other unforeseen circumstance, a person coming in contact with the tube might receive a very disagreeable shock. Therefore, always remember when installing any electrical apparatus that efficient earthing is the best preventive against shock and greatly reduces the risks of fire.

As the wiring of a house has to follow various routes and branch out at numerous points, the conduit system includes a number of fittings such as elbows, couplings, tee-pieces, junction boxes, etc., all of which must be fitted to the tubes in such a way as to make the system electrically continuous.

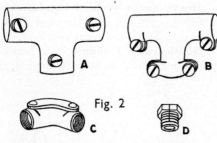

Fig. 2

Fittings commonly used with light-gauge conduit have projections or lugs which form sockets into which the ends of the conduit are inserted. Continuity is obtained in various ways, the most popular being, perhaps, the set-screw method, whereby electrical contact is acquired by means of set-screws fitted in the lugs, which press on the tube when in position, as illustrated in Fig. 2, at A. Another type of widely-used continuity fitting is shown at B. It is known as the lug grip fitting. Continuity is obtained by tightening up the screws at the side of the lugs, which causes it to grip the tube. The fitting shown at C is the one used on the grip socket system. In this system each outlet of the fitting has internal screw-threads. Contact between the fitting and the tube is obtained by contact nipples (D) screwed slightly taper and split along one side, which, on being screwed into the fitting and the end of

the conduit placed in the nipple, tighten up and securely grip the tube. In this system it is necessary to use the next larger-size screwed fitting to the normal size of the tube. Thus, a $\frac{3}{4}$-in. screwed fitting would be used for a $\frac{5}{8}$-in. plain tube.

Heavy-gauge conduit is used in conjunction with screwed fittings, as illustrated in Fig. 3, perfect continuity being attained by the screwed junctions.

There are two distinct types of conduit fittings in general use, namely, the solid and the inspection. The former is used when the tubing and wiring is done at the same time and the tubes are threaded over the wires, while the latter is employed where the wires are drawn into the conduit after erection.

As there is only a slight difference in the cost between the solid and inspection fitting, the latter should always be used if possible, for not only does its use simplify wiring, but the conductors can always be easily got at for inspection or replacement should the necessity arise.

Although the conduit system is one of the most satisfactory and safest systems for the mechanical protection of conductors in house wiring, it has the disadvantage of not being flexible, which

Fig. 3

makes it somewhat difficult to run in awkward corners and the like, and it also looks rather unsightly when run on the surface, as is necessary when the wiring has to be installed in a house already decorated and inhabited.

The metal-sheathed system of wiring gets over the difficulty, for it is particularly adaptable to surface-wiring. It has the great advantage of being flexible, and at the same time provides a good mechanical protection to the wires. The cables—which may have one, two or three separate insulated wires, or cores, as they are called—are enclosed and protected by a thin sheath of lead alloy, continuity being obtained by special junction boxes with clamping devices, bonding clips, etc., as shown in Fig. 4.

Lead-sheathed cable needs very little skill to install, and when neatly fixed

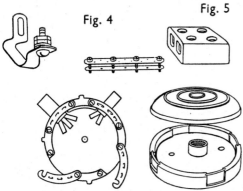

Fig. 4

Fig. 5

with the thin buckle-clips designed for the purpose, the appearance is not at all unsightly.

Another system which is being used extensively for house-wiring is the cab-tyre-sheathed system, generally known as the C.T.S. system. In the C.T.S. system the cables are similar to the metal-sheathed cables except that the metal sheathing is replaced by a thick layer of vulcanised india-rubber which renders it sufficiently strong to protect the inner conductors from mechanical injury. It can therefore be used without further protection and can be run under floors, between partitions and on the surface with equal ease and safety. When it is buried in plaster, however, it should be further protected by conduit tube. The C.T.S. system is extremely simple to install—in fact, almost as easy as installing bell-wires—and as the outer protective covering is an excellent insulator, it does not require earthing, thus obviating the necessity for bonding.

12*

Joints in C.T.S. cable are all made with china-insulated connecters and enclosed in bakelite junction-boxes, as shown in the illustration at Fig. 5, or in boxes having special connecters incorporated.

The Fittings or accessories, other than the conduit fittings, used in a simple electric-light installation of a private residence, comprise mainly one or more fuse-boards, switches, ceiling-roses, lampholders, and plug-sockets, as shown in the simple circuit illustrated in Fig. 6.

Current from the fuse-board is conveyed by the insulated conductors and feeds a certain number of "points" or outlets. At each of these outlets a suitable fitting must be provided in order to connect the lamp, heater, or other piece of apparatus to the circuit wires, the current being controlled by a switch fixed in a convenient position.

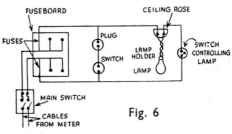

Fig. 6

Figure 7 at A shows a common type of ceiling-rose known as a two-plate rose. It is used for connecting an ordinary pendant light. It consists of a porcelain base having two brass terminal-plates each provided with two terminals. The through terminals are for connecting the circuit wires and the flat ones for joining to the ends of the flexible wire pendant. The terminals are protected by a screw-on porcelain cover having a central hole through which the flexible cord passes.

A three-plate ceiling-rose is illustrated at B in Fig. 7 and is similar to a two-plate

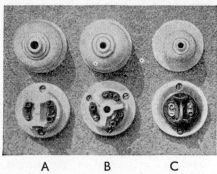

A　　　B　　　C

Fig. 7

rose but has an extra terminal-plate. It is used principally where two separate lamps are required in the same position, each controlled by a separate switch.

Porcelain ceiling-roses, which are usually mounted upon a hardwood block, are now being rapidly superseded by those made of bakelite, which can be fitted directly upon the ceiling without any intervening block; an illustration appears at c in Fig. 7.

Fig. 8 shows an illustration of the parts of a standard type of bayonet lampholder. It consists of a porcelain interior carrying two terminal blocks separated by an S-shaped insulating piece. The terminal blocks contain screws for securing the ends of the wires and also the spring-operated bayonet plunger-contacts which convey the current to the lamp-filament via the contact-pieces fixed in the end of the lamp-cap. The porcelain interior is enclosed in a cylindrical-shaped metal case, which is in two parts to enable the wires to be connected. The porcelain interior is slotted on each side, which enables a corresponding indentation in the holder to engage in the slots and keep the interior in the proper position. Two hook-shaped slots at the bottom of the holder engage in the projecting side pins of the lamp cap and thus keep

it in position. The top portion of the holder contains a small wooden cord-grip, kept in place by means of a screwed metal cap. The upper and lower parts of the case are held together by means of a screwed locking-ring, while another screwed ring—called a shade-ring—enables a shade to be kept in position.

Metal Lampholders can be obtained in several finishes such as polished brass, oxydised silver, bronze, etc.

Bakelite is now extensively used in the construction of lampholders. Such holders have the advantages of being practically shock-proof, not liable to corrosion as are metal ones, and they have fewer parts.

Three standard types of lampholders are in general use and are illustrated in Fig. 9. That shown at A is made of bakelite and is used with hanging

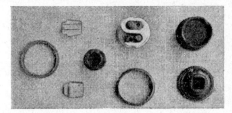

Fig. 8

Fig. 9

pendants, and that at B is fitted with an internal-threaded top to enable it to be attached to the screwed end of a bracket or other fitting. The holder at c is called a batten holder, and is used for screwing direct on to a wooden block or other support.

Fig. 10 at A shows an ordinary wall-socket and plug, which is used for connecting up such apparatus as standard-lamps, vacuum-cleaners, kettles, etc. It consists of a porcelain base having two socket terminals to which the main circuit wires are attached, the whole being covered with a hardwood or porcelain cap. The plug, which is connected through the flexible wire to the current-consuming device, is inserted

Switches play a very important part in an electrical installation, for their duty is to interrupt the current when a light or other apparatus in circuit is not required.

The type commonly used for ordinary domestic electric-lighting, where only

Fig. 11

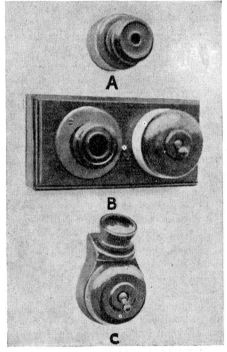

Fig. 10

into the socket and thus completes the circuit.

The disadvantage of such a socket is that it is always "alive," owing to the absence of a controlling switch. It is therefore good practice to install a switch at the side of the socket to control it, as shown at B, or better still, to fit a combination switch-plug such as that illustrated at C.

comparatively small currents have to be dealt with, is the quick-make-and-break tumbler-switch, as represented in Fig. 11.

The essential parts of such a switch consist of a copper bridge, which, when operated by a knob insulated from the current-carrying parts of the switch, connects two copper contacts attached to two separate terminal plates, to which the circuit wires are connected. The whole of the parts are supported upon a fire-proof insulating base such as porcelain, and protected by either a metal or other fireproof cover.

A few modern types of tumbler-switches are shown in Fig. 12. That illustrated at A represents a surface type switch used with a mounting block. The switch indicated by B is a semi-recessed switch where the base of the switch is sunk into the mounting block. This is a very popular type of switch as it has a much neater appearance than that of the ordinary surface type. This is due to its smaller projection from the surface of the wall or other support to which it is attached. The sunk

Fig. 12

switch shown at c is used with cover-plates which lie flush with the surface of the wall. Sunk switches necessitate the use of a wooden or an iron box sunk level with the surface of the wall. Owing to their extreme neatness, sunk switches with flush plates are particularly suitable for use in such places as living-rooms, halls and the like.

Numerous other kinds of tumbler switches are available for various purposes, the chief of which include two-way and intermediate switches used where more than one point of control is required.

Two-way switches are used where it is required to operate a light or lights from two points, such as, for example, a

Fig. 13

hall light, where it is convenient to operate it from either the hall or the first-floor landing, or that in a dining-room where there are two entrance doors.

Fig. 13 shows a two-way switch which is fitted with three terminals. It will be seen that the terminal on the left-hand side is common to both terminals on the right, that is to say, the left-hand terminal is always connected to either one or the other terminals whatever the position of the switch-knob may be.

A diagram of a light controlled by

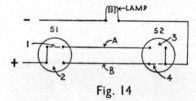

Fig. 14

two two-way switches, S_1 and S_2, is shown in Fig. 14, whence it will be clear that the current has alternative paths through the leads A and B. If the switch-arm of S_1 is put in position 1, shown by the dotted line, the circuit

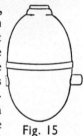

Fig. 15

is open at 3 in S_2 but can be closed by either replacing the switch-arm of S_1 to its original position or by moving the switch-arm of S_2 to 3.

The leads A and B are sometimes called channel wires or strapping wires.

The pear-shaped suspension switch shown at Fig. 15 is a particularly useful one, and is commonly used for operating bed-lights and other apparatus where a switch is required in a flexible cable. It is made for either single or two-way switching. The light is suspended from the ceiling over a bed or on the bed-rail, the switch being attached to a flexible cord suspended from either a ceiling-rose fixed high on the wall or on the ceiling in such a position that it can be easily operated from the bed.

The two-way pear switch is generally used in combination with another two-way switch near the entrance door, for controlling the principal light of the room. This arrangement allows the light to be switched either on or off from the bed, a convenience which nobody will dispute.

Other important accessories used in domestic electric light installations include a distributing fuseboard, a main switch, and a pair of main cut-out fuses.

The Fuseboard may be justly termed the heart of the installation, as all conductors forming sub-circuits radiate from this point.

Although there are many types of fuseboards, the standard type depicted in Fig. 16 is the one commonly used. It consists of a wooden case containing the necessary fuses for protecting the sub-circuits.

As it is compulsory to have a fuse in both poles to protect the conductors, etc., constituting a sub-circuit, the board is divided into a number of double-pole ways, the positive and negative sets of fuses being separated from each other by an insulating and fireproof material, such as porcelain asbestos.

The Fuse or safety-valve of the circuit consists of fine wire capable of carrying the normal current of the circuit but melting when the current flowing through the conductors rises above a certain degree, due to an overload, short-circuit, or other cause.

The rule for fuses is that when the working current does not exceed 10 amperes, the fuse must be of such capacity as to melt at not more than twice the working current of the smallest cable which it protects.

Fuse-wires for small currents, such as those flowing in sub-circuits in lighting installations, usually consist of a lead alloy, but where the current exceeds 10 amperes it is usual to employ a copper wire or a special cartridge fuse.

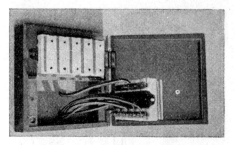

Fig. 16

The following table is helpful for ascertaining the correct size of fuse-wire to use.

TABLE OF FUSE-WIRES

Size of Wire S.W.G.	Lead Alloy Lead 75%; Tin 25% Approx. Fusing Current in Amps.	Tinned Copper Approx. Fusing Current in Amps.	Pure Tin Approx. Fusing Current in Amps.
16		166	26
18		108	17
20	9·42	70	11
22	6·46	48	7
24	4·50	33·4	5
26	3·33	24·7	4
28	2·48	18·4	3
30	1·90	14·0	2
32		11·5	1·75
34		9·04	1·50
36		6·79	·75
38		4·76	
40		3·41	

The fuse-wire is held in position by screw terminals provided in the porcelain fuse-carrier, the carrier being kept

Fig. 17

Fig. 18

Whilst dealing with the subject of fuseboards it may be pointed out that one of the rules to be observed is that the amount of current allowed per sub-circuit for lighting purposes is limited to a maximum of 5 amperes with pressures up to 100 volts and 3 amperes for circuits above this pressure, 250 volts being the maximum voltage permitted for lighting.

The following practical example will make this clear. Suppose that the "load" on the sub-circuit is composed of, say, three 60-watt lamps in a dining-room centre fitting and four 25-watt lamps in the brackets, also one 100-watt lamp and four 40-watt lamps in the lounge. The total current taken by these lamps is 180 + 100 + 100 + 160 watts. Since the current is equal to the watts divided by the voltage—in this case assumed to be 200—the current taken is

$$\frac{540}{200} = 2 \cdot 7 \text{ amperes.}$$

From this it will be seen that the current in such a circuit is below the ampere limit allowed.

If in the above example the voltage is 100, the current flowing will be 5·4 amperes, which is just above the limit allowed to suit such a pressure. In practice it is not considered good policy to feed more than eight or nine points from one pair of sub-circuit cut-outs, although the current may be well below the limit prescribed. This is done with the object of convenience, because it is a nuisance to have a large number of lights suddenly extinguished should a fuse blow at any time.

It is also necessary to have adequate fuses and a switch operating on both the positive and negative conductors at a point near to where the supply cable enters the premises. Such apparatus is known as the consumer's main

in place by metal sockets fixed to a small porcelain slab or base, as shown in detail in Fig. 17. This arrangement allows the fuse-carrier to be withdrawn easily should the fuse-wire need replacing.

A standard lighting fuseboard is designed to carry safely a current of five amperes per way.

switch and fuses. The combination double-pole fitting shown in Fig. 18 admirably satisfies this requirement, although in some small installations two single-pole tumbler-switches coupled together, so that they both operate at the same time, and two single-pole fuses, as indicated in Fig. 19, are allowable. The ironclad main switch should, however, always be installed where possible as it has the great advantage of preventing a person from gaining access to the fuses unless the switch is in the off position.

The object of the main switch is to cut off the entire supply should the need arise. The main fuses have to carry the total current of the whole installation and are therefore larger than those used in sub-circuits. The sub-circuit fuses should " blow " first and thus prevent the whole of the premises being thrown into darkness.

Fig. 20 shows a diagram of the connections, and the order in which the main switch is placed in relation to the supply cable and the distributing fuseboard.

The incoming supply cable terminates within the premises in a pair of ironclad boxes containing fuses, calculated to melt should the current flowing rise to a dangerous degree. The fuse-boxes are the property of the Supply Authority and are sealed in order to prevent unauthorised persons gaining access. In the event of the supply fuses melting it is necessary to communicate with the Supply people, who will send one of their representatives to replace them, a charge being usually made for the service.

This inconvenience can easily be avoided by giving due attention to the consumer's main fuses, which should always be adjusted to melt before the supply fuses.

The electric supply meter comes

between the supply main fuse and the main switch, and, like the service fuses, it is sealed to prevent unauthorised persons from interfering with it.

From the main switch, the conductors

Fig. 19

are connected to the consumer's main fuses and so to the distributing fuseboard from which the various sub-circuits radiate.

In the conduit system of wiring the conductors employed are of the vulcanised india-rubber variety, usually known as V.I.R. cables. Such a conductor consists of one or more strands of tinned copper wire insulated with a layer of pure rubber, then vulcanised rubber, both vulcanised together, then taped and braided and served with a preservative compound.

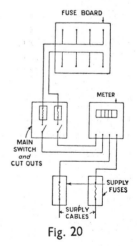

Fig. 20

The cables are supplied in 100-yard coils, and finished in either red or black colour, which allows the cables to be easily distinguished during the process of wiring. By convention the red-coloured conductors are connected to the positive side of the supply and the black ones to the negative.

As already pointed out, the core of a cable may consist of one or more strands of copper wire to which has been given a definite standard size.

A cable whose size is 1/·044 means that it consists of a single strand of wire having a diameter of ·044 in., and a 3/·029 cable has three strands of wire, each strand having a diameter of ·029 in., and so on.

The table below gives particulars of the various sizes of conductors commonly used in electric light and domestic power installations.

Size.	Nearest equivalent S.W.G.	Current-carrying capacity: amps.
1/·044	1/18	6·1
3/·029	3/22	7·8
3/·036	3/20	12·0
7/·029	7/22	18·2
7/·036	7/20	24·0
7/·044	7/18	31·0
7/·052	7/17	37·0
7/·064	7/16	46·0
19/·044	19/18	53·0

Reference to the table will show that the only single-strand wire used is the 1/·044 and this or its nearest stranded equivalent, a 3/·029 is the size generally employed for wiring lighting sub-circuits.

The current-carrying capacity of a conductor is governed by its voltage-drop and its rise in temperature.

One of the rules indicates that the voltage-drop must not exceed 2 per cent. of the supply voltage, and that the permissible temperature rise of V.I.R. cables must not exceed 20° F.

Fig. 21

The voltage-drop due to the resistance of the wires given in the table when the maximum current is flowing is approximately one volt for every five yards lead and return—that is a total length of ten yards. Since the average length of the runs of the electric wiring in a moderate-sized house is not very great, and as the permissible current for every sub-circuit at the common pressure of 200 volts is only 3 ampères—which is about one-half the maximum carrying capacity of a 1/·044 cable—it follows that the voltage-drop in such an installation is negligible.

Lights and Plugs.—The first thing to settle in planning an electric-light installation is the handiest positions of the various lights, plugs, fittings, etc., and the controlling switches.

This preliminary should be carried out with due care and consideration, as it is upon the careful arranging of these points that the convenience of electric light depends.

The best way to go about it is to prepare a schedule of the proposed lights, mentioning the position, candlepower, the type of fitting to be used, type of switch, and method of control; as quoted in the example given on pages 370 and 371, which represents the average requirements of a moderate-sized house.

Fig. 22

The object to be aimed at in efficient lighting is to obtain well-diffused yet sufficient illumination, and, in order to get a pleasing effect, the artistic arrangement of the lights should also be kept in mind.

This is not a difficult matter in these days when almost every type of electric-light fitting can be obtained at a reasonable figure.

In determining the number of lamps required to light a room efficiently the scheme of decoration must be taken into consideration, remembering that a light wallpaper reflects a greater amount of light than a dark one, and that the reflecting power of a cream ceiling is not so great as that of a white one.

In order to point out various details with regard to the positions, of lights, etc., of a proposed installation, it will perhaps be an advantage to explain the model schedule in detail, step by step.

The example given is not governed by any hard and fast rules and may of course be altered and modified to meet individual requirements. For instance, if the house is already decorated and furnished it is not advisable to fit sunk switches, as their use involves the cutting away of walls. In such a case, semi-recessed switches can be substituted in conjunction with a surface system of wiring.

Starting on the ground floor, the first item is the porch light. In a great many instances this convenient light is omitted,

Fig. 23

much to the regret of those people who have to grope their way to the entrance gate on a dark winter's night.

The fitting used for this purpose is usually in the shape of a lantern, an illustration of which appears in Fig. 21.

Apartment	Position of Fitting	Type of Fitting	No. and Wattage of Lamps	Switch
Ground floor				
Porch	Centre of ceiling	Lantern	1–40	1 sunk switch in hall
Hall	,,	Bowl	1–60	1 2-way sunk switch in hall and also operated from landing
Cloaks	,,	Pendant	1–40	1 sunk switch, shockproof
Lounge	,,	Bowl	1–100	1 sunk switch, by door
	4 on wall, side of fireplace and other wall	Brackets	4–40	2 ,,
	1 on skirting for piano	Standard	1–40	Combination switch-plug
Dining Rm.	Centre of ceiling	3 light counterwt.	3–40	2 sunk switches, by door
	2 on wall, side of fireplace	Brackets	2–40	1 ,,
Maid's Room	Centre of ceiling	Pendant	1–40	1 semi-recessed switch by door
Kitchen	,,	,,	1–40	,, shockproof
Coals	,,	,,	1–25	,,
Lavatory	,,	,,	1–25	,,
Garage	Over entrance door	Watertight Bracket	1–40	,,
	Ceiling, over engine	Pendant	1–40	,,
	Ceiling, over bench	,,	1–40	,,
	1 on wall	Handlamp	1–40	1 Combination switch plug, 3 pin
Larder	Centre of Ceiling	Pendant	1–25	1 surface switch

It should be fitted to the ceiling as high up as possible to protect it from the weather. If such a position is not practicable a plain watertight bracket fitting, as that illustrated at Fig. 22, fixed to a wall, may be substituted.

The switch operating such a light should be fitted in the hall, near the front entrance door.

As the hall of a modern house is usually more or less square, a small opalescent bowl fitting (Fig. 23) of the same tint as that of the wall decoration, or a fancy fitting of pastel-coloured glass, gives a very pleasing effect, and is much more distinctive-looking than the old-fashioned lantern, although the latter would suit an oak-panelled hall with half-timbered ceiling. The light should be arranged, if possible, with two-, or better still, three-point control, one switch being fixed near the front door to enable the light to be operated as soon as one enters or leaves the house. Another switch should be fitted at the back of the hall at a point easily reached from the kitchen and the third switch on the landing or at the top of the staircase.

Apartment	Position of Fitting	Type of Fitting	No. and Wattage of Lamps	Switch
1st Floor				
Bedroom 1	Ceiling, over dressing table	Fancy Pendant	1–60	1 sunk switch, by door
	Ceiling, over bed	,,	1–25	1 pear switch, by bed
Bedroom 2	Ceiling, over dressing table	,,	1–60	1 sunk switch, by door
	Ceiling, over bed	,,	1–25	1 pear switch, by bed
Bedroom 3	Ceiling, over dressing table	,,	1–60	1 sunk switch, by door
	Ceiling, over bed	,,	1–25	1 pear switch, by bed
Bedroom 4	Ceiling, over dressing table	,,	1–60	1 sunk switch, by door
	Ceiling, over bed	,,	1–25	1 pear switch, by bed
Study	Centre of ceiling	Bowl	1–100	1 sunk switch, by door
	1 on skirting	Standard	1–60	1 combination switch-plug
Landing	Centre of ceiling, over newel post	Fancy Pendant	1–40	1, 2-way sunk switch on wall and also operated from hall
Bathroom	Centre of ceiling	Enclosed fitting—white enamelled	1–60	1 sunk switch, shock-proof, by door
	1 on skirting	Shaving Mirror	1–40	1 combination switch-plug, 3-pin
Lavatory	Centre of ceiling	Pendant	1–25	1 sunk switch, by door
Attic	Near trap door	Handlamp	1–25	1 combination switch-plug

The cloak-room is usually a small apartment, but nevertheless a good light is required. The switch should be fixed near the entrance door, about 4 ft. 6 in. above the floor level—the usual height for switches. A white semi-recessed shockproof switch may be used here with advantage, and a white porcelain-finished bracket fitted over the hand-basin is generally in keeping with the decorations of such a room.

If a bracket cannot be conveniently fixed, a good alternative is a small, enclosed, white-enamelled ceiling-fitting with a white opal totally-enclosed shade fixed close up to the ceiling, as shown in Fig. 24. Such a fitting is much to be preferred to the ordinary hanging flexible pendant and conical glass shade.

The lounge, which has now almost completely taken the place of the drawing-room, calls for a soft yet plentiful supply of light. This can be achieved by means of a centre light and wall brackets. Two lighting combined switch-plugs should also be included and fixed on the skirting: one for supplying a tall standard lamp and the other for a piano

Fig. 24

Fig. 25

recesses at the side of the fireplace, may be installed with advantage.

The general light of a kitchen may be obtained by a fixed enclosed ceiling light similar to the cloak-room fitting, but larger, while a plug for an electric iron should not be overlooked; but here again, if power is to be installed, the iron should be fitted to that circuit.

light. If an all-electric wireless receiver is also to be installed in the room, it is as well to provide an additional plug for this; but the radio receiver is generally run off a power-plug, when such a plug is available.

Fig. 25 shows a modern design of bracket suitable for lounges, etc., while a modern centre-light fitting is shown in Fig. 26.

Three switches should be fitted at the lounge door, one for controlling the centre light and two for controlling each pair of bracket lights.

The usual position for a dining-room light is over the centre of the table and, as a concentrated light is usually needed in this position, a three-light rise-and-fall fitting will answer these requirements. Such a fitting is shown in Fig. 27, and as it is fitted with a counterbalance it can be adjusted to any height required. In addition to a centre light a couple of wall brackets, fitted with imitation candle-lamps, fixed in the

The kitchen switch should be of the shockproof type, with a brown or white bakelite cover, as this type of switch is easily cleaned with a duster.

The scullery light should be fixed over the sink and can be an ordinary plain hanging pendant with an opal shade. A pearl or inside frosted lamp can be used here with advantage, to prevent glare.

The switch should be of the same

type as that used in the kitchen, as also can be the lights and switches for the lobby, lavatory, coal cellar, maid's sitting-room and larder.

The Garage Lighting is of no less importance than the lighting of any other part of the house, for in here a good many jobs may be required to be carried out in connection with the car.

The chief light should be suspended from the ceiling over the bonnet of the engine and it should be of the rise-and-fall type—so that its height may be adjusted to a convenient height—fitted with an enamelled iron shade to prevent breakage.

A wall plug should not be overlooked as it allows a portable inspection lamp to be used for lighting awkward places when carrying out repairs or other work upon the car.

If a workbench is fitted in the garage another light will be needed over this, and another refinement is a light outside the main entrance door.

If the garage is accessible by a door from the house, the main light should be controlled by two-point switching, one switch being fitted at the main

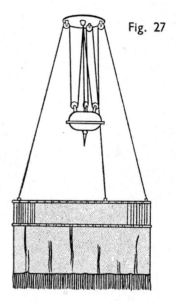

Fig. 27

entrance door and the other at the house entrance door.

As the floor of a garage is generally composed of concrete, the inspection lamp referred to should be of the shock-proof type where the whole of the electrical parts are protected in such a way that it is impossible for anyone to receive a shock should a fault occur in the lamp. The inspection lamp, shown in Fig. 28, should be connected to the plug with heavy flexible cab-tyre cable as the ordinary twisted flex as used on pendants is entirely unsuitable.

Bedroom Lighting generally calls for at least one light over the dressing-table, suspended in such a position as to avoid shadows being cast on the blinds. The switches for such lights are usually

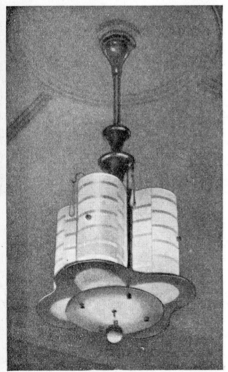

Fig. 26

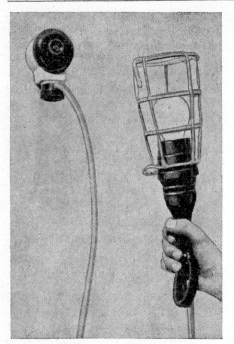

Fig. 28

As the bathroom is now considered one of the most important rooms in the house, it is not surprising to find that numerous special light fittings have been designed to conform with its significance.

The chief light may be a white, porcelain-finished, totally-enclosed unit, fixed to the ceiling, similar to that suggested for the cloak-room, while a shockproof combined switch-plug for feeding an illuminated shaving mirror is a great convenience which can only be proved by those who have used it.

A Shockproof Switch should always be used in a bathroom and it should be fixed in such a position that it is impossible for any person in the bath to

Fig. 29

fixed at the entrance door of the apartment.

In the best bedrooms it is now usual to provide an additional light, operated by a suspension switch, over the head of the bed or by a plug fixed on the skirting near the bed, to enable a small table standard lamp to be used.

Where the rooms are small, however, and do not need a bed light, it is a convenience to have the general light controlled by two-way switches operated from the bed and the door.

A suitable type of dressing-table fitting is shown in Fig. 30; while Fig. 29 represents a popular type of bed light fitting fixed at a foot or so above the head of the bed.

The landing light, which may consist of a plain hanging pendant with a fancy shade, should be controlled by two-way switches fixed at convenient points on the landing and in the hall.

operate the switch. This absolutely necessary precaution refers not only to the switch but also to all other electrical apparatus installed in a bathroom, for should a person in a bath touch a leaky piece of apparatus he would possibly receive a dangerous if not fatal shock, due to the leakage current passing through the body which is connected to earth through the large volume of water. It is for this reason also that a

Fig. 30

three-pin plug should be used with the shaving mirror mentioned above to enable the metal case of the mirror to be efficiently connected to earth via the third pin on the plug. This is connected to the earthed conduit tube or other metal protecting system of the conductors.

The General Lighting of a Study— which in the case under review is on the first floor—may be by means of a bowl fitting carrying a 100-watt lamp, operated by a switch located near the entrance door. At least one lighting plug should be installed in such a room to enable a small portable standard lamp, such as the one illustrated in Fig. 31, to be used on the writing-desk, when, for economy, the main light is generally switched off. A plug at the side of the fireplace will also be found useful as it allows a tall floor standard lamp to be used for reading purposes. The standard lamp should be arranged to come behind the reader, which is the best position for preventing eyestrain.

The lavatory light calls for no other comment except that a small enclosed white ceiling fitting is to be preferred to the usual hanging pendant and that the switch should be a shockproof one.

The last item on the schedule refers to the attic—usually the store for junk in general and also the home of the supply tank of the water system.

A plug installed in the attic is a great boon and enables a portable shockproof lamp, similar to the garage portable lamp previously referred to, to be used. Moreover, the plug can also be used for supplying current to a small portable heater, which will prevent the water in the supply tank from freezing when heavy frosts occur.

The Lamps now commonly adopted in private-house installations are those known as gas-filled or $\frac{1}{2}$-watt lamps. The $\frac{1}{2}$-watt lamp consumes half a watt of electrical energy for every standard candle-power emitted. The candle-power of an electric lamp, however,

Fig. 31

has not the illuminating power of a similar number of ordinary wax candles.

The ordinary paraffin wax candle often emits double the amount of light of the "standard" candle, known as the International Candle, which is the practical unit of luminous intensity used in this country.

The first successful incandescent electric lamp was introduced by Thomas A. Edison in 1880, when bringing out the carbon filament lamp. This type of lamp had a thin carbon filament enclosed in an air-exhausted glass bulb, and, owing to its low efficiency, namely,

about $3\frac{1}{2}$ watts per candle-power, it is seldom used to-day except for special purposes. The carbon filament lamp was superseded by a lamp having a metallic filament of tungsten, also enclosed in a vacuum bulb, but this has been more or less replaced by the present-day gas-filled lamp.

The gas-filled lamp is filled with an inert gas—nitrogen or argon—which allows the tungsten filament to be run at a much higher temperature and therefore greater brilliancy than the vacuum type; hence its greatly increased efficiency.

Gas-filled Lamps can be obtained in voltages ranging from 100 to 130 and from 200 to 250 in standard wattages of 25, 40, 60, 75, 100 and 150 for fitting ordinary standard bayonet lampholders and from 200 watts up to 1,500 watts for fitting special lampholders, but lamps of above 150 watts are rarely used for house lighting purposes.

Gas-filled lamps can be obtained either with clear-glass bulbs for use with obscured shades, such as bowl fittings, or obscured on the inside surface of the bulb, known as pearl. The latter are very useful as a protection from glare and should therefore always be used with open type fittings.

A very useful type of lamp which is becoming increasingly popular is the two-filament lamp having two filaments which can be brought into operation separately by simply pulling a cord, which operates a two-way switch within the lamp-cap. For normal lighting, one filament consuming 25 watts is used, but when only a small subdued light is required, such as a night light, a 5-watt filament is brought into action. Such a lamp is particularly useful in such places as halls, corridors, bedrooms, etc.

While on the subject of electric lamps, it may be pointed out that intending purchasers of lamps should be very careful when buying lamps of unknown origin. There are at present huge numbers of cheap foreign-made lamps on the market whose life and efficiency leave a lot to be desired. Whenever installing lamps, it is important to use only those whose efficiency has been proved by time and experience.

The Wiring System.—When the number and the positions of the lights constituting the installation have been definitely settled, the next step is to decide upon which system of wiring —that is, conduit or otherwise—is to be adopted, and then to give attention to the general layout of the runs.

If the building is in course of erection, the conduit system is strongly recommended, in which case the conduit tube and its fittings are erected and fitted before the floor-boards are laid or the plastering started. This allows all conduit to be completely hidden under the floor-boards and buried under the plaster so that when the work is complete, all that meets the eye is the switches and fittings and other necessary accessories.

In a similar way, if the house is an old one and is going to be redecorated, the conduit system may be installed with advantage as some of the floor-boards can easily be lifted and the walls cut away where it is necessary to run down to switches and the like, and made good after the tubes are installed.

In a furnished and decorated house, the choice generally rests between a metal-sheathed system and the cab-tyre-sheathed system. The former system should be given the vote if it is not a matter of price, for lead-covered cable makes a better job, and looks much neater when completed.

For the purpose of explaining the method of wiring on the conduit system, the case of the unoccupied house will be considered, as the wiring of a house in course of construction is substantially the same. The specification already dealt with will also serve as a basis upon which the work is to be carried out.

The method of house-wiring usually adopted in this country is known as the multiple circuit distribution system and is common to electric light and to domestic power installations.

The system begins at the main switch and fuses and feeds one or more distributing fuse-boards, where the main

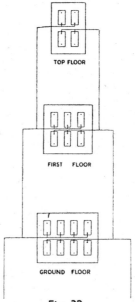

Fig. 32

circuit is split up into a number of sub-circuits, each protected by a pair of fuses on the distributing fuse-board, as already mentioned. The position of the fuse-board should be as near to the centre of the branch circuits as possible in order to keep the runs as short as practicable.

In some installations where there are a large number of lights it is usual to install a fuse-board on each floor to feed the circuits controlling the lamps on that particular floor as indicated in the diagram at Fig. 32.

As the conductors between the main

switch and the first fuse-board have to carry the whole of the current taken by the total number of lamps, they are necessarily of greater current-carrying capacity than those forming the branch circuits.

Where two fuse-boards are used, however, the cables joining the first and second fuse-boards may be reduced in size because they only have to carry the current of the particular sub-circuits they feed. To make this clear, suppose there are 30 40-watt lamps or their equivalent connected to the first-floor fuse-board and 40 60-watt lamps fed from the ground-floor board. The total current taken by all the lamps is:

$$\frac{30 \times 40}{200} + \frac{40 \times 60}{200} = \frac{1200 + 2400}{200} = \frac{3600}{200}$$

= 18 amperes.

Hence the cables between the main switch and the ground-floor board must safely carry a current of 18 amperes, while those joining the first to the second fuse-board need only be of sufficient size to carry six amperes.

The system adopted in the early days of electric lighting is shown diagrammatically in Fig. 33. In this system, known

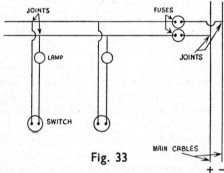

Fig. 33

as the "tree" system, wood casing was used for protecting the conductors, and a heavy cable was employed between the main switch and the first branch of lamps and a smaller one to the next set, gradually decreasing in size to the farthest lamp. Among the many disadvantages of this obsolete system was the large expenditure of time necessary for making a great number of soldered joints, which all had to be properly insulated after the joints had been

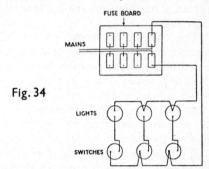

Fig. 34

made. Such joints, and their insulation, however well made, were a continual source of trouble. The tree system also involved the use of numerous fuses scattered all over the premises, usually in very inconvenient places.

The modern method, known as "looping-in" the wires, entirely eliminates the use of soldered joints, and can be easily understood by referring to the diagram in Fig. 34, which shows a typical sub-circuit wired on the loop-in principle.

It will be seen from the illustration that a single conductor runs from the positive terminal of the fuse and is connected to a terminal of the first switch. From this terminal the conductor is joined to a terminal of the second switch, and so on to the last switch in the circuit. Similarly, the wire from the negative fuse-terminal is taken to a terminal on the ceiling-rose and then on to the next rose, all roses being connected up in the same way. A single wire between each switch and ceiling-rose completes the circuit.

The conductors connecting the switch terminals are known as "switch feeds" or "positive feeds" while those connecting the roses are termed "light feeds" or "negative feeds." The wire connecting the ceiling-rose to the switch is called the "line."

Sometimes it is more convenient or necessary to make a joint—a joint often means the saving of a considerable amount of wire—in which case special connecters insulated with porcelain may be used, but they must be enclosed in a proper junction-box. Such a junction-box and connecters are shown in Fig. 35.

Fig. 35

It is here necessary to study the schedule, already mentioned earlier in this article, and the plans of the two floors, illustrated on page 377. The plans are not drawn to scale, but have been prepared with the object of pointing out important details, such as positions of the lights and the tube runs, the sizes of the wires, and how to split up the lights to form the sub-circuits.

On totalling up the number of lights it will be found that the total number of watts is approximately 1645, and as the voltage is assumed to be 200, the maximum current, with all lamps on, is:

$$\frac{1645}{200} = 8.23 \text{ amperes.}$$

To allow for the possibility of extension, etc.—it is better to over-estimate than under-estimate—call it 10 amperes. Referring to the table of the sizes of

conductors previously given, it will be seen that the nearest-sized cable safely to carry 10 amperes is a 3 /.036, which carries a maximum of 12 amps., and this is the correct-sized main cable to use.

As the smallest cable allowed safely carries a load of 6 amps., the sub-circuit wiring can be carried out with a 1/·044 or its equivalent a 3/·029, and as the single-strand conductor is a little cheaper than the stranded, the former can be decided upon.

With regard to the grouping of the lamps to form sub-circuits, it may be pointed out that although the maximum current allowed per sub-circuit is 3 amps., and that the number of points should not exceed eight or nine, it is not always good policy to adhere rigidly to these figures provided the values specified above are not exceeded.

Starting with the first floor and work-

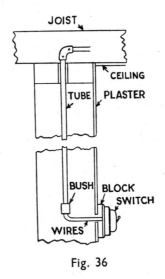

Fig. 36

ing downwards, the sub-circuits could be conveniently arranged by having two circuits to feed the first-floor lamps and three circuits for the lights on the ground floor, arranged as follows:

Circuit	Apartments	Points	Watts	Current in amps.
1	Bedrooms 1, 2, 3, and 4 . . .	8	340	1·70
2	Landing, Study, Bathroom, Lavatory, Attic	7	350	1·75
3	Lounge, Maid's Sitting-room, Larder	8	365	1·83
4	Dining-room, Hall, Porch, Cloaks .	6	340	1·70
5	Garage, Kitchen, Coals, Cellar, Lavatory	7	250	1·25
	Total	36	1645	8·23

This arrangement necessitates the use of a five-way, double-pole fuse-board.

Referring to the plan, it will be seen that the supply cable enters the garage. In order to prevent damage to the meter and the main switch, they should be fixed on the wall as high up as possible. The fuse-board is shown at the other end of the garage on the opposite wall, as this is the nearest convenient point to the centre of the building. The fuse-board, like the main switch, should also be kept up as high as practicable. From this point, all conduit tubes carrying the branch circuit wires radiate to all parts of the building.

The main cables from the main switch to the fuse-board can be run in conduit fixed on the surfaces of the walls and fastened thereto with saddles, as there is no object served in burying them in the walls.

The Conduit runs should now be set out, bearing in mind that the shorter the runs the less cable, conduit, and fittings required, which, of course, means so much money saved.

In a small installation, such as the one under review, it is as well to keep to one size of conduit as much as possible for the main portions of the runs, and only reduce the size where the conduit drops down to switches, where the use of a smaller-sized tube may save a little labour in cutting away. Hence, $\frac{5}{8}$-in. diameter conduit can be used for runs under floorboards, etc., and $\frac{1}{2}$-in. tubes for the switch drops, when the number of wires in such a tube does not exceed three.

As the cost, in these days, of conduit fittings used on the installation does not involve a great outlay, it is preferable to use fittings of the "inspection" type, and as the use of pin-grip fittings makes quite a satisfactory job if proper care is taken to screw the contact-screws up tightly on the tubes, it is assumed that these will be used.

If the nature of the supply is alternating current, there is a rule that the wires protected with a metal protection device must be run in such a way that the sum of the current flowing in the wires is zero. This means, in so many words, that the positive and negative wires run in the same tube, because a single conductor, carrying a heavy current, when protected with a metal tube or sheath, induces a current in the metal protection due to the alternating or fluctuating nature of the current.

A skeleton plan of the conduit "runs" for supplying the lamps on the first floor is shown in Working Drawing No. 23.

As all the tubing and wiring is carried out from the floor above the rooms to

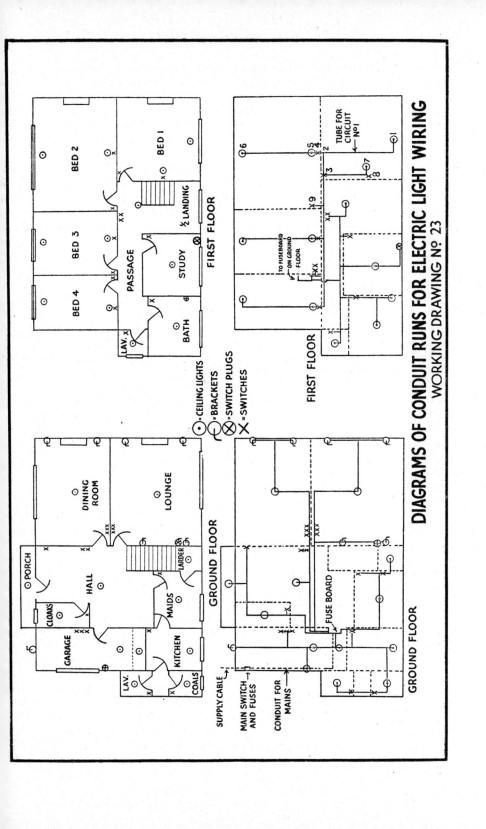

BED 2

BED 1

BED 3

BED 4

PASSAGE

STUDY

½ LANDING

BATH

LAV.

FIRST FLOOR

⊙ = CEILING LIGHTS

= BRACKETS

⊗ = SWITCH PLUGS

✕ = SWITCHES

TUBE FOR CIRCUIT NO 1

TO FUSEBOARD ON GROUND FLOOR

FIRST FLOOR

DINING ROOM

LOUNGE

LARDER

PORCH

HALL

CLOAKS

MAIDS

GARAGE

KITCHEN

LAV.

COALS

GROUND FLOOR

FUSE BOARD

SUPPLY CABLE

MAIN SWITCH AND FUSES

CONDUIT FOR MAINS

GROUND FLOOR

DIAGRAMS OF CONDUIT RUNS FOR ELECTRIC LIGHT WIRING
WORKING DRAWING No. 23

be lighted, the runs for the first-floor lamps will be carried out from the attic. As this space is usually devoid of floor-boards and other obstructions, the tubing of these circuits should present little difficulty.

The runs shown on the plan need not, of course, be rigidly adhered to; they are only shown for the purpose of explaining the methods of tubing and wiring.

In laying and fitting the conduit it is a wise plan to complete one circuit at a time. Thus, a start would be made by tubing No. 1 circuit, commencing at the dressing-table light in bedroom 1 and working back towards a point where it drops down to the fuse-board in the garage below, as indicated by the arrow.

Before fitting any tubes the positions of the various light outlets and switch outlets must be marked out and the walls prepared for accommodating the tubes running down to the switches, etc.

When the correct positions of the light-points have been found and duly marked on the ceilings below, holes should be made through the ceilings at these points to enable the exact spot to be easily located from the floor above. This can be easily done by first making a small hole in the ceiling with a bradawl and then gradually enlarging the hole with the blade of a screwdriver or other tool with a fairly large shank. Care should be exercised not to damage any laths supporting the plaster and the hole should only be of sufficient size to allow the wires to pass through comfortably.

With regard to the switch-points, the approximate positions of each may be found in the same way, that is to say, by piercing the ceiling with a bradawl at a point opposite to where the tube drops down to the switch.

After each hole has been made, a great

deal of time may be saved by placing a piece of white paper over each hole from the floor above to show the various positions, as it is somewhat difficult to locate a small hole quickly, especially if the light—as is usually the case in attics—is indifferent.

As the walls upon which the switches are fixed are not always composed of solid brickwork, but are sometimes hollow and composed of lath and plaster, which precludes them from being cut away to receive the down tubes, it is usual to drill the wall-plate above the studs which support the laths, and then

Fig. 37

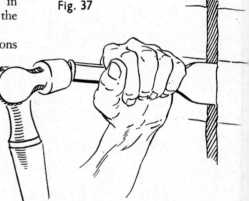

to insert the tube in the hollow space between the plaster faces in the manner shown in Fig. 36.

The holes in the wall-plate can be drilled with either an auger or a brace and twist-bit. They should be of sufficient size to allow the conduit with a bush on the end to pass through easily and when fitted can be held in position by means of a wooden wedge set between the side of the hole and the conduit. The switch wires are then drawn through an aperture made between the laths, as indicated in the sketch.

Where the walls are solid the surface of the plaster should be accurately marked out with vertical lines spaced

Fig. 38

little wider than the diameter of the tube, and then neatly chased out to form a narrow channel, deep enough to bury the tube completely when the wall is made good with plaster. The cutting away can be executed with a bricklayer's bolster chisel in the manner shown in Fig. 37. At the outlet of each switch-point a square wooden fixing block should be let into the wall and fixed with cement in order to obtain a firm fixing for the switch, in the manner indicated in Fig. 38.

As electric-light wiring requires to be carried out in a methodical and systematic way, it is advisable to get all the cutting away of walls, etc., on the first floor, finished before any tubing is put in hand, as, by so doing, the debris can be removed and the floor left clear when the time comes for tubing the ground-floor lights.

The strength of the laths should never be relied upon for fixing fittings, ceiling roses, etc. A piece of board or batten, having a hole to correspond with the outlet in the ceiling, should be prepared and fixed between the joists over each light outlet, as illustrated in Fig. 39. If, however, the outlet wires are close up

to a joist, the joist can be used for fixing purposes, rendering the use of fixing battens unnecessary.

The actual tube-fitting may now be commenced, and as it is unnecessary to sink the conduit below the level of the ceiling joists in the attic, the tubes are simply fastened to the tops of the joists.

Reference to circuit No. 1, in the plan of the first floor (Working Drawing No. 23) shows that the first length of tube to be prepared is that running from the light-point marked 1 to the first branch at 2, where a tee-piece should be inserted to join the switch drop-pieces at 3 and 4. At the end of the tube at the light-point 1, an elbow and a short piece of tube should be fitted to protect the wires right down to the outlet.

The conduit is cut with a triangular file by first filing a deep nick across the joint and then running the cut round the tube. If the tube is then placed across the knee and strained it will break at the filed position. The jagged edges at the ends of the tube must be entirely

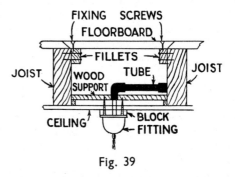

Fig. 39

removed and filed perfectly flat. It is also a wise precaution entirely to remove the enamel from the ends of the tube to ensure perfect contact between the contact-screws of the fittings and the tube. Fig. 40 shows the operation of breaking the tube at the filed position. When this is completed the tube can be lightly nailed in position and the tube joining the tee at 2 to the tee at 4 can be prepared in the same manner. The tee at 4 is to connect the short switch-drop for the bed light in

Fig. 40

bedroom 2, and therefore one of its outlets turns downwards.

When connecting fittings to close-joint tube, it is necessary to see that the contact-screws bear on a solid part of the tube and not between the joint. Failure to take this precaution will possibly cause a sharp indentation inside the conduit, which may injure the insulation of the conductors when drawn in.

The Switch Tubes may either be fitted as the main portion of the tubing proceeds, or they may be fitted after the main horizontal runs have been completed. The writer prefers to fix all switch-drops after the main runs have been finished. Having settled the matter one way or the other, the tube joining 4 and 5 can be fitted and another tee inserted for the bed-light outlet at 5, following with the length joining 5 and 6.

This procedure is carried on until the whole of the tubing is complete up to

a point where it drops down to the fuse-board, when No. 2 circuit can be tubed in a like manner.

Where the tubes of the two top-floor circuits meet, i.e., the point where they drop down to the fuse-board, they can be coupled together with a tee, which enables a single tube to be used for carrying the two pairs of circuit-wires down to the fuse-board.

When the tubing of the first floor is complete, the ground-floor circuits may be proceeded with in the same manner as that just explained.

There are certain points, however, to be observed when carrying out work on the ground floor, one of the chief being that the conduit has to run under the floorboards, which necessitates their removal, and that the joists have to be slotted in order to allow the tubes to be sunk in them to a depth just below the top surface of the joists.

As the notching of joists in the centre of a room considerably weakens the floor they support, the runs should be arranged to come as near a supporting wall as possible. This may be clearly understood by referring to the illustration at Fig. 41, which shows the correct way of running conduit across the joists under floors.

A great deal of time may be saved in setting out the runs and locating the positions of the floorboards to be taken up by calling upon the help of a second person.

When the positions of the lights, etc., have been marked, and the holes in the ceiling have been made, as previously explained, a thin metal rod about 15 in. long should be inserted into the holes to reach the floorboard above. If the rod is now tapped from the bottom, the particular floorboard above it can easily be located and marked with a piece of chalk by the person above.

Plain floorboards may be easily lifted by first punching down the nails with a proper nail set and then prising them up

Fig. 42

by means of cold chisels in the manner indicated in Fig. 42. Great care should be taken to prevent damage to the board.

When the floor consists of tongued and grooved boards, the tongue must first be removed by the use of a pad-saw.

In order to avoid taking up more floorboards than is absolutely necessary, it is sometimes found that a trap cut in the board will answer the same purpose as removing a whole board. In preparing such a trap, the board should be cut across on the bevel, as indicated in Fig. 39, and two wood fillets nailed to the sides of the joists will support the trap and enable it to be screwed down when the floorboards are relaid.

Another important point refers to the switches.

By consulting the schedule it will be seen that the switches in the best rooms and the hall are to be of the sunk type. As these switches are to be fitted with flush plates, it is necessary to protect them with wooden boxes sunk into the walls, flush with the plaster.

The boxes should be drilled to take

the particular size of conduit, and great care should be exercised to prevent the end of the tube projecting into the interior of the box, as this may prevent the switch from operating. Such a defect is very difficult to remedy after the wall has been made good.

The Boxes should be sunk in the wall to a sufficient depth to allow the front edges of the box to lie about $\frac{1}{8}$ in. below the surface of the finished plaster. They can be held in position by wooden wedges and then cemented in with a mixture of cement and sand, leaving sufficient depth to allow it to be neatly finished off with a facing of plaster, in the manner shown in Fig. 43.

When the whole of the tubing is complete, the ends of the tubes terminating at the fuse-board should be bonded together with proper earthing clips designed for the purpose. It is almost unnecessary to say that the enamel on the tubes must be removed to ensure a good metal-to-metal connection. A bare 7/22

Fig. 43

copper wire should then be connected to the tubes and the nearest main cold-water pipe to ensure a good earth. Under no consideration whatever must a gas-pipe

13

be used for earthing purposes, and it is as well to point out here that all conduit runs, etc., must be kept clear of gas-pipes and not allowed to touch them.

In order to make sure that the conduit system is continuous it should now be tested for continuity. This may be done by means of an electric bell, a single cell, and connecting wires, which, when connected to the system, as shown in Fig. 44, should ring the bell normally.

If no ring is forthcoming it shows that there is a break in the continuity and it is therefore necessary to trace and rectify the fault. This can be done by the process of elimination, with the aid of the electric bell and battery, by first testing the continuity of the conduit containing the mains, and then each section of tubing forming a sub-circuit. When the particular run containing the break is found, the fault should be localised by testing each joint which, when found, can easily be rectified.

Threading the Wires.—The next process consists of drawing or threading the wires through the tubes. This should be carried out methodically, starting from the furthest point in circuit

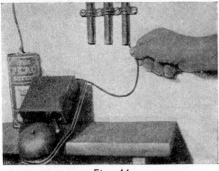

Fig. 44

No. 1, and completing each circuit as the work proceeds, in the same manner as that adoped for the tubing.

It is unnecessary to go into the details of the wiring of every circuit, so a few

brief observations will be given with regard to the first circuit, which is typical of the rest.

The first procedure is to remove all the inspection covers of the conduit fittings of the circuit to be wired, placing them on the plaster of the ceiling just below the fitting to which they belong, in order to prevent them from being mislaid.

Now measure the length of the switch-tubes from the fittings—that is, the elbow or tee—above, down to each switch outlet, in order to know the amount of wire to allow at these points when they are being wired from above. In the case under review the switch wires will all be of the same length, as there is no difference in the floor level below. Assuming that the length of the tube is 4 ft., it is well to allow an extra 9 in. for connecting up to the switch, always bearing in mind that it is obviously better to have the wires a little too long than too short. The same amount of extra wire should also be allowed at the ceiling-light outlets.

Starting with bedrooms Nos. 1 and 2, we shall require the following black wires feeding one terminal of each ceiling rose. One from 1 to 5, 5 to 6, 5 to 7, and another feeding back to the bed-light in bedroom No. 3. The red wires required for looping to the switches are 4 to 3, 3 to 8, 3 to 9, and another looped back to the bed switch in bedroom No. 3. The following lines connecting the lights to the switches will also be required and these should be wired in red-coloured cable. From 1 to 3, 7 to 8 in bedroom No. 1, and 4 to 5 and 6 to 9 in bedroom No. 2.

From this the number of wires at each outlet should be as follows: One red and one black at the dressing-table light outlet at 1 in bedroom No. 1, and 4 reds at the switch by the door, consisting of 1 line for controlling the dressing-table light, one switch-feed from 9, one loop to 8 and one loop to 4. At the switch outlet at 8 there should be two reds—one from 3 and the other the line connecting the light at 7. At 7 there should be one red and two blacks; the red is the line from switch 8 and the two blacks from 5 and from the light outlet over the bed in bedroom No. 3 respectively.

In bedroom No. 2 the number of wires at each outlet will be as follows: A red and a black at 6—the red being the line from the switch outlet 9, and the black from 5. At the bed-light outlet there should be three blacks and a red, the red being the line from the bed-switch at 4, and the blacks from 1, 6, and 7. At the switch outlet 4 two reds should be seen, one a line from 5, and the other a feed from 3. At the switch outlet by the door three reds should be observed, one being the line controlling the dressing-table light at 6, another a loop from 3, and the remaining one a feed from the switch over the bed in bedroom 3.

In order to distinguish the lines from the switch feeds it is a good plan to nick the insulation at the switch end of the wire.

The wiring is carried out in the same manner throughout the installation, which is much easier to do than write about.

The wires are simply threaded or drawn through the conduit from each inspection fitting.

When the whole of the wiring is complete it is a good plan to check all the wires to see that none has been omitted.

This done, the making good can be proceeded with, and then the switches, fittings, and other accessories can be erected and connected to the circuit wires.

Before the switches and fittings are actually connected, however, the ends of the insulated wires must be properly prepared, for if any braid or tape is allowed to come in contact with the metal terminals, leakage is likely to occur, which will probably affect the insulation test when the installation is ready for a supply of current.

The ends of wires should be stripped

Fig. 45

of insulation, leaving sufficient bare wire exposed for making the connection to the switches and other fittings, and then the braid and tape removed for at least $\frac{1}{2}$ in. down the insulation, so that only the vulcanised rubber is allowed to come in contact with the terminals, as shown in Fig. 45. Sufficient slack wire should always be left behind the fittings, switches, and other accessories, so that at any time a replacement is required it can be carried out with the minimum of trouble.

Switches and fittings should not be mounted directly upon a wall, but should be mounted upon a suitable hardwood block, screwed to the wall or other support. Thus, in surface switches and ceiling roses of the porcelain type, a 3-in. by 1-in. round, white-enamelled block, suitably drilled to allow the wires to project, is first screwed to the wall or ceiling, and the accessory mounted upon it.

Where semi-recessed switches are used, the block is kept in position by a flange on the porcelain base, which, when fixed by screws screwed into the wooden fixing-block sunk in the plaster, holds the mounting block tightly between the flange and the plaster surface of the wall.

When fitting semi-recessed switches, always remove the plaster under the base of the switch to a depth of about ¼ in., so as to prevent the wires from being pinched, and also to allow a certain amount of slack wire to be tucked away in the recess so formed. This is easily understood by referring to Fig. 46, which shows the correct method of fixing a semi-recessed switch.

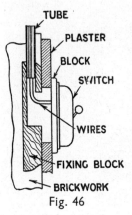

TUBE
PLASTER
BLOCK
SWITCH
WIRES
FIXING BLOCK
BRICKWORK

Fig. 46

In fitting sunk switches the chief point to observe is that they must be fixed in the centre of the box, and their height adjusted to enable the screwed fixing ring to be tightened up sufficiently to keep the cover plate in position.

All special fittings, such as bowl fittings, fancy brackets, etc., should be connected to the sub-circuit wires by means of proper porcelain-insulated connecters, inserted in the recess at the back of the mounting block.

The flexible wire for pendants, etc., should be of the double-vulcanised class, as flexibles are generally the weakest wires in the whole installation, except, of course, the fuse-wires.

Flexible wires can be obtained in almost all colours, finished in either glacé cotton, or silk, to suit various decorations.

Care should be taken when connecting flexibles to make sure that all the strands

composing the wire make proper contact under the screw terminals. Failure to observe this simple precaution may cause a short-circuit or other fault due to a stray strand bridging across the terminals.

The fuse-board should be mounted

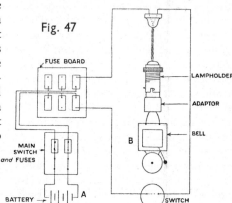

Fig. 47

FUSE BOARD
LAMPHOLDER
ADAPTOR
BELL
MAIN SWITCH *and* FUSES
B
BATTERY
A
SWITCH

upon a properly made mounting board, fitted with battens at the back to clear the tubes. The board is then fixed to the wall by means of wood screws driven into wooden plugs inserted into the wall.

The same thing applies to the main

Fig. 48

switch and cut-outs, which should never be mounted directly upon a wall.

When the whole of the fittings, switches, and other accessories are in position, and the fuses inserted in the fuse-board and main cut-outs, the conductors should be tested for continuity, in order to verify that all the components are working correctly, and that no wires have been cross-connected.

The only necessary apparatus for making such a test is a three-cell battery —a $4\frac{1}{2}$-volt flash-lamp battery will answer the purpose—an electric bell and a lampholder adapter.

The battery is connected up at the ends of the main cables in the manner indicated in Fig. 47 at A, and the adapter is connected up to the bell as at B.

All sub-circuit switches should be in the "off" position and the main switch closed. The adapter is then inserted into each lampholder in turn and if the bell rings when the switch controlling the particular lampholder is placed in the "on" position, it shows that the light is correctly wired. Although this test may show that all the wires have been connected up in a perfectly satisfactory manner, it does not prove that the wiring is all that it should be, for such a test does not indicate faults such as earths and leaks, nor is it possible to obtain the insulation resistance of the wires.

To carry out an insulation test, a proper testing instrument, known as an ohmmeter (Fig. 48), is generally employed, and, as one of these instruments can usually be hired at a few shillings per day from a local electrical contractor, it is well worth while to take advantage of this to enable these important tests to be carried out.

The insulation test is the most important test applied to the installation by the supply authorities, who insist—and rightly so—that the insulation resistance must be up to a certain standard, according to the number of lighting or other points installed, before they will connect up the installation to the supply cables.

Briefly stated, the ohmmeter consists of a hand-driven generator, usually supplying a small current at a pressure of 500 volts, which, by a suitable system of magnets and coils within the instrument, registers the resistance in megohms (1 megohm = 1 million ohms) on its scale when the circuit under test is connected to its terminals and the handle driving the generator is revolved.

To carry out an insulation test of all the wires to earth, all lamps must be in place and all switches in the "on" position, so that all circuit-wires, flexibles, fittings and switches are included in the test. The instrument is then connected up to the two main cables, which are connected together at the main switch, and connected up to one terminal of the instrument, while the other terminal is connected by a wire to a good earth, such as a main cold-water pipe. The generator is then cranked up to speed, causing the index needle to move across the scale and indicate the value of the resistance. Fig. 49 at A shows how to connect up the instrument for making an insulation test of the wires to earth.

The insulation resistance must not be below that specified by the rules of the supply authorities, which generally state that the insulation resistance of the installation when connected to earth shall not be less in megohms than 25 divided by the total number of points.

Thus, as the installation under discussion has 36 points, the insulation value must not be less than $\frac{25}{36} = \cdot 7$ megohm (approx.).

As the earth test only indicates the value of the insulation between the wires and fittings when connected to earth, and does not show whether any leakage is taking place between the wires or the terminals of the fittings, another test between poles is necessary.

This test is carried out in a similar way to the earth test except that the two main cables are connected up across the terminals of the testing set, as shown at

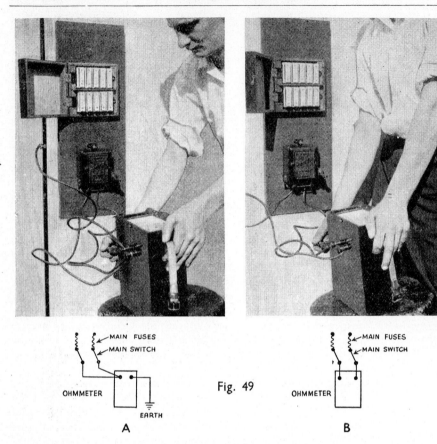

Fig. 49

B in Fig. 49, and all lamps removed from their holders. The results of such a test should not be below the value of the earth test.

Should the pointer of the testing instrument indicate a zero reading when the earth test is applied, it shows that there is an "earth" on one or more conductors of the installation.

This fault may be due to various causes, such as a screw or nail driven through a tube into the insulation of the wire, generally caused by the carelessness of the person relaying the floorboards. An earth fault may also be due to the neglect of taking the proper precaution to see that the ends of the tubes are filed perfectly smooth when erecting the con-duit, whereby the sharp edge has cut through the insulation and allowed the bare wire to come in contact with the tube. Whatever the cause may be, the fault must be located and remedied.

To do this the process of elimination should be applied.

Remove the fuses from the fuse-board and the lamps from their holders, and test each main cable from each bus-bar separately, as shown in Fig. 50, at A. If these are found to be in order, test each sub-circuit wire as indicated at B. When the particular sub-circuit wire is found, make a note of the circuit it feeds and also the colour of the conductor, that is, whether it is a red or a black. If it is a black one the fault is in one of the wires connecting the ceiling-rose or light points; on the other hand, if it is a red one, it indicates that the fault is either on a switch-feed or a line.

Assuming the fault to be on a red conductor, open the switch controlling the farthest or first light in the circuit and test again. This eliminates the line of the first light. If the fault is not relieved, test each line in turn in the same manner. If the defect is still on when the lines have been tested, it shows that the lines are clear and that the trouble is on a switch-feed. Proceed by testing each switch-feed in turn, commencing at the first switch in the circuit. This will necessitate the removal of the switches in order to isolate each length of feed-wire as the test proceeds. When the faulty wire has been found, it should be carefully drawn out of the tube and examined in order to ascertain the position and the cause.

To find the cause of the trouble the position of the fault in the cable should

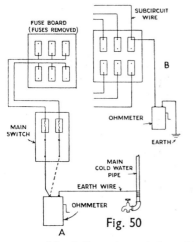

Fig. 50

be measured back from the switch outlet, and the measurement so obtained can then be applied to the tube, which will give the approximate position of that point of the tube likely to be causing the trouble.

The tube should be examined carefully. If it is found to be pierced with a nail or the ends not properly filed, the remaining wires should be drawn out, after which the offending conduit can either be properly prepared, or renewed if necessary. When this has been done the wires should be replaced, including a new one to replace the faulty one.

If a fault occurs on a black wire, proceed in a similar manner.

It sometimes happens that although the earth test may be of a high value the between-poles test is low. This may be due to condensation or moisture at the switches, ceiling roses or other fittings, especially when a test is carried out on a damp, humid day. If the insulation resistance, as read on the instrument, is not too low, it may be safely assumed that dampness is the cause. In such a case it is as well to make a further test on a day when the atmosphere is dry and crisp, when, in all probability, the results will be found to be much more satisfactory.

A low test between poles is also very often caused by failure to remove the protecting tape and braid of the wires when preparing them for connecting to the fittings, etc., whereby the covering is allowed to touch the terminals of the switch and other devices. In this case the only remedy is to remove the cause, that is, by baring the tape and braid back so that only the bare wire and the rubber insulation are allowed to touch the terminals.

From what has been written above, it will now be seen that it is good policy to hire a testing set in order to make sure that the installation is in perfect order before the supply authorities' inspector pays a visit, because not only will he refuse to connect up the installation unless it is up to prescribed standard, but a charge—usually 7/6—is made for each subsequent test.

When the whole of the installation is complete and satisfactory, all lamps should be inserted into their lampholders and all switches left in the "on" position, ready for the supply authorities' representative when he comes to test and connect it up to the supply mains. Two short pieces of main cable should

Fig. 51

be left to enable him to make the necessary connections to the meter.

Where a lead-covered surface system is installed, it is carried out, in the main, on the same lines as those described in the

foregoing pages, except, of course, that it is subject to various modifications.

It is very much simpler to install a lead-covered system as there are no protective conduits to fit, and as the system is essentially a surface system, the cutting away of walls, etc., is eliminated.

The Circuits should be planned in the same manner as those already described, and the main runs should be run under the floorboards where possible, exposing the wiring only in such places as the switch-runs.

In order to save wire and to eliminate the unsightliness of a number of wires being shown on the surface, it is customary to employ joint-boxes—a standard size metal box being used throughout—and, in some cases, three-plate ceiling-roses. This arrangement dispenses with the loop-in method used with a conduit system.

Fig. 51 shows a typical circuit where lead-covered conductors are used, and from it will be seen clearly the usual method adopted for feeding the switches and lights.

ELECTRICAL HEATERS AND COOKERS

As a great many electrical appliances, such as heaters, cookers, etc., take a much heavier current than can be safely carried by the lighting wires, it is necessary to have a separate power-circuit for supplying these devices. Even if it was possible to run apparatus taking a large current from the lighting circuit, it would be false economy, as the price charged per unit for heating and running other domestic apparatus is very much lower than that charged for lighting.

The system adopted for wiring a domestic power-circuit is substantially

the same as that for electric lighting, that is, the conductors may be protected by conduits, metal-sheathed cables or the C.T.S. system.

Electric Radiators and other portable apparatus are usually connected to the main circuit wires by means of a flexible lead having a plug connected to a combined switch-controlled socket, fixed on a skirting or other convenient position. Each plug should be separately protected by a fuse in each pole of the conductors, to form an individual sub-circuit on the distributing fuse-board.

When planning a domestic power-installation for supplying current to portable heaters, vacuum cleaners, etc. (apart from cookers and other heavy current-consuming devices) it is advisable to use conductors and sockets of one standard size throughout. The sizes of these should be based upon the

Fig I

A

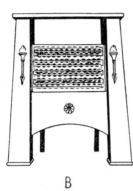

B

amount of current taken by the most heavily loaded apparatus in view, as such an arrangement allows the heater, etc., to be used with safety with other power-sockets that may be installed in different rooms.

In determining the size of the conductors it is as well to remember that there are three standard loadings for electric heaters, known as the one, two and three kilowatt (one kilowatt equals 1,000 watts) sizes respectively. A 1 kilowatt fire consumes one unit of electricity per hour and is usually of sufficient size to warm a small room having a cubic capacity of approximately 1,000 cubic feet, or a room of, say, 12 × 10 × 9 ft.

A 2 kilowatt heater under the same conditions would suit a room of 16 × 14 × 9 ft., while the largest size— viz., a 3 kilowatt, would suit a room 20 × 14 × 9 ft.

As the 3 kilowatt fire is now commonly fitted with switches to obtain three degrees of heat, it is sometimes an advantage to use this size, although a smaller one

13*

would perhaps answer the purpose, for by so doing the apartment can be heated up quickly by having it first switched on to its full capacity and then regulating it to suit requirements.

Electric Fires can be obtained in numerous designs and finishes to suit modern decorations, two of which are shown at A and B in Fig. 1.

The one shown at A represents an imitation coal fire suitable for a dining room or lounge. By an ingenious flickering arrangement worked by a lamp placed under the "coals" the effect produced is almost identical with the real flickering glow obtained from a real coal fire.

A light portable electric stove made of sheet iron is shown at B. This type of stove is extremely light in weight and is fitted with a handle which makes it easy to carry from room to room. The current taken by a 3 kilowatt stove varies, of course, with the voltage of the supply. Assuming that the supply pressure is 200, the current taken will be:

$$C = \frac{\text{watts}}{\text{volts}} = \frac{3000}{200} = 15 \text{ amperes.}$$

Referring to a table of the current-carrying capacities of conductors it will be seen that a 7/·029 carries a maximum of 18·2 amps. and is therefore the correct sized cable to use.

In such an installation, 15-ampere combined switchplugs should be used, preferably of the 3-pin type, for earthing purposes as a precaution against shocks. It is absolutely essential to fit a 3-pin switchplug in the bathroom, and it is also necessary to see that the heater is placed in such a position that it is impossible to operate it from the bath. An illustration of a neat and

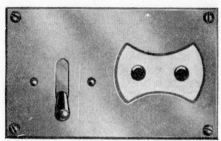

Fig. 2

efficient switchplug of the 2-pin type appears in Fig. 2.

Before installing a domestic power-circuit the supply authorities should always be consulted because in some districts they insist upon the power installation being split up into two separate circuits in order to balance the load on their mains.

When the balancing of power-circuits is insisted upon, it is necessary to have two distributing fuse-boards and two main switches and cut-outs. A three-core cable is brought into the premises and connected up to the installation in the manner indicated in Fig. 3, which shows the lighting installation circuit and the power-sockets for the first floor connected between A and C and the power-sockets supplying the ground-floor circuits between B and C.

When balanced circuits as described above are used, the main switches, etc. and the distributing fuse-boards, etc., must be fixed in a position at least 6 ft. from each other so that it is physically impossible for a person replacing a fuse in one switch or board to touch the live terminals of the other.

This precaution is necessary because the voltage between the live sides of the apparatus is possibly over 400 volts, a pressure which may cause a dangerous shock to a person coming into contact with any parts.

With the advent of cheap electricity, electric cooking is no longer an expensive

novelty but is now a formidable competitor with other methods of cooking. Judging from the increasing number of cookers that are being installed in both new and old homes, electric cooking bids fair to become in the no longer distant future the premier method of preparing meals.

Cooking by Electricity is convenient, clean and dependable, and as there is an entire absence of fumes and dirt, the food is prepared under perfect hygienic conditions.

Fig. 4 shows a modern type of electric cooker suitable for preparing food for 4–6 persons. The cooker is finished with a special leadless black and white vitreous enamel which can be easily cleaned with a cloth.

The cooker illustrated has a total consumption of 5,650 watts, which is

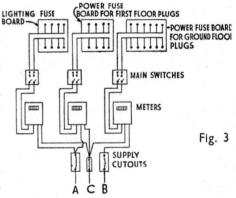

Fig. 3

distributed in the following way. The top and bottom elements for heating the oven each consume 1,100 watts and are controlled by one switch to obtain three degrees of heat. The boiler-griller is also controlled by a three-heat switch and takes 2,240 watts, while the boiling-plate also has three degrees of heat. The cooking equipment includes a thermometer, ventilator, splash plate, etc., and a number of cooking pans.

An electric kettle is a separate item fed from a switchplug on the main switch control unit.

The circuit for supplying an electric cooker is quite simple to install, and may be carried out on the conduit or lead-covered system. Before installing a cooker the supply authorities should be interviewed with the object of finding out whether the existing service cable (if any) is large enough to carry the additional load and also whether there are any special regulations other than the usual ones to be complied with.

Fig. 4

As with other electrical apparatus, the size of the cable used for connecting the cooker to the supply depends upon the supply voltage, which will, in this case, be assumed to be 200 volts.

As already stated, the total loading of the cooker shown in Fig. 4 is 5,650 watts, which gives a current value of $\frac{5650}{200} =$ 28 amperes approximately. A 7/·044 cable will safely carry a current of 31 amperes and is therefore a suitable size to use.

As it is extremely unlikely that more than about 70 per cent. of the total current taken by the cooker will be switched on at a time, a 30 ampere main switch and fuses will be of sufficiently large capacity to serve the cooker. The main switch and cut-outs should be fixed as near as possible to where the supply cable enters the premises and mounted upon a board securely fastened to the wall.

Although it is possible to connect a cooker directly off the circuit wires it

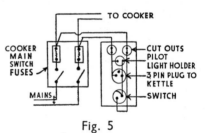

Fig. 5

is much better practice to fix either a 30 amp. combined switch-fuse or a proper controlling panel at a convenient height at the side of the cooker.

If an ordinary ironclad combined switch-fuse is fitted, it is a good plan to provide a pilot-light protected by a pair of 5 ampere cut-outs to enable the operator to see at a glance whether the cooker is switched on or off. It is also an additional advantage to fit a 5 ampere 3-pin combined switchplug on the same mounting board to allow a self-contained electric kettle to be used from this point. Fig. 5 shows a diagram of connections of the above arrangements.

The specially designed cooker control-panel shown in Fig. 6 is quite inexpensive and is well worth the small additional outlay. It consists of a 35 amp. double pole main switch which completely disconnects the cooker from the electric supply. A small pilot-light is incorporated in the panel and lights up when-

Fig. 6

ever the main switch is on. A 5/7 ampere 3-pin catch socket operated by a switch allows an electric kettle to be used. The whole of the gear is protected by a neat cover finished in black.

The wiring running from the main supply switch to the cooker can be carried out either in V.I.R. cable protected by enamelled steel conduit tubing, run under the floor, or in lead-covered cable where it is to run on the surface. The first method, especially if carried out in screwed tubing, makes the best job, while the latter looks much better when it is necessary to run on the surface, as its flexibility allows it to be bent round awkward corners and the like.

Whatever system is adopted, it is essential that the whole of the protective metal covering of the wires, together with all metal-covered accessories and the cooker itself, should all be bonded together and efficiently connected to earth. If screwed tubing is used the continuity will be maintained by the screwed joints as also will a grip system of conduit, if the enamel is properly removed from the ends of the tubes to enable the nipple, contact screw or other device to make good contact with the tube. When lead-covered cables are used the ends of the sheathing should be fitted to the main switches by a proper lead-cover-to-iron-nipple screwed into the outer case of the switch, or, failing this, a thick stranded copper wire should be attached to the sheathing by suitable earthing clips and attached to the switch by the earthing screw usually provided for the purpose.

When fitting the earthing wire under

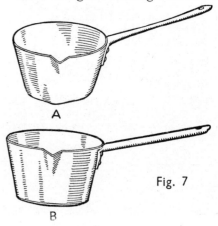

Fig. 7

the earthing screw of the switch it is important to see that all enamel and paint is removed to ensure a perfect metal-to-metal contact. The cooker is also provided with a terminal for earthing purposes, which should be connected up to the lead sheathing or conduit in a similar manner. The whole of the system should then be connected by a thick stranded copper wire to the nearest main cold-water pipe—previously scraped perfectly clean—using a proper earthing clip for the purpose.

Before leaving the subject of electric cookers it should be pointed out that in order to get the maximum efficiency from the hot plates it is important to use perfectly flat-bottomed cooking utensils. The reason for this is easy to see by referring to A at Fig. 7, which

shows an ordinary cheap aluminium saucepan—produced from one piece of metal—which has become badly distorted during use and therefore only makes contact with the hot plate at irregular places. This results in a great loss of current owing to the time taken to boil the liquid. The saucepan at B, however, is fitted with a bottom of $\frac{1}{4}$ in. thick aluminium having a thinner gauge body built into it and therefore makes perfect contact with the plate.

WIRING FOR ELECTRIC BELLS

B EFORE going into details of the methods adopted in installing electric bells, it will not be out of place to give a brief description of how an electric bell works.

This can be easily understood by referring to Fig. 1, which shows an illustration of an electric bell worked from a battery and connected to a single push.

The bell consists of the following essential parts:

    A.—The base, which may be either of wood or bakelite.

    B.—The frame.

    C.—The electro-magnet.

    D.—The armature with the contact-spring and hammer.

    E.—The adjustable contact-maker.

    F.—The gong.

When the two pieces of metal forming the contacts of the push are pressed together, current flows from the carbon or positive terminal of the battery, through the push to one terminal of the bell. From here, the current travels through the windings of the electro-magnet by way of the contact-maker to the other terminal and from thence back

to the zinc element of the battery, thus completing the circuit. As soon as the current energises the magnet, however, the armature with its contact-spring is

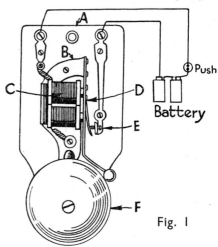

Fig. 1

attracted to the poles of the magnet, thus automatically breaking the circuit. Consequently the magnetic pull is released, causing the armature to fly back to its original position, due, of course, to the influence of the spring. This rapid alternate making and breaking of the circuit causes the armature and the hammer to tremble against the edge of the gong and give an audible signal.

Fig. 2

It is obvious that if one push only is required to ring a bell, two main wires are all that are needed, namely, one to conduct the current from the bell and another from the bell back to the push, with a break in this wire to allow the battery to be inserted in the circuit.

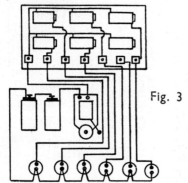

Fig. 3

In modern installations, however, it is usual to have a bell-press in every important room as well as one at the front and back doors all to ring one bell in the kitchen.

The Indicator.—Fig. 2 shows a pendulum indicator commonly used in a private residence. It consists of a number of simple electro-magnets, each of which is normally connected to a push and to the bell, so that when a current

flows it causes a freely suspended, soft-iron armature, to which a cardboard flag is attached, to vibrate rapidly in sympathy with the bell and thus forms a distinctly visible signal.

The indicator movements are mounted upon a hardwood base and are enclosed in a dust-proof case having a glazed front. To avoid confusion, either the names of the rooms are usually written on the front or the flags are numbered.

Fig. 3 shows a diagram of the connections employed when such an indicator is used.

Starting from the positive or carbon terminal of the battery it will be seen that one wire, called the "push-feed," is common to one terminal of each push. Independent wires, known as "lines," run back from the other terminal of the push to a corresponding terminal on the indicator. One end of each magnet winding is connected to a common terminal which in turn is coupled to one terminal of the bell. The other bell terminal is joined to the negative pole or zinc element of the battery.

Having briefly described how an ordinary electric bell installation works, a typical installation will now be explained to enable the amateur to carry out the work himself.

For this purpose it is assumed that seven pushes, situated in different apartments, are required to ring a bell and work an indicator in the kitchen.

When such an installation is contemplated it is an excellent plan to do the job when the house is being redecorated, for by so doing, it will then be possible to conceal all the wires by cutting narrow channels in the walls and burying the protecting tubes, where the wires run down walls to pushes, etc., finally "making good" the plaster when the tubes are fixed in position, in the same way as that described in ELECTRIC LIGHTING.

If this is done as suggested, not only will a great deal of wire and time be saved, but it will obviate the necessity of running the conductors around skirtings, through door frames and the like, which, however neatly done, does not improve the appearance of a room.

The first thing to be settled is whether the conductors are to be protected throughout by means of conduit tubes, as in electric lighting, or whether the wires are to be installed without such protection under the floorboards, etc.

If expense is not the primary consideration, the former method is to be recommended, as it is the system adopted in all high-class work. On the other hand, if this is thought to be an unnecessary expense, quite a good job can be made by threading the wires through the joists or stapling them along the joists as the case may be.

If the conduit system is chosen, $\frac{1}{2}$-in. diameter close-joint enamelled conduit should be used. The fittings, such as elbows, tees, etc., should be of the inspection type as their use allows the wires to be drawn in after erection.

Another point to consider is the positions of the bell-pushes, bell, indicator and batteries.

Fig. 4

In the living-rooms, the most convenient position for bell-pushes is usually at the right-hand side of the fireplace. The pushes may either be of the simple surface type, as shown at A in Fig. 4, of brown or white bakelite to suit the decorations of the room, or they may be of the flush type, that is, sunk flush with the surface of the wall as at B, so that only a flat metal or bakelite plate with a press-button is exposed. The latter is to be preferred as such pushes look very much

Fig. 5

neater than the former. A white push looks well in a bathroom, and it should be fixed at the side of the bath in such a position that it can be easily reached in the case of emergency. In the bedrooms, the most convenient position, of course, is at the head of the bedsteads. The best type of push to use is the suspension push, consisting of a small pear-shaped "tassel" suspended by a flexible wire from a connecting rosette, fixed just below the picture rail. The front and back door pushes should be of metal, and where they are exposed to the weather, they should be watertight.

It is a good plan to have the front and back door pushes finished in oxydised copper or steel bronze, as polished brass pushes require frequent cleaning. There are numerous designs to be had, and a suitable pattern can usually be chosen by referring to a catalogue. A good position for a front door push is at the right-hand side of the door, at such a height that it can be easily operated by a child. The same applies, of course, to the back door push.

Before leaving the subject of pushes, it may be mentioned that a foot-press (Fig. 5), fitted at a convenient position under the dining-room table, is a refinement well worth the small extra trouble of installing it.

The position of the indicator and bell in the kitchen must be left to the discretion of the installer; suffice it to say that they should be kept as far away as possible from the influence of gas fumes and steam. If this precaution is not taken, corroded terminals and rapid deterioration of other parts will take place, which will ultimately result in a complete breakdown. A position favoured by electricians is over the entrance door as it is usually far removed from a gas stove.

The Battery.—We now come to this important item. It should consist of two or more No. 2 size cells of the Leclanché type. The best place for housing the battery is on a shelf, not too high off the ground, in a cool and dust-proof cupboard, as near to the indicator as possible. Avoid putting the battery in a coal cellar as this is the last place in which a battery should be accommodated. Fig. 6 shows the batteries installed on a shelf, as suggested.

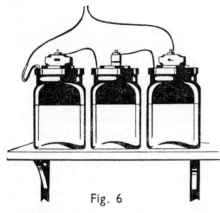

Fig. 6

Needless to say, if a supply of alternating current is already available in the house, by all means use a transformer for the source of current. A transformer is much to be preferred to a battery, as not

only is it more efficient but there will be no further renewals required of porous-pots, zincs and sal-ammoniac.

Remember that a transformer can only be used with alternating current, and in no circumstances must it be connected to a direct-current supply.

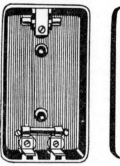

Fig. 7

If you are in doubt as to the nature of the lighting supply, either look at the meter, which usually has a metal label giving the necessary information, or ring up the local supply company, and ask them.

Bell Transformers.—Fig. 7 shows an illustration of a bell transformer—with cover removed—for connecting up to the electric light supply. It should be fitted near a distributing fuse board and the primary terminals connected to the positive and negative terminals of a pair of sub-circuit fuses to ensure that the fuse will "blow" in case of failure. It is a good plan to insert a switch into this circuit so that the current can be interrupted if necessary. The secondary or low-voltage terminals are equivalent to the terminals on a battery, so all that is necessary is to use one terminal to feed the pushes and the other to feed the bell. Bell transformers are provided with three low-voltage tappings to give 3, 5 or 8 volts, to enable the voltage to be adjusted to suit the installation. Fig. 8 shows a diagram of connections.

Having settled the numerous details suggested above, the next thing is to measure roughly the length of the runs to arrive at the quantity of wire, conduit (if used), and other items for carrying out the job, bearing in mind that the runs should be kept as short and direct as possible.

The approximate cost of the material for an electric bell installation of seven points, using steel conduit and a transformer, is summarised as follows:

	£	s.	d.
150 ft. ½-in. close-joint conduit . @ 8/-		12	0
1½ doz. ½-in. inspection elbows . @ 4/-		6	0
1 doz. ½-in. inspection tees . . @ 5/-		5	0
½ doz. ½-in. couplings . . @ 2/-		1	0
1 bell transformer .		7	6
1 transformer bell .		5	0
1 7-hole pendulum indicator per hole @ 3/-	1	1	0
1 indicator . .		3	0
2 flush bell pushes with boxes and plates for dining-room and drawing room . @ 4/6		9	0
1 foot-press for dining room (if used)		3	9
1 front-door push .		5	0
1 back-door push .		2	6
1 bathroom push .		2	6
2 bakelite suspension pushes with flex and rosettes. @ 2/6		5	0
300 yds. 1 R.D.C.C. bell-wire 1/20 gauge . . @ 5/-		15	0
Sundries . .		3	6
	£5	6	9

If the work is carried out without conduit, except, of course, where the wires run under plaster, plain bell-pushes in the living-rooms, and ordinary batteries, the above cost would be reduced by approximately £1 4s. 0d.

Assuming that the necessary materials are to hand, the following tools should be got together in order to make a start:

Padsaw, for cutting floorboards; tenon-saw for cutting slots in joists; ½-in. wood chisel; brace and ¾-in. twist bit; 10-in. triangular file for cutting the conduit; large and small screwdrivers; pair of pliers for cutting the wire, etc.; an electrician's bolster chisel for cutting chases in walls; and one or two cold chisels for prising up floorboards.

Fig. 9 illustrates the modern method of electric bell wiring, known as the "loop-in" system. It is vastly superior to the old-fashioned way of jointing the wires,

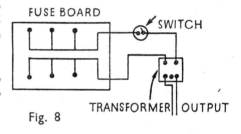

Fig. 8

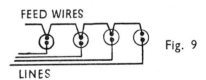

Fig. 9

which is invariably a source of breakdown. The loop-in system has also the advantage that each wire can be tested individually should a fault occur.

As this system of wiring is fully dealt with under the heading of ELECTRIC LIGHTING, repetition is unnecessary.

In professional practice it is usual to use coloured conductors to distinguish a push feed, while the lines running to various rooms are readily known by a distinguishing colour.

The class of bell-wire used for internal work consists of a single No. 20 gauge tinned copper wire insulated with a layer of pure rubber protected by a double cotton covering coated with paraffin wax. It is sold in coils of 100 yards.

As the pushes, etc., serving rooms on both floors will have to be wired from the floor above, it is sometimes more convenient to start by setting out the runs for the ground-floor pushes first, by marking and lifting the floorboards on the first floor. This will leave the less laborious task of fixing and fitting the tubes (if used) in the attic to a later stage.

The first thing to do is to mark those floorboards which come immediately above each push-point and also above the indicator, etc. It will then be readily seen which other floorboards it will be necessary to lift to complete the run,

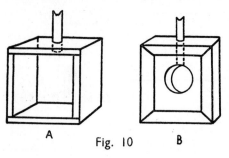

A   Fig. 10   B

bearing in mind that the main portion should be kept, if possible, under the boards in a passage where they can be easily lifted at any time with the least disturbance.

When the chases in the walls (as described in ELECTRIC LIGHTING) have been prepared, make the slots in the joists just deep and wide enough to take the tube. When this is finished, the next operation—consisting of cutting and fitting the conduit—may be taken in hand.

To Cut the Conduit, file a deep groove round the tube at the desired position, using the edge of the triangular file for the purpose. The tube may then be severed by placing it across the knee and applying pressure at each side of the groove, with the hands. The jagged ends of the conduit must now be filed perfectly smooth, otherwise the sharp edges will damage the insulation of the wires when they are drawn in.

When fitting the elbows, tees, etc., do not forget to place them right side up— that is, with the inspection covers uppermost, and also remember to leave an outlet at a convenient position for joining up the rising tube for the top floor circuits. This can often be arranged for in a linen cupboard where there is no need to conceal the tube.

If flush pushes are to be fitted in the living-rooms, the wooden boxes should be so fitted that they do not project above the level of the plaster. It is a wise plan to sink them a little below the surface line, say $\frac{1}{8}$-in., so that the plaster can be made good up to the inside edges of the box. Be careful to see that the end of the tube does not project into the interior of the box. The correct way of fitting the tube into the box is shown in Fig. 10, at A. Where plain pushes are to be used, a piece of wood about $2\frac{1}{2}$ in. square and 1 in. thick should be sunk and fixed below the level of the plaster to provide a good fixing. The blocks should be drilled down from the centre of the top edge to take the end of the tube, to meet a 1-in. hole in the face, as shown at B in the illustration (Fig. 10). Fixing-blocks should be sunk into the wall to a depth of at least a $\frac{1}{4}$ in. below the surface to allow the plaster to be finished flush.

The conduit run for the top floor is proceeded with in exactly the same manner as that adopted with the ground floor, but as the space above the bedrooms, etc., is generally an attic, devoid of floorboards, there is no necessity to go to the trouble of sinking the tubes into the joists.

As some of the walls of the rooms on the first floor are very often constructed of lath and plaster and are thus hollow, there will be no need to cut these walls, as the wooden wall-plates above these walls can be drilled with a $\frac{3}{4}$-in. twist bit and a short length of tube fitted down within the partition to a point where it has been decided that the rosette or the bell-push is to be fitted.

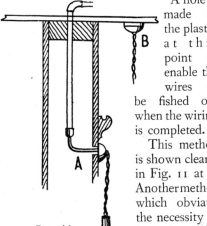

Fig. 11

A hole is made in the plaster at this point to enable the wires to be fished out when the wiring is completed. This method is shown clearly in Fig. 11 at A. Another method which obviates the necessity of burying the tubes, if solid walls are encountered, is to fix the rosettes on the ceiling, close to the wall, as shown at B.

Wiring.—When all the tubing is finished, this can be put in hand. This is quite a simple and straightforward job, and consists of drawing the wires through the tubes via the inspection fittings. Start at the top floor and gradually work downwards, finally completing at the indicator. When measuring off the wire do not forget to allow sufficient wire at each outlet to enable the pushes, etc., to be conveniently connected. It is a good practice to leave a short length of wire at the back of each push, and at the indicator in case trouble is encountered at these points at any time.

The indicator should be securely fixed to the walls by screws driven into wooden wall-plugs; nails should never be used.

When fixing the pushes, take great care not to bare the wires behind the pushes, otherwise trouble from short-circuits will most likely arise; also, do not penetrate the insulation of the wires when screwing in the fixing screws.

It sometimes happens when connecting the conductors to the indicator that the wires get mixed up, especially so when distinctive coloured wires have not been used for the lines. In such a case each line can be easily tested out by connecting it up to a bell and battery, as indicated by the dotted lines in Fig. 12.

In carrying out a bell-wiring job without protecting conduit, all that is necessary is to drill through the joists and thread the wires through the holes. Keep the centres of the holes down at

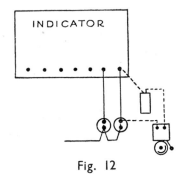

Fig. 12

least 2 in. from the tops of the joists and drill the holes so that they come beneath the centres of the floorboards. Where the wires run along the sides of joists, care must be taken not to drive the supporting staples in too hard. Failure to observe this precaution may cause a short-circuit which is difficult to locate when the installation is complete.

MAKING AN ELECTRIC BELL

To make an electric bell does not require a high degree of skill, and it is one of those small but interesting things that the practical man can construct in a few hours with a few tools and inexpensive materials.

A carefully constructed home-made electric bell will give very much better service than one of the cheap foreign-made articles which are now on the market.

The following is a list of the simple materials required:

A piece of $\frac{3}{8}$-in. hardwood, $5\frac{1}{2}$ in. by 3 in. for the base.

A $2\frac{1}{2}$-in. length of $\frac{1}{4}$-in. round soft iron for the cores of the electro magnet.

A piece of flat soft iron, $\frac{3}{32}$ in. thick and $1\frac{1}{2}$ in. long for the magnet yoke.

Four hardwood or fibre discs, $\frac{3}{4}$ in. diameter by $\frac{1}{8}$ in. thick for the ends of the magnet bobbins.

A piece of $\frac{1}{8}$-in. soft iron $1\frac{1}{4}$ in. long and $\frac{1}{2}$ in. wide for the armature.

A 2-in. length of thin clock-spring $\frac{1}{4}$ in. wide for the armature spring.

A $\frac{3}{4}$-in. length of $\frac{1}{4}$-in. round brass rod for the contact pillar.

A gong taken from an old alarm clock or an old electric bell.

Two brass terminals.

Two ounces 24-gauge enamelled or cotton-covered copper wire.

A small block of hardwood for supporting the spring and armature.

A few wood screws, small copper rivets and No. 4 B.A. screws.

A supply of cigar-box wood for the cover.

Cut the base to the dimensions given in the drawing (Fig. 1) and finish it off with glass-paper.

Next, prepare the electro-magnet, details of which appear in Fig. 2. File the ends of the cores perfectly flat and square, and then drill and tap one end

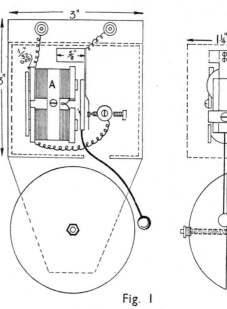

Fig. I

of each to take a No. 4 B.A. iron screw. Prepare the yoke first by filing to the correct size and then drill two clearing holes $\frac{7}{8}$ in. apart to take the fastening screws of the cores.

Fix the cores to the yoke in order to verify that they are perfectly square. If they are not true, file the ends until the desired result is obtained. Now remove the cores from the yoke and fit the bobbin discs.

The discs should fit tightly on the cores, so the holes should be drilled a trifle smaller than the diameter of the core and then they can be gently forced into place.

Allow $\frac{1}{32}$ in. of the core to project at each end of the discs, and drill a small hole in each left-hand disc as shown at A in Fig. 3.

Winding the Wire on to the bobbins is the next process. Wrap two layers of cartridge or similar stiff paper over the cores and fasten them with liquid glue or paste. To wind the bobbins, first push 6 in. or so of wire through the hole for connecting purposes and then wind the wire in a clockwise direction to form even layers until the bobbins are nearly full, that is, about $\frac{1}{16}$ in. below the tops of the discs. Now make a tiny hole for anchoring the wire and leave sufficient free wire for connecting. The magnets are now completed by assembling the cores to the yoke.

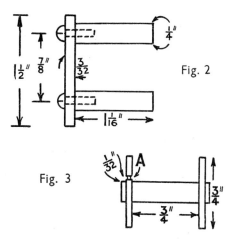

Fig. 2

Fig. 3

To Make the Armature, file the piece of soft iron flat and square to the size given at A in Fig. 4 and then drill two small holes in the positions indicated to suit the diameter of the small rivets used for fastening the spring, B. Drill a small hole about $\frac{3}{16}$ in. deep at the end to take a piece of stout wire to which the hammer is attached, the wire being

soldered in its place after the spring has been fitted. The spring should now be drilled and bent to shape. Before this can be done, however, the steel must

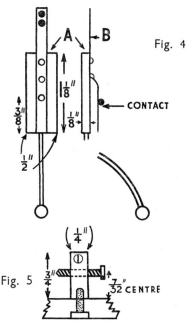

Fig. 4

Fig. 5

be softened by heating it up to redness and allowing it to cool slowly.

When the drilling and bending is complete, reharden the spring by heating it up to redness and then quenching it quickly in cold water.

Before riveting the spring to the armature a small silver contact consisting of a silver rivet should be fitted in the position indicated in Fig. 4, and filed to give a flat surface.

The Contact-pillar is made from a piece of $\frac{1}{4}$-in. round brass. File the metal to the size shown in Fig. 5, and drill and tap a hole in the side to take a No. 4 cheese-headed brass contact-screw. Drill and tap a hole near the top to take a similar-sized screw. This screw is used for locking the contact-screw in position when it has been adjusted. Now place the pillar in a vertical position between the jaws of a vice and make a saw-cut from the top to meet the contact-screw hole. The pillar is complete when a hole has been drilled and tapped in the bottom to take a No. 4 B.A. screw for fixing purposes.

To make the contact-screw, drill a small hole in the end of the screw, insert a small piece of 20-gauge silver wire, and solder it in place.

The silver wire and the rivet can be obtained at almost any jeweller's for a few pence.

The gong support or spindle can be made from a length of No. 2 B.A. screwed rod cut to length to suit the gong, the gong being held in position by suitable nuts, as shown clearly in the drawing.

When the baseboard has been drilled to receive the various fixing-screws and the small hardwood block for support-ing the armature glued and screwed in position, the parts can be assembled.

Reference to the drawing (Fig. 1) shows that the magnet is kept in position by means of a hardwood or a brass clamp (A), which is simply screwed down to the base by means of a wood screw placed between the bobbins of the magnet.

If brass is chosen for the clamp it is well to insert a small piece of cardboard or similar soft material between the metal and the coils to prevent damage to the wire.

Connect up the wires as shown and test with a single cell. Adjust the contact-screw until the maximum ring is obtained.

The bell is complete when a cover has been made to fit over the magnets, as indicated by the dotted lines, Fig. 1.

FAULTS IN ELECTRIC BELL SYSTEMS

FAULTS common to electric bell installations may be summarised as follows:

1. Battery failure.
2. Defective bell, indicator, pushes, etc.
3. Broken wires, bad contacts.
4. Leakage of current.
5. Short circuits.

When a total breakdown occurs in an ordinary domestic bell installation where batteries are used as a source of current, the first thing to do is to ascertain the condition of the battery, as the majority of failures are traceable to this part of the equipment.

If dry cells are used and are found to be "exhausted," they must be replaced by new ones, because dry-cells cannot be recharged.

When current is derived from wet cells of the Leclanché type, which is the type generally employed, it will probably be found that the liquid has evaporated, in which case they must be recharged.

To do this, procure sufficient powdered or crystal sal-ammoniac, allowing $\frac{1}{4}$ lb. for each 3 pint cell. Place the proper quantity of the salts into each glass jar and pour in a pint of warm water—not hot, otherwise it may crack the container. Stir the liquid to dissolve the sal-ammoniac, and then allow the solution to cool. Replace the porous-pots and zincs, taking care to keep the liquid level with the bottom edge of the pitch on the porous-pot. Fig. 1 shows the operation.

Although recharging the battery usually has the desired effect, the addition of fresh electrolyte does not always answer, because the porous-pots or zincs, or both, may require renewal.

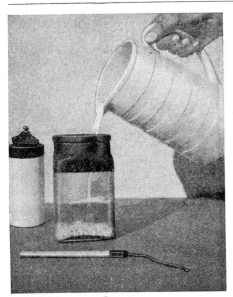

Fig. 1

If a porous-pot smells strongly of ammonia it is usually a sure indication that the active materials within it are spent, in which event it is wise to discard it and substitute a new one.

When Fitting New Porous-pots to a battery a great deal of time may be saved by making a small hole in the bottom of each pot as indicated in Fig. 2. This procedure allows the liquid to flow quickly into the pot, with the result that the normal amount of current can be taken from the cells almost as soon as the pots are immersed in the electrolyte. Without such holes it takes a considerable time before the liquid percolates through the porous walls and thoroughly saturates the materials within, which means considerable delay before a current is available.

The hole may be conveniently made with a small, sharp bradawl, by applying slight pressure and twisting the blade back and forth in the fashion of a drill. Care must be taken not to force the point of the tool too quickly through the pot, or disastrous results may occur in the

shape of a broken pot. The size of the hole must, of course, be small, otherwise the active material will fall out.

As a new porous-pot naturally absorbs a great deal of the liquid when placed in the glass container for the first time, it is important that more liquid be added to make up for the deficiency.

Zinc Elements that are slightly corroded, due to normal use, should be scraped clean, rubbed with mercury and replaced in the cells; but if they are badly deteriorated they should be discarded and fresh ones substituted.

Creeping.—A common trouble with regard to wet cells arises from "creeping." This defect is generally caused by filling the jars with too much electrolyte, with the result that the liquid creeps up to the terminals of the pots, which not only causes corrosion, but very often "eats" through the connecting wires. The obvious remedy for this defect is to keep the liquid at the correct level.

Sometimes the solution creeps over the

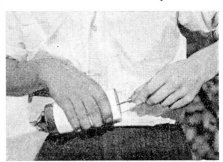

Fig. 2

tops of the jars and forms a crust of sal-ammoniac on the exterior surfaces of the containers. This condition is brought about either by the pitch flaking off the top portion of the jar, or by failure to wipe the jars quite dry after the cells have been recharged. In the former case, creeping may be prevented by "painting" a band of either melted

Fig. 3

paraffin wax or hot pitch round the top edge and upper portion of the jar (as shown in Fig. 3) while in the latter case the remedy is always to wipe the jars perfectly dry after recharging.

Corroded Terminals are another source of trouble. When found in this condition they should be scraped perfectly clean and a thin film of vaseline applied before replacement, bearing in mind that too much vaseline may cause greater trouble by producing imperfect contact between the terminals and the connecting wires.

If the bell still refuses to act after having examined the battery and put it into perfect working order, the next step is to examine the bell.

A preliminary test can be made by disconnecting the wires from the terminals and then joining the wires together so that the bell is cut out of circuit (as shown in Fig. 4). Assuming that the wires, pushes and indicator are in good order, on pressing a push the current flowing in the particular circuit should cause the indicator flag to operate. If such is the case, it is obvious that the bell is at fault.

The defects common to battery-operated bells are want of adjustment between the contact-screw point and the contact on the armature, dirty contacts, corroded terminals, and broken wires.

First examine the terminals, and if they are dirty or corroded, scrape them perfectly clean. Reconnect the bell into circuit, and if it rings when a push is pressed, it follows that the defective terminals were the cause of the interruption. If this fails, the contacts should be attended to. First, clean the contacts, using fine glass-paper for the purpose. To adjust the screw, a push should be short-circuited by bridging the terminals with a piece of wire to close the circuit (as shown in Fig. 5). With a small screwdriver unscrew the

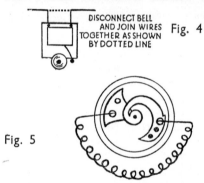

DISCONNECT BELL AND JOIN WIRES TOGETHER AS SHOWN BY DOTTED LINE   Fig. 4

Fig. 5

locking-screw at the side of the pillar and then give the contact-screw a turn or so, first in a clockwise direction and then in the reverse way. This operation will increase or decrease the pressure between the screw point and the armature contact and may have the desired result. Fig. 6 shows the adjustment being made.

Should there be no response to this treatment, there is no alternative but to take down the bell and trace for a broken wire. A likely place for a break is under a terminal pillar or the contact pillar.

Faults in Indicators can usually be traced to corroded terminals or broken wires. If the common wire joining the electro-magnets is broken in the position indicated between A and B in the diagram, Fig. 7, it will put every circuit, that is Nos. 1 to 8, out of action, as it will form an open circuit to each bell-push. If, however, the break occurs between B and C, only circuits Nos. 1 to 4 inclusive will cease to operate.

Broken Wires occurring between a "line" terminal and its magnet will, of course, only affect the particular push to which it is connected.

Breaks in indicator wires generally occur at the terminals and also at the sharp bends, where it is a common practice to twist the magnet wires over small nails to keep the wires in position.

It sometimes happens that although a battery has been recently recharged, it fails after very short service. On examining the battery it is found that the zincs are considerably blackened and corroded. This condition is a symptom of a leakage of current in some part of the wiring, which causes the battery to be in a continuous state of discharge. The cause in a great many instances is a corroded staple which partially short-circuits the wires.

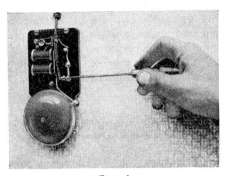

Fig. 6

This type of fault usually occurs in places subject to dampness, for instance, where the wires have been run under ground floors.

Such a fault requires some patience to locate, and it is usual to use a galvano-meter for the purpose. Such an instrument, employed for detecting minute currents, may possibly be hired from the local electrician for a small fee.

Connect up the instrument as shown in the diagram (Fig. 8). If the needle is

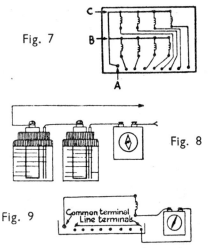

Fig. 7

Fig. 8

Fig. 9

deflected when so connected, it indicates that a current is flowing and that there is a leakage somewhere in the installation.

The first step is to ascertain in which circuit the fault lies. When an ordinary indicator is included in the installation it is not a very difficult matter. Disconnect the wire joining the common terminal of the indicator and the bell, keeping the "galvo" connected up at the batteries. If no deflection is recorded on the instrument, it shows that the wires between the batteries and the indicator are clear, and that the fault lies somewhere in the indicator circuits.

Test each line wire by inserting the instrument as shown in the diagram (Fig. 9). Start with circuit No. 1 and test each line in turn until a deflection is obtained which will indicate the faulty circuit.

Assuming that the fault occurs in the dining-room circuit, for instance, remove the push and examine the wires where they come out of the tube, as the covering of the wires may be partially cut through, causing a high-resistance leak of insufficient strength to operate the bell. If the wires are found to be in good order the chances are that it is a corroded staple that is causing the trouble.

If the run of the wires is known, the floorboards should be lifted and the wires examined, step by step, until the fault is located and put right.

As this part of the procedure may prove a difficult and tedious job, it may be easier and quicker to insert an entirely new line wire (if this should happen to be the faulty part) on the surface from the indicator terminal to the push, and disconnect the old wire.

When this is completed, the "galvo" should be inserted at the battery end of the installation, and if no indication is recorded on the instrument, you can be assured that the trouble has been rectified.

If, for some unapparent reason, the bells start ringing on their own accord, that is, without anyone operating a push, the cause may generally be put down to a short-circuit. This kind of defect is usually much easier to trace than a leak, because the current flowing is generally sufficient to operate the indicator which, of course, gives a visible means of ascertaining the faulty circuit.

When such a fault occurs, do not wedge the bell with paper as is so often done to stop it from ringing continuously, but remove the zinc element from the battery. This method will save the battery from becoming exhausted.

Short-circuits arise from several causes, the chief of which include the cutting through of the coverings of the wire due to the sharp edges of the tube at a push outlet, or a staple driven in too tight and doing similar damage. Short-circuits may also be attributed to such minor defects as worn flexibles, a broken push-contact, or a stray strand of flexible wire bridging across the terminals of a suspension push.

To cure the trouble, examine the pushes carefully to see that they are in proper working order. If the push happens to be one of the suspension type, see that all the strands are screwed down tightly under the terminals. In the case of an ordinary bell-push appearing to be in order, it is as well to remove it from the wall to examine the circuit wires at the back. If the insulation of the wires is cut through, repair the covering with electrician's adhesive tape.

If the push, etc., are in order, you may take it that a staple is causing the short, in which case it should be traced and the circuit relieved in a similar manner to that suggested for leakage.

ELECTRIC LIGHT EXTENSIONS

IT sometimes happens that an extra light or two is required in a workshop, garage or shed situated at some little distance from the house.

The method of carrying out the work will naturally depend upon the distance between the building to be supplied and the house supply. If this is only short,

the conductors can be run in a few lengths of screwed galvanised tube fastened to a fence or other convenient support. On the other hand, if the distance is greater than say about 30 ft., it is much better to run a cable underground.

To carry out the latter, a special

armoured and watertight cable must be used to protect the inner conductors. Such a conductor consists of an ordinary twin-core, lead-sheathed cable embedded in jute, over which a steel armour of either tape or galvanised wire is wound spirally and then finished with a braid covering served with a bituminous compound.

Whether the extra lights are supplied by an underground cable or by conductors run in conduit-tube above otherwise the particular sub-circuit feeding the extra lights might be overloaded.

To do this, all that is necessary is to remove the ceiling-rose and switch—not forgetting to cut off the supply current before doing so—and to connect the bared end of a length of single-conductor lead cable to the black or negative wire joining one terminal of the ceiling-rose and to run it down to the switch, leaving sufficient wire for making a connection behind the switch-block.

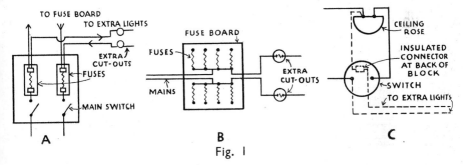

Fig. 1

ground, a pair of cut-outs should be fitted at both ends to protect the wires, and also to provide a convenient means of connecting up the main installation at one end and the extra lights at the other.

The extension cable can be connected up to the house supply by one of several methods. If the main switch is within reasonable distance of the extension cable's cut-outs, a lead-covered twin-cable can be looped out of the consumer's main fuses and run to the supplementary cut-outs as shown at A in Fig. 1, or if the distributing fuse-board is near at hand, the lead-covered cable can be connected to the bus-bars as indicated at B.

Other Extension Methods.—Another method, shown at C, is to take a supply of current from a nearby switch and light point, but this should only be done when not more than a couple of lights are required in the out-building, Another length of twin cable is run from the switch to the extension cut-outs. One end of this wire is connected to the positive or feed terminal of the switch, and the other is connected by means of a china connector at the back of the switch-block to the wire from the ceiling-rose, as shown clearly in the diagram at c in Fig. 1.

Laying the Underground Cable.— A trench about a spade wide and about a foot deep should be prepared for laying the armoured cable and a hole made in the wall of each building to receive the ends of the cable. The holes should be large enough to allow plenty of play, as the armouring on the cable prevents it being bent to a small radius. The cable is then simply laid in the trench and requires no further protection than the reinstated earth.

To prepare the ends of the armoured cable for connecting purposes, remove the outside covering for a distance of about 9 in. from the ends of the cable. At this point, bind a length of strong wire round the armouring to keep it in place. If the cable is protected with

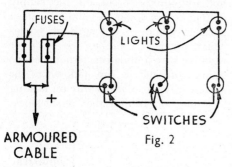

FUSES
LIGHTS
+
SWITCHES
Fig. 2
ARMOURED CABLE

wire armouring, cut the wire neatly at the binding wire, with a pair of cutting pliers. Should the cable be armoured

with steel tape, however, cut the tape round by means of a hacksaw, taking care not to cut too deep or injury to the conductors may result. Next, remove the jute bedding and then strip the lead sheathing by nicking it round with a knife—again taking care not to nick too deep—when it will break off at the nick when bent. The lead can then be removed by pulling it from the conductors. Bare back the insulation for about an inch and remove the tape. When the armouring at the binding wire has been bound round with electrician's adhesive tape, the cable is ready for connecting to the cut-outs. The method of connecting and wiring the extra lights in the outbuilding is indicated in Fig. 2.

INSTALLING AN IMMERSION WATER HEATER

THE problem of ensuring an adequate supply of hot water without using the ordinary coal-fired boiler during the summer months is easily solved by installing a thermostatically controlled immersion heater in the storage tank.

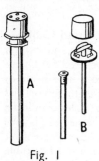

A

B

Fig. I

The installing of such a heater should present little difficulty to the practical man who has a slight knowledge of electric wiring and mechanical work in general.

The electrical equipment includes a tubular immersion heater and a suitable thermostat, shown at A and B respectively in Fig. 1. The latter is for automatically cutting off the current when the temperature of the water has reached a predetermined degree,

likewise switching it on when the water gets below a certain temperature.

There are numerous excellent makes to be had, all of which will give good results provided they are installed in the correct manner.

As most modern medium-sized houses are provided with a storage tank or cylinder of about 25 gallons capacity, either a two or a three kilowatt heater can be used, the latter, of course, heating the water the more quickly. A two kilowatt heater, together with a suitable thermostat, costs about £3.

The first thing to do before installing an immersion heater is to make sure that the hot water system is connected up in the correct way, that is, that the hot water taps are connected to the expansion pipe as shown in the diagrammatic sketch (Fig. 2). If the system is not in accordance with the diagram, but connected to the flow pipe, it should be altered, otherwise satisfactory results cannot be obtained. The necessary alteration may be quite a simple job, but if it is deemed beyond the scope of the amateur, a competent plumber should be called in to do the work.

Assuming that the pipe system is in order, the cylinder or tank must be

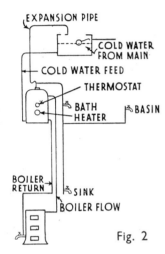

Fig. 2

emptied. Before doing this, however, turn off the cold water feed at the tap, if such a tap is provided; if not, the outlet of the feed pipe of the supply tank should be stopped up by plugging it with a tapered piece of wood shaped to suit the bore of the pipe. The storage tank and boiler are emptied by turning on the tap usually to be found in the boiler return pipe at the side of the stove.

The First Operation on the supply tank consists in boring a couple of holes to take the fixing flanges into which the heater and the thermostat are screwed. Although this appears to be a formidable job, it is indeed quite simple provided a patent adaptable boss, known as the "Essex," is used, an illustration of which appears in Fig. 3A, which represents the front and 3B the back. By using this device there is no need to remove the cover plate of the storage tank, as the

boss can be fitted directly into the hole made for its reception. A cardboard template is included with the flange, and this is placed at the position required and a guide-line marked with a pencil or a scriber. The hole is then drilled either by a suitable-sized cutter or by drilling a series of small holes close together inside the guide line and removing the unwanted piece by means of a small, sharp cold chisel, care being taken to see

Fig. 3a

Fig. 3b

that the piece does not fall into the inside of the tank. The jagged surface is then finished off carefully with a file.

Having completed the hole, the

flange is placed on a wide holder—supplied with the flange—and slipped into position, still retaining hold of the holder. A split metal washer is then worked into the hole and slips over the threaded portion of the flange. A special heat-resisting packing washer is then placed on the boss and this completes the work on the inside of the tank.

Fig. 4

A similar packing washer and a metal washer are placed over the projecting portion of the flange and the whole boss is kept in position by means of a locknut which, when tightened up, forms a perfectly efficient watertight joint. It should be noted that this type of boss can be used for other purposes, such as connecting up extra pipe outlets, and can be used on either a flat or curved surface. Fig. 4 shows the operation of fitting the boss.

The Best Position for the Heater is approximately one-third the height from the bottom of the tank or cylinder and placed horizontally as indicated in Fig. 5. The thermostat should be fitted about 6 in. or so above the heater. If it be found that a horizontal position is impracticable, then the heater can be

placed on top, but the heater and thermostat should be sufficiently long to reach at least two-thirds of the way down. A two kilowatt heater is usually provided with a $1\frac{1}{4}$-in. gas thread, while the boss of the thermostat casing is threaded $\frac{1}{2}$-in. gas.

All that is necessary to fit the heater and thermostat, after the bosses have been fixed to the tank, is to place a heat-resisting washer over the ends and carefully screw them into their respective flanges in the tank.

Before proceeding any further, it is a good plan to turn on the water-supply to make sure that no leakage takes place at the joints. If the work has been properly done, the joints will be perfectly watertight, but should any leakage occur, it must be attended to and put right.

The next procedure consists in wiring and connecting up the heater and thermostat to the electric supply.

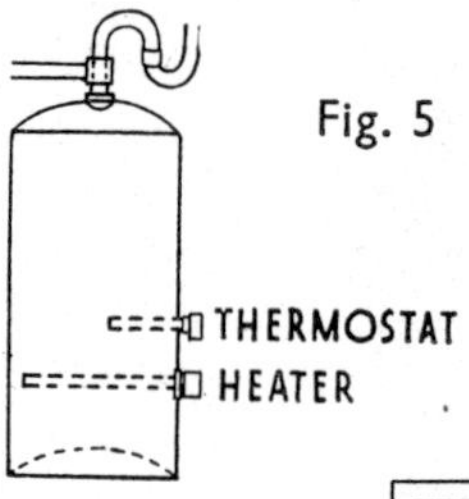

Fig. 5

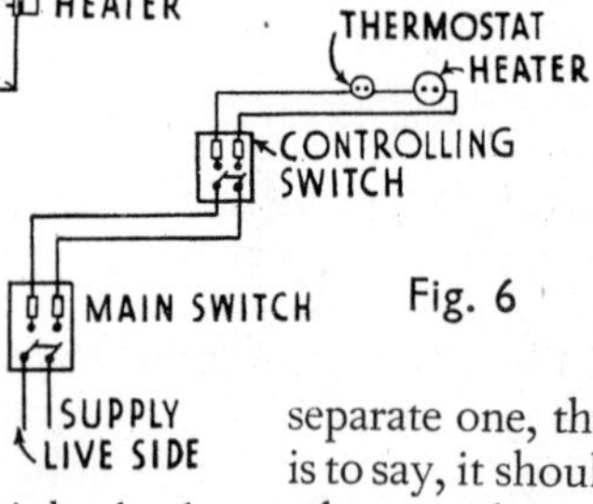

THERMOSTAT
HEATER

THERMOSTAT
HEATER

CONTROLLING
SWITCH

MAIN SWITCH   Fig. 6

SUPPLY
LIVE SIDE

This circuit should be a separate one, that is to say, it should be run right back to the supply and protected at that point with a double-pole main switch and fuses. A similar switch with fuses should also be fixed in a convenient position near the storage tank.

The wires can be protected with enamelled steel conduit, or twin lead-covered cable may be used; but whatever kind of metallic protective covering is chosen, it is of the utmost importance to earth the whole system efficiently, including the thermostat, heater and switches.

The amount of current taken by the heater is, of course, determined by the size of the heater and the voltage of the supply. In the case of a two-kilowatt heater supplied at 200 volts, the current taken will be $\dfrac{2000}{200} = 10$ amperes and a three kilowatt size will take $\dfrac{3000}{200} = 15$ amperes.

As it is better to have a larger cable than is strictly necessary, a 3/·036 cable should be used with the smaller heater, while a 7/·029 will safely carry the current for the larger one.

The electrical connections are of a very simple character, the heater being connected in series with the thermostat, as indicated in the wiring diagram in Fig. 6.

If everything is found satisfactory on test, the tank should be efficiently lagged with a non-conductor of heat to prevent loss of heat. This should present little difficulty, as convenient-sized sections of suitable material can be had which only require to be bound on to the tank or the cylinder.

In conclusion, it is necessary to say that whenever any adjustments are being made to either the thermostat or the heater, always turn off the main switch.

HOME-MADE LIGHTING FITTINGS

O F the many useful and artistic articles which can be easily and cheaply constructed at home, electric-light fittings are among the most profitable and extremely interesting.

The construction of the fittings from the designs illustrated and described in the following paragraphs and the Working Drawings, requires no exceptional skill on the part of the constructor beyond the ability to use a fretsaw, soldering iron and a few commonplace tools.

The illustration shown in Fig. 1, details of which are shown at A in the Working Drawing, is a lantern suitable for a small entrance hall. The body of the fitting is constructed of $\frac{3}{16}$-in. plywood, while the top is of similar material, $\frac{3}{8}$ in. thick.

First accurately mark out and cut two pieces of the $\frac{3}{16}$-in. material $5\frac{1}{2}$ in. long by $4\frac{1}{2}$ in. wide for two sides and two pieces of similar material, but $4\frac{1}{4}$ in. wide for the others. A piece of $\frac{3}{8}$-in. stuff should also be cut $5\frac{1}{4}$ in. square. With a pencil, mark out the outline of the design on the side-pieces to the dimensions shown and carefully cut out the waste with a fretsaw. If reasonable care is taken to support the parts well, the risk of breakage will be negligible. After having cut out the pattern, remove any irregularities at the angles, etc., with a fine file and then finish off with fine glass-paper.

The Top is the next item to prepare, and requires no further work than making a $1\frac{1}{8}$-in. diameter hole in the centre for taking the lampholder, boring four $\frac{1}{2}$-in. ventilation holes and cutting off the corners.

Four pieces of thin frosted or mottled glass, each 5 in. long by $3\frac{15}{16}$ in. wide, should be obtained. These can be bought for a few pence, including cutting. The glasses are fastened in position by means of small brass clips cut and shaped to the size shown. If desired, pieces of tracing cloth or parchment, glued in, will serve equally well. If glass is the chosen medium, fit the top clips next, as these are difficult to fasten after assembly.

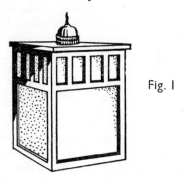

Fig. I

The parts can now be assembled. Place one of the narrow side-pieces lengthways in the vice so that its edge just projects above the tops of the jaws and then apply a thin film of tube glue to the edge. Place one of the wide pieces squarely on top and fasten them together by means of ½-in. fine panel pins, taking care to see that they are driven in the centre of the edge of the bottom piece of plywood and also that the top edge does not overlap the bottom. Fix the other two sides together in the same way and then fasten the two members—each consisting of two sides —together, not forgetting to apply a small quantity of liquid glue at the edges.

The next operation consists in fixing the top and then finishing the fitting with stain, paint or enamel as desired. If a metallic finish is required, a small bottle of bronze, gilt or aluminium paint can be obtained for a few pence, but before applying this it is an advantage to give the fitting a coat of gold size. The fitting shown in the illustration (Fig. 1) is finished in aluminium. When the paint is thoroughly dry, slip the glasses in position and fix them with the bottom clips, spaced in the centre of each piece of glass at the bottom.

An artistic electric-light fitting suitable for a lounge, dining-room or a large hall is shown at Fig. 2, details of which appear at B in the Working Drawing. The making of such a fitting calls for the use of a soldering iron and its accompanying materials in the shape of flux, solder, etc.

As will be gathered from a glance at the illustrations, the shape is hexagonal and the glasses are supported in a frame made of brass strip about $\frac{1}{16}$ in. thick, which is suspended from the ceiling by means of three chains and a ceiling-plate.

To make the fitting, procure 8 ft. of $\frac{3}{8}$-in. wide L angle brass $\frac{1}{16}$ in. thick. This length allows sufficient material for

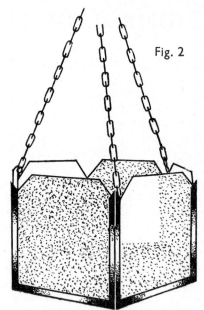

Fig. 2

waste. Suitable angle brass can be obtained at most shops dealing in metals, or it may possibly be stocked at the local ironmonger. If possible, obtain one piece in a single length of 45 in. as this will save making an extra joint in the

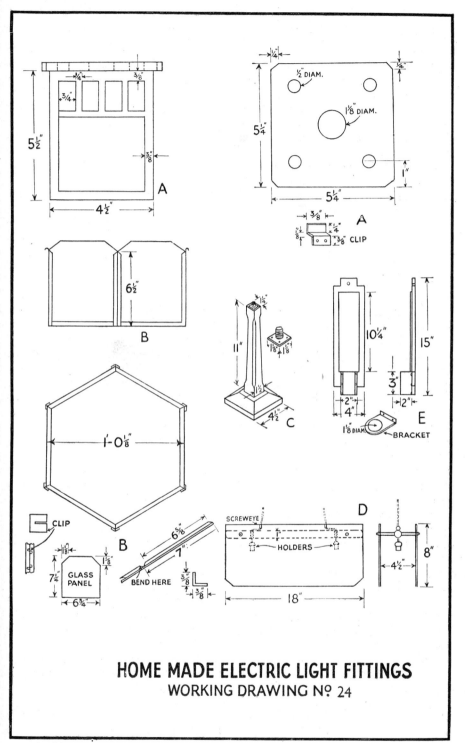

HOME MADE ELECTRIC LIGHT FITTINGS
WORKING DRAWING Nº 24

base of the frame. Mark out this length to the dimensions shown in the detailed drawing and cut out a series of notches in one web of the metal to enable it to be bent at the corners to form a hexagon. The cutting may be accomplished with the aid of a hacksaw or a triangular file.

Now cut 6 pieces of the same material $6\frac{1}{2}$ in. long for the vertical corner-pieces; file the tops to give a finish, and bend the webs to form the corner angles, as shown in the Working Drawing. Cut 12 $\frac{5}{8}$-in. square pieces of thin sheet brass or tinplate and split them at the centre to a depth of $\frac{1}{2}$ in. to form clips for supporting the glass panels in the inside of the frame.

The next process consists in soldering the parts together. Start with the base frame and sweat the ends together to make a good sound joint. Next solder the two fixing clips for the glass to each upright. The positions for these are $1\frac{1}{2}$ in. from the top and bottom, in the centre of the angle. Then thoroughly tin the outside faces of the hexagonal corners of the bottom frame and the inside lower surfaces of the uprights. With a very hot iron—not red hot, of course—sweat each upright to its respective corner, taking particular care to keep each vertical piece truly upright. Form three neat hooks having loops about $\frac{1}{2}$ in. in diameter from a piece of stout wire and sweat one to the top of every other upright, keeping the shank between the angles of the inside face. This finishes the frame.

If the metal parts are to have a brass finish, the frame should be thoroughly cleaned and polished and given a good coat of cold lacquer to prevent it from tarnishing. If another finish be desired, a metallic paint, as that suggested for the hanging lantern, could be used.

In order to gauge the size of the glass for the base of the fitting it is a wise precaution to make a cardboard template of the shape, allowing $\frac{1}{16}$ in. play all round. This is a better method than measuring, as it allows certain adjustments to be made in the event of the frame not being quite correct. The template method might be used to advantage for the side panel glasses, but the size shown on the drawing will allow sufficient play between each piece and leave ample room between them for the fixing clips.

The Glasses are then cut from either frosted or mottled glass, the bottom piece being placed in position first and then the side panels. The latter are kept in place by bending over the clips—half on one side and half on the other.

The final items consist of a suitable length of chain of the desired finish, a ceiling-plate for suspending the fitting, a cord-grip lampholder and electric flexible wire. Suitable chain, fitted with $\frac{3}{4}$-in. oval links, costs about 10d. per yd.; the length required must be ascertained by measuring from the ceiling. A ceiling-plate having three hooks can be obtained for about 8d., or a $3\frac{1}{2}$-in. round white-enamelled wooden block, having three round cup-hooks, can be used if desired. The hooks should be spaced equally apart at a distance of $\frac{3}{4}$ in. from the face edge of the block. A good quality lampholder costs about 9d., while suitable flex can be obtained at most electrical stores at 4d. per yd.

A serviceable table standard lamp in oak is illustrated in Fig. 3 with dimensioned drawings at C in the Working Drawing. Two pieces of oak $\frac{3}{4}$ in. thick are required for the upright and a piece of similar material $4\frac{1}{2}$ in. square by 1 in. thick for the base. A screwed brass nipple, $\frac{1}{2}$ in. long by $\frac{1}{2}$ in. in diameter, a key switch-holder, and flex complete the list of principal parts.

To make the standard, true up the two long strips and cut a channel $\frac{1}{8}$ in. deep and $\frac{1}{4}$ in. wide along the centre in one wide face of each piece and glue the two prepared faces together so that a $\frac{1}{4}$-in. hole runs through the entire length. Mark out the length and plane it to the tapered shape shown, that is, $1\frac{1}{2}$ in. at the base and $1\frac{1}{4}$ in. at the top. Cut a shoulder at the bottom $\frac{1}{2}$ in. deep and $\frac{1}{4}$ in. wide for fixing into the base.

The sharp corners of the upright should be stop-chamfered to within a distance of 1 in. from the top and the bottom in order to give the fitting a pleasing appearance.

Now prepare the flange for fixing the lampholder to the top of the wooden upright. This is shown in detail in the drawing. To do this, cut a piece of sheet brass $\frac{1}{16}$ in. thick by $1\frac{1}{8}$ in. square and neatly smooth the edges with a file. Drill a $\frac{1}{2}$-in. diameter hole in the centre and four $\frac{1}{8}$-in. holes near the corners, as shown, to take fine brass fixing screws.

Countersink the screw-holes and then solder the nipple to the base or flange, taking care to keep the nipple square with the flange. Having completed this, screw the part to the top of the standard, using thin $\frac{1}{2}$-in. brass screws for the purpose.

The next thing to do is to prepare the base. Cut and plane the wood squarely to a finished size of $4\frac{1}{2}$ in. by $4\frac{1}{2}$ in. by 1 in. and then mark it out by scribing a centre line round the sides and also a $1\frac{3}{4}$-in. square in the centre of the top face. Now cut a 1-in. square hole in the centre of the base by first boring the wood with a 1-in. diameter bit and removing the remaining waste with a sharp chisel. Bore a $\frac{1}{4}$-in. hole in the centre of one of the sides just below a marked line to meet the square hole. Slightly countersink the mouth of the hole to prevent the flexible wire from chafing when wired up.

Next, neatly form the chamfers between the marked sides and the $1\frac{3}{4}$-in. marked square on the top face. The post can now be fitted to its base by

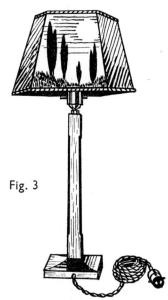

Fig. 3

inserting the shoulder of the former into the square hole of the latter, after having applied a small film of tube glue round and underneath the shoulder.

Smooth the surfaces with fine glass-paper and then stain the fitting to the desired shade, finishing it off with a good quality wax polish.

When dry, the standard can be wired up by passing the flex through the hole in the side of the base and up through the standard. The bottom portion of the lampholder is removed and screwed tightly to the nipple. The ends of the flex are then bared, the strands of wire inserted into the respective terminals of the holder and firmly secured by means of the tightening screws, after which the other parts of the holder are replaced. A plug top should be fitted to the other end of the flex, to suit the size of the supply socket.

A piece of thick sheet lead, about $\frac{1}{8}$ in.

thick, covered with a piece of baize and screwed to the underside of the base, will make it sufficiently heavy to prevent the fitting from being easily knocked over when a suitable shade is fitted. A parchment swivelling shade can either be made or bought. Its design must be left to suit the taste of the individual user.

A Two-light Bedroom Fitting of modern design, as that shown in Fig. 4,

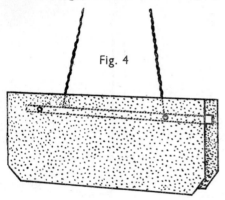

Fig. 4

can be easily made from the drawings appearing at D in the Working Drawing. The fitting consists of two pieces of frosted glass 18 in. long by 8 in. wide, an 18-in. length of broomstick, two pieces of $\frac{3}{8}$-in. diameter dowel rod $4\frac{1}{2}$ in. long, cordgrip lampholders, two $\frac{3}{8}$-in. diameter screw-eyes and a suitable length of white silk twin flexible electric-lighting wire.

The Frame for supporting the glasses is made by drilling a $\frac{3}{8}$-in. hole 2 in. from each end of the thicker rod to take the two pieces of dowel at right-angles, as shown. Great care must be exercised in drilling the holes to keep them "dead" in line, otherwise the edges of the glasses will not be parallel when fixed. Drill a $\frac{1}{4}$-in. hole 1 in. away from the cross-pieces and towards the centre, to take the flex and lampholder, and fix the screw-eyes 1 in. away from these holes, as shown.

Carefully round the ends of the thick rod and give it and the dowels a rub over with fine glass-paper. Then insert the dowels into the holes in the main member so that the ends project equally, and fix them by means of fine screws, after having drilled small holes for their reception. The frame can now receive a coat of white paint thinly applied, followed by a coat of art enamel, the former coat being allowed to dry, of course, before applying the second.

The next procedure requires patience and care as it consists in drilling the fixing holes in the glass. To do this, a very hard $\frac{3}{16}$-in. twist-drill will be required, together with four blocks of $\frac{1}{2}$-in. thick hardwood, a small quantity of water and some emery powder.

Mark the glass where the holes are to be, namely, 2 in. from the ends and 1 in. from the top edge, and then drill a $\frac{3}{16}$-in. hole in each hardwood block. Glue the blocks to the glass so that the centre of each hole registers with the centres of the marked positions on the glass and allow the glue to set. If in doubt as to the hardness of the drill, is a wise plan to heat it up to a cherry red and immediately quench it in cold water.

When the glue is perfectly dry, place the glass on a perfectly flat surface, pour a small quantity of emery powder down the hole in one of the blocks and then a few drops of water, and rotate the drill by means of a small hand stock, applying only a little pressure, when the emery will eventually wear a hole through the glass.

If desired, the drill can be replaced by a piece of brass or copper tube of the same diameter, the business end of which must be serrated. Having finished the drilling, the glasses should be placed in lukewarm water to soften the glue and thus enable the blocks to be removed. Drill a small hole in the end of each projecting dowel piece in order to prevent splitting when driving in the fixing screws for the glass.

Four each of ⅜-in. and ¼-in. diameter felt washers and four ¼-in. metal washers will be needed in order to give a soft bearing surface to the glasses when fixed in position. Thin round-headed brass screws are used for fixing the glasses. A metal washer and a small felt one are threaded on each screw, which is then passed through the hole in the glass and a large felt washer is inserted between the back of the glass and the end of the dowel. Do not drive the screws right home, otherwise you will probably crack the glass.

The Ceiling-Plate consists of a 3½ in. by 1 in. thick round white, enamelled block having two ¼ in. holes in line to take the flex, the ends of which are connected in parallel to a two-way china insulated connecter and connected to the main circuit wires at the back of the block.

An opal tubular lamp is employed instead of the usual spherical bulb in the wall bracket shown in Fig. 5 and at E in the Working Drawing.

The back plate consists of a piece of hardwood, such as oak, ½ in. thick, and is cut out to the shape and dimensions shown. An overlay of ⅛-in. thick plywood, painted with aluminium

paint, not only relieves the otherwise somewhat plain appearance but acts as an efficient reflector. If desired, a mirror can be substituted, in which case the edges should be covered with a small, neat moulding.

Fig. 5

The lampholder is supported by means of a sheet brass or a tinplate bracket 1/16 in. thick, cut and bent to the dimensions shown. A 1⅛-in. hole is cut in the centre and the bracket is fixed to the back plate with small round-headed brass screws.

A shaped piece of thin sheet brass is cut and bent to surround the holder to hide it from view. Its ends should be bent at right-angles to form fixing flanges which are secured to the back plate by means of small screws.

The lampholder is wired up in the usual way and the flex taken through a ¼-in. hole just below the cord grip. As the main circuit wires will probably come in the centre at the back of the fitting, it is advisable to cut a narrow channel to enable the flex to lie flush or just below the surface.

MENDING AN ELECTRIC IRON

THE best type of electric iron for general household purposes is perhaps one weighing about 5 lb. and designed to work at a fixed voltage to suit the supply. An iron of this weight will be found easy to work without having to exert undue pressure. Such an implement is shown in Fig. 1.

When purchasing an electric iron it is wiser to spend a shilling or two more for a good British-made article, which usually carries a guarantee, than to buy a cheap foreign-made iron of doubtful qualities.

Whatever the type of iron may be, they all work on a common principle, which involves the use of a suitable heating element within the iron. The current passes through the element and heats the iron.

Fig. 2 shows the internal parts of an ordinary household electric iron. The

Fig. I

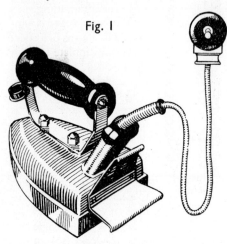

top portion (Fig. 1) carries the handle and the terminal pegs or pins to which the flexible connecting cable is attached. The lower portion contains the heating element A (Fig. 2), which usually consists of a resistance wire wound on a flat mica former. The former is enclosed between sheets of mica to insulate the resistance wire from the body of the iron. Two tags are generally provided at the broad end of the element for connecting the resistance wire to the terminal pins. The element is shown in detail at B. This part is kept in close contact with the bottom of the iron by a heavy cast plate, c, which is held in position by nuts screwed on two projecting studs fitted to the bottom portion of the iron, D. Connection to the main circuit is made by a flexible cable fitted with a suitable connecting-piece to fit the pins of the iron at one end, the other terminating in a plug top or an adaptor to fit a plug socket or lampholder, as the case may be.

However good an electric iron may be there comes a time when it ceases to function. When this occurs it is not a very difficult matter to locate the fault and repair it.

The chief causes of breakdown are as follows:

1. Short-circuit of flexible connecting wire.
2. Broken circuit due to break in flexible wire.
3. Bad contacts in iron connecter or plug or adaptor.
4. Bad contacts between terminals and the heating element within the iron.
5. Burnt out or broken resistance wire in heating element.

It is hardly necessary to say that the first thing to do when a failure occurs is to disconnect the iron from the main circuit by pulling out the connecting plug, or the adaptor.

A Short-cir-

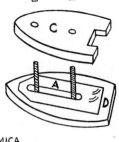

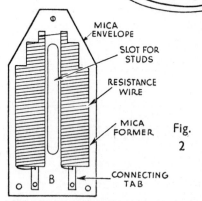

MICA ENVELOPE

SLOT FOR STUDS

RESISTANCE WIRE

MICA FORMER

CONNECTING TAB

Fig. 2

cuit in the flexible is usually caused by worn or broken insulation, which allows the naked wires to touch each other. Such a defect is easily discernible for, when a short-circuit occurs, a spark is usually emitted at the points of contact. The obvious remedy for this is to fit new cable. Procure from your local electrician a suitable length of 70/40 gauge double-vulcanised twin cab-tyre flexible cable. This is the best kind of connecting wire to use and is much to be preferred to the ordinary twisted flex as it does not kink, and further, owing to its toughness, has superior wearing qualities. Before beginning operations it is advisable to spread a large sheet of white paper on the table. This will not only enable you to see better, but also save a good deal of time in hunting for lost screws. Open the iron connector—which in these days is usually made of bakelite and is in two halves—by removing the fixing screws. It will then be readily seen how to disconnect the old and to connect the new wire by referring to Fig. 3. Remove about an inch and a half or so of the rubber sheathing to expose the two insulated wires enclosed within it and bare the ends of these, so that ½ in. of the naked wire is exposed. Twist the strands of each wire tightly to form a loop and fix one underneath the head of each contact-screw, taking care to see that the loops are placed in a clockwise direction to prevent them from being forced out when the screws are tightened. It is also important to see that none of the strands of one wire is allowed to come in contact with any of those forming the other wire, otherwise a short-circuit will take place within the connector, which will necessitate the work being done over again, and a possible replacement of a fuse. Now place the spring top, which supports the flex, in position and refix the two halves of the connector.

Having accomplished the work at the more difficult end, proceed with the other. Unscrew the top of the plug—

or adaptor—from its base, remove the old wire, bare the wires of the new as explained above, fix them under their respective terminals and refix the plug. The iron is now ready for a test. Before connecting up to the circuit replace the fuse which should have blown when the short-circuit occurred.

If it is found that the defect is not due to a short-circuit then the flexible should be examined for a break or bad connection.

Remove the flexible with its connectors from the electric iron and test

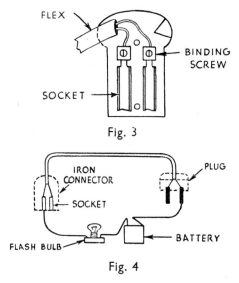

Fig. 3

Fig. 4

each conductor with an ordinary flash-lamp battery and suitable bulb. Connect up the battery and lamp as indicated in Fig. 4. If the lamp remains alight when the flex is pulled and twisted it may be taken that the flexible and its connectors are in order. Should there be no light, however, or if the light is intermittent, it points to either a broken wire or a bad contact. A break in the flexible usually occurs where the wires enter the connectors. This is due to the constant bending of the wires at these points when the iron is in use.

If the flex is found to be out of order the iron connector and the plug top will now have to be opened and examined as previously explained. Look at the connections and if these are found to be satisfactory, test the ends of the flex again for about 3 or 4 in. up, by pulling each wire in turn. If a fair amount of pressure is exerted in so doing, it will generally reveal the break by the insulation parting company.

Assuming that the above tests have been carried out in accordance with the instructions and the flexible connection is found to be in perfect order, the next thing to do is to open the iron and examine the contacts and the element within. Unscrew the nuts under the handle and remove the top part of the iron. Examine the connections between the element and the bottom of the terminal pins. In some irons the connection between the pins and the element is made by the ends of the pins pressing on the metal tabs of the element. In such an iron a breakdown is likely to occur at these points owing to a bad contact between them. The contacts therefore should be carefully looked at to make sure that they are perfectly clean and that there is sufficient pressure between the parts to prevent heating at these points.

Irons in which the element is connected to the pins by screws do not often cause trouble at these parts.

Assuming that the contacts are satisfactory the next procedure is to unscrew the nuts on the studs and remove the iron plate. This will reveal the element. Disconnect the element from the terminal pins and thoroughly examine the resistance wire. If it is broken close to the connecting tabs it can easily be put right by joining it up again, but if the break is elsewhere it cannot be satisfactorily repaired, which means that a new element is necessary.

Spare Elements can now be readily obtained to fit almost any iron at most electrical stores. They are not expensive to buy. When purchasing a new element it is a good plan to have the old one to hand to enable the assistant to gauge the size and also the correct loading.

To fit a new element is a matter of only a few minutes' work. Place the element over the studs and refix the plate. Then connect up the tabs to the terminal pins and fit the top of the iron, taking care to keep the tabs from touching the body of the iron. The job is completed when the handle is fixed. The iron should now give months of satisfactory service.

A DOMESTIC TELEPHONE

IN these days when every conceivable labour-saving device can be readily obtained at a reasonable figure, it is surprising that house telephones, as distinct from those operated by the Post Office, are not more widely adopted than they are. This may be due to the idea that they are difficult to instal and costly in upkeep. House telephones can be installed by any intelligent practical man who can use a few simple tools, while the upkeep involves nothing more than the occasional recharging of the batteries.

As most modern houses are fitted with an electric-bell installation, there is no necessity to have separate wiring for operating the telephones; the wires can be used for ringing the bell in the ordinary way and also for conveying the minute speech-current.

It must be noted that should the bell system be worked from an alternating current transformer supplied from the electric lighting system, the transformer must be replaced with a battery, as telephones will not work with alternating current.

Briefly stated, a simple telephone system consists of three principal parts, namely, the receiver, transmitter and a suitable signalling device in the shape of a bell or buzzer in order to call attention when it is desired to speak.

The Receiver, a diagrammatic sketch of which appears in Fig. 1, consists of a

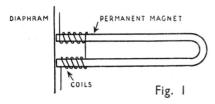

Fig. 1

strong permanent magnet, each end of which is embraced in a coil of very fine wire. Just above the poles of the magnet, but not quite touching them, is a thin iron diaphragm which vibrates when acted upon by sound-waves, such as the human voice. As the distance between the disc and the poles of the magnet varies according to the intensity of the sound waves, so also does the intensity of the magnetic field, and in doing so causes minute currents to be induced in the coils. This current, if connected by wires to a similar instrument, will cause its diaphragm to vibrate in sympathy and produce sound-waves which can be heard if the receiver be placed to the ear. From this it will be observed that a receiver can be used as a transmitter, but such a magnetic transmitter is very inefficient.

14*

The Transmitter in practice consists of a thin carbon plate or disc which presses very lightly upon a number of small, highly-polished carbon balls housed in a suitable case. If a small current be

applied to the disc and granules, and the disc be caused to vibrate by means of sound-waves, the pressure of contact alters the electrical resistance in accordance with the intensity of the vibrations and causes a fluctuating current to flow through the coils of the receiver magnet to which the microphone is normally connected and consequently makes the diaphragm vibrate.

In simple telephones such as those used in conjunction with the electric bells in private houses, the microphone or transmitter and receiver are usually incorporated in one instrument,

Fig. 2

as shown in the illustration, Fig. 2. The cost of such an instrument is about 17s. 6d.

If the illustration is studied carefully, it will be seen that in the handle is included a press switch, whose function is to cut out the speech circuit when not in use.

Fig. 3 shows how a pair of instruments is connected to an ordinary electric-bell system having the usual pendulum-type indicator and bell in the kitchen. The only alteration of the wiring needed is to alter the circuit near the bell and extend the wires down to a special automatic switch in the form of a rosette. A bell-push fitted with plug sockets, as illustrated at A in Fig. 4, is fitted in place of the ordinary push in any other room where telephonic communication is desired.

The switch in the kitchen consists of a spring-controlled hook upon which the receiver hangs when not in use. The weight of the instrument keeps the hook

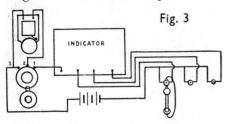

Fig. 3

in its down position which allows current to flow across the contacts when a push is operated and thus causes the bell to ring. When the instrument is lifted from the hook it breaks the bell circuit at this point, but it is remade on gripping the lever switch in the handle of the receiver.

After pressing the push at the dining-room end, the instrument is removed from the hook and the handle switch operated, which connects the two instruments in series.

The advantage of this system is that only two instruments are required as the dining-room receiver can be used in other rooms provided such rooms are

fitted with suitable plug pushes. Only one-way ringing is possible, that is to say, from the various rooms to the kitchen, and not vice versa.

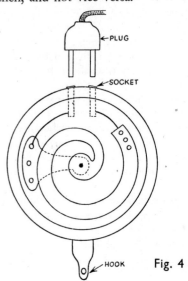

Fig. 4

Where ringing is desired both ways a separate circuit should be used, while for operating telephones over a distance exceeding about 200 ft. better-class instruments having transformers should be employed.

WIRELESS

ALTHOUGH the number of wireless receiving licences taken out by owners of sets increases enormously year by year, there are still thousands of homes without the necessary apparatus for taking advantage of this fascinating modern form of entertainment.

In these days, the would-be listener who contemplates installing a radio receiver has a choice of instruments which leaves little to be desired in efficiency, quality of reproduction and ease of control, but such sets should always bear the stamp of a reputable manufacturer and be obtained from a dealer who specialises in electrical and radio work, whose interest generally lies beyond the mere making of a sale.

Much disappointment and annoyance will be obviated if a reasonable price is paid for a set, and it is a great mistake to rely on the beautiful outward appearance of a receiver and take it for granted that the internal parts correspond in quality.

Although there are numerous types of radio receivers, all of which are useful for their particular purpose, they may be graded into two classes, namely, those taking current for their operation from the supply mains, commonly known as mains sets, and those obtaining current from batteries, or, as they are termed, battery sets.

In cases where an electric supply is available, advantage should be taken of this valuable source of current, as its use eliminates the somewhat costly up-keep of batteries and the running costs of an all-mains set is negligible, especially if run off a power-circuit. On the other hand, if mains current is not available, the only alternative is a battery set, which may be of the portable type of the more or less permanent kind.

A few years ago the majority of wireless sets consisted of a receiver, separate loud-speaker and a conglomeration of wires and batteries usually placed outside the set. In these days a wireless receiver is self-contained: that is, the receiving apparatus, loud-speaker and batteries are all incorporated in one cabinet, which generally adds to the appearance of a room than otherwise.

There is little reason why the purchase of a radio set should be delayed on account of the initial cost and disturbance of capital, as most of the leading manufacturers are prepared to accept a small initial payment, leaving the balance payable in instalments spread over a period of nine months to a year. This concession is, of course, only granted to responsible householders and those who can find a guarantor to guarantee the payments when they become due.

Speaking generally, a good quality modern three-valve set—mains- or battery-driven—will not only allow the majority of the programmes transmitted from the British Broadcasting Corporation's stations to be heard at good loud-speaker strength at any point in the British Isles, but such a set will generally "bring in" numerous Continental ones, especially during the winter, when receiving conditions are very much better than in the summer.

At the moment, a good many makers are using the superheterodyne method of reception, which allows more distant stations to be received and is, in addition, more selective than the ordinary

Fig. I

type of set. An excellent example of this type of set is illustrated in Fig. 1.

A fair price to pay for a mains-driven set of the superheterodyne type varies from about £12 upwards, according to the number of valves, while reliable battery sets can be obtained for about £10, including batteries.

The requirements of the amateur constructor are amply catered for in kits of all the necessary parts to build a first-rate receiver. These constructors' outfits can be obtained for either battery or mains operation. Such a kit can be assembled by the merest tyro in a matter of a few hours with the aid of a pair of pliers and a screwdriver. Fig. 2 shows

an efficient set being built from a kit of parts supplied by a reliable manufacturer.

Before, or immediately after, installing a wireless receiver, a Post Office licence must be obtained from the nearest Post Office. The icence is available for a period of one year and costs but 10/–. One licence covers the use of one or more permanent sets belonging to the same owner and, in addition, a portable set. If the latter is used away, it is necessary to carry the licence. The licence is not transferable, that is to say, that anyone purchasing a second-hand set must take out a new licence for it, irrespective of whether the licence belonging to the original owner is still in force or not. It should be noted that it is a punishable offence to use an unlicensed wireless set.

Aerials.—To obtain the best results from a radio receiver an efficient aerial and earth system is necessary, except in portable sets, where the aerial is incorporated in the set. Portable sets, however, are not so popular as they used to be a few years ago owing, possibly, to their comparatively heavy cost of upkeep due to the number of valves required to operate the set efficiently.

The outdoor type of aerial is undoubtedly the most efficient and should consist of about 40 ft. of insulated aerial wire, including the "lead in," which is the more or less vertical portion of the aerial connecting the horizontal component to the set. The earth connecting lead should be as short as possible and, if practicable, made directly to the earth by means of a proper earth-tube. Failing this, a connection made to a nearby main cold-water pipe may be used, as shown in Fig. 3, provided the connection is perfectly clean and properly made by employing either a special earthing clip or solder. A hot-water pipe or a gas-pipe should never be used for earthing purposes. The best posi-

Fig. 2

tion for fixing the earth-tube in the ground is below the aerial and about a couple of feet out from the wall.

A stranded, insulated wire, consisting of 7 strands of 22 gauge copper wire should be used for the aerial in preference to a single wire in order to provide ample surface for the reception of the incoming minute high-frequency currents, which only flow on the surface and not in the interior of the wire.

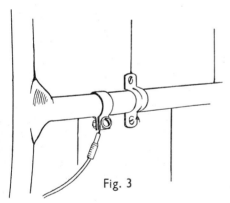

Fig. 3

Fig. 4 shows an efficient type of outdoor aerial. The wire is suspended from the top of a 25-ft. mast by means of a couple of insulators, while the other end goes down to the set. An insulator is placed at the junction between the horizontal part of the wire and the down lead, and this insulator is anchored to a

convenient spot, such as the top of an upper floor window-frame or the large board under the eaves of the roof.

In erecting an aerial of this type, pulleys should be fitted to the top of the mast and also at the house end, to enable the aerial to be lowered if required. The pulley halyard should be in one continuous piece and fastened to a cleat fixed at the lower end of the mast. The same thing, of course, applies to the house end of the aerial, the cleat being fixed to the wall.

An important point to observe when installing an outdoor aerial is to bring the lead-in wire down at an angle and clear of the house, as the efficiency of the aerial will be reduced if allowed to

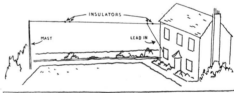

Fig. 4

touch the house. In addition, a proper earthing switch or a lightning arrester should be incorporated in the aerial circuit, so that in the event of a thunderstorm, any charge induced in the aerial may pass freely to earth without traversing any part of the receiver. If a switch is used, a single- or a double-pole throw-over switch will suffice. The switch should be fixed outside and protected from the weather by means of a waterproof box. A diagram of the switch connections of a single-pole throw-over switch is shown in Fig. 5. The disadvantage of such switches is that they have to be operated from outside and

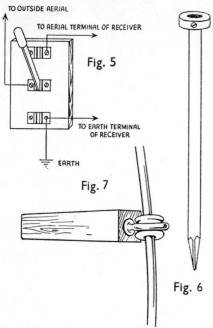

Fig. 5

Fig. 7

Fig. 6

that the contacts, etc., are likely to become corroded. To obviate these disadvantages, a proper lightning arrester can be used. There are several types of inexpensive arresters to be had, all of which are entirely automatic in action. Such a device does not need to be disconnected from the set as any static charge in the aerial is discharged safely to earth.

The Earth-tube shown in Fig. 6 is an excellent type to have. By its use the ground is kept moist in dry weather by simply pouring a bucketful of water down the tube. The water is evenly distributed in the soil by means of a series of holes in the wall of the tube.

In cases where an outdoor aerial is impracticable due to lack of space, or is objected to on account of its somewhat unsightly appearance, a good substitute is an aerial installed in the attic space or loft between the top-floor ceiling and the roof that is usually to be found in modern houses.

Such an aerial consists of the same kind of insulated wire as that employed for outdoor purposes. About 60 ft. of wire, including the down lead, will be found sufficient, but if found to be too long, it can be reduced. If possible, suspend the wire between two rafters as far apart as possible, in order to keep the wire from touching masses of woodwork. The down lead to the set can usually be run outside by drilling a hole under the roof at a point immediately above the window of the room where the radio receiver is situated. In order to keep the down lead from touching the wall, a piece of wood about 12 in. long, having an insulated screw-eye, can be fixed in a joint in the brickwork, as shown in Fig. 7. The earth lead is connected to the set, taken through the window and joined to the earth-tube in the usual way.

Satisfactory results are sometimes obtained by running an insulated wire round the back of a picture rail, using insulated staples to keep the wire in position, as illustrated in Fig. 8, but its efficiency is very much lower than that of an outdoor aerial or one fitted in an attic. This is due to a screening effect which greatly reduces its capabilities of "picking up" long-distance transmissions, and it should therefore only be employed where conditions preclude the use of a better aerial.

Certain precautions should be taken when installing a radio receiver. In the case of a mains set just received from the makers, the printed instructions which are invariably sent out with the apparatus should be carefully read and carried out to the letter. Under no consideration whatever must the set be connected to the mains until all internal and external connections have been made and checked, and the back of the receiver replaced. Great care should be taken to see that the valves are placed in their correct valve-holders and if the

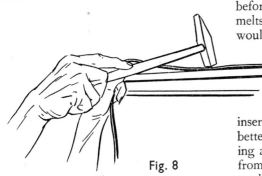

Fig. 8

set is of the alternating current type, to make sure that the mains transformer is connected to suit the voltage of supply. This is necessary because the majority of modern alternating current receivers are fitted with a tapped mains transformer, the primary or input winding of which is tapped at certain intervals to suit the voltage of the mains. As the majority of supply voltages in these days are between 200 and 240 volts, three tappings are usually available, namely, 200, 220 and 240 volts respectively. If the supply pressure lies between the voltages marked on the terminal plate, the connecting plug should be inserted into the one of higher value. Thus, if the supply voltage is 230 volts, the 240-volt tapping would be used; similarly if 210 volts is the mains pressure the lead would be plugged into the 220-volt socket. Reference to the diagram in Fig. 9 will make this clear.

Another very important point refers to the use of a power plug for obtaining the mains current in order to operate

the receiver. The normal use of such a plug is for operating apparatus taking a comparatively heavy current as, for instance, an electric stove. As the current taken by a wireless receiver is very much less than that necessary to work a stove, it follows that should a fault occur in the set or in the connecting leads a very large current will flow before the safety-fuse of the circuit melts. This current in all probability would be large enough to damage the set badly by burning out the mains transformer, if nothing worse. It is therefore of the greatest importance to see that suitably sized fuses are inserted either in the connecting leads or, better still, a special fuse-point box, costing about 2/6, fitted at the side, looped from the power plug and feeding a smaller switch-plug to which the supply lead of the set is connected, as shown in Fig. 10, and in the wiring diagram, Fig. 11. A lighting plug is generally fused— or ought to be fused—up to carry a much smaller current than that of a power plug, and, although a smaller current would flow, should a fault occur, it is far wiser to spend a shilling or two on a proper safety device than run the risk of ruining a costly set. However, the majority of manufacturers now fit fuses inside their mains sets to guard against trouble of this kind.

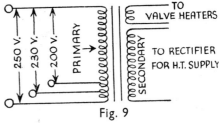

Fig. 9

Having satisfied yourself on these points, the aerial and earth can be connected up to their respective terminals, the current switched on, the set

Fig. 10

tuned to the wavelength of the desired station and the volume control adjusted to give the desired degree of sound.

Do not be surprised if the instrument does not respond immediately after having switched on the current. A slight delay of a few seconds is quite normal and is due to the fact that the cathodes of mains-operated valves—with a few exceptions—being indirectly heated, take some little time to warm up and do their work.

A Battery-operated Set is perhaps a little more complicated to connect up than a mains set as there are usually two dry batteries and an accumulator to install, apart from placing the valves into their respective holders.

The current for heating the filaments of the valves is commonly derived from an accumulator, which, of course, must be filled with sulphuric acid and charged before its current is available. A high-tension battery, usually of about 120 volts, is needed for supplying the plates or anodes of the valves with a high-tension positive charge. The amount of current taken from this battery is very small and is regulated by the fluctuating current of the grid of the valve. A small battery termed a grid battery is employed to give a small negative charge to the grid of the valve, thus also influencing

the amount of current drawn from the high-tension battery.

Fig. 12 shows an illustration of a high-tension battery with its outside wrapper removed. It will be observed that it consists of a number of small dry cells of the Leclanché type, connected up in series to obtain the necessary voltage. The tops of certain cells are provided with a plug socket to enable various voltages to be obtained. This is necessary because the plate voltage varies with different types of valves; for instance, a detector valve usually requires a pressure of about 60 volts, while a power valve generally needs at least 120 volts.

Unfortunately, high-tension batteries of the dry cell type cannot be re-charged, which necessitates their replacement when exhausted.

When connecting up a battery-operated set for the first time, proceed as follows: First connect up the high-tension battery and then the grid bias

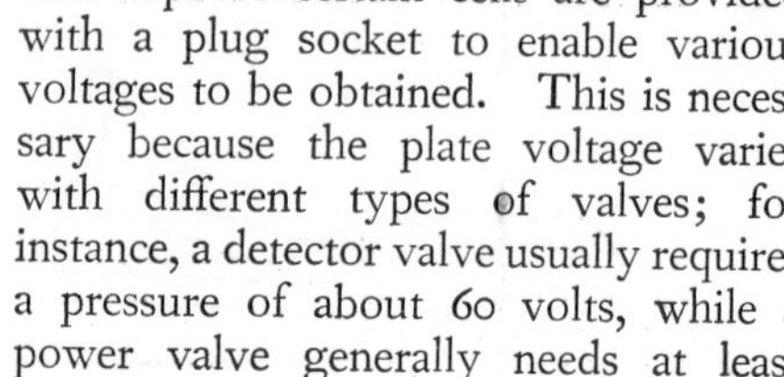

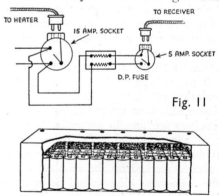

Fig. 11

battery, taking particular care that the connecting plugs are inserted into their correct sockets. The leads connecting these batteries are usually labelled showing the correct voltage, or sometimes they are distinguished by differently coloured plugs, the colours of which are indicated in the instruction chart.

Fig. 12

Next connect a fully charged 2-volt accumulator, but do not insert the valves at this stage, as it is a wise precaution to test the valve-holders in order to make sure that the connections have been properly made. The test can be easily accomplished with the aid of a 2-volt flash-lamp bulb and a miniature holder, both of which can be obtained for an outlay of about sixpence. Connect two insulated wires to the terminals of the lampholder and insert the bulb. Switch on the set and insert the free ends of the wires into the filament sockets of the first valve-holder, as shown in Fig. 13. If the wires have been connected up properly the test bulb should light normally and "go out" when switched off by the controlling switch. Test each valve-

Fig. 13

holder in turn by the same method and, if correct, further operations may continue, but if no light is forthcoming when the switch is in the "on" position, check over the connecting leads, when

it will generally be found that a mistake has been made by cross-connecting them. If all is found correct, switch off the filament current, draw out the high-tension positive plugs, insert the valves and re-insert the plugs.

It sometimes happens that the owner of a battery-operated radio set removes

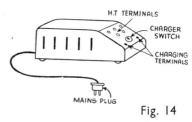

Fig. 14

to a house in which a supply of mains current is available and wishes to work his set from this source in order to eliminate the inconvenience of having to send the accumulator away at frequent intervals to be re-charged, and also to obviate the necessity of purchasing a new high-tension battery from time to time. If the set is of a fairly modern type and is in a satisfactory condition it is well worth while to install a combined high-tension eliminator and trickle charger, an illustration of which appears in Fig. 14. If, however, the set is very much out of date, it will be better to sell the old set for what it will fetch, and purchase a new one.

The use of a high-tension battery eliminator in no way interferes with the internal parts of the receiver other than the removal of the high-tension battery.

High-Tension Battery Eliminators can be obtained for use with alternating and direct current, but before purchasing a direct-current instrument it is a wise plan to find out whether the supply is likely to be changed over to alternating current in accordance with the new "grid" system of electrical distribution. Assuming that an alternating current

H.T. eliminator is required, several things will have to be specified in order to obtain an instrument suitable for the receiver. First there is the voltage and the periodicity of the current. These particulars may be found by consulting the label on the supply meter, or failing this, by inquiring at the Supply Company's office. The output of the eliminator must also be stated as this will vary according to the type of set and the number of valves. An output of about 12–15 milliamperes will generally be found sufficient for operating the average three-valve set. Such an eliminator should have at least three tappings, one for the screened grid valve and a second for the detector, giving about 60–80 volts, and a third giving from 120 – 150 volts for the output valve. If in doubt, take the set to a qualified radio engineer who will, no doubt, put you right on these points.

As the plates or anodes of the valves must be supplied with a unidirectional current and not an alternating one, either a valve or a metal rectifier is incorporated in the eliminator to convert the output current of the transformer into a unidirectional one. Before the rectified current is available for use, however, it passes through a filter circuit which smoothes the current and renders it suitable for operating the valves.

An H.T. battery eliminator incorporating a trickle charger is generally of the metal rectifying type and has an additional rectifier for supplying the accumulator-charging current.

The High-tension Leads of the receiver are connected up in the same way as those for connecting up a high-tension battery, while the ordinary type of grid battery is usually employed, as such a battery will generally give satisfactory service for about nine months. The positive and negative leads of the charger are connected to the positive and negative terminals of the accumulator respectively. A plug or a lamp socket adaptor is attached to the input terminals of the eliminator, which, when inserted into a plug socket or lampholder, connects the instrument to the supply.

A switch controls the charging circuit, cutting off the charging current when the set is in use, and connecting it for charging purposes when the set is switched off.

As the charging current of such an eliminator is usually only about $\frac{1}{4}$ ampere and the current required for heating the valves of an average 3-valve set is about $\frac{1}{2}$ ampere, it follows that the accumulator must be charged for at least double the period of time the set is in use, to which must be added extra time to allow for the inefficiency of the cell. Thus a 3-valve receiver, having been in use, say, for 4 hours, should have its accumulator on charge for at least 10 hours to bring it up to its normal capacity.

The owner of a charger of this description will find it pays to send the accumulator to a local charging station about every three months to have the specific gravity of the acid tested and adjusted, and a good charge given at its normal rate of charge.

Many battery-operated receivers fitted with the old type of balanced armature loud-speakers can be improved by substituting a moving-coil speaker of the permanent magnet type, an illustration of which is shown in Fig. 15. The reproduction obtained from these speakers is practically perfect, and they can be obtained at a reasonable figure.

In this type of speaker, a low resistance speech-coil is attached to the diaphragm or cone and its movement is regulated by the current flowing in the coil and the intense magnetic field across the air

Fig. 15

the skirting of the wall. Fig. 17 shows a circuit diagram of such an arrangement, and, as will be seen from it, all plugs are connected in parallel and fed from a master-plug. This plug should be fixed · in a convenient position on the skirting as near to the output terminals of the set as possible.

The removal of the floorboards is quite a simple matter and can be undertaken by anyone handy with carpenters' tools. The lead-covered cable, consisting of two separate insulated wires of 20-gauge tinned copper, should be clipped up to the joists with buckle clips or the joists bored and the cable threaded through the holes, as the case may be. In order to save wire a special junction-box, as used for electric lighting installations, can be used to advantage, and the wires connected by means of china-

gap. Owing to the comparatively low resistance of the speech-coil a, suitable transformer is necessary. The primary winding is wound to match the output valve and the secondary winding to match the impedance of the speech-coil. A suitable transformer with tapped primary windings to suit a power, a super-power and a pentode valve is usually included with the unit. All that is necessary is to connect up a suitable pair of transformer terminals to the output terminals of the set, as illustrated in the diagram, Fig. 16.

It frequently happens that a loud-speaker is required to operate in a room other than that in which the receiver is installed. A temporary expedient would be to connect up a suitable length of insulated flexible wire to the output terminals of the set and the speaker terminals. This arrangement has many disadvantages, the chief of which is its liability to kink and soon wear out.

The best way to operate a loud-speaker in other rooms is to install a proper circuit, consisting of cable run under the floorboards and connected to a number of standard-sized plugs fixed on

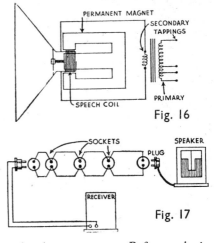

Fig. 16

Fig. 17

insulated connectors. Before relaying the floorboards, the lead-covered sheathing should be efficiently earthed by connecting it to a main cold-water pipe. The cost of the material is not excessive, twin lead-covered wire costing about 4d. per yard junction-boxes, 1/–; and plugs in the neighbourhood of 1/6, all of which can generally be obtained at the local electrical stores.

Two separate wires without a lead cover are better for speaker extension from the point of view of reproduction, but many people like to have lead-covered wire when it is to go beneath floorboards and out of sight.

Like all other apparatus of a similar nature, wireless sets and their components are not immune from faults which are almost bound to occur sooner or later.

Much annoyance will be obviated and money saved if simple faults can be located and remedied by the owner. With this object in view, the amateur radio enthusiast cannot do better than invest in one of the many little inexpensive testing instruments that are to be had from most electrical stores. For

Fig. 18

an outlay of 12/6 an efficient testing instrument, as that shown in Fig. 18, can be obtained. Such an instrument consists of a low- and a high-reading voltmeter, a milliameter, while a miniature dry cell fitted in the body of the meter enables valves and other components to be tested.

The most likely faults to occur in a wireless receiver are those which cause the complete failure of the set to respond

to signals, falling-off of volume and intermittent and noisy reception.

In the event of a total cessation of signals, the trouble may be due to a fault in the aerial system, in the set itself, including the loud-speaker and batteries, or in the connecting leads.

The first thing to do in this case is to see whether the set is "alive" or not. This may be ascertained by switching on the filament current and pulling out the high-tension positive or negative plug and just touching the socket with the plug. If a distinct "plop" is heard in the loud-speaker it may be taken that the set is functioning normally and that the fault is in the aerial. Test the aerial and earth system for breaks, short-circuits and bad connections. It may be that the earthing device is making bad contact, or that the earth lead has come adrift from the connecting terminal of the earth-tube.

In the event of the receiver being absolutely dead, first look to the high-tension fuse, if fitted, and if found in order, make sure that the accumulator is not below 2 volts when the filaments are switched on. If necessary, replace it with a freshly-charged one. Possibly the ends of the leads connecting the accumulator are dirty, or the accumulator terminals are in a like state. If this is so, thoroughly scrape the ends of the leads, or the accumulator terminals, or both, as the case may be. Assuming the connecting leads, including those of the high-tension battery, etc., are in order and that the voltages of the high-tension and grid batteries are normal, try the loud-speaker leads for short-circuits, breaks and faulty connections. If possible borrow a loud-speaker and substitute this. If the loaned speaker works, the defect obviously lies in your speaker. As it is not always possible to obtain a second speaker, the suspected

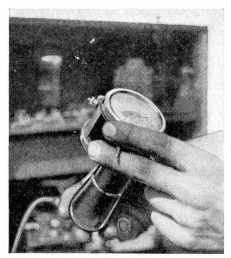

Fig. 19

pointer moves on the scale on the front. A movement of the pointer shows that the filament is intact, while no such movement indicates a broken filament. Note the type of the defective valve and replace. Fig. 19 shows the operation of testing a valve.

The next test consists in examining and testing the continuity of the internal wiring. Examine the switch carefully as this component is a common source of breakdown. Clean the contacts, make sure that the switch is making proper contact and adjust if necessary. Then go over all the wiring and test for continuity from point to point, making sure that all terminals are perfectly tight and making proper contact with the wires under them. Do not omit to test all soldered joints with the fingers, because it sometimes happens that a soldered connection, although appear-

one can be tested by momentarily connecting it in series with four or six volts of the high-tension battery and a pair of headphones. If no sound is forthcoming when the circuit is made and broken, it can be assumed that there is a break in the windings, in which case the loud-speaker should be sent to the makers for repair.

Test the Valves next, in order to ascertain whether the filaments are intact. With the filament current switched off and the high-tension leads removed from the battery sockets, take out the valves from their respective holders. To do this, grasp the lower portion of the valve and not the glass, otherwise the two may part company. The valves should be plainly marked so that they can be replaced into their correct holders. As the bases of valves cannot usually be marked distinctly owing to their glazed black surface, gummed paper will overcome this difficulty.

Assuming that a test meter, as suggested in the earlier part of this article, is to hand, place each valve in turn into the sockets provided at the back of the instrument and observe whether the

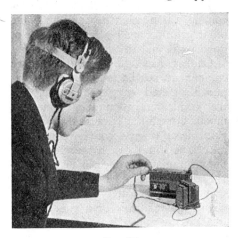

Fig. 20

ing in order by visual examination, proves otherwise when tested mechanically.

Assuming that all the internal wiring is as it should be, the other components should be tested. Try the transformer first, as this item is frequently a source of trouble, especially the primary winding, which consists of thousands of turns of extremely fine wire, scarcely thicker than a hair. An easy method of testing a transformer is to connect a pair of wireless headphones in series with the high-tension battery plugged up to about 10 volts, as illustrated in Fig. 20. If a distinct click is heard on touching one of the terminals with the free end of a connecting wire, it may be taken that the transformer is in order. On the other hand, a burnt-out transformer

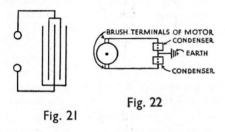

Fig. 21

Fig. 22

is indicated when no sound is forthcoming. If nothing happens scrap the old transformer and replace it with one of good make and of the same ratio.

Chokes and other high-resistance components can be tested by the headphone method suggested above, but the condensers require a somewhat modified treatment because they do not pass direct current between their terminals, as will be seen by referring to the diagrammatic sketch in Fig. 21.

Should a reading be observed when a voltmeter and battery are connected across the terminals of a condenser it indicates a short-circuit, and if the condenser is of the fixed type it should be discarded and a new one of the same value substituted. Besides short-circuits, condensers are likely to become leaky, that is, they will not hold their charge for any appreciable length of time. Fixed condensers of a comparatively high capacity, say, from ·01 microfarad upwards, can be tested for leakage by first charging up the plates by means

of the high-tension battery, leaving the condenser in this state for a few seconds and then placing the free ends of the headphone leads across the terminals. This causes the condenser to discharge and impart a pronounced click in the headphones. If no such click is heard it shows that the charge has leaked away and that the condenser is therefore useless. In the event of a small fixed condenser being suspected as defective, the best thing is to substitute a new one.

One of the chief causes of lack of volume and distortion is a run-down high-tension battery. The battery should be tested with a high-reading voltmeter and if found more than about 30 per cent. below its normal voltage, the old battery should be replaced with a new one. Another cause of lack of volume and of distortion can often be traced to a run-down grid battery—a necessary item which is often overlooked. It is a wise plan to fit a new grid battery every second or third time a new high-tension battery is installed, as a worn-out grid battery tends to drain the larger one.

Poorness of quality of reproduction is often occasioned by the loss of efficiency of one or more valves. This defect applies particularly to radio receivers that have been in commission for some considerable time. The obvious remedy for this failing is to replace the valve or valves with new ones. When purchasing new valves, always obtain those of well-known British manufacture and do not begrudge the small extra cost asked for a good article, especially radio valves, which form the heart of a radio receiver.

Much annoyance is frequently caused when listening-in by various objectionable noises, such as crackles, hisses, whistles, etc., which are emitted from the loud-speaker. Atmospherics or, as they are sometimes called, "static," are responsible for a great deal of crackling noise and are due to atmospheric disturb-

THE FASCINATING MECHANISM OF RADIO

ances which charge up the aerial and discharge to earth via the set. Atmospherics are more prevalent during the summer months—particularly during thundery weather—than in the winter and are usually predominant on the long-wave band rather than the short. A practised ear can usually detect atmospherics by their intermittent hiss and crackle. Another type of static—commonly known as "man-made" static—is generally caused by nearby electrical machinery, such as a motor dynamo, or it may even be due to a vacuum-cleaner being used by a neighbour.

Crackling Noises.— To ascertain whether these are due to outside interference, simply disconnect the aerial lead from the receiver. If the noises cease on doing this, it proves that the interference is not caused by any defect within the set.

Unfortunately, noise due to atmospheric disturbances cannot be cured, but static caused by an electric motor or a dynamo can be greatly reduced, if not entirely eliminated, by connecting two large-capacity condensers in series across the brushes of the machine and making an earth connection between the two condensers, as shown in the diagram, Fig. 22.

Whistling Noises and shrieks are often caused by a nearby neighbour fooling about with his old-fashioned set and allowing it to get into oscillation. If this annoyance persists and the owner of the offending set can be traced, a few friendly but firm words will generally put matters right.

Noises traced to defects within the set may be due to faulty components, etc. A run-down high-tension battery is a frequent source of intermittent cracklings, or even the gas-bubbles from a freshly-charged accumulator may be found guilty. A faulty transformer will also produce unpleasant crackling noises in the loud-speaker, as will dirt and dust between the plates of a variable condenser.

The same method of procedure for tracing simple faults can be applied to mains receivers, except, of course, that battery troubles are dispensed with.

Do not fall into the more or less common trap of spending a considerable time in trying to trace a defect in the set, only to find in the end that you have forgotten to switch the current on.

When testing the internal parts of a mains receiver always disconnect it from the supply, otherwise you may receive a dangerous shock. Finally, if it is necessary to disconnect any internal wires, always mark them so that they can be easily refixed in their correct places.

HOUSE DECORATION AND REPAIR

DISTEMPERING

HOME decorating offers a pleasant and profitable occupation to the practical man who has a few odd hours at his disposal. Those readers who have not yet "tried their hand" at decorating are advised to start operations on a small scale by working on a more or less unimportant room, such as a small bedroom, before attempting anything more ambitious. By so doing a great deal of valuable experience will be gained in handling tools and in the general scheme of operations.

Preliminary Decisions.—When the entire redecoration of a room is contemplated, it is as well to consider one or two points before actually starting the work. For instance, the addition of a picture rail, if not already fitted, greatly improves the general appearance of a room as it tends to make the apartment look larger. Also, a sunk switch with a neat flat cover plate (as shown in Fig. 1) could be fitted with advantage, to replace an unsightly projecting one. All such things as these should be definitely decided upon so that the necessary work can be put in hand and other operations followed in proper sequence.

When all these points have been settled and assuming that the room under discussion is to be entirely redecorated, that is, the ceiling to be distempered, the walls papered or colour washed and the woodwork, etc., to be painted, the initial operation consists in washing off the old distemper from the ceiling and then removing the old distemper or the paper from the walls.

As it is almost impossible to carry out the numerous operations without a certain amount of splashing, the first thing to do is to remove all furniture and other articles into another room for the time being. This will not only

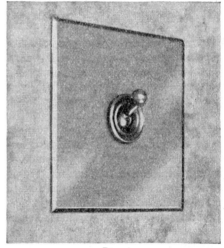

Fig. 1

prevent damage to the furniture but will enable the work to be carried out comfortably without loss of time and temper and save the laborious task of having to shift the articles to a new position every few minutes. If this suggestion cannot be fulfilled in its entirety, the contents not removed should be carefully protected with dust sheets, or old newspapers conveniently pinned together to form large "sheets."

The Tools necessary for preparing the ceiling include an old distemper brush as in Fig. 2 for washing off the old distemper—a new one should never be used for this purpose, otherwise it will be ruined—a bucket of clean water, preferably warm, decorator's sponge, two pairs of good steps and a strong scaffold-board.

As it is unusual to find two pairs of steps in the average household equipment it is very often possible to borrow a pair, while a suitable scaffold-board can generally be hired from a builder.

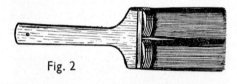

Fig. 2

It may be asked why two pairs of steps and a scaffold-board are necessary. The answer is that greater comfort in working is obtained than by working from a single pair of steps and much wearisome labour is also saved.

If an extra pair of steps and a scaffold board are not available, then the alternative is to use a high box on which to stand the bucket and work from a single pair of steps. Assuming that the scaffold board arrangement is used, the board should be placed at a convenient height across the opened steps.

Washing the Ceiling.—Having donned an old suit or a pair of overalls and an old cap, the operation of washing off the ceiling may be proceeded with. Start at one end of the room. Place the bucket of water at your side and dip the brush into the water and, using the least amount of water possible, apply it to the ceiling with the brush held edgewise. When an area of about a square yard has been treated go over it again from the starting point, this time rubbing vigorously. This will gradually

soften the distemper and render it more or less plastic. It is then removed by applying more water and well rinsing the brush. Go over this two or three times if necessary and then wipe the surface perfectly clean, using a damp sponge for the purpose. Continue the process, step by step, until the whole ceiling has been washed perfectly clean, not forgetting to change the dirty water as many times as are necessary. When finished it is a wise plan to survey the ceiling to satisfy yourself that the whole of the distemper has been removed. If any remains, clean it off at once, before it is forgotten, otherwise the surface of the new wash will be unsatisfactory.

Mending Cracks.—For this you will require a small quantity of plaster of Paris or some Keene's cement, which is a pinkish powder, obtainable at most oil-shops; a small bricklayer's trowel, costing about sixpence at one of the cheap stores; and a "hawk" on which to place the stopping. The latter consists of a flat piece of wood fitted with a handle, as shown in Fig. 3. This handy device can be made almost as quickly as it takes to write about it by merely nailing a flat piece of planed wood about 7 in. square by $\frac{5}{8}$ in. thick to a piece of broom-handle or a short length of 1-in. by 1-in. batten with its sharp edges removed.

With the hawk held in the left hand, place a small quantity of the plaster in the centre of it to form a mound. Make a crater in the centre, using the point of the trowel for the purpose and then pour a small quantity of water into the depression. Gradually work the point of the trowel round the crater until the whole of the plaster assumes a plastic mass of about the consistency of very thick cream.

The plaster must be applied to the cracks immediately after being made, as it dries off very quickly and is then useless.

To apply the stopping, moisten the brush with water and run it along the cracks, as plaster will not adhere permanently to a dry surface. Now take a

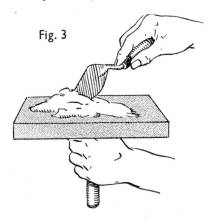

Fig. 3

small quantity of stopping from the hawk by inserting the point of the trowel with its bottom face up and press it firmly into the crack, as indicated in Fig. 4. Smooth it down evenly with the trowel and remove any surplus.

Old cracks which have been previously stopped should be tested to see that the stopping is tight. If loose, the old stopping should be entirely removed and refilled afresh. In dealing with wide cracks, the ceiling plaster should be undercut a trifle with the point of the trowel to form a dovetail or key for the new stopping.

The ceiling must now be allowed to dry thoroughly, a process which will be hastened by opening the door and window if the weather is favourable or by lighting a fire if the outside atmosphere is damp.

Sizing.—This operation is necessary because the ceiling is now in a very porous state and unless the condition is reduced to a minimum the water in the distemper to be applied later will be absorbed almost as soon as it is put on.

The size solution is made by dissolving $\frac{1}{2}$ lb. concentrated powdered size in $\frac{1}{2}$ gal. of hot water. A small quantity of distemper—just enough to colour the solution—can be added to advantage as it enables the otherwise colourless liquid to be easily seen and therefore helps to prevent any portion of the ceiling from being missed when applied.

The solution should be applied hot and it should be spread evenly over the surface to be covered, taking great care not to miss any portion of the surface, otherwise an unsightly, patchy appearance will result after the distemper has been put on.

Distemper.—The home decorator has the choice of either buying the distemper ready made or mixing up the wash himself. The former method is to be recommended as it is both cheap and of excellent quality, especially if it is one of the well-known proprietary brands. Those who prefer to make up their own material, however, will find the following mixture gives good results and will make sufficient distemper for covering a surface of approximately 80 sq. ft.

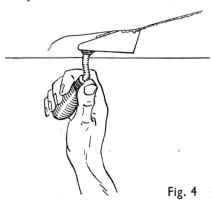

Fig. 4

Obtain the following ingredients which may be bought from an oil-shop: 7 lb. of whitening, $1\frac{3}{4}$ lb. of powdered size and $\frac{1}{2}$ oz. of ultramarine blue. The addition of the blue is to improve the colour which would otherwise be a yellowish-white.

Break the whitening into small fragments, place them in a clean bucket and add sufficient water to cover. Allow it to soak for at least twelve hours. Draw off the water and thoroughly stir the mixture with a stick, or knead it well with the hands, and then add the blue in liquid form by mixing it with a small quantity of water. Place the powdered size into a saucepan, add water according to the instructions printed on the label and heat it up sufficiently, but do not let it boil. Mix the hot size to the whitening and add sufficient water until the resultant mixture assumes the consistency of thick cream and then strain it through muslin to remove all lumps. This is important.

As good results cannot be obtained from freshly made distemper, it is a good plan to let it stand in a cool place for at least twelve hours before it is applied to the ceiling, not forgetting to cover it up to exclude dust, grit and other foreign matter. At the end of this period, the distemper, if properly made, will have become jellified, and to it a suitable quantity of water must be added to enable it to be worked.

Applying the Distemper.—For this you will require a good quality two-knot distemper brush as shown at Fig. 2. When purchasing such a brush do not choose a cheap one as they are usually far from satisfactory. It is a much better policy to pay a little more for a good article because the extra outlay is more than justified by knowing that it will give years of good service, provided, of course, that it is properly looked after. A new brush should never be used until it has been allowed to soak in water for a few hours.

Before starting the actual distempering, make up your mind where you propose to start, bearing in mind that it is always best to work across the narrowest part of the ceiling, and from the back towards the window.

Having mounted the platform formed by the board across the steps, and with the bucket of distemper in a convenient position, load the brush by dipping the tip into the wash and apply it quickly to the ceiling. Avoid painting it on, but slap it on as the professional does, with bold even strokes applied in all directions; that is, to and fro and across. When a small section of the surface has been covered, shift your position and carry on in the same way with another portion, joining each section whilst the surface is wet, as the work proceeds. Make sure that no part of the ceiling is missed, as the fault cannot be rectified when the surface is dry.

A common fault with most beginners is that they overload the brush, with the result that the liquid runs down the handle of the brush and not infrequently up the sleeve of the worker. The remedy for this is obvious; do not dip the brush too deeply into the distemper. If the brush becomes overloaded, remove the surplus by drawing the tool across the edge of the bucket.

Distempering Walls.—The amateur decorator has the choice of two distinct kinds of colour wash with which to decorate his walls, namely, ordinary size-distemper of the same constituents as that used for the ceiling and the washable variety.

Ordinary size-distemper is unsuitable for covering the walls of living-rooms and its use is generally confined to such places as coal-cellars, outhouses and the like. Its great disadvantage lies in the fact that it easily rubs off and cannot be washed. Size-distemper used for covering walls should have a larger proportion of size incorporated with the whiting than whitewash to render it of a more durable quality.

This kind of distemper is applied to the walls in the same way as it is applied to ceilings and as this has already been explained there is no need to recapitulate.

Water-paint or washable distemper should always be used in living-rooms for reasons already stated and if one coat is found insufficient to cover the surface of the walls efficiently, another coat may be easily applied after the first one has been allowed to dry. Another feature about washable distemper from the practical point of view is that it is easier to apply than size-distemper because it does not dry so rapidly.

There are numerous excellent proprietary brands of water-paint to be had which are usually stocked by shops dealing in decorating materials. Some of these paints are in powder form and sold in packets, while others are in the form of a paste contained in tin cans; all of them are inexpensive although, of course, a little more costly than ordinary size-distemper. In some cases water only is needed to make the paint ready for use, while others require the addition of a special petrifying liquid. Whatever kind of water-paint is decided upon the instructions are usually to be found on the container and these must always be strictly adhered to.

Preparing the Walls.—In cases where the walls to be treated have a previous coat of size-distemper, the whole of it must be removed in the same manner as that already described for removing old distemper from a ceiling. When the surface is perfectly clean and dry, stop up any holes and other defects and apply a coat of size to stop the pores, then allow it to dry. The water-paint can then be applied.

A wall which has previously been water-painted should, if in good condition, be thoroughly washed with soap and hot water and should the new colour be of a different tint, a coat of size should precede the water-paint to prevent the colours running.

Washable distemper can be applied to a papered wall, although it is not usual unless the paper is in very good condition. If the paper is not too badly damaged, any little tears and other blemishes should be repaired and loose pieces stuck down. This treatment should be followed by a good coat of size which, once dry, the surface is ready.

Generally a much more satisfactory job is obtained by entirely stripping off the old paper from the walls. The extra time spent on this process is well repaid and is not time lost. Instructions

Fig. 5

for stripping will be found under the heading of PAPERHANGING.

When the walls are entirely bared of paper all defects in the surface should be made good with either Keene's cement or plaster of Paris. After making good has been completed and allowed to dry thoroughly it is a wise precaution to give the repaired parts a thin coat of thin ordinary oil paint of the same tint as that of the water-paint, followed, when dry, with a coat of size solution over the entire surface.

Applying the Distemper.—Having mixed the distemper according to the maker's instructions the work of applying the water-paint may be proceeded with by using a perfectly clean brush— the tool used for the ceiling will do.

The best place to start is at the top of a corner of the room, working downwards towards the skirting. Cover a section of about 18 in. wide at a time. If you cannot conveniently reach to the top without undue stretching, stand on a box or an old chair, for there is no need to work uncomfortably. Load the brush fairly full but not excessively, by dipping it into the wash, and then flow it over the surface, using the tip of the brush only in long vertical strokes. When one section is completed, start on the second and so on until one side is finished. Then start on the others and proceed in the same way.

Stippling.—A very much better finish will be obtained and all brush marks eliminated by stippling the surface of the wet distemper. Stippling consists of dabbing the wet surface with a special brush, known as a stippling brush. Such a brush (Fig. 5) is provided with short coarse bristles and an arched handle. The tool is manipulated by simply dabbing it lightly on the surface in short pronounced "taps" which leave impressions of the bristles and incidentally obliterate the brush marks.

The best way to carry out the stippling is to cover a wall at a time and then stipple the whole surface. Care must be taken to wipe the brush from time to time as the stippling proceeds to prevent it becoming clogged.

If a stippling brush is not available, excellent results can be obtained by

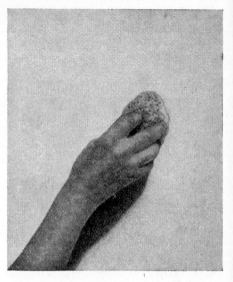

Fig. 6

carefully using a sponge as a substitute, as indicated in Fig. 6. Charming effects can be produced by sponge stippling, first applying a background coat of any desired colour and then dabbing the sponge on the wet surface of the final coat, which should be of a colour to harmonise with the background. In doing this the flat face of the sponge should be patted gently but firmly on the wall, care being taken not to twist or turn the sponge as this would mar the surface and spoil the effect.

PAPERHANGING

WHERE paper is the chosen medium for decorating the walls of a room, the paperhanging should follow after the ceiling is finished and one or more coats of paint have been applied to the woodwork. The finishing coat can then be applied after the paperhanging is completed.

Although new wallpaper can be hung on top of old paper, it is a very much better plan entirely to strip off the old material and start afresh by hanging the paper on clean, bare walls. The little extra time and labour involved in stripping the walls is more than compensated by the satisfaction of knowing that a perfectly sanitary job will result.

Materials and Tools.—For carrying out a paperhanging job you will require, besides a sufficient quantity of paper, a few tools and miscellaneous items, a selection of which appears in the illustration (Fig. 1).

The list includes a stripping knife for removing the old paper. This is shown at A and can be purchased for about 6d. at any of the cheap stores. A pair of paperhanger's scissors (B), preferably those having 12 in. blades, will be required for trimming the paper. If this item is considered an unnecessary expense, the alternative is to use the largest pair of household scissors you have, bearing in mind that the larger the scissors used the straighter the trimming will be.

A special shaped brush (as that shown at C) is necessary for smoothing down the paper on the walls. This is an inexpensive accessory and the expenditure of a shilling or two on this tool is money well spent. If put to it, a soft clothes brush could be used, but this is not advised.

A small rubber roller, about an inch or so wide, is useful for rolling the seams. Such a roller is seen at D. A flat brush about 6 in. wide, illustrated at E, is used for applying the paste.

The remaining items consist of a 2 ft. rule (F) for measuring, a plumb line (G), and piece of coloured chalk, a supply of paste and a pair of steps.

A kitchen table may be used as a support when pasting the paper, but a much better and more convenient arrangement is to have a proper lightweight trestle board as shown in Fig. 2, especially if several rooms are to be decorated. Such a board can easily be constructed in a very short time by using three 6-ft. lengths of 8-in. by $\frac{5}{8}$-in. planed boards held together with battens screwed to the underside and supported by a pair of legs at each end. The legs can be made of 2-in. by 1-in. battens strengthened by cross battens near the feet and fixed to the top pieces by means of screws, the legs being kept from spreading apart by light cords, as indicated in the sketch. This arrangement has the great advantage that it allows the board to be easily transported from place to place as required and also to be conveniently stored until needed again.

Choice of Paper.—Probably the most difficult part of the whole process of redecorating a room is that of selecting a suitable paper, and as this is a matter of individual taste the choice must be left to the discretion of the people concerned. At the outset it is well to remember that the colour of the paper should blend with the immediate surroundings such as the paint, furnish-

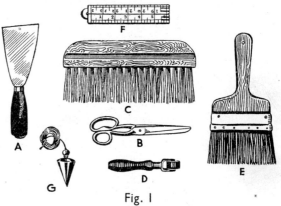

Fig. 1

ings, etc., and further, that a large pattern tends to make a room look smaller, while a smaller figured paper has the opposite effect.

Where practicable always choose a bright coloured paper in preference to a dark one, as a dark paper is not only depressing but its reflecting power is small.

It is a good plan to pay a visit to one of the numerous shops to be found in almost every town, who specialise in wallpapers. Here the paper can be chosen from a roll and a good idea obtained of the finished effect by un-rolling a portion and holding it up to a wall. This method is much to be preferred to the old-fashioned and un-satisfactory way of choosing a pattern from a sample book.

Always get as good a paper as your pocket will allow, because cheap papers

Fig. 2

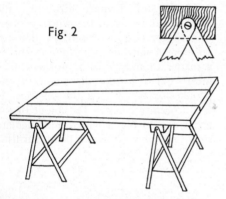

will not give such good service as those that cost a little more, besides which, a cheap paper is generally of the thinnest nature and difficult to hang.

Wallpaper is sold at so much per piece or roll. Most English papers are supplied in rolls of 12 yds. or 36 ft. in length and 22 in. wide, which includes two plain edges or selvedges $\frac{1}{2}$ in. wide, to allow for trimming. French papers are smaller than the British standard and are usually 9 yds. in length and only 18 in. wide. As there is such an excellent selection of British papers to choose from in these days, there is little need to revert to foreign makes.

Calculations.—To ascertain the number of rolls required for papering

the walls of a room, all that is necessary is to measure its height in feet from the top of the skirting to the bottom of the picture rail, or the ceiling if the room is devoid of a picture rail, adding three extra inches at the top and bottom for waste and then calculate the number of 21 in. widths that will go round the walls. Obviously the total length required will be the product of the number of widths multiplied by the length, and if the result is divided by 36—the number of feet in a roll—the result will be the number of rolls required. For example, in a room 14 ft. long, 10 ft. wide and say 7 ft. 6 in. from the top of the skirting to the bottom of the picture rail, the total measurement round the room including the door, window, etc., is $(14 \times 2) + (10 \times 2)$ ft. $= 48$ ft. or $48 \times 12 = 576$ in. From this measurement, the space occupied by the door and window must be deducted, which, allowing 8 ft. or 96 in. for this, will give a total of $576 - 96 = 480$ in. This result divided by 21 gives the number of strips, which in this instance is $\frac{480}{21} = 23$. As the total length of each strip is 8 ft., in-cluding 3 in. at each end for trimming, the number of rolls required will be $\frac{8 \times 23}{36} =$ just over five. To this figure thus obtained you should add at least another roll in every six to allow for unavoidable waste due to matching, etc., and where the pattern chosen is a large one it is a wise plan to allow one extra roll in every four and thus avoid the inconvenience of run-ning short of material whilst the work is in progress.

Stripping.—As previously suggested, before beginning the actual paperhang-ing the old paper should be removed from the walls. To do this you will require an old distemper brush or, failing this, a sponge, also a bucket of warm water and a stripping knife.

Start at a convenient corner by applying a copious supply of warm water with the aid of the brush to soak the paper thoroughly. When sufficient time

Fig. 3

has elapsed to allow the paper to soften, it can be easily scraped off with the aid of the knife. In doing this work it is sometimes advisable to give the whole of the paper a preliminary soaking before attempting to use the stripper. When this method is resorted to, the work can be carried out by stripping a section at a time, first giving the paper another supply of water and following it up with the stripping tool.

The stripper should be held at an angle of about 30° to the surface with its edge flat on the wall as illustrated in Fig. 3, otherwise damage may be caused by the blade digging into the plaster.

If the soaking operation has been properly done, very little effort is needed to remove the paper, which will simply peel off in long narrow strips. In some instances, especially if the

15

paper has been well soaked, it may be possible to remove large pieces without the aid of the stripper.

To remove a varnished paper is a somewhat tedious and unpleasant job as its surface is waterproof, which renders water ineffectual until the surface has been removed. The varnished surface can be removed by brushing the surface vigorously with a stiff wire brush or a piece of file card sold by most ironmongers for cleaning engineers' files. The file card should be fastened to a small block of wood as shown in Fig. 4. In order to prevent an unhealthy dust, it is advisable to use a small quantity of water in conjunction with the brush. When the whole of the primary covering of varnish has been removed, the paper may be dislodged by the usual method of soaking and stripping.

When all traces of the old paper have been entirely displaced, any cracks and other imperfections in the bare plaster should be made good either with Keene's cement or plaster of Paris, as already explained in dealing with distempering a ceiling.

Do not forget that plaster of Paris and Keene's cement do not adhere to dry surfaces, therefore water must be applied to the defective places before the stopping material is used.

When the making good is thoroughly dry, smooth

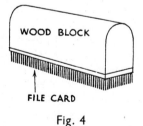

WOOD BLOCK

FILE CARD

Fig. 4

the parts down level with the surface of the plaster, using a piece of fine glass-paper wrapped round a block of wood.

The next step is to give the walls a coat of thin size and water in the proportion of $\frac{1}{4}$ lb. concentrated size to two quarts of water. Put this on evenly and thoroughly without leaving any parts uncovered. Allow the walls to dry before attempting to fix the paper, which is the next process.

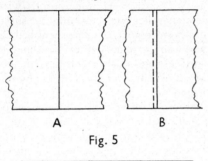

A   B

Fig. 5

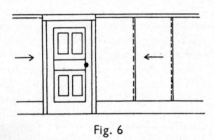

Fig. 6

Trimming.—Before applying the paper to the walls one or both trimming edges must be cut off. Where a thick paper is employed it is customary to remove both selvedges, as the finished edges are butted up to one another when hung, in the manner indicated at A in Fig. 5. In ordinary thin papers it is only necessary to trim one edge, as the prepared edge of one length is lapped over the unprepared edge of the next as shown at B.

Professional paperhangers invariably hang paper in such a way that a person entering the room cannot see the front edges of the paper and, as the novice should always follow the experienced, it is best to start in a corner farthest away from the door and work towards it as the illustration in Fig. 6 shows. This procedure will necessitate the removal of the right-hand edge in some pieces and the left-hand edge in others.

The modern method of trimming wallpaper is to use a little cutting instrument, which, when run along the edge of the paper, removes the waste, but as these desirable instruments are rather expensive to buy, the amateur is generally limited to the use of a pair of scissors. If a pair of paperhanger's scissors is available, so much the better, as a longer and straighter cut can be obtained by their use than that obtained by a short pair.

Fig. 7 shows a convenient method of trimming paper which is a much better way than carrying out the trimming

Fig. 7

operation on a table. To do this, you will require a chair or box to sit on. With your legs stretched out and your heels touching the floor and toes turned up, place the roll across the feet in the manner shown and unroll the paper step by step by pulling the paper towards you with the left hand. This leaves the right hand free to manipulate the scissors. As the cutting proceeds, wind up the paper with the left hand and this will, of course, unroll more paper from the bottom roll.

Pasting.—The paste may either be made up at home or bought ready for mixing. There is an excellent preparation on the market—obtainable at most wallpaper shops—made from rye flour, which only requires the addition of clean cold water. As it is cheap it is hardly worth spending the time preparing your own.

For those who prefer to make their own paste, however, the following recipe will give excellent results. Place half a quartern of wheaten flour in a clean, wide bowl or bucket and add sufficient water to make it into a paste. To this, slowly add boiling water and then place the receptacle over a gas-stove burner until the mixture boils, stirring it well all the time to prevent burning. The paste is ready when it is cold and has been strained through a piece of muslin to remove all lumps. The consistency of the paste must not be too thick otherwise difficulty will be experienced when applying it to the paper. The addition of a small quantity of alum will prevent the mixture from turning sour.

When the necessary preliminaries have been attended to, the paste board fitted up and the requisite tools and paste to hand, the paper may be cut into suitable lengths, pasted and hung on the walls.

Assuming that a plain paper, that is, a paper devoid of pattern, is to be fixed, cut off a length to reach from under the picture rail or cornice, as the case may be, down to the top of the skirting, allowing about 3 in. at each end for trimming after the paper is hung.

When cut, offer the piece up to the wall to verify that no mistake has been made. Now cut as many pieces of a similar length as are necessary for one wall, taking care to cut them square. Next, place a piece face downwards on the table, which, of course, should be perfectly clean, keeping the bottom edge of the paper to the left hand and allowing the surplus length to hang over the right, as pasting is started from the left.

In order to prevent any paste getting on the surface of the table—which would ruin the faces of subsequent pieces of paper—pull the paper forward so that its front edge overlaps the edge of the table by about a ¼ in. The paste is prevented from getting on the back of the table surface by shifting the paper,

Fig. 8

after it has been partially pasted, so that its back edge overlaps the back edge of the table in the same manner as that adopted for the front.

Dip the brush into the paste and apply it evenly to the paper, starting at an inch or so from the left hand edge. Work outwards from the centre, taking care to see that every part is well covered except, of course, a small margin at

Fig. 9

the back which should be pasted after the paper has been shifted to overlap the back edge of the table. When you are satisfied that all is correct, grasp the paper at the left hand edge and carefully fold it over on itself as indicated in Fig. 8, so that the pasted faces stick together lightly. Care must be exercised to see that the narrow edges are not allowed to overlap. This method of folding will facilitate the handling when hanging the paper on the wall. Now pull the pasted portion towards the left to bring the remaining length on the table, allowing the folded part to hang over the left hand edge if necessary. When the remaining section is pasted to within an inch or so of the end, fold it over itself in exactly the same manner as that mentioned above, allowing a small gap of about 3 or 4 in. between the two.

Using the Plumb-line.—It is now necessary to make a perpendicular starting line on the wall where it is proposed to start from, as the walls, especially in old houses, are not always quite vertical and square. For this you will require a plumb-bob and a piece of dark-coloured chalk. Fix the line firmly to the top of the wall by using a small brad or the end of a carpenter's bradawl and rub the string with the chalk. When the line has come to rest—it generally swings to and fro at first—press the bottom end of the string hard against the bottom of the wall, holding it in this position with the left hand. Now grasp the string with the forefinger and thumb of the right hand and pull it gently an inch or so from the wall. If the string is now released quickly it will fly back and leave a distinct line on the wall. Fig. 9 shows clearly how this is accomplished.

Hanging the First Strip.—Have the smoothing brush and scissors close at hand and place the steps in position. Place the folded paper over the left arm or hold it between your outstretched

Fig. 10

hands, whichever is the more convenient, and ascend the steps. Carefully unfold the top section of the strip by holding it at each corner between the forefinger and thumb of each hand and then apply the top of the paper to the under edge of the picture rail so that an inch or so overlaps above the rail. Take care to get it into as correct a position as possible and make sure that the long edge coincides with the marked vertical line. If everything is as it should be, stick the top section down by giving it a few gentle sweeps with the smoothing brush, working from the centre towards the narrow edges.

Now remove the steps and unfold the lower section by holding it away from the wall and gently pulling it. Keep the paper away from the wall by holding the bottom edge with the left hand and gradually brush obliquely across the paper from the top to the bottom, finally releasing the paper a few inches or so before the top of the skirting is reached.

The top and bottom edges of the

Fig. 12

picture rail and the wall, in the manner shown in Fig. 10, taking particular care not to damage the paper when so doing. This will score the paper and leave a distinct mark across it. Gently pull the paper away from the wall for a distance of about 6 in. and cut along the guide line. Replace the paper, using the smoothing brush for the purpose, and then repeat the process at the top of the skirting.

Prepare the second piece of paper and hang it in exactly the same manner as the first, taking care to cover the margin of the first piece completely if a lap joint is used, or butting the edges closely together if both selvedges of the paper have been trimmed off. Fig. 11 shows the operation. If you are entirely satisfied with the appearance of the joint, run the roller lightly down the seam, using a little pressure only.

Proceed in precisely the same manner until the last strip. At this juncture measure the distance from the edge of the piece previously hung to the angle

Fig. 11

paper should now be trimmed. To do this, run the rounded nose of the scissors along the top of the paper in the angle formed between the bottom of the

formed by the adjacent wall and cut the last piece to this width plus an extra inch margin for turning at the angle in the manner indicated in Fig. 12, and continue in the same way right round the room until complete.

Patterned Papers are a trifle more difficult to cope with than plain ones inasmuch as a little more care is necessary at the outset in arranging the general "lay out."

With a view to obtaining the best effects it is worth while spending a few minutes in studying the pattern to help you to decide how such results may be obtained. For instance, you should take care to see that when hanging the first piece the full pattern appears below the ceiling line (or picture rail) as nothing looks worse than only a portion of the pattern appearing at this point. Another important point is to make sure that the pattern of the next piece registers with the first. To attain this result and to avoid unnecessary waste it is a good plan to offer up each piece as the work progresses, before cutting it from the roll.

Papering a Ceiling is not so easy to accomplish as papering a wall, owing to the somewhat difficult task of having to manipulate the material from underneath instead of in a more comfortable position.

Before the paper is actually hung, the ceiling must, of course, be thoroughly prepared by entirely removing the old distemper, stopping up cracks and other imperfections with either Keene's cement or plaster of Paris, and giving the bare surface a good coat of size solution in the same manner as treating a ceiling in good condition.

If the ceiling only is to be decorated and not the walls, the necessary precautions as to covering the walls with dust-sheets or other suitable material should be taken to prevent any unavoidable splashes, due to washing down, etc., spoiling the decorations.

A scaffold-board, resting between pairs of steps or trestles, should be arranged at a convenient height to suit the height of the worker. This should be neither too high nor too low for comfortable working; a convenient height being such as to allow a space of six inches or so between the operator's head and the ceiling.

Lining Paper, that is, a plain paper, is not usually trimmed at the edges unless the edges are in a damaged condition, but a patterned paper is provided with selvedges which, of course, are trimmed off should a butt joint be employed in the hanging.

To enable the paper to be hung squarely, it is an advantage to mark a guide line on the ceiling preparatory to hanging the paper. This can be done in a similar way to that employed in making a vertical guide line when dealing with wall-paper, by stretching a chalked string across the ceiling 21 inches away from and parallel to a wall as starting-point. The line is stretched and fastened to a couple of carpenter's bradawls—one driven in at each end of the ceiling. The string is then pulled down squarely for an inch or so in the centre and then quickly released, which makes a bold line on the surface of the ceiling.

As a rule the paper is hung so that the joints run at right-angles to the window, that is to say, in the same direction as the light, and, where practicable, the pieces hung in individual lengths, allowing a couple of inches at the ends for trimming afterwards.

Pasting.—The paper is pasted in the usual way, taking care to see that the paste is of the right consistency and devoid of lumps. Special attention must also be given when pasting not to allow any paste to come in contact with the face of the paper.

When pasting the paper, start at the left-hand end as in pasting wall-paper, and when a convenient length has been pasted, fold it over pasted face to pasted face, as illustrated at A in the diagram (Fig. 13). Then continue the pasting and fold again as at B. Now turn the

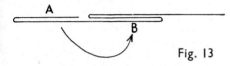

Fig. 13

top of the first treated piece as indicated by the arrow and proceed in a similar manner to the end of the piece.

Great care must now be exercised as the paper is in a somewhat limp condition and therefore requires delicate handling. A good method is to slip the left forearm under the middle of the paper, mount the staging board at the window end of the room, carefully open the first fold and with the right hand offer a corner of the paper up to the ceiling so that the narrow edge overlaps the wall by a couple of inches, and the long edge registers exactly with the marked line. Work the hand across the paper to enable a sufficient area to adhere to the surface and then smooth the paper out gently with the smoothing brush, working it from the centre to the edges. Continue in this way until the entire length of the strip is hung.

Trimming.—The next operation is to trim off the ends by first marking the paper with the rounded nose of the scissors run in the angle between the ceiling and the wall, and then gently pulling the paper down for about a foot and cutting it across the marked line. The paper is then replaced with the aid of the brush.

Follow on with the next piece and so on until the whole of the ceiling is covered. When sufficient time has elapsed to allow the paper to dry, apply a coat of size solution, and when this is dry, the distemper may be applied.

In dealing with a patterned paper, which obviously is not distempered, the same method of procedure is followed as that mentioned above, except that due regard must be paid to the correct matching of the pattern.

INDOOR PAINTING

A GREAT many people imagine that painting is one of the simplest processes—little but the purchase of a tin of ready-made paint, to be indifferently applied with a cheap brush. It is not surprising that such people are bitterly disappointed with the results obtained when they put their theories into practice.

Painting, like every other process in home decorating, requires skill, care and forethought to obtain satisfactory results, which are only acquired by practical experience.

Before going into details as to the methods adopted in painting, it is as well to know something about the constituents of paint ordinarily used for home decoration and coming under the category of oil paint.

Oil Paint consists of a "base," "vehicle," "pigment" and "drier." The base, which constitutes the body or foundation of the paint, is usually composed of white lead in the form of a paste ground in oil. In some paints zinc oxide is used as a base, while in some dark paints the colouring pigment itself forms the base. In order to render the plastic base sufficiently liquid for application, a vehicle or binder, consisting of linseed oil, is necessary and in addition to this a thinner of either turpentine or white spirit is generally used to enable the mixture to flow more easily. The pigment is the colouring matter to give the paint the desired hue; it may consist of yellow ochre, venetian red, etc. A suitable drier is

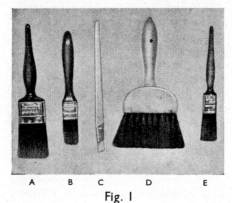

A   B   C   D   E

Fig. I

required to assist the paint in drying hard and quickly. Patent driers in the form of a paste are used in some instances, while in others, terebene, or an oil drier, is employed.

These ingredients must be mixed in definite proportions suitable for the work in hand, otherwise satisfactory results cannot be obtained. If the paint lacks the correct amount of base, its covering power is considerably reduced, and if there is a deficiency of vehicle and thinner the paint will be thick and difficult to work. Lack of the proper quantity of driers holds back drying and thus causes considerable delay.

In these days it is questionable whether it pays the home decorator to mix his own paints, as it is possible to obtain paint of excellent quality with the ingredients mixed in correct proportions ready for use. Such paints are reason-

able in price. Buying ready-made paint certainly has the advantage that it saves a considerable amount of somewhat messy work, and if the paint is made by a reputable manufacturer, the user has the satisfaction of knowing that it can be thoroughly relied upon.

In purchasing ready-made paint, always buy the best, as it is a great mistake to buy a very cheap one of unknown origin. Such paint very often contains as a base a large proportion of whiting which is useless as a protective medium, while the other ingredients are usually of the poorest quality.

As a rough guide in estimating the quantity of prepared paint required for a particular job, 1 lb. of paint is generally sufficient to cover an area of about 35 sq. ft. when used as a priming coat on a smooth surface. The same quantity of paint used as a second or third coat should cover 50 sq. ft., and when used as a final coat, about 60 sq. ft.

High class work not only depends upon good quality paint, but the paint must be properly applied with good tools. It behoves the worker to obtain brushes of a better quality than those supplied by some of the cheap stores.

Brushes.—For ordinary work, such as painting the woodwork, etc., of a room, five brushes, as shown in the illustration, Fig. 1, should be provided: four for applying the paint, etc., and one for dusting down the surfaces. The former should consist of a "ground" brush (A) of suitable size for dealing with comparatively large broad surfaces, a "sash" tool (B) for applying the paint to narrow work such as mouldings, sash-bars and work of a similar nature, and a "lining" tool (C) for cutting in straight lines. These brushes should be made of hog's hair set in rubber and metal bound. The dusting brush (D) is a different type of tool and should have long, soft bristles. If the finishing coat is to be of enamel, a special flat brush having very soft hairs and a wedge-shaped tip will be required. Such a brush is seen at E.

Before a paint brush (not an enamel brush) can be brought into requisition it should be soaked for about twelve hours in clean cold water to rid the body of grit, dust, etc., and swell the bristles. It should then be thoroughly dried, as the slightest amount of moisture, if allowed to remain, is detrimental to the work.

To obtain the best results, a new brush should never be used on important work, but should first be applied on work of lesser importance in order to "break it in."

As good brushes will give indefinite service if properly treated, the worker should always make a practice of thoroughly cleaning them when they are temporarily put out of commission. This can be done by removing the paint with turpentine and then submerging them in raw linseed oil up to the top of the bristles. To keep the ends of the tools from touching the bottom of the container—which would eventually ruin the brushes if permitted—it is a good plan to drill a small hole in the handle, pass a strong wire through it and suspend the ends on the edge of the receptacle as illustrated in Fig. 2. In the event of the brushes not being required for an indefinite period, the best plan is first to remove the paint with turpentine, wash them well with soap and water and store them in a dry place.

Other Materials.—Besides brushes and the necessary covering medium in the form of paint, the worker will require several other items for carrying out certain preliminary work before applying the paint. These include a suitable can for holding the paint, scraping knife for removing old paint, putty knife for applying putty when filling cracks and other imperfections, a sponge, chamois

15*

leather for cleaning-purposes, glass-paper for smoothing down surfaces, and a pair of steps. To this list must be added linseed oil, turpentine and putty.

Before beginning the actual work there are several points to be considered, such as whether the paint is to be applied to the bare wood or on a surface previously painted; the number of coats and the kind of finish desired.

Preparing the Surface.—In the case of new wood the first thing to do is to smooth the surface down well with glass-paper. The work should then be dusted down with the dusting brush and all knots treated with knotting to prevent any resin extruding from the knots—and there are many in most soft woods—staining and therefore spoiling the finished work. This substance is a mixture of shellac and methylated spirit, and threepennyworth purchased from an oil-shop will be sufficient to cover hundreds of knots. In applying the knotting, a

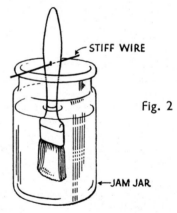

Fig. 2

STIFF WIRE

JAM JAR

small soft brush or mop should be used, and it should not be applied too thickly. In cases where very bad knots are to be treated it may be necessary to give them two or even three coats of the medium. When going over the work, make sure that none of the knots is missed, otherwise a stain is sure to appear on the finished surface at some future time.

Fortunately, knotting does not take very long to harden—the spirit will evaporate in the course of half an hour or so. When dry, the first coat, known as the "priming" coat, is applied. This coat generally consists of white lead, driers, linseed oil and a small quantity of red lead. Priming paint, like other paint, can be bought if desired, but if the home decorator prefers to make his own he can do so by mixing 2 lb. of white lead ground in oil, 1 oz. red lead and 1 oz. driers, with ¾ pint of raw linseed oil.

Priming.—It should be noted that the priming coat is of the utmost importance, as the quality of the finished work depends almost entirely on how the foundation coat has been applied.

Apply the paint evenly and thinly over the surface, and do not imagine that a thick coat is necessary. Covering power is not required in this operation as the paint is only needed to provide a key to the wood and subsequent coats.

The work must now be allowed to dry thoroughly, which will probably take a day, when the next operation of stopping any holes, crevices and other inequalities may be proceeded with. A small quantity of ordinary putty, consisting of whiting and linseed oil, will be required for this operation, as well as a putty knife for applying it. The putty should be in a fairly plastic state and if it is inclined to be hard it can be easily softened by kneading it in the hand. The stopping should be forced into the holes with the top of the knife, any surplus material remaining being removed with the blade. When all imperfections have received treatment, sufficient time should be allowed to enable the putty to set hard, after which any unevenness can be smoothed down with fine glass-paper.

The work should then be well dusted down with the dusting brush and subsequent coats applied in the same manner as that to be mentioned later when dealing with work that has already been painted.

Treatment of Old Paintwork.—In dealing with old paintwork, the question arises as to whether it is in a sufficiently good condition to receive the new coats of paint or whether it is too badly cracked, worn or blistered to be of further use. If the old paint is merely discoloured and its surface otherwise unimpaired, there is no need to remove it, but in other cases it is by far the wisest plan entirely to remove the old by stripping down to the bare wood and start afresh; any attempt to patch it up being worse than useless.

Before painting old work whose condition is such as to warrant further coats, the surface should be thoroughly cleaned with a copious supply of hot water and a good household soap—or better still, sugar soap—to remove all traces of grease and dirt. This should be followed with water only, applied with a sponge and then wiped over with a damp chamois leather. When dry, the surface should be rubbed down with fine glass-paper to remove the gloss to form a key for the next coat. Ordinary glass-paper may be used, but it is much better to use a waterproof paper in conjunction with water as its use prevents the formation of objectionable dust. If this method is adopted the whole of the surface should be washed down afterwards and gone over with the leather.

Before applying the new paint, the prepared surfaces of the old must be allowed to dry, as paint applied to a damp surface results in the formation of blisters, cracks, etc.

If found necessary to strip off the old paint, it can either be removed by burning off or by using a strong solution of caustic soda. The former is perhaps the better as it eliminates the use of a powerful chemical, which, if not very carefully handled to prevent it from coming in contact with the hands or other parts of the body, is liable to burn them.

Burning Off.—In burning off, the flame of the blow-lamp is played upon the surface and thus softens the paint, which is removed with a scraper as the softening proceeds. In the chemical process, the caustic soda is the solvent and the plastic paint is also removed with a scraper. After treating the surfaces with caustic soda, they should be thoroughly washed and gone over with vinegar and water to neutralise the effect of the alkali, after which a further application of clean water applied with a sponge completes this part of the work. The surface is ready for preparing for the new paint when it is quite dry and not before.

Burning off the old paint requires some experience before proficiency is attained. The chief points to observe are only to have sufficient flame to melt the paint and not so intense as to burn the woodwork underneath, and to apply the heat to only a small area at a time. The blow-lamp is held in the left hand and is followed up with the knife held in the right, as shown clearly in the illustration, Fig. 3.

The Number of Coats to be given to a particular piece of work depends upon the nature of the work. For painting new interior woodwork, three good coats including the priming coat should be the minimum, while four coats will, of course, give better results. At least two coats should be applied to old painted surfaces in good condition, but three coats are necessary where the surfaces are not quite so good. In cases where the old paint has been removed, it is best to treat it in the same way as new work, that is, the bare wood should

be knotted, primed and a further couple of coats applied.

If ready-prepared paint is to be used, all coats except the last should be of the "flat" variety, devoid of gloss. Such paint is known as undercoat paint and is readily obtainable at most domestic and paint stores. Should the usual glossy finish be desired, a good quality gloss paint is needed.

Mixing.—Those readers who prefer to mix their own paint can obtain good results by using the following: For the

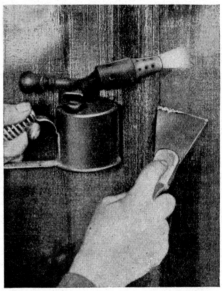

Fig. 3

coat following the priming coat—the proportions of ingredients of which have already been mentioned—white lead, 4 lb.; driers, 2 oz.; best American turpentine, $\frac{1}{2}$ pt.; linseed oil, 1 pt. The third coat may consist of white lead, $3\frac{1}{2}$ lb.; driers, 2 oz.; turpentine and oil, $\frac{1}{2}$ pt. of each.

If the room is being entirely redecorated the actual painting should be done after the ceiling has been distempered and the walls stripped.

Some workers prefer to apply the

finishing coat of paint after the paper has been hung, while others like to get the whole of the painting completed and then hang the wallpaper.

To facilitate the work as much as possible, it is a good plan to remove all fittings such as door handles, etc., as it is difficult to paint round these small objects without soiling them.

As a general rule it is advisable to start painting the window sashes and frames. This should always be done in day-light, if possible. A sash tool should be used for the majority of this work, and a lining tool for cutting in the lines be-tween the glass and the sash. As this part of the work is somewhat difficult because extra care is needed to keep the paint off the glass, a rectangular piece of thin cardboard placed over the pane at the edges in the manner shown in the illustration (Fig. 4) will obviate this to a great extent, but if any paint should get on the glass it should be removed before it hardens.

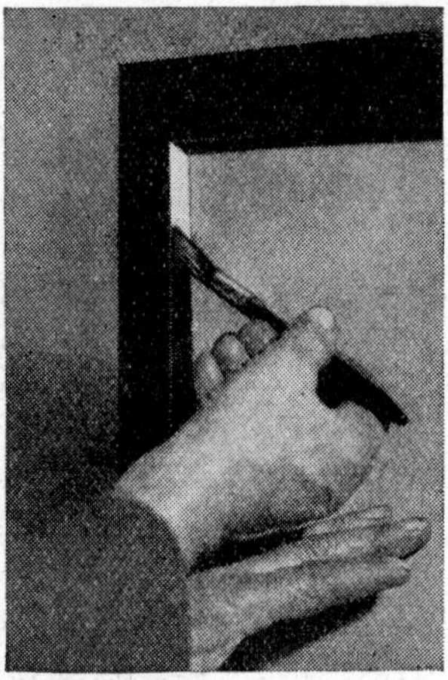

Fig. 4

The paint should be well stirred, strained through muslin or a paint-strainer and poured into a wide can—not used from the maker's container.

Application.—In applying the paint, be careful not to overload the brush and do not put it on too thickly. A thick coat of paint takes a considerable time to dry, is uneconomical and is not conducive to a good finish. This evil can easily be prevented by just dipping the tip of the brush into the paint can, which should never contain more than an inch or so of paint. If the brush becomes overloaded, remove the surplus by placing the body of the tool on the edge of the can and gradually drawing it away, or better still, fix a stout wire across the handle supports and wipe the brush across this. (*See* Fig. 6.)

Use gentle upward and downward strokes, but it is as well to push the brush where angles and narrow strips are to be negotiated.

In the case of a panelled door, it is customary to start with the panels, includ-ing the mouldings which hold the panels in place. The panels should be followed with the middle vertical members, known as muntins, and then the middle, top and bottom "rails" or cross pieces and finally the "stiles" or outside vertical mem-bers. The sequence of operations in painting such a door is shown alphabetically in the dia-gram at Fig. 5. A ground brush is the best tool to use for a door, as the latter presents a large, more or less unbroken surface. When painting the door do not forget to paint the opening and closing edges. The former should be painted at the same time as the inside of the door, and the latter when the outside is being treated. The door jamb and archi-trave should then be painted, and when this is finished, the open door should be wedged underneath to prevent it closing and thus spoiling the work.

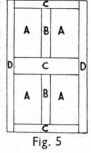

Fig. 5

The Skirtings should be left till last. In painting these, care should be exercised to see that the surfaces are well

Fig. 6

paint from spoiling the floor surface, especially if it happens to be parquet.

It is an advantage to paint the bare plaster for 1 in. or so above the top edge of the skirting, for by so doing, any little inequalities in trimming the bottom edges of the wallpaper will not be so conspicuous.

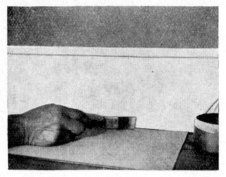

Fig. 7

covered. It is a wise precaution to cover the floor with a piece of newspaper, cardboard or sheet metal placed immediately under the part being painted, as shown in Fig. 7, to prevent the brush collecting dust, grit and other foreign matter, and also to prevent the

Each coat of paint should be allowed to harden thoroughly and then be carefully rubbed down with glass-paper before the next coat is added.

OUTDOOR PAINTING

HOME decorators who can make a successful job of indoor painting will have little difficulty in making an equally successful job of exterior work, as it is carried out in much the same way.

The usual items associated with painting the exterior parts of a house include gutters, pipes and the general woodwork such as barge boards or facia boards, windows, doors, etc. As exterior painting necessitates the use of a ladder sufficiently long to enable the gutters and facia boards to be easily reached, it may be necessary to hire one from the local builder, who generally makes a

charge of a few pence per day for the accommodation.

Ladders.—Those workers who have had little or no experience with ladders should make a point of seeing that they are properly erected before ascending them. A little extra time expended in this direction is not time wasted, as it may be the means of avoiding an accident.

A ladder should always be so placed that its feet are perfectly level; moreover, it should not be placed at too acute an angle to a wall nor too sloping, but should be placed at a safe angle such as

TOO STEEP   TOO WIDE   CORRECT

Fig. I

shown in Fig. 1. When working on gutters and other parts which are at a considerable height from the ground, it is a wise precaution to get a helper to stand on the bottom rung of the ladder to prevent it from shifting. Failing this, a couple of stakes driven firmly into the ground with a board placed across them against which the foot of the ladder can rest, in the manner indicated in Fig. 2, is an excellent substitute.

To judge the approximate length of a ladder required to reach a certain height, add up the number of brick courses of the wall (these are generally 3 in. deep) and divide the result by four. This gives the height of the wall in feet. An extra foot or so should be added to allow for the slope of the ladder, etc. For example, suppose the wall has 68 courses of bricks, its height is therefore $68 \div 4 = 17$ ft. and the minimum length of the ladder $17 + 1 = 18$ ft. As the length of a ladder is usually measured in terms of the number of rungs, which are spaced 9 in. apart, it follows that the number of rungs is $18 \times 12 \div 9 = 24$. The nearest standard-sized ladder to this would be a 25.

If after examining the old paint carefully it is found to be in fairly good condition, that is, it is not badly blistered and cracked, two good coats applied after it has been carefully prepared will usually give satisfactory results; but should the surface of the old paint be so bad as to expose bare wood, etc., the best plan will be entirely to remove the old paint and replace it with at least three coats of new paint, as it is a sheer waste of time and money to put new paint on badly damaged surfaces.

Preparation.—Having settled this important point, the first thing to do is to start at the top and remove all dirt, moss and other litter which may have collected in the gutters. The condition of the gutters can also be examined at the same time and if found perfectly sound and firmly fixed, they can be prepared for painting.

Assuming that the condition of the old paint is sufficiently good to receive further coats, the gutters, facia boards and pipe work should be thoroughly washed with clean water and sugar soap and then rubbed over with a wet sponge. When dry, the surface should be well rubbed down with fine glass-paper and carefully dusted with the aid of a dusting brush, after which it will be in a suitable condition to receive its first coat of paint.

If two coats only are to be applied and the final coat is to be a dark colour, such as a brown, grey or green, ordinary white lead paint may be used, but it should be tinted to suit the last coat. This can be done by adding a suitable amount of black prepared paint, or, if desired, a tin of grey paint can be purchased for the purpose.

When working aloft it is a good plan to suspend the paint-can by means of a hook placed over one of the rungs and at the back of the ladder. This arrangement frees the left hand and thus enables a firm hold to be obtained on the ladder.

The paint for the undercoat should be of the "flat" kind and should not be applied too thickly. If it is found necessary to thin

Fig. 2

it down a trifle to enable it to flow easily, use equal quantities of turpentine and linseed oil.

As the next coat cannot be applied to those parts of the work until they are properly dry and hard, which under normal conditions usually takes about twenty-four hours, other parts such as window sashes and frames, etc., should now be thoroughly washed, glass-papered and dusted.

It is usual to have these parts of a lighter and different colour to that of the gutters and pipe work. If white or cream is the colour chosen for the final coat, the ordinary white lead paint can be used as an undercoat, but in the event of a stone or a buff colour—which generally gives pleasing results—being preferred, the undercoat should be tinted to suit the finished shade.

When preparing the window sashes, make sure that the putty surrounding the glass is in good condition. If unsatisfactory it is wise to remove the old putty and replace it with new, in which case the rebates should receive a priming coat of paint and be allowed to dry before applying the putty.

Assuming that there is no need for re-puttying, the paint should be applied to the sash-bars first, the rails next and finally the stiles. Next, paint the reveals and the window sill, and follow on with the outsides of the doors.

The Final Coat.— When you are quite satisfied that the first coat is quite hard, the final coat may be proceeded with. Start with the gutters, facia boards, and pipe work as before and rub the surfaces down lightly with fine glass-paper and remove the dust.

The final coat should be a high-class quality gloss paint especially prepared for outside work and should be applied in the same way as the previous coat.

In cases where it is necessary to strip off the old paint, all woodwork, etc., should be treated as new wood, that is to say, after the old paint has been removed by the use of a chemical solvent or by burning off and then thoroughly cleaned as already mentioned in the article dealing with interior work, the bare wood should be well smoothed down, knotted, a priming coat applied and then all imperfections stopped with putty. The primary coat consisting of white lead paint, to which sufficient red lead has been added to turn it to a dark pink colour, should be covered with a further two undercoats, followed by the final one, allowing sufficient time for each to harden before applying the next.

The secret of success in all painting may be summarised as follows: Always use good materials and tools and apply the paint to perfectly clean and dustless surfaces. Apply the paint thinly consistent with covering power—a thick coat is wasteful both as regards cost and time. Allow sufficient time for each coat to harden thoroughly, which means that the oil has oxidised and the turpentine evaporated, and always lightly rub down the surface of each coat before applying another.

ENAMELLING AND VARNISHING

IN high-class work, enamel is widely used as a finishing medium for interior woodwork, etc., as it produces a much smoother and more durable surface than ordinary paint. Enamel also has the additional advantage of being able to withstand a considerable amount of washing without its having a detrimental effect upon the surface, provided this is done carefully with a clean chamois leather.

A good quality gloss enamel consists of a zinc oxide base, a suitable quantity of varnish and a small quantity of linseed oil. Such an enamel is expensive, but its purchase is a worthwhile investment compared with many cheap enamels now on the market. Inferior enamels give inferior results.

As a rule enamel is applied to the flatted coats of oil paint. It is not applied in the same way, nor is it so simple to apply as paint, but no difficulty should be experienced provided certain precautions are taken. For instance, enamel is more or less flowed on the surface in more liberal quantities and does not require so much brushing as in painting. Another point of importance is that of temperature; it is unwise to use enamel in very cold weather unless suitable means are provided to heat the room to at least 65°, to enable the enamel to flow properly. Enamel cannot be worked successfully in a damp atmosphere, as this condition produces a kind of unsightly film. Draughts must be avoided.

Brushes.—Paint brushes are useless for enamelling; a special enamel brush, having long, springy yet soft bristles terminating in a wedge-shaped end, being the correct tool to use. Great care must be exercised to exclude dust—the bugbear of enamelling—and all surfaces to be treated must be thoroughly dusted.

Number of Coats.—If a very high gloss and an exceptionally hard and durable surface is required, two coats of enamel should be given and better results will be obtained if the finishing coat contains very little or no linseed oil at all, and a very small quantity of turpentine and gold size is added. The undercoat should not be in its glossy state, but flatted when it is thoroughly hard before applying the finishing coat. The best way to do this is to sponge the surface with clean cold water and rub it evenly and carefully with a piece of soft material dipped in fine pumice powder which must, of course, be entirely devoid of grit. After the whole surface has been carefully gone over in this way, it must be thoroughly washed over with a soft sponge and clean chamois leather until the surface is entirely free from pumice.

Application.—The art of enamelling lies almost entirely in judging the proper amount to apply to the surface being treated. If the correct amount is applied, any streaks will disappear in due course. Too much enamel is not only wasteful, but results in the formation of blobs and waves; on the other hand, too little prevents the proper flow and is conducive to brush-marks. Great care should be taken not to overload the brush and only a small area should be treated at a time. Before starting to apply the enamel be particularly careful to stir up thoroughly and pour out a small quantity only from the maker's container into a clean, dustless can sufficiently wide to allow easy access of the brush. After having done this, replace the lid of the container to exclude air and dust.

It sometimes happens that the enamel has been stored in a cold place, rendering it difficult to work. In such a case it can be easily rendered workable by partially immersing the container in warm water.

Varnishing.—In many instances varnish applied to painted surfaces not only greatly enhances their appearance but provides an excellent protective medium against wear and tear and tends to greater cleanliness than a painted surface, as it can easily be cleaned with a damp cloth.

The varnish used as a finishing medium for paint is that known as oil varnish, made from various gums, linseed oil and a small quantity of suitable thinners. Such varnish must not be confused with the rapid-drying varnish consisting of certain gums dissolved in methylated spirit, called spirit varnish, which is unsuitable for applying to painted surfaces and is used for an entirely different purpose.

Oil Varnishes can be obtained in various qualities and vary in colour from an almost transparent liquid bearing the name of pale copal varnish—which is the kind that should always be used for covering light paint—to a pale oak colour which could be used on a darker coloured paint such as brown, although it is always better to use the more expensive paler variety as pale oak varnish is really intended for use on more or less bare wood.

If the surface of the paint to be varnished is in a good, clean condition, the varnish can be applied without preliminary treatment except, of course, that it must be thoroughly dusted down. On the other hand, if it is intended to varnish new work, the various undercoats should consist of flat paint, that is, paint without gloss, applied in the usual manner.

Varnish is applied in very much the same way as enamel—that is, it is flowed on and not "painted" on, and the same precautions to be taken apply in both cases. A clean, broad special varnish brush is a necessity, a paint brush being utterly unsuitable.

One of the important points to observe when applying varnish is not to over-load the brush; and it is a great mistake to work the brush too vigorously, light, delicate strokes only being necessary. If the brush is pressed too hard on the surface it tends to produce minute bubbles which, when dry, result in the formation of minute holes.

Varnish is not only an excellent finishing medium for painted surfaces, but it can be used to good advantage on ordinary wall-paper.

Paper Varnish is used for this purpose and can be obtained at most wall-paper shops. The paper is hung in the usual way and allowed to dry. It is then treated with a warm solution of size and water in the proportion of an ounce of concentrated powdered size to a pint of water.

The varnish is applied in the same way as ordinary oil varnish, light strokes only being taken, so as to prevent the formation of tiny bubbles.

Cellulose Paints have the advantage of drying rapidly but they cannot be satisfactorily applied on top of enamels or varnishes.

The work must first be stripped, either with a blow-lamp or a solvent composed of equal parts of benzol and methylated spirits. The paint is applied with a rubber set brush. Begin at the top, then with the second stroke begin lower down and work up, so that the first and second strokes flow into each other. This is continued to the bottom when a continuous stroke is carried smoothly upwards over the whole. Continue this over the whole area to be covered.

FITTING A PICTURE RAIL

ANY room fitted with a picture rail not only looks higher but is much lighter owing to the white surround. The walls are much easier to re-paper, and the positions of pictures may be changed without damage to the walls.

The addition of a plate rail or narrow shelf provides accommodation for antique plates and similar ornaments.

Materials.—The following tools should be put ready for use: A mitre block and tenon saw for cutting the corners, a square, bradawl, hammer, nail punch and rule.

Measure round the room where the moulding is required, leave out windows and cupboards, and to allow for waste in cutting add 6 in. for each corner.

The selected shape of moulding should be ordered in lengths of not less than the length of the longest side of the room plus the extra 6 in. for cutting the two ends. About half a pound of 2-in. cut nails will be required for fixing. These are wedge-shaped and hold better than wire ones.

The following example of a room (Fig. 1) will serve as a guide, to illustrate the method of determining the quantity of wood moulding required.

The longest length of unbroken flat wall in this case is wall A. Wall B has a doorway at the end, C has the fireplace, and D contains a window and a doorway almost at the extreme end. It was decided to run the picture rail level with the top of the door frames. The top edge was 1 ft. 10 in. down from the ceiling. To make a total of the added lengths we have (allowing 6 in. per end):

Wall	ft. in.	in.		ft. in.
A	10 6 +	6 for cutting ends		11 6
B	13 3 +	6 „ „ „		14 3
C	13 0 +	60 (10 ends) „		18 0
D	13 3 +	24 (4 ends) „		15 3
		Total feet		59 0

From this we must deduct door and window spaces, a total of 10 ft. 9 in., which gives us 48 ft. 3 in., so if 50 ft. is ordered there will be ample and a piece to spare for the odd 4 in. in the corner by the door in wall D.

Depth of Frieze.—In the case mentioned above some difficulty was experienced in getting the picture rail to hold to the wall. The nails buckled up after a few blows, which indicated that they were striking the bricks behind and not entering the mortar joints between the rows of bricks as they should do for proper fixing. For the sake of appearance, the top of the door frame had been taken as a fixing-level.

Similar trouble will be avoided if the position of the longitudinal joint between the row of bricks can be located. The first line of mortar is usually about 2½ in. below the surface of the ceiling, and the rows are 3 in. apart down the wall. The wood moulding is generally about 2 in. wide and the nails are put in ½ in. or so below the top edge; the

bottom of the frieze should be 1 in. less than a convenient multiple of 3 in.: 20 in. is a good depth. The joints between the bricks are shown at detail drawing X in Fig. 1.

A pencil line may be marked at intervals round the room before starting the actual fixing, and another good plan is to drive a fine nail or a bradawl to locate the joint. If the position is not correct the tiny hole may be patched with plaster should it be likely to show when the rail is in position.

Cutting and Fixing the Rail.—Examine an existing picture rail if possible,

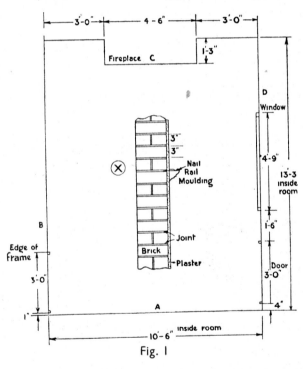

Fig. 1

and note how the corners are cut. The moulding is cut on the slant or mitred at the corners. When the rail fits into a corner the internal mitre is required, and where it fits round a corner of a projecting wall such as the chimney breast the external mitre is cut, as shown clearly in Fig. 2. For accurate work a slotted cutting-block or mitre block is essential.

Start at a wall which requires an internal mitre at each end, such as wall A in Fig. 1.

Measure the length of wall from corner to corner, mark this on the *back*

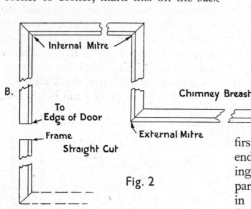

Fig. 2

Internal Mitre

B.

To Edge of Door

Frame

Straight Cut

Chimney Breast

External Mitre

of a length of moulding, and add about $\frac{1}{8}$ in. for cutting. With the square mark a pencil line across at right-angles to the top edge where the length is marked. Have the beginning of the measured length about 1 in. from the end of the piece. Place the moulding in the mitre block with the flat side vertical against the back, in the manner shown in Fig. 3. The mark on the right-hand end should be set opposite the right-hand slot in the block; hold the wood firmly, insert the saw in the slot and start the cut, lift the wood clear to see if the cut is on the marked line, and then finish sawing through. The left-hand end is treated in the same manner by setting the mark against the left-hand slot in the block. When the length is held with its back face in position on the wall, the two ends should fit snugly

into the two corners of the wall. If too tight, a little may be eased off with a rasp or glass-paper, or by a fine saw-cut.

Two or three nails should be started in the wood before it is put up, the

Rail

Door Frame

Brad

first one being about $1\frac{1}{2}$ in. from the end, in the thickest part of the moulding, and with the broad side of the nail parallel with the grain. Hold the piece in place with the top edge against the frieze line marked on the wall and drive the nails in almost to the head. With the nail punch finish driving the nails in so that the heads are well below the surface of the wood. Any nail that bends should be taken out, otherwise it will force the wood away from the wall.

For cutting the external mitre, square a line across the back of the wood

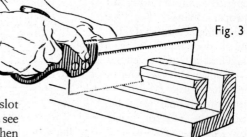

Fig. 3

about 3 in. from one end, measure the wall and mark the distance on the wood as before, and cut the left-hand end of the moulding in the right-hand slot of the mitre block, and the right-hand end in the left-hand slot. To secure the corner, nail through with an oval brad, as illustrated in Fig. 4.

To make a joint in a straight run of moulding the two ends must be spliced, one being cut with an internal mitre and the adjacent piece with an external mitre end. This will not show when painted.

The heads of the nails and any cracks or joints may be filled with plastic wood or putty; the latter being applied after painting on the primary coat.

Partition Walls.—Fixing picture rails to breeze slab walls should not present any difficulty, as they are comparatively soft and hold nails well, but the lath and plaster type will not hold nails except at the solid vertical timber members or studs, which must be located. These run vertically from floor to ceiling and are from 18 to 24 in. apart. There will be one in the wall at each side of a door, behind the architrave of the door frame. Tap the

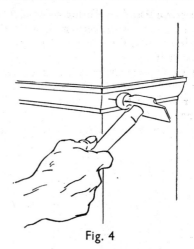

Fig. 4

wall and it will sound hollow, so proceed along the wall until a more solid backing is found. Prick through with a fine bradawl to find if this position is correct. Having found two, the other positions can be located and marked.

MENDING BLINDS

SPRING roller blinds are quite simple to fix, and if properly taken care of, do not cause much trouble. Most faults with existing blinds are due to inaccurate fitting at the start.

There are two general types in the various makes available: one is fitted with a side cord, for pulling to release the ratchet on the end of the roller, allowing the spring to roll up the blind. When the cord is released the ratchet comes into contact with teeth on the metal end fitting and stops the blind. The other type requires no side cord. Two small ratchets engage and hold the blind. A slight pull on the blind disengages them, and when released the turning motion, as the blind runs up, keeps them apart until it is checked, when they engage once more. In both types the spring is inside the wooden roller.

Fitting the Brackets.—The first thing to do in fitting a roller blind is to fix the bracket, which has an open slot, to the woodwork on the left-hand side of the window, by means of screws, as illustrated in Fig. 1. Then, using the roller to gauge the distance, place the other bracket on the end of the roller, and mark the fixing holes for this side, taking care that the roller is horizontal, otherwise the blind will run over to one side.

Fitting Blind to Roller.—When new fabric is necessary, setting the material squarely upon the roller will not prove difficult if the top and bottom edges of the fabric are cut square at the onset. Lay the blind out on a clear space on the floor and see that the sides are parallel along the length. If the width varies, rule a line, using a long straight-edge

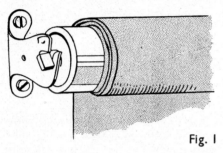

Fig. I

for a guide, and cut carefully with a large pair of scissors.

Now turn the bottom end over to the top edge but do not make a fold as this will leave a crease. See that both edges are exactly parallel to each other, and cut a small nick through both thicknesses, as near to the end as the uneven end will allow. Open the material flat, and rule a pencil line across top and bottom between the two nicks.

A more perfect edge can be obtained if a sharp penknife is run along the straight - edge which, of course, should be done on a flat piece of wood. Each end should now be a true right-angle with the sides.

The bottom edge may now be turned up to make a hem or pocket for housing the wooden lath. This should not be a tight fit. When running it up on the sewing machine the ends may be left open. The lath is slid in and secured by the two small screws which fix the metal fitting that retains

the knot of the cord to the bottom of the blind.

The top end of the fabric is placed with the edge in and parallel to the groove in the roller, keeping in mind that, when in use, the blind hangs between the window and the roller and that the left-hand end is the end of the roller with the square peg projecting. Patent rectangular pins with four points should be used as these fit the groove and will not tear the material. When these are not available small drawing pins may be used as their thin heads cover a fairly large surface, while a strip of tape placed along under the heads as indicated in Fig. 2 will prevent any liability to tear. Ordinary tacks are not suitable, because the heads are not sufficiently flat, and the points may not only split the wood at the spring end but damage the spring as well.

Roll the blind up and place the right hand end with the round peg into the bracket, wind the square peg up a few turns and slip it into the left bracket. This ensures that the spring starts with a certain amount of pressure. Pull the

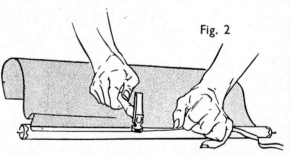

Fig. 2

blind down and see if it will roll up properly without running to one side or sticking part way. The ratchets should be given a spot of oil occasionally and kept free from dust and fluff.

If the roller obtained is too long for the particular window for which it is required, it can be shortened by removing the metal fitting opposite the spring end, and sawing a piece off the roller to give the required length, slightly longer than the width of the blind. Replace the metal end and drive in the pin if this is not part of the end fitting. Support the other end on two pieces of wood so that the square peg and the spring are not damaged.

Roller Blinds With Cord.—A roller blind having a cord at the side which when pulled causes the blind to roll up is very simple and the only thing to cause trouble is the cord. Where an endless cord is used it is passed round the pulley once or twice to make it grip. As this soon stretches it does not maintain sufficient pressure to make the roller wheel rotate. In the other type if the cord is not of a suitable size it fills the spool and runs over on to the teeth of the ratchet. The latter is released by a slight forward pull on the cord, which passes through an eye on the side of the locking pawl. The cord is fixed by passing the end through the hole in the flange and making a knot at the back and winding it on when the blind is down, so that pulling it off winds up the blind.

PELMETS AND CURTAIN RODS

THE more elaborate pelmets are only suitable for large rooms, but there are many styles suitable for smaller rooms, such as the plain pelmet shown in Fig. 1, which can be easily made at home, to improve the smartness of the interior. These are generally faced with material similar to the hangings, but plywood is also used, painted to match the woodwork of the window, the curtains, or the walls. Nicely grained wood may be stained and polished to harmonise with the furniture, e.g. a walnut or limed-oak pelmet with similar furniture.

Box-shaped Pelmets are the easiest to make, and suit the ordinary square window, and in cases where its size and shape do not seem in proportion with the remainder of the room the pelmet and curtains may be arranged to correct this fault. A window that is too long and narrow should have the curtains carried well out at each side to conceal the woodwork, but they should not hang down lower than the window sill as this only counteracts the wider effect produced by the pelmet. The appearance of a very

Fig. 1

broad window may be greatly enhanced by keeping the curtains well towards the outer woodwork of the frame and extending them right down to the floor.

The general working procedure is more or less the same whatever shape or type of pelmet is being made. First measure across the window for the front of the pelmet. The rule should be held from the outside edge of the architrave, or woodwork round the window, to the opposite edge. The pelmet board is usually 4 in. wide and should be made

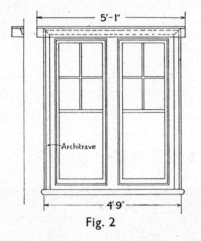

Fig. 2

4 in. longer than the measurement taken across the window, as indicated in Fig. 2. This gives 2 in. at each end, and may be more if required, according to the kind of curtains used. For the pelmet board, use timber $\frac{1}{2}$ in. thick, and in the case of the window shown in Fig. 2, it is 4 in. wide by 5 ft. 1 in. long. The corners are either left square or may be rounded off if a curved end is required. If the whole of the board is made smooth, and painted the same colour as the woodwork, it is much easier to keep clean.

Three light metal brackets will be required, about $\frac{1}{8}$ in. thick and $\frac{1}{2}$ in. wide with flat surfaces both sides, $2\frac{1}{4}$ in. long one side by 2 or $2\frac{1}{2}$ in. the other, as indicated in Fig. 3. These are usually supplied ready drilled and countersunk for wood screws, two holes in each side. Only one bracket is used at each end, the third one is to provide similar material for making the two small extra brackets for supporting the curtain rod.

From the spare bracket cut off near the bend a piece 1 in. by $\frac{3}{4}$ in., to include the bend as indicated in the large details (Fig. 3) and from the spare flat metal left over make a similar bracket, making the bend as near as possible the same. Holes are now drilled in each bracket, one in the $\frac{3}{4}$-in. side to pass an $\frac{1}{8}$-in. diameter metal screw, and 3 in the 1-in. side. The centre hole in the latter is countersunk for the fixing wood screw, and the two—one above and one below—are for $\frac{3}{32}$- or $\frac{1}{8}$-in. diameter rivets. Three similar holes must be drilled in the end of each larger bracket, and the two for the rivets slightly countersunk so that the rivets can be hammered flat on the back face. The two complete brackets are screwed to the flat surface of the window frame, one at each side, and to ensure that they are in the correct position, the pelmet board is held in the right position with its back edge against the wall and resting on the ledge of the woodwork along the top of the window. Make sure that an equal amount projects beyond the frame at each end, and mark on the underside the positions for the brackets; at the same time mark along the top and near the back edge the positions of the first and last fixing screws which pass through the board into the top of the window frame. These should well clear the top back screws fixing the brackets.

The top of the board is now drilled to clear the wood screws and slightly countersunk to take the heads, and the brackets screwed into position on the underside at the correct distance forward from the back. These screws will hold the board in place while the other screws are driven in through the top near the back edge.

A length of metal tubing about $\frac{1}{2}$ in. diameter will be required for the curtain rod, and electric light conduit is quite suitable and inexpensive. The overall length is such that the end of the tube is

1 in. beyond the centre of the metal screw in the bracket at each end. At this distance from each end a hole is drilled right through the tube, large enough to clear a metal screw $\frac{1}{8}$ in. diameter, fixed in the bracket by means of a thin nut. Metal end caps as shown are obtainable with a wood screw end to fit into a wooden plug driven into the end of the tube. The last curtain hooks fit into the eye of these end caps, small

corner ends and the size of the sides, also the depth from top edge to bottom. Fold the paper over at the centre and cut through both thicknesses with a pair of scissors; both halves will now be exactly alike, and the piece may be pinned up as a trial.

If the depth and shape are satisfactory the actual pelmet may be made, and if there is more than one window of the same size to be done a stiff cardboard

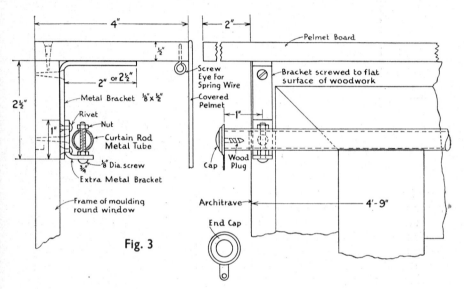

Fig. 3

curtain rings with eye tabs being used for the other hooks.

Fabric Pelmet.—It is advisable to cut out a paper pattern of the outline before cutting the actual materials, so that the general shape may be studied and altered without wasting any material.

Only one-half of the pattern need be drawn, but the paper should be in one piece, long enough to go right round the edge of the board. Stiff brown paper or a piece of old wallpaper will do. Outline the design of the edge by using any convenient articles about the house, such as the edge of a plate, the lid of an oval tin, etc. Leave ample space all round and mark the positions of the

template for half of the front should be made from the paper pattern, and this used to mark the outline directly on to the back of the material; but before cutting, a margin parallel with the outline must be marked outside the original shape to indicate the extra amount of material needed all round for turning in, and a strip at each end also for turning in.

The pelmet consists of three thicknesses of material; the front piece of the same material as the curtains, the centre stiffening of buckram, and the back or lining, that is, the side which shows from outside the window.

Silk and cotton curtain materials may

be made up on a stiffening of strong calico sheeting, but heavier materials require stiffening with pelmet buckram, which is thin canvas treated with glue.

Calico centres are cut with the same margin for turnings as the other two

or braid is to be sewn on also, the material will only be tacked first, and the final stitching carried through the gimp as well.

The finished pelmet may be fixed to the edge of the board by means of tacks inserted under the gimp, or a wide tape is stitched to the back edge along the top and the tacks put through this into the top surface of the board. If there is a picture rail or moulding round the walls

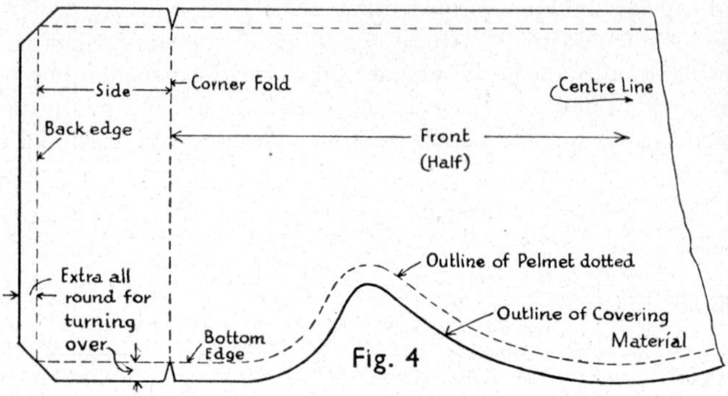

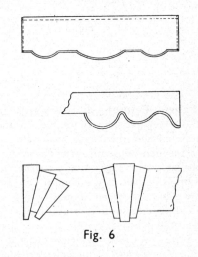

Side — Corner Fold   Centre Line

Back edge   Front (Half)

Extra all round for turning over   Bottom Edge   Outline of Pelmet dotted   Outline of Covering Material

Fig. 4

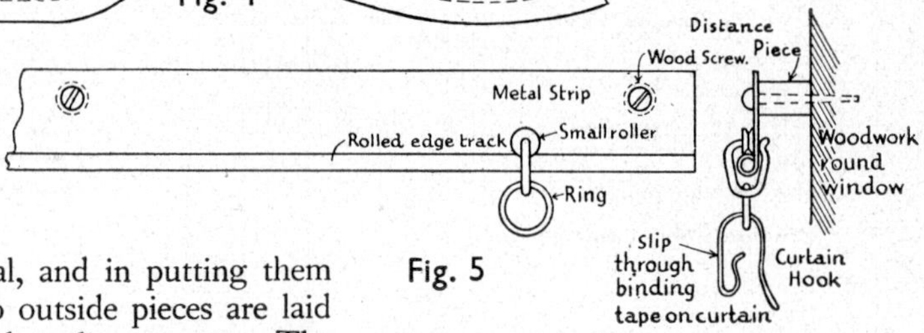

Distance Piece

Wood Screw.

Metal Strip

Rolled edge track   Small roller

Ring

Slip through binding tape on curtain

Woodwork round window

Curtain Hook

Fig. 5

pieces of material, and in putting them together the two outside pieces are laid face to face and the calico on top. The whole is then machined about $\frac{1}{2}$ in. from the edge all round, except for a space of about 18 in. along the upper edge. Small slits must be made in the turnings at all curves and inside corners, without cutting the stitches. These slits will make the pelmet edge lie flat when finished.

The bag thus formed is turned inside out and the 18-in. opening sewn up.

When buckram is used it is cut to the exact shape and size of the finished pelmet, that is, the inside dotted lines on Fig. 4, including the sides. The facing material is laid pattern side down on the table and the buckram on that, and the facing material may be cut out, leaving the border for turnings, which must be nicked with the scissors, so that they lie flat when sewn. The lining is turned in and tacked on the reverse. If a gimp

Fig. 6

butting up to the window and therefore in the way of the back edge of the pelmet, a small piece of the moulding must be cut away, with a small saw, just

Fig. 7.   A MODERN FABRIC PELMET

wide enough to pass the pelmet edge. Where extra side curtains are required they may be hung on a taut length of spring wire hooked into a screw-eye at each end of the board. Such wire can be obtained at most of the cheap stores. In place of the tubular curtain rod there is obtainable the metal-strip type of curtain runner, as shown in Fig. 5.

This is screwed to the woodwork through distance pieces, and may be bent or curved if required. The rings for the curtain hooks are fitted with small rollers for free movement, and the hooks are slipped through a special binding tape sewn to the curtain.

Modern designs are shown in Figs. 6 and 7.

PLUGGING WALls

AMONGST the various fixtures added to the house from time to time for the kitchen, scullery, or bathroom, we have the medicine chest, plate drying rack, soap dish, shaving mirror, or small cabinet for shaving gear with mirror door, towel rail, etc. To make a sound

thicker than the mortar joint between the bricks may be used. These are cut from $\frac{1}{2}$ in. to $\frac{3}{4}$ in. wide, and driven into suitable holes made with a cold chisel, between the joint where the screws are to be fixed. The plug is made longer than required as the head

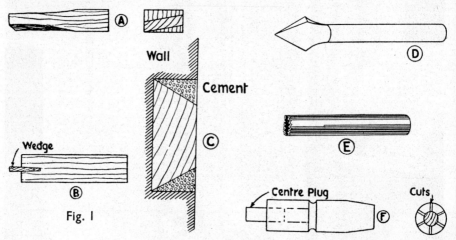

Fig. 1

neat job plugs are fixed in the wall in the positions where the article is to be screwed, and as the construction of walls may be different the type of plug used is varied to suit the wall and the weight of the fixture.

Wood Plugs in Brickwork.—For supporting comparatively heavy articles on brick walls wood slips, slightly

which may become broken through hammering is sawn off after the plug has been driven in. Figure 2 shows the operation. The end entering the wall should be cut tapered and slanting, as shown at A in Fig. 1, to ensure a good grip.

For heavier articles larger holes for square plugs are cut in the brickwork with a cold chisel, making the back of the opening larger than the front, so that when the plug has been driven in tight, the small wedge shown at B will spread the back to fill the hole. An alternative method is to shape the

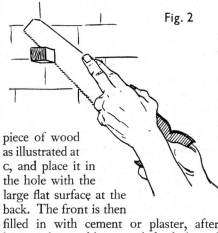

Fig. 2

piece of wood as illustrated at C, and place it in the hole with the large flat surface at the back. The front is then filled in with cement or plaster, after having thoroughly wetted the hole and the block.

Round holes, if small, can be made with a pointed drill sharpened as shown at D. This may either be rotated in a carpenter's brace or held in the left hand and turned slightly at each tap of the hammer. Only light blows are necessary, with constant rotation so that the drill does not become fixed. This type of drill is also useful for drilling stonework.

Large round holes are more conveniently made with a "jumper" E, consisting of a length of iron pipe or steel tube with walls about $\frac{3}{16}$ in. thick, cut at one end to form teeth. These are cut with a thin file and should be spaced as equally as possible. The other end may be screwed and fitted with a metal cap fitting to take the hammer blows. The jumper is held on the spot where the plug is to go, and struck with a hammer, and is rotated at each blow. The wood plug is first cut square, slightly larger than the diameter of the hole. The

corners are then pared off with a chisel until the shape approximates that of the hole but with a slight taper so that the plug will loosely fit the hole at the back only, for about $\frac{1}{2}$ in. from the end. This plain taper plug may be driven in and the projecting end sawn off, or a central hole is bored part way from the front end and saw cuts made round the outside, as represented at F. A smaller plug to take the screw is then driven down the centre and causes the outer wood to expand and grip the wall of the hole.

For heavier fixtures such as fixing the end of a partition to an existing wall, where bolts are to be used, a suitable diameter is obtained in what is known as "rag bolts." These have a thick square end covered with spike projections, and this end is cemented into the wall. The same type of bolt is often used in concrete floors to secure woodwork, electric motors and other machines.

For bedding in stonework it is usual to fill the space round the bolt with lead, poured in hot, while the bolts are held in position by frames or pieces of wood fixed over the holes, the threaded ends passing through the wood and secured with the nuts.

Plastered walls should have the plaster round the hole position cleared before the proper hole is cut. About $\frac{1}{8}$ in. all round larger than the hole is enough. This will prevent the working of the jumper or other tool from shaking or bulging a larger area of plaster loose.

Patent Wall Plugs.—There are several specially prepared plugs for domestic uses. Most household sets contain a special steel tool for making the holes, a supply of special hollow fibre plugs, and a variety of wood screws, etc., all suitable for the general run of domestic jobs.

These plugs are suitable for use in brick, concrete, or stone, and any tiled surface. The tool is used in the same way as the jumper (Fig. 3) and is rotated at each blow. The hole is made a trifle deeper than the length of plug to be used so that the end does not project beyond the wall surface. When

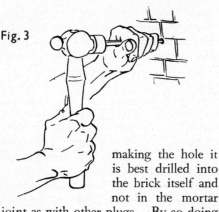

Fig. 3

making the hole it is best drilled into the brick itself and not in the mortar joint as with other plugs. By so doing the holes can be made in any desired position without having to find any joints or move the article out of place in order to find a good spot.

Partition Walls.—The outer walls of the majority of present-day houses are constructed of bricks; some of the ground-floor dividing walls may be of brick also, but they are usually those in positions where another wall is directly above, dividing rooms on the next floor. Some of these upper walls are of lighter construction and are either made of coke breeze moulded into slabs, or with a timber framework covered on both sides with laths and plaster. Slab parti-

tion walls are often used on the ground floor, between kitchen and scullery, or along a passage. An alternative form of construction between living-rooms, kitchen, and scullery, is the wooden frame filled with brickwork, known as a "brick-nogged" partition.

The use of plugs in a coke breeze partition is not necessary as the material will, in most instances, take nails or even screws quite easily. A brick-nogged wall can be treated as an ordinary brick wall unless one happens to find one of the timber uprights, when the screws may be driven into it in the ordinary way.

A lath and plaster partition, however, cannot be plugged owing to the space between each surface. It will be necessary to locate at least two of the upright timber members for fixing large articles. Tapping the wall should give a more solid sound where the timber is, and a trial can be made with a fine bradawl or a very thin drill. The studs, or vertical members, are about 3 in. by 1½ in. to 4 in. by 2 in. in section, spaced at an average distance of 12 in. apart. Any article with fixing holes at less than this may be first fixed to a wood panel, and then this fixed to the wall by means of two larger screws top and bottom, into the studding of the wall.

The framed and braced type of partition has horizontal members also and the positions of these may prove convenient.

LAYING LINOLEUM AND CARPETS

Any form of floor-covering will give longer and better service if it is properly laid, and especially if some time is spent on the preparation of the floor surface.

Preparing the Floor.—Whenever

possible clear the room of all articles of furniture before starting to prepare the floor. With a nail punch and hammer punch all nail heads to sink them below the surface of the wood. At the same time look out for old tacks and remove them. Any loose boards should be made secure. There may be one in every room, where the pipe for the gas supply comes through to a gas fire, or for the lighting. As these boards may have to come up at some future time they should be fixed with screws in place of nails. Knots in the boards should be cut level with a wood chisel. Warped boards, and those with raised edges should be attended to, otherwise the lino will wear in lines corresponding to the board joints below. Remove the worst edges with a chisel and finish off with a small plane. Wide gaps may be plugged with lengths of strip wood, or folded paper tapped well into the cracks.

Concrete or stone floors must be covered with some damp-resisting under-lay.

An uneven floor should have the worst places filled up with layers of paper, and then covered with thick felt paper underlay. Even with a good boarded floor this underlay felting is advisable. This material is obtained in rolls, and should be placed across the floor at right-angles to the run of the boards.

Having measured the size of the room, calculate which is the most economical way of laying the lino, bearing in mind that the rolls are made 6 ft. wide. Try to arrange it in such a manner that there will be only a single joint where most wear takes place.

Fitting the Lino to the Floor.—Few walls are perfectly square, so do not expect the skirting boards to be the same distance apart at any position across the room. Start by laying the width opposite to the fireplace. At this end of the room there is usually an unbroken run of skirting. Unroll the lino and try the long edge against the long edge of the wall. If there is very little uneven-ness it is best to leave it and not try to cut off a little here and there to get a

dead fit. One cut will often result in many. Assuming that the back left-hand corner, as shown in the diagram, Fig. 1, fits well but that there is a gap of about $\frac{1}{4}$ in. at the front edge (B), tapering back as indicated by the dotted line, this portion must be trimmed across the 6 ft. width. Use a lead pencil or other convenient marking tool, moving the point along the skirting, and cut the lino to the mark produced. If this is carefully done the lino will be found to fit perfectly. The same method can be

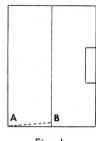

Fig. 1

used with other edges, provided the lino is kept in the same position.

When the first width is in position the second width is laid to match the pattern. Starting from the end of the room as before, cut the end of the lino and slide it up to the wall. Allow the long edge to overlap the first piece by $\frac{1}{8}$ in. and allow it to remain like this to give it sufficient time to expand. Later this strip is trimmed off.

The actual cutting is done with a special knife having a hooked blade.

Fig. 2

These tools are inexpensive. It is therefore well worth while to invest in one instead of using a makeshift, which is usually unsatisfactory. The illustration, Fig. 2, shows the knife in use.

Fixing Lino.—The actual fixing is by means of headless lino tacks or sprigs, placed about $\frac{1}{4}$ in. from the edge and 5 to 6 in. apart. If the material buckles after this the nailed joint need not be undone: either of the far ends are trimmed.

Preserving.—As most cleaning soaps contain a large percentage of soda, and hard scrubbing has a damaging effect on lino surfaces and colours, an application of liquid surfacing preparation will prolong the life of the pattern and the whole lino. When this has been allowed to dry, the lino should be cleaned with some form of polish with a wax base.

Carpets.—A fitted carpet, which completely covers the floor, is best laid by the firm who supply it, as the cutting and stretching will be done by an expert with the proper tools.

The ordinary carpet in conjunction with a lino or other surround has the advantage of being removable. It should be turned about at intervals so that the extra wear near a door or fireplace comes over a fresh section of carpet. A felt underlay below the carpet is also recommended.

Stair Carpets.—Where a staircase has one or more bends some difficulty may be experienced in setting the carpet neatly.

The easiest method is to start at the top of the stairs, fix the end, and work downwards, keeping the carpet central and straight at the sides. Insert a rod at each stair, and on reaching a bend keep the edge of the carpet firm and straight down the outer or wider edge, and do the same at each turning, step and rise. This will bring it right on the straight stairs again, and a neat fold may be made at the narrow edge of each turning, a tack or two generally being necessary to keep it in place.

SIMPLE FURNITURE REPAIRS

IN every home there will be found some article of furniture in need of repair, and too often it is dumped in some out-of-the-way place and left to become spoilt with the damp and dirt. If the damage is dealt with promptly and properly, such articles may be given an extended and useful life.

Broken Back Leg.—To repair a chair with a broken back leg, put the broken parts together, and if not too splintered, drill holes through at right-angles to the break, perhaps two each side, to just clear No. 8 wood screws without being too slack, and countersink the holes to let the heads into the wood as shown at A in Fig. 1. The heads of the screws may be covered with stained plastic wood when fixed. Apply strong glue to the broken surfaces, and drive the screws home tight, from opposite sides, and the leg will be quite strong.

Front Leg.—In the event of a break in a front leg of a chair, as illustrated at B, the remains of the broken part (A) should be cut off to leave a flat surface, and, if not too damaged, the circular piece may be glued to the top of the leg and left to dry hard. If in very bad condition, the part (B) containing the break may be cut off and a new piece made and fitted in its place to make up the correct height, and the two pieces glued together to complete the top of the leg.

When set, the hole for the dowel rod may be bored in each part, well up into the square portion, and also down into the leg, as shown. The dowel should be of hardwood, about ¾ in. or 1 in. in diameter, according to size of leg. Both the dowel and the inside of the hole should be well glued.

Chair Back and Frame.—The curved part of the back of a chair, if only loose at the joint, should have the surfaces cleaned, the old dowels carefully

brace may be used across the corners of the frame to make it firm. The bracket form, indicated at D, may be marked on a piece of suitable wood, getting the correct angles from the frame after it has been tapped back into its correct position. Clearance holes for the screws are drilled in the bracket only. If the tenons are loose it would be as well to

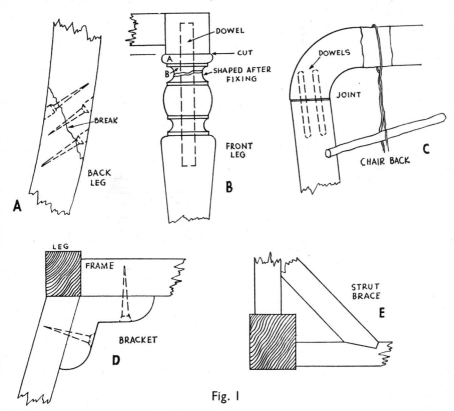

Fig. I

drilled out in both pieces, and new ones fitted. Glue holes and dowels, and fix into position. It may be clamped as shown at c by covering the wood with a piece of cloth, tying a double string round it and the frame and twisting a piece of wood in the string until it is strained tight.

Loose Seat Rails.—Loose seat rails are a defect common in most chairs subject to rough usage. Two forms of

"blind wedge" them. Two small wedges of hardwood are cut just thick enough to give the required spread to the tenon, the mortise holes being shaped with a chisel to a slight dovetail.

The strut brace (E) is fitted in the same manner as the solid bracket, screws being used as before.

Kitchen Chairs.—When any other job about the house has to be done, the

16

first thing demanded is "a chair out of the kitchen." It may be to stand upon, for use in sawing wood, or to dry clothing before the fire. This, and the fact that such chairs are usually made in large quantities from wood not thoroughly seasoned, results in the whole of the joints becoming loose; and the various rails and legs fall out. If the repairing is properly done, the old chair will prove more durable than a new one, one reason being that the wood has become thoroughly shrunk; therefore the joints are not likely to work loose.

To make the chair serviceable, take out all the rails of the back that are loose, and clean off the old glue, if any. Treat the legs in a similar manner, and, if necessary, fit a new spindle rail to replace a broken one. A simple piece like this is not worth mending because any piece of suitable wood can be shaped with a plane or spokeshave.

If a little is cut off the tops of the legs to enlarge diameter, they can be made a tight fit. The same would be possible when the back consists of all-round bars. The slight reduction in height would not matter. Rectangular uprights may be tightened by small wedges driven in to spread the tenon.

Tables.—Fig. 2 shows the underside of a type of dining table with removable centre leaf. The chief cause of these getting out of order is the over-winding of the screw by putting too much strain on the key handle after inserting the loose leaf. This causes the plate at the winding end to strain and bulge away from the frame until the screws become loose or even wrenched out. The opposite end holding the cover tube may come adrift, and in a few cases the

joints of the frame are found to be loose, but on the whole the construction of this class of table is very sound. To strengthen the frame, glued and screwed blocks can be added to the corners and to the sides under the cross straps. The one with the dovetail ends, if loose, may be strengthened by means of a T-shaped metal strap fixed over the top. These are obtainable in several sizes, ready drilled.

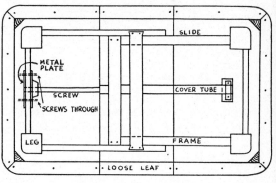

DINING TABLE   UNDERSIDE

Fig. 2

The tube end-bracket is fixed to the underside of the table top, so longer screws should not be used or they may come through. The old fixing holes should be carefully plugged and the metal piece re-fixed with new screws. The winding end-plate may be removed and tapped flat again where bulged, and as plugs are liable to pull out here, it is possible to turn the plate a little and to insert screws into a fresh position. A much stronger and more lasting job is made of this end if long Whitworth or B.A. thread metal screws are fixed right through the frame, to secure the plate by nuts on the inside. A brass or other metal plate with a central hole to take the winding key should be used on the outside of the frame, otherwise it has been found that in time the screw-heads

Fig. 3

pull into the wood and that end works loose again.

The top, if badly scratched and dented, may be rubbed down with fine glasspaper, re-stained to the correct tint, and polished with french polishing materials.

Furniture With Padded Seats.— Settees and chairs with stuffed seats, with or without springs, are not difficult to make good, even if they are in such a bad condition as the chair shown in Fig. 3. The work should be supported, bottom upwards, on two boxes or chairs.

First remove the outer canvas by tapping out the tacks, using an old screw-driver and light hammer. Strike in the direction of the grain and they will come out easily and not split the wood. Fig. 4 shows an armchair with the canvas removed. Remove the webbing in the same manner, and as the springs possibly will be found bound to the webbing with twine, they must be cut free and any distorted ones removed and discarded. One should be taken as a sample when buying new. Also, see whether the inner canvas over the tops of the springs requires replacing. If this is in good condition it may be left and new web-

bing put on by folding over the end, tacking it to the frame and straining it tight by folding the surplus round a piece of wood and using this as a lever against the frame. Interlace the rows of webbing at right-angles across the frame, under and over the first lengths, as indicated in Fig. 4. The springs may now be pushed down into position under the webbing and bound with uphol-sterer's twine, which is exceptionally strong without being thick. An ordinary packing needle will serve very well for doing this. Make sure that the springs are upright and do not touch each other. Finish the bottom by replacing the canvas, folding in the rough edges. An illustration showing the springs in position ready for the covering canvas appears in Fig. 5.

If the inner canvas needs replacing and the seat is a bad shape, the outer

Fig. 4

cover should be carefully taken off and kept as the pattern for cutting new material. If the stuffing is not disturbed it can be removed in one piece for putting back later. Cut the twine holding the springs, but not that which is stitched across the front edge of the chair.

Remove the canvas and old webbing as before, and start by re-webbing, interlaced as already described. Bind the heads of the springs as previously suggested, and cover them with canvas. The stuffing may be freed from dust by beating carefully, in the open, with a light cane. The top layer of wadding, if very dusty, can be renewed, and the pad of stuffing pulled out a little to lean forward in the front.

Fig. 5

Tack the top covering into position along the front edge first, but only in one or two positions in case it needs altering. Strain the cover over to the back, and then from side to side. When all is set as required, drive in tacks about every 2 in. A final finish is given by adding gimp to hide the tacks, using covered pins of a colour to harmonise with the covering material.

REMEDYING ILL-FITTING DRAWERS

A DRAWER in a new piece of furniture may develop the annoying habit of sticking after it has been installed in the house a few days. This may be due to the newness of the wood or the article may have been placed in too warm a position. A damp atmosphere would have the same effect.

If the drawer can only be opened a little way, apply a little grease to as much of the exposed parts of the runners as possible, and if accessible do the same to those at the back. Close the drawer and re-open it a few times, and if it comes forward more each time, without using undue force, apply more grease to the newly exposed parts of the runners and drawer surface.

When the drawer is free and removable, wipe off the grease and rub the sliding surfaces with a piece of sand-paper folded round a block of wood. Rub over the whole length evenly. Note if the tightness is on the bottom edges or on the surface of the sides.

Easing Down.—Before easing down too much with sand-paper, and thus making the drawer too free, see that the article, such as a wardrobe cupboard with a drawer under, is standing level and even on all of its four feet. The piece of furniture may not be inaccurate, but the floorboards may be uneven, and with a certain amount of weight due to the contents, the framework has become slightly twisted or lowered at one corner, thus throwing the drawer opening out of shape slightly, but just enough to make all the difference between it and the shape of the drawer. The legs may be standing on the stained boards of the surround at the back, and on the linoleum at the front, so this difference of level may be the cause. This can be put right by cutting two small squares of lino to the shapes of the bottoms of the feet, and pushing a piece under each back leg. If this is found to be the correct height they can be fixed in place by means of a small quantity of liquid glue or a few lino sprigs. For correcting uneven legs plywood is very convenient as the thickness can be reduced by paring off one layer of ply.

Another cause of distortion of the frame may be too much weight placed in a drawer or drawers.

In very bad cases where such distortion is permanent, a few shavings must be taken off the runners with a small sharp plane in the manner shown in Fig. 1, taking care to plane in the direction of the grain of the wood.

Lubricants.—Candle grease is a good material to rub on the drawer and

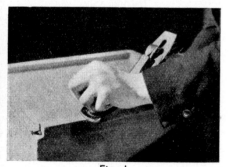

Fig. 1

runner surfaces as it retains its lubricating properties for a considerable length of time. Soap is frequently used but fails to be of use after a time because it

becomes hard and dry. French chalk, a finely-ground powder, is satisfactory as a lubricant for some woods, but should never be used if the wood is damp, because it will fill the pores and seal the

Fig. 2

moisture in. Oil such as raw linseed may be used as a lubricant for the sliding surfaces and will preserve the wood. It should be well rubbed in, and the surfaces allowed to dry before putting the drawer back, otherwise the slightly swollen wood will cause trouble. A loose drawer or one that has dropped at one end requires a new runner. The edge of the drawer may have become worn thin or have broken; or if of hardwood may have rubbed the guide piece inside into a groove, allowing the edge to fall lower and leave an unsightly gap round the front opening. Fine wood dust will be found at the sides and at the back of the opening, indicating hard wear, and deep scratches will show where this has taken place most.

The damaged edge of the drawer is planed off and a length of suitable section wood fitted in its place, as shown in Fig. 2, using glue and panel pins. The heads of the latter should be set below the surface with a fine nail punch.

New runner bars may be fitted in the same manner, always selecting a hardwood for the purpose.

HOUSEHOLD REPAIRS

UNDER this heading it is proposed to deal with some of the numerous odd jobs that the handyman is called upon to do in order to prolong the useful life of various articles about the house.

Folding Clothes-horse. — With frequent use the web hinges of a clothes-horse tear away from the uprights.

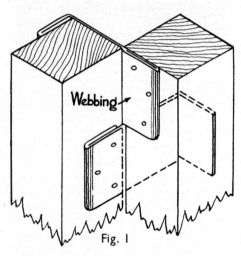

Fig. I

These may be renewed with strong webbing as used for chair repairs. Cut a piece equal to three times the thickness of the wood frame, fold the end over and tack to the wood as shown in Fig. 1. This will allow the frame to be folded in either direction.

Cover Plate Round Range Flue Pipe.—When the sheet metal flue pipe of a kitchen stove has become old and burned thin, the new one, purchased ready-made, may not be a good fit in the hole where it passes through the metal below the chimney opening. If there is a gap the fire will not burn so well as before, and smoke may issue in considerable quantities at this point.

The fault, as indicated in Fig. 2, may be corrected by cutting a sheet metal plate to lay over the hole. This has a central opening cut to fit the new pipe at that point in its diameter.

Fit the new pipe to the top of the cast-iron box part of the range flue, mark on it where it passes through the hole, and on removing the pipe measure the diameter at that point. The pipe will probably be oval in shape so that a cardboard template must be made as shown in the sketch, Fig. 3, using a tracer to obtain the correct curve. A template made to one-half the shape will do as it can be reversed to obtain the full shape.

A piece of sheet metal is required—the lid of a biscuit tin will do or a piece cut from an old tray. Mark the shape of the hole on this, and then mark another line, about $\frac{3}{4}$ in. from and inside the first one, as shown. This inner piece may be removed by drilling a circle of small holes and breaking the middle out with a small cold chisel. One with a cutting edge about $\frac{3}{8}$ in. wide or less as used by mechanics is best. With this type of metal-cutting chisel, the metal may be cut without drilling, if carefully used. Trim the rough edge all round with a file, and cut a series of slits outwards as far as the outer line. Place a block of wood under the sheet and tap these pieces round to set them at right-angles to the sheet, as illustrated in Fig. 4. Fit this over the pipe down to the mark to test it for fit. The next job is to open the slide, push the cut sheet through over towards the hole, to keep it in position while the pipe is pushed up from below. A wire hook may be of assistance in holding the piece down while this is being done, and a little patience may be required before the pipe is set back in position with the new flange down tight on to the inner side of the original hole. The illustration at Fig. 2 shows the completed job.

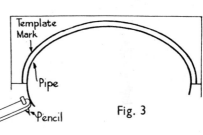

Fig. 2

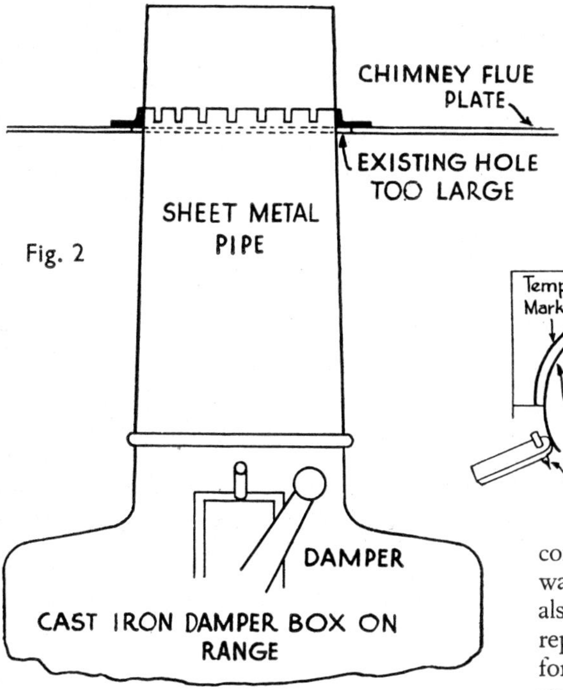

CHIMNEY FLUE PLATE

EXISTING HOLE TOO LARGE

SHEET METAL PIPE

DAMPER

CAST IRON DAMPER BOX ON RANGE

Broken Lug on Range Trivet.—The cast iron trivet in front of the ash-pan of a kitchen range sometimes suffers from the loss of a fixing lug through being dropped. In such cases, there is no need to discard the trivet, for a repair as shown in Fig. 5 can be easily made by bending a piece of metal about $\frac{3}{16}$ in. or $\frac{1}{4}$ in. thick by $\frac{1}{2}$ in. wide to turn down to match the other lug as near as possible. Two holes to clear $\frac{3}{16}$ in. or $\frac{1}{4}$ in. Whitworth screws are drilled in

the flat end in positions where they will come over some convenient opening in the trivet top. Two nuts on each screw underneath the trivet will keep it firm.

Mending Holes in Enamelware.—To stop a small leak in enamelware the hole should be enlarged with a drill about $\frac{1}{8}$ in. diameter, a copper or aluminium rivet pushed through and the stem hammered flat on the outside. The rivet will spread and close the hole. Small screws

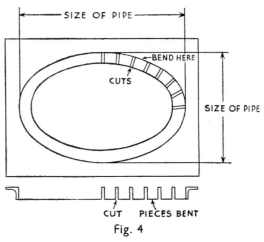

Template Mark

Pipe

Pencil

Fig. 3

complete with nut, two metal washers and a disc of cork are also obtainable for these small repair jobs but are not suitable for use on pie dishes and utensils used for food. These,

SIZE OF PIPE

BEND HERE

CUTS

SIZE OF PIPE

CUT PIECES BENT

Fig. 4

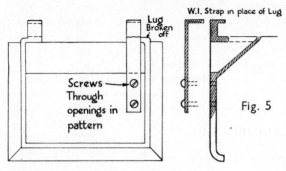

Fig. 5

and the rivet method, should be used for a pail or bowl.

Coal Shovels.—The thin broken edge of a small coal shovel makes it hard to use. The edge can be reconditioned by cutting off the worn portion with a cold chisel and then trimming with a file.

Household Steps.—Cords should be replaced immediately they show signs of fraying. A loose strut between the frames, if too bad, should be replaced by a new piece with the tenon cut large enough to make a tight fit. Wedges can be driven in to tighten the tenon, care being taken that the surrounding wood is not split in doing so. The whole job will be spoilt if this happens. Hinges may work loose, and replacing with longer screws will, in the end, cut the wood to pieces, so the hinges should be refitted to a new batten let into the frame, if it is not possible to fix them in new positions.

OVERHAULING A SEWING MACHINE

To meet the needs of a family, the sewing machine may be called upon to deal with a variety of materials and jobs, so that periodic cleaning and oiling will be necessary. New materials shed a fine dust from the dressing, and there are always short ends of cotton and fluff from each piece of work to accumulate round the working parts near the shuttle.

The movement of the shuttle varies in different machines; in some a boat-shaped carrier takes the long spool, on which the cotton is wound, backwards and forwards in a straight line. In others the cotton is wound on a small circular spool, and a special shaped outer ring moves in a semi-rotary motion, first to the left and then to the right, to carry the cotton to the needle.

Cleaning.—The fluff is picked out with a long needle, from the underside and from the top by sliding the plate to one side, working the movement at intervals to carry any loose pieces forward to where they may be removed. All dust and fluff may be wiped from the few moving parts, the underside of the metal base, and the inside of the recess in the wooden base with a piece of old linen, damped with petrol. Do not use paraffin for a sewing machine, or any similar mechanism. Parts and corners that cannot be reached with the rag can be cleaned with a small brush, in the manner shown in the illustration, Fig. 1. The same applies to the parts above the base on the outside.

Oiling.—Only sewing-machine oil should be used for lubricating purposes. This is a special preparation which will not dry into a hard film on the various parts, or retard their motion by a sticky deposit. Small holes, made in the correct places where oil should be applied, will be found in various parts of the machine, inside and out. Use a long needle to clear these of dust, and use a clean oil-can; one with a small screw-on cap is the best as this will keep the oil and the very fine bore of the spout free from dust.

Under the claw foot is a small moving plate with teeth, to feed the material

Treadle Machines.—These few points on cleaning apply to the treadle-type machines, and, in addition, the belt sometimes needs attention. This is usually of round-section leather with patent metal hook and eye ends, or a simple wire clip passed through the butting ends of the belt. These points should be examined to see if the leather is fraying. A new belt will stretch after a short period of use and a satisfactory

Fig. 1

along; this should be kept clear or the material will not move forward.

Any trace of oil round the shuttle and needle movements must be removed to prevent soiling materials and cotton.

The spool-winding attachment may need attention; the rubber tyre on the driving wheel occasionally works loose and may be secured with one of the many reliable liquid glues. If the tyre is badly worn or perished it is advisable to replace it with a new one.

drive will not be obtained unless it is tightened. This is done by cutting a short piece off the end and re-fitting the fastening. It will now require some straining to get it back into the pulley grooves, but if it is held firmly against the edge and guided while the pulley wheel is turned by hand it will soon slip into place.

Oiling-points will be found on the treadle bearings, the foot-rest plate, and the crank arm.

16*

OVERHAULING A GRAMOPHONE

THE gramophone, like all mechanical devices, requires adjusting and cleaning at intervals, if it is to give lasting and efficient service.

The mechanism is made by specialists, and calls for a degree of skill and accuracy equal to that required for clock- and instrument-making. Adjustments are therefore very sensitive, and should

Fig. I

be followed by frequent tests until satisfactory results have been obtained.

Two of the main troubles are, failure to wind up, and slow playing speed, often convulsive, with a bumping noise at intervals.

When the winding handle turns freely and the motor does not respond, the end of the spring has either slipped from its peg, or the spring has broken. This usually happens while winding, and the noise of something suddenly loosened is unmistakable. To the experienced ear

the sound of a break is perhaps more pronounced, but the average owner need look no farther than the spring drum to locate the trouble.

As both faults sound alike, there is a chance that the inner end of the spring has slipped from its catch or peg on the spindle. In winding up, tension is applied to the centre of the spring, *i.e.* the inner end, and to lessen the risk of this becoming too slack, in the normal way no spring-driven motor should be allowed to revolve until it will turn no more. Always leave it wound a little, and on no account spin the turntable round in the reverse direction. On the other hand, never wind to the utmost limit of the handle; gramophones are as sensitive to this maltreatment as clocks.

The Spring.—Every make and type of gramophone motor has its own special size spring. When fitted, they are packed with a graphite mixture, and in use a certain amount works out owing to the coiling and uncoiling of the spring. Fixing a new one is rather a messy job, and for this reason it is as well to be provided with plenty of old newspaper to work on and to wipe the grease from the parts as they are removed. If it is not desired to do this work, remove the spring drum and take it to a gramophone dealer, giving the name or make of machine, if possible.

Cleaning.—It is astonishing the difference that a regular cleaning will make to the quietness and efficiency of a gramophone. Annoying background noises are almost completely eliminated by this simple little service. To clean a gramophone first remove the turntable. This is a push-on fit on the taper top of the spindle, and should be carefully prised upwards from two opposite points at once, in the manner illustrated in Fig. 1. Next unscrew the catch-plate on the top board, retaining the end of the lid support. The four corner wood screws are easy to remove, and the top board, complete with motor, is lifted off and placed motor side up on two pieces of wood to keep the spindle clear.

The motor is generally fixed to the top board by means of three screws passing into tapped holes in the metal frame, and rubber pads are placed between the frame and the top board. If these screws are too tight the pads are pressed, the buffer effect is lost, and the motor will be noisy when running.

For replacements, take a sample to a rubber stores or ironmonger. Some pads have a rivet-shaped head only, and others have a $\frac{3}{8}$ in. diameter stem to pass through the board and surround the screw as a buffer against vibration.

Remove the motor on to a sheet of paper, and wipe off as much of the black grease as possible. Afterwards, the quickest and least messy procedure is to wash the whole thing as it is with petrol, out of doors or anywhere away from a fire, of course, using a stiff brush. Paraffin is not suitable.

The Winding Spindle is geared to the springs through a suitable gear, the latter being contained in a single drum. The drum shaft has a gear wheel driving a pinion to which is fixed a larger wheel: the large one drives the turn-table spindle. Higher up on the turn-table spindle is a fibre gear, for silent running, which engages with a polished steel worm thread at the end of the spindle carrying the governor, as clearly seen in the illustration (Fig. 2). This is the most delicate part of the mechanism. The governor spindle has been ground and polished to very fine limits of accuracy, including the worm thread, therefore it should not be held by pliers.

This also applies to the turntable spindle. The only damage that can happen to the governor is broken springs caused by running the motor too fast. It will

Fig. 2

be noticed that as the speed is increased the three weights move outwards on the bow springs. As these are all fixed at one end to the shaft, the opposite ends cause the sliding sleeve with the large flange to move along the shaft. The amount of travel allowed along the shaft

Fig. 3

is adjusted by the speed regulator arm extension-piece carrying the small felt pad which acts like a brake block.

The brass flange should be cleaned and the felt pad soaked in sewing-machine oil and always kept moist. If dry, the action is jumpy. Dirty felt is easily replaced; the material is the same as that used in pianos. New governor springs are obtained from a gramophone dealer, and should be of the same length and thickness as the one to be replaced. In manufacture, the springs and weights are sorted into sets of equal thickness and weight, otherwise the governor would not work satisfactorily.

The coiled spring on the winding spindle prevents it from running back after winding. This may slip out of its setting or break, but being of stiff steel piano wire, a new one is difficult to wind at home unless a lathe is available. Home-made check springs should be exact reproductions of the old one as regards number of turns and gauge of wire.

Fitting New Spring.—To fit a new spring the top metal plate of the motor must be removed. The fixing is either by nuts or screws screwed on or into the corner pillars. The spindle complete with spring drum unit is then lifted clear. The illustration appearing at Fig. 3 shows the springs in place. The lower bearing sometimes contains a steel ball: this must not be lost in the cleaning, but should this happen, one as used in cycle ball-bearings can be tried, $\frac{1}{8}$ in. size or less.

A small taper pin through a collar on the drum fixes it to the shaft in some cases, but the drum is soon taken off, and the cover plate unscrewed. The spring, although broken, will fly out and cause some damage if great care is not taken to prevent it. One method is to hold the open end of the drum inside the mouth of a sack, and to prise the spring out with a screwdriver pushed through.

The outer end of the spring slips under a catch-piece in the drum and the inner end of the spring fits over a peg or projection on the spindle and may need easing over to get it to catch. Vaseline is quite suitable for packing, and is spread over the open ends of the spring and pushed in with a knife blade, but it must not be allowed to clog the worm or governor parts.

MAKING USE OF A RECESS

THE existing recess between the fire-place and the side wall of any room may be made quite easily into a useful cupboard. Both labour and materials are saved because sides and a back are not required.

The type of fitment built will depend upon the room. For a bedroom it may be a design suitable for a wardrobe on modern lines, with full length swing doors, shelves and coat-hangers. A sitting-room may need a book-case with doors, open shelves only, or, where a large quantity of books are not kept, the lower part may consist of a closed-in cupboard with open shelves above. In a kitchen, cupboard accommodation is always in demand, so that the fitment may follow a variety of designs and each recess be used.

The cupboard, details of which appear in Fig. 2, extends the full height of the room from floor to ceiling. The top part is enclosed by a pair of doors with glass panels, and contains shelves for china, and battens with hooks for cups and jugs. Below this is a store cupboard with shelves.

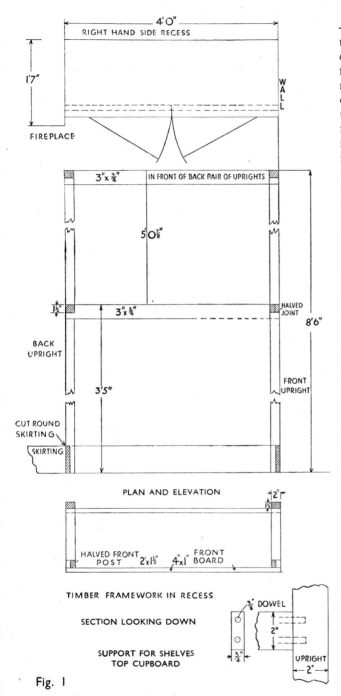

RIGHT HAND SIDE RECESS

4' 0"

1'7"

FIREPLACE

WALL

3" x ¾"   IN FRONT OF BACK PAIR OF UPRIGHTS

5' 0⅞"

BACK UPRIGHT

3" x ¾"

1½"

HALVED JOINT

8'6"

FRONT UPRIGHT

3'5"

CUT ROUND SKIRTING

SKIRTING

PLAN AND ELEVATION

2"

1½"

HALVED FRONT POST   2"x1½"   4"x1"   FRONT BOARD

TIMBER FRAMEWORK IN RECESS

SECTION LOOKING DOWN

SUPPORT FOR SHELVES TOP CUPBOARD

⅜" DOWEL

2"

¾"

UPRIGHT

2"

Fig. 1

The Framework. —The first stage of the work consists in cutting and making a framework to fit the recess. Two uprights of 2 in. by $1\frac{1}{2}$ in. timber are cut to the full height of the room and are fitted into the back corners with the 2 in. face towards the front. If there is a picture rail on the wall round the recess this part is taken down and part may be used later along the top of the front board. At the bottom end the face of the upright is cut to clear the existing skirting boards along the sides and back so that the back faces go flush against the wall. The boards which form the top of the lower store cupboard and 5 in. wide shelf in front of the china cupboard are $\frac{7}{8}$ in. thick, and at a height of 3 ft. 5 in. from the ground, as shown. At the back, the shelf is borne on the top edge of a length of 3 in. by $\frac{3}{4}$ in. timber screwed to the outer faces of the back posts at the required height. A similar length is fixed to their top ends.

Two front posts 3 ft. 5 in. long are

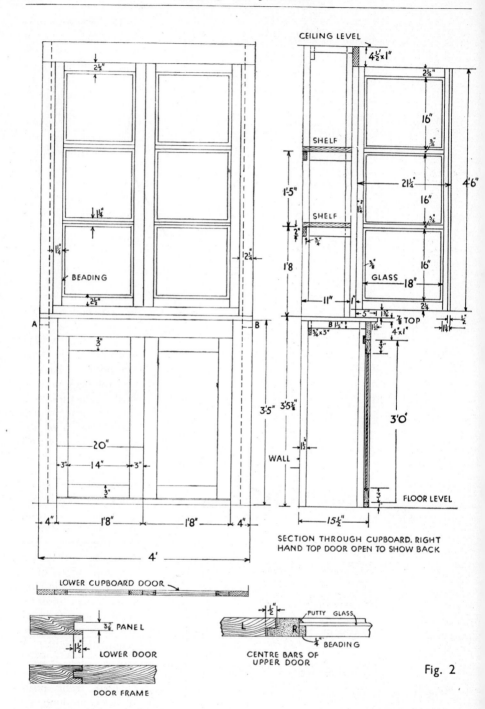

SECTION THROUGH CUPBOARD. RIGHT
HAND TOP DOOR OPEN TO SHOW BACK

LOWER CUPBOARD DOOR

PANEL

LOWER DOOR

DOOR FRAME

CENTRE BARS OF
UPPER DOOR

PUTTY GLASS

BEADING

Fig. 2

needed to complete the framework for the bottom cupboard. These are also 2 in. by $1\frac{1}{2}$ in., and the same section timber is used for the horizontal members. The back ends of these rest on the edge of the cross rails where cut away, and may also be nailed through from the backs of the uprights. The front ends have a halved joint with the front posts, and similar pieces may be used at the floor level and nailed or screwed to the floor.

The front uprights for the top cupboard are set back 5 in. from the front edge of the shelf and are fixed to the horizontal side rails A and B (Fig. 2). The boards of the division between the two cupboards are cut to fit round the uprights.

The support rails for the back and ends of the shelves in the top cupboard are 2 in. wide by $\frac{3}{4}$ in. thick and fitted between the uprights by means of dowels as shown in the detail (Fig. 1). The corners of the shelves are cut to fit round the uprights; the top, side horizontal rails are supported at the back as before, and the joints with the front uprights halved. A top front board 1 in. thick by $4\frac{1}{2}$ in. wide completes that end of the frame and a similar board 4 in. wide with two side pieces of the same material is made into a frame for the front of the lower cupboard, a strip 1 in. square being fixed to the floor along the bottom. A similar strip at the back will prevent the doors from pushing inwards.

The lower doors have 3 in. by 1 in. thick frames, with plain panels let into grooves all round. The panel members are also grooved and tongued as shown in the detailed diagram (Fig. 2).

Six pieces of glass each 16 in. by 18 in. are required for the top doors. The frames are mortised and tenoned, and a thin beading is fixed round each opening towards the front, to leave a ledge all round inside for the glass, which is put in at the back and finished with brads and putty.

Recess Wardrobe.—A suggestion for a recess wardrobe is given in Fig. 3. The existing picture rail is left in place and used with the front frame to support the roof or top of plywood. The dimensions of the recess will vary, so that no exact dimensions can be given, but the general construction may be followed. The frame members are cut to clear the skirting boards and the picture rail, and the horizontal rails are joined to the uprights by means of dowels. These rails support the shelves at the back and sides on the left- and right-hand sides of the recess, the centre edges being supported on runners screwed on each side of the centre partition, which is secured to the plywood top and the floor. Only one half need be fitted with shelves so that the other is left clear full length for dresses, etc., or if a recess is available on the other side of the fireplace this could be used for a similar wardrobe, one fitted for a lady and the other for a gentleman.

The four side rails are made of 2-in. by $1\frac{1}{2}$-in. deal, and as they may not be in convenient positions for shelves, lighter runners are fixed to the partition and dowelled to the back and front frame members. Extra support may be arranged along the back if necessary.

The picture rail is usually about 6 ft. 8 in. from the floor, and the uprights are level with the top edge. A sheet of $\frac{1}{2}$-in. or $\frac{3}{4}$-in. plywood is nailed to the picture rail at the back and sides, and to the front frame of the wardrobe. Three pieces of $1\frac{1}{2}$-in. by 3-in. scantling are required for the front frame—two lengths from floor to top of picture rail, marked A and B, and the top piece, C, between. On the floor level the front board, D, should be the same height as the surrounding skirting. The door frames are mortised and tenoned together in the usual way, or they may be dowelled, and the panels either sunk in the front or raised, with a bevel or moulding all round. The general finish should be in keeping with the remainder of the room.

Shelves.—This arrangement is indicated in Fig. 4. The height and number of shelves depend upon the quantity of books to be stored. Heavy volumes should occupy the bottom shelf, and it is suggested that a compartment of suitable size is partitioned off and enclosed with a drop flap door so that newspapers, etc., may be kept handy but tidy. A similar compartment might be used to accommodate a home-made wireless set, as indicated, so that the usual tangle of unsightly wires and batteries is hidden from view.

Uprights of 2-in. by 1-in. timber extend from the floor level to the top of the picture rail, in each corner of the recess. The lower, outer edges are cut to clear the skirting board on each side of the recess, but as the timber is only 1 in. thick, the back pair need not be notched to clear the back skirting board, but may be screwed to the face of it and packing pieces fixed behind the upright to fill the small gap to the back wall. When the spacing of the shelves has been decided, the left-hand back and front uprights are clamped together and marked for the runner positions. The runners are 1 in. by 1½ in. deep and are let into the outer edges of the uprights

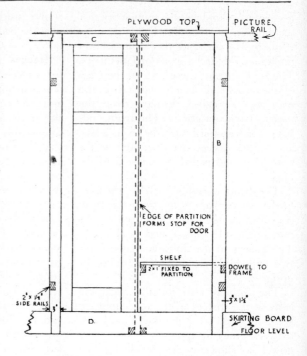

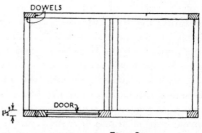

Fig. 3

as shown. They are screwed. This means that the ends of the runners will show at the front, and must be hidden by a length of moulding fixed round that edge wide enough to cover this part of the construction. The runners on the other side are fixed in the same manner, and the moulding should be carried round the top and sides, with mitred joints at the corners.

A raised floor is provided by fixing a 3-in. by 1-in. board on edge behind the front uprights, and a 2-in. by 1-in.

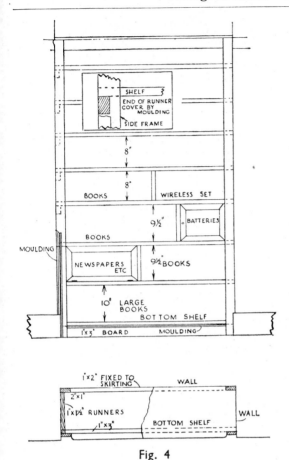

MOULDING

Fig. 4

batten at the same height, to the back skirting. On this the bottom shelf or platform boards are laid and fixed, and finished with a length of moulding.

The shelves are cut at the corners to clear the uprights so that they go right back to the wall at the back and sides.

Thick plywood is used for a top and is secured to the top edge of the picture rail all round and the tops of the uprights, the edge being hidden as before by a suitable moulding.

The Doors for the battery and newspaper compartments consist of plain pieces of $\frac{1}{2}$-in. plywood, accurately cut to fit flush with the shelves and partitions. If a more ornate door is desired the addition of strips of wood, $1\frac{1}{4}$ in. wide and $\frac{1}{4}$ in. thick, with mitred corners and front edges slightly bevelled, glued to the face of the plywood background will give a good imitation of a panelled door, as shown in the drawing.

FITTING AN EXTRA DOOR

THE cutting of an extra doorway, or the changing of the position of a door, is really not difficult, and, with a little care, may be completed without having the room repapered; but unless one has done similar work before it is as well to leave such jobs until the room requires redecorating. This is certainly the best time, because the old door and framework, if carefully taken down, can be used n the new opening. The original opening can be either filled in and a plaster surface formed to correspond with the wall, or the old doorway may be closed on one side and the other side converted into a book-case, with or without doors. If a new door is not being made at home, it may be possible to obtain a second-hand one from a local builder.

The Wall.—It is first necessary to ascertain how the wall is built, and for an example we will assume that it is a lath and plaster partition.

When the general position of the proposed opening has been chosen, tap the wall with a hammer to locate, by the more solid sound, just where the studs or uprights are. A very common form of construction for a lath and plaster partition is shown in Fig. 1. The studs may be spaced from 12 to 15 in. apart, centre to centre. At intervals, horizontal pieces or "nogging" are fixed. These are usually fitted between the studs, as shown. The laths, spaced about ¼ in. apart, horizontally, are nailed to the face of this timber framework to form a key for the plaster surface. Let us

suppose that it is desired to have the new door as near the end of the room as possible. To save cutting a number of studs the position is fixed between the second and fifth studs. When a doorway is built in a partition during the construction of the house, it is usual to make the two side posts of thicker timber than the studs. In a partition of the size shown these would be 3 in. thick on the face and 4 in. deep, forming the thickness of the wall, but in this case 1 in. thick by 4 in. wide timber in the form of a frame or rough backing is used and nailed to the inside faces of the existing studs. By cutting the two studs marked Nos. 3 and 4 a width of 3 ft. between centres is obtained. Allowing for 2 in. for the sides of the

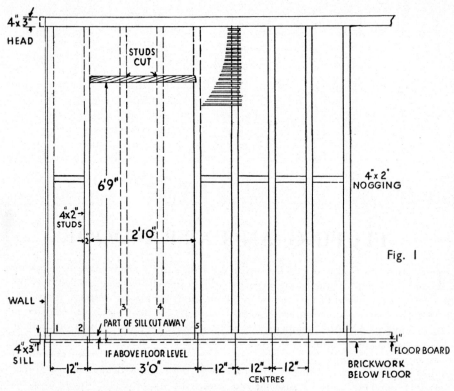

DOOR OPENING IN LATH & PLASTER PARTITION WALL

rough backing and a final lining 1½ in. thick on each side and at the top, it is possible to use a ready-made door 2 ft. 6 in. wide by 6 ft. 6 in. high. The jamb member is rebated ½ in. deep by 1½ in. wide, as shown in Fig. 2, to suit the dimensions of the door. The head of the door opening is 2 in. by 4 in.

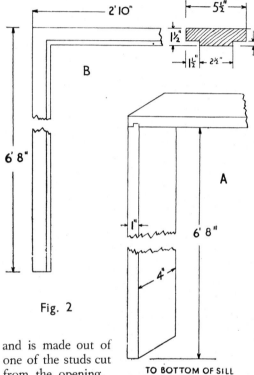

B

6' 8"

A

Fig. 2

6' 8"

4"

TO BOTTOM OF SILL

2' 10"

5½"

1½"

½"

1½" 2½"

edges. From these two pairs of marked holes the centre-to-centre distance of the studs is determined. Now mark on the wall the position of the edge of the next stud to right and left. These will form the side posts of the opening. Make sure with the bradawl that the edge has been found and mark a line down the wall at each side. Before cutting into the wall check from the dimensions just obtained to make sure

Fig. 3

¾ LATH & PLASTER NAILS

JAMB LINING

STUD

JAMB

4"

2" 1" x 1½"

1½"

GROUND STRIP

that the opening will correspond with the size of door selected and the jamb members and lining. It is now necessary to cut the plaster very carefully to the lines representing the inner edges

and is made out of one of the studs cut from the opening.

Making the Opening. — Having marked the outline of the desired opening, next find the two centre studs, which must be removed. This is done by pressing the blade of a thin bradawl into the wall. Little resistance indicates that the hollow space between studs has been penetrated. A solid obstruction about ¾ in. below the face of the wall is a stud, and you must find the two edges representing the thickness, and, having found one, move the bradawl along about 12 in. and locate the other stud

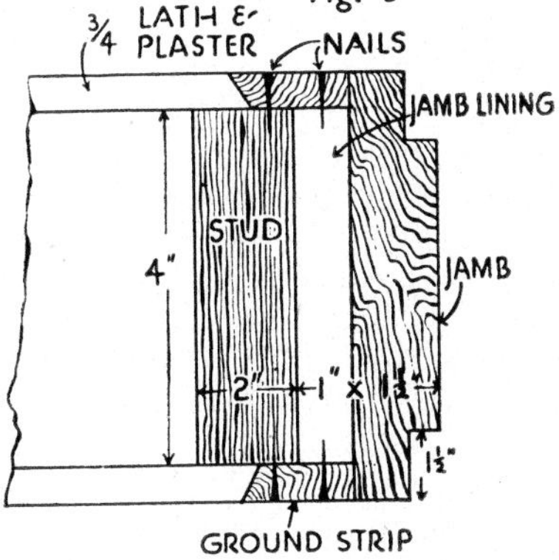

of studs Nos. 2 and 5 (Fig. 1). An old wood chisel will do, care being taken that only a little is removed at a time, so that the plaster does not break back beyond the lines of the opening. A space all down the wall, about an inch wide, will be enough to expose the laths and the edge of the stud behind. A keyhole saw, or a small handsaw with fairly fine teeth, may be used to cut through the laths, keeping the blade close to the edge of the stud without cutting into it. It will also be necessary to remove one or more floorboards, according to the direction in which they are laid, so that the sill or bottom plate of the partition can be cut through, as indicated in Fig. 1. If, while sawing, the laths and plaster are inclined to pull away from the studs and tend to become jagged at the edge, fix a length of board down the wall close to the cut. This should prevent the plaster from breaking out beyond the line.

The other edge is cut in the same manner, and the laths with the plaster can then be pulled off almost up to the line of the top edge of the opening. Here the plaster should be cut away first, and the laths cut carefully so that the plaster above is not damaged. The next step is to cut away the laths and plaster on the other side of the partition. The position can be located by piercing a few holes through the plaster from the prepared side, using the edges of the studs as a guide. It should then be possible to mark the other side of the wall, and to proceed as already described. When all the laths and plaster have been removed the tops of the studs may be sawn through, as well as the sill. The cross-piece should be either notched or housed into the studs. The remaining short pieces of studding supporting the lath and plaster over the door are secured to the head by means of nails driven in from below.

The rough frame or lining of 4-in. by 1-in. deal, as indicated at A in Fig. 2, is now fixed into position, and the narrow front strips or ground, $\frac{3}{4}$ in. thick by 2 in. wide, nailed to this and the studs. To enable these pieces to lie flat on the faces of the studs the laths and plaster must be cut back an inch to the centre of the studs. The double rebated jamb shown in detail at B in Fig. 2, is in turn nailed or screwed to the lining. The arrangement is shown in Fig. 3.

A moulding with mitred corners forming the architrave is then cut and fixed to the grounds all round the opening on both sides and the top of the doorway. In fixing the jambs and the door hinges it is essential to see that they are upright and level, otherwise the door will not hang properly. A piece of wood the thickness of the floorboards will be required to make up the floor level between the two rooms. Defects in the plaster are made good and the door and frame are ready for priming and painting.

Doorway in Brick Wall.—To make a doorway through a 9-in. brick wall between two rooms, the size of the opening is first marked on the wall and the plaster cut down the lines with a hammer and chisel. The exposed brickwork is also marked, but before cutting out any of the bricks, provision must be made for bridging the opening at the top to take the weight of the brickwork above the door. This support takes the form of two timber lintels or small beams, each 4 in. wide by 3 in. deep. These should be long enough to span the opening and extend at least $4\frac{1}{2}$ in. at each end for letting into the wall, as shown in Fig. 3. Before removing the main portion of the brickwork, cut away one course where the lintels will come and remove the cement from the underside and the top surface of the $4\frac{1}{2}$-in. recess. Cut the lintels and fit them in position, with their outer faces flush with the face of the bricks on each side of the wall, as shown. The space of about an inch between the lintels need not be filled, but wedges may be driven in between the ends of the timber and the wall, if required.

The same size of door is used in this case as in the partition, but instead of a solid backing, packing pieces 1 in. thick are substituted. With brick walls the

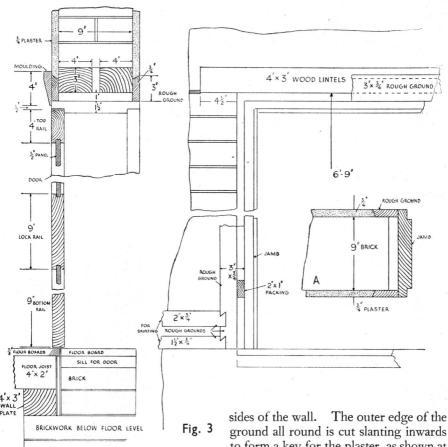

Fig. 3

sides of the wall. The outer edge of the ground all round is cut slanting inwards to form a key for the plaster, as shown at A in Fig. 3. Architrave moulding is fixed to the rough grounds to finish the doorway, the corners being mitred. The brick wall will, of course, continue down below the floor level, and if the surface of the existing floorboards is level with the top of a row of bricks below, these, to the width of the doorway, must be taken up and a timber sill fitted of such thickness that the addition of a piece of floorboard will make the two floors level.

usual practice is to fix the packing pieces in the form of strips about 2 in. deep, fixed at intervals to the lintels over the doorway, and at intervals to the jamb members, but secured to the wall by means of wood plugs driven into the joints between the bricks.

The jamb member is $1\frac{1}{2}$ in. thick, double rebated as before, but $10\frac{1}{2}$ in. wide. The grounds are nailed to the lintels and to the backing pieces on both

FIXING A NEW SASH-LINE

EVERY house owner or tenant whose house is fitted with sliding sash windows should make a periodic examination of the condition of the cords supporting the sashes as failure to do so may result in damaged fingers should the lines give way when one opens or closes the window.

Fig. 1 shows the principle upon which an ordinary sliding sash works. It will

removed, allow access to the weights. The illustration seen at Fig. 2 shows the pocket with its cover removed.

The tools required for carrying out the repair consist of a light hammer, chisel about 1 in. wide, pair of pincers, and a bradawl, while the materials, etc., include a suitable length of best quality sash-cord, a few galvanised clout nails, a piece of thin string about 6 ft. in length,

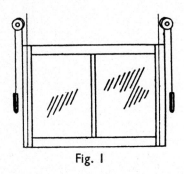

Fig. 1

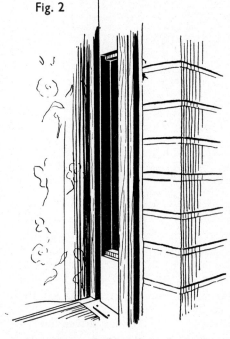

Fig. 2

be seen that the sash is kept in any desired position by means of the balancing action of weights attached to the sides of the sash, through the medium of cords running over pulleys provided on each side of the window frame; the weights, being housed, slide up and down in narrow channels or boxes formed in the sides of the frame.

If you examine your window-frame carefully you will find that the sashes work in grooves formed by a guard bead fastened round the frame at the back, or that portion facing the inside of the room, and a fixed wooden projection running round the outside which forms part of the frame. The sashes are separated by a narrow parting bead.

At each side of the frame near the bottoms of the grooves will be found the covers of the pockets, which, when

and a piece of thin sheet lead about 2 in. square.

If the bottom sash-line is the one that needs attention, that sash only need be removed from the frame, but if the cord of the top sash requires replacement, both sashes will have to be taken out.

Defective Top Line.—Assuming that the top line is defective, the first thing to do is to remove the parting bead. This is not a fixture but is simply wedged in a housing or groove running down the centre of each side of the frame. Insert the edge of the chisel between the housing and the bead, at a distance of about 6 in. or so from the bottom, and prise it up. It will then spring out of its groove. Patience should be exercised in doing this to prevent undue damage to the wood and paint.

Next, remove the guard bead on one side of the frame. This is lightly bradded to the frame and can easily be taken out by prising it up with the chisel, starting in the centre and gradually working to the ends. When the nails have been partially withdrawn, the bead can be sprung out of the corner mitres by gripping it with the hand and pulling the bead up.

Now take out the bottom sash from the frame by giving it a gentle pull at the side where the guard bead was removed. If this cannot be easily done owing to the sash having insufficient play between the frame sides, the opposite bead must be taken out.

When this has been accomplished remove one cord from the sash groove by withdrawing the nails, and let it stand aside for the time being.

It will now be possible to draw the upper sash out. If you are working without the aid of an assistant, allow the sash to hang by the unbroken cord, making sure that the line is sufficiently strong to withstand the strain.

The next procedure is to remove the pocket cover. This is done with the bradawl or a strong penknife by simply inserting the blade into the wood at the bottom joint and then prising it open. The cover should come out without much trouble, but if it sticks, a few gentle hammer-taps round the joint will help to loosen it.

At this stage it is a good plan to examine the pulleys to see that they are in good order and work freely. If they revolve stiffly a few spots of oil should be applied. It sometimes happens that a pulley needs replacement owing to its centre hole being worn, in which case it is wise to fit a new one—sash-pulleys being procurable for a few pence at almost any ironmonger's.

To resume, take out the weight from the pocket and remove the broken piece of cord attached to it, and also disconnect the fellow piece from the cord-

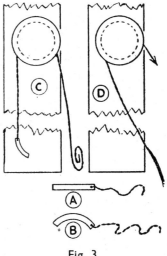

Fig. 3

groove in the sash by the use of the pincers. Make a pencil mark on the face of the sash to coincide with the bottom end of the groove.

The next operation consists of threading the new sash-line over the pulley and through the narrow compartment in order to attach the weight.

Roll the lead to form a thin cylinder round one end of the string as indicated in the drawing at A in Fig. 3. Now bend the lead to enable it to pass freely over the pulley as at B. Put the "mouse"—as the device is called—over the pulley and feed in the string.

This is shown at C. When the mouse has arrived at the bottom of the pocket, pull it out and make fast the free end of the string, otherwise you may have to repeat the operation.

Take one end of the new line—which should have been thoroughly stretched —and tie it to the string after having removed the mouse, in the manner indicated at D in Fig. 3. Now haul on the free end of the string until sufficient length of line is pulled over the pulley and then make a temporary knot to prevent it slipping back.

Fix the weight to the line by threading it through the eye and out of the hole at the side, and then knot the end and tuck it into the recess which will be found at the side. It is important that the knot should not protrude outside the weight, otherwise it may foul the interior of the channel and prevent the weight from sliding freely up and down.

Replace the weight into the pocket, put back the sash between the sides of the frame and keep it in its lowest position in order to mark the frame, to gauge where the cord is to be cut. Now make a pencil mark on the frame opposite to that made on the sash and cut the cord to this length when the weight is pulled up about an inch or so above the bottom of the pocket—to allow for clearance.

After cutting the line to length, pull the weight up as far as it will go and fix the cord for the time being by either driving a nail through it into the frame or inserting a wedge between the top of the pulley and the woodwork above.

Fix the new line temporarily in place in the cordgroove by driving in a couple of clouts. Again replace the sash into the frame to test whether the weight is working freely and does not hit the bottom of the pocket when the sash is pushed up to the top. The latter defect is easily seen as the sash will not remain closed when unsupported by the hand, but will drop an inch or so according to the excess length of line. The sash is taken out, the cord permanently secured into the groove by driving in a few more clouts, and when the guard, parting beads and pocket have been refixed into their respective places, the job is complete. A little Russian tallow rubbed over all sash-lines will not only make them pliable but will also help to preserve them and thus increase their useful life.

DRAUGHT PREVENTION

IN any draughty room the windows and doors should be examined for faulty fitting, and at the same time other faults corrected.

Fig. 1 illustrates a few sources, not only of draughts, but of dampness leaking through to the walls, so stopping one fault will often cure another. The points to look over are:

1. Between the wall and the window frame down the sides where the cement may have fallen away, leaving a gap wide enough for the fingers to be inserted for some distance behind the brickwork. This exposes the woodwork to wind and rain and should be made good with cement.

2. Between the sash and the head of the window.

3. Between the wall and the head of the window frame.

4. Between the top of the lower sash and the transom or bar of the window frame.

Shrunken Frames.—In cases where

the frame has shrunk, leaving a gap at the top between the wood and the wall, the cavity must be filled with cement, the lower edge of which should be made to project outwards to form a lip to carry the rain-water forward clear of the frame. Where the woodwork has shrunk, leaving a gap between the top edge of the window and the frame, the defect may be remedied by adding a strip of wood to the window edge, using fine nails for fixing, and tapping the heads well below the surface so that any surplus wood may be planed off until a perfect fit is obtained. The edges, either the hinge side or the other, may be treated in the same manner, the window fitted to the opening, and the hinges refitted. This method is much easier than trying to plane up strips to fit round the frame, with repeated fitting before the desired result is obtained.

The sash may bind on the frame, owing to the wood swelling, and not allow the window to be closed properly. In dry weather it may shrink and rattle with wind and vibration, causing draughts. A window tight in dry weather requires immediate attention. If left until the damp season the trouble will be so much worse that in trying to obtain a proper fit the possible result will be the removal of too much wood, and when dry weather returns the window will rattle.

A Casement Sash should be examined to see exactly where it is tight, and whether there is any slackness on the opposite side, as it may be possible to alter the position of the sash and make use of the slackness by refitting the hinges. The old screw-holes must be filled before trying to fit new screws near the old positions. A little packing behind one of the hinges, or sinking one a little deeper into the frame may so alter the position of the frame

in the opening that it fits better without need for further work on it. Unseasoned timber is so often used that new houses generally give the most

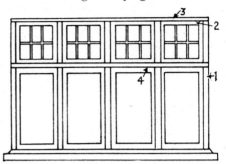

Fig. 1

trouble and such windows should be treated with care. As a general rule the frame should not be interfered with too much. Make any necessary adjustments to the window, the part most easily removable. Do not remove too much material at a time, and once or twice try the sash in position, and do not forget the coatings of paint to go on afterwards.

A Leakage Along the Transome may be corrected by nailing a length of picture-moulding upside down to the face so that the groove, coming now along the bottom edge, will make the water drip off before coming into contact with the frame. Open joints should be filled with putty.

Doors.—A door may be the main cause of draughts owing to poor fitting and unseasoned wood. This will prevent the door from shutting properly all along the edge. Any of the tenons may be projecting as in Fig. 2, either on the opening edge or the back edge. The surface should be levelled with a wood chisel and finished with a small plane, where possible. The same treatment is applied to the fault shown in Fig. 3, where the bottom of the style rubs on the floor as at A and the bottom rail shows a gap as at B. To effect a repair, the door must be removed from the hinges and enough wood taken off the bottom of the style to clear the floor,

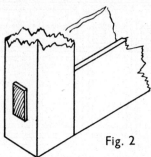

Fig. 2

and the bottom edge of the rail made up to correct thickness by means of a thin strip of wood, tacked so that the surface may be trued up with a plane to just clear the line.

Hinges.—Fig. 4 shows the effect of a strained or broken hinge at the top edge of the door, allowing the door to droop and scrape the floor. A new hinge should be fitted, otherwise the door will be a bad fit when closed. Unseasoned wood will often warp until gaps show between the centre rail and the

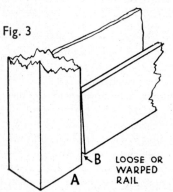

Fig. 3

B LOOSE OR WARPED RAIL
A

edges of the panels as in Fig. 5. When the door has been taken down, and it is found that the parts cannot be knocked back into the correct position with a

mallet, the gaps may be covered by fixing a suitable beading all round the edges of the panels.

Steps.—A worn step, as illustrated in Fig. 6, either at an outer door, or the wood floor in any inside doorway, will allow a draught to pass underneath. An outside door may have a sloped weather-board fitted to the lower outside edge to throw the water away from the step (A), and another piece fitted

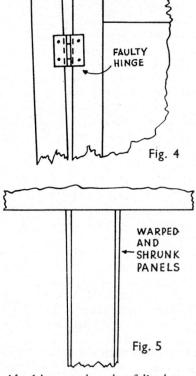

FAULTY HINGE

Fig. 4

WARPED AND SHRUNK PANELS

Fig. 5

inside (B), or a length of linoleum, to stop the draught.

The small piece of worn board in the doorway of a room can be lifted and replaced the other way up, with the worn surface below.

Rubber strip, folded so that one edge forms a hollow tube, as in Fig. 7, will prevent any draught coming through a badly fitting door, provided it is tacked round the opening in the correct manner. When the tubular part is pressed together it covers the crack between door and frame.

Draught-Preventing Curtains suspended from a rod fitted across the doorway may be fixed by means of various types of simple fittings, some of which are arranged to lift the curtain as the door is opened. Only two fittings are required in cases where the curtain is pushed back to allow the door to open. A bracket with a projection on which one end of the rod swivels is screwed to the door-frame on the hinge side, and a bracket with a loop top screwed to the top edge of the door on the catch or lock side. The end of the curtain-rod passes through the loop end and is left free. On opening the door the curtain-rings are pushed towards the hinge side of the door.

Re-hanging a Door may prove a trying undertaking, even for two people, unless it is wedged up to the correct height to bring the holes in the hinges in line with the existing holes in the frame.

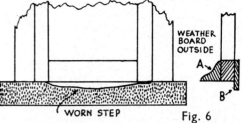

WEATHER BOARD OUTSIDE

A

B

WORN STEP

Fig. 6

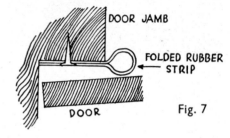

DOOR JAMB

FOLDED RUBBER STRIP

DOOR

Fig. 7

Hold the door half open with the hinged edge touching the frame. Place a strip of wood under the bottom edge, then, while one person holds the door steady, the other fixes the screws through the hinges. An occasional spot of oil on hinges and locks will keep them in good working condition.

RE-GLAZING A SASH

THE tools and materials necessary for carrying out a simple glazing job, such as replacing a broken pane of glass, are as follows:

A hacking knife, which is a knife fitted with a pointed blade having a thick back, used for removing the old putty. Its cost is a few pence only.

An old chisel, useful for removing any superfluous putty left by the hacking knife.

A putty knife, having a blade specially shaped for applying putty.

A light hammer.

A small quantity of putty.

A few thin brads.

A small quantity of paint and a brush for applying it.

In some cases it is easier to execute the repair by removing the sash from its frame and carrying out the work on a bench.

If a ground-floor window needs attention, the re-glazing may be done with the window in situ; on the other hand, should replacement be necessary to a window above the ground floor, it will be generally found more con-

Fig. 1

venient for working to remove the sash, and thus obviate the necessity of using a ladder.

Removing the Glass.—Having decided these points one way or the other, the next step consists in removing the old putty and glass; and it may be mentioned that when doing this it is advisable to wear an old pair of gloves to protect the hands.

The old putty is removed with the aid of the hacking knife and hammer by inserting the pointed end of the blade between the rebate—or recess for holding the glass—and the putty, in the manner shown in the illustration, Fig. 1. Care must be exercised when using the knife to prevent damage to the rebate by cutting into the wood.

When the whole of the putty has been removed and the recess thoroughly scraped clean and free from lumps— the chisel will come in handy for this— the measurements for the new glass should be made. These measurements must be accurately taken, preferably with a wooden or steel rule, as a tape-measure is unsuitable for the purpose, due to its liability to stretch. The length and width of the new pane should be $\frac{1}{8}$ in. smaller than the opening between the rebates, for if the glass is

a tight fit, it will crack in the not-far-distant future.

A visit should now be made to the local builder or hardware merchant, who will cut the glass to the desired size, and also supply the putty.

You will probably be asked whether 15, 21 or 26 oz. glass is required, which is the technical way of expressing the thickness equivalent to so many ounces per square foot.

If you are not familiar with these terms it is a good plan to take a sample piece to enable its thickness to be determined with accuracy.

As the glass must not come in direct contact with the wood at the back of the rebate, it is necessary first to prepare a bed of putty on which the edges of the glass can rest, in the manner shown in Fig. 2, but before this can be put in hand, the whole of the rebate must receive a coat of paint. The reason for this is that if the putty is applied to the bare wood the wood absorbs the oil

Fig. 2

from the putty and renders it useless; in fact it would simply crumble away after a few hours.

The paint should be allowed to dry thoroughly before puttying is proceeded with.

As ordinary lead paint takes some hours to dry, a great deal of time may be saved by using knotting as a substitute, in which case the puttying may be proceeded with in about a quarter of an hour or so after being applied.

Puttying.—Take a lump of putty and knead it well between the fingers and also roll it between the hands to render it soft and pliable. If the material does not readily respond to this treatment, add a spot or two of linseed oil, which usually has the desired effect. All hard lumps present must be removed.

Now take a small piece of putty and apply it to the back of the rebate, working it into position with the thumb.

Bedding-in.—Place the glass in position—the glass must be perfectly dry—and drive a couple of thin brads or panel pins into each side of the rebate, to hold the glass temporarily in place. Take great care when driving the brads not to break the glass. The best way to insert the brads is to keep the hammer head against the glass as indicated in Fig. 3.

Press the glass round the edges to squeeze out as much of the back putty as possible. Do not attempt to do

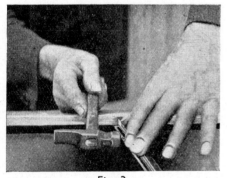

Fig. 3

this by pressing the middle of the pane or disaster will result.

When the process of "bedding-in" is complete the next operation is to apply the "top" putty to the front of the glass and the rest of the rebate. Start at the top or side and follow all

Fig. 4

round, spreading the putty evenly by drawing the putty knife along to form a neat bevelled edge as indicated in the illustration, Fig. 4, and then trim off the surplus putty at the back. The top edge of the bevel should be level with the top edge of the rebate.

When the putty is hard it should be given a coat of paint, the colour of which should match the rest of the frame.

Glass Cabinet Doors.—In fitting glass to such articles as cabinet doors, etc., where a thin wooden fillet or bead nailed to the rebate is employed instead of putty for holding the glass in position in the frame, the fillets can be easily removed by inserting a thin knife-blade between the beading and the rebate. Start in the centre, near one of the fixing brads, and gradually prize it up by twisting the blade, taking care not to damage or disfigure the wood. When the new glass is in position, the beading strips should be replaced in the same positions they previously occupied, so that the nail-holes in the fillets coincide with those in the rebate.

It is a good plan to use slightly longer brads than those originally used, for by so doing the fillets will be more securely held.

Leaded Windows.—The replacement of a broken pane in a leaded window can usually be effected by first cutting and then opening up the lead

Fig. 5

jagged edges should be removed with a glass cutter, and it should be stored for use at some future time.

Glass Cutting.—Although professional glaziers use a diamond-pointed tool for glass cutting, a wheel cutter, fitted with a small hardened steel cutting wheel, can be used with good results, especially if lubricated with paraffin oil. The glass to be cut should be placed on a perfectly flat surface, such as a table, while the cutter should be held between the first and second fingers of the right hand as shown in Fig. 5. The wheel of the cutter is then drawn across the glass, and, if cutting properly, leaves only a slight scratch on the surface. A rough irregular scratch indicates that the cut is incorrect. The glass is then placed at the edge of the cutting board with the unwanted piece overlapping the edge, and given a gentle tap, which causes the piece to part and leaves a clean edge.

strip which supports the glass. When the new glass is placed in position the lead is then carefully bent over it and replaced into its original position. Should the corners get broken during the process, apply solder to the joint.

If an old pane of glass which has been broken is not too badly damaged, the

LAYING A TILED HEARTH

IT will be found that the cement of the existing hearth is flush with the surface of the floorboards, so that if the tiles are required to be level with the floor, the cement face must be chipped away to the concrete underneath, or at least to a depth equal to the thickness of the tiles and the cement used to fix them.

A cold chisel and a 1-lb. hammer will be required for removing the top layer of cement, and a start should be made along the front edge of the hearth, chipping towards the back and always away from you so that the pieces do not fly about the room or into your face. It would not be necessary to go back right under the bottom of the grate unless this small section comes adrift, as thin layers of cement are liable to do where there has been considerable heat.

While this preliminary work is being done the tiles should be placed in a pail of water to soak, as dry tiles will not adhere properly to the cement.

After cutting the surface to the required depth, the chipped bottom surface should be checked and any too-shallow places made deeper.

Preparing the Cement.—A mixture of Portland cement and sand in equal quantities is prepared with water to form a stiffish plastic mass. The surface of the concrete must be thoroughly wetted with a brush dipped in water, and the cement carefully floated over the damp surface with a bricklayer's trowel to make it level. The level must still be kept lower than the surrounding floorboards, that is, sufficient room must be kept for more cement in which to lay the tiles, and the tiles themselves. This recessed space should be left to set hard. When dry the tiles may be placed loosely in position to see how they fit in. This will show if it is possible or better to start the work from the front edge and work back in straight rows from side to side, finishing level with the iron skirting of the fireplace or mantel surround, or to start laying the tiles with the back edges under the ironwork and work to the front. With long narrow tiles, where the width may be half the length, and to save cutting to produce half lengths in order to preserve the bond, that is to avoid all the joints from back to front coming in continuous lines through each row, it may be possible to lay the outer rows, or two to three side rows, at right-angles to the main run, on each side.

In Fig. 1 the front outline of the grate and the ironwork of the mantelpiece has been shown in plan, and the dimensions taken from an actual grate. The tiles in this case are 4 in. square.

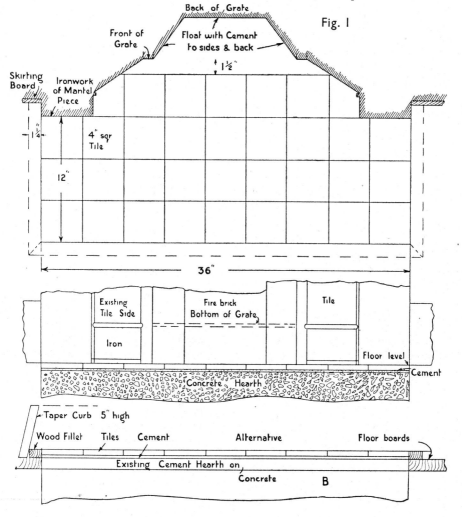

Fig. 1

Laying the Tiles.—Having settled how the tiles should be laid, they may be placed, in the selected formation, on a large tray, a piece of plywood, or a large sheet of paper, near at hand.

Some neat cement—not too wet—is now prepared and spread evenly over the surface. Into this the tiles are pressed or tapped down with the handle of the trowel, checking them for level as the work proceeds, with the aid of a straight-edge laid across the floorboards surrounding the hearth. The top surface of the tiles must be level all over with the floor. If it is not desired to cut the cement away to enable the tops of the tiles to lie flush with the floor, they may be laid in cement, on top of the existing hearth surface, but this surface must be chipped all over to provide a key for the new cement. As the tiles will stand up above the surrounding floor-level it is usual to finish off round the tiles with a stained wood fillet of or about the same thickness, as indicated at B in the illustration. The width of this strip may be made to any convenient dimension and if a modern curb in oxidized copper is to be used, the *inside* dimensions where it rests *on the floor*, should be noted, together with the outside dimensions of the mantelpiece. The amount of space between the two will fix the size of the wood strip. In the example of hearth shown, the dimensions of the curb at the bottom are $38\frac{1}{2}$ in. long and 15 in. back to front, so a $1\frac{1}{4}$-in. wide strip just keeps the curb in trim position and prevents it from being moved out of place in any direction.

The tiles are arranged in the same manner as before, and the space at the back, under the grate, is filled with cement or fireclay to the level of the tiles.

SIMPLE GAS-FITTING

APART from the cleaning and adjustment of gas-burners for fires, cooker and lights, there are several simple gas-fitting jobs which the amateur gas-fitter is quite capable of doing, such as extending a run of pipe to another room for a gas fire and a gas copper, as instanced in the following paragraphs.

Extension for Gas Fire and Copper.—In the example shown by the plan, Fig. 1, which is typical of many jobs, the gas supply is already fitted to an existing cooker in the recess of the kitchen, and it is proposed to run extra piping under the floor, from the lower end of the gas pipe feeding the cooker, to supply a gas fire on the hearth in the living-room. At the same time a new gas copper is to be placed in the adjoining scullery, and to connect this the most convenient will be to take a pipe through the wall into the kitchen and to connect on to the spare connecting point on the cooker. A great number of gas cookers have a long cast box or a specially shaped pipe right along the front, under the top plate, to which the various rings, grill, and oven pipes are joined. Each end of this main feeder terminates in a threaded barrel, so that the cooker can be connected to the supply pipe either on the left-hand or right-hand side, whichever happens to be the most convenient, the unused one being plugged.

However, some modern gas cookers are fitted with one main gas inlet only, in which case the connecting pipes would have to be cut to suit.

As the total length of the run is com-

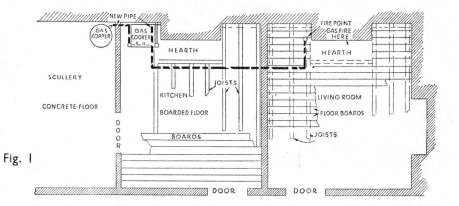

Fig. 1

paratively short, $\frac{3}{4}$-in. gas barrel will suit the job admirably. Such pipe can be bought roughly cut to lengths, and then sawn to the correct sizes at home. A stock fitted with a $\frac{3}{4}$-in. die for cutting the threads will also be required, together with a gas-fitter's pipe-vice for gripping the tube. These tools can generally be hired for a small sum, or perhaps the ironmonger will cut the threads for a small fee.

If you decide to cut the threads yourself, the pipe should be securely fixed to a bench, or a convenient post, as it is essential that the pipe be quite rigid while it is being cut and threaded.

Special care should be taken to keep the hacksaw perfectly straight while cutting, as any twisting of the tool invariably results in a broken blade. The correct method of using the tool can be seen clearly by referring to the illustration, Fig. 2.

Having sawn off the waste, round the outer edge slightly with a file to allow the die to start easily.

In cutting the thread, lubricate the die with machine oil, and do not cut the thread to a greater distance from the end than the depth of the threaded portion of the T elbow, or other fitting it has to fit. Fig. 3 shows the threading operation.

The scullery floor is of concrete and is not touched; the only cutting here is the hole through the kitchen wall, the hole being on a level with the burner under the copper. The other two floors are of wood, and from the position of the fireplace the joists will run in the direction indicated, and the floorboards across these at right angles. Those near

Fig. 2

the hearth in each room must be taken up, and channels cut in the joists to allow the pipe to sink in to just below the level of the underside of the boards. Having worked across the kitchen, the hole is made through the dividing wall of the living-room, and the other joists grooved as far as the trimmer in front of the hearth.

17

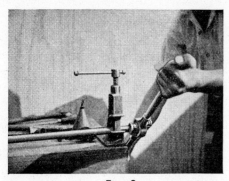

Fig. 3

Here the pipe will turn at right-angles, and can be fixed along the outside of the joist. In both rooms the boards near the corner will have to come up, and the cooker must be moved from its

place while the new pipe is being installed.

Tools.—The following tools will also be necessary: 2 pairs "Footprint" adjustable grips, hacksaw and blades, tenon-saw and chisel for woodwork, and adjustable spanner.

Fitting.—The first length can be fitted with the elbow, EI (Fig. 4), and this screwed in to the existing T, to finish tight with the open end facing the correct way. The second length is fitted with elbow E2, and this screwed into place.

The third length is the longest, but can have the elbow screwed on, and the end pushed through the wall to the kitchen; it is then screwed tight into E2, and the same proceeding carried

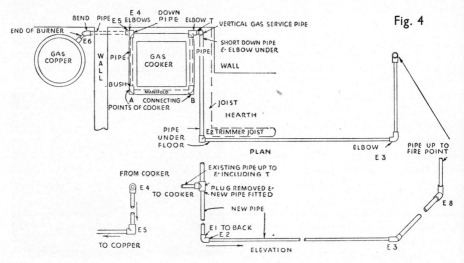

Fig. 4

Materials.—To connect supply-pipe to fire, the following material will be required:

1 length pipe from existing T down to elbow EI   ¾ in. diameter
1   „   „   „   elbow EI to E2   „ „   „
1   „   „   „   „   E2 to E3   „ „   „
1   „   „   „   „   E3 to E8   „ „   „
1   „   „   „   „   E8 vertical up to fire point „ „   „
1 Reducing piece, or bush.
1 Gas-fire point with flange for fixing to floor.
4 Elbows, for ¾-in. gas pipe.
    These are shown in the plan and elevation in Fig. 4.

out to the end, making each joint absolutely gastight with thick red lead paint, as indicated in Fig. 5.

The hole in the wall will be below the skirting board level and can be made good, if desired, with the brick removed or a new piece, although it is not usual to make these parts good, provided the holes have been neatly made. When replacing the floorboards see that they are level and use wood screws for the purpose.

Extending the supply to the copper calls for the following materials:

3 elbows for $\frac{3}{4}$-in. gas pipe, E4, E5, E6.
3 lengths of „ „ „
1 reducing piece from pipe to burner.
1 „ bush from cooker point to pipe.

Cleaning and Adjusting a Gas Fire.—To clean and adjust a gas fire, remove and clean the fireclay tubes, and

Cracks in the fireclay back may be mended with plastic cement, which is supplied ready mixed and can be applied straight from the tin.

Fig. 6

On some fires the air and gas adjustment is by means of two separate locked screws, and these are varied in or out to obtain a silent flame. Other types have only a tap to control the gas, and the air supply is varied by moving a loose sleeve over the opening in the casting.

Gas Burners for Lighting.—To ensure a good light the gas burners should have a thorough cleaning at intervals. First remove the mantle, unscrew the fitting from the pipe, as shown in Fig. 6, and clean all the parts, paying special attention to the needle regulating valve and the gauze to free them from dust. The air-adjusting sleeve may be fitted with a locking screw, which, if missing, should be replaced.

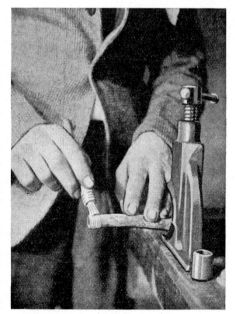

Fig. 5

brush all dust away from the burners. Clear the burner tubes and make sure that the gauze is clean and replaced in each.

Cooker Burners.—The burners of gas cookers are best cleaned by putting tl em into a pail of strong, hot soda water, or even boiling them in a pail. When free of grease the replacement is easy. The air adjustment is by means of a sliding sleeve with locking screw. The gas supply is also regulated by locked screws, and once adjusted should be kept locked. New burners may not have the full supply of open holes owing to some being filled when the casting was made. These can be opened with a suitably sized drill. Other types with radial slots under a cap can be filed to a better shape with a thin file. The drip-proof type with gauze requires very hot water to remove the grease, which unavoidably accumulates even if splashing and spilling are avoided.

All care must be taken when laying new pipe to see that the many joints are perfectly gastight, especially those under the floor where a leak might take place over a considerable period before it was noticed. A final warning should not be necessary, but do not look for gas leaks with matches or a candle.

SMOKY CHIMNEYS AND THEIR CURE

Any fire that does not burn properly and causes inconvenience and annoyance by filling the room with smoke and soot-flakes every time a door is opened, or when a person walks by the fireplace, demands immediate attention. Not only will this nuisance rapidly spoil wallpaper, paintwork and the furnishings in general, but unhealthy invisible gases will take the place of the smoke when the fire appears to be burning normally.

In an ordinary-sized room a fire should burn brightly, and the flue draw the smoke and fumes away properly, aided by the air which enters the room through crevices round the windows and under the door, and even through the joints in the floorboards. There should be no need to open windows or door to help the fire to get started.

Before deciding that the flue is at fault, try the experiment of opening a window or the door when the fire is sluggish, and note if there is any improvement after a test of about twenty minutes. If an improvement is noticeable the flue is probably in order, but there is insufficient air entering the room from outside. An alteration to, or the complete removal of a draught-excluder (if fitted) from the door, will often effect a cure.

Cold Flues.—The fire may smoke owing to the flue being very cold, and perhaps a little damp through not having been used for a considerable time. This is a common cause of the trouble in new houses, and is especially noticeable in any room where the flue is built into an outer wall and exposed to the weather. Such a flue and the air in it will be colder than the outside air and cause a down-draught, because the cold air is heavier and sinks, only forcing its way out as it becomes warmer. This condition is only temporary and will cease with a bright fire.

Smoky Chimney Caused by Wind. —A large number of smoky chimneys are caused by the wind. Houses at the corners of two streets and those adjoining higher buildings are the chief sufferers.

In the first case, the wind swirling round the house causes down-currents of air, and in the latter case, the currents of air, striking the high building, are deflected back and downwards on to the lower chimney, thereby inducing a down-draught.

This may be overcome by fitting a metal extension-piece with a special shaped cowl. A more sightly method is to fit a special anti-down-draught chimney-pot, of which there are several types on the market. In general these pots are made with two or three rings of slits or louvres in the sides, so that if the wind blows on the side it is directed upwards and takes the smoke with it, while should it blow downwards on to the pot it escapes through the slits and does not press the smoke back into the flue.

Obstructions in Flue.—The most difficult case to deal with is a flue partly blocked by accumulated soot at a bend, or by a loose brick which has become wedged across the flue during the construction of the house. Fig. 1 shows how the flues are arranged in the average house. The walling containing the flues and fireplaces is termed the "chimney breast" and it rises straight up through each story of the house until it reaches the space under the roof, where it slants off sideways to finish into the "stack" of lesser dimensions, fitted with the chimney-pots. The flues themselves are 9 in. square and rendered inside with cement to make the passage airtight and to obtain a smooth surface offering little resistance to the ascending gases. Some of this lining or "parging" may have accidentally dropped inside when it is put on and, falling to a bend, accumulated and set hard, making a trap for soot, which if not removed may catch fire. Each flue is turned or curved to one side, as shown at A in the diagrammatic sketch, Fig. 1, to keep it from running into any of the other flues. If a brick has become lodged in the flue, a chimney-sweep may be able to move it by working rods up the flue, but care

must be taken that none of the lining is broken and brought down, as this is a protection against fire getting through the joints in the brickwork to any woodwork nearby. Fumes will probably find a way through the brick joints into the room, and be most noticeable in cupboards adjoining a fireplace.

If a loose brick cannot be removed by such simple means, the only practical

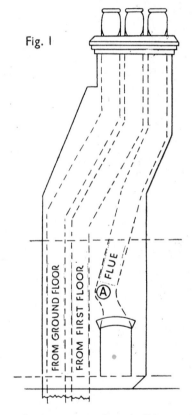

Fig. 1

remedy is to consult a builder and to have the wall near the bend cut away enough to allow the obstruction to be removed. The wall is then made good, and will of course need re-papering, but the expense and trouble of this must be balanced against the injury to health and home by the fumes and smoke.

In the daily cleaning of the fireplace

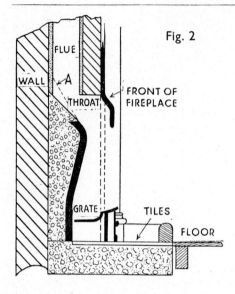

Fig. 2

FLUE

WALL   A

THROAT

FRONT OF
FIREPLACE

GRATE   TILES

FLOOR

it is essential to see that the ledge at the back of the grate is swept and all loose soot removed. This not only impedes

the draught but also causes smoke by smouldering.

Alteration to Throat of Grate.—Another cause of excessive smoke is that sometimes the space at the back of the grate is too large to allow the fire to draw properly. In this case an improvement may be made by cleaning the surrounding concrete and brickwork, roughening the surface, and building up the slope to reduce the size of the opening, as shown by the dotted lines at A in Fig. 2. In many cases this can be done without removing the mantel-piece or surround. With an old grate the packing material at the back and sides behind the ironwork may have crumbled away and formed pockets where soot collects. Fine concrete is then worked into place behind the iron, from the top and back, using a piece of iron or wood to ram it down before resetting the back firebrick into place.

DAMP WALLS AND THEIR CURE

THERE are many causes of damp walls, and it is often a difficult matter to locate and cure the trouble, especially in rooms above the ground floor, as a defect in the roof some distance from the wall may be letting the rain through to run down the rafters or under the slates until it reaches the wall. In such cases the damp shows along the ceiling line.

Where the house is in an exposed position, and in rooms with painted or distempered walls of an impervious nature, their coldness will cause a moist atmosphere to condense on the surface, especially if little or no fire is used.

Certain kinds of wall-brick are very porous, and the rain beating on the outside is able to soak through, to

evaporate on the inside, loosening the plaster and paper.

In other cases it is the mortar joints only which fail in the above manner but with the same results.

The most common cause of damp walls on the ground floor is a defective damp-course. Examination outside the house should show a layer of bituminous felt about 6 to 9 in. above the ground-level all round. Other materials are used, such as two layers of slates bedded in cement, asphalt and tarred felt. The idea is to prevent moisture from the soil from rising by capillary attraction up the walls. In modern houses this precaution is compulsory, and when the work of building reaches this stage an inspection is made by the local authorities and must be passed by them before the work is allowed to proceed. In old houses this damp-course may not exist.

In many cases the wall is covered with cement for a distance up to about 9 in. above the ground-level, like a skirting, and in no case should the soil of flower beds or garden be piled above this level or to cover the visible damp-course. Dig the earth away and level it to 6 in. or more below, all round the house.

While each different case has a remedy best suited to the conditions, the same treatment may be applicable to several defects.

Defective Roof.—The exact spot is often difficult to locate, but an examination should be made for missing or broken slates, or any that may be loose or have insufficient overlap which may be letting the rain through the joints.

Several good makes of plastic bituminous compound are obtainable for patching, which are applied with a trowel and it may prove less expensive to cover the roof with this material, rather than re-slate the whole roof. It may also be used for flat roofs covered with asphalt or similar material, though small cracks and seams may be closed by the application of a hot iron to make the material melt and flow together.

Condensation may be cured by improving the heating and increasing the ventilation within, covering the walls with some absorbent material, such as canvas under the wallpaper, or lining the walls with fibre or plaster compound boards. The latter method is easy and very effective.

A Porous Wall may be corrected by several methods. A good external coating of tar is effective, but very unsightly. There are also patent liquid waterproofing materials easily applied with a brush, two or three coatings being necessary, according to the condition of

the wall, but such applications must be repeated after a year or two.

A more permanent cure is to cover the wall either outside or inside with waterproof cement, in the manner indicated in Fig. 1. The walls must first be made rough by chipping the surface of the bricks and raking the old mortar from the joints. The waterproofing ingredient is in powder form and must be mixed dry with the cement, and the two well mixed again with the sand. Thorough mixing is essential both in the dry state and after the water had been sprinkled on from a can fitted with a rose. Too much water will take longer to dry out and the finished surface will crack.

The wall is wetted before applying the cement, and this is put on in two coats, each about $\frac{3}{8}$ in. thick. The first coat,

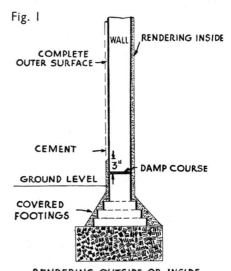

Fig. I

WALL — RENDERING INSIDE

COMPLETE OUTER SURFACE →

CEMENT →

$\frac{1}{3}$" — DAMP COURSE

GROUND LEVEL

COVERED FOOTINGS

RENDERING OUTSIDE OR INSIDE

when just set, must be made rough to form a key to hold the last coat, and is also wetted before the next is put on. There is a method of allowing a cement surface to dry slowly, called "curing," which increases the strength and imperviousness with the slowness of drying. The plan is to retard the drying by occasionally spraying the surface with water during a period of several days. Horizontal surfaces are covered with wet sacks, with the same results. Another essential feature, for sound work, is to use the cement as quickly as possible after mixing, and to complete the surface at once, avoiding the making of joints.

Re-pointing.—

POINTING

Fig. 2

Dampness due to imperfect joints between bricks can be remedied by re-pointing. The old cement is raked out of the joints between the bricks, and new mortar put in its place. After a few courses have been done, the edges are struck straight and clean with a trowel point run along a straight-edge. At the same time the surface of the joint is inclined backwards, as shown in Fig. 2; thus any water running down the face of each brick drips off at the edge and is deflected outwards to the top edge of the brick below, and not inwards to settle.

Damp Courses.—Where no damp course exists it is an expensive but not impossible job to put one in. Such work and the replacing of a defective damp-course takes time, because only about 3 ft. of brickwork can be removed at a time, the previous section being made good as the work proceeds. About three or four courses are taken out, and the material unrolled along the bottom surface thus exposed.

If this work is regarded as too expensive, the best plan is to render the inside wall with waterproofed cement. On outside work the coatings may be carried down over the footings to the concrete base of the wall. This will deflect any surface moisture away from the wall. To do the same inside the room would mean having most of the floorboards up.

Walls treated outside, and having defective plaster inside, will dry quicker if the old plaster is chipped off and a good fire made up.

Inside rendering is usually finished with a thin coat of skimming stuff, consisting of sand 6 parts, plaster of Paris 1 part, and lime putty 3 parts. This should prevent condensation.

DRY ROT: ITS PREVENTION AND CURE

D RY rot is a fungoid growth which thrives on timber such as floor joists, near ground-level. The chief places where it may be found are in damp cellars, basements, and those parts of the ground floor where the air under the floor is damp and stagnant through want of proper ventilation.

Symptoms.—In bad cases far advanced, the fungus may be seen on the woodwork, if not, the surface shows shrinking and cracks, and very little pressure is required to sink a knife blade well into the wood. There are several different forms; some show red or white spots, also red and black streaks. In all cases there is a very unpleasant smell and in the early stages the wood is discoloured with a white or grey film. This develops into a growth of fungus.

The disease will spread to other woodwork, even through the joints in the brick walls of adjoining houses. Timberwork in the upper floors is seldom attacked, unless dampness can be traced to a faulty roof.

Cure and Prevention.—The first step is to remove all timber without stint.

Any doubtful piece left in is liable to breed and spread the disease, so that, in about a year's time, or less, according to conditions, the new wood is in the same bad condition. The old wood must be burned to destroy the spore or germs, and all the wall surfaces and surrounding brickwork, including the joints, are then well scorched and burned with a blow-lamp.

Any adjoining timber passed as sound may be treated with sulphate of copper, creosote, or one of the many patent preparations to be obtained.

Air-bricks.—When air-bricks or metal grids (Fig. 1) can be found, see that they are clear. Two or more should be found in each outside wall. Some parts of the ground floor timbers may be supported on low brick walls, called sleeper walls, and if these contain no openings, several should be made by knocking out a full brick here and there to let the air through.

Air-bricks should be placed in all outside walls, at the back and front of the house, and at the sides if a semi-detached house. For these, a full brick must be removed from the face of the wall, in a position above the damp-course but below the level of the floor-timbers, and the opening carried right through.

The new timber used should be given a good coating of creosote or other similar preparation before use, not forgetting to treat the underside of all floorboards. Unventilated cupboards and the skirting boards round the ground-floor rooms should also be examined and if too far gone should be removed. In these last-mentioned cases, and in many others, damp walls may be the main cause. The damp is perhaps from a leaky roof, but

Fig. 1.

more often than not, from the ground. The damp-course should be above ground level, so if the garden soil has been piled up above it it should be raked or dug away and not allowed to rise higher than the level of two bricks below the damp-course. In old houses such a damp-course is sometimes non-existent. In common work bitumen or a form of tarred felt is used. To insert a new damp-course all round the house is a long and costly job, as it is not considered safe to cut away more than about a yard of the brickwork at a time.

BURST PIPES

BEFORE dealing with the methods of repairing a burst water pipe, let us consider what steps can be taken to protect the exposed sections of the supply system against a sharp frost, because pipes burst under the strain of the expanding formation of ice as the water freezes, and not when it thaws.

Prevention.—Outside lavatory cisterns may be covered with a piece of old carpet or sacking, taken right over the top, leaving sufficient room for bell and arm to move. Bind round the sides with stout string, and continue the covering of sacking strip round and round the pipe to the end. Straw is often packed round the pipe under the sacking. Other lengths of pipe may be treated in the same manner. While doing this it is as well to locate the stop-cock for turning off the supply from the main. In old houses this may be found in the basement or cellar, but in houses of more modern design it is usually below a small iron flap somewhere between the entrance gate and the front door. If a proper key has not been obtained, one can be made by cutting a notch in the end of a piece of hardwood. This trap may also be packed with straw in frosty weather.

Some houses are supplied direct from the main, but others have a cistern situated under the roof. This should also be protected and fitted with a wooden cover to keep out dust.

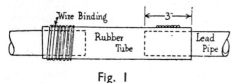

Fig. 1

During frosty weather the pipes should be inspected and, if a split is found, flooding may be prevented before the thaw. First turn off the supply at the stop-cock. If the key cannot be found and a cistern is used, tie a string round the arm near the ball which operates the inlet valve, and fasten it so that it remains in the raised position, shutting off the water. To save emptying the tank the inner end of the outlet pipe may be plugged with a length of wood having a round, tapered end. Ease the faulty pipe away from the wall and drain the water out of the lower end, if it is free. In any case, the more serious matter of not having a proper water supply for some time needs attention, so a temporary repair should be made to enable the household to carry on while the necessary materials are being obtained,

or a plumber called upon to do the work.

Temporary Measures.—With a hacksaw or even an old tenon saw, cut out the damaged piece of pipe. Procure a short length of ordinary rubber hose, or, better still, a piece of canvas-covered car radiator hose from a garage, of a size just to fit over the lead pipe. File any rough edges off the ends which were cut, and ease the rubber into place on to one end and then ease it back to go over the other lead pipe so that there is about 2 to 3 in. of overlap at each end. Bind the ends with copper or other wire, keeping the turns tightly pressed to the rubber, and twist the ends to secure, as in Fig. 1. The service may be put into use at once if a thaw allows, or the ice may be gently melted out by using a blow-lamp carefully at a distance from the pipe.

An Active Burst Pipe.—The more familiar case is where the pipe has thawed and a stream of water threatens to damage ceilings and furniture. Desperate measures may be necessary at the burst before hunting for the stop-cock key or tying up the ball valve. The only quick way is to hammer the pipe flat at the split, closing the gap as much as possible and making the pipe quite flat on that side of the burst nearest the incoming supply. Cut the pipe above this point, i.e. towards the empty side, turn the end over and hammer the fold tight. This will stop the stream and provide time for turning off the water until a plumber can attend to it.

A temporary repair to a small hole emitting only a fine jet of water may be carried out by moulding a good thickness of plastic modelling clay round the pipe over the defective place, covering this with a piece of rag, and binding the whole with close turns of string. Putty can be used in the same way, or lengths of rag, like a bandage, smeared well with stiff red or white lead paint and bound on tightly. Electricians' adhesive tape will also be found helpful in effecting a temporary repair.

Repairing Lead Pipes.—To replace the piece of lead pipe cut out to remove the split section, as mentioned in a previous paragraph, prepare the two ends of the pipe by opening out the lower end as in Fig. 2, by holding a piece of metal bar inside for a short distance and working it round, pressing sideways to form a bell mouth. When opened sufficiently, scrape the inside clean and bright with a penknife. The top end is shaved to wedge in a similar bell-mouth. Now cut a piece of pipe to complete the length, and treat the ends in the same manner, as shown. Try the shaved end to see that it is a good tight fit.

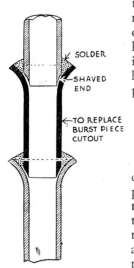

SOLDER

SHAVED END

TO REPLACE BURST PIECE CUTOUT

Fig. 2

A blow-lamp, powdered resin, and a strip of tinman's solder will be required. Heat the joint thoroughly all round with the blow-lamp, pick up a small quantity of resin on the end of the stick of solder and apply it round the joint, letting it melt round the joint by keeping the heat on the pipe, not by a close stream, but by flashing the end of the flame on and off the joint, up and down or sideways, provided there is no woodwork in the way. Dip the solder frequently into the resin and melt in enough to fill the space round and extend well over. If care is taken there is little chance of the

pipe melting. When cold the pipe may be replaced in its original position. Fig. 3 shows such a repair being carried out.

Repair to Small Split.—For a pipe not subjected to much internal pressure, as one fed from a tank, the repair may be made without cutting.

Carefully tap the swollen part back to near its normal diameter, using a light hammer, and close up the crack. But do not forget to mark the spot. Scrape the metal bright all round the crack and bevel it out. Use the blow-lamp and

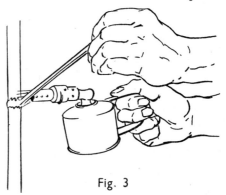

Fig. 3

solder, as previously described, and fill the crack, letting the solder extend well over on each side. With a vertical crack start at the bottom and fill by building up. The usual light-weight domestic soldering iron is too small for the purpose as it does not hold the heat long enough, and if one is purchased in preference to a blow-lamp it should be of the 1-lb. type.

Repairs to Iron Pipes.—The only satisfactory way to deal with a defective iron pipe is to replace it. Owing to the practice of using as long a length of pipe as possible between any two points, joints are not frequent. The complete length need not be replaced, but as any fresh-made end must be screwed with a suitable size thread, the faulty pipe must be removed. This may be no easy job where it passes through a wall or woodwork, but it will come through much better if the unions or sockets and nuts are taken off. A pipe-wrench and an adjustable spanner will be required, one to hold the pipe and the other to turn the nut. When loose, ease the free end to one side and, having freed the far end, turn the pipe and withdraw it. Measure and note the overall length and cut the faulty part out with a hacksaw. The new piece to make up the length may be obtained threaded from an ironmonger, who will also thread the other piece and supply the union or unions cheaply.

FAULTS IN CISTERNS

THE flushing cistern is subject to periods of erratic action, and as the ball-valve controls the water inlet, much of the trouble can be traced to this part of the mechanism.

Figure 1 shows an illustration of the mechanism of a typical flushing cistern, and although there are many forms of

sufficient volume to push out the air, fill the pipe with water and create a syphon action. The cistern flushes itself empty until air is drawn in at the lower edge of the bell, which stops the

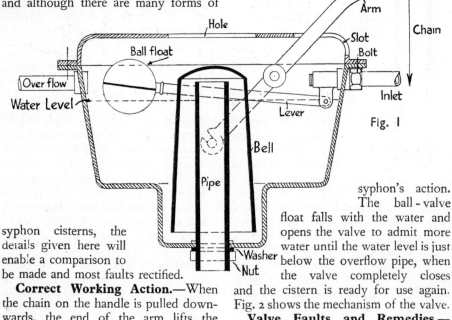

Fig. 1

syphon cisterns, the details given here will enable a comparison to be made and most faults rectified.

Correct Working Action.—When the chain on the handle is pulled downwards, the end of the arm lifts the metal cone or bell. Water flows into the well, and as soon as the handle is released, the bell drops. In doing this the lower part traps the water inside the well, where it rises up inside the bell and falls down the centre pipe with

syphon's action.

The ball-valve float falls with the water and opens the valve to admit more water until the water level is just below the overflow pipe, when the valve completely closes and the cistern is ready for use again. Fig. 2 shows the mechanism of the valve.

Valve Faults and Remedies.—Insufficient flush of water, making it necessary to pull the handle more than once, indicates that the ball-valve is shutting off the water too soon and not letting the cistern fill to its correct capacity. The ball end of the lever may have been bent downwards, thus giving too much lift, or the washer in the valve may have swollen. Both have the same result.

The quickest and easiest method of correction, if done with care, is to bend the ball end of the lever upwards to set the ball at a higher level, but this requires great care, otherwise the arm, being of brass, is easily broken, or the valve strained and the washer damaged. Note how high the water is before bending, as only a slight amount will make a lot of difference; if bent too much the water will rise too high and probably overflow down the wall outside.

From this it will be obvious what must be done when a cistern keeps overflowing. New cisterns are liable to both of these faults, but in an old cistern the bell may have become coated with rust and deposit from the water, making it a tight fit so that it will not drop quickly enough to force the water up the bell and down the pipe. In this case the bell must be taken out and well cleaned, and the lower edge made level and smooth with the aid of a file.

Noisy Filling.—Cisterns connected to pipes fed direct from the main are often under such pressure that the rushing water may be heard over most of the house when the cistern is filling. This nuisance may be reduced to a great extent by fitting a length of pipe on to the outlet of the valve. The pipe should be sufficiently long to reach nearly to the bottom of the cistern, where the end is soon covered with water, and the sound reduced.

Repeated Overflowing.—Overflowing is a common defect, and to remedy

this the ball float must be set by bending the lever to make the valve shut before the water reaches the overflow level. This arm, starting from a central position on the valve, has to curve round the bell to the ball which floats about the centre of the width, and the amount of space between the two parts is so

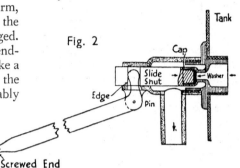

Fig. 2

little that in an old cistern a coating of rust and deposit which grows thicker with time, causes the lever to rub on the bell and catch. This may not happen every time the cistern is used, but at intervals, so the best remedy is careful cleaning to remove the rust and a slight bending of the lever to clear the bell. If the increased freedom of action does not stop the trouble a new valve washer should be tried. When the water has been turned off, the sliding plug is easily removed and the small cap screwed off. Do not use force as the metal is very thin, and it is therefore very easy to squeeze the cap out of shape.

A new cistern may work stiffly owing to the rounded end of the arm being too tight in the slot of the plug. A few rubs with a fine file, just enough to remove the rough edges, should make it free to work properly. A small quantity of grease applied at this point would be helpful.

The Ball Float is of very thin metal, and a pin-hole is enough to allow the water to enter very slowly until the ball will not float. This trouble should be looked for when the ball is seen very low in the water, as, under normal conditions it has very little of its surface below. To remove the ball, hold the arm and simply screw off the ball. Shaking it will show if there is any water inside. If water be present in the interior, dry the outside and, turning it about, note where the water comes out. Enlarge the hole a little with the point of a very thin nail, drain all the water out, and run a spot of solder over the hole, as shown in the illustration, Fig. 3. Wedge the ball at the bottom of a pail by means of a piece of wood wedged between the sides, fill up with water and let it remain for as long as possible. When taken out note if it floats lower in the water than when first put in. If the repair is watertight the ball can be

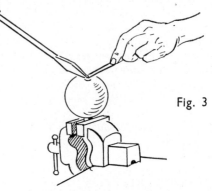

Fig. 3

replaced in the cistern. Hot water can be used with advantage for testing, if available.

Always see that the cover of the cistern is replaced in the correct position and properly secured, as failure to do this may prevent the bell from moving or prevent free action.

FAULTS IN WATER TAPS

IN most districts where a public water supply is provided, it is a punishable offence to leave water taps in a faulty condition so that they allow water to be

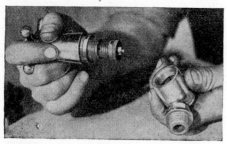

Fig. 1

wasted by continuous dripping. Many houses are supplied direct from the main, the water is under considerable

pressure, and so a very small defect in the tap can cause a large waste of water.

Some people, when turning off the tap, twist it round tightly after the water has ceased to run. With a tap in good condition this should not be necessary, as it destroys the washer and strains the jumper and seating. That this should be possible will be clearly understood by referring to Fig. 2, which shows the inside of the tap and the thin walls of metal. This form of construction is common to many types, and in all, the water is shut off by the leather or rubber disc being pressed over the opening or seat, which is machined dead true on its top surface. After much use the washer wears away until it will no longer make a watertight joint. The seating also wears, and if in a very bad condition will wear out new washers in a very short time. Leakage can occur at other points, such as through the cap and gland, owing to the deterioration of the packing, and at any of the joints if they are not screwed up sufficiently.

Fitting a New Washer.—In remedying any of these defects, the first step is to turn off the supply. If this is from the main, a stop-valve is usually found below a metal flap set in the front pathway or near by. Where the tap is on a pipe

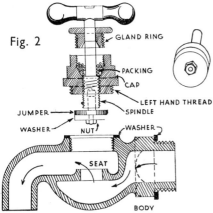

Fig. 2

CRUTCH HANDLE
GLAND RING
PACKING
CAP
LEFT HAND THREAD
SPINDLE
JUMPER
WASHER
NUT
WASHER
SEAT
BODY

from a storage tank the ball-valve must be tied up so that no more water can enter, and, to save wasting the contents of the tank, a pointed stick to fit the outlet may be prepared and tapped into the opening of the down pipe inside the tank. The water in the pipe is run off and the top part of the tap unscrewed by using an adjustable spanner. In many districts taps are supplied with this part threaded left-handed, and so to remove it, the turning motion must be opposite to that when undoing an ordinary nut. When free, the jumper part will be found either inside the body of the tap or in the end of the screwed extension below the handle (Fig. 1). In any case it is not fixed and therefore easily pulled out.

Release the small nut and replace the

old washer with a new one. This operation is shown in the illustration (Fig. 3). The usual size is $\frac{1}{2}$ in., and they are made from oil-treated, compressed

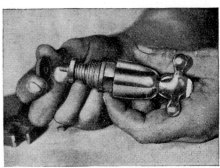

Fig. 3

leather for cold-water taps, and from vulcanised rubber for hot-water and bath taps. Emergency washers may be cut from odd pieces of leather with a simple cutter, as that illustrated at A in Fig. 4: simply a piece of $\frac{1}{2}$-in. bore iron

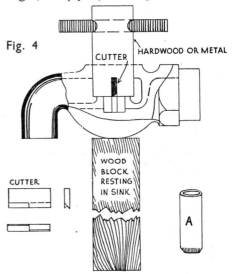

Fig. 4

CUTTER
HARDWOOD OR METAL
WOOD BLOCK RESTING IN SINK
CUTTER
A

tube, filed or ground, tapered to a sharp edge at one end.

Packing the Gland.—Leakage round the spindle can be prevented by unscrewing the ring nut when the tap is turned off, and picking out the old packing. Special packing string is obtainable, but two or three turns of soft string, well greased with lard, may be used as a substitute. Wind this round the spindle and push it down with a long match stick or piece of stiff wire. When nearly full, cut off the end and replace the nut. Turn the tap on and off several times to settle the packing into position and then give the nut a final turn, but do not make it too tight. When removing the cap to fit a new washer, do not lose the large washer at the back of the threaded part. A similar washer is fitted behind the flange of the hexagon end where the tap connects with the pipe.

Cutting the Seat.—As stated before, after long use the seat inside the tap wears unevenly and rough, causing new washers to last only a very short time. Providing there is a good thickness of metal, this fault may be corrected many times before the tap has to be replaced. Ready-made cutters to fit a drill brace or with a handle are obtainable. Only a thin shaving of metal is removed, and it is a good plan to support the body of the tap on a piece of wood when carrying out the work. Fig. 4 shows details of a home-made reseating tool, and the method of supporting the tap when using the tool.

MAKING AND FITTING A SHOWER ATTACHMENT

A SHOWER attachment to give hot, cold, or any variation of temperature between, complete with waterproof splash curtain, is readily made by the simple assembly of certain standard-sized pipes and fittings, as illustrated in the accompanying dimensioned drawings.

The whole of the piping and fittings used are standard wrought-iron gas-fittings: these are not quite so large as the steam fittings for the same size bore pipe. If desired, $\frac{5}{8}$-in. heavy gauge screwed electrical conduit could be used with the necessary screwed fittings.

In the plan view of the curtain rail (Fig. 1), the end is shown bent to half a circle, but a square end can be made if preferred. Width and overall length may also be altered to suit individual requirements.

The following materials are stock items:

 5 lengths of $\frac{1}{4}$-in. bore iron pipe, each
   7 ft.
 2 lengths of $\frac{1}{4}$-in. bore iron pipe, each
   1 ft. 6 in.

 5 $\frac{1}{4}$-in. gas tees. Wrought iron.
 5 $\frac{1}{4}$-in. gas flanges. Wrought iron.
 2 lengths of $\frac{1}{4}$-in. bore pipe, bent to
   18-in. radius.

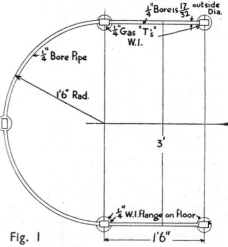

Fig. 1

If square ends are required, add 2$\frac{1}{4}$-in. gas elbows and four straight lengths of pipe, each 18 in. long, in place of the two curved pieces.

Both ends of each piece of pipe must be screwed with the standard thread for that size of pipe. Any ironmonger will do this after cutting the various lengths, for a small charge.

Construction.—Take each 7-ft. length of pipe and fit a flange on one end, and a tee-piece on the other. These parts form the uprights, details of which are shown in Fig. 2; they are screwed down to the floor.

Before the 18-in. horizontal pieces forming the curtain rail can be fitted, the curtain-rings must be placed on the pipe.

As the piping, etc., in its more or less rough state, would not only be unsightly but liable to rust, some kind of finish is essential. Enamel of the same shade as used for the bath or some other colour would do. The standards and the short lengths should be well cleaned, and given one or two coats of aluminium paint as an undercoating and protection against rust. The final coat of enamel could be left until the whole had been assembled and fixed to the floor. The two end tees are capped or plugged to finish off.

Spray Fitting.—The fittings for the spray attachment are standard gas parts in wrought iron and are quite strong enough, and less bulky than the steam pipe fittings your ironmonger may wish to provide in their place. The following materials will be required:

4 $\frac{3}{4}$-in. gas elbows.

1 $\frac{3}{4}$-in. gas tee.

2 $\frac{1}{2}$-in. bore iron pipes, each 4 in. long.

2 $\frac{3}{4}$-in. gas - to - $\frac{1}{2}$ - in. - gas - reducing bushes

2 connecting nipples for $\frac{3}{4}$-in. gas pipe.

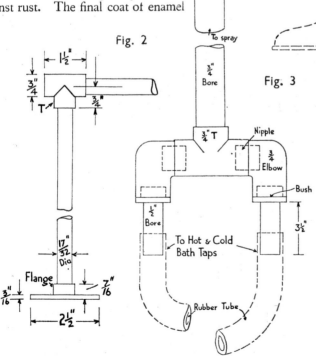

Fig. 2

Fig. 3

2 rubber hose to fit bath taps and the outside of item 3, length according to requirements.

2 $\frac{3}{4}$-in. gas pipes according to requirements.

1 6-in. rose spray.

Fig. 3 gives the necessary details of the assembly.

The assembled tee, elbows and ends for the rubber tube may be enamelled to match the bath. The vertical pipe and the length with the rose may also be finished in this way. Pipe clips will be required to go round the vertical pipe and the back standard of the curtain support, the rose part being supported from the ceiling, or an iron strap fixed across the two side pipes of the curtain rail.

To ensure water-tight joints, a mixture of gold size and red lead or thick paint is smeared on the screw-threads of each part to be fitted together. Turn the elbows at right-angles to the tee piece, so that the rubber connections hang down out of the way. These should be pushed well up the pipe ends towards the bush, and secured with plated clips or bound with tinned copper wire neatly wound on and nicely finished off.

For a cold shower it is obviously only necessary to turn on the bath cold tap, a warm spray being obtained by turning on the hot tap as well, and altering the flow to obtain the desired temperature.

The Curtains.—Material for the curtains, such as thin rubber, rubberised fabric or oiled silk should be long enough to hang a few inches below the top of the bath, and need not reach the floor. Brass eyelets may be fixed along the top edge of the material, and split rings through these and those already on the pipe rail, or S-shaped hooks can be obtained, the lower hook passing through the eyelet in the curtain, and the upper hook to go through a small eye-loop forming part of the ring.

HOT WATER SYSTEMS AND BOILER TROUBLES

ALTHOUGH this is an age of Gas and Electricity, there must be a great number of the old type saddle boilers forming part of the kitchen range still in use. Their general inefficiency and the increasing need of more continuous supply of hot water for domestic purposes have at last led to the introduction of more reliable types, usually quite separate from the cooking range. Some of the old type may be found in large houses that have been converted into flats, so that a few details may be of assistance when any troubles arise.

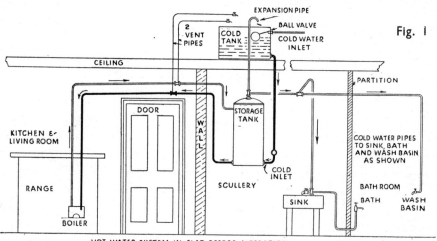

HOT WATER SYSTEM IN FLAT BEFORE ALTERATION

Poor Supply.—When the system has been installed on one floor as in a flat, the conditions are usually difficult. Fig. 1 shows a typical case where it has been necessary to carry the pipes over a doorway. The main trouble is the poor supply of hot water, and Fig. 2 shows the alterations made to correct this fault.

retarding the flow of cold water would have the same result. The supply pipe to any hot taps should be taken from the tank at the side near the top. Both flow and return pipes must have an air vent pipe extending above the cistern with open ends free of any air locks.

In some flats, the kitchen and bath-

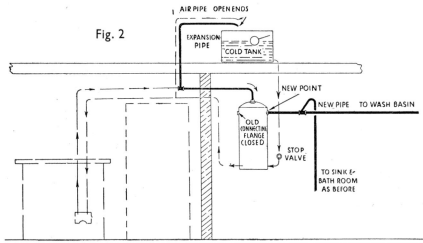

HOT WATER SYSTEM IN FLAT AFTER CHANGING POSITION OF PIPE CONNECTIONS ON CYLINDER

The cold water tank is not very high above the hot storage tank, thus the pressure will be very low and the flow from the taps is due to, and governed by, the flow of cold water down the supply pipe. A faulty stop-valve in this pipe would check the supply of hot water, many elbow bends and any feature

room are at the extreme ends of the building, so that a long run of pipe is necessary, and to avoid them showing in the living room and bedroom between, they are sometimes run above the ceiling, under the roof, as shown in Fig. 3.

Hot Water Slow in Arriving.—The usual trouble in this case is that a lot of

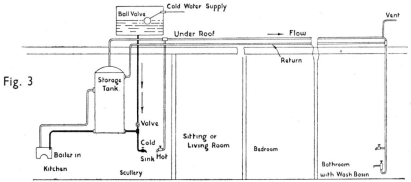

Long Pipe System in Flat with Bathroom at far end.   Before Alteration

cold water has to be run off before the hot arrives; the flow is slow, with air coming through at intervals.

This is due to lack of circulation in the long run of pipes in the roof. The return enters the cylinder near the top, and in a short time after starting the fire, the upper part of the storage tank is filled with hot water, and both flow and return pipes have high temperature water in them at that end. There is so little difference in the height, and the distance is so long, that there is little to induce the water to circulate.

The alteration, as in Fig. 4, is to fit

quantity as from the cold tap. This tank and the pipes must be covered with a non-conducting cement to prevent loss of heat.

Improving the Supply.—A modern combined cooker and heater, with the boiler forming part of the range, is sometimes used in small two-storied houses containing the hot water system shown in Fig. 5. The trouble experienced here is that the water takes a long time to heat and the supply is irregular and poor.

The fault is usually found to be with the method of connecting to the storage tank, as it is possible under certain

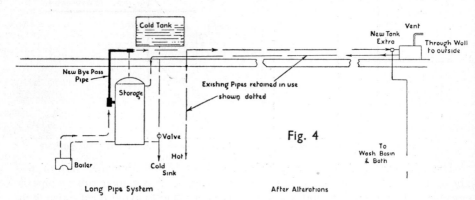

Fig. 4

Long Pipe System   After Alterations

a bye-pass pipe to stimulate the circulation, and at the same time increase the difference in the temperature of the flow and return.

Air in the Pipe.—The cold cistern, being low, provides only sufficient head of water for a cold tap, yet to move the hot, the cold water has first to go down through the storage tank, then up, pushing the hot water to the pipe under the roof, and along to the bath tap. The open expansion pipe gives the flowing water an injector or pump action, drawing air and discharging it at the open tap. A small 8 to 10 gallon storage tank should be added at the bathroom end as shown, with the result that the bath tap flow becomes free from air and improved to about the same

conditions for the tank's contents to be hot, yet it is not possible to draw it off at the taps, as in this case.

The cold water enters at the bottom of the tank and rises in a solid stream without spreading to the top. Turning on a tap results in an instant movement of cold water to the expansion pipe from which the tap pipe is taken, so it is impossible to draw more than a small quantity of hot water before the cold mixes with it. Fitting the cold supply to the side at the bottom, and making a new connection at the top for the pipe from the boiler improve the supply.

Boiler Cleaning.—Hard water necessitates frequent clearing of accumulated fur deposit from inside the boiler and pipe ends. To effect this, the water

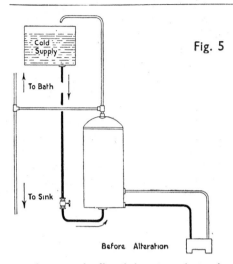

Fig. 5

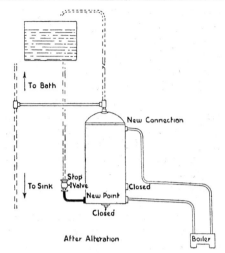

Before Alteration

After Alteration

must be turned off and the pipes drained. Remove the top plate of the range to expose the boiler. The hand hole cover is cemented over with an asbestos mixture which must be carefully chipped off. Have a pail and large swab-cloth handy in case there is no drain from the boiler. Loosen the centre nut on the cover a little, tap the cover to free it, and mop up any water that comes through. Remove the cover without breaking the joint ring. Feel all round inside and remove any loose fur, and tap the outside all over; also, chip over the inside with a long chisel, taking care not to damage the boiler. Insert a screwdriver or stout wire into the pipes to clear any deposit, and remove all loose pieces. When replacing the cover, a new ring may be required. This is cut from $\frac{1}{8}$-in. thick sheet asbestos, using a wood chisel and a piece of wood underneath to support it. Smear the inside with pipe joint compound.

Refix the cover and tighten the nut. The water may be turned on to test for leakage. Asbestos cement or fireclay is plastered over the cover to protect it from the fire.

CLEANING PIPES, DRAINS, ETC.

ALTHOUGH the drainage system and the various fittings connected with a modern house are arranged to be self-cleansing and are provided with suitable traps and grids to ensure that no solid matter will pass into the pipes to cause stoppages, they require proper attention and periodical assistance to keep them in good working order.

General Cleaning. —The bath, lavatory basin, and scullery sink, may all be kept sweet and clean if they are wiped round with a little paraffin on a rag and washed down afterwards. This will remove any soap, scum, or grease without scouring with gritty powders, which in time remove the glaze and leave the surface open to collect dirt and stains that are harder to remove. The same applies to lavatory pedestals. If badly stained and furred below the water level drop in a good handful of common washing soda last thing at night and let it stand. If the first application does not clear it, either repeat with more soda, or one of the patent solvents. Do not make a practice of using spirits of salts as this also removes the glaze, and once this happens the surface will never remain clean for long. This powerful acid also finds a way into the joints of the pipes and attacks the sealing material, and may eventually cause leaks underground.

Stoppages.—Most cases of stoppage can be put right if attended to at once, but as prevention is better than cure, it is advisable to see that all wash basins, sinks, etc., are provided with proper grids under the plugs and that all outside gullies have grid tops to keep out larger solids, leaves, etc.

Each waste pipe is usually provided with a screw cap at the bottom of the bent sealing-pipe, which will be found under each sink, bath and wash basin. This cap should be removed at intervals and the collection of foreign matter removed. Should the water be slow in flowing away after attending to this, it follows that a partial stoppage is in some part of the pipe. To remove the obstruction the suction method can be tried. A plunger device, consisting of a rubber cup fitted to a handle, is obtainable for this purpose, and such a tool should be included in the household set of tools. Fill the basin or sink with water and work the cup up and down over the outlet. A normal rush of water will indicate when the obstruction has been moved. If this method fails, use a length of wire, thin cane, or a special flexible pipe cleaner, and work it round the bends from either end. The waste pipes discharge into a gulley on the ground level, but in the case of upper floor rooms they discharge into the gulley via a hopper head outside the house fixed about first floor level (as shown in Fig. 1).

Some waste pipes, as from a lavatory, lead into a cast-iron pipe outside, and it is at this junction that a stoppage may occur. If a removable plate has not been provided at the bend to enable a rod to be inserted for removing the obstruction, a force pump should be obtained which can generally be hired from a local builder. Remove the manhole cover in the garden, locate the end of the waste pipe and cover it so that water can pass, but anything solid which

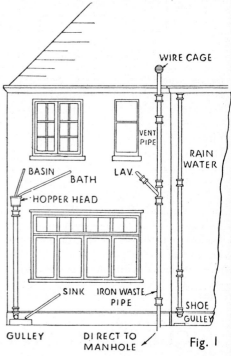

Fig. 1

has lodged in the pipe above cannot slip past down the other part of the drain. Half fill the pedestal with water and, holding the force pump in position, work it until the water sinks. Add more water to keep the cone part of the pump well covered so as to force more water down the pipe until the ease of pumping indicates that the obstruction has moved. If it has not reached the manhole end a good flush of water may possibly force the obstruction through, or a piece of wire pushed up the pipe may locate it.

Stoppage Beyond the Manhole.— A stoppage beyond the intercepting chamber, which is connected by a pipe to the sewer, is a serious matter, and may not be noticed until water overflows from the gullies and round the edges of the inspection and intercepting chambers. Having removed the cover of the latter and located the stopper and the outlet trap which is shown in the bottom left-hand corner of the illustration, Fig. 2,

and scrubbing brush are taken out first. In the scullery, use a sink-basket so that tea leaves and other small refuse are kept clear of the small grid over the outlet and not allowed to pass down into the trap bend. In spite of frequent flushing with water, grease will accumulate at the end of the waste pipe and in the gulley trap—a part of the drainage system often neglected. Strong soda solution will clear or loosen this, and with the tap water running in the sink inside, scrub the gulley with a stiff bristle brush made

Fig. 2

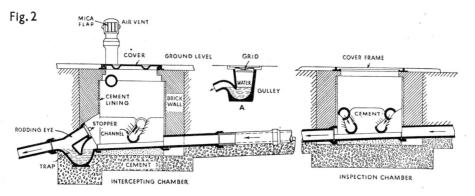

work it loose with a loop of thick wire or a stick, thus making an outlet for part of the surplus water. If the obstruction is in the trap it should be drawn back into the manhole and removed, and not forced the other way into the main drain. If the trap is found clear the obstruction is obviously in the main drain. The best plan is to consult a builder, as he generally keeps a set of flexible rods similar to those used by a chimney sweep, but with special interchangeable ends designed to deal with various forms of obstruction.

Prevention.—Many of the worst cases, which end in the expense of having the drains opened, can be traced to carelessness. After scrubbing floors, if it be necessary to empty the water down the lavatory, see that the cloth

on a wire handle so that it can be worked round the bend. Other such gullies, which take the rain or surface water from the gutters, may be cleaned in the same manner and well flushed with the garden hose or pails of water, especially in dry weather when the water seal (A in Fig. 2) is liable to dry up. A small ladle made out of a tobacco tin is very useful for removing soil and other matter from the bottom. The ventilating pipe which is connected to the soil pipe should be provided with a wire top to prevent birds from building a nest in it. The shorter ventilating pipe, connected to the intercepting chamber and usually fixed against a nearby fence or a wall, should be examined to see that the mica flap is unbroken and in working order. It should be able to blow open inwards to admit fresh air, but to keep closed with any current of air from the drain side. Some houses have a lavatory upstairs and another on the ground floor adjoining, say, the coal cellar. If this is seldom used the W.C. must be flushed with water at intervals to maintain the water seal whose object is to prevent any air from the drains passing up that way.

Drain Testing.—As indicated in Fig. 2 it is usual to have two manholes or inspection chambers in the line of drains to each house.

The one at the back or side of the house forms a collecting point for all the outgoing waste from the house, that is, from bath, lavatory and kitchen, and the car-washing space outside the garage, if any. The other, sometimes in the front garden, is an intercepting point for all these after leaving the first manhole, with perhaps one from a car-washing space if this happens to be to the front of the house. This last chamber isolates the whole house system from the main sewer, thus preventing any sewer gas and smell from coming back up the house drains, and also facilitating the removal of obstructions in general.

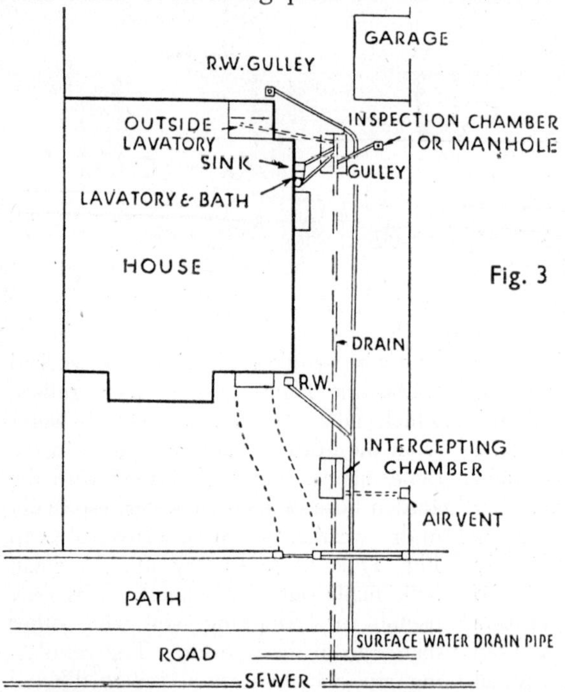

If a leakage is suspected there are several methods of testing the drains, section by section, but as they require smoke-making apparatus or strong-smelling chemicals they are not suitable for the householder to use. In both cases results are uncertain owing to the lack of pressure in the pipes to force the smell or the smoke through any fracture or defective joint.

A simple water test can be made if desired, and for this one or two expanding drain stoppers are required and a ladder. These can generally be hired from a local builder.

Washbasin and bath waste pipes usually discharge over an open hopper, as already mentioned, and are easily plugged with a cork to enable them to be filled with water. If the water level falls after an interval each length of pipe should be traced to see where the leak is situated. The lavatory is connected to the long iron pipe as shown in Fig. 1, so that if the end entering the manhole or inspection chamber is found and plugged, several flushings with water will fill this pipe and the pedestal itself. Note the water level after an hour or so, and if lower, and no leakage can be traced round the pedestal, mount the ladder outside and examine each joint in the waste pipe. It may be found that the water is working out round one of

Fig. 3

the joints indicated. Other sections may be treated in the same manner. To test the run of pipe between manholes, plug the inlet of the intercepting chamber and pour water into the inspection chamber. When the whole pipe line is brimming at this point, note if the water level drops after an interval, but make sure that none is leaking past the stopper at the far end, otherwise the test will be useless. If a leakage is certain it can only be located by removing the soil for the whole length between the two points and exposing the pipes to view. This requires very careful digging because the pipes are of stoneware laid in concrete up to half their diameter, and may easily be cracked or broken by an accidental blow. Some idea of their depth below ground can be judged by noting the depth of the openings at each manhole. Any damp patch located during the digging should be carefully investigated, as this indicates a most likely spot, and may save extra work.

Fig. 3 illustrates diagrammatically a typical lay-out of the drainage system of a small modern house. It should be noted that the surplus water from roofs, etc., does not discharge into the sewer, but into a separate surface-water drain pipe in the road.

ROOF AND GUTTER REPAIRS

A LEAK in the roof may not always be over the spot where the damp shows in the ceiling of the room below. The rain may drive under the slates or tiles well up the roof and the water will travel down the timber members or the underside of the slates until it reaches some obstruction which turns it away to drip on to the ceiling below, or it may go right on to the wall. The faulty side of the roof may be in a very exposed position, and the tiles or slates have been laid with insufficient lap. To remedy this defect the edges can be pointed with cement, as shown in Fig. 1, provided that the tiles have been laid on open battens and not on boards. This of course is done from the inside.

Broken Tiles or Slates within easy reach from a ladder may be replaced by pulling them out after the adjoining ones have been lifted a very short distance and carefully wedged. The new one is worked into position and secured by zinc, lead or copper strip bent to form a hook at each end. The top portion is placed over the supporting batten and the lower end bent over the lower edge of the slate, after which the wedges are removed. Work higher up the slope of

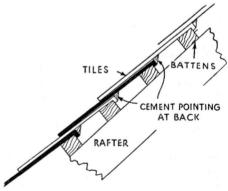

Fig. 1

the roof should be left to an experienced man with proper ladders and tools, as it is dangerous to attempt it yourself.

Flat Roofs.—Small cracks in lead-covered roofs may be closed by cleaning the place bright with a scraper, and running solder along the defective part, using a large hot iron and plumber's solder prepared with tallow to act as a flux to prevent oxide forming on the surface. A petrol blowlamp will be required for this. As it is necessary to heat up the part to be repaired, the flame must be kept moving and not played on one spot too long, otherwise the lead will melt. Keep the solder (plumbers') in the same spot as the flame and rub it about until it melts and the surface round the crack is well tinned. When the surface is thus prepared, run more solder along the crack, fill it well, and wipe it smooth with a piece of greased soft cloth. This more or less raised finish is of little consequence in some positions, but if a repair is to be executed across the bottom of a gutter channel the ridge may check the flow of water to a certain extent, and catch floating matter.

The procedure is altered in this case. The edges of the crack are raised to expose the woodwork below. In this, cut a small depression with a wood chisel and tap the lead back into the recess. Then scrape the surface clean, apply flux and solder, as previously described, but instead of leaving a high surface along the repaired crack, wipe the surface so that it is flush with the adjoining surface.

Zinc coverings or gutters are easily repaired by soldering, using a dilute solution of hydrochloric acid, commonly known as spirit of salts, as a flux. This chemical must be washed off after the process is completed as it will corrode the zinc if allowed to remain. The surface must, of course, be cleaned bright before soldering. A large well-tinned copper bit can be made hot in a blowlamp flame.

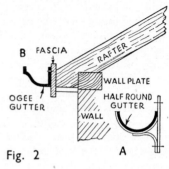

Fig. 2

Cast Iron Eaves Gutters.—In dealing with cast iron eaves gutters it will be found that rust is the chief cause of faults occurring with this type of gutter. Several layers of paint on the outside may hide the slow decay of the metal for years, until a high wind, heavy load of snow or rain causes a section to break loose, and down it falls. The danger of this to persons passing, or to windows, could be avoided by periodical inspection and cleaning. The dust collected during dry spells fosters the growth of moss and this retains a certain amount of dampness along the bottom to help the formation of rust.

The half-round type of gutter is fixed and supported on brackets, as indicated at A in Fig. 2, but the ogee type (B) is screwed direct to the fascia board, brackets being unnecessary under ordinary circumstances.

Fitting New Gutters.—If the existing gutter work is in a bad state, ladders should not be rested against any part, for fear of possible accident, but should rest against the brickwork below. Have two such ladders and set an assistant to hold the gutter section while the bolts and nuts through the jointing sockets are removed. These will possibly be found so rusted that the only way to get them loose is to strike off the ends of the bolts, or the nuts, with a sharp cold chisel, or they might be cut through with a hacksaw. The screws or the metal round the holes may be so rusted that the gutter only requires a pull to come clear away.

When a new section of the exact length required cannot be obtained, a longer one must be used, after having had the end cut off. Take the measurement from the old gutter and mark it on the outside of the new piece. The unwanted portion can be removed by cutting with a very sharp cold chisel, but such a procedure requires considerable care, as cast iron is extremely brittle, and therefore easily broken. The safer method is to use a good hacksaw fitted with a new blade and saw it through. The metal is only thin and no lubricant is necessary. The rough edge can be finished with a file, and a neat job is made without any worry about cracking or breaking the gutter. Holes for the gutter bolts are drilled with a suitably sized twist drill, a dent having been made first with a centre punch for the drill point to rest in.

The joint in the socket is made with red lead. The back of the gutter should be well painted before it is fixed, and the woodwork as well. Press the red lead putty under and over the screw-heads and

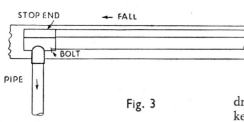

Fig. 3

paint the inside as well as all the outside surfaces. A priming coat of stiff red lead paint made with boiled linseed oil can be put on the inside first, or at any time the gutters are being cleaned and painted. Stopped ends are fitted in the same manner.

Round gutter-pipe may need cutting. After being marked either use a hacksaw or file a groove all the way round with the edge of a thin file and finish with careful taps with a hammer on a small cold chisel.

If a long run of iron gutter is examined thoroughly it will be seen that one joint towards the higher end is free of socket

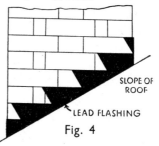

Fig. 4

bolts and joining material. This has been purposely left in this condition to allow for expansion and contraction, which may only be $\frac{1}{16}$ in. in the overall length, but this amount would be enough to strain the joints, cause a leak, and allow water to drip down the wall. The question of fall or slope (Fig. 3) is also important. If not sufficient the water will not flow away properly. The down pipe is usually at the end, so it is not difficult to check the slope when replacing an old section or putting up a complete gutter. Drive a nail in the fascia board at the high end, level with the top edge of the gutter, fix a length of string to this and stretch it to the outlet end and secure to a nail driven into the wood at that end, also keeping it level with the top edge. The line should drop compared with the top edge of the fascia board. If this is clear of guttering for complete renewal it is an easy matter to measure at each end, even where some gutter remains fixed it may be possible to work a very thin steel rule up behind the gutter to measure from the bottom edge of the fascia board to the top edge of the gutter. The amount of fall or drop should be ½ in. per 10 ft. of length. If the string is rubbed with chalk of suitable colour, drawn tight and plucked, it will fly back and strike the board, leaving a long straight chalk mark which can be used as a guide when fixing the gutter, or if more convenient the string can be left in position until the job is finished.

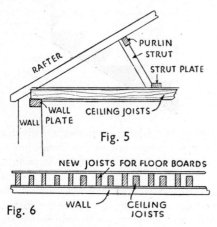

Fig. 5

Fig. 6

Brackets for half-round gutters may be positioned in the same manner.

Trough gutters behind a parapet wall or in the valley between two roof slopes should be cleaned at intervals, and if the house is near trees a wire-netting cover over the outlet will prevent a collection of leaves from blocking the pipe and causing an overflow up under the tiles or slates.

Side Flashing.—Another portion of the roof equipment which may give trouble at some time or other is the side flashing, as the sheet lead at the end of a roof where it joins a chimney-stack or brick gable-end is called. This follows the slope of the roof in steps down the brickwork, as shown in Fig. 4, the ends being tucked in to the joints and secured with lead wedges and pointed with cement to form a water-

tight joint. Any parts found loose or bulged from the wall should be carefully dressed back with a block of hardwood, and re-cemented, if necessary, to prevent rain from working its way down the wall.

Repairs to Roof Timbers.—The construction of the average house roof and the proportions of the various members have usually been well attended to by the architect and builder in compliance with the local building bye-laws, but there may be cases with old houses and out-buildings where the roof has sagged and the addition of new members is advisable to strengthen the roof.

The span of the rafters may be reduced by fixing extra horizontal pieces called purlins, and struts which support them, as shown in Fig. 5. Heavy timbers are not necessary and would be difficult to handle, so timber 3 in. by 4 in. is used for both members if they are spaced at not more than 4–5 ft. apart. Many houses have quite a large space under the roof which could be used for storage purposes or as an extra room capable of being made into a comfortable retreat or study for reading or writing, or as a workshop for light work. When planning such a job it must be kept in mind that ceiling joists are intended to support the ceiling below the loft, and not heavy boxes, etc. The common practice is to lay floorboards on top of the exposed ceiling joists to protect the plaster work below and to form a floor. This is liable to distort the small joists and bow them, so that the ceiling cracks and perhaps falls. The correct form of construction is to add floor joists at least 1 in. deeper than the existing ones for the ceiling, support the ends on the wall plate and space them apart between the others so that the floorboards are supported clear of the ceiling joists, which do not then carry any of the extra weight. This is shown in Fig. 6.

THE GARDEN
AND SMALLHOLDING

MAKING AND EDGING PATHS

A GARDEN, large or small, must have paths; and having planned where they are to come, proceed to make them up before going on with other digging and planting work. So many gardens just happen. Having received little or no thought by the house-builders, there remains plenty of work to be done from the time the owner takes over the weedy patch of land until it becomes something of beauty.

The first consideration in path construction is the amount to which it will be used. Paths in the front of the house carry more traffic and will need more care in making.

Types of Path.—The cheapest kind of path is a soil track covered with cinders. Such a path is inclined to lift after frost and needs as much weeding as the garden beds. If, however, the soil is removed to a depth of 9 or 10 in. for the whole length of the path, and the bottom rammed down hard and firm, a dry path may be completed by adding a 6 in. layer of larger clinkers, broken bricks and stones. Break up the old bricks on the site, spread each layer with a rake and roll well to give a good foundation. On this, a top layer about 3 in. thick is added of smaller pieces of broken bricks and cinders mixed. An all-cinder path looks very dull but if, from the old bricks, the dark reds and yellows are picked out and broken up in patches for the top layer, quite a bright effect is obtained. Such a path is shown in Fig. 1.

Instead of cinders the top layer may be of gravel about 4 in. thick, spread in layers and rolled well, keeping the middle higher than the edges to turn away the rain.

The path will keep in better shape and condition if it is edged in some manner. Bricks laid on edge as in Fig. 2 make a good edge for the kitchen and small garden.

For longer paths timber edging 3 or 4 in. wide by from $\frac{3}{4}$–1 in. thick, nailed to pegs as in Fig. 3, is easily fixed, and

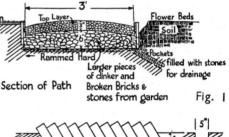

Section of Path

Larger pieces of clinker and Broken Bricks & stones from garden

Fig. 1

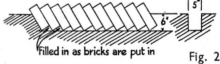

Filled in as bricks are put in

Fig. 2

if treated with creosote, wood preservative stain or paint, will last a long time. Prepared lengths of this edging, each about 10 ft. overall, are driven in at each side of the path when the bottom layer has been established. (Fig. 4.) Drive in a peg to mark the centre of the path; extend this centre up the garden by means of a marking-out line. Use a shorter line at right angles to start the path parallel to the existing fence, em-

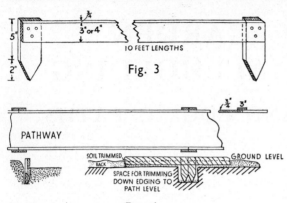

Fig. 3

PATHWAY

SOIL TRIMMED BACK   GROUND LEVEL

SPACE FOR TRIMMING DOWN EDGING TO PATH LEVEL

Fig. 4

the work proceeds will give a rounded finish.

Dry Walling. — Very effective and pleasing results may be obtained by the use of dry wall gardens leading up to the house at the back or front, with sunk flower beds, all on very simple lines. Cement and mortar are not required. The wall is built up with pockets of soil between each

ploying a square as shown (Fig. 5). The gauge board is cut as at A (Fig. 5), and with this it is possible to keep the edging boards the correct distance apart all the way along. A spirit-level placed on the top edge of the gauge board will indicate a side being lower than the other. Where the lawn comes to the path it is best to keep the timber edge below the turf level, thus making it possible to run the mowing machine right to the edge. Work along the length of the path, using an equal length of edging each side, keeping the pegs all to the back, out of the way of rolling operations when the top layer is added to finish the path.

Concrete edging also makes a very effective and lasting border.

The boundaries of the proposed path are staked out with pegs to which are fixed two 8 or 10 ft. lengths of edging timber; a piece each side to give a cavity $1\frac{1}{2}$ in. to 2 in. wide, into which the concrete is placed and worked down, as shown at A in Fig. 6. A variation of construction is to fix the edge boards to bridge pieces, as indicated, forming a handle for lifting. Pegs here and there between the boards keep the spacing correct and can be left in with the concrete. A shaped board (c) for working along the top edge as

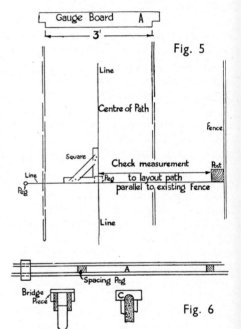

Fig. 5

Fig. 6

stone, the layers being set back and each piece of stone tilted down at the back.

This ensures that every possible drop of moisture finds its way to the roots of the plants growing on or in the wall. The various plants should be placed in position as the wall is built, thus allowing the roots to be spread out well into the wall.

LAYING CRAZY PAVING

O DD-SHAPED pieces of flat stone, fitted together in a kind of rough mosaic, known as crazy paving, is very effective as part of the garden design. As it provides a dry clean surface its use is not restricted to pathways only; it may be laid over larger areas surrounding the house or an odd corner of the garden surrounding a bird bath or seats.

Figure 2 shows a typical example of crazy paving.

The first essential feature of construction is to establish a firm, level ception-room, is to be covered. The existing soil on the site is removed to a depth of about 10 in. and the bottom rammed as hard as possible with a fairly heavy block of wood fitted with a handle, shaped as that shown in Fig. 3, at A. Now prepare a foundation of large clinkers and broken bricks, but before working this material into place drive into the ground five wooden pegs about 2 in. square, one at each corner and one in the centre as indicated in Fig. 1. Have them long enough to stand about 2 in. above the proposed

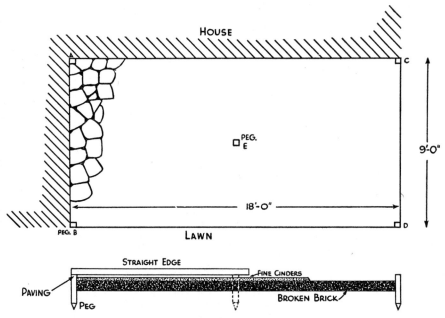

Fig. 1

foundation. As an example let us take the case illustrated in Fig. 1. Here a space measuring 9 ft. by 18 ft., behind the house and outside the main re- final level of the paving. Prepare also a timber straight-edge about 10 ft. long. The old bricks are most conveniently broken up on the site. An ordinary

Fig. 2

lengthways as suitable pieces come to hand. Tap each piece into place with a wooden mallet. As the laying proceeds test the surface between the pegs, both along and across the site, pressing down any high slabs and working a handful of small ashes under any that may be too low, using a trowel for the purpose.

Crazy paving for pathways is laid in the same manner, the width being set by either pegging down two tight lines or, what is more convenient to the average worker, a length of 3-in. by $\frac{3}{4}$-in. timber on each side to preserve the width (B in Fig. 3) while the slabs are being put down. After a good start has been made, and several feet of path finished,

2-lb. hammer is quite suitable. Work the larger pieces which will not break into smaller pieces to the bottom and rake the smaller stuff over the top, using the rammer frequently, keeping each layer as level as possible as the work proceeds. A depth of 6 in. should be enough.

Test the surface level with the straight-edge, ramming down the high places and adding more brick to the hollows where required. On the top of this spread a layer of fine ashes rolled or rammed down to give a depth of 2 in. Drive the pegs down until their tops project roughly 1 in. above this surface; this is about the thickness of the stone used for crazy paving. Take particular care that this final layer is both firm and level. Now for laying the stones. Use a length of wide board to stand or kneel upon to save deep foot marks in the prepared surface. Start in the corner from peg A towards the outer peg B, at the same time extending

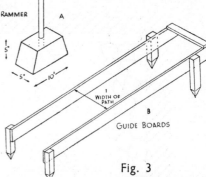

Fig. 3

these guide boards are moved along the prepared site.

A visit to a builder's yard will often locate a supply of broken cement slabs of varying sizes, obtained from repair work and the breaking up of old cement floors. This material makes up into excellent crazy paving pieces.

Dummy crazy paving is often seen on pathways leading to the front door of a house. An ordinary concrete path is made and, after the top surface has been floated smooth, the mosaic marks are drawn in the wet cement with the end of a large nail.

CRAZY PAVING STEPS AND GARDEN POOL
NOTE THE WIDE CRACKS LEFT FOR ROCK PLANTS.

18

CONCRETE AND CEMENT WORK

CONCRETE consists of cement, sand, aggregate and water. The cement is a manufactured greyish powder and is known commercially as Portland cement. It is imperative that the sand used should be perfectly clean and free from impurities, such as loam, as these greatly reduce the quality of the concrete. The sand should be sharp and consist of grains varying in size from about $\frac{1}{8}$ in. in diameter downwards. Silver sand consisting of fine equal-sized grains is unsuitable for concrete-making. Aggregate is the term used for the larger solid matter and may consist of broken stones, broken bricks, gravel or slag. The aggregate should not be regular in size, but should vary from about 1 in. to $\frac{1}{8}$ in. Like the sand, the aggregate should also be free from impurities, and clean water only should be used to obtain the best results.

Proportions.—The proportions of cement, sand and aggregate vary with different classes of work and it does not necessarily follow that the greater the proportion of cement the better the concrete will be, although an excess of sand reduces the ultimate strength.

A mixture of 1 part cement, 3 parts sand and 7 parts aggregate may be used successfully for work where great strength is not required, but concrete composed of 1 part cement, 2 parts sand and 4 parts aggregate is usually considered a suitable mixture, giving good results for all ordinary purposes.

In determining the quantities of materials required, ascertain the cubic measure of concrete required, bearing in mind that the cement and sand are proportioned to fill the crevices in the aggregate. Thus in a 1 : 2 : 4 mixture,

1 cu. ft. of cement, 2 cu. ft. of sand and 4 of aggregate will yield approximately only 4 cu. ft. of concrete.

Suppose you wish to make a concrete floor measuring 10 ft. long by 7 ft. wide and 6 in. thick, for a small garage or outside workshop. The cubic contents of such a floor is found by simple arithmetic by multiplying the length by the width by the thickness. In this case the cubic contents of the floor is 10 × 7 × $\frac{1}{2}$ = 35 cu. ft., or, as there are 27 cu. ft. in 1 cu. yd., $\frac{35}{27}$ = approx. $1\frac{1}{3}$ cu. yd., say $1\frac{1}{2}$ cu. yd.

It has been found that 1 cu. yd. of a 1 : 2 : 4 mixture requires 5 cwt. cement, 12 cu. ft. sand and 1 cu. yd. aggregate and, basing the example on this, it follows that $1\frac{1}{2}$ × 5 = $7\frac{1}{2}$ cwt. cement, $1\frac{1}{2}$ × 12 = 18 cu. ft. sand and $1\frac{1}{2}$ × 1 = $1\frac{1}{2}$ cu. yd. aggregate will be necessary for the work.

Preparing the Site.—If the ground has a tendency to be soft, remove the top layer of soil to a depth of 12 in. or so and drive in four corner pegs of about $1\frac{1}{4}$ in. square, pointed at one end to mark the size of the floor. Ram the bottom of the excavation well down to give a solid foundation and on this tip a quantity of "rubble" consisting of old bricks, stones and similar material; any large pieces of which should be broken into smaller fragments not exceeding 3 or 4 in. in diameter. A heavy hammer will be needed for this. Work the larger pieces into the bottom and, with the aid of a garden roller, roll well and add more broken pieces into the hollows. A layer 4 in. thick is sufficient.

Next, drive a peg into the ground to the level of the concrete surface required and level other pegs to this, using a straight-edge and spirit-level for the purpose. Nail thick side-boards to the pegs, as indicated in Fig. 1.

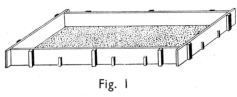

Fig. 1

Then drive in a number of extra pegs at short intervals to support the boards from the outside, otherwise the weight of the concrete will bend the boards outwards.

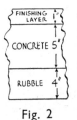

Fig. 2

Laying the Floor.—The best method is to begin with a 5-in. layer of coarse stuff and to finish the remaining thickness of 1 in. with fine cement and sand mortar floated level with a levelling board or "screed." Fig. 2 shows a section.

Mixing the Ingredients.—Assuming that the materials are close to the site to save unnecessary labour, the next step is to make the concrete by mixing the ingredients together. If this part of the work is done incorrectly the quality of the mixture will not be up to standard and good results cannot be expected.

For the mixing operation the following tools, etc., should be to hand: A garden spade or, better still, a shovel; a water-can with rose; a large, strong bucket and a mixing board or platform as shown in Fig. 3. The latter can be made of stout tongued and grooved boards fastened together with battens nailed on the underside. The size of this board should be at least 3 ft. 6 in. square; in fact, the larger the better. The object of the mixing board is to provide a smooth working surface to enable the shovel to be worked freely

and to retain the moisture which would be lost if mixed on the bare earth.

Place two measures (bucketsful) of sand into the middle of the mixing board and to it add one measure of cement. Mix the dry sand and cement well together by turning it over and over with the shovel. When the sand and cement are thoroughly incorporated, the mixture will assume an even greyish

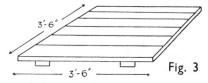

Fig. 3

colour. Then add four measures of aggregate, which, if of broken brick, should be damped with water. Place the aggregate on top of the dry sand and cement mixture and mix it thoroughly by turning it over and over at least four times from one part of the board to the other, as shown in Fig. 4.

Fig. 4

Now add water. Use a little at a time and turn the mass over well several times before adding more water. The more it is worked the more plastic it becomes.

Be particularly careful to avoid the common error of applying too much water. If the mass is too liquid the aggregate will sink to the bottom when placed in position, thus leaving the finer stuff at the top.

Laying the Mixture.—Wet the bed of rubble and tip the concrete into the middle of the site, spreading it to the sides with a spade or rake and ramming it down with a heavy block of wood to fill up any hollows. Continue mixing and filling until the level of the concrete is within 1 in. from the top edges of the frame and then allow the whole of the work to dry before attempting to add the finishing layer.

If the weather is cold and likely to be frosty, be sure to protect the freshly-laid concrete with boards and sacks or old lino placed on the top of them to prevent it becoming frozen. On the other hand, if the weather is hot, cover the surface with damp sacks or straw as this will ensure a slow, hard setting.

The Top Layer.—When the bottom layer of concrete is perfectly hard, sweep the surface with a stiff broom to remove all dust, sprinkle water over the site and proceed with the top layer.

Sand, cement and water only are required for this. The proportion of three of sand and one of cement will give excellent results. If an extra hard floor is required the quantity of sand may be reduced to two or even equal quantities of each.

Strips of wood 1 in. wide and about ¾ in. thick are now set lengthwise on the concrete bed and fixed in position with a small quantity of cement on each side,

as indicated in Fig. 5. The top edges of these should be perfectly level with the top edges of the frame. Make the strips slightly tapered from the top

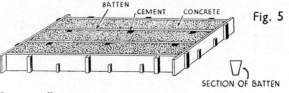

BATTEN   CEMENT   CONCRETE   Fig. 5

SECTION OF BATTEN

edge to the bottom to facilitate removal.

A levelling board or screed (Fig. 6) 4 in. wide, 1 in. thick and about 9 in. longer than the distance between the outsides of any two battens on the concrete, is required.

Fig. 6

Pour the cement and sand mortar—which should be somewhat wetter than that used for the bottom layer—between the two strips at the far end and spread it forward by pressing the screed down on to the wood strips and advancing it with a backwards, forwards and sideways motion. This moves the cement forward and fills the hollows and ensures a perfectly flat and even surface. Each section is treated in a similar way. A certain amount of water will accumulate on the surface, but this will soon disappear.

The final touches to the surface require a hand float—a metal tool designed for the purpose. A piece of planed board about a foot long, 4 in. wide and 1 in. thick, with a wooden handle, as indicated in Fig. 7, is a good substitute. This tool should be used for levelling any inequalities in the surface close to the edges.

Remove the wood strips before the cement sets hard and fill the recesses left with cement and sand mixture, using the float to make the surface flush with the rest of the work. Cover the surface as before to prevent damage and when quite hard remove the side boards.

Concrete Paths.—In making concrete paths the process is similar. The width is marked out with lines and pegs. Stakes, 2 in. by 1 in., are inserted at intervals of about 3 ft. and boards 1 in. thick by 4 in. wide are nailed on edge to them. The concrete is laid between the boards in sections of about 6 ft., each section

being separated by a cross batten. The wood dividing strip should be without taper and about $\frac{3}{4}$ in. thick.

As it is usual to make the path slightly higher at the centre than the sides to ensure a dry path, the working edge of the screed should be shaped slightly concave to suit the curve. It is used as previously described. The top edges of the wood dividing strips should be made a trifle convex to suit the surface of the path.

The wood strips dividing the sections are not removed after the work is

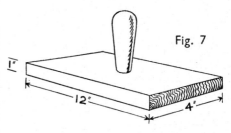

Fig. 7

complete but purposely left in to allow for expansion and contraction which, if not provided for, generally causes a cracked surface.

Renewing a Cement Surface.— When doing this it is essential to roughen or chip the old surface before attempting to apply the new cement. The roughened surface forms a key and must be well watered before laying the cement.

SIMPLE BRICKLAYING

MANY amateurs are deterred from attempting bricklaying for no other reason than that they consider it too difficult. Bricklaying as a trade is highly skilled work, but an amateur would not expect to build a house any more than an amateur engineer would be likely to construct a full-sized railway locomotive.

The Tools used for bricklaying are few and simple. They include a rule, spirit-level, plumb gauge, two trowels, bolster chisel and such items as a shovel, bucket, water-can with rose, and other odds and ends generally to be found about the home.

Before any bricklaying can be done a

proper concrete foundation must be made, the top surface of which must be flat and level, as the base or "footings" of the brickwork rest on this. The bed of concrete is formed below the ground

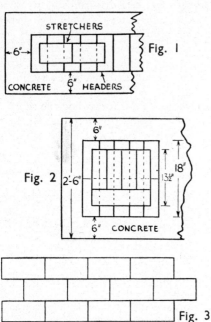

Fig. 1

Fig. 2

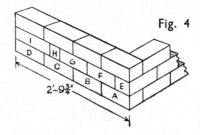

Fig. 3

level, and its thickness depends upon the nature of the subsoil and what the foundation has to support. A standard size brick measures 9 in. long, $4\frac{3}{8}$ in. wide and $2\frac{7}{8}$ in. thick, so that four courses, including the mortar joints, measure 1 ft.

Bricks are to be obtained in a great variety of qualities and degrees of hardness, such as Stocks, Flettons, etc. For amateur purposes the Fletton brick is, perhaps, the most suitable. It is hard, uniform in shape, comparatively cheap and has a rather pleasing light red colour.

The Foundation.—The width of this should be the width of the footings or base of the brickwork, plus 6 in. on each side. For a $4\frac{1}{2}$-in. wall ($\frac{1}{2}$-brick thick), the bricks forming the footings

are laid with their $4\frac{1}{2}$-in. faces to the front. Bricks laid in this fashion are called "headers," while those forming the wall are laid lengthwise on top of these and are termed "stretchers." Fig. 1 shows the arrangement. For a 9-in. wall (1 brick thick), the footings would consist of two horizontal courses of bricks, as indicated in Fig. 2. The bottom course is composed of two headers giving a total width of 18 in., while upon this is another course consisting of stretchers at the front and headers at the back. Upon this is built the first course of the wall.

Bonding.—If you examine a piece of brickwork you will invariably find that no two vertical joints in adjacent courses come together, but are separated by an intermediate course whose bricks are arranged to break the joint, as indicated in Fig. 3. This method of laying bricks is called bonding, as it interlocks or bonds the bricks together. This matter of bonding is very important, because the strength of the brickwork depends upon proper bonding.

As it is not always possible to obtain continuity of bond by the use of whole bricks, a piece of brick is inserted to

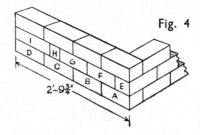

Fig. 4

overcome the difficulty. In some cases a half-brick ($\frac{1}{2}$-length) or "bat" is necessary, while in others a quarter-brick or "closer" is employed. A closer is shown at H in Fig. 4. Referring to the illustration, it will be seen that the bottom course consists of three full-length bricks, A, B and C, while D is a

¾-brick, making a total of 2 ft. 9¾ in. In the second course E is half a brick wide, F, G and I are full-length bricks, and H a closer (¼-brick), making the same total as before.

Mortar.—The amateur has the choice of two kinds of mortar with which to lay bricks, namely, that made from lime and that made of Portland cement. The latter, although more expensive than the former, is recommended, as it requires no more prepara-

boards about 4½ in. wide, securely fixed round three sides to form a three-sided tray, as indicated in Fig. 5.

Greenhouse Base.—An example of simple brickwork is a base for a small greenhouse measuring 10 ft. long by 8 ft. wide and 2 ft. 6 in., composed of 4½-in. brickwork, as shown diagrammatically in Fig. 6. The concrete foundation is 1 ft. 9 in. wide and 9 in. thick, as shown in Fig. 7.

Marking Out.—First mark out the

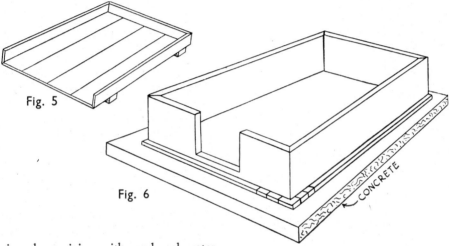

Fig. 5

Fig. 6

CONCRETE

Fig. 7

1st. COURSE   GROUND LEVEL

FOOTINGS

CONCRETE

3″
3″
9″

1′-9″

tion than mixing with sand and water. Lime mortar must be prepared before use by first "slaking" the lime with water, which takes several hours, then mixing it with sand, and even then it cannot be used for at least three days.

The Sand used in making mortar must be clean and sharp, any foreign matter such as loam being very detrimental to the quality. A mixture of four parts sand to one part Portland cement gives satisfactory results. The mortar should be mixed on a platform or "banker" consisting of tongued and grooved boards fixed together with battens underneath. For convenience of mixing and to prevent waste, the platform should be fitted with narrow

site by driving in four pegs—one at each corner, as indicated at A, B, C, and D in Fig. 8—to mark the centres of the walls. Test the angles to see that they are perfectly square. This can be verified by driving a nail in the centre of the top of each peg and measuring diagonally across with a piece of batten or a metal tape, as shown by the dotted lines. If correct, the distance from

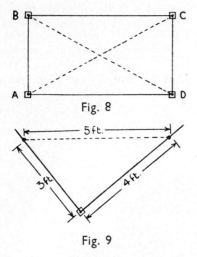

Fig. 8

Fig. 9

A to C should be exactly equal to that between B and D. Another method to obtain square angles is to measure 3 ft. along one line and 4 ft. along the adjacent one forming the angle, inserting pegs at these points and measuring the distance across, as represented by the dotted line in Fig. 9. If this distance is 5 ft., the angle is correct.

Assuming the centre line to be correct, use it for setting out similar parallel lines to indicate the width of the excavation, which should be 1 ft. 9 in. If the soil be hard and more or less solid and comparatively level, dig a trench 15 in. deep. This depth allows for 9 in. of concrete, 3 in. for the footings and 3 in. for the first course of the wall below ground level, as illustrated in Fig. 7.

After ramming down the bottom, drive a peg in the centre of the trench, leaving 9 in. exposed above the bottom. This represents the thickness of the concrete and the top of the peg indicates where the top surface will come. At a distance of about 30 in. from this peg, drive in another until it is exactly level with the first or master peg, using a straight-edge (both edges parallel) about 3 ft. long and a spirit-level for the purpose, in the manner shown at Fig. 10. Drive in similar pegs about 30 in. apart round the excavation, keeping them all level, each to the other.

If the soil is found to be soft and yielding at this depth, it is advisable to dig the trench deeper until a more solid bottom is obtained. This may necessitate two or three courses being below ground.

If the weather be dry and there is no likelihood of the sides caving in, the operation of mixing and filling in the concrete can be proceeded with. If, however, the sides are likely to fall, it is wise to support them with boards, as in Fig. 11, which are removed when the concrete has set.

Concrete for the Foundation.—A suitable grade of concrete for the

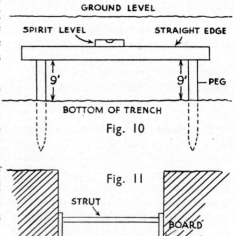

GROUND LEVEL

SPIRIT LEVEL　　STRAIGHT EDGE

9′　　9′　—PEG

BOTTOM OF TRENCH

Fig. 10

Fig. 11

STRUT

BOARD

foundation is one consisting of 5 parts of washed stone ballast, 1 part clean sharp sand and 1 part Portland cement. The ingredients should be mixed on the banker already mentioned, provided it is sufficiently large. Place 5 buckets of aggregate in the centre of the board, add 1 bucket of sand and thoroughly mix them together with a shovel. To this add 1 bucket Portland cement and incorporate it with the aggregate and sand mixture by turning it over and over several times. Then add a small quantity of water from a can fitted with a rose, and mix. Continue adding water and mixing alternately until a plastic mixture is formed—not too wet and not too dry.

Shovel the concrete into the centre of the trench and spread it outwards to the sides and along, patting it down firmly with the back of the shovel so that the top of the concrete is perfectly flat and level with the tops of the pegs. Before proceeding further, the foundation must be allowed to set, which possibly will take several days.

The Footings.—The foundation is now ready to receive the footings. Clear the surface of all dust and soil which may have settled upon it and, if the surface be dry, sprinkle it with water. This operation is omitted, of course, if the surface is damp.

The footings consist of a course of headers, the centres of which must come in the centre of the foundation. Set up

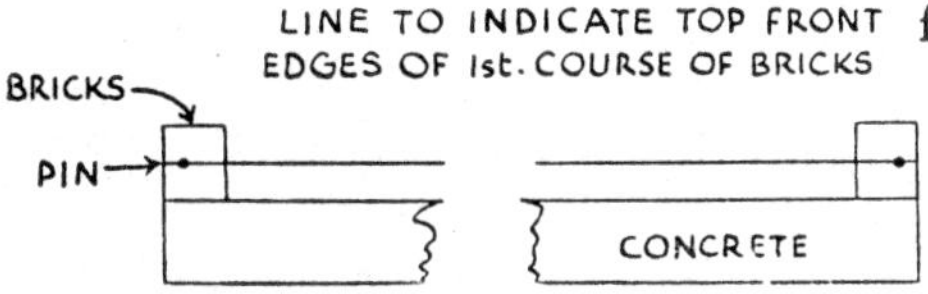

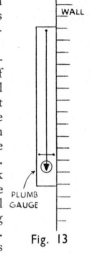

Fig. 13

inserting pins at the joints, as in Fig. 12. With the bricks and mortar to hand and the tools in readiness, the actual bricklaying can be started. If the bricks are dry it is advisable to sprinkle them with water—just sufficient to damp them—as this prevents too much absorption of moisture from the mortar. Damp bricks do not need this treatment.

Laying the Bricks.—Start at one corner of the foundation. Spread a bed of mortar about ¼-in. thick for a distance of about half a dozen bricks, using the large trowel for the purpose. Place the end brick "frog" or hollow side up, keeping it level and square and using the line as a guide. Against the side of this brick, where the next one is to come place a trowelful of mortar and lay the second brick. Continue in this way until the six bricks have been laid. With the straight-edge and spirit-level set on top of the bricks, check for level; any bricks standing high can be tapped down with the handle of the trowel by holding the tool vertically upside down. Proceed, step by step, until the whole of the bricks have been laid, checking each section as the work proceeds.

The First Course.—This and the following courses consist of stretchers. Alter the guide line and proceed as before by building up the corners, and test them from time to time for verticality and squareness.

A Plumb Gauge is necessary for testing uprightness. This tool can be easily constructed and consists of a piece of planed wood 4 ft. 6 in. long and about ¾ in. thick, planed true and parallel on

LINE TO INDICATE TOP FRONT
EDGES OF 1st. COURSE OF BRICKS

BRICKS

PIN

CONCRETE

Fig. 12

a string line representing the front top edges of the bricks. This can be done by setting two bricks at each end and 18*

edges. On one wide face a centre line is marked down its length. At a distance of about 4½ in. from the bottom, a pear-shaped hole is cut out in which a heavy plumb-bob can swing freely. A saw-cut about ¾ in. deep is made in the top edge and in line with the centre line and from this cut a string-line carrying the plummet is suspended. A piece of wire bent to form a rectangular staple is driven into the face at the lower end of the string which restricts the swing of the weight. A suitable plummet with a pointed end can be obtained for a few pence from a tool shop. In using the tool, the edge is placed against the brickwork in the manner shown at Fig. 13. If the string coincides with the marked centre line when so placed, it shows that the wall is vertical.

Assuming the corners are as they should be, the rest of the bricklaying is carried out, using the guide line, course by course, until complete.

Mention has been made of the use of bats and closers for obtaining continuity of bond. These must not be overlooked whilst constructing the wall.

Cutting Bricks.—The best way to cut bricks—although not the method adopted by a tradesman who uses a trowel—is to use a bolster chisel, which has a thin, wide blade. Mark a line round the brick where the cut is to be, nick round the marks, place the brick plain side up on a smooth surface and give it a smart blow with a club hammer.

Pointing.—To give a neat finish to the joints, they should be pointed. To do this, rake out the joints to a depth of about ¾ in. before the mortar becomes too hard. Fill up the gaps so made with "compo" consisting of equal parts of sand and cement, using a small trowel.

GARDEN POOLS

WHEN properly constructed, a lily pond or other type of pool will add distinction to the smallest garden, while those of greater extent give scope for more ambitious treatment as part of the ever-popular rock garden.

Many garden lovers who feel the enchantment of such a pool with its surrounding plants reflected on its surface, and the natural grouping of rocks and ferns, are deterred from making similar pictures for their own delight because of the impression that running water is necessary, whereas it is in many cases undesirable. Others, disregarding the fact that fishes are useful as well as ornamental, by omitting these, allow the pool to become a breeding place for midges and mosquitoes. Both fishes and purely aquatic plants are necessary

and in themselves add much to the interest of the garden.

There are various kinds of ponds and pools, which include those of well puddled clay, brickwork and concrete, apart from the smaller kinds forming part of the crazy-paving scheme, such as those fashioned from cisterns, old sinks, coppers and tubs, camouflaged with rocks, crazy-paving and plants.

Once a pool has been established on natural principles, it needs practically no attention except the periodical pruning of water plants which may spread enough to hamper the movement of fishes and generally choke the pool with vegetation of an unpleasant kind.

Site and Construction.—Often, some odd corner of the garden which is useless for growing plants proves suitable for a pool. It is essential that the site should not be fully exposed to a maximum of direct sunlight, as this will result in the development of rapid growths of microscopic plants which render the water opaquely green. On the other hand, water-lilies require sunlight, but as they are so very ornamental in bloom and provide their own shade with their large leaves, it is best to arrange the site so that part of the pool receives full sunlight whilst the other is shaded, but not by any type of tree which sheds its leaves in winter, otherwise the pool will soon be filled and the water plants will be uprooted in every attempt to rake them out. An excess of decaying leaves is also harmful to fishes.

Before starting any construction work it is necessary to decide if the pool is to be of formal, geometrical, ornamental design or the natural irregular type. It should be in keeping with the rest of the garden. For a formally arranged garden with straight paths a round or rectangular pool is more appropriate; for the average garden one more ornamental is preferable; while for the wild type of garden with rockery, an irregular pool edged by rockwork on natural lines is recommended. The latter may be more costly owing to the amount of stone required, but it is better to strive for as natural a setting as possible, even if the rock garden is altered in that part. Many such gardens are overcrowded with rocks, so a little careful selection and re-arrangement will do no harm.

Small Puddled Pond.—If the soil is of heavy clay, it is quite easy to make a puddled pond. A clay pond is particularly suitable for goldfish, carp and tench.

First peg out the margin to the desired shape and dig out to the required depth, arranging that one portion is not less than 18 in. deep for the fish to retire beyond the reach of frost; also make one or more sides slope gradually to very shallow water thus providing a refuge for the smaller fish out of reach of larger inhabitants. Make the excava-

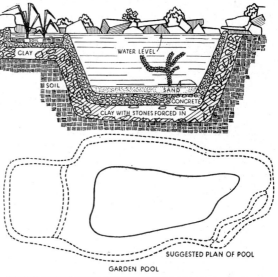

SECTIONAL DIAGRAM OF POOL SHOWING ROCKWORK OVERLAPPING CONCRETE EDGE, LEDGE FOR BOG PLANTS AND CLAY BACKING

Fig. I

tion with sides sloping about 20° outwards, and ram down the bottom and beat the sides until these are firm. Force into the sides and bottom any pieces of old concrete, stone and brick available, filling in the crevices with moist clay. Treat the edge in the same way, using as much natural stone and rockwork here as possible. To prevent worms burrowing through and causing a leak a 3-in. layer of soot in the bottom covered with a 9-in. layer of moist clay well pounded into place has proved successful. When this much has been completed, cover the bottom with a layer of coarse (not silver) sand which has been previously well washed in running water to remove dirt and other particles of matter, to a depth of 3 or 4 in.

Filling with Water.—To fill the pond with water, place a pail or basin on the bottom of the pool and pour the water into this and allow it to flow gently over the sides; this will not disturb the sand very much and prevents clouding the water. Let the water stand for at least three or four weeks to settle, then water-plants may be introduced, and fish added a week or so later when the plants have become established a little. Any reduction of these settling periods generally results in the death of the fish.

Concrete Ponds made on similar lines to that illustrated in Fig. 1 are not quite so simple to construct as the one just described, yet are not beyond the skill of the average practical man. When making use of an old bath for pool-construction purposes it is important to remember that galvanised iron is injurious to both fishes and plants, so it is essential that this be painted with two or three coats of waterproof enamel of any sombre tint, preferably dark brown. To save all this extra work it is perhaps cheaper in the long run to keep to concrete and cement only.

Before starting any cement work, the subsoil must be made firm by ramming the bottom and sides and working in rough pieces of slag, broken bricks, etc., as previously described; otherwise the weight of water may cause the pool to settle in parts. Do not economise over time, labour and material for this foundation work. Trying to repair a faulty pool after it has been finished and stocked is difficult and troublesome.

There is no need for the bottom to be dead flat or level. The finished depth may slope here and there from 18 in. to 24 in., with shallow ledges round part of the sides 6 in. to 9 in. below the surface line for marginal plants, which only require shallow water, and perhaps other pockets at or a little above the water level for bog plants. An average depth of 30 in. for the excavation will allow for the hole being lined with a 6-in. layer of well-puddled clay beaten down and shaped more or less to the desired form of the pool.

The proportions of concrete materials have been dealt with elsewhere but a mixture composed of one part Portland cement to two parts of clean, sharp sand and two parts broken stones or old bricks $\frac{3}{4}$ in. diameter has been used to advantage.

Having made the concrete, tip it into the centre of the clay-lined excavation, and spread it towards the sides, working it down to a depth of 4 in. with a trowel, building up the sides, sloping them outwards, keeping the upper part of the sides about 2 in. thick. Run the sides into the bottom by well-rounded curves to form a good bond. With fairly stiff concrete it may be found possible to dispense with any form of wood shuttering to hold the mixture in place while it sets. The work is considerably strengthened if oddments of wire netting, iron bars and old iron bed laths are embedded in the concrete when it is being laid, care being taken that no parts project through into contact with the water.

Quite a fair surface can be produced on the concrete by using a trowel, but if a very smooth surface is desired a final layer of fine sand and cement in equal proportions, mixed to the consistency of

Fig. 2

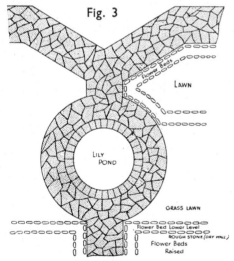

Fig. 3

Flower Beds

LAWN

LILY
POND

GRASS LAWN

Flower Bed Lower Level
ROUGH STONE (DRY WALL)
Flower Beds
Raised

mortar and made ½ in. thick would be suitable.

After allowing about a week for the concrete to set hard the pool can be filled with water, but unless the cement has been treated with some preparation of conditioning crystals which fill the pores with a siliceous deposit, converting any soluble poisonous compounds into insoluble ones, the soaking period must extend for quite a month with frequent changes of water, otherwise fish and plant life will suffer from poisonous emanations from the cement. This seasoning may be hurried by slaking a large piece of lime in the water, and stirring it well every few hours. The liquid should be drawn off after two days. Clean out well and fill up again. This process repeated for two weeks should be sufficient. When the pool is first filled a few minnows can be put in as a test before introducing more valuable fish.

The illustration appearing as Fig. 2 shows an excellent example of a garden pool constructed by an amateur, while that illustrated at Fig. 3 is a suggested lay-out for a garden pond.

LEVELLING AND DRAINING
A LAWN

IN the preparation of a new lawn, a combined process of levelling and draining has to be carried out. Only the simplest form of levelling which can be done by the average practical man will be described, while the system of drainage is quite simple to arrange and lay.

The two sections of the work cannot very well be started and finished, each as a separate job, although, of course, when an existing lawn or new site is regarded as already sufficiently well drained the work of levelling may be carried out as described.

The amount of levelling to be done depends on the existing site, and on whether it is desired to make the lawn in a true horizontal plane, or to reduce the site to a level in the general plane, that is, to follow the general slope of the garden, which may be on a slight incline down from the back of the house to the end of the garden. The most common variations of this condition are as follows. Where the slope is from the house end up to the far end, which is the higher. The left-hand side of the garden may be the higher side or vice versa. With this in mind it can only be left to the owner to decide which general plan to follow. Very often where the problem appears difficult owing to the steep slope of the ground, quite effective results are obtained by dividing the length of the garden into terraces.

Tools Required.—Before starting the work, obtain a wooden straight-edge about 12 ft. long, 5 or 6 in. wide, by 1 to 2 in. thick, a spirit-level at least 12 in. in length, two marking-out lines with iron pins, and a number of wooden pegs about 1-in. square by 1 ft. or more long,

pointed at the end. See that the tops of these are level and square and, with a carpenter's square, mark each peg with a line all round, 6 in. down from the top end. Such a peg is illustrated in Fig. 2.

Setting Out Position of Lawn.— Having decided where the lawn is to be, it is very convenient to use two marking-out lines, as indicated in the drawing (Fig. 2), to ensure that the edges of the proposed lawn are parallel, and the ends at right-angles to the sides. The short line A–B is pegged down taut. Next, by check measurements from some convenient fixed point, such as the square post supporting the boundary fence, fix the width of pathway on each side of the lawn, and the width of the lawn itself at the house end, and insert a peg at each corner. To fix the position of the two far corners extend the long marking-out line from the edge of peg B up the garden, and by moving the far end of the line either to the right or to the left, set the long line B–D at right-angles to the line A–B, checking the truth by means of a square. Measure off the length of the lawn and drive in peg D with its edge against the line. Do the same with the other edge and drive in peg C. All of these pegs are only driven a little way into the ground, just enough to set them firm.

By inspection, pick out the peg which stands at the highest corner of the ground and drive it in down to the 6-in. mark. This will be the chief peg from which the level will be taken.

As, in the course of building the house, much of the original top soil has been covered by clay and stones dug out by the builders, the best way is to clear a space right across the site and by digging a trench in the usual manner of gardening, bring as much of the top soil again to the surface as possible, bury the clay and throw out the stones. As much

Grass will never grow with any strength on sour sub-soil, and years of arduous fertilization will be necessary before the carefully prepared site gives its reward. When driving in the wooden pegs, the tops may be protected from the hammer

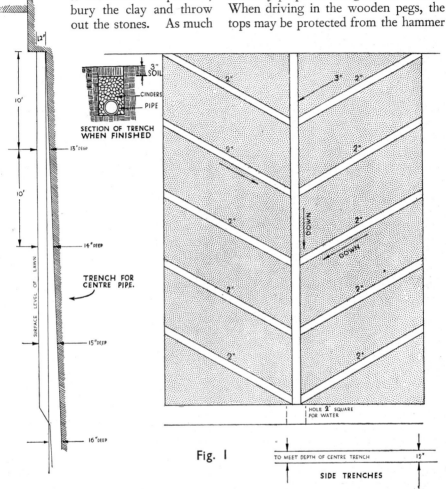

Fig. 1

of it will occur in patches, it is possible with care to distinguish the more fertile soil, on account of its darker appearance, and thus keep it at the surface, at the same time keeping the whole fairly level as the digging proceeds. The importance of retaining top-spit soil on the surface cannot be overstressed. For it is possible to waste all the careful levelling and draining work by ignoring it.

blows by holding another piece of wood on top of the peg and striking this and not the peg direct.

Setting the Pegs Level.—The next step consists in setting the marked pegs and levelling them. In a line across the site drive pegs into the ground at equal distances apart: about 8 or 10 ft. will do, to keep within length of the straight-edge. This gives a line of pegs along the line A–B. Then set up a line of pegs at equal distances along the line A–C, and the same along the lines C–D and B–D, and by using lines both ways from one set of edge pegs to the other, add the intermediate pegs to cover the area of the lawn, as shown in the illustration.

Before proceeding any further, fix the spirit-level to the top edge of the straight-edge by means of a piece of string.

Assuming that peg A is on the highest corner, and that the main slope of the ground is away from the house towards the bottom of the garden, with a slight slope from the A–C side towards the B–D edge, lay the straight-edge and spirit-level from the top of peg A to the top of peg A1 and hammer the latter down until the bubble in the level remains stationary in the centre. Peg A1 is now level with the chief peg A. The remainder of the levelling work is a repetition of this: Peg A2 is tapped down level with the top of A1, A3 from peg A2, until peg B is reached, then all the tops of the pegs in that row will be true and level. Each new row of pegs is treated in the same manner; Peg E is set from A, and having established that one the remainder, E1, E2, etc., are levelled as previously described. Occasional checking back to the preceding row, such as between F3 and E2 and E3 and A2, is well worth the extra trouble.

When the whole has been done there will be 6 in. more or less of each peg standing out clear of the ground, which allows for any high places in the surface, and permits the free use of the straight-edge.

The slight slope sideways may now be corrected by raking the soil over from the high side to make up the lower edge; this leaves the main slope to be dealt with, and we will assume that it has been decided to have the lawn in a true horizontal plane.

There are two ways of levelling in this direction. Either extra soil may be added at the far end to make it up to the same height as the house end, or some of the surface soil at the house end may be moved to the other end with the same result, but to save disturbing the best end, the recommended procedure, if possible, is to make up the low end with soil from another part of the garden. The soil should be applied to form layers of about 2 in. deep, and after each layer has been carefully raked over, it should be thoroughly rolled to ensure a firm foundation.

As the work proceeds, the level should be checked from time to time with the straight-edge, and any small depressions or bumps appearing on the surface should be either filled in or removed as the case may be.

In cases where additional soil is not available or cannot be spared from another part of the garden, the actual levelling must be done with the subsoil.

Remove Top Soil.—To do this, first remove the top soil for a depth of about 6 in., and make a heap of it at the side of the site. Now find the mean level, which, when worked from, will give enough soil from the high parts to make up the low parts. Where the fall of the ground is more or less regular, drive one of the pegs in to its marked line. This will indicate the main point where the high ground falls off into a hollow. This peg becomes the chief one for this particular case, and the procedure is the same as before. The tops of the pegs are levelled to this one and it is quite possible that, if the amount of earth to be removed from the high side is considerable, the top of the pegs in this section will come to the level of the earth at those parts, so the quickest way

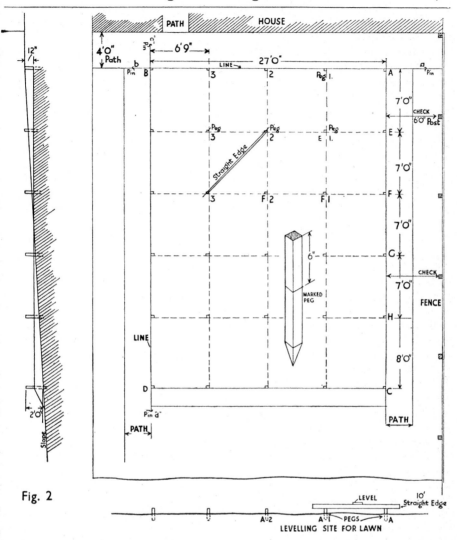

Fig. 2

LEVELLING SITE FOR LAWN

will be to start reducing the mound from here and work back, setting the pegs level a section at a time as progress is made. In Fig. 2, the shaded part represents the soil to be removed to bring the surface level down to the line B–C. All the soil removed from that part of the site to the left of peg D is used to fill the hollows on the right. If the two slopes indicated by the letters A–B and C–E (Fig. 1) are to be grass covered

they must be at an easy angle to allow a mowing machine to be used.

Having thus far prepared the site a final check-up on the levelling is left until the drainage work (if necessary) has been completed, as this will disturb the surface along certain lines.

Drainage is only necessary in cases where the soil is of such a nature that water in excess of that required for maintaining the grass in a healthy condition is so slow in running off or accumulates to such an extent that it prevents the free circulation of air between the particles—a condition which is fatal if a satisfactory lawn be desired. Thus, a deep sandy or gravelly soil forms a natural drainage, but in cases where the top soil is of a heavy nature and the subsoil composed of clay, the moisture is prevented from sinking into the ground and getting away, with the result that the ground becomes waterlogged. In the latter case it will be necessary to resort to artificial drainage by means of a system of drain pipes. It is important to arrange the pipes in such a way that the water can get into them, and also to have some efficient means of disposing of the water collected by the pipes. In the absence of a convenient ditch, a deep hole with puddled clay sides, dug at the outfall, will hold a useful supply of water for frequent use in the kitchen garden or elsewhere.

Drain-laying.—The actual work of laying the drains is no more complicated than levelling the ground. The most effective way of laying agricultural drain pipes, or field pipes as they are sometimes called, is on the herring-bone system shown in Fig. 2. This diagram shows the arrangement suitable for a flat site, or one which slopes down in the direction of the arrow. In general the pipes are placed as near as possible diagonally across the direction the water in the ground will flow, so as to catch as much of it as possible, and when leading it away to do so in the easiest direction. Do not connect the side pipes at right-angles with another as this will hinder the flow.

The pipes used are of unglazed earthenware, 12 in. long; the 3-in. diameter size is suitable for the main run, and the 2-in. diameter pipes for the side feeders. The latter are set about 10 to 15 ft. apart, according to the nature

of the soil and the area of the site to be drained. In very heavy wet ground they would be closer together than in other cases. As a preliminary guide to arranging a good system, sketch a rough plan of the site to a simple scale of say $\frac{1}{8}$ in. to equal 1 ft. Mark the oblong outline to represent the size of the lawn, then for a case like that indicated in Fig. 2, mark the centre line of the main pipe down the middle, divide the side length into five equal spaces, and the centre line in the same way only the junction point is in advance a distance about equal to the first division on the sides.

To put this into practice drive in pegs to mark the lines of pipes, and dig out the trench a spade wide to a regular depth, if the ground is on a slope, of 12 in. to 18 in. In the case of a level site such as the case dealt with when levelling, the depth at the start can be 12 in., with a fall or slope of 1 in. in 10 ft. This regular fall must be kept to the end of the pipe line and it is also important to see that the points of junction are on the same level, or a little above will not matter, but never below.

When all the trenches are ready, remove all the loose soil and, to be on the safe side, drive a peg in at every 8 to 10 ft. along the bottom of the trench, tap the tops level, and then, starting at the top end peg, note the increased depth at the next peg, 10 ft. along. At the end of the 10 ft. straight-edge the increase should be 1 in. at the next peg, another 10 ft. along the drop is 2 in. and so on.

Lay the pipes in the bottom of the trench in a straight line and see that the junctions butt together well, otherwise soil will work its way into the pipe and block it. To test them, pour water in at the top or high end of each branch pipe-line in turn and note if it runs freely from the outlet. If found in order, fill up the trenches with clean cinders to within 3 in. of the top and finish filling in with top soil. Rake off the surplus soil and check the general level of the site as before to finish the surface ready for turf or seed. The easiest way to complete the lawn is to dress the ground with a complete grass fertiliser at the rate of 3 oz. to the square yard, and sow with a good grade of grass seed at about 4 oz. to the square yard. Rake them in together and roll down. If this is watered well in very dry weather, a thick covering of grass should be available in about six or seven weeks. All weeds that come up should be pulled out as soon as they are large enough to handle, and not allowed to remain to become part of the turf.

WIRE NETTING AND ITS USES

G ALVANISED wire netting plays an important part in the construction of many structures for the garden and small-holding. Poultry-houses and runs, rabbit hutches, etc., all require wire netting.

The size of the mesh of this material varies from $\frac{1}{2}$ in. to 2 in., and the usual length per roll is 25 yards, while the width increases from 12 in. to 72 in. in steps of 6 in., eight widths being available.

A very convenient way of making poultry runs, and even light, net-covered parts of the houses themselves, is shown in Fig. 1. The run may be extended to any width or length by building sections as shown. Each section is made of three 6-ft. lengths of 2-in. by 2-in. square timber, pointed at one end for putting into the ground, and tarred to prevent decay for just over 1 ft. at the bottom. The top cross-bar is 2 in. by 1$\frac{1}{2}$ in., and 6 ft. long. The lower part of the frame is boarded up for a height of 1 ft. 6 in. to 2 ft. 6 in., as required, and the remainder is covered in with wire netting fixed to the back of

the frame by means of staples driven in at frequent intervals.

Such enclosures require a door. A suitable one, complete with a pair of hinges for fixing to the adjoining section, is shown on the right in Fig. 1. The door frame consists of two pieces of 2-in. by 2-in. timber for the sides, 5 ft. long, and a piece of 3-in. by 1$\frac{1}{2}$-in. for the top. The lower part is boarded up to the same height as the sections on either side, and with similar material.

As this part is the one most likely to

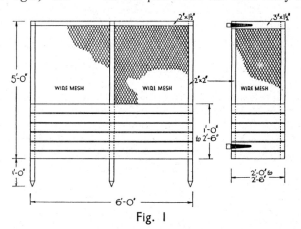

Fig. 1

come into contact with a person's clothing, it is advisable to cover the edges of the netting with strips of lath. Cut the netting to the size of the door at the back and nail it down by placing the laths on top, and nailing through them and the netting into the door frame. This will cover in any stray ends and edges. The finished sections and doors are treated with creosote or similar preserving solution.

Another indispensable addition to the

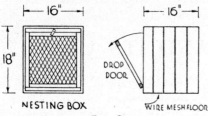

NESTING BOX   WIRE MESH FLOOR

Fig. 2

poultry-keeper is the nesting box, shown in Fig. 2. The bottom is of fine-mesh wire netting as a protection against rats and for easy cleaning. The door may be hung to open sideways or to drop as indicated, and consists of a light frame covered with 1-in. mesh netting edged round with light lath. The overall dimensions of the box are: height, 18 in., width 16-in., and depth 16-in. Tongued and grooved boards ⅝ in. thick would be suitable for this.

Wire Mesh Fence.—Another useful form of wire enclosure for poultry is made as in Fig. 3. The posts are 2 in. square, 5 ft. high above ground level, and 18 in. below. The bottom ends are pointed for driving into the ground, and are tarred. These are set up about 10 ft. apart and braced by means of No. 8 or 10 S.W.G. galvanised wire. Starting from the ground level at the first post, this wire is taken to the top of the next post and fixed by means of staples, then on down to ground level at the next post,

and so on right round the series of posts forming the enclosure. A second length of wire is also run in the same manner from post to post, starting from the top of the first post this time and crossing the first wire between each section, as shown. A roll of 2-in. mesh netting, 6 ft. wide, is suitable for this job. As there are no boards along the ground level, 12 in. or so of the bottom edge of the netting is buried in the ground, so that the live stock cannot make a way out. For rabbit pens, the height need not be so great and the extra amount over at the bottom is not only buried straight down, but the edge is also turned inwards, parallel with the ground level, so that the rabbits cannot burrow downwards and beyond the wire netting. A medium-size door such as used in rabbit-hutch construction, is shown in Fig. 4. The timber is halved at the corners and the edge of the wire netting covered with

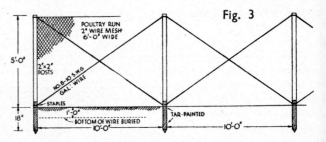

Fig. 3

light batten or lath strips to make a neat finished job and to prevent damage to clothing and the live stock.

Enclosure for Tennis Court.—The usual height of the wire netting round a tennis court is between 8 and 10 ft. and the posts of 3-in. square timber are spaced 10 ft. apart.

The intermediate posts may be plain and set in concrete in the ground, or braced on both sides in the direction of the fence, as shown in Fig. 5. Corner posts are braced in the same manner, but at right-angles. Between the tops of the

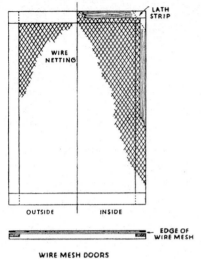

WIRE MESH DOORS

Fig. 4

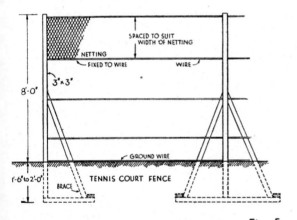

TENNIS COURT FENCE

Fig. 5

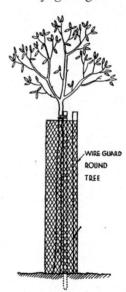

Fig. 6

often damaged by rabbits and other animals. If a light stake is not already used to support the tree, one can be driven into the ground near it, and a length of wire netting bent round to give a diameter of about 8 in. or 9 in., the two vertical edges being lapped and fixed to the stake with staples, as indicated in the sketch (Fig. 6).

Wire Guards for Gutters and Drains.—The ordinary eaves gutter can be reached for cleaning purposes by using a ladder, but there are many modern houses, and other buildings with flat roofs, where the gutter channel can only be reached by getting on to the roof.

posts and along at the ground level wire is stretched and fixed to each post. On this the wire netting is hung and secured at frequent intervals by means of wire ties twisted through the edge of the mesh and round the horizontal wires. If the width of netting used is 24 in. or 30 in., other wires are fixed between the posts, and the overlapped edges of each run fixed to these as before.

Wire Guards round Young Trees. —Wire netting is useful for protecting the bark of young fruit trees, which is

A guard of wire netting fixed over such a gutter will keep the outlet clear.

In some cases the rain-water down-pipe from the gutter is arranged to discharge over an iron grid, very often set low in a small wall of brick or cement. A small wire-mesh guard fixed to a light wooden frame fitted over the top will prevent the grid becoming choked.

FENCES AND FENCING

A LARGE variety of fencing may be bought ready-made but there is no reason why the amateur craftsman should not be able to make and mend his own when necessary.

The fence forming part of the house property is usually considered to be the one which is supported by posts in that garden. Look down your garden and you will notice that along one side the boundary fence shows its supporting posts in your garden, while on the other side only the fencing boards can be seen. If the property is your own you are only responsible for the care and upkeep of that length having posts on your side.

When repairing a section of fence the existing parts are the best guide as to the manner of cutting and fitting the new parts.

Posts rot away at the ground level, and if they become very bad, or a heavy gale snaps them off, the first job is to clear the ground along that section and to remove the old stump or butt.

With care this may be done without loosening the surrounding earth too much, thus leaving a good hole for the new posts, which will be much firmer than when a large hole is dug and loose soil rammed in.

To remove a butt which has broken off short at ground level first expose part of the top end of it and nail two pieces of strong wood on opposite sides. A block of wood is placed flat under each block on the butt so that by inserting a lever between, it may be lifted a little. Other pieces of wood are placed on the one on the ground to make up for the space the butt has been lifted until it is far enough out of the ground to be pulled out. Work first one side and then the other if working single-handed, or if help can be obtained both work together from opposite sides.

Wire Fence.—Details of several fences of simple construction are shown in Working Drawing No. 25. The wire fence illustrated in Fig. 1 can be easily erected by any practical man. All that is required for this type of fence is a number of posts 4 in. square for the end or main posts, which are usually spaced at about 9 ft. apart, and two smaller ones of 3-in. by 2-in. section, spaced between each pair of main posts. A suitable gauge of wire is between Nos. 8 S.W.G. and 10 S.W.G., galvanised.

The length of the posts for a low fence usually is 3 ft. above ground and 2 ft. below, but for a fence 4 ft. high an additional 6 in. should be allowed below ground. All the holes should be marked out and bored before erection, those in the main posts being larger to pass the stems of the eye-bolts used to secure the ends of the wire. By turning these the wire is tightened and locked by means of the nuts provided on each.

When a large number of posts has to be bored it is a wise plan to make and use a template for marking the positions of the holes.

With even a simple fence of this type it is essential to establish the posts firmly in the ground. The wire looks thin, but as there are three lengths strained taut there is considerable strain on the end posts, so that a spur leg is advisable, even if the post be set in concrete. To ensure long life, each post should be well tarred before inserting into the ground.

Cleft Chestnut Paling.—Cleft chestnut paling, as shown in Fig. 2, is very

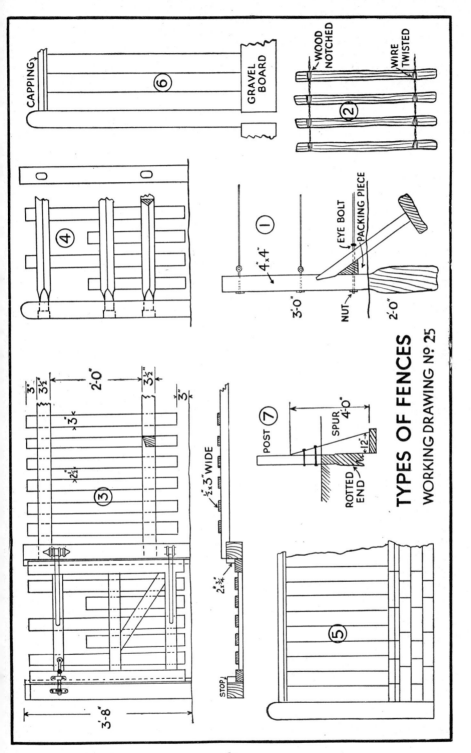

TYPES OF FENCES

WORKING DRAWING Nº 25

suitable for dividing gardens or parts of larger grounds. The cleft pales are bound together with tightly-twisted galvanised wire. The standard spacing between palings is either 3 or 5 in., and the height, 3 ft. 6 in., 4 ft. 0 in., and 4 ft. 6 in. The posts used at intervals are made 5 ft. 6 in., 6 ft. 0 in., and 6 ft. 6 in. for the above heights of fencing.

The two designs of simple fencing illustrated in Figs. 3 and 4 may be carried out without having to cut any intricate joints. As far as the fence shown in Fig. 3 is concerned, the work is only plain sawing and nailing up. The other type has the ends of the rail or "arris rail," as it is termed, reduced to fit into the mortise made by boring two or more holes close together in the post, and finishing with a chisel. The same kind of rails are used for a close-boarded fence. Two rails only are required for the close-boarded fence in Fig. 5, where the lower part consists of a low brick wall with splay bricks to throw off the rain. The top of the fence should always be finished with capping.

It will be noticed that many of the larger sizes of square post have a natural or log-shaped end which is the end that was towards the top of the tree. The sap flows towards this end, so if this part is put into the ground, it stops the moisture rising, and helps to protect the post against rotting.

Boarded Fence with Gravel Board. —A boarded fence with a gravel board (Fig. 6) is usually considerably higher than a paling one. The posts are generally set 9 ft. apart, and are mortised for three arris rails. If mortised by hand the best way is to make two holes with an auger, one above the other, and finish the sides with a chisel. Their position is not central, but towards the front face of the post, so that when the boards are in position they do not stand out beyond the face of the post. The ends of the rails are shaped to fit the mortises, and it is a good plan to coat both with red lead paint before fixing.

Making Holes for Posts.—The correct method of making the hole in the ground for the post is to remove as little earth as possible beyond that which is essential for inserting the butt. Three inches larger than the post all round is ample, care being taken to see that the sides are kept upright as the hole is deepened, and that it is not allowed to become larger at the top. When the post is in position, ram the earth in tightly with a heavy piece of wood, adding a small quantity of soil at a time. No amount of ramming can produce quite the same degree of firmness as exists in the undisturbed earth round the post hole, hence the reason for keeping the hole as small as possible.

Gravel Boards.—A thick board, called a gravel board, between the two posts saves the lower part of the palings from damage and is stronger to withstand the weather and damp near ground level. Short pegs are driven into the ground to support it, and a fillet is nailed to each post. In place of these fillets the side faces of the post are often cut-in from $\frac{1}{2}$ in. to $\frac{3}{4}$ in., the depth being the same as the thickness of the gravel board, which varies from 1 in. to $1\frac{1}{2}$ in. The width also varies between 6 in. and 12 in.

Boards for Fence.—The boards may be either ordinary or feather-edge, and should not be nailed too tightly together as they swell when wet. The cutting to length may be done before fixing, or after they have been nailed to the top rail. Capping is used along the top to protect the ends of the boards against the weather.

Oak fencing is the best for wear and appearance, and the method of construction is the same as the above. The pales are either sawn or cleft, the latter being the best as they weather better and have a brighter appearance. The usual size is $\frac{1}{4}$ in. thin edge to $\frac{1}{2}$ in. thick on the other edge.

Repair to Old Post.—Fig. 7 illustrates a simple method of repairing a post that has rotted away at the root. For this purpose a wedge-shaped balk of timber may be obtained from a timber yard, and is thoroughly tarred or creosoted before use. A hole is dug on one side of the post deep enough to take about half of the spur. Large nails or bolts are used for fixing.

Fence for Tennis Court.—To surround a tennis court either at home or at a club ground a high wire fence is required to prevent the balls from going over beyond the court. If tall wooden posts at the corners are regarded as too cumbersome, light iron supports are quite easy to make. The simple cutting is done with a hack-saw, and the drilling by hand with a drill brace and twist-drills.

A height of 6 ft. above ground is suitable for a private court, but can be increased on one or more sides if they adjoin a roadway or public pathway.

The supports are made from $1\frac{1}{2}$-in. by $\frac{1}{4}$-in. thick T-section angle iron, drilled for fixing bolts or iron rivets, and also for horizontal wires, to which the wire netting is secured by wire ties. The wire netting is obtained in rolls of convenient widths varying from 12 in. to 72 in., and is hung with a 1-in. overlap, the bottom edge being fixed down at intervals to wooden pegs driven into the ground.

TRELLISWORK AND PERGOLAS

ONE of the most common applications of trelliswork is that shown in Fig. 1, where diamond mesh trellis is added to an existing fence to increase the height, forming a screen over which climbing plants may be trained.

This type can be made from laths or, better still, obtained ready made in widths varying from 12 in. to 48 in. A framework of $1\frac{1}{2}$-in. square section wood, with strips of $1\frac{1}{2}$-in. by $\frac{3}{4}$-in. batten to take the edge of the trellis, makes quite a sound job. The method adopted for fixing purposes is clearly indicated in the illustration.

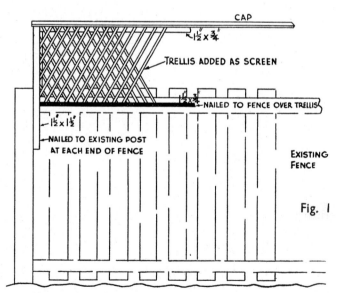

CAP

$1\frac{1}{2}'' \times \frac{3}{4}''$

TRELLIS ADDED AS SCREEN

$1\frac{1}{2}'' \times \frac{3}{4}''$ NAILED TO FENCE OVER TRELLIS

$1\frac{1}{2}'' \times 1\frac{1}{2}''$

NAILED TO EXISTING POST AT EACH END OF FENCE

EXISTING FENCE

Fig. 1

Fig. 2

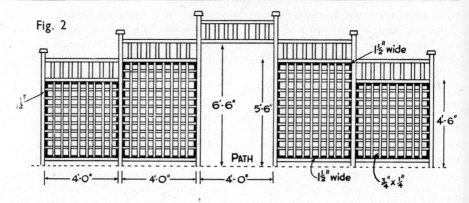

Square mesh trellis is easier to make and looks much better, lending itself to endless arrangements of panel and arch screens, such as that shown in Fig. 2. The essential points to keep in mind are that the whole construction must be made strong enough to carry the weight of the climbing plants and to resist the wind. Arches crowned with a flat grid construction of laths to support the blooms are best. When making arches and pergola frames avoid getting the very common ladder effect. There are plenty of other ways of arranging pieces of wood, even at right-angles, such as that illustrated in Fig. 3, where rough-sawn timber 3 in. by 2 in. is used for the uprights and 3 in. by 3 in. for the two cross bars supporting a grid of battens. The foot ends should be sunk 12 in. or more into the ground.

The once popular "rustic" work has given place to the more modern and stronger designs carried out with larch poles. As the bark will sooner or later fall off it may be removed as each piece is prepared, and the whole covered with wood preservative stain, such as creosote.

These poles are very suitable for rose pergolas, and if carried out on the lines suggested in Fig. 4, a pleasing structure will result. The main uprights are about 4½ in. diameter, and arranged to form single or double arches at intervals of 6 ft., thus allowing sufficient room for adjacent plants without overcrowding or overlapping the top foliage. The width of the span depends, of course, on the width of pathway, but a general projection of 12 in. on each side as shown is generally enough.

As regards actual construction, any cutting and drilling is done first. The

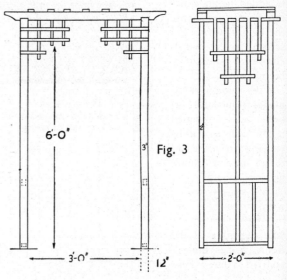

Fig. 3

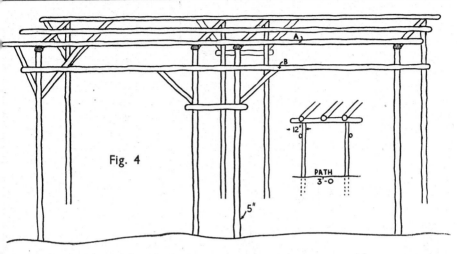

Fig. 4

PATH
3'-O

poles for the arches are then set up and the cross members fixed in position to keep them apart. Adding the side members, B, next will help to set the arches at the right distance apart at the tops, and adds considerable rigidity to the structure, while the top row of poles, A, are being fixed into place.

A pergola built of rough-sawn oak members secured by means of galvanised coach-screws or bolts, makes a lasting structure. Oak pegs left projecting not only add a certain amount of finish to the job but allow for weather-loosened joints being made firm. As a guide the following sizes are suggested. Uprights 3 in. to 4 in. square, with cross members 5 in. by 4 in., halved and notched into the main horizontal timbers. The remainder of the framework can be in 3 in. by $1\frac{1}{2}$ in. slightly notched into the other parts.

An alternative treatment is to support the open roof timbers on pillars of old red brick, or layers of brick and tiles in cement, random rubble, etc., to form pillars 9 in. square. This method is quite simple to carry out, and very effective when overgrown with blossom.

GARDEN GATES

ONLY gates of simple construction suitable for the amateur to make will be dealt with here.

The single gate in Fig. 1 is hung between two 3-in. by 3-in. posts set in concrete, 2 ft. 9 in. apart.

Cut the two stiles each 3 ft. long for the gate from a length of 3-in. by 2-in. timber. Lay the two pieces side by side with the 3-in. faces together, and mark out the $\frac{3}{4}$-in. wide mortice at 4 in. from each end and $\frac{1}{2}$ in. in from one face, as shown.

A pair of rails 3 in. by $1\frac{1}{2}$ in. by 2 ft. 9 in. long are cut half-way through at each end to form the tenons 3 in. long which go right through the stiles, where they are firmly secured by screws, or hardwood pegs. Six vertical pales of 2-in. by 1-in. planed batten may be fixed in position, and cut to even length at the top and bottom afterwards. The tops can be either pointed or rounded off as desired.

Suitable hinges for a light-weight gate of this type are the ordinary T kind, known as cross garnets.

Double gates of simple and effective design, suitable for a garage entrance, are shown in Fig. 2. The four stiles are each 4 ft. long and cut from 4-in. by 2-in. timber. Square the ends and place the cut lengths side by side with the 4-in. faces together for marking out the mortices, which are $\frac{5}{8}$ in. wide by 3 in. long and central on the 2-in. wide face. For the top pair of rails the tenons are taken right through, 4 in. deep, but the bottom four are only $2\frac{1}{4}$ in. wide, as shown in detail at A in Fig. 3. Six rails are required, each 4 ft. 5 in. long, cut from 3-in. by 2-in. timber. The two top pairs have a tenon cut 4 in. long by $\frac{5}{8}$ in. thick, and the bottom pair are the same thickness, but only $2\frac{1}{4}$ in. wide, as detailed. Screws or hardwood dowel pins may be used to secure the rails. The two top pairs of rails will require six rectangular holes cut $\frac{1}{2}$ in. deep to receive the 2-in. by 1-in. vertical pieces, spaced at

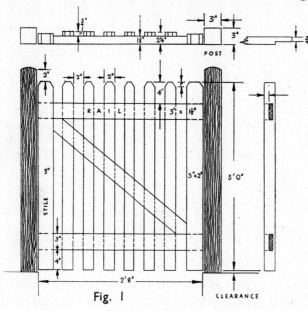

Fig. 1

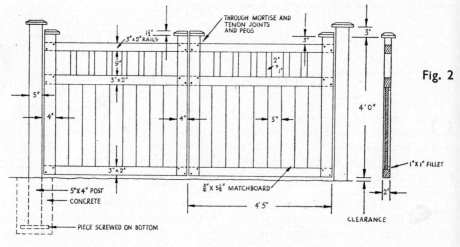

Fig. 2

equal distances. These are housed as shown at B in Fig. 3, and may be marked out in sets of six to ensure the lengths being equal.

Caps, made out of $1\frac{1}{2}$-in. thick wood are fitted to the tops of the posts and stiles, but those on the latter must be cut flush with the closing faces of the stiles and against the post face to allow the gates to open.

One of the closing stiles may be fitted with a stop strip fixed on the back so that half of the gate may be used as required.

A 1-in. by 1-in. fillet is fixed to the under edge of the middle rail, and another to the top edge of the bottom rail to form fixings for the boards. Nine widths of $\frac{3}{4}$-in. by 6-in. V-jointed tongued and grooved matchboards are cut to fit into the lower part of each gate, and nailed to the fillets.

The two main gate posts are 5 in. by 4 in. and are 3 in. higher than the stiles. They should be buried at least 2 ft. in the ground with a square piece of timber screwed to the bottom as indicated. The hole is filled in with concrete, care being taken to see that the posts are kept perfectly upright until the concrete has set hard.

Hinges suitable for these gates are of wrought-iron, 14 in. long by $1\frac{1}{2}$ in. wide and $\frac{3}{16}$ in. thick. A suitable catch should be fitted for fasten-

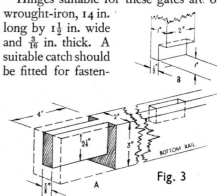

Fig. 3

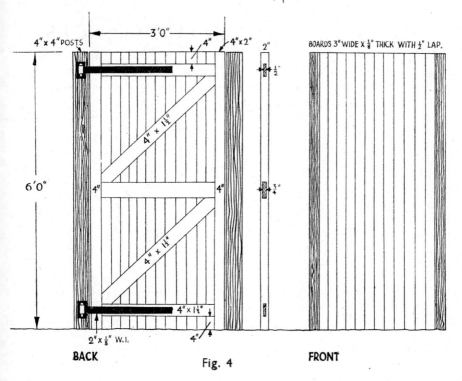

BACK   Fig. 4   FRONT

ing the gates, and a wooden stop driven into the ground to prevent the doors opening outwards. A ledged and braced gate, suitable for a side or back entrance, in a boarded fence between 5 ft. and 6 ft. high, is shown in Fig. 4. The stiles are 4 in. by 2 in., morticed for the three 4-in. by 1½-in. rails. The outer faces of these are flush with the back face of the stiles, so the mortices are towards the back edge, and not central on the 2-in. face of the stile. The boards are 3 in. wide and are placed with about ½-in. lap to fill the space between the side members and not to overlap on them. The rough lengths are fixed into position and a line is drawn to mark the top and bottom edges as a guide for sawing. Capping may be fixed to the top edge to match that on the fence, and the centre rail fitted with a lock.

The metal plates with the hinge pins are let into the side posts which are 4 in. by 4 in. The hinge is a simple iron bar with an eye formed in the end, so it is only necessary to lift the gate to remove it, or to drop it back. This type of hinge is known as the "band and gudgeon," and is fixed with one or more coach bolts driven into the rail in addition to the usual wood screws, after the manner of T hinges.

For the brace there is no fitting other than cutting the ends to fit the corners and skew-nailing.

All of these gates may be finished with wood preservative stain, which may now be obtained in a shade of green as well as the more usual brown, or if painted, one or more coats of priming paint are necessary before the colour is applied.

USEFUL GARDEN APPLIANCES

M<small>OST</small> amateur gardeners and allotment holders have a few home-made tools and appliances in addition to their usual equipment of digging fork, spade, rake and hoe. Many of these extra tools have been made for the purpose of avoiding unnecessary labour and to save time. Allotment holders at work during the day have to make the most of their spare time in the evenings and week-ends, and after the soil has been prepared on a full-size plot there is not so much time left for sowing and planting out as one would desire.

The various small articles described here, if not suitable in their existing form, will no doubt suggest variations which the practical man can adopt for his own particular purpose.

Three-peg Dibber.—The three-peg dibber illustrated at Fig. 1 is of great

service when planting. The holes are quickly made, accurately spaced and of uniform depth.

It consists of a stout bar about 2 ft.

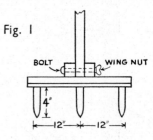

Fig. 1

6 in. long, to which pegs about 2½ in. in diameter are fixed. These may be of square wood, pointed at the lower ends and the corner edges trimmed off neatly with a wood chisel to form a round section. A length of 4 in. is shown, and the spacing apart is 12 in.,

but both dimensions may be altered to suit the spacing of the kind of plants for which it will be most used. The top of the appliance has two wooden blocks between which the lower end of the handle is fixed by means of a bolt and wing nut. This arrangement allows the handle to be adjusted to any desired angle.

For setting maincrop seed potatoes, for example, the planting of which takes

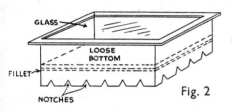

GLASS
LOOSE BOTTOM
FILLET
NOTCHES
Fig. 2

considerable time in the ordinary way, the dibber will be found exceptionally useful.

The usual spacing between plants is 12 in. apart, and the distance between rows is 2 ft. With the dibber handle down, use it as a rake, and drawing it across the ground mark three lines in the soil, using a string line as a guide. At the end of the row start back again, letting the end peg go over and along the last line again as a guide, thus marking out two new rows. Repeat this on reaching the end of the row, producing two new rows on each journey across the plot until the required number has been marked out.

Now slacken the bolt which passes through the handle and the two blocks of wood on top of the bar, and set the handle upright. Along the first line marked out make a series of holes by pressing the handle down hard, assisting the pegs into the ground by pressing the foot on the bar, and then pull it up. This leaves three holes in the ground at once. Hold the dibber with the last or left-hand peg over the last

hole made, and press down again. Repeat this to the end of the row, using the last hole made as a spacing guide, unless the distance between the last hole and the new position for the dibber can be judged by eye to enable three new holes to be made at once. To make the next row of holes the line previously made by the centre peg is missed and the holes made along the third line, which is, of course, 2 ft. from the first. In this way every other line on the ground, working back, is the one to make the holes in.

Seed Boxes.—Small light boxes in which to plant seeds in some sheltered spot, or in the garden frame to produce seedlings for planting out later, are always in great demand, and now that cardboard is chiefly used in the confectionery trade for packing sweetmeats, the once familiar light wooden box is not so readily obtainable. Suitable material is often at hand. The example shown in Fig. 2 consists of a fairly shallow-sided box having a small square fillet of $\frac{1}{4}$-in. wood tacked inside all round and about 1 in. up from the bottom edge. Resting on this is a loose bottom with the usual holes made in it. Notches or half-round openings are cut round the bottom edges of the rectangular frame to let the air circulate underneath. The overall sizes are left to the constructor.

A handy variation of this design would be to make a box with a loose bottom as previously mentioned, but with the back higher and the sides sloping from back to front. Two pieces of wood are nailed, one on each side of the box and projecting about $\frac{1}{2}$ in. above it, and a small block added on the front end to act as a stop. This prevents the piece of glass from sliding off or moving sideways. Any odd pieces of glass may be made to serve a useful purpose in this way and provide the gardener with a series of small frames. When planting out time comes the bottom board with the soil and small plants is easily pressed out by placing one hand under the box and easing the contents upwards. The board can be carried to the planting-out site and the seedlings carefully removed one by one. Spare bottom boards will allow the boxes to be prepared for use again without delay.

wire are stretched between the ends of the arms from pole to pole and another single wire is suspended about 3 in. above ground level. Vertical wires or strong strings are run from the bottom wire up to the top pair, the spacing of which is regulated by the directions given for spacing the plants. Starting from, say, the left-hand end of the row, the first plant will be trained up the first wire which goes up to the back wire at the top; the second plant is given the

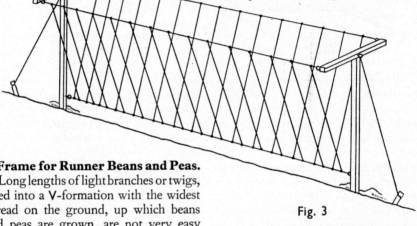

Frame for Runner Beans and Peas. —Long lengths of light branches or twigs, piled into a V-formation with the widest spread on the ground, up which beans and peas are grown, are not very easy to handle and put up. Many of the pods start to grow within this tangle of twigs and under cover of the stouter growth which has had the benefit of more air and sunlight. These seldom develop into anything worth picking and the crop is poor.

An easily erected frame which enables each plant to obtain the maximum of fresh air and light on both sides, back and front, is illustrated in Fig. 3. A length of timber about 2 in. square is used for the upright. Allowing 2 ft. in the ground, the height is made 6 or 8 ft. according to the class of plant to be grown. A cross-bar, about 18 or 20 in. long, is fixed on the top. One of these T-poles at each end of the row may be sufficient, but others may be spaced in between as required. Two lengths of

Fig. 3

next sloping vertical towards the front, and so on to the end of the row. This arrangement allows each plant plenty of room as it grows upwards, and the pods to be reached without difficulty from either side of the frame.

Protection of Seeds, etc., from Birds.—The old-fashioned method of stretching black thread over a seed-bed would be more effective if more attention was paid to guarding the edges. The guard shown in Fig. 4 is just a flat piece of wood, high enough to clear the small plants until they are well established, and sufficiently long to cover the extent of the bed, plus a little to spare on the width so that the first and last rows have as much protection as the centre. The two top corners are cut off and two long rectangular shaped pegs added outside for driving into the ground. Small flat-headed nails are driven in round the edge right down to the bottom edge of the end boards, leaving about $\frac{3}{8}$ or $\frac{1}{2}$ in. of each nail standing clear. With the two boards in position, one at each end

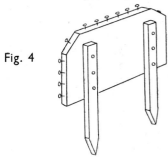

Fig. 4

of the bed, cotton or thread is stretched from each nail, and from end to end right down to ground level. Pieces of white or silver paper may be secured to the threads here and there if desired, to flutter in the wind. Wire netting may also be used in place of thread.

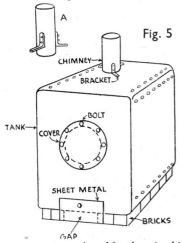

Fig. 5

Incinerator.—An old galvanised iron hot water tank makes an excellent incinerator. Such a tank is usually to be obtained for a few pence, or perhaps for the asking, at a builder's yard.

The apparatus is shown in Fig. 5. A series of large holes is punched in the

19

end that forms the bottom, and at the opposite end or top a single hole about 4 in. diameter is bored at 5 in. from the back edge for accommodating the chimney, which consists of a piece of gutter pipe about 18 in. long. The chimney is not a permanent fixture but is kept in position by means of three angle brackets as used for supporting shelves, in the manner shown at A. The brackets are fixed to the pipe by bolts passing through suitable holes, and in a position to allow about a couple of inches to enter the interior of the tank. The other ends of the brackets form feet and simply rest on the top.

To ensure adequate draught the bottom edges of the tank rest on bricks placed narrow edge upwards and butted

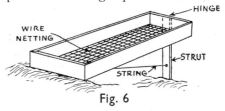

Fig. 6

closely together, a gap two or three bricks wide being left in the front. This aperture is covered with an odd piece of sheet metal, the lateral movement of which allows the size of the opening to be adjusted, and consequently the amount of draught.

Wire Screen or Sieve.—A wire screen or sieve as seen at Fig. 6, while not perhaps in everyday use, is a very convenient garden accessory to have about, and being shallow needs very little room when packed away. If re-making old paths the loosened material is often well worth sifting in order to separate the large stones, etc., from the finer stuff. Other uses in the garden will suggest themselves. The frame is of any convenient section of timber. Over this a piece of stout wire netting of small mesh is stretched and secured along the edges by staples. The side pieces are screwed or nailed on last, as these help to hold the wire and cover the edges. The leg is

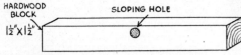

Fig. 7

fitted with a hinge, and a cord passing through the hole and knotted prevents the strut from slipping outwards.

Garden Rake.—One often feels the need of a rake, different in some detail from the ready-made article. It may be that a wide one is desired, or one with longer or closer-spaced teeth. Any of these possible features may be included in the one made on the lines of Fig. 7.

The bar is of ordinary black iron, which will not split when the teeth are driven in. A row of holes is drilled in the bar a shade less in diameter than the large nails used for the teeth, which are $\frac{3}{16}$ in. diameter and 4 in. long. With a larger drill countersink these holes slightly on one side, also drill three or four holes for the fixing screws. Cut out the head from a piece of hardwood. Then place the drilled metal strip on the flat edge and mark the teeth positions through on to the wood. With a small drill or bit bore small holes in the wood sufficiently deep to clear round the heads of the nails but only just deep enough to allow the metal bar to be screwed down to the wood, leaving no gap for the teeth to push back. Drill a slanting hole in the wood block for accommodating the handle, and fix the metal member to the underside.

OVERHAULING A LAWN-MOWER

A LITTLE understanding of the construction and action of the main parts of the mowing machine will be a great help when cleaning and adjustment are carried out.

Back Roller Machines.—Machines fitted with back rollers obtain their driving power through twin rollers, like a miniature garden roller, fixed at the ends of a pair of long handles which are adjustable to suit the user. As this roller passes over the ground its spindle conveys motion to the cutters, either by an enclosed chain or cog-wheels, arranged for the turning to be in the forward direction only, with a free-wheel action to allow the cutters to revolve after the machine has been brought to rest and

so free themselves of cut grass. Such a machine is shown in Fig. 1.

Side-wheel Machines, as illustrated in Fig. 2, derive their power through wheels on each side, which, in running along the ground, drive the cutters with the same forward motion only. The driving mechanism consists of internal teeth on the side wheels engaging with small toothed wheels on the cutter shaft. This type of machine being lighter than that with back driving rollers is easier to use, but as both wheels must be on the lawn it will not cut right up to the edges and therefore does not leave such a nice finish, owing to the absence of the roller.

The cutting action of both types is

similar to that of scissors. The rotating blades or "cylinder" make contact with the bottom blade, and as they are set on a twist or spiral, cutting action results.

Cleaning after Use.—Lawn-mowers, especially those of British manufacture, will give lifelong service if properly treated and regularly attended to.

No machine should be returned to the shed after use without being cleaned. Always brush off the loose grass and mould, and wipe away any moisture. Locate all the oil-holes and see that they are clear before introducing the oil; wipe the blades with an oily rag to prevent rust.

Replacements.—Any practical man can undertake the fitting of replacement parts. On most modern machines each part has a number, and as these parts are made to standardised dimensions it is an easy matter to replace a broken part without any troublesome filing and fitting.

The driving arrangements are generally the parts to require attention first.

Fig. 1

The ends of the driving pawls in the cutter pinions wear and become too short to engage properly. When replacing old ones or fitting new ones care should be taken that the flat end makes good contact with the clutch portion of the pinion. On renewing the pinions

themselves see that they are put on the correct side of the machine. This is important, because these parts are made left-handed and right-handed and any reversal of them would cause the drive to be taken up backwards instead of

Fig. 2

forwards. The side wheels themselves are interchangeable, so it does not matter on which side of the machine they are replaced.

The replacement of both chain and gear drives is very simple. The gears and chain wheels are generally fixed to the spindle by means of a metal wedge or key, which may be loosened by driving the wheel a little farther on the shaft by careful hammer blows round the centre. To replace, hold the wheel in position with the key notch in the side of its centre hole over the corresponding notch in the shaft and drive in the key. The drive between the wheel and spindle is by a sunk key between spindle and wheel or by a pin passing through the wheel boss and spindle.

Cutter Bearings may be in two parts, in which case they may be fitted to the spindle by accurate filing and scraping until the bore fits the spindle. A machine with loose cutter bearings will not give satisfactory results owing to the cutting cylinder moving away from the bottom blade. In this way the grass is not cut but bruised into some resemblance of flatness.

Ball bearings should not require much attention beyond cleaning. When removed for cleaning, use a tin box for accommodating the parts, and make sure that all small parts and thin washers have been collected. After cleaning, pack the ball bearings with good grease lubricant.

Roller brackets, and the wood rollers with spindles, should be replaced when much worn, because these parts gauge the height at which the grass is cut.

A worn bottom blade may require packing in position in one or two places. Thick brown paper may be used for packing purposes. This will set the blade in line and in true relation with the cutting cylinder.

Repairs to the cutters generally require the use of special machinery and skilled workmen, but hand grinding of the cutting cylinder and bottom blade may be done by the owners of certain makes of machine. The work consists in revolving the cutting cylinder backwards by hand after painting the edges of this and the bottom blade with a mixture of oil and emery powder.

Setting and Adjustments.—When the machine has been cleaned and all the parts have been replaced in position, we come to the final and important job of adjustment.

The setting and adjustment of the cutting units call for close attention and accuracy. One method is to adjust the rotary cutters to the bottom blade; or this blade may be lifted upwards to the cutters. The first method is that usually adopted for roller machines, and if very close and accurate cutting is desired fine adjustment is imperative. The second method is the one to use for side-wheel mowers. The tilting action

of the bottom blade is arranged by rocking points between the side-frames and the bottom plate carrying the bottom blade, screws being used on either side of this rocking point for adjustment.

The height at which the grass is cut is regulated by adjustments made to the small front rollers in back-roller machines and to the back rollers of side-wheel machines. The method of adjustment varies with different machines, but the general principles remain the same. In some makes hand-operated screws are fitted, or two sliding brackets, one on each side, secured by screws to allow the rollers to be moved either up or down, as the case may be.

The adjustment is made by tilting the machine backwards to clear the cutters from the ground.

For ordinary work the measured distance from the ground to the cutting-edge of the bottom blade should be about $\frac{5}{8}$ in. The adjustment can be tested by turning the machine on its side, holding a straight-edge on the back and front rollers or the back roller and side driving wheels, and noting their relative positions, which should be the same over the width of the machine.

If adjustment fittings are provided on both sides of the machine, care must be taken that both are adjusted exactly the same amount. If set out of truth the machine will work badly. The bottom blade must not scrape the ground, as this, besides damaging the machine and turf, would make it very hard to push.

The setting of the cutting cylinder and bottom blade is most important. The cutters of the cylinder should just touch the bottom blade as they pass, but so lightly that they will cut a piece of thin paper if held against the edge of the bottom blade at intervals to the full width of the cutter.

A HOSE-REEL

To keep the garden hose in good condition it should be kept coiled on a reel, and this is one of the useful things the practical man can make for himself.

The design shown in Fig. 1 is very simple. The device is provided with a and through the ends of the iron pipe so that a long nail may be driven through to prevent the pipe from turning. Next make the two A-shaped frames of 2 in. by 1 in. wood. Four lengths are required, each 2 ft. 2 in., notched at the top ends to fit the bearing blocks, and

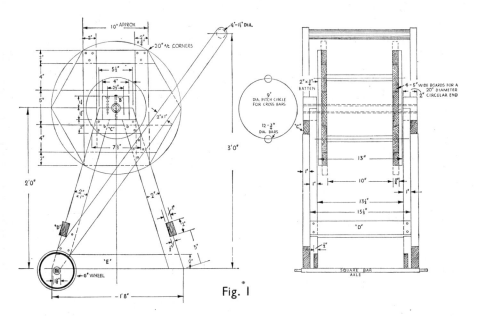

Fig. 1

pair of wheels and a handle so that it can be moved freely about the garden.

A length of iron pipe about ¾ in. outside diameter and 18 in. long is required for the spindle. First prepare the two bearing blocks. These are built up of four pieces of wood each measuring 1¾ in. by 4 in. by 2 in., and each pair may be screwed together and the hole bored to as near the outside diameter of the pipe as possible so that it will be a tight fit when the blocks are fitted together. Drill the central hole. B about ⅛ in. diameter in each block

halved at the bottom with the 1 ft. 8 in. long bottom bar E. The short piece c at the top also helps to support the blocks. Two pieces of batten 2 in. by 1 in., 3 ft. 9 in. long, will be required for the handles, also a length of 1¼ in. to 1½ in. diameter wood, such as a piece of broom-handle, for the round bar between, as shown. Two cross-bars D also help to brace the frames apart.

Between the two frames at the bottom at the front a square piece of timber is fixed, to which the iron axle is screwed. An odd piece of arris rail as used for fencing would do for this. The axle is from an old pram. The fixing holes in the square part of the axle will be ready drilled, also the holes in the round ends for split pins. The wheel is put on first, then a washer and a split pin, the end being covered with a screw-on cap. Quite small wheels about 6 in. diameter would be suitable.

The reel consists of two end discs made of boards about ¾ in. thick, secured by battens on the outside like a copper lid. If circular ends are required it is suggested that four 5-in. wide boards are used and a 20-in. circle marked thereon.

The shape can be cut nearly to size with a hand saw and the final finish done with a padsaw, small plane and a spokeshave, depending on how much time the constructor is prepared to spend on the job. If the circular ends are considered too difficult to form, the hexagon shape is not unsightly. To keep the overall size the same across the corners the ends are built up out of one 5-in. centre board, flanked by two 4-in. boards and completed with two 2-in. boards, as indicated. The central hole is bored a trifle larger than the pipe so that the reel will turn freely. Before boring the centre hole, mark out a circle for the cross-pieces on which the hose is wound.

Round pieces of wood are ideal, but square section wood can be utilised provided the corners are taken off. If possible use a large number of these bars because this will form a more perfect circle and the hose will not rest in a series of flats; each flat bend is liable to start a crack in the rubber at some time. It is well worth while to pad these cross bars with sacking or, better still, to tack on a length of old linoleum for the hose to be wound on.

A HOME-MADE GARDEN ROLLER

AN inexpensive roller for the garden may be made from a variety of common oddments which are not diffi-cult to collect if not all at hand at the time of building. Working Drawing No. 26 gives details of such a roller.

The standard sizes of commercial garden rollers are 13-in., 14-in., 16-in. and 20-in., the length being the same as the diameter. With these sizes as a guide obtain an empty paint or oil drum as near to the desired size as possible; the one selected should be of the type with the ends inserted towards the inside of the drum.

It will be necessary to find the centres of both ends, and for this a rough centre-square can be quickly made from two pieces of wood nailed together at right-angles as shown in the sketch. The head-piece has two short pegs of round wood of any convenient small diameter nailed on the back, or pieces of dowel rod driven through; these must be in line. Mark the centre line across the head between these two pegs, and fix the blade with one edge to correspond with this centre line. When this square is set across the end of the drum, a line marked along the edge, B, will pass through the centre, and by turning the square round and marking another line at right-angles, the centre is found.

Make a centre-punch mark on this centre-point and mark a circle large enough just to clear the outside diameter of the iron pipe which is to be fixed through the centre of the drum. By

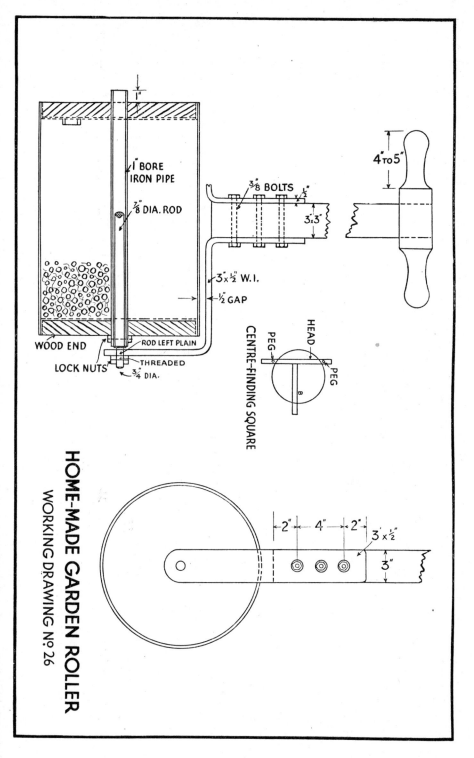

1" BORE
IRON PIPE

⅞" DIA. ROD

WOOD END

ROD LEFT PLAIN

LOCK NUTS

THREADED

¾" DIA.

⅜" BOLTS

½"

3.3"

3"×½" W.I.

½" GAP

4" TO 5"

CENTRE-FINDING SQUARE

PEG

HEAD

PEG

2"

4"

2"

3'×½"

3"

HOME-MADE GARDEN ROLLER

WORKING DRAWING Nº 26

drilling a circle of small holes round the marked circle the centre piece may be removed and the edge of the hole cleaned up with a file. At the same time it is well to note how the top end of the drum has been made round the filler cap. If the metal is turned in where the bung fits, it will not matter, but if it projects up towards the outside of the drum-end it must be removed by drilling small holes all round it and breaking it away.

Next cut two wooden discs to fit into the recessed ends of the drum and bore holes at the centres to take the pipe. A length of 1-in. bore iron pipe is required to pass through the centre as shown. The length will be the same as the drum plus an extra 1 in. at each end beyond the faces of the wooden ends. Have each end of the pipe threaded for a distance of just over 1 in. from the ends, and fitted with lock-nuts, four in all, each $\frac{5}{16}$ in. thick. Also, cut a length of 2-in. by $\frac{3}{4}$-in. batten and bore a hole in the centre to take one end of the pipe.

Pass the pipe through the ends of the drum and put the bottom disc of wood into place. A few long wood screws driven through drilled holes in the edge of the drum and into the disc will help to hold it in position. In place of the top disc, fit the piece of batten for the time being, screw the lock-nuts on and see that the pipe projects the same distance at each end. Stand the drum on end on blocks of wood to keep the end of the pipe clear of the ground.

Mix some concrete, but see that the stones are of a size to pass through the filling hole. Fill the drum and keep working the mixture down with a length of wood until no more can be packed in. Remove the top batten and fix the proper end disc in its place. Tighten up the two inner nuts and lock them with the outer ones. While the contents of the drum are setting hard, the remainder of the work can be prepared.

Get the blacksmith to cut, drill and bend the two iron side-pieces, and to make the axle-rod. The ends of this rod are reduced to $\frac{3}{4}$ in. and screwed with a standard $\frac{3}{4}$-in. Whitworth thread. The handle bar is of 3-in. square timber of a length to suit personal requirements. The holes for the $\frac{3}{8}$-in. fixing bolts are marked out from the finished ironwork.

By the time the handle part is ready the concrete will be firm enough for the drum to be placed on its side to complete the fitting, and the painting of the wooden ends and ironwork.

A WHEELBARROW

FOR garden work either at home or on an allotment, a wheelbarrow, such as that shown in the accompanying drawings, will save many laborious journeys.

The materials are usually ash for the handles and elm for the other parts, but the most convenient materials can be used.

The side frame members are 3 in. by 2 in. and 4 ft. 2 in. long. Handles are shaped as shown, and the other ends are rounded off. Both inner faces are grooved 1 in. wide by $\frac{1}{4}$ in. deep to take the edges of the front and back boards where they fit between the frame.

A piece of 3 in. by 2 in. stuff may be fitted between the legs, tenoned into the handle members to give extra strength,

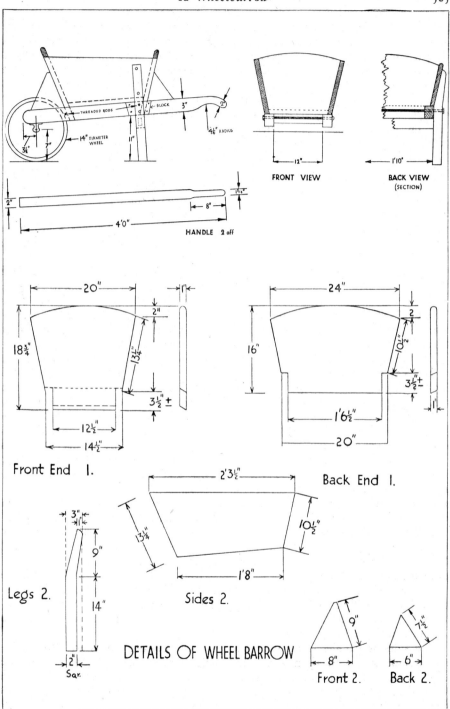

THREADED RODS BLOCK 3"

14" DIAMETER WHEEL 11" 4¼" RADIUS 2"

3¾" 7"

2" 1½" 8"

4'0"

HANDLE 2 off

FRONT VIEW

BACK VIEW
(SECTION)

12" 1'10"

20" 1" 2" 24" 2

18¾" 13¼" 16" 10½"

3½"± 3½"±

12½" 1'6½" 1"

14½" 20"

Front End 1. Back End 1.

2'3½"

3" 1" 13¾" 10½"

9" 1'8"

Legs 2. Sides 2.

14"

2" 9" 7½"

Sqr. DETAILS OF WHEEL BARROW 8" 6"

Front 2. Back 2.

19*

and the addition of two threaded rods passing from one side to the other ties the parts together. The tie-rods consist of lengths of $\frac{1}{2}$ in. diameter mild steel rod screwed for a distance of 2 in. at the ends with standard $\frac{1}{2}$ in. Whitworth threads, a washer being used at each end under the nuts. The bolts for fixing the legs may be standard $\frac{3}{8}$ in. Whitworth.

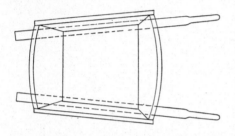

Four blocks are also fixed to the handle members to help keep the legs firm, and triangular pieces support the back and front boards.

The Legs are cut to the shape shown by using 23 in. lengths of 3 in. by 2 in. ash. Mark out the leg so that the top end is set over as in the detail sketch. Saw them parallel for a distance of 14 in. and then in from the top.

The Front Board is 1 in. thick, 20 in. wide at the top and tapering down to $14\frac{1}{2}$ in. at the bottom; the corners are 2 in. lower, the top edge being curved and rounded off slightly.

The Back End is 24 in. wide at the top and tapering down to 20 in. at the bottom. The corners also drop 2 in., as in the front board.

A pair of sides built up to the dimensions shown will complete the body work. Perhaps the most convenient way of marking out a piece where none of the sides is parallel is to mark out the straight edge 2 ft. $3\frac{1}{2}$ in. long, and then to take a length of fairly stout strip of wood and drive a nail through about $\frac{1}{2}$ in. from one end to use as a pivot point. On a marked centre line on the strip set off the distance $13\frac{1}{4}$ in. and carefully drive another nail through. With this scratch an arc and repeat the operation with the nails set at a radius of $10\frac{1}{2}$ in. and scribe the length of the back end edge. Now find the two points on these two arcs which are 1 ft. 8 in. apart; a line marked through these points will settle the position of the fourth edge. The dimensions can be checked with a rule after they have been marked out, before cutting.

The Sides should be completed by planing the long bottom edges to a slight angle so that they lie flat on the side frame members.

The next thing to do is to assemble the parts. Fit the front and back to the side frame members by placing their edges into the grooves and securely fastening them together by means of stout screws. Then pass the front tie-rod through the holes in the frame, place washers over the ends and tighten up the nuts. Fix the sides to the back and front, using screws for the purpose. The legs may now be added. Fit the tenons of the cross-piece into the legs and secure them by means of screws driven through the sides of the legs. Then add the back tie-rod and fix the strengthening blocks.

The triangular supporting pieces can then be fixed at the back and front, and the floor boards—which are 1 in. thick —cut and fastened down. These should be screwed and not nailed.

Iron-shod wooden wheels can be purchased quite cheaply, ready-made. The constructor is therefore recommended to purchase one in preference to making it.

Metal bearing blocks are also obtainable at a reasonable figure. These are much more efficient and durable than home-made wooden ones having holes bored to take the ends of the axle.

A GARDEN FRAME

A COLD frame is not only a great help to the owner of a small garden but a practical necessity when the gardener is an allotment holder as well.

A twin-light frame, as that shown in the working drawing, may be objected to on account of its size, but the overall dimensions may be varied to suit individual requirements.

The corner posts are of 2 in. square

two for the front and four for the sides without any cutting, except to obtain the specified lengths. To complete the sides and obtain the required slope two 6 in. wide boards are cut wedge-shape. To prevent the lights moving sideways a 4 ft. 4 in. length of 5 in. by 1 in. timber is fixed to the sides, allowing 1½ in. to 2 in. to project above the top board. The central dividing bar

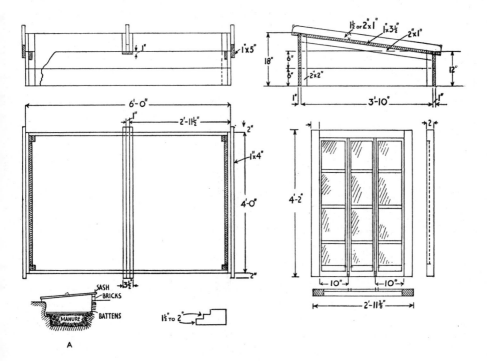

section timber. The back ones are 18 in. long and the front ones 12 in. At the sides a top rail 3 ft. 10 in. by 2 in. by 1 in. is halved into the top ends of the corner posts as shown. Tongued and grooved boards 6 in. wide by 1 in. thick are used for the body. Three such boards will be required for the back,

is built up to form supports and guides for the lights. The lower portion of the bar consists of a piece of 3½ in. by 1 in. stuff, 4 ft. 4 in. long, while the piece forming the rebates is of the same overall length, 1½ in. wide by 1 in. This is fixed, narrow edge upwards, along the centre of the lower member, the latter being let in flush with the front and back top edges as shown in the elevation.

The lights are 4 ft. 2 in. long by 2 ft. 11¾ in. wide and have three sections for glass. Each light consists of a main frame of 4 in. by 2 in. good quality deal. These may be constructed by either one of two methods. The first consists in forming the rebate in the inner faces by the use of a plane and making mortised and tenoned joints at the corners, and the alternative is to have false rebates and halved joints at the corners. The false rebates are formed in a similar manner to that adopted in the centre bar of the body, using ½ in. square strips for the purpose. The division or sash bars are also built up. These consist of lengths of 2 in. by 1 in. stuff upon which 1 in. square strips are fixed by means of screws driven in from the underside of the lower member. The ends of lower parts of these members are let in flush with the top face of the frame, while the lower ends of the strips are carried right down to the lower top edge of the frame, as shown.

The Glass.—Twenty-one oz. horticultural glass is the kind generally used, but often there are odd pieces available which may be cut and fitted to the frame. The pieces are placed in the rebates so that the one above overlaps the one below in the same manner as tiles on a roof. This enables water to run down to the bottom and not into the frame. A priming coat of paint must be given to the lights before applying the putty, otherwise the putty will not hold. After glazing, the whole of the body, inside and out, as well as the lights, should be given at least two coats of paint.

Glazed lights can be obtained ready made, the stock sizes of which are, in feet, 2 by 3, 3 by 4 and 4 by 6. If ready-made lights are used in preference to home-constructed ones the body could be built on similar lines to that already described.

It will be noticed that the glazed sections are not hinged, but are free to slide open within the guides. To prevent from sliding shut, a few holes should be made in the centre bar to take round, tapered pegs. These will hold the frames in the desired positions. Stepped blocks, as shown at the foot of the drawings, are also very useful for keeping the top ends lifted to enable a current of air to pass under the sash and through the frame.

To prepare the frame for use, place the whole in a warm situation and upon a firm foundation, preferably a layer of ashes 3 or 4 in. deep. Having made the frame firm, cover the bottom with a 2 in. layer of half-decayed leaves, levelled and trodden firm. Over this place enough light soil to ensure that, after being well trodden, there is a depth of at least 3 in. Rake this level and then cover it evenly but not deeply with fine sharp sand. The frame is then ready for use.

Another method of preparing the site to obtain a certain degree of warmth for seeds started in small boxes or pots is shown at A in the illustration. Here, a pit is dug somewhat smaller than the inside dimensions of the frame and deep enough to accommodate large pots if required. These stand on a framework of open battens resting on the step in the soil. The soil is removed from under the battens and replaced with stable manure and covered with a thin layer of soil. The manure gives off heat which will help the young seedlings. Spare sashes may be used over a pit of this kind if a complete frame is not available, provided it is supported all round on a single layer of bricks in the front and a double row at the back to give a slope. If bricks cannot be obtained, pieces of turf can be substituted.

GARDEN SEATS

A SEAT is certainly desirable in any garden, and the smaller the garden, the less obtrusive should be the seat, either in size or in colour. It is often the case that a seat is wanted to fit into a special corner, or else its construction must harmonize with special surround-

pattern shown. This gives a slanting back. A framing between the back legs consists of a top rail $2\frac{1}{2}$ in. by $1\frac{1}{2}$ in., a seat rail $4\frac{1}{2}$ in. wide by $1\frac{1}{2}$ in. thick, and two uprights of the same section enclose the 12-in. wide panel of $\frac{5}{8}$-in. tongued and chamfered board 4 in. wide. The

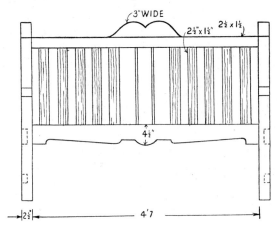

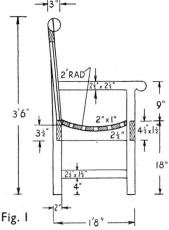

Fig. I

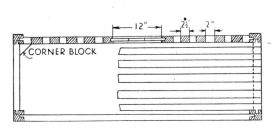

ings. The best thing then is to vary the construction of an average seat to suit the case. 4 ft. to 5 ft. is a good length, and while white enamel looks well in some surroundings, green and brown are good colours and suitable for a town garden.

The example in Fig. 1 is not difficult to make in either deal or oak.

The back legs are 3 ft. 6 in. long, and cut from 3-in. by $2\frac{1}{2}$-in. stuff to the

shaped piece at the top of the back is cut from a 3-in. wide board, $1\frac{1}{2}$ in. thick.

The top and seat rails are tenoned into the legs, as are also the short uprights near the centre. Four $2\frac{1}{2}$-in. by $1\frac{1}{2}$-in. rails, spaced at 2 in. intervals on each side of the centre panel are tenoned into the top and seat rails.

The two front legs are $24\frac{1}{2}$ in. long by $2\frac{1}{2}$ in. by 3 in., joined at the front by a $4\frac{1}{2}$-in. by $1\frac{1}{2}$-in. seat rail with bottom edge cut to shape as shown. Between the front and back legs at the ends two shaped rails are fixed. These are $3\frac{1}{2}$ in. wide where they join the legs and $2\frac{1}{2}$ in. at the narrow part. A radius of 2 ft. will give a suitable curve to make the seat battens. A plain rail should be fixed between the front and back seat rails to support the centre of the seat, and blocks or metal angle brackets will add strength to the corners. The bottom side rails are tenoned into the legs at 4 in. from the ground, as shown.

Small Seat: Rustic Style.—A single seat in the modern rustic style is shown in Fig. 2. The back should be in one

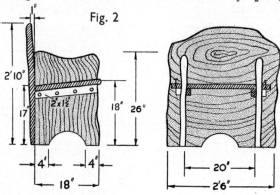

Fig. 2

lengths of $\frac{5}{8}$-in. by $1\frac{1}{2}$-in. stuff, cross-braced with two lengths of $\frac{3}{8}$ in. by 1 in. and 18 in. long. Holes to pass $\frac{1}{4}$-in. bolts are drilled at the centres shown. The back frame consists of two 38-in. lengths of $\frac{5}{8}$ in. by $1\frac{1}{2}$ in. with two 18-in. lengths of $\frac{3}{8}$ in. by 1 in. for cross-braces as before. There is only space for two back rest rails, and these are $\frac{1}{2}$ in. by $1\frac{1}{2}$ in., the same section timber being used for the seat rails. All of the parts are fixed by means of wood screws. If hardwood is used it is as well not only to drill suitably sized holes in the members that are to be fixed to another and to countersink to take the heads of the screws, but to drill a hole smaller than the screw diameter for a little way into the piece which receives the

piece, if possible. Straight planed legs are avoided and the edges left as sawn. Runners support the seat at a slight backward slope and the reduced ends are passed through slots in the sides and secured tight by wedges.

Folding Chair.—A very handy and simple type of folding chair, suitable for use in a small garden, where there is not enough space for larger pieces of garden furniture, is shown in Fig. 3. Hardwood is used, with bolts and washers at the pivoted joints, the whole being arranged so that the seat and two side frames fold flat. The front frame is made out of two 26-in.

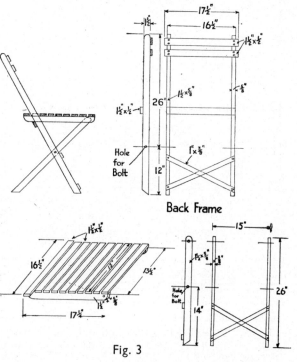

Back Frame

Fig. 3

end of the screw. By doing this the screws are not so hard to get in, and there is less likelihood of the wood splitting. The seat has two side rails which must be drilled at the front end for the hinge bolts. To these are screwed 9 battens of ½-in. by 1½-in. stuff, spaced ¼ in. apart, and one long one at the back to support the back of the chair when in use.

popular "deck" chairs which may also be folded up and stored away when not required.

Fig. 4 shows the assembly of the three frames which make up into the deck chair.

The back frame consists of two sides 4 ft. long, of 1½-in. by 1-in. hardwood with a top rail 2 in. by 1 in. The bottom rail is 1 in. square.

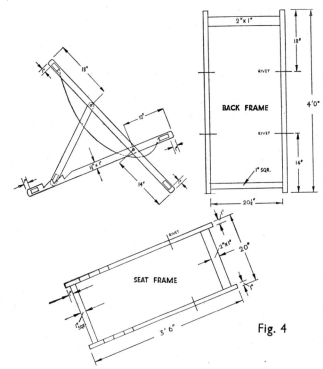

Fig. 4

The seat frame has the back end notched to give the usual adjustments of height. The two sides are 3 ft. 6 in. long and 1½ in. by 1 in. section. A front bar 2 in. wide and a bottom rail 1 in. square completes this frame.

The prop frame is 2 ft. long, and a bottom rail 1 in. thick by 2 in. wide is cut to fit the notches at the back of the seat frame.

When putting the chair together, place an iron washer under the head of the bolt, one between the two frames and a third on the outside, under the nut. When tightened up to the right degree to allow easy opening, the nuts may be prevented from working loose by spreading the end of the bolt outwards all round over the edge of the nut, using a centre punch for the purpose.

The real comfort of the garden is perhaps not complete without the ever

All square edges should be neatly rounded off, also the ends of each frame. The bars and rails are tenoned and glued into the sides of the frame, and further secured with nails. Iron rivets, ¼ in. diameter, are used to fix the frames at the pivot points, an iron washer being inserted under the heads on both sides and between the members of the frames.

Seat canvas is tacked to the flat rails of the back and seat frames, as indicated.

A RABBIT HUTCH

THE construction of the hutch shown in the accompanying drawings (Fig. 1) does not involve the cutting of any special joints in the woodwork. Two compartments are shown, side by

with a piece of wood to prevent it blowing aside. If a wood floor is desired it is suggested that it be made in sections which can be removed for cleaning, and that each section be made

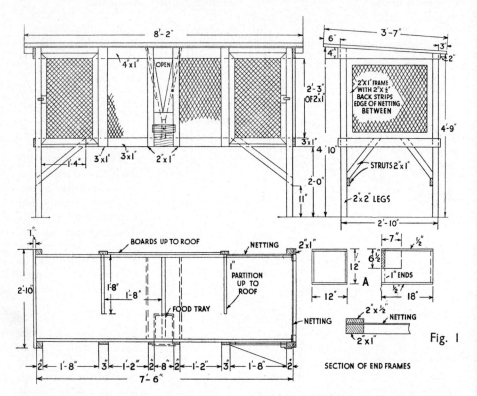

Fig. 1

side, to make one structure 7 ft. 6 in. long by 2 ft. 10 in. wide, raised 2 ft. from the ground. The centre division is arranged as a feeding hatch, thus saving disturbing the rabbits or opening the doors. One section of the back in each hutch and both ends are enclosed by wire netting to provide ample light and air. In cold weather or at night, any of these may be covered with a sacking cover weighted at the bottom

up of 1-in. wide bars with a $\frac{3}{8}$ or $\frac{1}{2}$ in. space between each, but not wide enough to allow a rabbit's foot to slip through, perhaps resulting in a broken leg. The same applies to a wire netting floor, which is much easier to keep clean. This is of small mesh or the thick straight bars in sections as used in aviary construction. The roof after boarding may be covered with tarred felt or other suitable roofing material.

Construction.—To construct the hutch start with the legs, which are 2 in. by 2 in. by 4 ft. 10 in. long. All four may be cut to the same length and the back ones shortened when the top side boards which taper from 4 in. to 2 in. are fixed. Cut two lengths of 3 in. by 1 in., 7 ft. 6 in. long, and two lengths, 2 ft. 10 in. long, for the bottom, back, front and side members, and fix them to the legs. The top front board is 4 in. by 1 in. by 7 ft. 6 in. long, and the two side boards, also 1 in. thick, are cut 4 in. wide at the front and taper to 2 in. at the back, as shown. Eight struts are required, of 2 in. by 1 in. timber. Four are 2 ft. 2 in. long for the back and front, while the side ones are 1 ft. 6 in. long. The vertical members which frame the door and wire-covered openings are 3 in. by 1 in. by 2 ft. 10 in. long for the front, and 2 in. by 1 in. at the sides of the feeding hatch. The back central section may be boarded with weatherboards or grooved and tongued matching. The central and two inner partitions are carried right up to the roof, and any exposed edges may be covered with metal strip to prevent damage from gnawing.

The fixed sections of wire mesh are fitted inside the main frame and the edges covered and secured by lath strips nailed on. The two hinged doors and the two end frames are of 2 in. by 1 in. wood, with laths to cover the mesh inside the doors, and 2 in. by ½ in. back strips for the end frames. All netting is 1 in. poultry wire mesh. Other details and full dimensions are shown in the drawing.

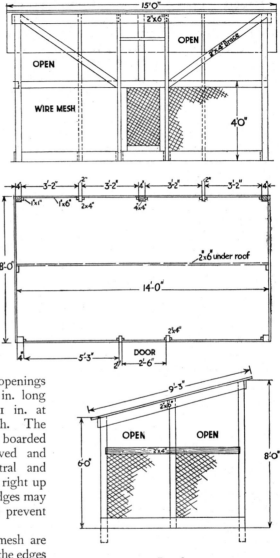

Fig. 2

Nest Box.—The type of nest box shown in detail at A in Fig. 1 allows the doe to get in and out without jumping and reduces the chances of accidents and injury to the young ones. Either the front or back should be removable for cleaning purposes.

Rabbit Pens.—Anyone starting rabbit breeding on a small scale will find that his stock will grow and develop faster in a pen than in breeding hutches, as there is ample space for exercise and sunlight. Both types of accommodation have their uses, and very young stock can be kept in hutches until strong enough to go with the older ones in the pen. The detailed drawing of a small pen (Fig. 2) shows a construction on the same simple lines as the hutch; all special joints common to carpentry work have been avoided, and the pen may be extended later if desired. Quite a suitable site would be in a small orchard so that the fruit trees would give some shelter from the wind and also provide shade in very hot weather.

The choice of roofing material is left to the constructor, but the ground should be covered with wire netting fixed to the frame to prevent the rabbits from digging a way out.

Sleeping and feeding boxes may be placed inside, and part of the back boarded in to a height of 4 ft. A hutch could be added to the pen but it should be raised off the ground and arranged so that the rabbits can get in when they want to.

Construction.—The corner posts are 4 in. by 4 in. by 6 ft. high at the back and 8 ft. high at the front. The boards round the bottom are 1 in. by 6 in. wide cut to fit between the posts. At a height of 4 ft., 2 in. by 4 in. timber is used all round, and the spaces all round to ground level are covered with 1 in. wire mesh. The doors are made in the same way as for the hutch but are of 2 in. by 4 in. timber with thick backing strips to cover the edge of the wire. The front and back top members of the main frame are 2 in. by 6 in. and should be in one length if possible. The side pieces are fixed on the slant with the top edge level with the top of the uprights at each end and the ends cut off flush with the face of the posts.

A CHILD'S SWING

THE garden swing shown in the accompanying working drawing is of quite simple construction and the little trouble expended will be amply repaid by the pleasure given to the younger members of the family.

In place of the usual large baulk of wood for the top cross-piece a built-up construction is employed. Two lengths of 4 in. by 1¼ in. board, 4 ft. 10 in. long, are spaced apart by means of four blocks, 5 in. by 4 in.; two screwed near the ends and two more central but 1 ft. 6 in. apart to carry the metal ring-bolts for taking the hooks of the ropes.

The two uprights are approximately 10 ft. long and 5 in. wide by 3½ in. thick. These are notched at the lower ends, as shown, to form bearings for the struts which are of 4 in. by 3 in. stuff butting against a 4 in. by 2 in. block fixed at each end of the sole plate. The sole plate is 4 ft. long of 4 in. by 2 or 2½ in. material. The strut ends of the posts should be buried about 3 ft. in the ground and the soil rammed down hard.

To protect the tops of the posts and rails a cap board, shown in the end view in the drawing, with bevelled top surface, is added. This is made to overlap about an inch beyond the edges of the cross-member and posts.

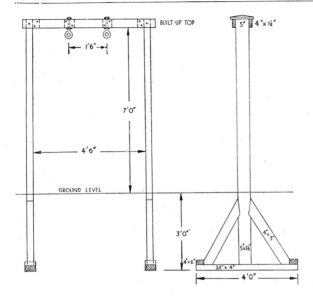

A groove should be made all round on the underside at a distance of about $\frac{3}{8}$ in. from the outer edge to prevent water creeping underneath. The cap board is fixed to the tops of the posts by means of screws, one at each end.

Metal ring-bolts and hooks for the ropes can usually be obtained from an ironmonger's. If hooks are used in lieu of ring-bolts the loops of the rope should be formed round metal eyelets to protect the rope from friction. A little grease applied to these parts will make for better working.

The seat is a plain rectangular board of oak. It should be sufficiently long to accommodate two children sitting side by side. The edges should be rounded and the sharp corners removed.

One advantage of the built-up head is that the whole can be bolted to the uprights through two holes bored lower down. This reduces the effective height of the swing to enable a safety swing for an infant to be attached.

Good quality yellow deal is suitable for all the parts. The portion above ground should be given at least two coats of creosote or three coats of good quality lead paint. The parts below ground are best protected against rot by a liberal coat of tar.

WINDOW BOXES AND PLANT STANDS

THE window box should commend itself to the town householder who has little other space in which to grow a few flowers, and to those who desire to brighten up the outside of the house.

Boxes on the lines of the design illustrated in Fig. 1 need not have a back board if it is intended to grow the plants in pots for the convenience of frequent changing, but if they are to be grown in soil a back is added.

Length and width will depend upon the size of window-sill. The overall length of the box is made a loose fit between the two inner faces of the brickwork, and the front extends beyond the corners and down over the edge of the sill. The bottom board is cut $\frac{1}{2}$ in. longer than the inside length of the box, so that the ends may be housed into grooves cut in the lower part of each side, $\frac{1}{4}$ in. deep. The back of the front board may be treated in the same manner if desired, or both back and front can be secured with wood screws. Hooks and staples are also added where convenient

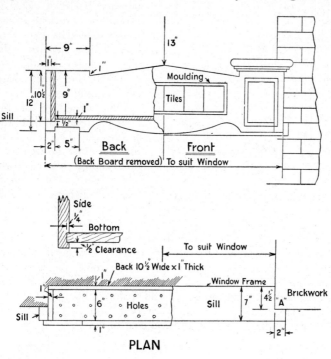

Fig. 1

the back garden or in the front one to hide an odd corner or to brighten a section of blank wall where a concrete or crazy paving surround prevents plants from being grown in the ground.

The box is 12 in. deep by 13 in. wide by 2 ft. long outside. Square timber of $1\frac{1}{4}$ in. section and 1 ft. 5 in. long is used for the two front legs fixed at the edges of the front of the box. A piece of $\frac{1}{2}$-in. or $\frac{3}{8}$-in. batten is curved as shown, and the ends let into notches cut at the sides of each leg near the top, and nailed or screwed down in the centre to the top edge.

The Trellis Screen is constructed of two $1\frac{1}{4}$ in. square uprights, 4 ft. long, spaced 2 ft. apart for fixing to the sides of the box, flush with the back edge. Caps about $2\frac{1}{2}$ in. square are made for the tops, and the trellis work

at the back to prevent the box from being moved off the sill. Suitable beading or light moulding is fixed on the front to give a pleasing effect, and glazed tiles are often fixed behind these mouldings to break the monotony of a plain front. Shades of green or green and white are suitable colours for painting, with tiles to match. The bottom is provided with holes for drainage, which are, of course, necessary for pot plants as well as soil-filled boxes.

The type of plant box shown in the drawing (Fig. 2) is very useful either in

is made of $\frac{3}{4}$-in. by $\frac{1}{2}$-in. batten, the vertical pieces having the broad side to the front and the horizontal lengths with the narrow edge showing. The latter are fitted first, with the ends just housed into the sides of the uprights.

Front and sides are finished with either plain strips, or moulding to form a mock panel. The latter looks best, especially with the ends cut to a mitre joint, and in any case the joints are well filled and covered with paint. Drainage holes are made in the bottom.

Plant Box to Hide Manhole Cover.—One of the most unsightly but unavoidable features of a house garden, back or front, is the iron cover over the drain inspection chamber. As this may have to be taken up at some future time it must not be covered with soil or part of the rockery, but may be effectively hidden by means of a flower box of shallow depth, easily removed when required.

As the cutting and fitting of sloping sides may prove awkward, small wedge-shaped pieces are first fixed to the legs to give the sides the necessary slope, but straight sides may be used if desired. The usual size of an iron manhole cover is 21 in. long by 21 in. wide, so if the box is made to the dimensions shown in Fig. 3 the cover will be well hidden. Some covers may be longer, but the dimensions shown can be altered to suit. Only two of the sides are shown grooved to take the edge of the bottom boards, but the other two members forming the front and back can be trenched if desired. Boards 1 in. thick are used for the bottom, and ⅜ in. thick boards for the sides. Two handles are screwed to the opposite sides for lifting, and a moulding with mitred corners is fixed on all four sides.

Tub Stand.—A plant stand, made on similar lines to that seen in Fig. 4, is a delightful acquisition to any garden or conservatory.

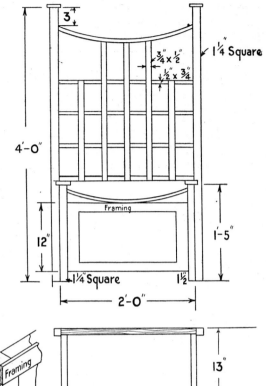

Fig. 2

It can be used to lift rare plants in the house or conservatory into a position where they can be easily and admiringly examined. Outside, it will serve to raise a tub of colourful flowers against an unsightly wall. Many other uses will occur to the amateur gardener.

The most important point is to see that the timber used is neither so heavy that it makes moving the stand an arduous task, nor so light that the tub of plants is insecure.

Any shallow or medium depth tub may be used for the centre, and should be provided with drop handles for lifting. The stand and the top rim may be made either round, square, or hexagonal in shape, and not only keeps the tub in position but serves as a shelf for a ring of small pots containing trailing plants which will hide most of the stand.

The pedestal has a centre about 3 in. square; into this and the base four brackets are fixed, with mortice and tenon joints.

Two-tier Box for Indoor Use.— Many kinds of plants and ferns may be grown indoors, and the stand shown in

Boards $\frac{7}{8}$ in. thick (finished) are used for the sides of the two boxes, and are fixed with the inner face flush with the back corners of each leg as shown, so that in each piece the side, back, or front is set back $\frac{1}{4}$ in. from the front face of the leg. All dowel pins project $\frac{3}{4}$ in. from the ends of the sides, fronts and backs, and are sunk in corresponding holes in the legs, etc., to the same amount. There is no wooden bottom to either box, but a galvanised iron container is

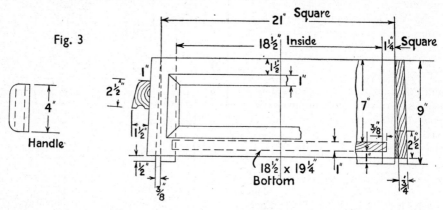

Fig. 3

Handle

Working Drawing No. 27 (in envelope with this volume) has been designed for this purpose. If the finished stand is varnished, and made of nicely grained wood, it will not look out of place in any hall or living-room to fill an odd corner.

Four legs are required and two centre posts, all made from $1\frac{1}{4}$ in. square timber. The back pair of legs is 2 ft. 7 in. long, and the front ones 1 ft. 11 in., while the posts are 1 ft. 3 in. in length. Care must be taken in marking out and drilling the dowel holes in these parts, remembering that there are dowel holes in adjacent faces. No dowel hole should show on any outer surface. The dowel rod is readily obtainable in convenient lengths, and 38 pieces are required, all of which are $\frac{3}{8}$ in. diameter and $1\frac{1}{2}$ in. long.

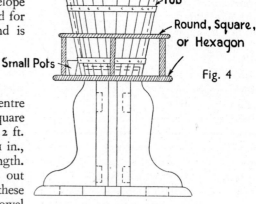

Fig. 4

supported in each, on 8 $\frac{1}{4}$-in. diameter iron rods pushed into holes in the back and front of each box, in a line and $\frac{5}{8}$ in. up from the bottom edge.

The marking out of each piece of sheet metal is shown clearly in the detailed drawing. The lines where the metal is to be bent or folded should be clearly marked with a scriber to scratch the metal, as pencil marks would soon be rubbed out. The narrow border, $\frac{1}{2}$ in. wide on all edges, marked A, should be folded over first and then hammered flat on the inside. The sides and ends of the container may then be bent up at right-angles to the bottom; also the $\frac{1}{2}$-in.-wide tabs on the sides, marked B. The two surfaces coming in contact must be well cleaned and these corners soldered to keep the box together. More solder is run along the corners, inside.

The best method of assembly is to build and glue up each end first, complete the centre rail, the two sides and the two rails. The iron rods for the lower box are then driven into the holes in the back panel. This and the front of the upper box may then be placed in position with the dowels just entering their proper holes in the centre post at each end. The front of the lower box is added and the rods are eased into place. The back of the top box is left until last and the whole may be eased together to make tight joints everywhere. The rods for the top box are inserted from the back and a cover strip fitted to hide the row of holes.

BIRD BOXES

VARIOUS birds may be encouraged to frequent the garden by providing a feeding perch and small nesting-boxes. The designs shown, besides serving this purpose, will, if made to look as natural as possible, give a charming effect in any garden for a small outlay.

The Feeding-perch shown in the detailed drawing in Fig. 1 has a small roof covered with narrow rough-sawn boards with unfinished edges, and fitted with a bottom board, thus forming an enclosed compartment with two sections in which small birds may make their nests, a small opening being left in each end for their entrance.

The bottom board of the enclosed portion is cut $21\frac{1}{2}$ in. wide by 24 in. long. Each long edge has a chamfer to match the slope of the end pieces. Three of the latter are required $\frac{3}{4}$ in. or $\frac{7}{8}$ in. thick, either nailed or screwed to the bottom board, one at each end and one in the centre. To complete this part the roof boards may be cut to length.

These overlap the ends by 2 in. at each end. The ridge piece is prepared ready for fixing when the other parts are finished.

Eight brackets, shaped as shown, made from 1-in. stuff, are tenoned, or merely nailed to the pole; four at the top flush with the squared end, and the other four to support the feeding-tray, which is fixed at 6 ft. 6 in. above ground level to allow food and water to be placed on the tray.

A tapered pole or post 8 ft. long would be suitable and should measure 3 in. square at the top. Holes to take $\frac{1}{2}$-in. diameter dowel rod for perches are bored through the pole between the tray and the roof compartment.

The tray is made 16 in. wide by 20 in. long, with fillets round the edge. These may be strips of board to match the roof. The centre hole is made to the size of the pole at the point where the pole passes through.

When assembling, the four lower

brackets are fixed to the pole first, then the tray is slipped down and secured. Two perches are added and then the four brackets at the top. To these, the bottom board with its three triangular pieces is fixed. The roof boards are then added, allowing each piece to overlap as with weather boards, and lastly the ridge piece or cap.

On completion, the whole is treated with a wood preserving solution, which

a fairly large nut or other convenient weight on the end. When the post has been lifted into the hole this string will indicate any departure from the vertical. Earth is now rammed into the hole round the post by using a heavy piece of wood.

If it is desired to bed the post in concrete it will require supporting while the concrete sets hard. This may be done by nailing to the pole two or three lengths

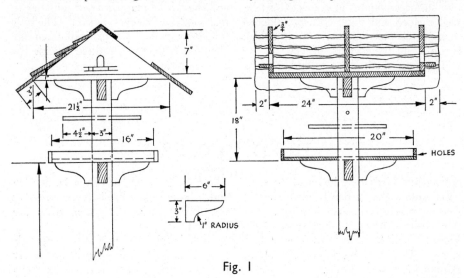

Fig. 1

looks more natural than paint. The lower end for a distance of 2 ft. 6 in. should be coated with tar to prevent rot.

The hole in the ground to receive the pole is 2 ft. deep. Make it about 3 in. larger all round than the post and keep the sides upright if possible, without getting the top larger than the bottom. If, in removing the soil, a little undercutting cannot be avoided and the bottom is larger than the top this will not matter, as it forms a wedge.

When erecting the post, drive a long thin nail into one of the faces at a distance of 3 or 4 ft. above the ground, and hang on this a length of thin string having

of wood at an angle to act as temporary struts and fixing the lower ends of these to pegs. Driving pegs into a lawn may be objected to, but if a small square of turf is carefully cut and rolled back at the peg positions the soil and turf can be replaced when the pegs are taken out.

A Hollow Log Nesting-box.—A neat design is illustrated at A, B and C in Fig. 2, in which A shows a side view; B, the front; and C, a plan.

To make this, select a sound log about 5 or 6 in. in diameter by 7 or 8 in. long, and leave parts of some of the side branches on to serve as perches and to retain a natural effect. Remove the

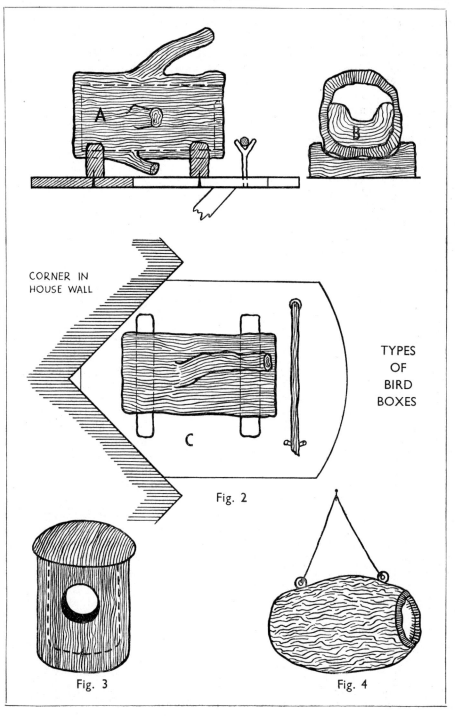

A

B

CORNER IN
HOUSE WALL

TYPES
OF
BIRD
BOXES

C

Fig. 2

Fig. 3

Fig. 4

centre wood by using a large-size twist bit, drilling a series of holes as close together as possible all over the portion to be removed, thus leaving a wall all round the edge of the log about $\frac{1}{2}$ in. or less thick, as shown by the dotted lines. Cut out the remainder of the wood to the bottoms of the drilled holes with a gouge, and use the brace and bit again to go deeper, cleaning up with a gouge as before. A rough disc of wood cut from the end of a log is then cut and fitted, as at B, into the open end, leaving a space for entrance.

This nest may be fixed to a feeding tray set into the corner angle of the house wall as indicated, or can be hung to a tree branch or set firm in a convenient fork.

A smaller nest box (Fig. 3) is made in the same manner, but used in a vertical position under the gutter of the roof or suspended from a tree in the garden. The entrance hole is about $1\frac{1}{2}$ in. diameter, which is quite large enough for very small birds, such as blue tits, who like these nests.

The shells of coconuts and the larger outer shells which have contained brazil nuts, if provided with an opening at one end (as illustrated in Fig. 4), make excellent nests for hanging in the garden and are seldom without tenants.

PIGEON COTES

A PIGEON cote gives quite a rural touch to the suburban house or garden. The smaller one with four compartments may be mounted on a pole or a bracket standing well out from the wall, and the other design is suitable for fixing to the wall itself, but could be fixed to a pole if required.

The small-pole type of cote illustrated in Fig. 1, consists of a tray 36 in. square, with an edging of $\frac{1}{2}$ in. thick beading, supported by four brackets 1 in. thick, the tops of which are let into the baseboard and the bottoms into the top of the square pole, as shown in the elevation.

The cote is made up of two sides 18 in. high by 27 in. long, to which 1 in. square battens are screwed or nailed, 1 in. in from the edges, as indicated in the plan. The two remaining sides are 18 in. by 25 in. Each side has a round-top opening 4 in. wide by 7 in. high, cut in the position shown, so that each compartment has its own doorway. The partition is built up to 18 in. by 25 in. with a 1-in.-wide slot cut half-way, as shown. These two pieces fit together and form the four inner walls, which are secured to the outer walls by thin nails or screws. All of these pieces are $\frac{3}{4}$ in. or 1 in. thick.

The Roof is supported on a baseboard 3 ft. 6 in. square. Mark a line across from corner to corner, as indicated by the dotted lines in the drawing of the roof, and set the central finial post of 2 in. square wood as shown. Drill six holes along each line in the baseboard for the fixing screws, and then cut the four triangular pieces, which support the roof boards. Having screwed the roof supports in position, fix the square roof board to the body before the roof is covered in. The covering boards may be narrow strips of weather-board or roughly sawn boards with their long edges left in their natural state.

The completed work should be treated with wood-preserving solution, or painted either all one colour, or the roof dark red, body green, and the tray and post brown.

The larger gable-end type of pigeon cote, illustrated in Fig. 2, has six compartments arranged as shown. The first part of the work should be to make the inner ridge block. This is 16 in. long, 8 in. high and 7 in. at the base, as indicated in the detail. The ends are cut back 2 in. wide for a depth of ¾ in. The apex of the end frames is fixed to this block. If the bottom board is cut next these two parts can be used as a guide for setting out the remainder of the work. The next step is to make two A-shaped frames out of 2 in. by ¾ in. wood, halved at the apex and resting on the battens fixed underneath the bottom board. The corners of the latter are cut away so that the face of the frame members is flush with the long edge of the bottom board. It will help

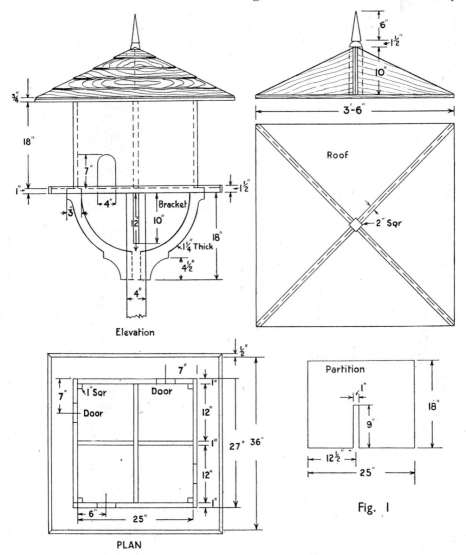

Elevation

Roof

PLAN

Partition

Fig. I

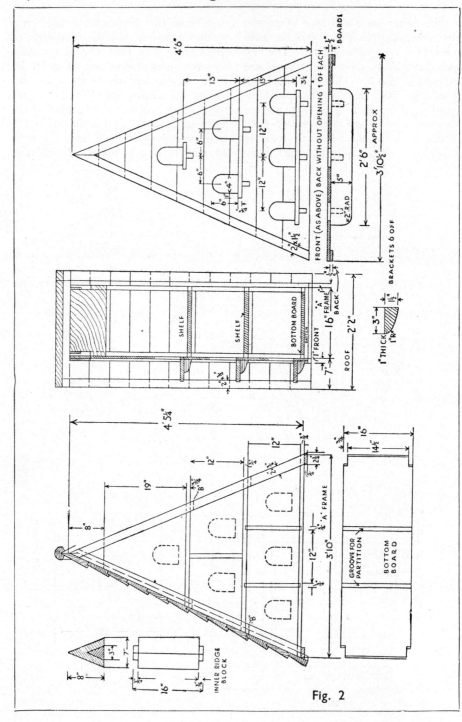

Fig. 2

a great deal with the accurate cutting of the shelves and the fixing of the battens between the frames (marked B), if the two **A** frames, the inner ridge block and the bottom board are fixed together for the time being. The battens are ¾ in. thick and just housed into the **A** frames. With these in position, the construction so far will look like a pair of steps standing on a baseboard. From this the two shelves may be marked out and cut.

The baseboard will require two grooves ¾ in. wide by about $\frac{3}{16}$ in. deep for the partitions. The first shelf, which forms the roof of the bottom three sections, has two grooves underneath, 12 in. apart, and one central on the other side for the central partition between the two compartments above. The two lower partitions are screwed to the baseboard first, then the first shelf is put in with the central partition ready fixed, the top shelf being added last. If the job is laid front face downwards on the bench, the back **A** frame can be removed to allow these parts to be placed in position and then put back when they are all secure.

For the back, boards 6 in. wide, with grooved and tongued edges are used,

eight widths of which will just fit into the height. Battens of 2 in. by ½ in. are fixed down at each edge on the outside, and holes are drilled down the centre of these battens and countersunk for the fixing screws.

For the front the same construction may be repeated, and the six openings, 4 in. wide by 6 in. high, marked out and cut after the boards have been fixed with the battens outside, as before.

Six small brackets, 3 in. by 1½ in. by 1 in. thick, are required to support the landing shelves. The latter are all ¾ in. thick and 5 in. wide. The top one is 6 in. long, the double one underneath is 18 in. long, and the bottom one is 30 in. long.

The roof is covered with 26 in. lengths of rebated weather-boarding, with 2-in. by ¾-in. battens inside, and completed with a ridge piece to cover the top joint.

Brown wood-preserving solution is the best finish for this type of cote. The structure is usually fixed to a wall. This could be done by cutting out two bricks a convenient distance apart, two known as "headers" being chosen for removal, and fixing in their place two timber bearers 3 in. by 4½ in. or 5 in. section on which to rest the base.

AN OUTDOOR AVIARY

Many different kinds of beautiful and interesting small birds may be kept out-of-doors if a suitable aviary is built for them.

The design shown in the illustration would not look out of place in any garden, and besides providing a sheltered house for the birds there is space for them to fly about or to perch in the open air under cover.

Light, natural branches of trees are

set about inside and suspended from the roof for perches, and small nesting-boxes are fixed in any convenient place, such as the fork of the struts or towards the top of the main posts, for the birds to use. Food-trays are also hung where convenient and a shallow cement bird-bath with water is included. This has a waste-pipe taken through the wall and a plug for cleaning and re-filling.

The construction of the lower sur-

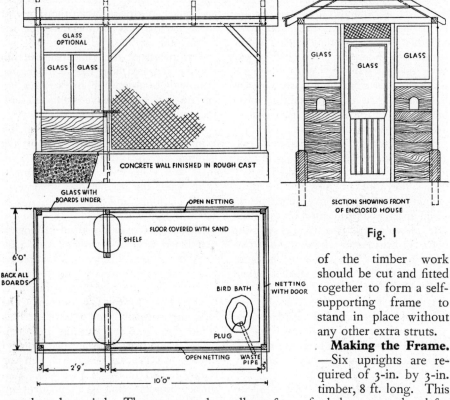

GLASS OPTIONAL

GLASS | GLASS

CONCRETE WALL FINISHED IN ROUGH CAST

GLASS WITH BOARDS UNDER

OPEN NETTING

3'2"

BOARDED INSIDE

GLASS   GLASS   GLASS

SECTION SHOWING FRONT OF ENCLOSED HOUSE

FLOOR COVERED WITH SAND

SHELF

BIRD BATH

NETTING WITH DOOR

PLUG

6'0"

BACK ALL BOARDS

OPEN NETTING   WASTE PIPE

3"   2'9'   3"   3"

10'0"

Fig. I

round can be varied. The posts may be set into the ground in concrete and enclosed with weatherboards, matched boards, or rough sawn boards with their natural edges to match the other parts of the house. Rough stone walling would blend well with other parts of the garden construction, or a wall is very easily made of concrete and finished in rough-cast with small stones and sand.

A concrete wall is made by pouring the wet mixture in between two timber surrounds spaced 5 or 6 in. apart to give the necessary thickness and 18 in. above ground level to fix the height. A very firm structure is made if the posts are fixed in position before the concrete is mixed and placed, so, in this case, part

of the timber work should be cut and fitted together to form a self-supporting frame to stand in place without any other extra struts.

Making the Frame. —Six uprights are required of 3-in. by 3-in. timber, 8 ft. long. This allows for 1 ft. below ground and for cutting the tenon at the top to fit into the horizontal members at the top, sides and ends. The horizontal pieces are also 3 in. by 3 in., halved at the corners. Two side members are 10 ft. long, and the end ones 6 ft. long. Struts of 2-in. square timber are fixed at each post, two on each side of the aviary and two at each end.

When the timber work has been completed and fixed together, the whole is given one or two coats of creosote.

Concrete Work.—The next part of the work, consists in excavating a trench, 6 in. wide, all round the site to a depth of 12 in., and where the posts will stand it is advisable to increase the depth to 14

A MULTIPLE-SECTION PIGEON AVIARY

in. for a space of 6 in. Ram the bottom of the trench hard with a heavy piece of wood, and check the depth to see that it is level at the bottom all the way round. Pieces of broken brick rammed into the bottom of the post-holes will help to make a firm foundation. Mix a small quantity of concrete, enough to fill the post-holes to the level of the bottom of the trench, and leave it to set. Meanwhile, the shuttering can be made. Two 9-in. wide boards 10 ft. long are fixed together on edge with battens. This will give the required 18 in. to the top of the wall. A second pair for the inside is made in the same way and secured in place along the edge of the trench by fixing them to 2-in. square pegs driven into the ground at intervals, or by struts splayed outwards. The two long side-walls can be formed first, and the boards reduced in length and re-used for the ends.

Suitable proportions of materials for the concrete are 4 parts of aggregate, consisting of clean stones or small pieces of broken brick, 2 parts clean, sharp sand and 1 part Portland cement. The next step is to place the timber framework in position and to see that it is standing perfectly level and central in the trench. Now fix the shuttering in position and the first section may be made by filling in with concrete. When this has set, the shuttering is removed and set up on the other side, and when this wall is complete the construction of the two end walls may be put in hand.

The finishing of the walls consists in applying a thin coat of cement and sand to give a fairly smooth surface to the walls, inside and out, and chamfering off the top edges. If rough-cast finish is desired, small stones and sand are applied before the surface becomes set.

The Roof.—Four roof-trusses are required, one to span each pair of uprights, one fixed central in the middle of the enclosure and the fourth to span the end pair of the wire-covered enclosure. They are of the collar-beam type with 3-in. by 2-in. rafters, 3-in. by 2-in. collar beam, and 5-in. by 2-in. ridge piece.

Where the rafters rest on the top side members, a birdsmouth joint is made, so that the ends of the rafters overhang 6 in. at the sides. To these ends a gutter or facia board, 1 in. by 4½ in. wide, is fixed.

The roof is boarded inside and outside; the latter being either lime-washed or painted white. The choice of material for the outer covering is left to the builder. Red asbestos tiles look well, but other forms of covering such as Ruberoid are easier to fix. Ordinary tarred, sanded felt is not recommended.

The whole of the back of the house is covered in with boards, but a small door can be made in this, if required. Another perhaps more suitable position for the door would be in the wire end, but in any case it need only be just enough for cleaning and feeding purposes.

Glass panels are used in both sides and in front of the house portion, the remainder of the space being covered with boards. Two openings are left in the partition for the birds to pass in and out, and a shelf is fixed to each, outside and in. The door opening is 2 ft. wide, but this could be altered to suit a ready-made door. All of the woodwork should be treated with creosote or other wood preservative.

The wire netting should not be larger than 1-in. mesh, and the edges are secured under battens along the top and sides and to a timber sill between the posts along the top of the concrete wall. Each width of netting overlaps the one below and the edges are bound together with wire. Special wire screens of stouter wire, arranged in straight lines, and in sections, are obtainable if ordinary wire netting is objected to.

ROOFING MATERIALS

EACH form of roofing material requires its own method of fixing, and each kind of material is best suited for one or more particular purpose according to restrictions of slope of roof, cost and appearances.

The structures amateur constructors are chiefly concerned about are workshop

Fig. 1

sheds, poultry-houses, cycle stores or perhaps small garages. It is a curious thing that most structures of this kind are admirable in the walls but poor in the roof. And yet modern materials for roof covering are varied and easy to use.

Roofing Felt.—A wooden shed or poultry house is cheap and easily roofed by boarding the top over and then covering it with roofing felt, obtainable under various trade names. Although so simple and suitable for amateur use, there are correct methods of fixing, and provided these are followed, no trouble should arise which would result in the felt lifting and becoming torn with the first strong wind, or bulging with the heat.

Bitumen roofing felt, suitable for the above kind of work, is obtainable in rolls containing 12 sq. yd., the width being 36

20

in. There are two grades, medium and heavy weight.

In fixing these materials, start at the eaves, i.e., gutter edge, and always lay the felt lengthwise, parallel with this edge, if possible. The cutting will often have to be done out of doors, and in this case a piece of board should be placed on the ground underneath the part to be cut and a lino knife used against a straight-edge, as shown in Fig. 1. Galvanised roofing nails or "clouts," with very large heads, are used, and these are obtainable in various lengths.

Each length of felt should overlap the piece below by at least 3 in. and the nails driven through the two thicknesses of the lap at intervals of about 2 in., as illustrated at A in Fig. 2. When cutting a length always allow about 2 in. more at each end extra to overlap the ends of

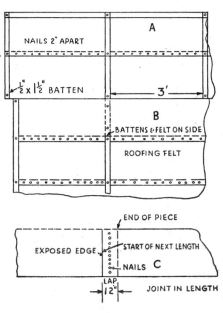

Fig. 2

the roof. Where it is necessary to use vertical joints to prevent unnecessary waste in covering a long roof, make an overlap of 12 in., and drive the nails in the exposed edge at 2-in. intervals, as indicated at c.

After covering both sides of the roof up to the ridge, a narrow piece is cut 5 to 6 in. wide and fixed over the exposed edges along the ridge. Battens of $\frac{1}{2}$-in. by $1\frac{1}{2}$-in. wood may then be

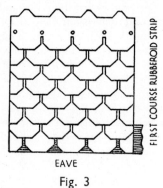

FIRST COURSE RUBBEROID STRIP

EAVE

Fig. 3

added, starting from the edge and fixed from the ridge downwards, by means of wood screws, spacing the battens at intervals of about 3 ft. or the nearest equal sub-division of the overall length, for neatness. A roof covered in this manner will stand any strong wind, and give service for years.

To repair a torn piece of felt, insert the new patch piece underneath the tear and nail along the edges.

The sides and ends of the shed may be covered in the same manner, if desired, by starting at the bottom and allowing the same overlap as that on the roof. Battens are also used on the sides if required, and in all cases they should be painted with creosote before fixing. The method adopted is shown at B, in Fig. 2.

Similar material is to be obtained in red and green colours, and has a surface of an imitation of crushed, natural slate

rolled into the surface, which gives a very pleasing appearance; it is just as easy to fix. The rolls are 3 ft. wide and contain enough to cover 100 sq. ft. of roof surface. The same material (Ruberoid) is also supplied in strips with the edges cut like tiles as in Fig. 3. They are laid on close-boarded roofs with nails, five tiles to a strip. These also hold the strip below, so there is no doubt about security. The holes are ready punched, and a good overlap is obtained. Very effective results are achieved by combining the two colours. These and the slate-surfaced material are suitable for garages, bungalows and even houses.

In fixing the strips of imitation tiling, a strip of ordinary Ruberoid is fixed along the roof as a first course, at the eaves. The bottom edges of the "tiles" are then placed over this course so that they register with the edge of the eaves, and then laid in horizontal courses up to the ridge.

Corrugated Iron.—Galvanised corrugated roofing sheets in 26-gauge iron are obtainable 2 ft. wide by 5-ft., 6-ft., 7-ft., and 8-ft. lengths. Sheets 9 ft. long are 3 ft. wide. Galvanised screws and washers are required for fixing, and the usual overlap is 6 in.

The sheets are laid from the gutter up towards the ridge, and the screws are driven through holes punched in the ridge or top of the iron and never in the valley between ridges. The first row of sheets should each overlap along the long edge by 3 in. or one corrugation, and the short ends, where the sheets of the next row lie over the first, extending to the ridge, should overlap the lower sheets by 6 in.

Tiles.—An important building such as a motor garage can easily be covered with ordinary roofing tiles. Such tiles are $10\frac{1}{2}$ in. by $6\frac{1}{2}$ in., and 7 in. by 11 in., laid to a $2\frac{1}{2}$ or $2\frac{3}{4}$ in. lap. A roof slope of less than 40 degrees is not recommended; the usual is 40 to 45 degrees. Some tiles have a turned-over end along the whole width, for fixing purposes, others only have two small projections called nibs.

The roof frame timbers consist of rafters, purlins and struts, with battens on which to lodge and fix the tiles. The best lap is obtained if it is made $2\frac{3}{4}$ or 3 in., and the battens must be spaced to suit this and the size of tile. It is common practice to nail tiles every fourth row only; some work is only nailed every fifth or sixth row, but as each tile is made with the necessary holes, each one could be nailed if desired.

Slates are not ordinarily used by the amateur, perhaps because they appear to be difficult to fix. This is a mistaken idea, and there is no reason why the novice should not make use of this excellent roofing material.

There is no nib on a slate and, being flat, each one has to be nailed either to boards or battens. No fixing holes are provided, as these have to be made on the job according to the method of fixing and size of slate.

Of the variety of sizes the following are the most common:

8 in. wide by 16 in. long. Known as "Ladies."

10 in. wide by 20 in. long. Known as "Countess."

12 in. wide by 24 in. long. Known as "Duchess."

Methods of Fixing.—Slates are laid in bond so that the edge joints do not run in continuous lines. Each slate is covered partially by two others and the visible portion of any slate is a little less than half its area. The minimum overlap is 3 in.

Centre Nailing.—Two methods of fixing slates are available, known as centre nailing and head nailing. The method of centre nailing is more general as the slates are more rigid, and not easily lifted by the wind. Should the margin break, the nail-hole of the slate below is exposed to the rain which may find its way through underneath, but as only one nail is used, repairs are more easily made. The first course near the gutter-

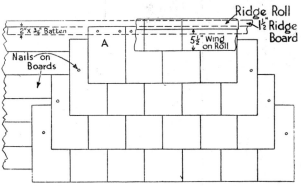

Fig. 4

ing is laid with 24-in. by 12-in. slates, lengthwise, in order to start the lap. The fixing nail holes are punched $1-1\frac{1}{4}$ in. from the top edge and $1\frac{1}{2}$ in. or more from the sides for this course only, all the others are nailed near the centre, that is, just clear of the head of the slate below. Details of centre-nailed slating appear in Fig. 4, which shows the slates fixed on plain battens and also on a boarded roof.

Head Nailing.—The alternative method (A in Fig. 4) is to nail them about 1 in. from the head and $1\frac{1}{2}$–2 in. from the sides. The nails are well covered, and the slate is not so easily strained in nailing, but being near the top the slates are liable to lift with the wind and break near the head; snow and rain drift farther up the roof between the coverings. Less surface is covered than with centre nailing, having the same nett lap.

THE AMATEUR PHOTOGRAPHER AT WORK

AMATEUR
PHOTOGRAPHY

THIS article is intended to help the beginner whose desire is to make good photographs, to turn out his own prints, without having to go into the

Fig. 1

theory and technicalities of chemistry and optics.

Modern equipment for amateur use has done much to remove the disapproval of photography as a hobby. This was due to the variety of chemicals collected, and the increasing amount of space required as time passed for the large number of bottles and other equipment. The mixing of these chemicals to suit developing of plates and papers involved much mess, many smells and stains and no small knowledge of chemistry.

All this may now be avoided by the use of prepared developers, and even a dark room is not necessary when a developing tank may be used in an ordinary room. The beginner is able to use the results of some of the finest research-work that has ever been done

with a view to improving every detail of the art. Camera, lens, shutter, plates, films and printing papers have all been improved in order to make photography as easy and trouble-free as possible.

One of the advantages of this fascinating and popular pastime is its elasticity. A start can be made in a very limited and simple way. At first, the novice may not attempt more than to select the subjects, to judge the exposure for each case, and to have the developing and printing carried out by a local photographic specialist. The advantage of

Fig. 2

this method is that he will be learning one thing at a time, and will know that the failures are due to his mistakes in selection and exposure, and can learn how to correct them. Improvements in this direction will enable him to be more certain about good results, and

Fig. 3

then development and printing may be undertaken.

The Camera.—The determination to begin photography presents the problem of selecting a camera, and this is not an easy matter to settle. There are so many cameras, and he will require one that will answer his purpose, without knowing very definitely what that purpose is beyond a general desire to take snaps of familiar scenes, holiday views and recreations, and portraits of friends. A little experience will show in what respects his camera suits or fails, so for a start the best advice is to get the simplest form that will do all he requires of it, and to buy the best of its kind he can afford from a reliable source, so that he can depend upon the quality of the design, materials, and workmanship. Later this may be disposed of in favour of something more suitable.

Box Cameras.—The simplest form of camera, costing a few shillings, is the box type shown in Figs. 1, 2 and 3, fitted with all-distance lens, eliminating focusing and enabling sharp definition to be had of any subjects at any distances upwards from 6 ft. from the camera. Two settings of the shutter are obtainable, for instantaneous or time exposures

as required, and two lens-stops are provided, for ordinary and for bright light. Pictures are taken on roll films, each measuring $2\frac{1}{4}$ by $3\frac{1}{4}$ in. A better model of the same class has a clear stop-indicator round the lens-front for different kinds of weather, landscapes, groups, portraits, etc. Other types of box cameras are obtainable for 6 or 12 plates, each held in a metal sheath. The movement of a lever drops each plate, after use, to the bottom of the camera, and the next one is brought into correct position by means of a spring. All of these have two view-finders set in the body of the camera, each with a miniature lens and ground-glass screen to assist in pointing the camera correctly, and showing the amount of subject that will come on the plate or film. Another convenient form of view-finder, fitted to some cameras, gives direct vision of the subject through an adjustable wire frame and an eye-piece at the back.

Folding Cameras.—A more compact form of camera using roll films is the folding type shown in Figs. 4 and 5. Such a camera is perhaps the most popular because when closed it measures

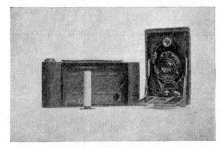

Fig. 4

only $6\frac{3}{8}$ in. by $3\frac{1}{4}$ in. by $1\frac{1}{4}$ in., which enables it to be carried in the pocket. The front is hinged and forms a base or stand upon which the front of the bellows rests. There is no focusing arrangement other than two marked positions, for views and close-ups.

Fig. 5

The shutter is of a superior type to those used in cheap box cameras, several speeds being provided for snaps, while time exposures can also be made. In addition, there are several adjustable stops for light. The lens is a single one of the rapid meniscus type. A thoroughly reliable camera of this type can be obtained for about a couple of guineas.

Numerous models, types, and sizes of folding pocket cameras are to be had, costing anything up to £20 or so, according to the quality of the lens and other refinements.

Another excellent type of folding camera is one with a leather-covered wooden body, rack-and-pinion adjustment for focusing, leather bellows, etc. This type of camera enables plates, film packs, and roll films to be used. All models have at least one screwed fitting to take a tripod, and also sometimes one at the side, for horizontal work.

More advanced work may be undertaken by means of a reflex camera, as shown in Fig. 6, so made that it is possible to watch the subject on a ground-glass screen at the bottom of the hood extension, and to make focus adjustments up to the moment of operating the shutter. This makes it ideal for dealing with moving objects, sport events, etc. The picture is seen at actual finished size and right way up (although reversed from right to left) owing to the mirror. The shutter of such a camera usually has a range of speeds from 1/25 to 1/500 of a second on the standard type and up to 1/1000 sec. on others. Both have time setting, and may be used on a tripod, but the usual method of support is by shoulder-straps.

There are many other forms and styles of cameras besides those mentioned here,

Fig. 6

but although all differ in design and detail, their general principles are the same.

When studying catalogues and reading through the various specifications, certain features may call for some explanation of their purpose and use.

Rise-and-fall Front and Cross Movement.—For example: The panel carrying the lens, on some models, can be moved upwards so that the lens is raised above its normal position exactly opposite the centre of the plate or film, with the result that some of the foreground is cut off and more of the trees, tall buildings, or sky included in the picture. This is an extremely useful feature, and can be used in the other direction by lowering the lens below the centre, to include more foreground than sky.

The cross movement is used in the same manner when taking landscape pictures with the camera on its side for horizontal views.

Infinity Catch.—In cameras where the front is pulled forward along runners, as in Fig. 7, and can be clamped

Fig. 7

in various positions according to the distance of the object focused upon, there is often a catch for stopping the front automatically at the point which will give the best results for the given distance, and all objects to within a certain distance of the lens. For

nearer objects the front is released from this catch and moved to the necessary mark on the focusing scale.

Extension.—The terms single and double extension are explained as follows: The lens commonly used for a given size of plate or film has a focal length roughly equal to the diagonal dimension (corner to corner) of the plate or film. If the lens is placed in the right position for focusing both near and distant objects, the camera is said to have single extension. To copy anything full size, the lens must be exactly twice its focal length from the screen used for focus adjustments, and a camera allowing this movement has a double extension.

The Lens.—It is essential that the novice should know something about the lens, which is the most important part of the camera, in order that he may use to the best advantage the one he has, or be enabled to select a suitable lens for any special purpose.

The term "lens" is used in general for what is often a complete and elaborate instrument containing several glasses which are, strictly speaking, the lenses. One or more pieces may be fixed in a metal tube or mount fitted with a device for varying the size of the opening through which the light passes. Even the simple lens is seldom a single piece of glass. It may be two, three, or more separate glasses, very accurately ground and polished and cemented together. According to the grinding and construction and to special characteristics in the results they give, lenses are given a variety of names: doublet, anastigmat, etc.

It is impossible to give even a brief description of lenses without referring to "stops" and "focus." In front of the lens there is usually an ingenious construction of thin metal plates working over each other in such a way that the turning of an outer ring or moving of a small pin round a scale, enlarges or diminishes the aperture, which remains circular and central at all settings. No light-rays reach the lens except those passing first through this hole. This device thus acts as a stop for the light-rays, but before going into this we must consider focus. A lens may be used to concentrate rays of light in such a way that they fall upon one small spot at a certain distance from the lens. The familiar experiment with the rays from the sun will be called to mind; provided the heat at this small spot is sufficient, the substance on which it is concentrated will ignite. In a similar way, the camera lens collects light-rays and brings them to a focus, or point of concentration, so that a sharp image is shown.

It will be very helpful at this stage if the beginner will make use of his camera for a few simple experiments to illustrate, by actual results, the effects of stops and focus. The camera is required in an unloaded condition, and if not fitted with a focusing screen, one should be improvised by using a spare film-pack holder or plate-sheath with most of the centre cut out, and fitted with a piece of ground-glass of the same size as the film or plate used. The prepared sheath containing the glass is placed in the camera in the usual position occupied during exposure, with the rough or frosted side towards the lens.

If a single lens is placed at a suitable distance from the flat surface of the screen to give upon it a sharply-defined image of distant objects such as clouds, the lens is at its principal focus. The focal length of the lens is the distance between the lens and the screen, which is termed the focal plane. If this distance from lens to focal plane were 6 in., the lens would be called a 6-in. lens. If the camera is now pointed to a near object, it will be found that the image is not

20*

clear, and can only be made so by moving the lens nearer to the object, and therefore farther from the focal plane. The image is always proportional to the focal length of the lens, so if the image of a person were 1 in. high with a 4-in. lens, it would be 2 in. with an 8-in. lens; 3 in. with a 12-in. lens, and so on.

The focus and stop experiments may be carried out in a room where objects at various distances are visible outside, and if present, lace curtains at the window will form a convenient ground to compare focus adjustments with.

At first, use the largest or most open stop, open the shutter, and examine the picture showing on the ground-glass. It will be found perhaps that the curtains and certain objects outside are sharply defined, and if the camera is carried slowly towards the window, it will be noticed that at certain distances the various objects lose their sharpness, there being one particular distance where it is possible to obtain the image of the curtain mesh still sufficiently clear. This distance should be measured and made a note of, as being the nearest distance an object may be to the camera, and still be sharp when using that stop. Now use the next smallest stop and it will then be possible to approach a little closer to the curtain without the image of the mesh appearing less distinct. This distance should be noted and the process repeated for each stop. With the second stop the image on the ground-glass will not be so bright, in fact half the light has been shut out; and this diminished light will again be reduced by half when the third stop is used. Thus we learn how near it is possible to go to objects with each stop and why it is necessary to double the time of exposure each time one passes to a smaller stop. The lens front is set at the infinity mark for these tests, which may be repeated with the lens set for distance and moved along its scale by the rack movement, if one is provided. On obtaining a sharp image of the curtain, it may be found that objects just outside the window may also be sharp and the more distant ones blurred, and it is evident that objects both near to, and far from, the lens, cannot always be got into sharp focus at the same time. If the ground-glass is watched carefully as the stop is changed to a smaller and smaller size, the definition of objects beyond the curtain gradually improves; and it may be possible to obtain everything sharp right up to the extreme distance.

The distance between the nearest and the farthest objects that are sharp at the same time, is the *depth of focus,* or briefly, *depth.*

When the lens, instead of being at its principal focus, is moved out farther from the focal plane to obtain a sharp image of a near object, the depth may be very little, especially with a large stop. A long-focus portrait lens with a large stop may not have sufficient depth to show both the ear and nose of a sitter sharp at the same time.

The principal use of stops is to obtain greater depth of focus, and to give good definition in every plane where required. Another point to be considered is that the image projected is contained within a circle, and if the focus is adjusted to give the best definition in the centre of the circle, it becomes worse towards the edges. The patch over which any light at all falls is called the *area of illumination,* and that part in which the definition comes up to the required degree of sharpness is the *circle of definition.* Good definition may be only in a small part at the middle, or may extend almost to the edges of the area of illumination. A smaller stop will increase the area of good definition, but does not increase the area of illumination.

The usual marking of the stop is to indicate the relation between the diameter of the stop and the focal length of the lens, and is therefore only correct when the lens is used at its principal focus; the relation becomes altered when the lens is out farther from the focal plane. The markings against the stops, such as $f/8$, $f/11$, etc., where f stands for the focal length, give the numbers by which it is to be divided. A given opening has different values according to the focal length of the lens used with it: $f/8$ with a 4-in. lens would be an opening of $\frac{1}{2}$-in. diameter, with a 6-in. lens it would be $\frac{3}{4}$-in., the diameter in every case being $\frac{1}{8}$ of the focal length.

As previously mentioned, the stops are generally arranged so that each smaller opening requires double the exposure given with the previous next larger stop, and some lenses have the stops marked to indicate this doubling. This method, known as the Universal System, may be compared with the fractional focal length markings of the Royal Photographic Society System, given below, and in comparing them it is useful to recall that U.S. 16 is the equivalent of R.P.S. $f/16$.

| Universal System | } | 4 | 8 | 16 | 32 | 64 | 128 |
| R.P.S. System | } | $f/8$ | $f/11$ | $f/16$ | $f/22$ | $f/32$ | $f/45$ |

Speed of Lens.—The speed or rapidity of a lens is often mentioned, and this depends on the value of its largest stop. A lens working at a full opening of $f/6$ is more rapid than one with $f/8$ for its largest stop; $f/4$ is still more rapid, because the larger the stop, the shorter, or more rapid, the exposure.

A landscape lens of normal focus for a given plate will not generally cover the plate or film sharply at a larger stop than $f/11$, and will therefore be rather slow. Straight lines coming near the edge of the field become more or less curved.

A rectilinear lens renders straight lines

without this distortion, and may cover the picture at f/8, so is more rapid, but it often requires stopping down to obtain good definition at the sides as well as in the centre.

A portrait lens may be constructed to work at f/4 or larger. It is therefore very rapid so as to be suitable for indoor use, but gives little depth without stopping down.

The anastigmat lens projects its image on a plane surface, instead of one that is saucer-shaped, so it will give a good definition all over the plate, even with a large stop, and as it is often as rapid as a good portrait lens, it is the best all-round type obtainable.

Lenses must be treated with great care and kept clean and bright, but not with hard rubbing. A gentle dusting with a clean, soft, camel-hair brush to remove all grit and dust should be enough. A very dirty lens should be moistened with methylated spirit, and carefully cleaned with a piece of old soft linen or chamois-leather.

Accessories.—The average photographic catalogue is packed with a great variety of accessories, but the absolute necessities for photography, developing and printing, are comparatively few in number, and depend to a great extent on the scope of the work undertaken. Many items that are convenient to have may be dispensed with or substitutes can be found, and necessary items may be obtained as progress is made. A guiding factor that will settle many points of equipment depends upon one's selection of negative material—plates or films.

Which are Better—Plates or Films?—In solving the problem as to whether plates or films should be used, it may be mentioned that both have their advantages and disadvantages; one or the other may be preferable in particular circumstances. There is a wide range of plates of excellent quality, varying in speed, but for general work the beginner should select a good brand of medium plate with a speed number of about 270. Nothing will be gained by attempting to use a much higher speed than this, and any below are unsuitable for general work, which includes instantaneous exposures.

Plates are, of course, more easily broken and are certainly more bulky to store away. For convenience of packing and carrying spares on holidays, with ease of daylight loading, the roll film is more suitable and immensely popular. It is light, small in bulk, not easily damaged.

Fig. 8

Modern films are capable of giving results as perfect in every way as those obtained with plates. About the same useful speeds are obtainable as with plates, and are orthochromatic, that is, sensitive to yellows and greens through being specially treated. Actual colours are not reproduced, but variations of tone, light or dark, corresponding to the appearance of the colours seen by the eye. The ordinary dry-plate does not do this so well, because the light-rays that affect the plate most are those in the violet group, with the result that, in a print, any bright yellow or red object appears much too dark, while blue and violet objects appear too light. This may not matter in some cases, but in others the result is so false that it is unsatisfactory. Even the plates and films treated with dye are far too sensitive to blue and violet rays, and to counteract this, colour-screens are used over the front of the lens. As longer exposures are then necessary, the colour-screens are given values such as a 3-times screen, and so on. A screen used with an orthochromatic plate will give much better results as regards tones of blue sky, green foliage, etc., and for flower-subjects or any objects where there are strong colour-contrasts. With a hand camera, longer exposures are not so

Fig. 9

convenient to manage, and only very pale screens are possible. All colour-corrected plates, orthochromatic, iso-chromatic, self-screen, and anti-screen, require more careful handling in the dark-room.

Films are almost free from the fault known as "halation," so common with glass plates. With the latter, very bright light will pass through the emulsion coating, and be reflected back by the glass on to the sensitive film, giving a spreading of the dense parts representing high lights. The windows in interiors give familiar examples of this; the light spreads all round over the wall round the window. If an object against a window is the item to be photographed, a backed plate should be used; but if the object can be moved into a good light, the camera should be used with its back to the window. In other cases, such as the interior of a church, where the object is a carved screen, or some special old tomb or other centre of interest, try to obtain another view-point where the camera will include the

wanted picture without facing towards a window.

Portrait Attachment.—Many useful lens attachments can be obtained for cameras having a more or less fixed focus. For portrait snaps and other photographs where sharp "close-ups" are required, an extra lens in a mount is slipped over the front of the camera lens, as indicated in Fig. 8. This will not in any way interfere with the operation of the camera or the exposure, but simply brings the subject into sharp focus at closer range. A similar form is also available which gives a "soft" result, instead of being critically sharp. This is known as the "diffusion portrait attachment"; a third model for pictorial work, landscapes, etc., gives a pleasing softness to the picture without loss of brilliancy.

Sky Filter.—The sky filter is another inexpensive and useful device. It is not an extra lens but is fitted and used in the same manner as the above attachments. The upper part of it is yellow. Its object is to reduce the effects of the glare of the sky while allowing the other portions of the picture to get full exposure, with the result that the delicate cloud detail is saved and recorded, often making all the difference between a commonplace snap and a real picture of the scene.

Exposure Meter.—No photographic enthusiast should be without an exposure meter as its use invariably saves disappointment.

One of the simplest exposure-calculators for the beginner to master and use is the Watkins Bee Meter (Fig. 9), which resembles a watch. Round the edge is marked a scale of numbers, and against these are other numbers on the dial part, which may be moved round. In place of the small seconds dial on a watch, there is a small circular opening under the glass, half covered with a tinted strip, and behind the open half is a piece of sensitive yellow-tinted paper. To measure the value of the light, the back of the meter is turned to bring a fresh surface of yellow paper into the opening, the meter is then held in the position of the object to be photographed, and exposed to the light falling on the subject. The time of this exposure must be taken in seconds—from a wrist-watch will do—from the instant of exposure until the yellow patch matches the standard-tinted half. We now have a figure for light-value which is set against the other figures on the meter, which include "H. & D." plate or film speeds, stops, and exposures, so that with the light-value figure in seconds set against the film-speed number, it is possible to read off, against the stop proposed to be used, the amount of exposure to give, or what stop to use with a selected film-speed and exposure. Full instructions are given with each type, and will save any guesswork. Their use often means a great saving in plates and films.

The Dark-Room.—Few people can command a properly-arranged dark-room, and by adopting certain processes, such as developing by tank, where time and temperature are the controlling factors, the dark-room may be dispensed with.

At the same time it is very convenient to have, for occasional use, some place from which daylight can be entirely shut out. A large cupboard or, better still, a bath-room, can generally be converted with a little trouble into a temporary dark-room. A wooden frame, covered with thick cardboard, plywood, or other convenient opaque material, can be made to fit over the window and secured by means of thumb-screws or wing-nuts for easy removal. A thick curtain may be hung over the door, and where electric light is available, special ruby bulbs for

photographic work are available for fitting into existing fittings, or into a specially-constructed dark-room lamp. A two-way adapter in the existing fitting is handy to have, as either a ruby lamp or an ordinary lamp can be used, as required. Electric-light bulbs can also be obtained in other colours for special purposes, such as dark green for panchromatic material, amber for gaslight papers, etc. With a little ingenuity, pails for waste, and jugs for fresh water can be used for dark-room operations, and the prolonged washing after fixing done elsewhere. A temporary dark-room is frequently required when transferring plates into a developing tank. Once this has been done, everything else can be carried through elsewhere.

Developing Dishes.—It is not advisable to use domestic utensils for photographic chemicals, unless they will be retained for that purpose only. A much better plan is to purchase articles designed for the purpose. For developing purposes bakelite, xylonite, and porcelain dishes are available in a variety of sizes, and those with grooves at the bottom should be chosen to permit of raising the plate easily. As far as possible any one dish should be used for the

Fig. 10

same purpose only. One used for hypo solution should never be employed for anything else. Dishes may be identified by colour, size, or material.

Glass measures are also necessary and should have a large base, and if the bottom is coated with white enamel it will be readily seen in the dim light of the dark-room.

A clear-reading thermometer will be required for time and temperature developing, and film-clips are handy on the ends of the films to provide a grip during developing if a dish is used, and a means of hanging them while drying. The illustration (Fig. 10) shows a collection of accessories and materials for carrying out the developing process.

Printing frames are supplied complete with glass, which is taken out if plates are used. These are made in a variety of sizes to suit standard sizes of films and plates. The backs of such frames generally consist of two sections hinged together and held in position by spring clips. This feature enables part of the back to be opened and the print to be inspected occasionally during the printing process.

Chemicals.—Practically all the necessary chemicals are obtainable, ready made up, in the form of tablets, solutions and powders that only need dissolving in a stated quantity of water to make developers, toners, intensifiers, etc. Hypo solution made from crystals is required for "fixing" developed plates, films and printing papers. The real action of hypo is to facilitate the removal of the silver salts from such parts of the coating of the film or plate as have been unaffected by light-action and development. To form the image, perhaps only one-quarter of the silver has been used; the remainder must be removed entirely from the gelatine or future exposure to light will ruin the negative. The same happens with printing-papers; the silver salts not darkened according to the lights and shades of the negative must be cleared, otherwise the print will fade.

Developing.—A plate or film that has been exposed in the camera shows no visible change, but the light admitted through the lens, even for the instant during which the shutter flicked open, has actually had an influence on the sensitive silver salts in the gelatine. Some of these have to be reduced to a state of metallic silver by means of a suitable solution, called a "developer." The metallic particles produced are more or less numerous in proportion to the light-action, so that the parts on which most light has fallen show the greatest density, while others show less, and perhaps some will show none at all. The lights and darks are therefore the reverse of those in the subject photographed, and the image is a negative one.

The aim in making a negative is to obtain the same proportions of light and shade contrasts as in the subject, so that they may be reproduced accurately in the picture printed on paper from the negative. This depends to a great extent on the exposure given, but development also plays an important part. If this process is not carried far enough, there will not be sufficient contrast in the results; if too prolonged, the negative will be dense, the contrasts harsh, and printing will take longer.

There are so many different developers, all giving good results, that it may seem difficult to choose a particular one. The actual one chosen is of less importance than how it is used. With a given plate or film, one will act quickly at first, another brings out the first signs of the image very slowly, and then makes up density quickly, while a third will work with more even progress throughout. It is therefore unwise to change from one kind to another, and much better to keep to one so that its particular working can be understood and used to the best advantage. Suitable developers and strengths will be found mentioned in the papers with each packet of plates or films. This information, based on the makers' experience, will give the

Fig. 11

beginner something dependable to start with.

The main factors which govern development are: The kind of plate or film used; the character of the negative required; the composition and strength of the developer; the temperature at which it is used. In general, development becomes prolonged when the developer is diluted or weakened with previous use; when the temperature is low; when the plate or film is of high speed, and when considerable density or contrast are required. Reverse conditions shorten the process.

In all cases it is important to know when to stop development; and this is simplified by using the same brand of plate or film, and the same developer, and in the correct proportions, as stated by the makers. Guess-work in making up solutions for use, even from powders, tablets or prepared solutions will not do, and the same applies to the fixing bath. The very worst way is to make up a solution, just before it is required, by putting an unknown quantity of developer or fixing crystals into an unmeasured amount of water and trusting to chance. It may be too strong or too weak to do its work. As the ingredients mix, the temperature falls, which prolongs the development. Blisters and frills are formed when the gelatine comes into contact with solutions too warm, and

when transferred from a liquid of one temperature to one of another.

A very easy and safe system of development is the "time and temperature" method. Makers of proprietary developers generally include a table with these goods showing the time a normally-exposed negative should be left in the solution, according to its temperature, which is taken by inserting a thermometer into the dish or tank before adding the plates or films. For developing plates in a dish in the dark-room, the plates are usually treated singly, although it is possible to manipulate more if a large dish is available, as shown in Fig. 11. Place the plate, film-side (dull) up, in a clean dish, and have the developer ready in a beaker or a large measure. If it has been prepared some time ahead and well stirred, it will have taken the same temperature as that of the dark-room. Note the thermometer reading, consult the table in the instructions, and pour or flood the developer over the plate in such a manner that all the surface is covered at once. Cover the dish with a piece of cardboard and rock it gently

Fig. 12

for the time specified, without any examination. Greater or less contrast can be secured by varying the time. The plate must then be quickly removed from the developing dish, rinsed for a moment or two in clean cold water, immersed in the hypo bath and kept there until all traces of the yellowish tint of the film has entirely disappeared when seen from the back. The next procedure consists in getting rid of the hypo from the plate by "washing" it in clean water.

Fig. 13

Developing Tanks to hold six plates at once can be used in the same manner after being filled in the dark-room. The advantage of the tank method is that the operations of developing, rinsing, and fixing can be done in daylight, as the tank, when shut, is light-tight. After the prescribed time, the developer is drained off and water run through to rinse the plates. The fixing solution is poured in and allowed to remain for a certain time and then drained off. The final washing, which can be carried out in daylight, is most important. The plates must not be left in a heap at the bottom of the dish, bath or bowl used, because, normally, the hypo oozes out of the gelatine and falls to the bottom, and it obviously cannot do so if the surfaces are together. A proper washing-tank with a rack should be used. This appliance has a free space between each vertical division and keeps the plates off the bottom. The tank is designed so that the flow of water passes through and not against and round the end plates. Complete washing, be it said, does not depend upon the quantity of water used, but the correct use of a steady, ever-changing stream. If a rack only is used, it should be lifted out at frequent intervals, the bowl emptied, rinsed, filled and the rack replaced.

Roll Films may be developed by hand by holding the two ends and "see-sawing" it through a dish of developer, as illustrated in Fig. 12, making sure that all the surface is covered as quickly as possible. It will be a great help if the film is dipped through a dish of water before being placed in the developer. As the negatives are in one long length, this may prove a messy method, and involves at least some portion being out of the solution, and possible direct exposure to the dark-room light. Those who use roll films will find a special film-developing tank a boon, using the temperature and time method as already described. When washing and drying films it must be remembered that both sides must be protected against scratches. Fig. 13 shows a simple method of suspending roll films for drying. A paper clip is fastened to a shelf and grips the upper end of the film, while a similar clip at the bottom acts as a weight and prevents the film curling up.

Intensification and Reduction.—If

the exposure has been cut down to such an extent that the light-action was insufficient to do the necessary work—a common fault with beginners—nothing can be done in development to compensate for it. Some improvement may be possible in some cases, but the result will never be as good as it would have been with correct exposure. On the other hand, if the exposure has been longer than necessary, the character of the negative may, to a certain extent, be altered, and the resulting print be quite satisfactory.

A thin negative, that is, one in which the image is weak, has the densest parts not sufficiently opaque to keep the highlights bright when printing, say, on self-toning paper. A print is obtained quickly, but the picture is dull and looks "washed-out."

A strong negative is the reverse; it has too much density. Such a negative will take a long time to print, and if very dense in parts, and very clear in others, the prints will be hard and full of contrasts.

Papers are made, both for daylight and for artificial light printing, to suit negatives that are either too weak or too strong, so that it is possible, to some extent, to suit the paper to the negative, but it follows that the negative itself must be treated to fit it for use.

A negative with plenty of detail, but with the image thin and lacking in density, may be treated with a ready-prepared intensifier. It is first soaked for about half an hour and then bleached in a bleaching solution till the whole image is changed to a yellow colour. When the change is complete, it is put to wash until all the stain has been removed and there is no trace of yellow in the washing water. The negative is then re-developed in any developer that gives a clean, black image, but not pyro in any form. The negative is then well

washed and dried in the usual way. The whole process may be repeated if found still lacking in strength, and can be carried out in daylight.

A fogged negative can be cleared by first soaking it in water and then placing it in a bath of stock hypo (not acid-hypo) mixed with an equal quantity of water. A crystal of potassium ferricyanide (poison) is placed in this and stirred till the solution is a very pale yellow, when the crystal is taken out. The solution is poured over the soaked plate and the dish rocked. The action is rapid and must be watched by holding the plate up to the light, and just *before* sufficient clearing has taken place the negative must be quickly rinsed, and then thoroughly washed. Take it out in good time as the action continues for a time and the delicate detail may be lost.

A very dense negative may also be due to over-development and can be restored to the condition it would have been in had development been stopped at the proper time. A stock reducer solution may be kept for these cases. The defective negative should be soaked in water before being placed in this bath. When the bright colour of the solution changes it should be poured off and fresh applied, until the action has proceeded far enough. Then the negative is quickly rinsed, and washed by using two or three changes of water only, as prolonged washing in this case is detrimental.

Printing by Daylight.—Whatever light is used for making prints with the paper in close contact with the negative, a printing frame is required, and for daylight work, more than one will maintain a steady flow of prints ready for fixing. Care should be taken when examining the frames that the fingers are not greasy or damp with hypo solution, otherwise finger-marks will spoil the paper. The best paper for the beginner to start with is that known as "self-toning." The printing is carried on to a deeper shade than required for the finished print because it will become much lighter during the fixing. Only a hypo bath is required for the operation, and should be made up to the proportions given in the printed instructions in the wrapper containing the paper. Thorough final washing is necessary, keeping the pieces clear of the bottom of the bowl where all the hypo falls, as with negatives.

Gaslight Printing.— "Gaslight" paper is the simplest and most suitable for making prints in the evenings, and all the operations can be carried out in an ordinary room illuminated by gaslight or other artificial light.

Apart from certain grades of surface, matte, glossy, etc., there are three types to suit various kinds of negative. For thin negatives one would use a vigorous grade paper; then there is the medium for general work, and the soft.

The paper must be protected from the light, and only one sheet taken out at a time for use. Load the frame and do the developing in a red or a yellow light.

The exposure is made close to the light but not too near, otherwise the lighting will not be evenly spread over the frame. Instructions as to exposure will be found in the packet containing the paper.

Special developers are to be obtained for use with gaslight paper, and as most of them can be used only once, it is better to use a dish only large enough to take a sufficient quantity of solution to flood the whole surface at once when it is poured over.

The fixing bath should be larger, to hold plenty of hypo and give room to move the prints about. Acid-hypo is usually advised as it instantly stops development and prevents stains.

It is particularly necessary to get the exposure for printing correct within very narrow limits. If this can be done, the print will develop rapidly to just the right depth, when it can be removed, rinsed quickly in clean water, and placed in the fixing bath, where it must be kept moving for a time. It is useless to take an over-exposed print from the developer to prevent it becoming too dark, or to leave an under-exposed print in longer to try and strengthen it, Correct exposure alone will give the desired results.

PREPARING WORKING DRAWINGS

M<small>ANY</small> amateurs who take up carpentry and other forms of woodwork, and metal-work also, are often at a loss when called upon to work from a drawing, and are unable to "read" or clearly understand a sketch or scale working drawing to the extent that they are able to visualise the shape and proportions of the finished piece or complete article.

This difficulty becomes more real when they start to measure up for making out a list of materials required, and when marking off pieces ready for cutting. Much material is thus often wasted, and more pieces are liable to be cut incorrectly when working out an idea straight on to the wood, without making even a rough sketch first.

If a dimensioned drawing can be prepared first and checked, it will show if the proposed construction is practical or possible, especially when making something to fit into a given space which cannot be altered, or if moving parts are used.

It sometimes happens that certain parts may be beyond the skill of the worker, or suitable appliances may not be available in his workshop for him to make these for himself, so they must be ordered from an outside source; in such cases even a rough sketch is of great service to make clear to others what is required.

Draughtsmanship is really very much easier than the average home worker imagines. Since the earliest times,

before any form of word-language was spoken, man has expressed his thoughts and requirements, and even written the history of his life and times, by means of drawings. The Egyptian work in our museums is a familiar example of this, and it is interesting to note how they made use of accurately marked squares when preparing a panel, in order to preserve the proportions of the human and other figures cut in the stone. Enlarging and reducing were carried out by making the squares larger or smaller. With the human figure, certain proportions were always kept the same, for example, the foot was always made one unit in length, no matter how large or small the figure. This method has its parallel in the use of squared paper for sketches and small drawings, a regular practice in large engineering workshops to-day. The professional draughtsman's work consists of more than actual drawing. There are stresses and strains, mechanical movements, methods of construction and other technical problems to solve which need not be gone into here. The home worker will obtain a knowledge of methods of construction connected with his hobby by the frequent study of existing articles and drawings, and develop the ability to think in the graphic language, to visualise shape and size and the best methods of completing the work with the tools at his disposal.

Instruments and Materials.—The study of drawings requires the making of them, and for this purpose equipment of some kind is necessary. Many of the instruments used by the professional draughtsman are expensive, but there is no need for the amateur to go to so much expense. Only a simple collection of drawing instruments is necessary, and we suggest the following:

Pair of dividers about 6 in. long.

Pair of compasses about 7 in. long, with pencil and pen points for drawing.

Pair of pencil-bows for very small circles.

45° and 60° set-squares. Transparent celluloid.

Protractor for angles, circular or semi-circular.

India-rubber. HB and 3H or 4H pencils. Small drawing-pins.

Cardboard or wood scales.

Drawing-board and tee-square.

A useful size of drawing-board is the Imperial (23 in. by 31 in.), but the size should be according to the kind of work to be done.

Drawing-boards.—The best quality "Engineer's" drawing-board is made of selected dry pine, with raised ebony edge at the left-hand side for the tee-square. The back is grooved and fitted with hardwood battens having brass slots for the screws, to allow for expansion and contraction.

A less expensive type, known as "Students'" boards, are made of ply-wood, or solid wood panel with clamped ends. The standard sizes of drawing-boards to correspond with sheet drawing-papers are:

16 in. by 23 in.	29 in. by 42 in.
23 in. by 31 in.	32 in. by 54 in.

A very serviceable board can be made out of a large piece of multi-ply wood about ½ in. or more thick. It can be cut to any size to suit individual requirements, and fitted with parallel or taper battens, as shown in Fig. 1. The advan-

HEADS OF WOOD SCREWS SUNK BELOW SURFACE & COVERED WITH PLASTIC WOOD

48"x 30"

1" to 1¼" thick

6"

½"

Fig. 1

tage of making one's own board is—provided that the board is made larger at first to allow for it—that the sides can be reduced in size when the corners become very pitted and broken, due to the small holes made by the drawing pins. The new edge is trued up for the tee-square to slide along. Quite a lot of work can be done before this becomes necessary, and a board constructed on these lines will give more or less constant use for several years.

It is very helpful to have a work table on which to rest the drawing-board firmly while drawings are being made. A very convenient drafting table can be made as shown in Fig. 2. This is constructed from a suitable-sized kitchen table which can usually be purchased for a very small sum at most auction sales. The whole of the top is removed and fitted with strengthening battens at the back, and re-fixed to the front edge of the frame with stout hinges to enable the top to be tilted at the back to any desired angle. A batten fixed along the front edge prevents the drawing-board from sliding off, while an adjustable arm at each side, as shown in the sketch, keeps the top at the desired angle. The most comfortable angle for general work is 15°.

Tee-squares.—The tee-square (Fig. 3) must be as long as the board, and the type with a taper blade is much steadier to use than a parallel one. They may be obtained in pearwood, and are inexpensive. A better quality instrument has a body of polished mahogany with an ebony working edge. Some tee-squares are fitted with transparent celluloid edges, but they are liable to become damaged with the slightest knock. As this edge is used to produce straight, horizontal lines, and to form a base along which the set-squares are moved and held while drawing vertical lines and angles, it is important that the edge and stock are treated with all possible care.

round the blade at the stock end, with a slight amount of tension to keep it in place. Fig. 4 shows how a tee-square is held and used.

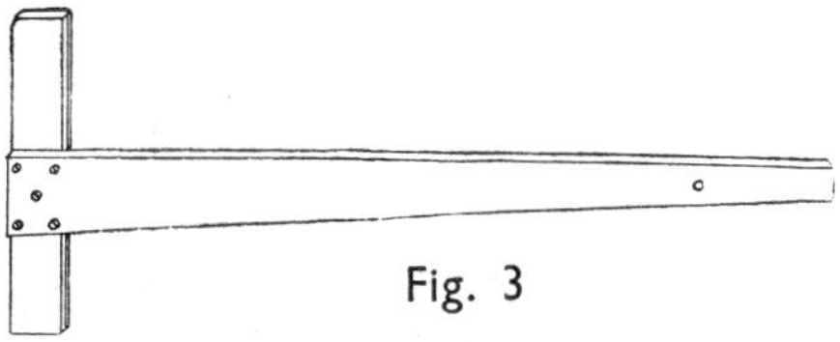

Set-Squares.—Transparent celluloid set-squares are the most serviceable, because they do not warp like the cheaper pearwood ones, and the transparency enables the draughtsman to see the lines of the drawing underneath. The square is used along the tee-square edge. Apart from forming a perfect edge along which to draw vertical lines at right-angles to the tee-square blade, one of the set-squares has its sides cut to an angle of 45°, as shown at A in Fig. 5, and the other square has an edge at 60°, as at B. The latter, when used with its long edge on the tee-square, also gives an angle of 30°. As this is the set-square with the longest edge, it is used a great deal for projecting views from others above or below, such as laying out a plan view from an elevation.

Fig. 2

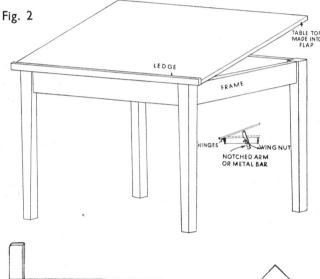

Fig. 3

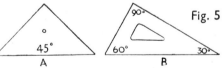

Fig. 5

45°
A

90°
60°
30°
B

Owing to its polished surface and size, a tee-square has a tendency to slide down a sloping board the moment it is left free, and although various expensive attachments have been brought out to prevent this, they are all a great hindrance to quick, free movements. The most effective method of preventing sliding, yet one that will keep the square free for instant movement, is to fit a simple rubber band about ⅛ in. wide

Adjustable Set-Squares.—There are two or three patterns of adjustable set-squares. One of these would take the place of the usual 45° and 60° squares, and also a protractor. The advantage of such an instrument is that it can be set quickly to any required angle. An ivory-grained scale is fully divided in half-degrees from 0° to 45° one way, and then reads back to 90°, and is locked firm at any point by means of a simple milled nut.

Fig. 4

French Curves.—French curves are used for the neat drawing of curves which cannot be struck with compasses. There is a large variety of transparent shapes similar to that illustrated at A in Fig. 6. The method of using them is shown at B, where a reverse curve has to be drawn through 7 points. Apart from odd curves in general drawing, electrical experimenters will find such curves of great assistance when plotting curves on graphs similar to those giving characteristics of radio valves, etc.

Scales.—On most drawings it is advisable to work to the largest size possible, but it frequently happens that on a large assembly of parts, or big details, the drawing cannot be made the same size as the finished article, so the drawing is made half-size, quarter-size, or one-eighth full-size. Smaller scales are used for plans of buildings, but for carpentry or mechanical details it is advisable not to work to a smaller scale than eighth full-size, that is, $1\frac{1}{2}$ in. to the foot. For full-size details a thin steel rule, 12 in. long, will give excellent service for years, and if kept clean will never leave dirty marks on the paper. On such a rule the whole of the top edge is usually fully divided into sixteenths. The bottom edge is fully divided into thirty-seconds up to the 3-in. mark, and sixty-fourths are

given in the first half of the fourth inch; the remainder of the bottom edge being divided in eighths.

Scales are obtainable in a variety of patterns with different arrangements of divisions accurately divided on flat or oval section boxwood. The type best suited for any drawing is that which is the clearest to read, even if this means purchasing one or two extra scales to obtain the required range. Some types of scales have two scales on each edge, front and back, making eight in all. Such scales should be avoided by the amateur, as their use is likely to lead to confusion and incorrect laying out of dimensions.

For amateur use there is, perhaps, nothing better than scales printed on varnished cardboard. These scales are sold in sets of eight each measuring 1 ft. Each strip has two scales, one on each front edge only, thus providing 16 variations of size. The markings are as follows:

Scale A.   Full-size and half-size.
  ,,   B.   4 in. to 1 ft., and 2 in. to 1 ft.
  ,,   C.   3 in. to 1 ft, and $1\frac{1}{2}$ in. to 1 ft.
  ,,   D.   1 in. to 1 ft., and $\frac{1}{2}$ in. to 1 ft.
  ,,   E. $\frac{3}{4}$ in. to 1 ft., and $\frac{3}{8}$ in. to 1 ft.
  ,,   F. $\frac{1}{3}$ in. to 1 ft., and $\frac{1}{6}$ in. to 1 ft.
  ,,   G. $\frac{1}{4}$ in. to 1 ft., and $\frac{1}{8}$ in. to 1 ft.
  ,,   H. $\frac{1}{5}$ in. to 1 ft., and $\frac{1}{10}$ in. to 1 ft.

Drawing Instruments.—Dividers, compasses and bows may be purchased as a complete set in a case, but this is not recommended as such sets often include unwanted items, or at least some which may be done without. A much better plan is to acquire the instruments separately as they can be afforded, and it is not a difficult matter to make a suitable case and to line it with velvet or similar material, if one is felt to be necessary. A great saving in cost is effected by obtaining good quality re-conditioned instruments from reliable factors who undertake repair work of this kind. Such instruments are in sound working condition, and there need be no doubts about their accuracy and the long service they will give.

A typical half-set of drawing instruments consists of a compass fitted with needle-points to save making large holes in the paper, divider-point, pencil and ink pen-points, and lengthening bar. The latter is fixed into the compass and then either the pen or pencil point, as required, which enables large circles to be drawn. For the ordinary run of work the pen or pencil-point is inserted in the compass without the bar. Both legs are jointed so that the instrument may be set correctly with both points vertical for use. Dividers, if required, are more convenient as a separate instru-

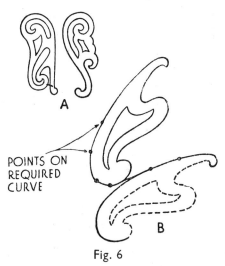

POINTS ON
REQUIRED
CURVE

Fig. 6

ment and certainly save repeated changing of the compass points.

It is advisable to examine the knee-joints to see whether they open and bend uniformly, and that these and the top joint do not move too freely. A certain amount of stiffness is essential, otherwise there will be unwanted movement while the instruments are being used and,

perhaps, more than one circle will be the result. Fig. 7 shows the correct method of using compasses.

Spring Bow Compasses.—Spring bows, for making small circles, are usually made in sets of three, either with side adjustment or centre adjustment, as

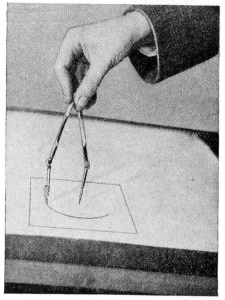

Fig. 7

pen, pencil, and dividers, but separate ones may be obtained. They are amongst the most convenient instruments one can possess, as it is impossible to do any satisfactory work without bows for very small circles, especially if the draughtsman is an amateur engineer.

Drawing Pens.—Special pens are made for inking-in pencil drawings and making ink tracings, and of the various designs, those with a hinged blade are best for cleaning and resetting. The pen is sent out with the points finished ready for use, but after prolonged use the points require resetting, because, although made of tempered steel, there is a certain amount of wear, and the pen will not produce clear or fine lines.

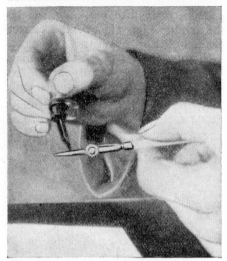

Fig. 8

The thickness of the line is adjusted by means of a set-screw, which opens or closes the small space between the blades, thus allowing more or less ink to flow as the case may be. Only a small quantity of ink should be placed between the blades, otherwise it may drop and make a blot or run from the edge on to the tee- or set-squares and be spread over a large area of drawing. Prepared waterproof drawing-ink is supplied in bottles with a piece of quill fixed in the cork for dipping into the ink when filling a pen. Fig. 8 shows the method of filling the pen, while Fig. 9 shows how the pen is used.

Pencils.—Drawing pencils are made in a variety of degrees of hardness, ranging from B, which has a soft lead, to 8H, which is very hard.

The best degree to use is more or less a matter of personal choice, but a lot no doubt depends upon the kind of paper employed, and amount of pressure used. It is just a question of finding a suitable grade of lead that will give the clearest, blackest line without requiring re-sharpening too often. An HB, F, or H with ordinary point is suitable for

sketching, making notes, and printing dimensions and notes on the drawing. For laying out the first pencil work a 4H or 6H will give a clear, fine line, easy to rub out if not drawn in too heavily, as a hard pencil produces quite a groove in the paper, which, of course, cannot be removed. When the drawing is finished and all corrections have been made, it is usual to go over the lines with a 2H or 3H pencil to darken the lines, but with practice and care, and by keeping the pencil point sharpened in the correct manner, it is possible to make a large drawing throughout with only one grade of pencil, by altering the pressure from light to heavy, according to whether one is making a trial line or a finished one, known to be correct. Practice alone will solve many of these small problems. A pencil drawing that is to be inked in needs no lining in provided the original pencil lines are clear and correct.

Short ends of pencils are useful when cut open, as they provide suitable pieces of lead for use in the compasses and bows.

Fig. 9

When sharpening a drawing pencil, enough wood should be removed to expose about $\frac{1}{4}$ in. to $\frac{3}{8}$ in. of lead. This is sharpened to a chisel point on a small 4-in. or 6-in. smooth file or a piece of fine glass-paper, kept for that purpose;

the corners are just eased off to save cutting the paper. This shape of end, if given an occasional touch on the file, will be found to produce fine lines without wearing thicker, for long periods of use. A chisel-shaped point is also much easier to use along the tee- and set-square edges. This cannot be done properly with an ordinary conical point, even if kept sharp with a pencil-sharpener. Fig. 10 shows a pencil correctly sharpened.

India-Rubbers. — Even the best draughtsmen make mistakes, so do not spare the use of a piece of rubber in order to get the drawing correct. On the other hand, do without it as much as possible because it will remove a certain amount of sur-face from the paper. These patches pick up the dust and blacklead from the drawn lines and give a patchy, dirty appearance to the paper. One piece of hard, green eraser and a piece of soft will answer all requirements, while for cleaning up a drawing that has been inked in, "Art Gum," a soft, almost transparent rubber, is the best. An erasing shield is also of great service and may be home-made from a piece of thin celluloid. Incidentally, a rubber should be used in one direction only.

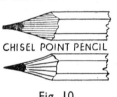

CHISEL POINT PENCIL

Fig. 10

Drawing Paper.—With regard to a suitable drawing paper, the most econo-mical practice is to select the paper according to the nature of the job in hand. Whatman paper is often recom-mended to beginners, regardless of cost, but is more suitable for architects for drawings that are to be coloured. Cartridge paper is quite suitable for all general requirements, provided it will take drawing-ink without running, which often happens on cheap paper.

"Imperial" size (30 × 22) is about 1½d. or 2d. per sheet, and will take ink and colour quite well. Thinner white paper, known as "Detail," is sold in rolls and may be cut for large or small jobs as required.

To Copy a Drawing, a sheet of trans-parent tracing paper is pinned over the pencil drawing and the lines copied through, using the instruments as for the original. Many grades of tracing paper are subject to patches of greasiness, which makes ink-work difficult, and even pencil does not show plainly on these parts. It is also very liable to crack and tear.

A very serviceable paper for all-round use is the type of greaseproof paper used by butchers for wrapping purposes. It has a dull, unglazed surface on both sides, is easy to work on with almost any grade of pencil, will take drawing-ink without running, and is tough enough to stand a good deal of rough handling. Being nearly transparent it may be used for tracings. This is also an advantage when drawing out a design where the main outline of the assembly is repeated on another sheet for detailing. A second sheet may be fixed over the first, and the required parts traced, thus saving measuring and plotting out a second time. The sheets are about 30 in. by 20 in., and can be obtained from any large stationers, in the unfolded state. Similar paper is sold folded, but this is not suitable. As it is not expensive (usually 4d. per quire of 24 sheets) it is very suitable for home workshop use, and for roughing-out ideas and designs as a preliminary to making more elaborate drawings either on the same, or better paper.

Making a Drawing and Using Instruments.—The necessary equip-ment having been described, it is advisable for the beginner to obtain some varied practice on details before proceeding with complete jobs. In elementary work, as taught in schools, much of the time in the early stages is devoted to geometrical constructions and the projections of views of cubes, cones and prisms, but as space does not permit this to be shown here, we will endeavour to deal with these points as they appear in actual work, because most objects are a combination of the regular solids in some form or the other, and the beginner will be drawing real parts from the first,

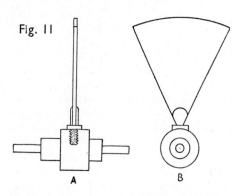

Fig. 11

A   B

which is always more interesting than plain cylinders, cones and cubes.

Preparing the Board.—Before starting operations of a practical nature it is advisable to fix a full-size sheet of cartridge drawing paper on the board under the one to be worked upon. This backsheet keeps the board clean and also makes a very substantial protection against the small drawing-pin holes that soon develop all over the board and spoil lines as the pencil slips into them.

One edge of the work sheet is placed parallel with the left-hand edge of the board and a small drawing-pin inserted in the top left-hand corner, then one in the bottom corner. Stretch or smooth the paper carefully and pin the other corners. Other pins half-way along top and bottom may be used if the sheet is a large one.

Dust the tee-square; rub the set-squares on smooth paper until they leave no mark, and they are ready for use. Sharpen the pencils away from the board and have everything handy. If the drawing is likely to be removed from the board several times, a "setting-up" line at the two extremes of the sheet will be of assistance.

A draughtsman's earliest efforts usually have a dirty appearance, but much of this can be avoided by keeping the hands clean, and wiping them constantly with a clean duster to remove perspiration. Wipe the tee- and set-squares at frequent intervals to remove the particles of blacklead dust picked up from the pencil lines, and dust everything after an interval, away from the board. This will soon become a natural habit and only noticeable by the unsullied drawings produced.

Arrangement of Views.—In arranging the views, the best practice, at first, is to make full-size drawings of simple pieces found about the workshop and home, such as the various joints in woodwork, a small bolt, washer, nut, simple tools, wireless parts, etc.

If possible, use a thin steel rule, 12 in. long, with $\frac{1}{4}$-in., $\frac{1}{8}$-in., and $\frac{1}{16}$-in. divisions, to measure the articles with; make a sketch, putting in all the dimensions, and use the sketch to work from when making the drawing.

In many cases a single view is not enough in which to show all the details of shape and dimensions. The piece shown in Fig. 11 (A) has another piece fixed to it, and in this view it appears to be a thin pin with a larger screwed end. It is only by reference to both views (B) that we see that this pin is a wedge-shaped fin of metal with a screwed end. Two views at least would also be necessary for the tenoned end on a piece of timber (Fig. 12). The second view shows the thickness, and a plan view is the clearest. This kind of detail lends itself to treatment in another manner, and combines two views in one illustration, simple to grasp in its detail, and being drawn to scale, is in correct proportion. A photograph shows a part in perspective, and the lines taper off into

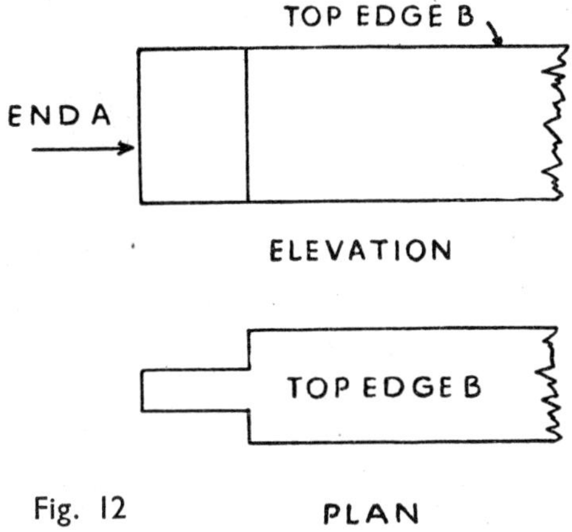

TOP EDGE B

END A

ELEVATION

TOP EDGE B

Fig. 12   PLAN

the distance. The modified form of perspective is called isometric projection, and is a conventional method of drawing used to obviate two or even three views by making a picture of the piece it is desired to represent. It is used chiefly in sketching parts when taking particulars from any device, for reproduction as working drawings later. The object is presented cornerwise to the observer, and the sides are drawn at 30° from the horizontal. Fig. 13 shows a piece of timber cut at the end; it is usual to make the lines equal to the correct lengths for scaling purposes. The lines of the top face and side are at the same correct width and depth at the front and at the back. Circular holes and cylindrical surfaces are difficult to show in this form of projection, because they assume an elliptical form, so the isometric drawing is more suited to views of objects without curves and circles, and is only used by engineers in freehand sketches.

For circular parts, "oblique projection" is more suitable because one face or end view may be drawn exactly as an ordinary elevation, a circular end retains its true shape, and compasses may be used for all circles. The side lines are often extended to one-half or one-third the scale of the front face, but may be made true length if desired. The oblique lines are at an angle of 45°, but it

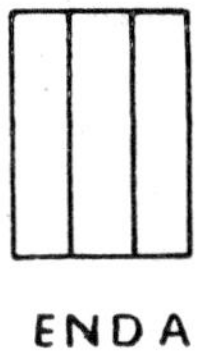

END A

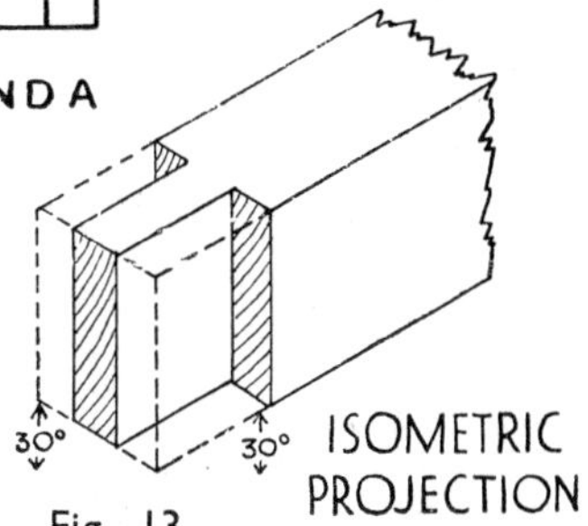

ISOMETRIC PROJECTION

30° 30°

Fig. 13

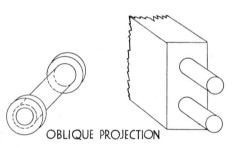

OBLIQUE PROJECTION

Fig. 14

is not essential to adhere firmly to this angle if more or less slope gives a better effect. Drawings in oblique projection are illustrated at Fig. 14.

View Conventions.—Every mechanical drawing—that is, one made with the use of instruments—will be found to consist of several "views," each sighted from a different direction. Few objects can be adequately represented in one view, because there are three dimensions to every solid, namely: length, breadth,

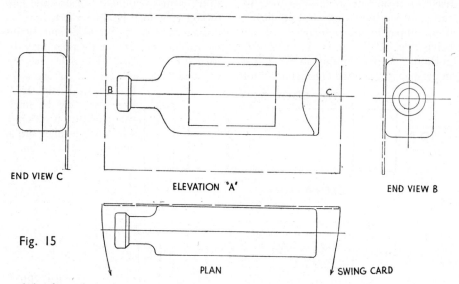

END VIEW C

ELEVATION "A'

END VIEW B

Fig. 15

PLAN

SWING CARD

and depth, and any one view will always contain two of these three dimensions; thus there must be at least two views to determine fully the shape of the piece.

For an example, take an ordinary medicine bottle, fixed on a piece of thick card, as shown in Fig. 15. Now stand the card on edge directly in front of you and the plain elevation A will be seen. Still keeping the same view-point, and using the bottom right-hand corner of the card as a pivot, swing the card round to the right so that when the edge is in a direct line, i.e. the card at right-angles to its first position, the cork end of the bottle is seen as at end view B. The card is now replaced in its original position, and to see the true end view of the bottom of the bottle, the card must be turned to the left, using the bottom left-hand corner as the pivot point. This gives view C. Return the card again to the first position and swing the top edge forwards until it is in line with the eyes, this gives a plan view as distinct from the elevation. The same plan

view would be seen if the observer stood over the card looking down on the top edge. In a correct working drawing of this bottle it would, of course, be shown in the most usual position, that is, with the cork end as the top, the labelled face as the front, and the narrow face as the side, but as a convenient object, with which to illustrate the viewing of unlike ends, it served the purpose better placed in the manner shown.

Fig. 16 shows four views of a wooden fretting vee. They are correct as regards projection, but the end view A, although correct, is unnecessary because it does not convey, even if dimensioned, as much information as the plan view, which gives the position of the two holes, the shape of the "Vee" end, and the extent of the channel for the clamp used to fix it to the work bench. A view of the other end is essential because it gives the width and depth of the channel, the overall width, and thickness of the piece. The long edge view above the plan shows, by means of dotted lines, that the holes pass right through the piece. This saves making a sectional view.

Sectional views often render other views unnecessary, particularly where many of the parts are cylindrical, as in the assembly (Fig. 17). In such views, shafts, spindles, bolts, keys, nuts, etc., are not sectioned, for greater clearness, and if there is any special feature at any

to the end viewed, and the rules of projection illustrated by the bottle in Fig. 15. The *plan* shows horizontal faces by looking downward vertically. This corresponds to a "bird's-eye view," and as regards a house would show the roof as seen from directly above the house, but this outside view of the roof is not always shown on building drawings unless the

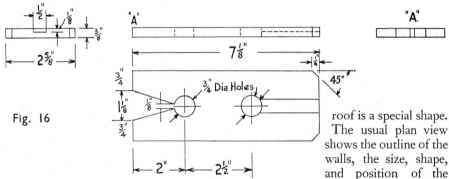

Fig. 16

roof is a special shape. The usual plan view shows the outline of the walls, the size, shape, and position of the

point, such as a drilled and counterbored hole, it may be shown by full lines and shaded round with section lines, as shown.

Generally, the views are understood as follows: The *elevation* shows the vertical faces by looking at the object horizontally, but at its widest and most important face, for example, the front of a house. *End elevations* and *side elevations* show vertical faces, but at right-angles horizontally to the elevation, projected to the left or right according

various rooms, and the position of the doors, windows and fireplaces, etc., as would be seen if it were possible to lift the top part of the building clear. Such a view is actually a section, or "sectional plan," but would be marked: "Ground floor plan" or "First floor plan," according to position. Similarly, a back view of a house would be marked "Back or Rear Elevation."

It may be required to show a view looking at the underside of a piece, as well as the usual plan: this is usually

Fig. 17

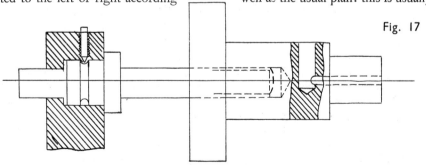

USE OF PART SECTION ROUND SMALL **DETAIL** SHAFT NOT SECTIONED

termed a *bottom view* or *underneath view* or *plan,* and Fig. 18 is a typical case, where a piece of metal has to be drilled and machined on both faces in order that

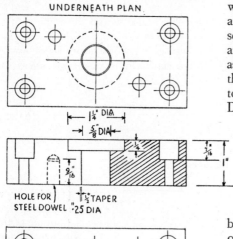

PLAN

Fig. 18

it may be fixed to a machine, and at the same time have other pieces fixed to its top surface.

Use of Breaks and Section Lines.— Long objects, even when drawn to a small scale, need not be shown full length if only the ends or certain points require certain operations performed upon them, while the remainder of the length between is left plain or as cut. To save space, conventional lines are drawn to indicate a break in the length, and the ends only, or parts calling for special note, are detailed. In Fig. 19 we have a length of pipe 12 ft. long, threaded at both ends for a specified distance, and fitted with two "Tee pieces" at certain distances from one end. To avoid

drawing a long length of plain tube or pipe, rod, timber, etc., the lines are broken as shown in Fig. 20.

As very few drawings can be produced without sections, it is customary to show any piece cut by a section plane by a series of lines "cross hatched" at an angle of 45°. Contiguous pieces should as far as possible be sectioned so that the lines come in the opposite direction to distinguish one part from another. Different materials are indicated by various forms of sectioning, as in Fig. 21, but as there are no standardised rules about this and the sectioning for brass in one engineering works may be the same as used elsewhere to indicate cast iron, the material required should always be specified on the drawing. The angle of the hatching may also be changed to 30° or 60° if, by so doing, confusion of sections is avoided.

Colours for Drawings.—It was a common practice at one time to use different colours to indicate various

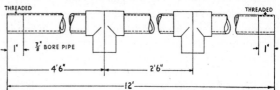

Fig. 19

materials, but this has died out owing to lack of time and mistakes involved. It is still used on occasion for special show drawings, and by architects. A list of suitable water-colours is given here for those who may care to use them, as it is no uncommon thing to find amateur craftsmen who, for some reason or other, are unable to follow the practical constructional features of their favourite hobby for a time, but are able, through the medium of making drawings, to keep alive their interest, to add to their store of knowledge, and to derive much pleasure from pencil and paper only, by planning and detailing various jobs, each in all its stages to complete assembly, thus creating on the drawing-board those things that they are unable to make at the moment, but hope to do later. Even if these plans never take concrete shape the time is regarded as well spent.

Colours Used on Drawings

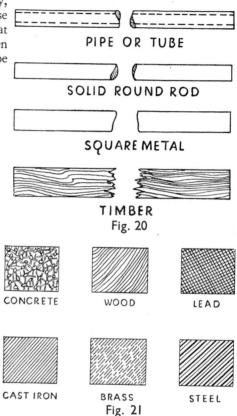

PIPE OR TUBE

SOLID ROUND ROD

SQUARE METAL

TIMBER
Fig. 20

CONCRETE   WOOD   LEAD

CAST IRON   BRASS   STEEL
Fig. 21

Material	Water Colour
BRICKWORK	
Elevations .	Yellow Ochre.
Sections .	Crimson Lake.
STONEWORK	
Elevations .	Light wash of Sepia.
Sections .	Dark wash of Sepia.
PLASTER	
Elevations .	Light Prussian Blue.
Sections .	Neutral Tint.
CONCRETE	
Elevations .	Light wash of Neutral Tint.
Sections .	Dark wash of Neutral Tint.
CAST IRON .	Payne's Grey.
STEEL . .	Purple (Crimson Lake and Blue).
WROUGHT IRON	Prussian Blue.
LEAD . .	Indigo.
BRASS . .	Gamboge.
OAK . .	Sepia.
FIR . .	Burnt Sienna.
MAHOGANY .	Crimson Lake, Sepia, Burnt Sienna, mixed to tint.
TILES . .	Venetian Red.
SLATES . .	Green with Grey.
GLASS . .	Cobalt, thin wash.
EARTH . .	Vandyke Brown or Burnt Umber.

In general, sections have a darker tint of the same colour as the elevations, and only a light, even wash is required.

The drawings dealt with so far have been used to illustrate the arrangement of views and other points to be clearly understood before a drawing can be made. Let us now assume that everything is to hand, and the drawing-board has a clean sheet of paper pinned on it ready to start work. Fig. 22 is a rough sketch of a knife-box, and from this we are going to make a working drawing. The free-hand sketch is typical of what a sketch should be after taking particulars from an existing object. It must be borne in mind that, when making such a sketch, nothing should be left out, as it may not always be possible to see the actual object again should it be found that some dimension is required, or other information is missing.

Having completed the sketch, the next step is to determine roughly what the

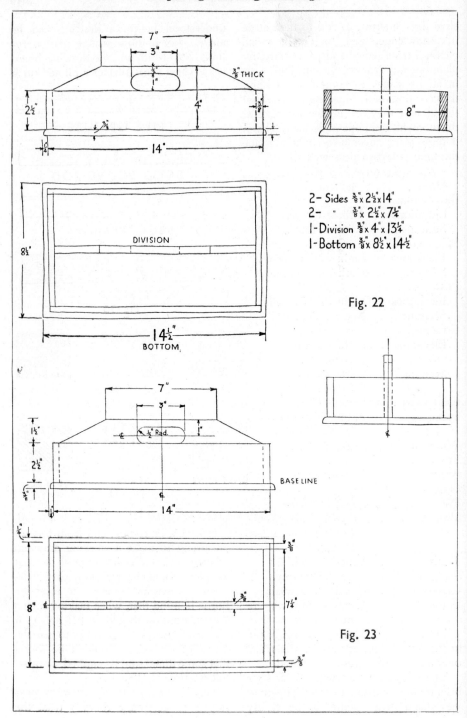

3/8 THICK

2- Sides 3/8"x 2½"x14"
2- "   3/8"x 2½"x 7¼"
1-Division 3/8"x 4"x 13¼"
1-Bottom 3/8"x 8½"x14½"

Fig. 22

DIVISION

BOTTOM

Fig. 23

BASE LINE

extreme limits of each view are likely to be. Only one end-view is necessary, so the elevation may be placed on the left, the end-view to the right, and the plan below the elevation. The overall dimensions are: length $14\frac{1}{2}$ in., width $8\frac{1}{2}$ in., depth $2\frac{1}{2}$ in., so a base line and centre lines may be laid out lightly as in Fig. 23, allowing space between each view for dimensions.

Work on All Views at Once.—In drawing a more complicated article than the example given here, it is advisable that one view should not be completed, or proceeded with to any great extent, without a certain amount of work being done on the remaining views. This applies especially when laying out a new design, even from rough sketches, because the designer is not entirely in a position to decide on many of the proportions in one view only, or whether the three or four views contain all the necessary information, without placing certain portions in section also. All lines should be drawn lightly in pencil, and section lines not added until last, when all the views are lined in darker.

Selecting a scale of 3 in. to 1 ft. for the knife-box, and regarding the main divisions as inches, the elevation may be started by laying out a distance on the base line of 14 of these divisions. At these two ends draw verticals with the set-square, $2\frac{1}{2}$ divisions high, and join them with a line for the top edge. The bottom of the box is $\frac{1}{4}$ in. larger all round, so this may be marked on the base line and the thickness of $\frac{3}{8}$ in. by a line below. As the main divisions on the scale are sub-divided into 12 parts, $\frac{3}{8}$ in. is shown by placing a mark against the distance equal to one-quarter, plus half of the next quarter division. The spring bows are set to $\frac{1}{4}$-in. radius and the rounded edge drawn as shown. The thickness of the ends of the box is shown by dotted lines, and the division piece

and slot are marked in, the centre line being used to space the dimensions an equal amount on either side. For the slot, draw a short horizontal centre line 1 in. down from the top edge of the division, mark off $1\frac{1}{2}$ in. on either side of the vertical centre line, set the bows to $\frac{1}{2}$-in. radius, and from each end of the slot strike a very small arc on the centre line, set the point of the bows at these points in turn and draw the half-circle for the slot. Join these with horizontal lines with the tee-square.

In the plan view, the width is marked off 4 in. on either side of the centre line, and the length of the sides projected downwards from the elevation by means of the set-square. The size of the bottom may be drawn round the edge of the box and the thickness of the sides shown by full lines. An end view has the width marked on a base line, and the heights projected across from the elevation.

All dimensions should be put in as shown; outside the object drawn as often as possible, and only placed inside when there is no other way. The lines leading out to indicate the limits of the dimension are always made thinner than the lines of the drawing, and those of the dimension line may be the same thickness, finished with neat arrow-heads at the ends. With practice it will soon be possible to choose a scale suitable to the job in hand, and to measure up any article and make a drawing from it, or from other persons' sketches.

Sketching. — Freehand sketching plays an important part in drawing routine; much of the finished drawing work cannot be started or carried through without it, so it is advisable to practice at every opportunity and to make drawings from the sketches. The making of the drawing will reveal any omissions or defects in the sketches and will afford the best kind of practice.

21

Any sketch should have all the essentials of a working drawing, the relative proportions being shown as near as possible, complete with all dimensions and notes necessary for the construction of the article. Sections are freely used, otherwise the doubtful position and shape of hidden parts shown by dotted lines may lead to mistakes.

A good method to follow is to show the object by as many views as considered necessary. With this much completed, a better idea of the construction and action of any moving parts will be gained, and will be a guide in distinguishing between dimensions that are essential and those that are not so important, or those useful only for the purpose of establishing other dimensions and laying out the drawing.

Squared paper is of great assistance in sketching, especially when developing the proportions of some new part or device. It is not good policy to rely too much on its aid for general work, because a sketch may be required quickly, perhaps to illustrate some point under discussion, when only an odd piece of paper such as the back of an envelope or letter is available. Train both eye and hand by plenty of practice on plain paper.

In conclusion, it may be stated that symmetrical objects do not require a complete sketch, and only part need be drawn as in Fig. 24. Sketches of more complete devices, etc., are conveniently arranged with the assembly views in the centre of the paper, and the details added at suitable points nearby.

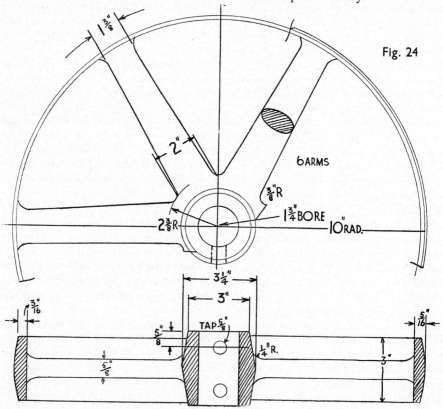

Fig. 24

MODEL MAKING

PLANNING A MODEL RAILWAY

MANY a spare hour might be less profitably employed than in building a model railway. The planning and carrying out of the work not only offer an extremely interesting and inexpensive pastime to the constructor, but when completed it has the additional advantage of giving endless pleasure to the younger members of the family. Model railway engineering also offers enormous scope for the ingenuity of the constructor; it differs from a good many other forms of model-making because once the preliminary work has been finished, the system can be added to as time and inclination allow.

To go deeply into this fascinating subject is beyond the scope of this volume, but a general brief survey of the work entailed and details for making various simple accessories such as stations, bridges, signal boxes, etc. suitable for an indoor miniature railway system of the popular 1¼ in. gauge will be found in the following paragraphs. Any of the models mentioned can, of course, be modified to suit individual requirements.

The Locomotive.—The first point to be considered when planning a miniature railway is to decide whether the locomotive is to be operated by steam, clockwork or electricity. Of the three, an electric locomotive has the great advantage of being clean, easily operated from the track, and run for hours without having to be constantly

wound up or replenished with water and fuel as do clockwork or steam engines, respectively.

Assuming that the vote is given in favour of adopting the electric system, it may be mentioned that excellent little models can be readily obtained from

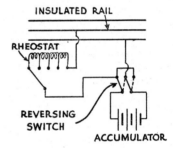

Fig. 1

about 10/– upwards, depending upon the quality of the mechanism and the amount of detail.

For operating a small railway system employing, say, a couple of locomotives, the direct-current system is perhaps the best, as the permanent magnet motor with which the miniature engines are usually equipped can be easily reversed without any more complicated apparatus than a simple reversing switch to alter the polarity of the current in the rails. Moreover, the speed can be controlled by means of a simple variable resistance. Fig. 1 shows the simple connections employed in this system.

The direct-current system requires a

battery of accumulator cells giving a pressure of 6 volts—6 volts being the standard voltage for the type of locomotive previously mentioned. If the electric lighting supply is direct current the accumulators can be readily charged from the source by passing the current used for normal lighting through the accumulators when the railway is not in operation. On the other hand, if alternating current be available the accumulators can be recharged by means of a small static transformer for reducing the supply voltage to a suitable pressure and a rectifier to change the alternating current into a unidirectional one, as accumulators cannot be recharged with alternating current.

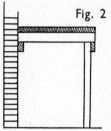

Fig. 2

The Site.—The next question that arises is whether the lines are to be laid out on the floor with its obvious disadvantages, or whether the proposed railway is to be raised above the floor-level. The latter method is recommended, as a superstructure not only forms an excellent base upon which to fix the permanent way, but is much easier to operate and a much more realistic appearance can be obtained. If it is possible to devote a spare room or a large shed for the exclusive use of the undertaking, so much the better, as the superstructure can then be made of a more or less permanent nature by attaching it to the walls round the room, a hinged section only being necessary at the doorway. Such an arrangement is shown in the diagrammatic sketch, Fig. 2.

Suitable lengths of batten, $1\frac{1}{2}$ in. by $\frac{3}{4}$ in., are fixed to the wall by means of screws so that the top edges of the battens are 2 ft. 9 in. above the floor-level, and cross-pieces of $1\frac{1}{2}$ in. square-section deal, 2 ft. long, are screwed to similar battens supported on legs 2 in. by $1\frac{1}{2}$ in., spaced at convenient distances apart. Planed boards 8 in. wide by $\frac{5}{8}$ in. thick are screwed to the cross members and form a rigid structure.

To give a realistic finish to the tops of the boards they should be sanded by applying plenty of hot glue and then pouring a quantity of clean dry sand on top, pressing it down firmly with the hands as the sand-laying proceeds. Still more satisfactory results can be obtained if one section or part of a section is made at a lower level than the adjacent ones, as this allows a bridge to be built to span the intervening space. In fact, the arrangement of the superstructure is adaptable to numerous methods of treatment, the general layout of which must be left to the discretion of the constructor.

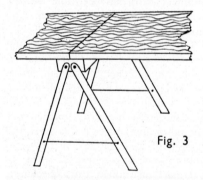

Fig. 3

A model railway constructed some years ago by the writer was arranged in sections of sanded boards 6 ft. in length, supported by folding trestles made from common slating battens as illustrated in Fig. 3. The rails were permanently fixed to each section, and the system was erected and in working order within a period of half an hour. The undersides of the ends of each section were provided with dowel-pins which fitted into corresponding holes in the tops of the trestles and thus locked the whole of the structure together. The system was operated electrically from model signal boxes situated at each end of the track. When done with, the sections were simply taken apart and stored in convenient racks in a cellar.

The Track.—The needs of the model railway engineer are well catered for as regards suitable track. This may consist of the familiar ready-made tinplate rails suitable for clockwork and steam-operated locomotives, while the same type of track fitted with an additional insulated centre rail can be readily obtained for electric working. Another popular form of track, an illustration of which appears in Fig. 4, can be obtained

in separate parts. The components consist of convenient lengths of steel rail of the correct section, which are supported on spring steel chairs fixed to wooden sleepers, the lengths of rail

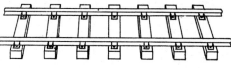

Fig. 4

being fitted together by means of spring steel fishplates. Although this type of track is a little more expensive than the tinplate variety, the extra outlay is more than compensated for by allowing curves, point formations, etc., to be easily carried out according to the desire of the constructor.

A WAYSIDE STATION

THE first model to construct after having completed the superstructure and arranged the track will un-

Fig. 1

doubtedly be a miniature station. A pleasing and simple design of a wayside station is shown in the Fig. 1. The model consists of a sanded platform, having fences and destination name-

boards and a detachable building fitted with booking-hall, booking-office and waiting-room.

The majority of the parts can be constructed of good quality $\frac{1}{4}$-in. yellow deal, free from knots and other defects. This wood will be found quite good enough as the whole structure is painted afterwards.

The Platform.—Start with the platform, shown in Working Drawing No. 28, the dimensions of which appear in Fig. 2. The sides consist of two strips of $\frac{1}{4}$-in. deal, 36 in. long by $1\frac{1}{4}$ in. wide, sloped off at the ends as shown. The top board is supported by the two long strips just mentioned and is 30 in. long by $3\frac{1}{2}$ in. wide. Two pieces of wood of the same width are bevelled at the ends to form the slopes, or "ramps," as they are called. The overhang at the front top edge of the platform is obtained by pinning $\frac{3}{8}$-in. by $\frac{1}{4}$-in. strip along the front, as shown at A. Four cross-pieces, or stays, each $2\frac{3}{4}$ in. long by $1\frac{1}{4}$ in. wide and $\frac{1}{4}$ in. thick, will be needed for strengthening and keeping the sides at the correct distance apart, as shown by the vertical dotted lines.

As the appearance of the finished model depends to a great extent upon the neatness of the paintwork, the paint should be applied to the parts before assembly. By so doing, clear cut, defined lines can be obtained which would be almost impossible to get if the parts were to be put together and then painted.

Ordinary oil paint, as used for house-painting, etc., should not be used, as it is impossible to obtain the beautiful matt finish which greatly enhances the appearance of models such as the one under review. The best results are obtained by using a high-class oil-bound water-paint which, when applied, will retain its colour and freshness for years.

The choice of colours must, of course, be left to the taste of the constructor. Suffice it to say that a charming effect will be obtained by painting the sides a light grey and the overhanging strip white. There is no need to paint the top of the platform, as this is to be sanded after the parts have been assembled, except the white front strip which is pinned on after the sanding operation.

Having assembled the parts, using $\frac{3}{4}$-in. panel pins for the purpose, obtain a few handfuls of clean, dry silver sand and have a small quantity of liquid glue at hand.

The best way to sand the platform is to spread a large sheet of newspaper on a table and place the heap of sand in a convenient position for handling. Brush some thin glue over the top surface of the platform and spread the sand over the entire surface, pressing it down firmly. Great care should be taken not to disturb the sand more than necessary during the operation, otherwise a patchy job is likely to result. When completed, allow the sand to remain for a few minutes, after which it may be tipped up and the surplus material allowed to fall on the paper. Then place the platform in a convenient place to dry. This process of sanding can be used in all instances where a sanded surface is required.

The Fences.—Two of these will be required. Each of these consists of a strip of $\frac{1}{4}$-in. stuff, $1\frac{1}{4}$ in. wide and $9\frac{3}{8}$ in. in length. The end corner posts are of $\frac{3}{8}$-in. square-section material, $1\frac{3}{8}$ in. high, while the imitation intermediate posts are simply pieces of $\frac{1}{16}$-in. by $\frac{1}{8}$-in. strip glued on after assembly. The fence capping is $\frac{3}{8}$ in. wide by $\frac{1}{16}$ in. thick. Dowel-pins, formed by cutting off the heads of stout panel pins, are used for attaching the fences to the platform, the top of the latter being drilled with small holes to correspond and receive the ends of the pins.

The fences will look well if painted a dark brownish-grey, with white posts, while the name-boards can be painted white with black supporting posts to give contrast.

The Destination Name-boards are made from 1-in. by $\frac{1}{4}$-in. wide strip supported by $\frac{1}{4}$-in. by $\frac{1}{4}$-in. section uprights, the bottoms of which are fitted with pin dowels and fit into corresponding holes in the tops of the fences.

The construction of the building (Fig. 3) is carried out on similar lines, that is, the parts are first cut accurately to the dimensions shown in the elevations and plan, painted, and then assembled, using fine panel pins for the purpose. The tops of the panel pins can be easily obliterated by spotting them with suitably coloured paint.

Before assembling the parts together,

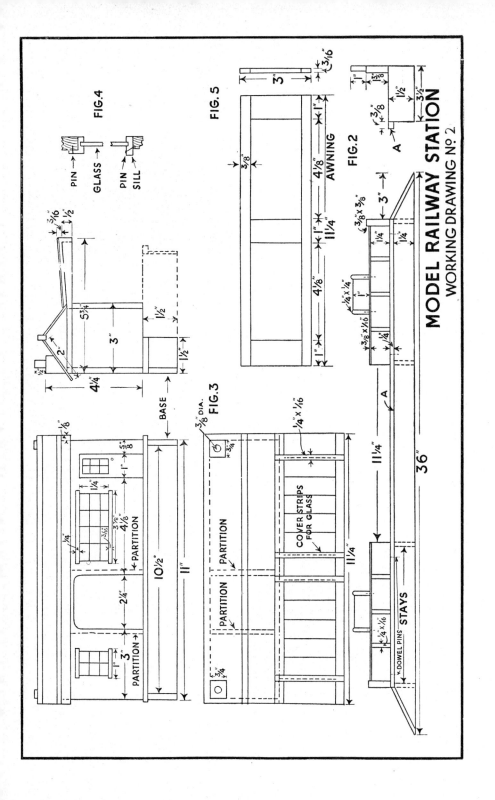

FIG.4

PIN → GLASS
PIN → SILL

FIG.5

³⁄₁₆″
3″
³⁄₈″
1″ 4⅛″ 1″ 4⅛″
AWNING
11¼″

FIG.2

1″ ³⁄₈″
³⁄₈″ ½″ 3½″
A
½″

³⁄₁₆″
½″
5¾″
2″
3″
1½″
½″
4¼″
½″
1½″
BASE

FIG.3

³⁄₈″ DIA.
³⁄₄″
¼″ × ¹⁄₁₆″
PARTITION
PARTITION
COVER STRIPS FOR GLASS
PARTITION
11¼″
11¼″
¼″ × ¹⁄₁₆″
¾″ DOWEL PINS STAYS
⁵⁄₄″

⅛″
5⁄₈″
1″
¼″
³⁄₁₆″
¼″
3⁄₁₆″
4⅛″
2¼″
PARTITION
10½″
11″
3″
1″
PARTITION →

³⁄₈″ × ³⁄₈″
3″
¼″
¼″
¼″ × ¹⁄₄″
1″
³⁄₈″ × ¹⁄₁₆″
¼″
A
11¼″
36″

MODEL RAILWAY STATION
WORKING DRAWING Nº 2

cut out the glass window-panes and mark the lines with thin white paint, applied with a draughtsman's ruling pen. The glasses are then fixed in the apertures by means of small slotted pieces of wood forming the tops of the windows and the sills, as shown in Fig. 4; they are simply pinned into the main structure.

To facilitate assembly, the parts should be put together in the following sequence. First make the base and the glass awning (Fig. 5), and then fix the sides to the front and back, following this by fitting the partitions. Next pin on the roof ridge and roof pieces, the awning supports at the sides, and then the awning. Then fit the base and finally the chimney stacks.

The following colours are suggested for the building. Walls, light stone; roof, slate grey; roof edge, black; chimney pots, red with black tops; base, to match sides of the platform; and other parts white.

Fig. 6 shows another neat and

Fig. 6

realistic type of model railway station building constructed on the same lines as the one just described. The chief dimensions of the model are as follows: Length, 14 in.; width, 5 in.; height from platform level, $4\frac{3}{4}$ in.

A SIGNAL BOX

S IGNAL boxes form a very important feature in the construction of a model railway.

The model shown in Fig. 1, although

Fig. I

not based on any particular railway company's design, has nevertheless a neat and realistic appearance and has been designed with a view to simplicity of construction.

The main structure is mounted upon a detachable base to which the levers and their blocks are attached.

A noticeable feature of the model is the pull-down window section at the back, shown in Fig. 2, provided in order to allow access to the interior for the purpose of operating the levers. This window is pivoted to the main structure, as shown in detail in Fig. 3.

The floor and outside landing are in two pieces, the former portion being provided with a series of $\frac{1}{4}$-in.-wide slots to enable the tops of the levers to project above the floor-level.

Four corner posts of $\frac{1}{4}$-in. hardwood having grooves $\frac{1}{16}$ in. deep, $\frac{1}{16}$ in. wide, and $1\frac{1}{2}$ in. long, provide a ready means of keeping the windows in their proper position.

Like the station previously described, the material used for the construction of the signal box is best quality prepared yellow deal, $\frac{1}{4}$ in. thick, although a better wood such as satin walnut could be used, if desired, as the small amount will not make an appreciable difference to the cost.

All parts should be carefully marked out and accurately cut to the dimensions given in Fig. 4. A fretsaw will come in extremely handy for this.

All painting should be done previous

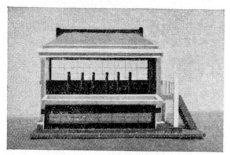

Fig. 2

to assembling the parts to ensure clean-cut lines. The colour of the paint should harmonise with the majority of other buildings used in the miniature railway system. As stone colour was suggested for the station, this colour should be used for the body of the signal box. The roof should be slate grey. The plinth surrounding the bottom of the model can be painted brown and the base and floor a brownish-grey. Levers look well in black, while the strips under the windows should be white. Use oil-bound water-paints, as suggested for the station.

Assembling the Parts.—The first items to assemble are the small door-posts, shown at A in the landing-end view, using a very small quantity of liquid glue and $\frac{3}{4}$-in. thin panel pins for the purpose. Then fix the two corner posts (B) to the ends of the front piece by using liquid glue and two panel pins driven in each post, one about $\frac{1}{2}$ in. from the bottom and the other about $2\frac{1}{2}$ in. above it, and repeat the operation by fitting the corner posts C (Fig. 3) to the back member.

Now fit the pull-down door at the back by driving a pin through each upright in the positions indicated in Fig. 3 to form the pivots on which the door works.

The next procedure consists in assembling the front, back and end portions together, and, after having accomplished this, the floor should be tested to see whether it fits correctly into its position. If it is a trifle too large it is an easy matter to remedy the defect.

Drill the holes in the fence posts for the tiny wire railings and then fix the posts in position on the projecting landing piece. Note that the pinning of the posts should be done from the underside, and a touch of liquid glue will further strengthen the joints. Fasten the plinth round the bottom of the building and

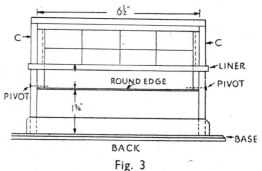

Fig. 3

fix the window sills which consist of strips of wood, $\frac{1}{4}$ in. by $\frac{1}{8}$ in., as shown.

The Windows.—The next step consists in cutting and lining the glass windows and fitting them into their respective grooves. Then drill a minute hole with the aid of an Archimedean drill to receive the bottom pivot of the miniature door and then fasten the floor in position.

Make up the frame which covers the top of the windows as shown in Fig. 4, and fasten it down to the tops of the corner posts. Great care is needed when fitting the frame as only a small amount of wood is available in the tops of the posts for fixing purposes, due to a

Make up another frame of $\frac{1}{2}$-in. wide by $\frac{3}{16}$-in. strip and fix it down to the lower frame, so that the outside edges overlap $\frac{1}{4}$ in., as shown at x in Fig. 4. Fix the two triangular-shaped roof supports in position, shown dotted in the plan view, Fig. 4, and then fix the roof ridge to the top of them and carefully fix the roof pieces, which are of $\frac{1}{8}$-in. plywood.

The Steps should now be assembled. A little patience will be necessary in order to carry out the operation in a

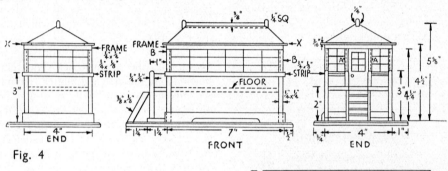

Fig. 4

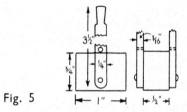

Fig. 5

PLAN

Fig. 6

portion having been removed to form the grooves. The window top frame should be accurately drilled with a very fine drill in positions to correspond with the four corner posts and the door posts. Now put a small blob of glue on the top of each post, and, after having placed the frame in position, drive a fine $\frac{3}{4}$-in. panel pin through the holes and into each post, taking care to keep the pins perfectly upright, otherwise the posts will probably split.

Hold the door in position and put a very fine panel pin in the top corner of the door to form the pivot.

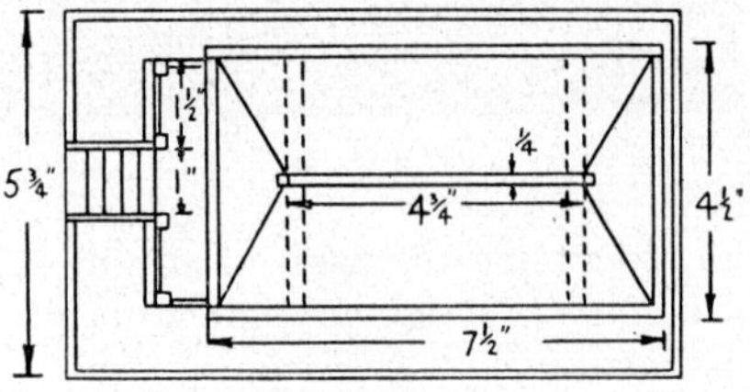

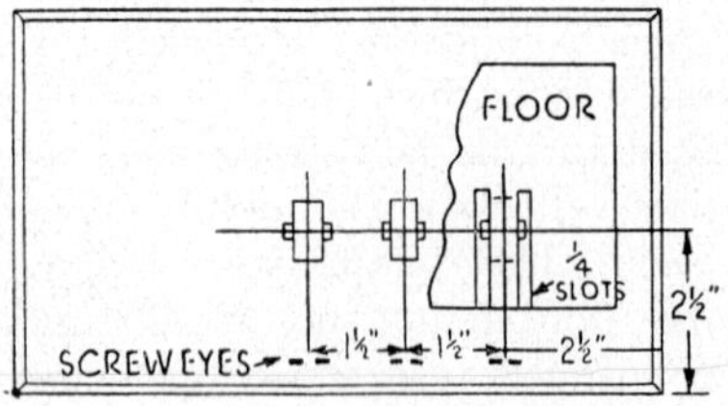

successful manner. One good method of fixing these small parts together is to take one of the side pieces—after having marked out the positions of the treads on one face—and place it face upwards flat on the bench or table. A couple of pins driven into the table and bent over will keep it from shifting. Apply a small quantity of tube glue on the end of each tread and stick them on to the marked side piece. When sufficient time has been allowed for the glue to set, a smear of glue can be applied to the remaining ends of the treads and the other side member carefully placed on top, taking care to see that the ends of the side members are perfectly level.

When dry, the steps should be painted a greyish-brown colour.

The steps are removable and are fastened to the landing platform by means of hooks, formed with ordinary pins minus their heads, driven into the tops of the side members of the steps. The hooks fit in corresponding loops—also formed with bent pins—driven into the edge of the landing.

Small pieces of thin wire are then cut to form the handrails and fitted into the holes of the landing posts.

The last step consists in fitting the levers to the blocks, details of which appear in Fig. 5, and then fitting them to the base, using fine screws driven in from the underside of the base. The spacing of the blocks on the base is given in Fig. 6.

To prevent the signal box from slipping out of position when the levers are being operated, a strip of $\frac{1}{4}$-in. by $\frac{1}{4}$-in. wood should be pinned securely to the base in a position to correspond with the inside bottom edges of the ends of the structure.

Finally, screw in six No. ooo brass

Fig. 7

screw eyes, or drive in pins bent to form eyes, opposite the levers to enable the "wires" (thread) from the signals to pass through, the wires being threaded through the holes provided in the lower part of the levers and then tied securely.

A model signal box of a somewhat simpler type appears in Fig. 7.

This model is not a working one and is only intended for show purposes.

BRIDGES

THREE interesting and easily constructed model railway bridges are illustrated in the accompanying illustrations, Figs. 1, 2 and 3. Fig. 1 represents a steel girder bridge for carrying a single track and is purposely kept low in height to give an easy gradient and thus enable a miniature train to pass over it with little effort.

The bridge depicted in Fig 2 is a small bridge for pedestrians and can be used as a platform over-bridge or placed at track level. The road bridge (Fig. 3) makes quite a good model although the approaches are rather steep. This feature is necessary, however, in order to keep the structure within reasonable dimensions.

The " Steel " Bridge.—Details of the "steel" bridge are given in Figs. 4 and 5,

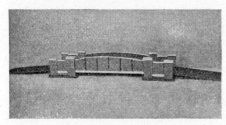

Fig. 1

Fig. 2

Fig. 3

plan view, in order to simplify the drawings.

The girder section, abutments and ramps are all separate items which allow the model to be assembled or dismantled in a few moments and packed in a minimum amount of space.

The base of the middle section (Fig. 4) is 10 in. long by $3\frac{1}{8}$ in. wide with sanded upper surface. The bow-shaped "girders" are cut to shape as shown, and have vertical pieces of $\frac{1}{16}$-in. square section wood stuck on to represent T section steel. Strips of thin wood $\frac{5}{16}$ in. wide by $\frac{1}{16}$ in. thick cover the tops of the girders, while strips of similar material $\frac{1}{4}$ in. wide are pinned along the bottom edge, as shown at A.

Having cut the girders to shape they should be painted a stone colour, and the vertical pieces and strips glued on after having been painted. The vertical pieces look well if painted black, the strips being painted white.

Care should be taken when fixing the girders to the base to see that the ends of the latter project exactly $\frac{1}{2}$ in., as these projections fit in one end of each abutment, as indicated by B in Fig. 5. The two abutments should be built up as

which show the middle or "girder" section and an abutment respectively, while the illustration at A in Fig. 5 shows details of the ramp or slope for carrying the track up to the ground level of the bridge. Reference to the side elevation of the abutment (Fig. 5) will show that capping pieces are provided at the tops of the two pillars, while this item has been purposely omitted in the end elevation and the

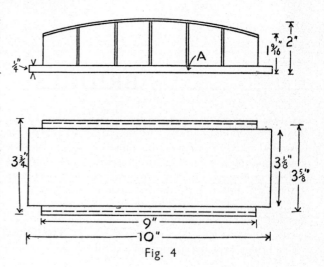

Fig. 4

shown in Fig. 5. The pillars consist of pieces of 1-in. by ½-in. hardwood or good quality yellow deal planed and

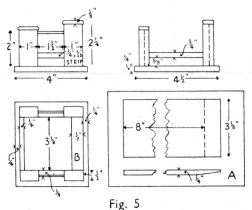

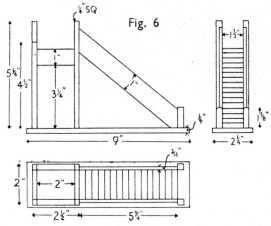

Fig. 5

tops by $\frac{1}{16}$ in. all round. A strip of wood $\frac{5}{16}$ in. wide by $\frac{1}{16}$ in. thick should be glued to the top of the piece adjoining the pillars and a similar strip $\frac{1}{4}$ in. wide should be glued on the side as shown.

Details of the ramps appear at A in Fig. 5. These consist of flat pieces of wood $\frac{1}{4}$ in. thick, 8 in. long by $3\frac{1}{8}$ in. wide. One end of each is chamfered on the underside to correspond with the slope, and the top surface is sanded.

The pillars of the abutments will look well if painted a bluish-grey, the intermediate piece stone, the base brownish-grey and the caps and strips white.

smoothed with fine glass-paper. The base is 4 in. long by 4½ in. wide, the pillars being fixed to it by means of ¾-in. panel pins driven in from the underside. A piece of ⅜-in. thick planed wood, 3½ in. long by 3⅛ in. wide, is placed on top of the base and between the pillars, while on top of this is a piece of ¼-in. material of the same width and 2¾ in. in length. The top surface of this piece is sanded to correspond with the base of the girder section. The tops of the pillars are fitted with caps ⅛ in. thick as shown in the side elevation, and should overlap the pillar

Fig. 6

The foot-bridge, details of which appear in Figs. 6 and 7, consists of three units, namely the right-hand and the left-hand stairways and the cross-piece spanning the stairways.

To construct the model, first make the standards which support the stairs and the base. Paint the

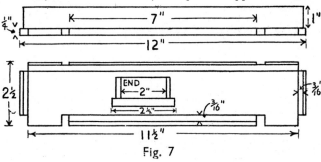

Fig. 7

standards white and the base brownish-grey and when dry fix the two together by means of $\frac{3}{4}$-in. panel pins driven in from the underside of the base into the four uprights.

The Stairs.—Next prepare the stairs, which are made from pieces of $\frac{1}{4}$-in. by $\frac{1}{4}$-in. section hardwood, planed to form triangular-shaped strips. The triangular pieces are then cut into lengths of $3\frac{1}{4}$ in. and glued down to a base of about 6 in. long by 3 in. wide by $\frac{1}{8}$ in. thick. This allows the two stairways to be formed in one operation. The projecting ends are cut off with the aid of a fretsaw, and the piece divided by cutting along the centre.

Fig. 8

The stairs are then cut off to length, painted white, and the side members—having been painted—fixed to them.

The next operation consists in fastening the stairs to the bases and standards. This is accomplished by driving in $\frac{1}{2}$-in.

panel pins at the tops and bottoms. The top or cross-member—details of which are shown in Fig. 7—calls for little comment. Suffice it to say that it consists of a base 12 in. long by $2\frac{1}{2}$ in. wide, having $\frac{1}{4}$-in. by $\frac{1}{4}$-in. recesses as shown, to take the uprights of the standards. The side members are strips of 1-in. wide by $\frac{3}{16}$-in. thick hardwood. Paint the base brownish-grey and the side pieces stone colour.

The final operation consists in fitting the miniature posts at the feet of the stairs. These should be painted white, and then fixed with $\frac{3}{4}$-in. panel pins driven in from the underside of the base and also with pins passing through the posts into the side members of the stairs.

The Road Bridge.—Lack of space prohibits more than a brief survey of the road bridge, Fig. 3. This model is made in three sections—the two approaches and the member spanning the track. The approaches are sanded and then given a very thin coat of stone-coloured paint, while the side fences are also of the same colour, capped with white strips. The top surface of the middle section is sanded and the sides are painted stone with capping on the top.

An illustration of the three separate sections is shown in Fig. 8, giving a general idea of its construction.

A GOODS DEPOT

THE accompanying illustrations (Figs. 1 and 2) show a front and a back view of an interesting model of a goods depot, a necessary adjunct to any miniature railway.

No high degree of skill is required in the construction of the model, which can

easily be put together in the course of a few hours.

Sliding doors at the back and front allow access to the interior, while a small platform in the front enables miniature trucks to be loaded or unloaded. A loading bank is also pro-

Fig. 1

Fig. 2

vided at the back by a recess cut in the floor.

The roof is partially glazed, a feature which greatly improves the appearance of the model, and a written facia board at the top of the ridge also adds to the general effect.

Construction.—Start by cutting out the various parts, following the dimensions given in Figs. 3, 4, 5 and 6. The size of the front is $11\frac{3}{4}$ in. long by $5\frac{1}{2}$ in. by $\frac{1}{4}$ in. thick. Its top edge should be chamfered to correspond with the slope of the roof. An aperture 5 in. long by $3\frac{1}{4}$ in. wide is cut in this, as shown in the front elevation (Fig. 3). The doors slide along at the back by means of a grooved strip of wood fixed at the top and a corresponding groove made in the long edge of the floor below. The top grooved strip is represented by the dotted lines shown at A in the front view (Fig. 3), while the

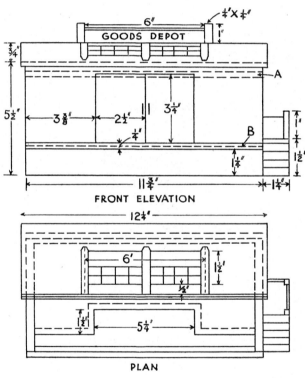

FRONT ELEVATION

PLAN

Fig. 3

bottom groove is indicated at B. The grooves should be $\frac{1}{8}$ in. wide and $\frac{1}{8}$ in. deep, which allows sufficient play for the doors, which are $\frac{3}{32}$ in. thick, to slide along easily.

The back is built up in sections, details of which appear in Fig. 4. The parts should be cut perfectly square and fastened together with liquid glue. The bottom member is grooved, and a strip similar to that used at the top of the front member is employed for keeping the doors in place.

The two ends (Figs. 5 and 6) are $5\frac{1}{4}$ in. wide by $5\frac{1}{2}$ in. high to eaves, and to take the bottoms of the sliding doors, as previously mentioned. The back edge of the floor is supported by five pieces of $\frac{1}{4}$-in. wood, $1\frac{1}{4}$ in. wide. These are represented by the dotted lines in the lower half of the plan view (Fig. 3).

The roof pieces are made with $\frac{1}{8}$ in. thick material. A 6-in. by $1\frac{1}{2}$-in. hole is cut in each of these members to receive the glass, the latter being supported by

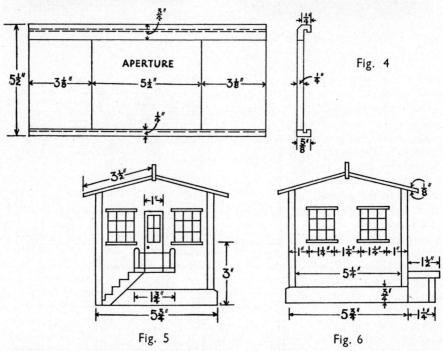

Fig. 4

Fig. 5

Fig. 6

$6\frac{1}{4}$ in. at the ridge. These should be carefully marked out and the window apertures cut out with the aid of a fretsaw. The four windows are all of one size, namely, $1\frac{1}{2}$ in. by $1\frac{1}{4}$ in. One end is fitted with a door, so do not omit to cut the doorway.

The floor is $11\frac{1}{4}$ in. long, $4\frac{3}{4}$ in. wide and $\frac{1}{4}$ in. thick and has a recess $5\frac{1}{4}$ in. long by $1\frac{1}{2}$ in. wide, cut in the back edge as shown clearly in the lower half of the plan view illustrated in Fig. 3. The top of the front edge of the floor is grooved

small strips or fillets, $\frac{1}{16}$ in. thick by $\frac{1}{4}$ in. wide, glued across the narrow ends so that $\frac{1}{8}$ in. overlaps the edges.

A plinth $\frac{3}{4}$ in. wide by $\frac{1}{8}$ in. thick is fitted to the bottoms of the ends and runs round the back as far as the opening for the doors.

The Loading Platform in front is $11\frac{3}{4}$ in. long and $1\frac{1}{2}$ in. high, and is constructed from $\frac{1}{4}$ in. thick material. Note that the top member projects $\frac{1}{4}$ in. beyond its support, as shown in the end view (Fig. 6).

The small landing at the top of the steps is 1¾ in. long, 1¼ in. wide and ¼ in. thick, upon which two 1-in. by ¼-in. square posts are fixed, the handrails being pieces of wire threaded through holes made in the posts and the structure.

Small steps may be made by planing ¼-in. square-section wood diagonally, and gluing the pieces to a thin piece of wood.

The roof ridge and facia board is built up. The base is a strip of ¼-in. square wood 12¼ in. long. Another strip 6 in. long by ¾ in. wide is pinned to the base and the end posts are attached to the ends of the boards by means of fine ¾-in. panel pins.

Assembling the Model.—Having cut the parts the next operation is to paint them. Oil-bound water-paints of similar colours to those suggested for the models previously described should be used unless, of course, any other colour is desired.

When the parts are perfectly dry, fit the windows, etc., in their respective apertures before actually beginning the main assembly, not forgetting to fix the tiny pane for the small door.

The roof glasses are kept in position by means of thin wood fillets as shown in the plan view, Fig. 3. The fillets look well if they are painted white.

It is better to assemble the component parts of the door end member before proceeding any further. Carefully remove the long sharp edges of the door with a small sharp plane to enable it to open and close easily, and then partially drive a thin headless panel pin into the top and bottom edges on the hanging side, to form pivots. Make a tiny hole at the top of the door opening to take the top pivot. The lower pivot fits into a minute recess cut with a penknife. The landing in front will prevent the pivot from slipping out of place.

Having fixed the landing, steps, posts and handrails, the main assembly can be begun.

Fix the front and back members to the ends, and then fit the floor by driving in ¾-in. panel pins from the outside of the structure. The top of the floor is 1½ in. above the bottom edges. Next fit the front sliding doors into the groove in the floor and fix the grooved strip at the top. Do not fasten this down tight on to the top of the doors but allow about 1/16-in. play to enable them to slide easily. Repeat the operation with the doors at the back and fasten the strips with ½-in. fine panel pins.

Now fix the supports under the back edge of the floor and then fasten the plinth, the ends of which should be neatly mitred at the right-angled joints.

The next step is to fix the roof ridge and then the roof pieces, and finally the loading platform in front of the structure.

A LEVEL CROSSING

THE model illustrated in Fig. 1 consists of a framed base, the middle of the sides of which are recessed to represent the slope of the roadway. Two gates constructed of ¼-in. by ¼-in. section hardwood are drilled to receive the wire "bars" as shown. The gates are supported by means of ¼-in. round dowel-posts which are glued into holes made in the base for their reception. The fence is made of ¼-in. by ¼-in. material and horizontal wires, while the

Fig. 1

top rail of the fence is composed of wood strip $\frac{1}{4}$ in. wide by $\frac{3}{32}$ in. thick.

Construction.—Procure two pieces of yellow deal 15 in. long by $3\frac{1}{2}$ in. wide and $\frac{3}{4}$ in. thick. Mark the top faces for the recess, cut out the waste with the aid of a tenon-saw and sharp chisel, and chamfer the edges as shown.

The underside has two recesses $1\frac{1}{2}$ in. wide and $\frac{3}{16}$ in. deep, into which the cross-members are fitted to keep the two main portions of the base at the correct distance apart.

Having completed this, sand the top surface of the recess, and paint the rest of it green. Then bore the holes and fix the fence standards, after having drilled the standards to take the wires.

The Gates (Fig. 2) should be carefully painted white and lettered on the top rails: "Beware of the Trains."

As the appearance of the gates will be spoiled unless the "bars" are perfectly straight, it is a good plan to make these from bird-cage wire, which can be procured at most ironmongers' shops.

After having threaded the wires through the holes in the uprights of the gates, two small discs or diamond-shaped pieces of tinplate should be pinned to the centre upright—one on each side—of the gate, and painted bright red.

A single or a double-armed signal near the gates will greatly add to the attractiveness of the model.

To enable the gates to open and close easily, an end upright of each gate is pivoted in the manner shown at A, in Fig. 2. The bottom pivot fits into a hole drilled in the base, while the top one is formed by driving an ordinary stoutish pin through the post and then bending the pin over at right-angles.

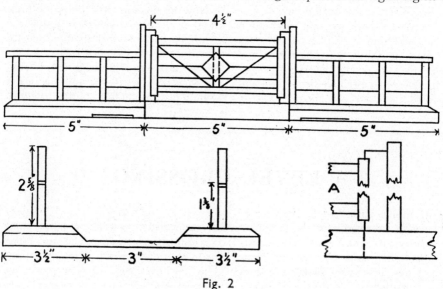

Fig. 2

SIGNALS

MINIATURE signals are a vitally important feature in any model railway system.

Fig. 1 shows an illustration of three common types of signals. That on the left is a single-armed signal post, the central figure is a two-post gantry, while the one on the right depicts a double-armed signal.

The signal arms used in all the models to be described are made to standard dimensions, an illustration of a typical arm appearing in Fig. 2. The arms are made out of tinplate taken from tobacco tins, etc.

Where a number of signal arms are required it is a good plan to make a cardboard template of an arm and then trace the outline from it on the tinplate.

Painting the Signals.—The arms should be painted in the following colours. The main portion of the front from the end to the edge of the post, should be painted vermilion, and from this point the rest of the horizontal portion of the arm, including the spectacle, black. The red and green "glasses" can be painted in carefully over the black when the latter is dry. A white vertical stripe should be made at the position indicated by w in Fig. 2. The reverse face is painted white from the end to the edge of the post and the rest black, while a black stripe is painted as on the front. Tube water-colours with only a small quantity of added water can be used, but the metal must be thoroughly cleaned before application.

The lever weights for operating the arms consist of lead seals $\frac{3}{8}$ in. in diameter. A piece of punched bar, as used for making bird-cages, is pushed into the recess in the seal and

then hammered flat to fix the lever. This component should be painted black.

The signal posts are all made from $\frac{1}{4}$ in. by $\frac{1}{4}$ in. stripwood, which can be obtained cheaply at almost any shops catering for amateur woodworkers' requirements.

No. 18 gauge tinned copper wire bent to suitable shapes is used for the

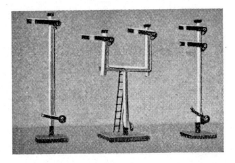

Fig. 1

"rods" joining the arms to the weighted levers, and $\frac{1}{4}$ in. gimp-pins, as used by upholsterers, are employed for attaching the arms and levers to the posts.

The tops of the posts are fitted with small capping pieces, $\frac{1}{8}$ in. thick and $\frac{3}{8}$ in. square, the sharp top edges of

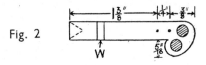

Fig. 2

which are removed to improve the appearance of the model. These should be painted black.

In order to prevent the arms rising beyond the horizontal position, the pointed ends of ordinary pins are driven into the posts just above the arms. The heads are then removed with a pair of cutting pliers, allowing $\frac{1}{8}$ in. to project above the surface of the post.

Headless pins, bent to form loops, are used for keeping the "rods" in position.

It is necessary to point out that all component parts of the signals should be

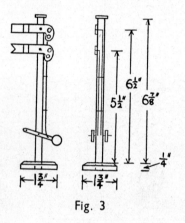

Fig. 3

painted before assembly, as it is practically impossible to obtain any degree of neatness if the finishing be postponed until after the parts have been put together.

The Single-armed Signal. — The simplest type of signal to construct is, of course, the single-armed one, dimensions of which can be obtained from the details shown in the drawing of the double-armed signal (Fig. 3). The base is a piece of wood, $1\frac{3}{4}$ in. square, $\frac{1}{4}$ in. thick, having a $\frac{1}{4}$-in. hole drilled in the centre into which the bottom of the signal post is fixed with liquid glue. The base can be either sanded or painted a dark green as desired. The post is painted white, except at the foot, which is black for a distance of $\frac{3}{4}$ in. up the post.

First fix the arm to the post, taking care to see that the pivot pin is exactly

in the centre and $\frac{3}{8}$ in. from the top of the post, measured from the underside of the cap. Then fix the arm stop and the weighted lever. Next cut off a piece of wire sufficiently long to reach from the hole in the arm to the hole near the weight in the lever, adding $\frac{1}{4}$ in. at each end for bending over at right angles, thus allowing the ends to pass through the holes. Fix the two loops—made from ordinary pins—at the side of the post for keeping the wire in position, and glue on the cap. A similar loop is fixed immediately below the free end of the lever, into the base.

The Double-armed Signal is carried out on similar lines to those of the single-armed signal. Fig. 4 shows constructional details of a two-post gantry. The bottom post, cross-piece, and the two side posts should be glued and pinned together and then painted, after which the back landing-stage at the top of the ladder can be attached by means of panel pins driven through from the front of the cross member.

The centre of the back edge of the landing-stage has two saw-cuts, $\frac{1}{8}$ in. deep and spaced $\frac{1}{2}$ in. apart, to provide a

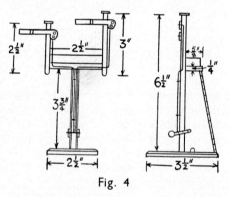

Fig. 4

means of fixing the top of the ladder. Similar saw-cuts in the back edge of the base fix the lower end. A handrail surrounds the top of the landing-stage,

is fixed to the base in the same way as that adopted for the single-armed signal.

The final operation consists in making and fixing the ladder. Punched bar, having small holes at intervals of $\frac{1}{2}$ in., is used for the sides. The sides are spaced $\frac{1}{2}$ in. apart and the rungs, consisting of bird-cage wire, are soldered into the holes. Any projecting ends of the wire can then be removed with a file. The ladder should be painted black and is fixed by springing the ends into the saw-cuts previously mentioned.

Four-post Gantry.—An illustration of a four-post gantry appears in Fig. 5, while a detailed drawing showing the chief dimensions is shown in Fig. 6. This model is constructed on similar lines to those previously dealt with.

The gantry is mounted upon a detachable framed base to facilitate storage. The ladders are also detachable and are kept in position by means of hooks

Fig. 5

except at the opening at the top of the ladder. This is formed of No. 18 gauge tinned copper wire and is supported by means of vertical pieces of wire forced

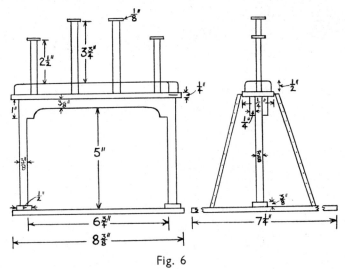

Fig. 6

into tiny holes drilled near the outside edges of the landing-stage. Solder is used for fixing the handrail to the tops of the uprights.

Next fix the arms, levers, operating wires and caps, after which the gantry

soldered to the ladder tops and thin wire staples, or bent pins, driven in the sides of the landing-stage.

The bottoms of the main posts are rounded and fit into hardwood sockets mounted on the base.

SMALL ACCESSORIES

A N interesting group of miniature railway accessories consisting of a fogman's hut, platelayer's hut, coal merchant's office, telegraph pole, etc., appears in Fig. 1. Constructional details of these models will be found in the accompanying diagrams.

The Fogman's Hut is made of hardwood, $\frac{1}{8}$ in. thick, and is provided with a small seat inside.

The chief dimensions of this model, shown in Fig. 2, are $3\frac{1}{8}$ in. high in front and 3 in. at the back. The front is $1\frac{1}{2}$ in. wide and the sides $1\frac{3}{4}$ in. in width,

Fig. I

while the base is 2 in. by $1\frac{3}{4}$ in. Small strips of $\frac{1}{16}$-in. by $\frac{1}{16}$-in. hardwood are stuck on the roof from front to back, which greatly enhances the appearance of the model. Dark grey paint is used for the base, and the main structure is painted black. Vertical lines are scratched on the sides and back to represent joints in the timber. The scratches are produced by means of a filed end of a nail.

The Platelayer's Hut (Fig. 3) is $3\frac{1}{4}$ in. wide by $3\frac{1}{4}$ in. deep; the height at the front is 2 in. and at the back $2\frac{5}{8}$ in. The roof overlaps the walls by $\frac{1}{8}$ in. A small pivoted door $1\frac{1}{2}$ in. by 1 in. is provided in the front. A chimney-stack, made

from a piece of soft wood $2\frac{7}{8}$ in. long, $\frac{5}{8}$ in. wide and $\frac{1}{2}$ in. thick, is fitted to the side of the structure, and a small imitation chimney-pot consisting of a $\frac{3}{8}$-in. length of $\frac{5}{16}$-in. diameter dowel is fitted at the top of the stack. The model stands on a base 4 in. long by $3\frac{1}{2}$ in. wide by $\frac{1}{8}$ in. Black paint is used for the main structure, dark grey for the base and light grey for the stack. Red is the colour used for the chimney-pot, with a spot of black on the top.

The Coal Merchant's Office (Fig. 4) is constructed of $\frac{3}{16}$-in. material. The front and back are $4\frac{1}{2}$ in. long by a trifle over $2\frac{1}{4}$ in. high, the top front edges being chamfered to suit the slope of the roof. A doorway and window are provided in the front, the door being $1\frac{7}{8}$ in. high by 1 in. wide. The window aperture is 2 in. wide and 1 in. high and fitted with a lined glass window. The width of the model is 3 in. and its height 3 in. to the bottom of the ridge. A facia board, 3 in. long by $\frac{3}{4}$ in. wide, is fitted to the ridge, while two square posts give a finish to the ends

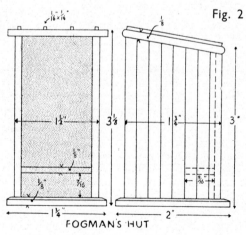

Fig. 2

FOGMAN'S HUT

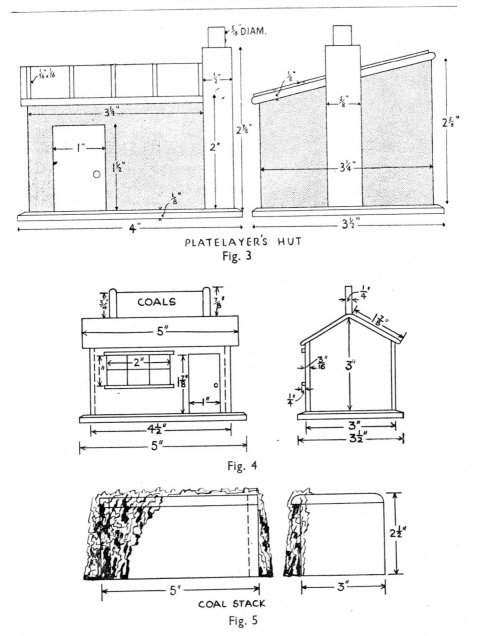

PLATELAYER'S HUT
Fig. 3

COALS

Fig. 4

COAL STACK
Fig. 5

of the board. The size of the base is 5 in. long by $3\frac{1}{2}$ in. wide, and the length and breadth of the two sloping roof members are 5 in. and $1\frac{7}{8}$ in. respectively. The bottom of the window is fitted with a sill $2\frac{1}{4}$ in. long by $\frac{1}{4}$ in. wide by $\frac{3}{32}$ in. thick. The model is finished in the following colours: Main structure, mid stone; roof, slate grey; facia board and sill, white; base, dark grey; and the posts at the ends of the board, black.

The Miniature Coal Stack is simply ordinary coal glued on an inverted box without a lid, with the top edges rounded or chamfered, as shown in Fig. 5. A

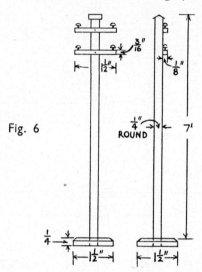

Fig. 6

coat of hot glue is brushed on the box and a small quantity of finely-powdered coal pressed on the surface. When this is dry a further application of glue is given, upon which small lumps of coal about $\frac{1}{4}$ in. in diameter are stuck.

Telegraph Poles (Fig. 6) can be constructed with $\frac{1}{4}$-in. diameter hardwood dowels, painted black, and hardwood cross-pieces $1\frac{1}{2}$ in. long by $\frac{3}{16}$ in. wide

and $\frac{1}{8}$ in. thick, also painted black. Imitation insulators on the cross-pieces are formed by partially driving in upholsterer's gimp pins, the heads of which are painted white. The bottom of the pole is glued into a $\frac{1}{4}$-in. diameter hole

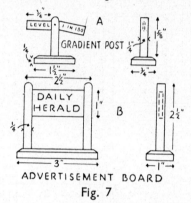

ADVERTISEMENT BOARD
Fig. 7

drilled in a $1\frac{1}{2}$-in. square base, $\frac{1}{4}$ in. thick. The base is painted dark grey.

Many other pleasing little accessories can be made out of odds and ends.

Gradient Posts, as illustrated at A in Fig. 7, can be constructed with $\frac{1}{4}$-in. square stripwood and pieces of tinplate for the arms. Neat miniature fences can be made with stripwood and wire, while name-boards and advertisement boards, as at B in Fig. 7, only require stripwood for the posts, thin hardwood for the boards and bases, a small quantity of tube glue, a small quantity of fine panel pins and paint of suitable colours.

A MODEL YACHT

To make the model racing yacht illustrated in Fig. 1, procure a flawless piece of soft pine about 19 in. long by a trifle over $4\frac{1}{2}$-in. wide and $2\frac{3}{8}$ in. thick and plane it up perfectly square to a finished size of 19 in. by $4\frac{3}{8}$ in. by $2\frac{5}{16}$ in. Draw a centre-line down the entire length of one of the wide faces and divide this line into 18 1-in. sections. With a try-square and pencil

Fig. I

draw lines across the face at the marked positions at right angles to the centre-line and carry them down the narrow sides, as shown in Fig. 2.

The next step is to number the section

Measurements of yacht hull taken at intervals of 1 in.

Half width of Deck in inches	Number of Section	Full depth of Hull in inches
0 (Bow)	0	$\frac{1}{2}$
$\frac{9}{16}$	1	$\frac{7}{8}$
1	2	$1\frac{1}{4}$
$1\frac{5}{16}$	3	$1\frac{9}{16}$
$1\frac{9}{16}$	4	$1\frac{13}{16}$
$1\frac{3}{4}$	5	2
$1\frac{7}{8}$	6	$2\frac{1}{8}$
2	7	$2\frac{7}{32}$
$2\frac{1}{16}$	8	$2\frac{1}{4}$
$2\frac{1}{16}$	9	$2\frac{1}{4}$
$2\frac{1}{16}$	10	$2\frac{7}{32}$
2	11	$2\frac{1}{8}$
$1\frac{7}{8}$	12	$2\frac{1}{16}$
$1\frac{3}{4}$	13	$1\frac{7}{8}$
$1\frac{5}{8}$	14	$1\frac{11}{16}$
$1\frac{7}{16}$	15	$1\frac{3}{8}$
$1\frac{1}{4}$	16	$1\frac{1}{16}$
1	17	$\frac{3}{4}$
$\frac{11}{16}$	18 (Stern)	$\frac{1}{2}$

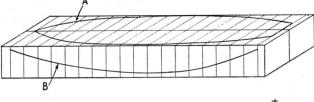

Fig. 2

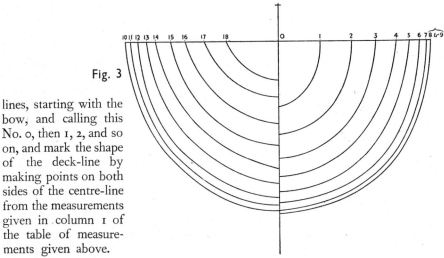

Fig. 3

lines, starting with the bow, and calling this No. 0, then 1, 2, and so on, and mark the shape of the deck-line by making points on both sides of the centre-line from the measurements given in column 1 of the table of measurements given above.

Having marked the points, trace a curve cutting the points. This is shown at A in Fig. 2. Turn the block over on its side and mark the corresponding depths as indicated in column 3 in the table. Trace the depth-curve as at B in Fig. 2, and repeat the process on the other side.

A supply of thin cardboard is now needed to enable a set of templates to be cut out to correspond with the shapes at the various sections of the hull. These shaped pieces are used as guides when shaping the wood.

Fig. 3 is a reduced drawing of the shapes at various sections. The ones at

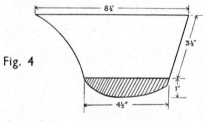

Fig. 4

the right-hand side represent the shapes from the bow to the mid-section, while those at the left are those from the mid-section to the stern. In setting out each outline should be traced on a separate piece of cardboard and then cut out with a pair of sharp scissors.

Shaping the Hull.—Remove the waste from the bottom down to the curved depth lines on the sides of the hull, using a sharp, wide chisel for the purpose, and then remove the waste material round the deck lines.

Mark a centre-line from bow to stern on the curved bottom of the hull and with a chisel pare off as much of the waste as possible, and finally obtain the correct shape by means of a spokeshave and the use of the templates, which should be tried at all sections as the work progresses. Rub the surface perfectly smooth with fine glass-paper.

As the next process consists in removing the waste from the interior of the hull, it is necessary to fix it down to a board having blocks to support the stem and stern. A flat board about 1 ft. 8 in. long by 6 in. wide and ⅝ in. thick should be selected. Make a centre-line down its length and drill two screw-holes near the middle and drive a couple of 1-in. screws from the under-side of the board into the bottom of the hull. The screws should be accurately centred so as to come in the portion of the hull where the keel-plate will be fixed. Shape a couple of blocks to correspond with the curved end sections of the hull, line them with felt or other soft material to prevent bruising the hull, and place them firmly in position.

Now fix the base-board with the hull to the top of the bench, using screws for the purpose. Run a guide-line parallel to and ¼ in. from the outside edge of the deck-curve and then remove as much waste as possible with a brace and bit, finishing it off with a sharp gouge. Great accuracy is not required, as the interior is hidden by the deck. This completes the most difficult part of the model,

The Keel.—Shape out the keel-plate, which is ⅜ in. thick, as indicated in Fig. 4, not forgetting to form a sharp edge at the front to cut the water. The lead at the bottom of the keel can be cast at home by first making a plaster-of-Paris mould and then pouring the molten metal into it, and when cool, finishing it off with a file. The lead is then fixed to the bottom of the keel-plate by means of long, thin nails, driven in after the metal has been drilled to receive them.

A ⅜-in.-wide slot should now be made at the bottom of the hull to take the keel-plate, and the plate inserted into the groove and secured with screws driven in from the interior of the hull.

The Rudder.—Drill a ¼-in.-diameter hole in the hull to take the stem of the rudder, and then make the rudder from a strip of wood $\frac{1}{8}$ in. thick. The rudder should be painted to match the hull and fitted after the deck has been fixed. Give the exterior another rub down with fine glass-paper and then apply a coat of gold size to fill up the pores of the wood, before painting. When dry, apply a thin coat of flat paint—that is, a paint without gloss—and then give a finishing coat of good quality gloss paint or enamel of the desired colour. A dark-coloured band about $\frac{5}{8}$ in. deep should be made below deck-line and the lead keel also painted black in order to give the hull a good finish.

The Deck consists of a piece of $\frac{3}{16}$-in. thick pine. The wood should be cut out to follow the curves of the deck-line of the hull, allowing $\frac{1}{16}$-in. overlap all round. Smooth the deck with fine glass-paper, round the edges, and draw neat pencil-lines $\frac{1}{4}$ in. apart to represent joints in the planks. Give the deck a coat of gold size, followed by a coat of good varnish.

The Mast.—Bore a $\frac{3}{8}$-in. hole in the centre of the deck, $6\frac{1}{2}$ in. from the bow, to take the mast. Then fix the deck to the hull by means of fine brass brads, taking great care not to split the wood. The mast consists of a piece of dowel-rod, 15 in. long, $\frac{3}{8}$ in. in diameter, tapering gently from the foot upwards, while the bowsprit and boom are made of similar material. The gaff is of $\frac{1}{4}$-in. dowel. These parts should receive a coat of gold size and then varnish.

The Sails should be made of best quality linen. Paper patterns must be prepared, allowing sufficient margin for the hems. When the sails are ready, rig up the yacht, using fishing line for the lines and halyards. The shapes of the two sails are shown in Fig. 1.

The foot of the mast is fitted with a spike, consisting of a headless nail, which fits into the wood at the bottom of the interior of the hull. No. 000 brass screw-eyes are used at the sides of the deck for fixing the stays, while ordinary pins, bent to form hooks, are fastened to the ends of the stays to enable the mast, etc., to be removed as required.

A DOLL'S HOUSE

THE main part of the doll's house illustrated in Fig. 1 and the accompanying Working Drawing is built up of yellow deal boards, $\frac{3}{8}$ in. thick after planing. Windows of a standard size are employed, except the small one in the front, which is made narrower than the rest.

Square-section grooved uprights are used at the corners for supporting the walls, a feature which not only greatly strengthens the structure but eliminates the unsightly appearance of a lap joint. The whole of the exterior is finished in rough-cast, which presents a much better appearance than the usual "brick" paper stuck on the surface. The rough-cast is formed by sanding the surfaces and then painting them with thin paint.

As it is not possible to obtain cheap boards of sufficient width to construct the front, etc., in one piece, glued and nailed dowel-joints are used, while the base is further strengthened by means of cross battens.

The roof pieces are made from material $\frac{1}{4}$ in. thick, and as these are $8\frac{3}{8}$ in. wide, they can be cut from 9-in. boards.

Materials Required.—The following is an approximation of the principal material required, including waste. Ten ft. run of 9 in. by $\frac{3}{8}$ in. for the front and back, 9 ft. 6 in. run of similar material for the sides, gable ends and roof supports. The base will require a length of 5 ft. 6 in., while 5 ft. run will be needed for the floor. A 3-ft. 6-in. length will suffice for the partitions. The top ceiling is made from material $\frac{1}{4}$ in. thick, as are also the roof pieces. The former will take a length of 5 ft. 6 in., while the latter requires 6 ft. To this list must be added 6 ft. of $\frac{3}{4}$-in. square-section deal, 4 ft. of 3-in. by $\frac{1}{2}$-in. planed batten for the underside of the base, and several other miscellaneous items, such as strips of wood, glass, etc.

Construction.—Start by forming the grooves in the square-section pieces of the corner uprights, which are $17\frac{1}{2}$ in.

Fig. I

long. The grooves are made in two adjacent faces in the two back uprights, and are $\frac{3}{8}$ in. wide by $\frac{1}{8}$ in. deep, while one groove is needed in each of the other two lengths.

Having cut the grooves, paint the pieces white, using an oil-bound water-paint or high-class washable distemper. Glossy oil paint should not be used.

Now cut all the boards to their respective widths and lengths, taking care not to get them mixed up, and mark and cut out the window apertures, etc., with a fretsaw. Join the boards together to form each unit, using plenty of hot glue and dowels formed out of headless nails at the joins.

The Roughcast Surfaces.—Before proceeding any further, the front, back and sides—not the gable-ends, as these are to be painted white—should be sanded. Apply very hot glue to the outside surfaces and press a quantity of clean, sharp, perfectly dry sand on to the glued surface. If any sand has stuck round the sides of the window apertures, it should be removed before the glue has set. Put the sanded surfaces in a safe place to dry. Meanwhile, fix the battens to the underside of the base, and paint the whole grass-green.

The Floor.—Prepare the floor by cutting small recesses at the corners to allow the corners to clear the uprights when assembled, and also cut the opening for the stairs. Paint this member white on the underside as it forms the ceiling to the lower rooms, and colour the top surface with a dark grey paint, or any desired colour to represent linoleum.

The Partitions dividing the rooms should now receive attention. Four of these, all the same size, will be required. The members should be cut $\frac{3}{8}$ in. less than the inside width of the structure, to enable vertical pieces of $\frac{3}{8}$-in. square-section wood to be bradded to the front edges in order to hide the unsightly end grain. A doorway should be provided near the front of each partition. The partitions can be seen in Fig. 2, which is an illustration of the house minus the front.

The Gable-ends should be cut to shape and the outside faces painted white. Cut two similar-shaped pieces to form the roof-supports.

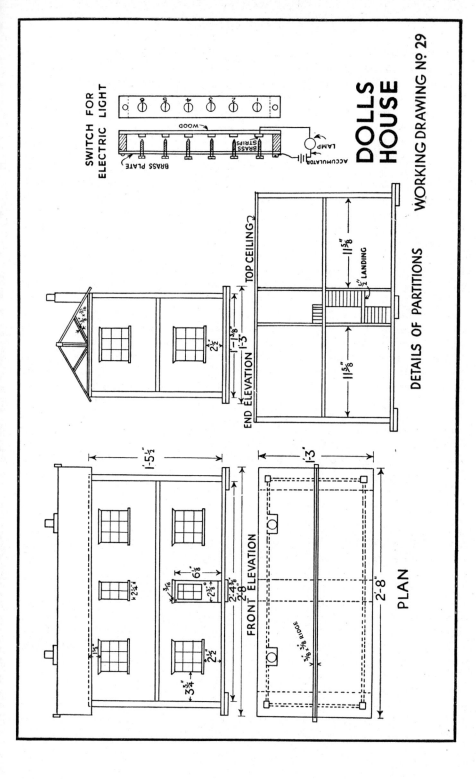

SWITCH FOR ELECTRIC LIGHT

WOOD

BRASS STRIPS

BRASS PLATE

LAMP

ACCUMULATOR

DOLLS HOUSE

WORKING DRAWING Nº 29

DETAILS OF PARTITIONS

TOP CEILING

11⅝"

½" LANDING

END ELEVATION

1-3

1-1⅛"

2½

11⅝"

FRONT ELEVATION

1-5½

2-8"

2-4⅜"

6⅝

2⅜

3⁄16

2¼

1¼

3½

2½

PLAN

1-3"

2-8"

3⁄16" ⅜ RIDGE

The underside of the top flat member, forming the ceiling of the upper floor, should be painted white. The roof-pieces and the ridge, the latter consisting of a $\frac{3}{8}$-in.-square length of wood, can be painted slate grey to represent slates, or a brownish red to imitate tiles, the latter colour being recommended as it gives a better effect.

Interior Decoration.—It is much simpler to paint or paper the walls before assembling. If paper is chosen, it should either have no pattern or a very small one. On the other hand, washable distemper can be used to advantage, as it can be washed without any detrimental effect to the surface.

In any case it is necessary to mark out carefully the partitions and the inside faces of the front, side and back members before applying the paint or the paper.

The Window Panes can now be put in hand. Old photographic plates with the gelatinous coating removed are ideal for this purpose, as they are of the correct thickness. Imitation sash-bars can be made by sticking passe-partout adhesive paper to the front surface of the glass, or they can be formed by the use of thin white paint applied with a draughtsman's ruling pen. The windows are fitted into the apertures by means of headless pins, carefully inserted into the corners of the wood on both sides of the windows.

The Stairs.—The next item to claim attention is the stairs. Two flights will be required, one from the ground floor to the half-landing and the other from the landing to the first floor. They are constructed by planing down $\frac{3}{8}$-in. square wood to form strips of triangular section. These are glued down to a base of $\frac{1}{8}$-in.-thick wood and then trimmed up to finished size. The posts and handrails are $\frac{3}{8}$-in. square-section wood and $\frac{3}{8}$-in. by $\frac{1}{8}$-in. strip, respectively.

Assembling the Parts.—When the front doors and windows are in position, and the half-landing has been fixed to the inside of the back member, fix the uprights to the two side members by inserting the ends into their respective grooves and fasten them securely by means of fine oval brads. Carefully mark out their positions on the base and secure the uprights to the base by means of 1-in. No. 6 countersunk-headed iron screws, driven in from the underside after having drilled the necessary clearing holes. Slide the back member into the grooves and fix with brads as before. Now fix the floor by driving in brads from the outside, taking care to see that the floor is perfectly level and that the brads are driven in straight.

Place the partitions temporarily in position and mark the positions for the pivots of the doors. Drill holes for the pivots, and then fix the partitions and doors. Fix the staircase next, and then secure the top board forming the ceiling of the first floor rooms to the tops of the uprights by driving in similar screws to those used in the base, and several finer screws of the same length into the top edges of the side and back members.

Next fix the end gables, keeping the outside edges flush with the ends of the top board. These should be fixed with screws as also should the roof-supports between the gable-ends.

The next step is to fix the roof-pieces to the gable-ends and the roof-supports, using 1-in. panel pins for the purpose. A long edge of the ridge-piece is placed between the angle formed where the top edges of the roof-pieces meet, and the ridge secured to the gables and roof-supports with panel pins 1 in. long.

A $\frac{3}{8}$-in.-square white-painted finial with rounded ends is required at each end of the roof-ridge, and these are also fixed with pins. White fascia boards

¾ in. wide by 3/16 in. thick should be fixed on the underside of the roof-pieces at the gable-ends, while a strip of white painted wood, ½ in. wide by ⅛ in. thick, is pinned to the end grain of the top board in order to hide it from view. A fan-shaped overlay, consisting of three pieces of similar material painted brown, should be pinned to each gable-end, while white strips of ¼ in. by ⅛ in. wood form the sills and the tops of the windows. The front doorway has covering strips, ¼ in. wide by ⅛ in. thick, at the sides, and a step and piece over the door of ⅜-in. square material.

A chimney-stack made from a block of wood is fixed near each end of the roof, while miniature chimney-pots made from ½-in.-diameter dowel, painted red, are provided at the tops.

Installing Electric Light.—Run the wires to the rooms and fix the accumulator and the operating switch in the space between the top board and the roof. Miniature lamp-holders, as used with flash-lamp bulbs, can be used, and these should be screwed to the centres of the ceilings. A pair of 22-gauge double cotton-covered wires is run from each holder up to the roof space. One lead of each pair is connected to a common terminal and from thence up to one terminal of the accumulator. The other

wires are connected to individual contact pieces mounted upon a piece of hardwood, or ebonite, while another wire is connected to the terminal plate fitted with screw contacts as shown in detail on page 669.

The wiring should be done while assembling the parts of the structure, as this enables the wires to be neatly

Fig. 2

stapled to the back member and the ceilings.

Special low-consumption 2·5-volt flash-lamp bulbs, obtainable at most electrical stores, should be used in preference to the ordinary cheap type, in order to save current.

The back roof-piece is, of course, hinged to the roof-ridge in order to gain access into the roof-space.